The Lessons
and Non-Lessons
of the Air and Missile Campaign
in Kosovo

Other Books by Anthony H. Cordesman

Transnational Threats from the Middle East, US Army War College, Carlyle, 1999

Iraq and the War of the Sanctions: Conventional Threats and Weapons of Mass Destruction, Praeger, Westport, CT, 1999

Iran in Transition: Conventional Threats and Weapons of Mass Destruction, Praeger, Westport, CT, 1999

Bahrain, Oman, Qatar and the UAE: Challenges of Security, Westview, Boulder, 1997

Kuwait: Recovery and Security after the Gulf War, Westview, Boulder, 1997

Saudi Arabia: Guarding the Desert Kingdom, Westview, Boulder, 1997

US Forces in the Middle East: Resources and Capabilities, Westview, Boulder, 1997

Iran: Dilemmas of Dual Containment, with Ahmed Hashim, Westview, Boulder, 1997

Iraq: Sanctions and Beyond, with Ahmed Hashim, Westview, Boulder, 1997

Perilous Prospects: The Peace Process and Arab-Israeli Balance, Westview, Boulder, 1996

The Lessons of Modern War: Volume Four—The Gulf War, with Abraham R. Wagner, Westview, Boulder, 1995, paperback 1999

Iran and Iraq: The Threat from the Northern Gulf, Westview, Boulder, 1994

US Defense Policy: Resources and Capabilities, London, RUSI Whitehall Series, 1993

After the Storm: The Changing Military Balance in the Middle East, Boulder, Westview, 1993

Weapons of Mass Destruction in the Middle East, Brassey's, London, 1991

The Lessons of Modern War: Volume One—The Arab-Israeli Conflicts, with Abraham R. Wagner, Westview, Boulder, 1990

The Lessons of Modern War: Volume Two—The Iran-Iraq Conflict, with Abraham R. Wagner, Westview, Boulder, 1990

The Lessons of Modern War: Volume Three—The Afghan and Falklands Conflicts, with Abraham R. Wagner, Westview, Boulder, 1990

The Gulf and the West, Boulder, Westview, 1988

NATO Central Region Forces, RUSI/Jane's, London, 1987

The Iran-Iraq War and Western Security, 1984–1987, RUSI/Jane's, London, 1987

The Arab-Israeli Balance and the Art of Operations, American Enterprise Institute (AEI)/ University Press of America, Washington, D.C., 1986

Western Strategic Interests and Saudi Arabia, Croom Helm, London, 1986

The Gulf and the Search for Strategic Stability, Westview, Boulder, 1984

Jordanian Arms and the Middle East Balance, Middle East Institute, Washington, D.C., 1983

Deterrence in the 1980s, Extended Adelphi Paper, International Institute for Strategic Studies, London, 1982

Imbalance of Power, Shifting U.S.-Soviet Military Strengths, with John M. Collins, Presidio, Monterey, 1978

The Lessons
and Non-Lessons
of the Air and Missile
Campaign in Kosovo

ANTHONY H. CORDESMAN

2001

Westport, Connecticut
London

Library of Congress Cataloging-in-Publication Data

Cordesman, Anthony H.
    The lessons and non-lessons of the air and missile campaign in Kosovo / Anthony H. Cordesman.
        p. cm.
    Includes bibliographical references.
    ISBN 0–275–97230–5 (alk. paper)
    1. Kosovo (Serbia)—History—Civil War, 1998—Aerial operations. 2. North Atlantic
    Treaty Organization—Yugoslavia. 3. Bombing, Aerial—Yugoslavia. I. Title.
    DR2087.5.C67 2001
    949.7103—dc21   2001021181

British Library Cataloguing in Publication Data is available.

Library of Congress Catalog Card Number: 2001021181
ISBN: 0–275–97230–5

First published in 2001

Praeger Publishers, 88 Post Road West, Westport, CT 06881
An imprint of Greenwood Publishing Group, Inc.
www.praeger.com

Printed in the United States of America

The paper used in this book complies with the
Permanent Paper Standard issued by the National
Information Standards Organization (Z39.48–1984).

10 9 8 7 6 5 4 3 2 1

Contents

Contents

1

The Lessons and Non-Lessons of the Air and Missile Campaign in Kosovo

Virtually every war leads to a rush to judgment in an effort to create "instant history," and then to find new lessons that apply universally to the chaos known as war. The victors are particularly prone to rush to judgment. So are those who feel the outcome of a given war serves their interests at the political and military level, proves the value of their strategic and tactical concepts, or can be used to advance the cause of their military service or some favorite weapon and technology. The losers are naturally defensive, and try to reinvent history to minimize their mistakes, losses, and the scale of their defeat. Success is claimed by those who are not responsible for that success, and blame is shifted to those who are not to blame. Data are manipulated and manufactured, and lessons are created as if planning to refight the last war could define the requirements set by future conflicts.

Some of the resulting analysis is useful and constructive. It provides a clearer path for shaping forces and military capabilities, and a better picture of the extent to which war can and cannot be used to serve political and strategic goals. At the same time, truth is not only the first casualty of war; it is often the first casualty of efforts to learn lessons from a given conflict. The search for lessons leads military analysts to go too far in drawing conclusions from limited or no data. There is a tendency to turn history into propaganda, and analysis into special pleading.

The war in Kosovo is a good case in point. At this writing, NATO and the US have both issued official reports on the lessons of the war. Nevertheless, there are many vital gaps in the unclassified data that are available. While NATO and its member nations reported with far more integrity and depth than Serbia, this is not a particularly high standard of comparison. Much of the data NATO provided during the war were originally intended more to serve propaganda purposes rather than be used for serious analysis. Even at the time they were highly suspect, and the information that has become available since the war raises even more doubts about much of their credibility.

The official studies issued since the war have a similar character. The one serious NATO attempt at a post-action study is largely a self-serving exercise designed to show that NATO aircraft did indeed do serious damage to Serbian land forces in Kosovo. It makes a reasonably credible case in this one area, but ignores virtually every other major issue.

The official US studies are short on substance and detail. The most thorough document, issued in January 2000, provides the most detail when it makes an argument for the funding of the programs the Department of Defense desires or for changes in NATO allied capabilities. It dodges around complex issues like the effectiveness of given weapons, the impact of the strategic bombing campaign, and collateral damage.[1] Senior US officers who played a leading role in the war indicate that such data were deliberately omitted from both the classified and unclassified versions of the reports on the lessons of the war at the direction of the Secretary of Defense. This has led to press reports that the US deliberately concealed the fact that NATO and US reports of damage to Serbian forces were grossly exaggerated, although senior USAF officers directly involved in the damage assessment reports deny this.[2] Other NATO allied countries have provided some individual studies that are of value, but they tend to be narrow in scope and have a highly political character.

Serbia has provided little more than post-war propaganda, efforts to prove that NATO air and missile power were relatively ineffective, and absurdist charges of war crimes. It is difficult to see the "other side of the hill" and to validate or disprove many of NATO's claims using meaningful information that is based on Serbian perceptions and analysis.

This lack of reliable and detailed data sometimes makes it difficult to determine what the lessons of Kosovo really are and when they are beyond the specific contingency involved. It is also far from clear that the military problems in Kosovo are really over. The cease-fire agreements did not resolve Kosovo's future, or provide a broad basis for stability in the Balkans. Since the cease-fire, the air and missile war has become a land-dominated peacemaking operation in which NATO has increasingly found itself caught up between the now dominant Muslim Albanian Kosovars and the Serbian minority that has remained in the province. The NATO air and missile war against Serbian forces may ultimately prove to be the prelude to a new low-intensity combat between Serbs and Kosovar Albanian, or to new fighting in the region.

The most that can be accomplished is to describe the broad course of the air and missile campaign, cite what original sources have said in enough historical context to help explain the reasons for such statements, and draw preliminary lessons from the unclassified material released to date. As this analysis shows, however, there are often more questions than answers and it is far from clear that some of the lessons of Kosovo will apply to the next conflict. As a result, identifying the "non-lessons" of Kosovo is as important as identifying the lessons. False or exaggerated conclusions, and false expectations, are worse than learning no lessons at all.

2

The Historical Background: The Course and Character of the NATO Campaign

The seeds of the conflict go back centuries, although today's memories and hatreds often have little to do with historical realities. The Serbs remember that Serb forces were defeated by the Ottomans at the battle of Kosovo Polje in 1389, and have made Kosovo the historical center of Serbia in Serb history and thinking. At the same time, the ethnic Albanians of Kosovo believe they are the "original" inhabitants and they have long been the majority population. Ironically, the historical evidence seems to be that both Serbs and Albanian Kosovars fought against the Turks in 1389, while other groups from both sides collaborated with the Turks.

The long series of Balkan wars that followed the decline of Turkey paid little attention to self-determination in the region. Kosovo became part of Serbia in 1913, despite an ethnic Albanian majority, and became part of Yugoslavia after World War I. These events led to a long period of Serbian repression of the Albanian Kosovars. While Tito promised members of the Albanian Kosovar resistance during World War II that Kosovo would be given a high degree of independence, this promise was only kept in part in the late 1960s. Kosovo remained one of the poorest areas in Yugoslavia, and received limited development funding. At the same time, the Muslim Albanian Kosovars had one of the highest birth rates, steadily increasing the percentage of the population that was Kosovar and reducing the demographic share of the Serbs.

Kosovo finally became an autonomous province within Serbia under the Yugoslav Constitution of 1974. It had its own assembly and a high degree of Kosovar participation in the government and the economy. This led to a Serbian nationalist backlash, however, while many Albanian Kosovars wanted independence. Economic development remained low, and some estimates indicate that the Kosovar per capita income was about half that of the Serbs in neighboring Serbia. The end result was a rise in both Kosovar nationalism and rising Serbian resentment over what many Serbs regard as the "corruption of the Serbian homeland."

The situation first began to degenerate towards violence in the late 1980s. Slobodan Milosevic gained power in Serbia in 1987 by exploiting Kosovo as a political issue and calling for Serbian control. He gave a speech from Pristina over Yugoslav television in April 1987 in which he stated that, "You will never be defeated again." The speech was a de facto pledge that Serbia would retain full control of Kosovo. At the same time, the fighting in Bosnia heightened Serbian nationalism, and led the Serbian leadership of the Federal Republic of Yugoslavia (FRY) to concentrate spending in Serbia and in the support of the Serbian cause in Bosnia.

Milosevic forced the Albanian Kosovar leadership in Kosovo to resign from power in November 1988. This led to a Kosovar general strike in February 1989, and Milosevic retaliated by sending the Yugoslav army into Pristina. On March 23, 1989, the Serbian-dominated forces surrounded the assembly building, and forced the Kosovar legislators to revoke the autonomy agreement. Milosevic then instituted direct rule from Belgrade. He directed the full revocation of the autonomy given to Kosovo in 1990, and the Kosovo Provincial Assembly and government were dissolved. Kosovo Albanians were removed from important state posts and jobs and a state of emergency was declared. His government sought to "Serbianize" the political control of the province, education, the media, the control of major industries, and the control of infrastructure and utilities.

By 1992, it was already clear that the situation could degenerate into another regional mini-conflict. As early as December 1992, President George Bush warned Milosevic that "the United States will respond in the event of Serb-incited violence in Kosovo."[3]

Albanian Kosovar unemployment reached levels in excess of 60% during the late 1990s. This led to even more Albanian Kosovar resentment and resistance to rule from Serbia. This resistance initially was largely peaceful. The Serbians, however, continued to treat Kosovar efforts to win autonomy or independence as a threat to a province they called the historical center of Serbia, and as a terrorist movement. As a result, peaceful protest and passive resistance came to appear more and more ineffective, and a new force called the Kosovo Liberation Army (KLA) emerged as a more radical organization that supported the use of violence in winning full independence.[4]

BOSNIA AND THE DAYTON ACCORDS BECOME THE PRELUDE TO WAR IN KOSOVO

In retrospect, Bosnia was a natural prelude to Kosovo. The long struggle in Bosnia, and its resolution in the Dayton Accords, helped convince Serbian nationalists and extremists that they were right in seeing Yugoslavia and Serbia as under siege by hostile ethnic movements and outside states. Bosnia also ended in a settlement that left Serbia with only one major non-Serbian ethnic element—the Albanian or Muslim Kosovars—and Serbia's leadership in a position where any further ethnic conflict challenged its right to lead as well as the entire basis by which Milosevic had come to power.

The Dayton Accords that "resolved" the conflict in Bosnia in 1995 accelerated the problems in Kosovo. They made no mention of the province and made no attempt to include Kosovo in a broader solution to the region's tensions. As a result, an over-reaching effort to create a multiethnic state in Bosnia created a growing impression in Kosovo that only violence could restore Kosovar rights while it gave Serbia an exaggerated view of its freedom of action in suppressing Kosovar rights and resistance.

The Dayton Accords also produced the legal illusion that the feuding Muslim, Croat, and Serbian factions had reached a serious agreement to create a true multiethnic state. The accords repeated many of the mistakes made after World War I by defining "self-determination" in ways where diverse and hostile ethnic groups were forced into new many states on the basis of outside judgements about geography. What the Dayton Accords really achieved was de facto ethnic partition enforced by a relatively large peacekeeping force and the threat of new NATO attacks.

UN, Western, and NATO efforts to deal with Bosnia failed to deal with ethnic tensions in the Balkans as a whole. The UN passed resolutions and attempted to use peace-keeping methods in a region where only the threat and reality of armed force—or "peace-making"—could halt ethnic violence. As a result, the de facto responsibility for action passed to the West and NATO. The West, however, pursued solutions that dealt only with the current crisis in Bosnia, rather than the region. When violence continued, the West threatened for a long time before it acted, often creating artificial deadlines it did not enforce, and making threats to use NATO forces it did not make good upon. The West also sought to create a multiethnic state in Bosnia that the Serbian population clearly did not want, and in spite of major tensions between the Bosnian Muslims and Kosovars.

This history provides a clear lesson about the dangers of expediency, and accepting quick and partial solutions to peace-making problems because they are politically convenient at a given moment in time. Peace-making efforts that are too expedient to solve regional problems simply set the stage for further fighting.

Bosnia also set a precedent in terms of Western moral illusions. Ethnic wars produce intense suffering and cruelty, but they rarely have a "good" side and a "bad" side. They instead have a strong side and a weak side. It is a grim reality in ethnic conflict that the stronger side often commits atrocities against the weaker side. The fact that winners punish losers, however, in no way means that the losers would not be equally vicious in dealing with their opposition if they were stronger.

The Serbians abused their initial strength in Bosnia in ways that include war crimes, ethnic cleanings, and crimes against humanity. At the same time, even Serbian victories could not force the Croats and Bosnian Muslims to work together until they suffered major defeats. The Croats and Muslims were equally prone to

ethnic cleansing and violence in those areas where they had local superiority—
often taking the form of fights between Croat and Muslim.

The West, however, reacted by demonizing the Serbs and sanctifying the
Muslims and Croats and to deal with the resulting violence as if criminal law could
be applied to ethnic conflict. This laid the ground work for both the false hope that
the Muslims and Croats would work together to create a solid multiethnic
state in Bosnia.

When NATO finally did use air power against the Serbs in Bosnia, it was only
successful in forcing a settlement because of a major Croatian and Bosnian Muslim
defeat of the Serbs in the Land War. Western diplomats, however, tended to claim
that limited amounts of air power had forced Serbia to settle and to underestimate
the levels of force that have been required to alter Serbian behavior. Equally
important, the West continued to underestimate the sheer depth and explosiveness
of ethnic hatred.

As was the case in Iraq, Lebanon, Somalia, Cambodia, Rwanda/Burundi, and
many other countries and regions, the West exaggerated the potential ease with
which diplomacy and force could reach lasting solutions, and demonized one side
against the others. It assigned too much blame to given political leaders and too
little responsibility to the festering hatreds that history had bred in entire peoples. It
saw the problem in terms of crisis or conflict resolution that could be accomplished
in months or a few years, and not in terms of exhausting exercises in armed nation
building that could drag on for a decade or more.

Seen from this perspective, neither the Serbian masters of the Federal Republic
of Yugoslavia nor the West were prepared diplomatically or militarily to deal with
Kosovo. Serbia lived in a world of illusions based on the thesis that only force
could solve its ethnic problems. The West lived in a world of illusions based on
multiethnicity and a false morality play.

In the event, these problems were then compounded by a divided UN, and by the
growing resistance of Russia, China, and other states to what they felt were
Western or US-imposed attempts to use the UN for peace-keeping missions and
justify Western intervention. Serbian ethnic cleansing in Kosovo began in an
international climate where the supposed "international community" had no unity
and other priorities.

THE DIPLOMATIC PRELUDE

It is questionable whether any diplomatic effort could have succeeded in
avoiding a bloody conflict in Kosovo, but the weakness and divisions in the
international community, and the grand strategic illusions in the West, scarcely
helped. Bosnia and the Dayton Accords helped exacerbate ethnic tensions and
created a climate of illusions about both diplomacy and the use of force. This, in
turn, made it almost impossible for the West, NATO, and the US to prepare
effectively for the risk of a new major ethnic conflict. It helped to create a
negotiating climate in which force had to be used to try to salvage a failed

diplomacy under conditions where no one was prepared to deal with the military realities that followed.

The blame for what happened must ultimately lie, however, with Serbia and its leadership. NATO neither caused the conflict in Kosovo nor took the kind of diplomatic action that "forced" Serbia into mass ethnic cleansing and countless scattered atrocities. It is unlikely that the conflict in Kosovo would never have approached the scale it did if President Milosevic had respected Kosovar autonomy in the first place or shown a serious interest in resolving the crisis once the Kosovars turned to force. At worst, the West's failures were based on good intentions, and a serious NATO attempt at conflict resolution.

The escalating clashes that ultimately triggered NATO military action started in 1996 and became steadily more serious until they first reached the crisis point in 1998. Serbian refusal to deal peacefully with the Albanian Kosovar leaders that advocated autonomy drove the majority of the Albanian Kosovars to support the use of force. The KLA began a campaign of low level attacks against Serbian security forces in 1996, who responded with military repression of the population as a whole.

There was little serious fighting until 1997, but the slow escalation of the fighting then began to reach the level where the international community began to react. The United Nations (UN), the North Atlantic Treaty Organization (NATO), the European Union (EU), the Organization for Security and Co-operation in Europe (OSCE) and the Contact Group, comprising France, Germany, Italy, Russia, the UK and the US, began to treat the situation as a potential crisis. In December 1997, NATO Foreign Ministers stated that NATO's interest in Balkan stability extended beyond Bosnia to Kosovo, and expressed their concern at the rising ethnic tension in Kosovo.[5]

The KLA stepped up its attacks on the Serbs, however, and this led to a major Serbian offensive in February 1998. Serbian forces conducted a major campaign against the centers of KLA power and killed many members of the Jashari clan—a key supporter of the KLA. In early March, FRY Interior Ministry security units (MUP Special Police) consistently used excessive force, destroying homes and villages and terrorizing the civilian population. The KLA retaliated with a major ambush of the Serbian army near Smolice on March 22, 1998, and other attacks near Drenica.

The North Atlantic Council (NAC) reiterated its concern over the deteriorating situation in Kosovo in March 1998, after Serbian forces killed some 30 Kosovo Albanians in response to the KLA attack near Drenica. On March 31, the United Nations adopted Security Council Resolution 1160, condemning the excessive use of force by Serbian security forces against civilians in Kosovo, and also established an embargo of arms and material against the FRY.

Serbia, however, continued to build up its regular army (VJ) and special police (MUP) forces in Kosovo. Serbian forces attacked villages in Drenica, Decani and Pec areas during March, April, and May. This led the Contact Group to make repeated diplomatic efforts to find a peaceful, negotiated solution. Ambassador

Holbrooke arranged the first meeting between FRY President Milosevic and Dr. Rugova, the leader of the shadow government in Kosovo.

Milosevic and Rugova met once in May to lay the groundwork for peace talks. Although Milosevic did appoint a negotiating team that participated in preliminary talks in Pristina, the dialogue process quickly broke down following a deliberate Serb offensive in Decani where several dozen Kosovar Albanians were killed. NATO Foreign Ministers also approved a series of steps aimed at deterring conflict spillover and promoting regional stability. These included Partnership for Peace (PfP) exercises in Albania and the FYROM, a NATO ship visit to Albania, and NATO preparations to assist NGOs in response to major refugee flows out of Kosovo.[6]

The violence did not halt, however, and the North Atlantic Council met at Foreign Minister level on May 28, 1998, and agreed on two major objectives for NATO:

- To help to achieve a peaceful resolution of the crisis by contributing to the response of the international community; and
- To promote stability and security in neighboring countries with particular emphasis on Albania and the former Yugoslav Republic of Macedonia.

The Defense Ministers of the North Atlantic Council met in London on June 12, 1998. The Contact Group (CG) issued a statement calling for: (1) a cease-fire; (2) effective international monitoring in Kosovo; (3) access for UNHCR and NGOs along with refugee return; and (4) serious dialogue between Belgrade and the Kosovo Albanians with international mediation. The Defense Ministers also tasked NATO military planners with producing a range of military options, both ground and air, for military support to the diplomatic process, and by early August the results had been reviewed by the North Atlantic Council (NAC). This led SHAPE to consider of a large number of possible military options. The implied military threat also helped lead to further negotiations, although they did not put an end to the fighting. NATO also undertook a series of air and ground exercises to demonstrate the Alliance's ability to project power rapidly into the region. Four RAF strike aircraft participated.

These actions helped lead to a meeting on June 16 between President Milosevic and Russian President Yeltsin during which Milosevic agreed to grant access to diplomatic observers—the Kosovo Diplomatic Observer Mission (KDOM). In late June, Ambassador Holbrooke continued his diplomatic efforts, meeting again with Milosevic in Belgrade and with KLA commanders in the Kosovo village of Junik. The KDOM was established, and then helped the international community assess the events on the ground.

Serbian attacks continued during the summer of 1998, however, and NATO estimates that resulting fighting between the KLA and Serbian military and police forces and Kosovar Albanian forces resulted in the deaths of over 1,500 Albanian Kosovars during this period. Rather than suppress the Kosovars, the Serbian attack led to steadily increasing Kosovar support for violent resistance to the Serbian effort. During the fighting, the Kosovar Liberation Army (KLA) grew steadily larger and better armed and emerged as a major force that continued to control some of the countryside and killed and abducted Serbs. This created a cycle of escalating violence that led the Serbian security forces to respond with even more attacks on the Kosovars in the countryside and this created a major refugee population. The fighting did so much damage to the civil population that the KLA declared a cease-fire during October-December, although this seems to have been largely a propaganda measure. The KLA continued its attacks on the Serbian security forces in spite of this declaration, and kidnapped and executed "collaborators."

The international community became gravely concerned about this escalating conflict, its humanitarian consequences, and the risk of it spreading to other countries. During a Clinton-Yeltsin summit meeting on September 2, Secretary of State Albright and Russian Foreign Minister Ivanov issued a joint statement on Kosovo calling on Belgrade to end the offensive and for the Kosovar Albanians to engage with Belgrade in negotiations. During September 5–7, John Shattuck, the US Assistant Secretary of State for Democracy, Human Rights, and Labor, and former Senator Bob Dole visited Kosovo to examine the conditions in the region. They then visited Belgrade and warned Milosevic about his treatment of prisoners and refugees in Kosovo.

By mid-September 1998, NATO and the UNHCR estimated 250,000 Kosovo Albanians had been driven from their homes and some 50,000 had no shelter as winter approached. As a result of these conditions, the UN Security Council adopted Resolution 1199 on September 23. This resolution warned of an impending human catastrophe in Kosovo, and demanded a cease-fire and the start of serious political dialogue. It expressed deep concern about the excessive use of force by Serbian security forces and the Yugoslav army, and called for a cease-fire by both parties to the conflict.

On September 23, the UN Security Council (with China abstaining) passed Resolution 1199 which called for a cease-fire, the withdrawal of all FRY security forces, access for NGOs and humanitarian organizations, and the return home of refugees and the internally displaced. NATO Defense Ministers met on September 24 and affirmed their resolve and determination to take action if required. NATO also agreed to begin the formal build-up and readying of forces to conduct air strikes. They approved the issuance of Activation Warnings (ACTWARN) for two different types of air operations, known as the Phased Air Campaign and the Limited Air Response.

Milosevic responded on September 28 by declaring victory over the Kosovo insurgency and announced the end of the FRY offensive—although NATO intelligence reporting indicated continued fighting in several areas and no significant changes to FRY security force deployments. The NAC responded by issuing an Activation Request (ACTREQ) for both air options on October 1.

On October 5, Secretary General Koffi Annan released a highly critical UN Security Council report on FRY compliance with the provisions of UNSCR 1199. As a result of this report, the US pushed NATO to issue Activation Orders (ACTORD) for both air options. While NATO reviewed this issue, a Contact Group meeting in London on October 8 gave US envoy Richard Holbrooke a mandate to go to Belgrade to secure agreement to the requirements of Resolution 1199. Holbrooke spent the next seven days in talks with both Milosevic and the Kosovar Albanians. On October 12, Ambassador Holbrooke reported to NATO that Milosevic was prepared to accept a 2,000 man OSCE ground verification presence and a NATO air surveillance mission to monitor FRY compliance with UNSCR 1199.

On October 13, Serbian President Milosevic issued a unilateral statement included a number of key principles that could form the framework of a peace settlement, including substantial autonomy, elections, and a local Kosovar police force. The statement included proposed dates for: (1) the achievement of an agreement which will comprise the basic elements of a political solution in Kosovo—November 2; and (2) general agreements on the rules and procedures of elections—November 9 (in reality, neither date was achieved).

In order to demonstrate NATO's resolve, and to maintain pressure on Milosevic backsliding, the North Atlantic Council proceeded to approve the ACTORD decisions the same day. However, it instructed SACEUR not to execute the Limited Air Option for 96 hours and authorized the execution of only the deployment phase of the Phased Air Campaign. NATO then communicated to Milosevic that it expected him to use the 96 hour "pause" to concretely demonstrate his commitment to complying with UNSCR 1199. As part of this commitment, Milosevic subsequently signed a Terms of Reference for a ground verification force with NATO Secretary General Solana. Additionally, FRY Army Chief Perisic and SACEUR signed a separate agreement allowing NATO aerial surveillance missions over Kosovo.

On October 16, an agreement between OSCE CIO Geremek and Yugoslav Foreign Minister Jovanovic paved the way for the creation of the OSCE Kosovo Verification Mission, or KVM. The OSCE Mission was endorsed by the UN Security Council (UNSCR 1203) on October 24, and the OSCE KVM was established under OSCE Permanent Council decision No. 263 on October 25. The primary mission of the KVM was to ensure FRY compliance with UN Security Council Resolutions 1160 and 1199.

As a result of these efforts, the NAC judged that enough progress had been made to justify an extension of the "pause" on the Limited Air Option until October 27. The air strikes were called off on October 27, after further diplomatic initiatives.

These initiatives included visits to Belgrade by NATO's Secretary General Solana, US Envoys Holbrooke and Hill, the Chairman of NATO's Military Committee, General Nauman, and the Supreme Allied Commander Europe, General Clark, to make the seriousness of the October 27 deadline clear to Milosevic. Clark and Nauman reached a comprehensive agreement for specific VJ and MUP withdrawals with the FRY leadership during this visit.

Ambassador Holbrooke reported to NATO on October 27 that Milosevic had agreed to the deployment of an unarmed OSCE verification mission to Kosovo and to the establishment of a NATO aerial verification mission. This report of FRY compliance led to an NAC decision to suspend execution of the Limited Air Option and Phased Air Operation. However, the NAC did not cancel the ACTORDs. Both would remain in place but would require a positive NAC decision for execution.

The Serbian-controlled authorities of the Federal Republic of Yugoslavia (FRY) authorities then negotiated with military representatives from NATO, and agreed to reduce the numbers of security forces personnel in Kosovo to pre-crisis levels.[7] These agreements formed the basis of UN Security Council Resolution 1203. NATO agreed to keep compliance of the agreements under continuous review and to remain prepared to carry out air strikes should they be required.

It was agreed that the Organization for Security and Cooperation in Europe (OSCE) would establish a Kosovo Verification Mission (KVM) to observe compliance on the ground and that NATO would establish an aerial surveillance mission. The establishment of these two missions was endorsed by UN Security Council Resolution 1203. NATO also deployed an Extraction Force to extract the KVM in case it was necessary to conduct a limited evacuation short of full withdrawal. This task force was deployed in the former Yugoslav Republic of Macedonia under the overall direction of NATO's Supreme Allied Commander Europe. The Extraction Force, under French command, was NATO's first deployment of combat troops to the area.

As a result, President Milosevic agreed to comply with the terms NATO proposed, began the withdrawal of some 4,000 special police forces, and the air strikes were called off. Limits were set on the number of Serbian forces in Kosovo, and on the scope of their operations, following a separate agreement with Generals Naumann and Clark.

The KVM began operations in November 1998. Several non-NATO nations that participate in Partnership for Peace (PfP) agreed to contribute to the surveillance mission organized by NATO. NATO established a special military task force in support of the OSCE to assist with the emergency evacuation of members of the KVM, if renewed conflict should put them at risk. This task force was deployed in the former Yugoslav Republic of Macedonia under the overall direction of NATO's Supreme Allied Commander Europe.

While these actions resulted in a brief period of peace, the fighting between Serb and Kosovar flared up again in early 1999. There were a number of provocative acts on both sides and the use of excessive and disproportionate force by the Serbian Army and Special Police. Some of these incidents were defused through the mediation efforts of the OSCE verifiers but in mid-January, the situation deteriorated further after escalation of the Serbian offensive against Kosovar Albanians.

In early January 1999, three Serb police were killed as a result of KLA ambush attacks on police patrols in the vicinity of Stimlje, prompting a significant build-up of Serb security forces in the area. On January 15, the KVM reported a serious deterioration of the situation in the area. KVM patrols witnessed VJ tanks and armored vehicles firing directly into houses near Malopoljce and Petrova, and noted houses burning in Racak. KVM units were initially denied direct access to these areas (late in the afternoon on January 15, a KVM patrol did get to the village of Racak—they noted one dead Albanian civilian and five injured civilians, and received unconfirmed reports of other deaths).

The KVM returned to Racak on January 16 and confirmed that Serb security forces had killed 45 Albanian civilians. The initial facts, as verified by KVM, included evidence of arbitrary detentions, extra-judicial killings, and the mutilation of unarmed civilians by the security forces of the FRY. FRY authorities took exception to direct comments made by KVM HOM Ambassador Walker, and declared him "persona non-grata" (PNG), ordering him to leave the country within 48 hours (an additional 24 hours was subsequently added to this order). In the face of intense international criticism for this action, Milosevic froze the PNG status of Ambassador Walker (allowing him to remain in Kosovo/Serbia), but did not lift it entirely.

These actions led to renewed international efforts to give new political impetus to finding a peaceful solution to the conflict. The six-nation Contact Group established by the 1992 London Conference on the Former Yugoslavia met on January 29. It was agreed to convene urgent negotiations between the parties to the conflict, under international mediation.

On January 28, 1999, NATO issued a "solemn warning" to Milosevic and the Kosovo Albanian leadership. NATO Secretary General Solana issued a statement indicating that NATO fully supported the early conclusion of a political settlement under the mediation of the Contact Group. The settlement would provide an enhanced status for Kosovo, preserve the territorial integrity of the FRY, and protect the rights of all ethnic groups. The statement called for FRY authorities to immediately bring the Yugoslav Army and the Special Police force levels, posture and actions into strict compliance with their commitments to NATO on October 25, 1998, and end the excessive and disproportionate use of force in accordance with these commitments.

On January 29, Contact Group Ministers met in London to consider the situation. The Ministers called on both sides to end the cycle of violence and to commit themselves to a process of negotiation leading to a political settlement. To that end, the Contact Group agreed to summon representatives from the Federal Yugoslav and Serbian Governments, and representatives of the Kosovo Albanians to meet Rambouillet, France and to begin discussions with the direct involvement of the Contact Group.

NATO supported the Contact Group efforts by issuing a statement by the North Atlantic Council (NAC) giving full support to the Contact Group Strategy. It agreed to the use of air strikes if required on January 30. The NAC further agreed to give NATO Secretary General Solana authority to authorize air strikes against targets on the territory of the Federal Republic of Yugoslavia.

Talks at Rambouillet began on February 6. The first round of talks was suspended on February 23, with both sides seeming to express broad agreement to the principle of substantial autonomy for Kosovo although they still had major differences. The Contact Group Ministers then met in Rambouillet on February 23, at the end of more than two weeks of intensive international efforts, and attempted to reach a signed Interim Political Agreement (IPA).

While neither side signed the agreement, it was felt that an agreed political framework was now in place, and the groundwork had been laid for finalizing its implementation. NATO made it clear that such a settlement would involve a NATO-led military force on the ground—which Serbia opposed—and that a settlement would defer any discussion of independence—which the KLA opposed. It specified that amendments would require the consent of all parties. The Kosovo Albanians ultimately accepted the NATO position at the Paris talks, but the Serbian side did not. This made it essential that the agreement on the interim accord be completed and signed as a whole, and the parties committed themselves to attend a follow conference in France, covering all aspects of implementation, on March 15.

In spite of this seeming agreement, the Serbs began an offensive west of Vucitrn on February 23 that caused 4,000 villagers to flee. Similarly on March 9, the Serbs attacked Ivaja and villages near Kacanic, burned homes, and displaced another 4,000 Kosovars. While the Serbian forces claimed to be in control of Kosovo, the reality was that the fighting went on and the KVM became steadily less effective.

Ambassador Holbrooke then met with FRY leadership in Belgrade on March 10 at the request of Secretary Albright. His trip supported the on-going negotiating efforts of the US envoy for Kosovo, Ambassador Chris Hill, and his Contact Group colleagues Ambassadors Boris Mayorsky and Wolfgang Petritsch. Ambassador Holbrooke conveyed to the authorities in Belgrade the necessity for full compliance with all of their commitments to the international community, and for maximum restraint in the period leading up to the March 15 conference in France.

The second round of negotiations took place at the Kleber Center in Paris during March 15–19. The Kosovar Albanians now signed the proposed agreement, but negotiations were suspended because Serbia did not agree. The Belgrade delegation left Paris without signing the agreement, and denounced the Western ultimatum as a violation of international law and the UN charter.

The violence in Kosovo continued to intensify. The Serbian security forces launched a new wave of arrests, and Serbian military and security forces built up a major presence in Kosovo and the surrounding border area. Serbian military and police moved new troops and modern tanks into the region, in a clear breach of compliance with the October agreement. By March 19, almost one-third of the FRY's total armed forces were massed in and around Kosovo, in preparation for an obvious offensive.

This offensive was so clearly imminent the OSCE Chairman-in-Office, the Norwegian Foreign Minister, Knut Vollebaek, announced the immediate withdrawal of the OSCE verifiers the same day as the Paris talks were suspended, and they withdrew from Kosovo during the night of March 19–20.

Only a day later, Serbian forces launched a major offensive in Kosovo and began driving thousands of ethnic Albanians out of their homes and villages. They summarily executed some Kosovars while displacing many others and setting fire to many houses. This Serbian offensive was named "Operation Horseshoe," and the scale of the resulting ethnic-cleansing campaign made it clear that it had to have been planned months in advance. As a result, tens of thousands of Albanian Kosovars fled their homes in the face of a systematic Serbian offensive.

Richard Holbrooke flew to Belgrade on March 22 in a last effort to persuade Milosevic to accept the terms of the Rambouillet Accords, but Milosevic refused. The talks failed to produce either a Serbian agreement or any delays in the growing Serbian military pressure on the Albanian Kosovars and Ambassador Holbrooke left the next day. This refusal, coupled to the increasing violence in Kosovo, led Javier Solana, the Secretary General of NATO, to consult with the NATO allies on March 23. He then told NATO's Supreme Allied Commander Europe (SACEUR), General Wesley Clark, to initiate air operations the same day. On March 24, NATO began the military campaign that became known as Operation Allied Force.

PEACE TALKS END IN WAR

Once again it is important to note that the West and NATO would almost certainly have failed to prevent the fighting in Kosovo regardless of what policies the West pursued. It is also clear that the West carried out a major effort to win support from the UN and Russia, and often had strong support from Secretary General Annan in its efforts to push both sides towards peace. At the same time, the West lacked the kind of unified international and UN support that might have confronted Serbia with a unified international community. Nothing the West could have done seems likely to have persuaded Russia not to tilt towards the Serbs or nations like China to support the principle of outside interference in internal ethnic quarrels.

Serbia's Grand Strategic and Tactical Mistakes

Serbia acted as it did for many reasons. The blind ambition of some of its leaders, the perceived weaknesses in the international community, the feeling that the Albanian Kosovars were conspiring against it, and because many Serbs truly believed in the justice of its cause and could not afford another defeat in dealing with Kosovar resistance for domestic political reasons. Serbia's leaders also seem to have drawn the conclusion from the diplomatic prelude to the war that the West and NATO were too divided to take sustained and decisive action. They concluded that Serbia could ride out the levels of force that NATO would bring against it, and that it could quickly achieve decisive military control of Kosovo.

Serbian commanders also seem to have misread the military situation on the ground in Kosovo. Serbia has scarcely been frank or open in discussing its side of the military planning that led to the conflict in Kosovo. Many Western intelligence experts, however, feel that Serbian military planners miscalculated the military situation in Kosovo as well as the seriousness of NATO's probable military response.[8] While some Serbian military officers strongly opposed a new confrontation with NATO, others greatly exacerbated the problem by exaggerating the "terrorist" nature of the KLA and creating unsubstantiated charges that it was a criminal organization that raised its funds by selling drugs.

More importantly, the Serbian military seem to have told Milosevic and the Serbian leadership that they could decisively defeat the KLA and bring total security to Kosovo in anywhere from 5–7 days to 2 weeks. Such a victory not only was militarily impossible—no guerrilla movement in history has ever been defeated so quickly—it created the military and political climate for an explosive effort at ethnic cleansing that had nothing to do with a focused campaign against the KLA. Once triggered, this mix of military action and ethnic cleansing was almost impossible to stop. As a result, the Serbian leadership and military combined grand strategic and tactical mistakes in a way that took on truly monumental proportions.

NATO's Blundering into Large-Scale War

The West and NATO ultimately has little choice in going to war other than ignoring the ethnic cleansing of hundreds of thousands of Kosovars. At the same time, NATO blundered into a massive ethnic conflict with inadequate diplomacy that made too many threats and took too little action. Its political leadership then operated under the military illusion that a limited number of focused air strikes could force a diplomacy based on political illusions to be successful.

NATO had a clear warning of what might happen in Kosovo based upon years of Serbian-sponsored ethnic cleansing in Bosnia. The ethnic cleansing and killing of up to 70,000 Muslim Bosnians in the UN "safe area" of Sebrenica in 1995 was only one tangible indication of how serious the fighting could become, and of the fragile and ineffective nature of agreements that were not backed by decisive force.

NATO also had clear reasons for preparing for a serious war if it was forced to act. These reasons were summarized concisely by US Secretary of Defense William Cohen, and were later included in virtually the same form in the Department of Defense report on the lessons of the war:[9]

The United States and its NATO allies had three strong interests at stake during the Kosovo crisis.

First, Serb aggression in Kosovo directly threatened peace throughout the Balkans and the stability of NATO's southeastern region. There was no natural boundary to this violence, which previously had moved from Slovenia to Croatia to Bosnia and then to Kosovo. Continued fighting in Kosovo threatened to: (a) scuttle the successful Dayton peace process in Bosnia; (b) re-ignite chaos in Albania; (c) destabilize the Former Yugoslav Republic of Macedonia, with its large Albanian minority; and (d) spill over into other neighboring countries, including Bulgaria and Greece. Instability in this region had the potential to exacerbate rivalries between Greece and Turkey, two NATO allies with significant and often distinct interests in Southern Europe.

Second, Belgrade's repression in Kosovo created a humanitarian crisis of staggering proportions. Dubbed "Operation Horseshoe" by the Serbs, this ethnic cleansing campaign was comprehensively planned months in advance by Milosevic as a brutal means to end the crisis on his terms by expelling and killing ethnic Albanians, overtaxing bordering nations' infrastructures, and fracturing the NATO alliance. NATO and other members of the international community responded to this crisis, preventing starvation and ensuring, ultimately, that the Kosovars could return safely to their homes.

Third, Milosevic's conduct leading up to Operation Allied Force directly challenged the credibility of NATO, an alliance that has formed the bedrock of transatlantic security for fifty years. The Federal Republic of Yugoslavia and the Republic of Serbia signed agreements in October 1998 that were to be verified by the Organization for Security and Cooperation in Europe (OSCE) and monitored by NATO. In the period leading up to March 1999, the FRY increasingly and flagrantly violated these agreements. Had NATO not eventually responded to these violations and other acts of the FRY, its own credibility, as well as the credibility of U.S. security commitments throughout the world, would have been called into question.

NATO did not fail to prepare for military action, but rather failed to prepare realistically for the level of conflict it might actually have to fight. NATO began to plan possible campaigns in June 1998, and produced some 40 different concepts of how to go to war before the fighting actually began. The US Department of Defense report on the lessons of the war describes this planning process as follows.[10]

Beginning in May 1998, internal NATO planning explored a wide range of military options, including the use of both air and ground forces to achieve NATO objectives. Target planning followed specific guidance provided by SACEUR and the North Atlantic Council, and continued to evolve with the dynamics of the situation in Kosovo.

. . . . In the early stages of NATO's operational planning for the Kosovo crisis, NATO considered a wide range of contingency planning options, including use of both air and ground forces, to achieve the alliance's objectives. In the period leading up to the initiation of the air campaign, there was not a consensus in the United States or the alliance to aggressively pursue planning for a ground force option in other than a permissive environment. At that time, we were exhausting all diplomatic initiatives while maintaining the credible threat of NATO air power. Following the failure to reach a settlement with the Serbs at Rambouillet and Paris, U.S. and allied leaders decided that execution of a phased air campaign was the best option for achieving our goals.

. . . . Military operations were originally planned to be prosecuted in five phases under NATO's operational plan, the development of which began in the summer of 1998. Phase 0 was the deployment of air assets into the European theater. Phase 1 would establish air superiority over Kosovo (creating a no-fly zone south of 44 degrees north latitude) and degrade command and control and the integrated air-defense system over the whole of the Federal Republic of Yugoslavia. Phase 2 would attack military targets in Kosovo and those Yugoslav forces south of 44 degrees north latitude, which were providing reinforcement to Serbian forces in Kosovo. This was to allow targeting of forces not only in Kosovo, but also in the Federal Republic of Yugoslavia south of Belgrade. Phase 3 would expand air operations against a wide range of high-value military and security force targets throughout the Federal Republic of Yugoslavia. Phase 4 would redeploy forces as required.

A Limited Air Response, relying predominantly on cruise missiles to strike selected targets throughout the Federal Republic of Yugoslavia, was developed as a stand-alone option. As originally planned, it was intended to be a short-notice, limited air response, to a serious, but limited incident in Kosovo, with the aim of preventing a further deterioration of the situation. The Limited Air Response was eventually integrated into Phase 1 of the air campaign. Within a few days of the start of NATO's campaign, alliance aircraft were striking both strategic and tactical targets throughout Serbia, as well as working to suppress and disrupt its integrated air defense system.

. . . On September 24, 1998, NATO Defense Ministers, meeting at Villamoura, Portugal, approved issuance of Activation Warnings for two different types of air operations. The first, a five-phased air operation, envisioned an air attack beginning with deployment of air assets and the suppression of enemy air defenses and moving through phases to ultimately eliminate major elements of Yugoslavian military and security force capability. The second option was known as the Limited Air Response and was designed to be a short notice, limited air response to a serious, but limited incident in Kosovo, with the aim of preventing a further deterioration of the situation. The Limited Air Response was eventually integrated into Phase 1 of the air campaign. As early as May 1998, well in advance of the activation warnings, planning staffs at all levels had initiated work to identify the classes, types, and specific characteristics of targets that would need to be attacked to meet the specific goals of these two alternatives.

The problem was that NATO should have realized that it faced the risk of having to fight a much larger scale war than it seriously considered. It also used to diplomacy to force a crisis point based on the threat of force, but failed to properly characterize that risk diplomacy might fail, and how serious the scale of the Serbian military response might be. As a result, NATO was unready to deal with the military realities that followed.[11]

Part of the reason for this failure was that NATO was deeply divided, and member countries simply were not prepared in peacetime to consider the costs of the kind of decisive military action that might have halted Serbian action or brought ethnic cleansing to an early end. NATO's analysis of the size of the land forces required to defeat the Serbian army during 1998 had called for a massive intervention by nearly two corps of land troops. This convinced virtually every member that the cost was too high both in terms of money and potential casualties. At the same time, overenthusiastic diplomats had concluded that a NATO show of diplomatic unity would be enough to force Serbian acceptance, or that only limited numbers of politically symbolic air and missile strikes would be required if diplomacy failed.

No one in NATO was prepared to employ decisive force when diplomacy failed. NATO had no on-the-scene military capability to deal with anything approaching a repetition of the ethnic conflict in Bosnia and initiate large-scale escalation of air and missile the moment it shifted to the use of force or even after massive ethnic cleansing began. Even the US side could not agree on the scale of strategic bombing that NATO should employ, and most European states took some time to gradually accept the need for the levels force necessary to deal with the fact it had made the wrong diplomatic diagnosis.

The end result was that NATO was not ready in terms of an agreed strategy for going to war, the number of aircraft deployed, full-scale targeting plans, and support capabilities It also publicly rejected the use of a ground option from the start. This inevitably weakened the credibility of the NATO threat to Serbia, and may well have convinced Milosevic that he could ride out a NATO air and missile campaign. NATO not only substituted gradual escalation for decisive force, it did not reserve the threat of decisive force are a credible option.

OPERATION ALLIED FORCE: THE AIR AND MISSILE CAMPAIGN

The NATO air and missile campaign in Kosovo began at 1400 EST (1900 GMT) on March 24. At this point, there were 112 US and 102 allied aircraft committed to the campaign, but only a relatively small number were "shooters" capable of delivering precision weapons effectively, particularly in poor weather or at night. NATO also had the US ships in the Adriatic capable of launching cruise missiles and one British submarine capable of launching cruise missiles.

The attacks began with air- and sea-launched cruise missiles that were targeted largely on air defense and communications targets. Two B-2 "stealth" bombers flew 30-hour missions from Whiteman Air Force Base in Missouri to drop Joint Direct Attack Munitions—an all-weather system with global positioning satellite (GPS) guidance. NATO tactical aircraft flew combat air patrol (CAP) and attack missions.[12]

The strikes began under the assumption that, using limited numbers of cruise missiles and air strikes, could rapidly force Serbia to concede in a short campaign of no more than 12 days.[13] While NATO never officially admitted how limited a campaign it initially planned for during the war—and NATO spokespersons repeatedly dodged questions on the subject—the Department of Defense report on the lesson of the war is more frank.[14]

As the peace talks broke down, the Supreme Allied Commander Europe directed that a new option separate from previous plans be developed. This option was envisioned to be a 2-day strike, hitting targets throughout the Federal Republic of Yugoslavia in an attempt to convince Milosevic to withdraw his forces and cease hostilities. This option was eventually translated into a list of specific targets. In addition to this option, planners developed two responses to Yugoslav actions that might follow strikes on these targets. The two options ultimately settled on were, first, a potential response to Yugoslav forces' acts of repression against the Kosovar Albanians, and, second, a response to Yugoslav attacks against NATO forces or countries. The limited 2-day strike with its two response options became the basis for new planning activities. During this time, the Secretary of Defense and the Chairman of the Joint Chiefs of Staff repeatedly cautioned allied leaders that the limited duration options would not guarantee success, and that NATO should not initiate these strikes unless the alliance was willing to escalate, if necessary, and persist until victory was secured.

As the US report all points out, this tenuous approach to war did not last for more than a few days. NATO was forced to rush into massive escalation, and was forced to take a completely new approach to the conflict by mid-April.[15]

Within a few days of the start of NATO's campaign, alliance aircraft were striking targets throughout Serbia, as well as working to provide freedom of maneuver for friendly air forces by suppressing and disrupting the Yugoslavs' integrated air defense system. At the NATO Summit in Washington on 23 April 1999, alliance leaders decided to further intensify the air operation by expanding the target set to include military-industrial infrastructure, propaganda-related media, and other strategic targets, and announcing the deployment of additional aircraft. This led to the development of additional target classes.

NATO began the campaign with only 50 pre-approved military targets—including air defense facilities, communications relays, storage deports, and ammunition dumps.[16] It then had to improvise a massive escalation involving a wide range of strategic, interdiction, and tactical targets throughout Serbia to stop a major Serbian military campaign that combined an all-out attack on the KLA with ethnic cleansing throughout Kosovo.

As a result, the size and impact of the initial NATO strikes bordered on tokenism. No targets of any major political significance were hit. NATO lacked the initial air strength to either inflict major damage on the FRY forces in Serbia proper or to strike hard at the Serbian forces in the field and limit ethnic cleansing. Weather made the problem worse, as did the lack of advanced sensor coverage and proper targeting. Serbia was already involved in a major war.

The Phases and Non-Phases of the Air and Missile Campaign

The initial phases of the NATO campaign were dominated by US missile and air power. The US had virtually all of NATO advanced intelligence, surveillance, electronic warfare, targeting, damage assessment, and battle management assets. It was the only NATO nation capable of launching significant numbers of cruise missiles, although Britain had a limited submarine-launch capability. It was also the only NATO power equipped and trained for demanding all-weather precision air strike capabilities. All-weather strike capability proved to be a critical mission capability during the early weeks of the campaign.

As a result, the US launched over 90% of the cruise missiles, and most of the actual strike sorties during the first month of the campaign. A number of European air forces lacked interoperable communications, secure communications to handle targeting information, and the sensors and avionics to deliver precision guided munitions in poor weather. This slow beginning helps explain why the US eventually flew half of the combat sorties, well over half of the strike sorties, and two-thirds of the support sorties during the 78 days of active fighting.[17]

As time went on, however, the fighting broadened to become a major multinational campaign that employed combat aircraft from 14 different countries. Belgium, Denmark, Netherlands, Norway, and Portugal contributed F-16s. The French Air Force flew Jaguars and Mirage aircraft, and Germany and Italy flew Tornadoes. Canada, Spain and Turkey contributed fighter jets, and the UK flew both Tornadoes and Royal Air Force and Royal Navy variants of the Harrier. These aircraft operated together under common command in fully integrated packages. U.S. and European early-warning aircraft provided protection, and their endurance was enhanced by air-to-air refueling aircraft that enabled NATO attacks to fly deep into the heart of Serbia and Kosovo.

During the war, NATO talked as if this build-up occurred in smooth phases and according to some orderly plan. Figure 1 shows a NATO summary of these phases in the war, but such distinctions are nominal, contradictory, and misleading. NATO did not execute a campaign that it had carefully planned before the fighting began; it improvised.

This was not the result of a lack of military foresight and planning. As has been touched upon earlier, the staff of SACEUR General Wesley Clark examined as

Figure 1
The Phases of the NATO Air and Missile War

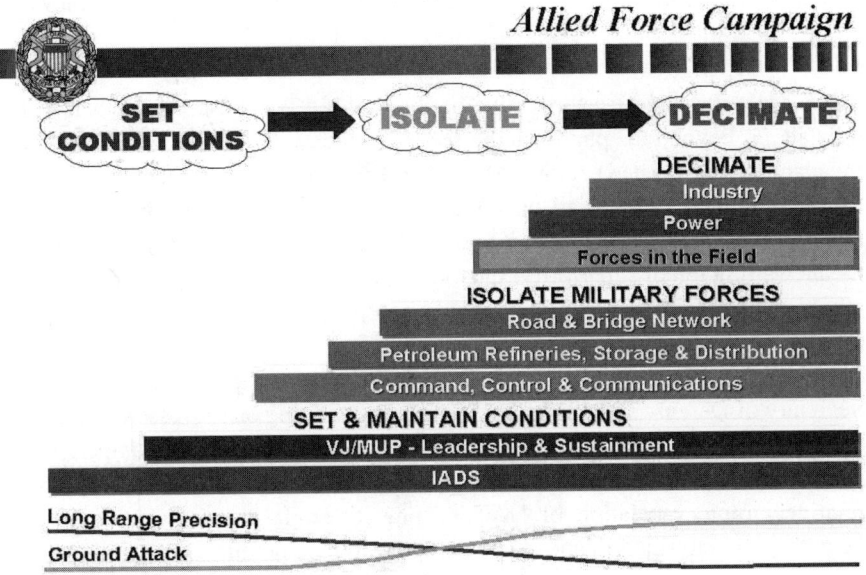

Source: Adapted from the Department of Defense press briefing for June 10, 1999.

many as 40 attack options before the fighting began. At the moment the war began, however, NATO's leadership had been debating two major options for going to war based on gradual escalation and the these that NATO did not face a serious conflict.

- One called for a limited air and missile response striking at fixed military targets such as headquarters, communications facilities, and ammunition and supply depots in a process of gradual escalation similar to the targets struck in Bosnia during Operation Deliberate Force in 1995.

- The other called for a phased air operation that would hit targets in Serbia to persuade the Serbs to negotiate and strike at Serbian operations in Kosovo to halt ethnic cleansing. This plan was phased to begin by creating air superiority over Serbia, Montenegro, and Kosovo (the three geographic regions of the FRY), then extend the strikes throughout the target area in proportion to the need to use force to coerce Serbia to accept NATO's terms.[18] *Phase 0* involved the deployment of air assets into the European theater. *Phase 1* was to establish air superiority over Kosovo (creating a no-fly zone south of 44 degrees north latitude) and degrade command and control and the integrated air-defense system over the whole of the Federal Republic of Yugoslavia. *Phase 2* was to attack military targets in Kosovo and those Yugoslav forces south of 44 degrees north latitude, which were providing reinforcement to Serbian forces in Kosovo. This was to allow targeting of forces not only in Kosovo, but also in the Federal Republic of Yugoslavia south of Belgrade. *Phase 3* was to expand air operations against a wide range of high-value military and security force targets throughout the Federal Republic of Yugoslavia. *Phase 4* would redeploy forces as required.

It was the first and least effective option that NATO chose, and it then had to escalate far beyond the phases in the second, which was more of an outgrowth of the planning NATO had begun in May 1998. Even NATO's phased battle plan was totally unrealistic and relied on a remarkable degree of passivity from a force already involved in ethnic cleaning. It ignored preparing for a ground option, meant waiting for air superiority, and did not take account of the risk of large-scale ethnic cleansing or that Milosevic would accept significant losses and try to ride out the NATO attacks.[19]

Neither NATO plan had much chance of surviving engagement with the enemy. Secretary of Defense Cohen made this clear in testifying on the lessons of Kosovo to the Congress, and it is interesting to note that he describes a campaign with slightly different phases from the one NATO summarizes in Figure 1, and a relatively rapid escalation of NATO's objectives. It is somewhat ironic that Secretary Cohen still talks about a five phase war, but does not even mention *Phase 0* and names only four phases.[20]

At the outset of the air campaign, NATO set specific strategic objectives for its use of force in Kosovo that later served as the basis for its stated conditions to Milosevic for stopping the bombing. These objectives were to: Demonstrate the seriousness of NATO's opposition to Belgrade's aggression in the Balkans; Deter Milosevic from continuing and escalating his attacks on helpless civilians and create conditions to reverse his ethnic cleansing; and Damage Serbia's capacity to wage war against Kosovo in the future or spread the war to neighbors by diminishing or degrading its ability to wage military operations. Although there were expectations on the part of some that this would be a short campaign, we made clear to our allied counterparts that Operation Allied Force could well take weeks or months to succeed and that the operation should only be initiated if all were willing to persevere until success was achieved.

Alliance leaders agreed in advance that if the initial strikes did not attain NATO's goals, NATO would have to persist and indeed expand its air campaign.

Operation Allied Force was originally planned to be prosecuted in five phases under NATO's operational plan, the development of which began in the summer of 1998. Phase 0 was the deployment of air assets into the European theater. Phase 1 would establish air superiority over Kosovo and degrade command and control over the whole of the FRY. Phase 2 would attack military targets in Kosovo and those FRY forces south of 44 degrees north latitude, which were providing reinforcement to Serbian forces into Kosovo. This was to allow targeting of forces not only in Kosovo, but also in the FRY south of Belgrade. Phase 3 would expand air operations against a wide range of high-value military and security force targets throughout the FRY. Phase 4 would redeploy forces as required. A limited air response relying predominantly on cruise missiles to strike selected targets throughout the FRY was developed as a stand-alone option, and was integrated into Phase 1.

Within a few days of the start of NATO's campaign, alliance aircraft were striking both strategic and tactical targets throughout Serbia, as well as working to suppress and disrupt the FRY's integrated air defense system. At the NATO Summit in Washington on April 23, 1999, alliance leaders decided to further intensify the air campaign by expanding the target set to include military-industrial infrastructure, media, and other strategic targets and announcing the deployment of additional aircraft.

The alliance also clearly outlined its political conditions to end the operation. As proclaimed in the NATO Statement on Kosovo, President Milosevic had to: Ensure a verifiable stop to all military action and the immediate end of violence and repression in Kosovo; Withdraw from Kosovo his military, police, and paramilitary forces; Agree to the stationing in Kosovo of an international military presence; Agree to the unconditional and safe return of all refugees and displaced persons, and unhindered access to them by humanitarian aid organizations; and Provide credible assurance of his willingness to work for the establishment of a political framework based on the Rambouillet accords.

The Road to Escalation

Once the process of escalation began, there was a continuing debate between NATO's political and military leaders over what to target and how fast to escalate, and senior NATO military planners called for a much more intense campaign than NATO's political leadership originally approved. For example, the NATO campaign did not reflect the thinking of Lt. General Michael Short, NATO's joint force air component commander in the Balkans. Lt. General Short had strongly recommended that a strategic campaign involving the decisive use of strategic bombing against Belgrade be launched at the outset of the war—somewhat similar to the campaign that the Coalition had launched against Iraq during the first day of the Gulf War.

The NATO alliance could not reach agreement on anything approaching this level of force, however, and the first day of NATO air and missile strikes only hit 53 targets, largely air defenses and radar sites. The strikes were designed more to show Serbia that it was vulnerable than to do major damage.[21] As General Short put it later, "It was not just apparent at the three star level that we were not following the classic air campaign. . . . It was just as apparent at the captain and major level that we were not using airpower the way we would have wished to use it."[22]

The strategy advocated by the NATO Supreme Allied Commander Europe (SACEUR), General Wesley K. Clark, also called for more intensive air strikes from the start—although Clark is later quoted as saying he thought there was a 40% chance the war would end within three days. Clark emphasized strikes on Serbian ground forces and the units involved in ethnic cleansing rather than relying on

strategic bombing. As a result, Clark pushed for both a rapid escalation of the attacks on targets in Belgrade and Serbia and for intensive air strikes on Yugoslav forces in the field, with a ground invasion as a back up.

While Clark and Short never reached mutual agreement during the campaign over the relative priority of strikes on Serbian ground forces versus strategic targets in Belgrade and Serbia proper, Clark did succeed in persuading NATO Secretary General Javier Solana to skip directly from Phase 1 to Phase 2, in spite of considerable reservations within some European countries and parts of the US State Department. From March 27 onwards, Clark also pressed for NATO to attack as many targets each night as it could hit, and he strongly opposed efforts to create a diplomatic pause in the bombing.

Much of the rationale for Clark's continuing efforts to escalate lay in the fact the sheer scale of the Serbian attack on Kosovo, and the intensity of Serbian ethnic cleansing, took NATO by surprise. While Serbia did not defeat the KLA in detail, it was successful enough to reduce it to limited pockets of organized resistance by April 3. Equally important, the number of refugees had increased from 210,000–240,000 to 500,000–600,000, and it was clear they would rapidly reach one million. While there was no way to accurately estimate ethnic murders, it was clear that the VJ and MUP had sharply stepped up their burnings and executions. Serbia was well on the way to creating "facts on the ground" little more than a week after the NATO campaign began.

Clark is reported having said at a NATO planning conference on March 27 that, "I don't want to get into something like the Rolling Thunder campaign, pecking away indefinitely. . . . We got to steadily ratchet up the pressure. . . . We also need to become increasingly relevant to the situation on the ground. Otherwise we are a risk of being paused indefinitely. We'll lose public support."[23] Clark seems to have successfully convinced Solana of the merits of his position on March 28, but did not have immediate success in convincing the North Atlantic Council (NAC) at a special meeting on March 30. The NAC instead left the decision to Solana, who gave Clark necessary authority several days later.

Expanding the Target Base and Scale of Military Action

For this time on, weather, initial limitations on the numbers of aircraft and cruise missiles, and political constraints on targeting did far more to shape the "phases" of the war than any strategic plan. The sheer scale of Serbian ethnic cleansing operations forced NATO to steadily expand the number and range of "strategic" targets. NATO also had to build-up to conduct a massive interdiction campaign against Serbian military facilities, resupply, and forces in the field. As the weather improved, strike aircraft flew lower, sortie rates rose, and more was made of "dumb" weapons launched by "smart" delivery platforms. As NATO increased the size of the force engaged, it had to steadily expand its basing, including the use of bases in Hungary and Turkey. At the same time, NATO did not face a major opponent and did not have to wait for air superiority to attack any category of target.

The range of targets NATO was allowed to attack also expanded. By early to mid-April, NATO's political leadership allowed them to include national command and control facilities; infrastructure including bridges; petroleum, oil, and lubricants (POL), central communications facilities, military factories and repair facilities, distribution systems. The electric power grid was added later. They also included targets related to Serbian forces, including assembly areas, key bridges in southern Serbia and Kosovo, command and control nodes, supply areas, POL pumping and storage facilities, and ammunition storage.

The initial broadening of targets focused on targets south of the 44th parallel, but was expanded to include targets north of the line.[24] The actual choice of target was often determined by a combination of politics and weather, however, and the weather problem was so severe in parts of April that the air and missile attacks came to a virtual halt. Nations like France vetoed some strikes while the aircraft were in flight and political review of sensitive targets took place on a case by case basis. Freedom of action in broadening the target list in no way ensured freedom of action in actual hitting the target.

NATO tacitly declared the death of its original war plans at the NATO Summit in Washington on April 23, 1999. The alliance leaders formally decided to further intensify the air campaign by expanding the target set to include military-industrial infrastructure, media responsible for promulgating propaganda, and other strategic targets, and by announcing the deployment of additional aircraft.[25]

At the same time, a series of political and diplomatic events and crises unfolded which also shaped the course of the campaign. These included the following events:

- *April 1*: Serbian forces capture three US soldiers in the Former Yugoslav Republic of Macedonia.
- *April 3*: NATO missiles strike central Belgrade for the first time and destroy the Yugoslav and Serbian interior ministries.
- *April 6*: The Federal Republic of Yugoslavia declares a unilateral cease-fire to commence at 1200 EDT and last until 1800 EDT.
- *April 11*: Belgrade claims that all FRY army and police actions in Kosovo would end and that the government is ready to negotiate with Rugova. NATO rejects the offer, with French President Chirac calls the proposed cease-fire indefensible without a political agreement and security package.
- *April 6–10*: The NAC approves the Concept of Operations and the Operations Plan for Allied Harbor, the NATO humanitarian effort in Albania.
- *April 10*: In discussion with the Organization for Security and Cooperation in Europe (OSCE), Russian Foreign Minister Ivanov says that a NATO-led Kosovo implementation force is "unrealistic" and calls for greater UN involvement.

- *April 14*: Germany unveils a plan for a 24-hour halt to the air strikes to give the FRY a chance to start pulling out of Kosovo. Russian President Yeltsin names former Prime Minister Chernomyrdin as his FRY peace envoy.

- *April 16*: The NAC approves the Activation Order for Operation Allied Harbor.

- *April 20*: U.S. Representative James Saxton meets with FRY Foreign Minister Jovanovic in Belgrade.

- *April 21*: All EU countries agree to back a proposed plan to stop oil product deliveries by or through member states to the FRY. NATO missiles in Belgrade hit the headquarters of Milosevic's Serbian Socialist Party and his private residence, both believed to have capability for command and control of VJ/MUP forces.

- *April 22*: At the NATO Summit, Alliance nations reaffirm the conditions that would bring an end to the air campaign. They also announce an intensification of the air campaign.

- *April 23*: NATO attacks the Serbian state television building in central Belgrade, a facility used for propaganda purposes. The FRY agrees to accept an international military presence in Kosovo after Chernomyrdin-Milosevic talks in Belgrade.

- *April 30*: The Reverend Jesse Jackson arrives in Belgrade and meets with the US servicemen that had been held captive by Serb forces for the past month. Russian envoy Chernomyrdin reports "progress" after 6 hours of talks with Milosevic in Belgrade.

- *May 1*: President Clinton extends U.S. sanctions to ban oil sales and freeze Belgrade's assets in the U.S. Following an agreement with NATO and FRY authorities on modalities, the ICRC announces plans to return to Kosovo. Reverend Jackson secures the release of the captured servicemen following a 3-hour meeting with Milosevic.

- *May 6*: At the Group of Eight meeting in Bonn, the West and Russia announce agreement over the basic strategy to resolve the conflict.

- *May 7*: NATO planes accidentally hit the Chinese Embassy in Belgrade, killing 3 and wounding 20.

- *May 8*: The UNSC convenes in an emergency session to debate the bombing of the Chinese Embassy. China implicitly accuses the U.S. and NATO of a deliberate attack while the Alliance apologizes for a "terrible mistake." Thousands demonstrate in front of U.S. diplomatic posts in China. Russian Foreign Minister Ivanov cancels his trip to London in the wake of the attack.

- *May 9*: President Clinton writes to Chinese President Jiang Zemin to offer regrets for the bombing, while Chinese demonstrations continued.

- *May 10*: Chinese demonstrations continue for a third day. China suspends contacts with the U.S. regarding arms control and human rights. Serbs announce a partial withdrawal from Kosovo. The FRY accuses NATO of genocide and demands that the World Court order an immediate end to NATO air strikes.

- *May 11*: Russian envoy Chernomyrdin meets with President Jiang Zemin in Beijing and labels the Chinese embassy bombing an act of aggression. China hints that it might hold up Western attempts to achieve a peace deal at the UN unless the bombing stops. NATO disputes FRY claims of a troop withdrawal from Kosovo, countering that FRY military and police have actually stepped up their actions against the KLA.

- *May 16*: Italian Prime Minister D'Alema proposes a NATO cease-fire on condition that Russia and China support a UNSC resolution imposing the G-8 terms on Milosevic.
- *May 17*: The EU announces that Finnish President Martti Ahtisaari will serve as the EU's new senior Kosovo envoy. The Greeks calls for a temporary cease-fire "to give diplomacy a chance."
- *May 23*: NATO began a bombing campaign of the Yugoslav electricity grid, creating a major disruption of power, creating a major disruption of power affecting many military related activities and water supplies.
- *May 27*: Milosevic and four other Serbian leaders are indicted by the UN War Crimes Tribunal (ICTY) for crimes against humanity.

NATO's Changing Objectives

While NATO initially had to react to ethnic cleansing without setting formal objectives for the air and missile campaign, NATO countries did agree on such objectives in April. NATO's objectives for the conflict in Kosovo were set out in the statement issued at the Extraordinary Meeting of the North Atlantic Council held at NATO on April 12, 1999 and were reaffirmed by Heads of State and Government in Washington on April 23, 1999. These objectives included

- A verifiable stop to all military action and the immediate ending of violence and repression;
- The withdrawal from Kosovo of the military, police and paramilitary forces;
- The stationing in Kosovo of an international military presence;
- The unconditional and safe return of all refugees and displaced persons and unhindered access to them by humanitarian aid organizations; and
- The establishment of a political framework agreement for Kosovo on the basis of the Rambouillet Accords, in conformity with international law and the Charter of the United Nations.

NATO's public goals were further refined when its heads of state and government held NATO's 50th anniversary summit meeting in Washington on April 25, 1999—although NATO never disclosed that some of its members were seriously considering a ground option. The heads of state discussed these goals, and met with the leaders of the countries bordering Kosovo including Bulgarian President Petar Stoyanov, Bosnian Foreign Minister Jadranko Prlic and Albanian President Rexhap Meidani. They established a process of individual consultations and discussions between the nineteen NATO countries and the countries of the region on a 19+1 basis and undertook to promote regional cooperation within the Euro-Atlantic Partnership Council (EAPC).

NATO's heads of state agreed to use the resources of the Partnership for Peace (PfP) to provide more direct and focussed assistance in addressing their security concerns. The Alliance also welcomed related measures being taken in other forums. These included the European Union proposal to convene a conference on a stability pact for southeastern Europe at the end of May 1999, recognizing the role of the G7 group of countries, and recognizing the role of financial institutions, like the World Bank and the International Monetary Fund, in the process of reconstruction which would have to follow the end of the Kosovo crisis.

NATO Moves Towards Decisive Force

Equally important, NATO agreed behind the scenes to go on with a full scale air campaign. Roughly one month after the beginning of the NATO air and missile campaign, NATO planners were given enough freedom of action to begin to apply decisive force. They also covertly began to seriously examine a ground option. The full effect of these decisions could not be tested until mid-May, however, because of weather. Late April continued to present weather problems that did not moderate until May 11. Good weather did not occur until late in the week of May 15–21.

At the same time, NATO operations were increasingly complicated by relief operations, which sometimes forced NATO to give air support of the relief operation priority over the combat effort. Tirana airport for example, was soon handling four times its planned load in C-17 shipments, and the relief effort—Operation Shining Hope—had already delivered over one million humanitarian rations by late April. The European relief effort was substantially larger, and involved a significant ground presence and sealift.

The weight of operations shifted strikingly after May 21. Although NATO had placed further political limits on targets in Serbia after a US B-2 hit the Chinese embassy in Belgrade on May 7, NATO forces were growing steadily and NATO had already destroyed all of the most important targets in Belgrade. There were 323 US and 212 allied strike aircraft in the theater by mid-May, and the shift in weather after May 18 allowed NATO to strike at Serbian forces in the field with growing effectiveness.

As a result, NATO damage assessment experts estimated that NATO more than doubled the number of tanks hit in the 10 days after May 22, tripled the number of other armored vehicles, and quadrupled the number of artillery weapons.[26] At the same time, the KLA launched an offensive, Operation Arrow, out of Albania. While this offensive was not particularly successful it both demonstrated that

Serbia had not been successful in destroying the KLA and forced Serbian units to concentrate in ways that made them more vulnerable to air power. There are still serious debates over the extent of Serbian losses, but Serbia almost certainly did take significant additional losses in the field. It had already taken major losses to its military facilities and production capabilities. Its economy was crippled by the loss of road, rail, and river traffic, shortages in POL, and interruptions in its power grid.

Ending the Air and Missile Campaign

These growing pressures helped put an end to what became a 78-day campaign in which NATO was locked in a war of attrition with Serbia in which NATO air and missile power was pitted against Serbian air and ground forces. General Shelton, the Chairman of the US Joint Chiefs of Staff, summarized the course of the air and missile campaign as follows at his press conference on June 10, 1999:

Many outside experts have criticized the NATO military campaign for being incremental or ruling out ground forces. And while it's true that U.S. military doctrine is geared toward hitting an adversary hard from the very start, it is also true in this instance that the strategy that NATO adopted, which was a phased air and missile campaign, increasing the frequency and the intensity of our air operations and our air strikes to reduce the Serb forces' capabilities, was successful. Successful first at achieving the military objective of disrupting and destroying a large number of Serb military equipment and facilities; and successful, ultimately, in setting the conditions for the achievement of the Alliance's overall policy objectives.

.... we basically started off with setting the conditions for the campaign, isolating the Serb forces, and then finally moving into the decimation phase. As we've talked from the beginning, we started off with the integrated air defense system, part of setting and maintaining the conditions to allow us to operate in what was a very robust, multi-layered air defense system, and at the same time starting to hit the leadership and sustainment targets for the VJ and the MUP.

Then we moved up into command and control, communications, petroleum, the roads and bridges as part of starting to isolate, to reduce his capabilities to be able to move about the battlefield, to sustain himself, or to move laterally to reinforce.

Then moving into the forces in the field. These two were shown as classified the last time you saw it, I think, but then ultimately going to the power and the industry. The power that would enable us to bring down some of his command and control, to reduce his military industrial facilities at the same time, as well as the integrated air defense. Finally, the industry that could allow him to sustain himself in some of these areas. So we started to attack the military industrial complex, and I'll show you the success of that in just a second. Of course, this is the phase we were in when the operation was suspended.

We started off initially, as you know, with long-range precision—TALCM, TLAMS, and then went [to] precision weapons brought in by the bombers including the B-2 from the United States. Then as we in further reduced his ability to operate, or increased our own ability to operate effectively in this integrated air defense system, we started bringing in more of the additional traditional types of fighters to continue to take it to him in each of these areas. That was the strategy from the beginning. That was the strategy we followed.

It should be noted that several of NATO's most senior commanders disagree with the idea that there was a smooth and orderly pattern to the escalation of the air campaign. In fact, the US Department of Defense has formally admitted to this fact in its report on the lessons of the war. These officers have said that political decisions prevented NATO from massing the air power that military officers requested, that France and several other NATO countries put political limits on the number and nature of the sorties flown early in the war, and that political constraints on targeting played a major role in limiting the impact of air strikes in creating the kind of "shock" and "compellance" that might have led to an earlier resolution of the war.

Nevertheless, the NATO air and missile campaign clearly did succeed in doing steadily greater damage to Serbian military capabilities during May and early June and made Serbian operations in Kosovo increasingly more difficult, which had a major impact on the Serbian economy.

Why Serbia Conceded

The success of the NATO campaign was one of four major reasons that Serbia was ultimately force to concede. These factors included

- The damage done by NATO air and missile power and NATO's continuing ability to attack any target with little or no loss,
- The fact Serbia alienated most of the world by its ethnic cleansing activities and lost all meaningful outside political support. Once Russia joined NATO in pressing for a peace settlement on terms that offered Serbia no hope of outside aid or that the world would learn to tolerate ethnic cleansing,
- Serbia's inability to defeat the ground operations of the Kosovo Liberation Army without exposing its forces to devastating air attack, and,
- The prospect that NATO would pursue a ground option if NATO air and missile power did not achieve decisive results regardless of denials that a ground option would take place by many senior officials in various NATO countries.

It is interesting to note that both the British and US governments stated that the impact of the air and missile campaign was only one important factor in bringing an end to the conflict in their respective analyses of the lessons of the war. Furthermore, neither government felt it was able to judge precisely why Serbia conceded.

The British Ministry of Defense provides the following estimate of the reasons why Milosevic conceded:[27]

Why did Milosevic concede? There is no simple answer, but a number of factors must have played a part. First, and contrary to his calculations, NATO unity, and that of the international community as a whole, including Russia and the other Balkan states, actually strengthened as the crisis and the air campaign continued. Second, the continued increase in tempo of the air operations, and the huge damage and disruption they caused to his forces' operations, was a highly significant factor. Third, his indictment by the International Criminal Tribunal for the Former Yugoslavia would have added to the psychological pressure on him. And, finally, the increasing pace of the build-up of ground troops in neighboring countries, and the announcement, underlined at the NATO Summit, that planning for all options including an opposed entry was continuing, must have played a part in convincing Milosevic that the only alternative to accepting NATO's terms was an even worse outcome for him. The Russians played an important part in bringing home to Milosevic the seriousness with which NATO was preparing and deploying its ground troops. Those troops eventually entered Kosovo on an agreed basis, but no doubt, in his decision to concede, Milosevic took into account the potential for them to form the nucleus of a force capable of entering despite opposition.

Secretary Cohen and General Shelton's report to Congress on the lessons of the war provides a broader list of reasons, but its focus is roughly similar to the British report.[28] Once again, the Department of Defense used virtually the same text in its report on the lessons of the war:[29]

Because many pressures were brought to bear, we can never be certain about what caused Milosevic to accept NATO's conditions to stop the bombing and instruct the Serbian military to sign the Military Technical Agreement with NATO embodying those conditions. Clearly, the mounting damage that resulted from the intensified air campaign against strategic, military-industrial infrastructure, and national command and control targets, as well as the attacks against Milosevic's fielded forces in Kosovo and Serbia's utter inability to cause any notable damage or casualties to NATO forces, had a major impact on Milosevic's decision.

However, other factors were also at work. First, the solidarity of the alliance was central in compelling Belgrade to accept NATO's conditions. Because Milosevic could not defeat NATO militarily, his best hope lay in splitting the alliance politically. Thus, it was not enough for NATO simply to concentrate on winning a military victory; at the heart of allied strategy was building and sustaining the unity of the alliance. NATO maintained its resolve even in the face of potential setbacks as serious as the inadvertent Chinese Embassy bombing and isolated incidents of unintended collateral damage and civilian causalities, and it became clear that Milosevic could not undermine NATO's unity and purpose.

Second, the alliance's continuous efforts to engage Russia in diplomacy proved critical to achieving the settlement. While Russia strongly opposed the air campaign, it sharply limited its practical support to the FRY and was prepared to work with the alliance diplomatically to end the conflict. The Russians agreed that the refugees should return, that Serb forces should leave, and that some form of international security force with NATO at its core needed to be deployed to Kosovo. When Finnish President Ahtisaari and Russian Special Envoy

Chernomyrdin met with Milosevic in Belgrade and spoke with one voice, Milosevic realized that he had become politically isolated and could expect no help from Russia.

Third, the buildup of NATO ground combat power in the region (e.g., Task Force Hawk in Albania, allied peace implementation forces in the Former Yugoslav Republic of Macedonia, and visible preparations for the deployment of additional forces), combined with the increasing public discussion of the possibility of and planning for the use of ground forces, undoubtedly contributed to Milosevic's calculations that NATO would prevail at all costs.

Fourth, the persistent military efforts of the Kosovar Albanians in the face of significant setbacks, particularly their resurgence in the latter weeks of the campaign—demonstrated to Milosevic that he would not be able to eliminate this threat.

Finally, NATO nations employed other economic and political means, enforcing economic sanctions, tightening travel restrictions, freezing financial holdings, that raised the level of anxiety and discontent within Belgrade's power circles.

In addition, the indictment of Milosevic by the international war crimes tribunal certainly helped persuade his most powerful supporters that the international political consensus against Serbia's actions would continue to strengthen rather than weaken. In sum, these factors all played important roles in the settlement of the crisis.

Estimates of the Overall Impact of the Air and Missile Campaign

Regardless of the exact reasons that Serbia withdrew, it is clear that many aspects of the NATO campaign were successful. By the end of the campaign, NATO succeeded in flying well over intensive combat missions over 78 days without suffering any casualties in combat, having lost a maximum of two aircraft to hostile fire, and without any losses to accidents or fratricide, weather, or problems in battle management.[30] The formal end to the campaign took place on the day that all Serbian forces withdrew from Kosovo.

While the success of NATO's strikes remains controversial, NATO claimed that it had destroyed over 80 percent of Yugoslavia's modern fighters and strategic surface-to-air missiles. It claimed to have severely crippled the Serbian military forces in Kosovo by destroying more than 50 percent of the artillery and more than one-third of their armored vehicles. A pause in bombing after the 79th day meant that these statistics still applied when the air and missile war was formally ended on June 20, 1999.

The debate over the precise count of Serbian vehicles destroyed during the war still continues, but the final estimates of the NATO and US team that investigated wartime claims after the war confirmed 93 direct tank kills after the war, with a suspected total of 181. It confirmed 13 direct other armored vehicle kills after the war, with a suspected total of 317. The figures for military vehicles were 339 direct kills and a suspected total of 800. The data for artillery and mortars were 389 direct kills and a suspected total of 857.[31]

NATO also claimed to have destroyed a significant share of the infrastructure Yugoslavia used to support its military, to have reduced Serbia's capacity to make ammunition by two-thirds, and to have eliminated all of Serbia's oil refining capacity and more than 40 percent of its military fuel supplies. Serbia reported that NATO damaged or destroyed 24 bridges, 12 railway stations, 36 factories, seven airports, 16 fuel plants and storage depots, 17 television transmitters, and several electrical facilities.[32] A later reassessment by the US Department of Defense, that was issued in January 2000, stated that NATO had destroyed or significantly damaged 11 railroad bridges, 34 highway bridges, twenty-nine percent of all Serbian ammunition storage, fifty-seven percent of petroleum reserves, all Yugoslav oil refineries, 14 command posts, over 100 aircraft, and 10 military airfields.[33]

INCREASES IN NATO FORCES AND LEVELS OF EFFORT

All nineteen NATO countries made some political, military, or economic contribution to Operation Allied Force by the end of the air and missile campaign. These countries include Belgium, Canada, Czech Rep, Denmark, France, Germany, Greece, Hungary, Iceland, Italy, Luxembourg, The Netherlands, Norway, Poland, Portugal, Spain, Turkey, United Kingdom, and the United States.

NATO deployed a total of some 27,000 men on the ground, and US alone had a total of 31,600 personnel committed to the operation, including 18,400 ashore and 13,200 at sea. While air and missile power dominated the campaign, NATO deployed significant ground forces in Albania and Macedonia, as well as significant naval forces.

NATO Naval Forces

During the air and missile campaign, NATO aircraft were supported at sea by some 20 naval ships within the environs of the Adriatic. They included aircraft carriers from the United Kingdom, France and the United States, which also provide further air combat assets. The NATO Standing Force (Mediterranean) provides 9 vessels from 8 countries.

From late April on, there were three carrier task forces in the area: The HMS *Invincible*, the US *Theodore Roosevelt*, and the French *Foch*. There were six US ships that could launch cruise missiles plus a British submarine, the HMS *Splendid*, with a total of 460 cruise missile cells in the surface and submarine based force, 358 of which were in the Roosevelt battle group and 90 in the US surface action group with the USS *Gonzales*. US and British ships launched many of the 329 cruise missiles, which allowed NATO to attack any target in Serbia without risking a manned aircraft.

The French carrier task force led by the *Foch* was in the area when the fighting began and stayed until June 1. It included the aircraft carrier *Foch* (with 14–16

Super Etendards, 4 Etendard IVPs, and 2 Super Frelon Helicopters), the frigates *Montcalm* and *Surcouf*, and the fuel and replenishment ship *L'Amethyste*. There was one nuclear attack submarine; first the *Saphir* and then the *Amethyste*. In mid-February, the carrier group was reinforced by the French frigates *Cassard* and *Turville*, and the British frigate *Somerset*. There were roughly 2,400 personnel about the task force.[34]

Table 1 shows the number of major combat ships that the US Department of Defense reported were deployed on May 13 (Day 50).

NATO Aircraft Numbers

The number of NATO aircraft rose sharply over time, as did the number of "shooters" and NATO sortie rates. The broad trend in US and allied forces is shown in Figure 2. The total number of aircraft rose from 334 aircraft in Europe (214 US and 130 allied) on March 24 (Day 1), to 550 aircraft on April 13 (Day 20). It then to rose 700 on April 27 (Day 34). The total number of strike-attack aircraft rose from 120 on March 24, to 250 aircraft on April 13, and then to 340 on April 27.[35]

As a result, the total number of aircraft committed nearly doubled during the first month of the air and missile war, and the total number of strike aircraft nearly tripled. Strike aircraft rose from 30 percent of the force at the beginning of the campaign to nearly 50 percent of the force on April 27. NATO reported that it had roughly 1,000 aircraft engaged by May 7, about one-third of which were now "shooters." It reported that it was in the process of deploying enough aircraft to raise this total to well over 1,100. The US reported on May 6 that a total of 916 aircraft were deployed, with 639 US aircraft and 277 allied planes. As of May 26, the US had deployed 717 aircraft, including 309 fighter/bomber, 261 support, 44 reconnaissance, and 103 helicopters. These figures do not, however, seem to have included some US aircraft based in the United States.

The US provided a more detailed breakdown of NATO planned build-up on May 13 (Day 50). By that time, the allied air effort included contributions from Belgium, Canada, Denmark, France, Germany, Hungary, Italy, The Netherlands, Norway, Portugal, Spain, Turkey, and the United Kingdom. The force strengths the US reported are shown in Table 2.

At the end of the conflict, the US was using a total of 24 European bases, including three in the UK, one in Spain, two in France, four in Germany, six in Italy, two in Hungary, one in Greece and two in Turkey.[36] It reported that it had about 650 aircraft committed to the NATO force. These included the following types of aircraft and missions:

- F-15 Strike Eagle: Air-to-ground attack aircraft

Table 1
NATO Major Combat Ship Strength in Mid-May 1999

Ships	US	UK/FR/GE/GR/IT/NL/SP/TU	Total
Carriers	1	2	3
Submarines	1	1	2
Cruisers	2	0	2
Destroyers	3	6	9
Frigates	0	10	10
Command Ships	1	0	1
Amphibious Ships	3	0	3
Minesweepers	2	0	2

On June 10, the US reported that it deployed one aircraft carrier, the USS *Theodore Roosevelt* (CVN 71); two cruisers, the USS *Vella Gulf* (CG 72) and *Leyte Gulf* (CG 55); three destroyers, the USS *Gonzales* (DDG-66), USS *Ross* (DDG-71), and USS *Peterson* (DD969); and two submarines, the USS *Albuquerque* (USS 706), and USS *Boise* (SSN 764). It also deployed the Kearsarge Amphibious Ready Group (ARG), which consisted of the USS *Kearsarge* (LHD 4), USS *Ponce* (LPD 15) and the USS *Gunston Hall* (LSD44). NATO European countries deployed two aircraft carriers (UK/FR), one submarine (UK), six destroyers (UK/FR/GR/IT), and 10 frigates (UK/SP/TU/IT/NL/GE/GR).

- F-16 Fighting Falcon: Multirole Fighter

- F-117 Nighthawk: Stealth fighter/attack

- B-52 Stratofortress: Heavy bomber

- B-1B Lancer: Long-range, multi-role, heavy bomber

- B-2 Spirit: Stealth multi-role heavy bomber

- A-10 Thunderbolt II: Close Air Support

- KC-135 Stratotanker: Tanker (refueler)

- KC-10A Extender: Tanker (refueler)

- F-14 Tomcat: Fighter

- AV-8B Harrier: Close air support

- EA-6B Prowler: Electronic Warfare

- AC-130H Spectre: Close air support, air interdiction and armed reconnaissance

- C-130 Hercules: Intratheater airlift

- C-141 Starlifter: Cargo and troop transport

- C-17 Globemaster III: Cargo and troop transport

- FA-18 Hornet: Strike fighter

- E-8C Joint Stars: Ground Surveillance

- RQ-1A Predator: Airborne Surveillance Reconnaissance and Target Acquisition (Unmanned aerial vehicle)

Figure 2
The Build-Up of NATO Air Forces

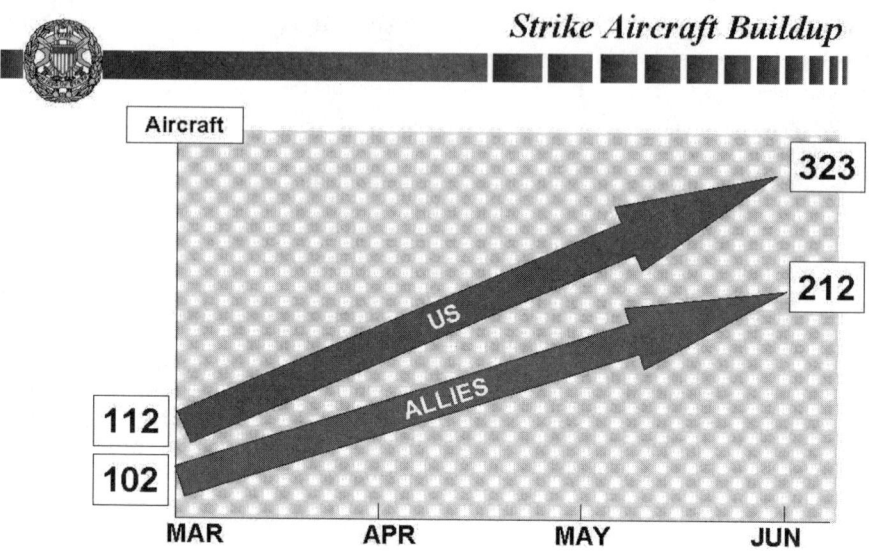

Source: Adapted from the Department of Defense press briefing for June 10, 1999.

- Hunter: Unmanned aerial vehicle
- AH-64A Apache: Attack helicopter
- C-5A: Intertheater Airlift

The Department of Defense summarizes the total US peak build up in June as follows:[37]

By June 1999, the total number of U.S. aircraft in Europe had grown to 731. These aircraft were based at the locations shown in Figure 5. During that same period, allied contributions more than doubled to over 300 aircraft. In addition, our NATO allies provided virtually all the basing facilities, air traffic coordination, and supporting elements to keep this air armada of over 1,000 aircraft functioning throughout the conflict.

A similar build-up took place in NATO European aircraft, and the peak number of non-US aircraft participating in Operation Allied Force is shown in Figure 3. Precise data are not available on all of the support and transport aircraft provided by other NATO countries. By June 10, however, other NATO powers had deployed a total of 277 aircraft to Operation Allied Force. These included 192 fighter/bombers, 19 reconnaissance aircraft, and at least 63 support aircraft, and 3

Table 2
NATO Air Strength in Mid-May 1999

Aircraft Mission	US		Allied	Total Planned
	Actual	*Planned*		
Fighter/Bomber	272	488	192	680
Support	246	358	63	421
Reconnaissance	27	30	19	49
Helicopters	100	106	3	109
Total	645	982	277	1,259

helicopters. This involved a massive beddown effort as well as an increase in aircraft numbers. The US alone conducted extensive beddown planning by surveying, preparing, and publishing new beddown assessments for 27 sites in 11 NATO and Eastern European countries.

Only limited unclassified data are available on the build up of individual European airforces during the conflict. The French Ministry of Defense reported that it used more than 100 aircraft between March 24 and June 1, of which 91 were directly assigned to NATO. It also reports that this was the second largest contribution to NATO by early June, when NATO had a total of 1,022 aircraft, and the US provided 720 out of this total versus 90 for France and 50 for Britain.[38] (Twenty of the French aircraft left the theater on June 3 when the carrier Foch returned to Toulon.) More detailed data on the French build-up are shown in the table in Annex One.

Detailed data are also available on the British air build up. The United Kingdom made an initial commitment of eight RAF Harrier GR7s based in Italy. These were supplemented by VC 10 and TriStar tankers, three E-3D AWACS aircraft and an RAF Nimrod. An additional four GR7s moved to Italy on March 28. Eight Tornado GR1s flew air operations from their base at RAF Bruggen, Germany. The Tornadoes later deployed to an air base in Corsica. Britain committed four more GR7s and four GR1s, together with additional tanker aircraft, in April.[39]

NATO deployed three aircraft carriers during the war: The USS *Theodore Roosevelt* (CVN 71), one British carrier, and one French. SHAPE reported on June 30 that a total of 912 NATO aircraft were deployed at the end of the air and missile campaign, with 312 more on the way. The British Ministry of Defense reported that 829 aircraft from 14 countries were available for tasking by the end of the campaign.[40]

When Britain sent the HMS *Invincible* Task Group from the Gulf to the Adriatic, this allowed its seven Sea Harrier FA2s to conduct combat air patrols over the region and freed other strike aircraft to concentrate on offensive operations. In addition Royal Navy ships, submarines and helicopters undertook other tasks, including participation in NATO Standing Naval Forces, the French carrier task

Figure 3
Non-US Aircraft Participating in Operation Allied Force

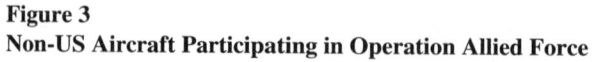

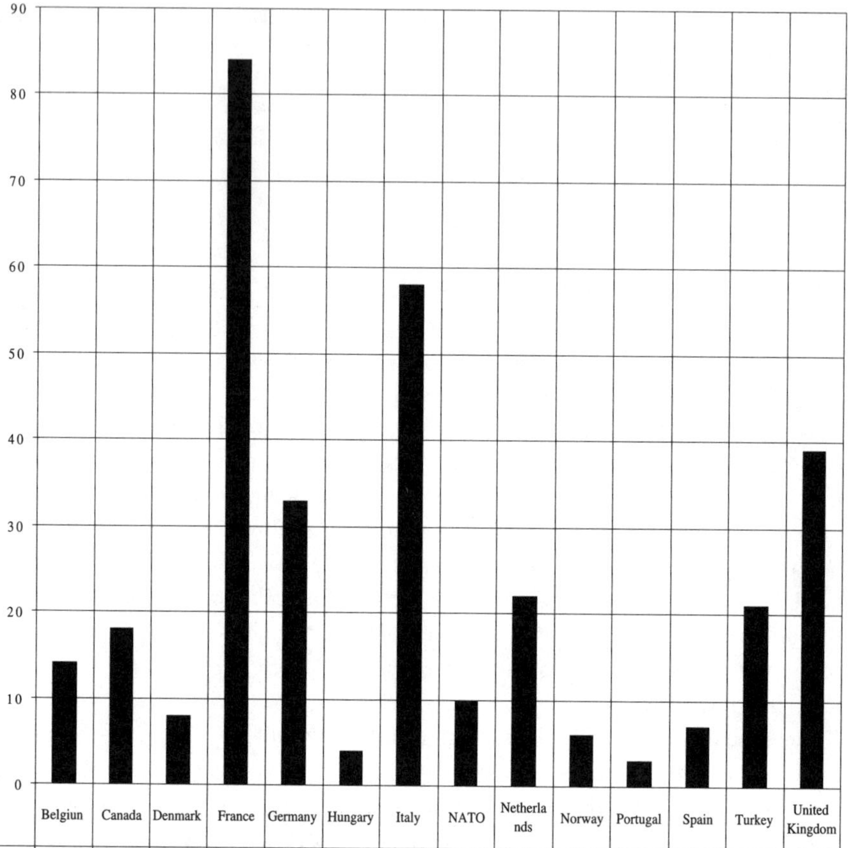

■ Aircraft	Belgiun	Canada	Denmark	France	Germany	Hungary	Italy	NATO	Netherlands	Norway	Portugal	Spain	Turkey	United Kingdom
	14	18	8	84	33	4	58	10	22	6	3	7	21	39

Source: Report to Congress: Kosovo/Operation Allied Forces After Action Report, Washington, Department of Defense, January 31, 2000, p. 78.

group, surveillance and ordnance clearance operations. The Royal Fleet Auxiliary provided strategic sea-lift shipping throughout and after the operation. The RAF Air Transport Force flew over 500 Hercules C-130, VC10 and TriStar sorties into theatre during the conflict.

Sortie Rates and Intensity

The data NATO, the US, and Britain provided on sortie rates is a statistical nightmare. The data provided at various times during and after the air and missile campaign often differed significantly and each source has reported data that were inconsistent at some point in the campaign. According to NATO, NATO had flown over 11,574 sorties as of April 27(Day 34). It had had only one loss in combat—an F-117—and no accidents costing the life of a pilot or destroying an aircraft. It had flown over 4,423 attack sorties under some of the most difficult weather and terrain conditions that can be encountered in modern warfare, and under extremely demanding rules of engagement designed to limit collateral damage.

NATO reported that it averaged about 340 sorties per day during the first 34 days of the air and missile war, and nearly 130 attack sorties per day. This compares with an average of 2,555 missions per day during the Gulf War, of which roughly 1,600 were strike-attack sorties.[41]

NATO sharply increased its activity over time. NATO flew only 5,926 sorties during the first 20 days of the war, of which 1,687 were attack sorties. It flew nearly 2 1/2 times the number of attack sorties per day during the fourth week of the air and missile war that it flew during the first three weeks. As a result, the total number of sorties rose by over 50 percent in the fourth week relative to the first three weeks, and the number of attack sorties rose by over 60 percent.

NATO reported on May 6 that it had flown about 17,000 sorties as of Day 43 (an average of 395 sorties per day) and some 5,670 strike sorties (an average of 132 per day). It was also able to fly over 600 sorties on a day with good weather, attack a total of more than 80 target groups, and hit 41 fixed targets. The British Ministry of Defense reported on May 9 that NATO had flown over 18,000 operational sorties, some 4,000 which had been flown in the past week. Of the total figure of 18,000 operational sorties, around 4,500 have been attack missions.

NATO reported on May 10 that it had now flown 19,000 sorties and that around one-third of the sorties were strike sorties. This meant the average sortie rate had risen to 404 sorties per day for the first 47 days of the campaign, and although the average number of strike sorties per day still averaged around 135.

The number of sorties had increased dramatically as of May 22 (Day 59), when 652 sorties were flown compared to only 245 the previous day. The US Department of Defense reported on May 19 (Day 56) that 22,626 sorties had been flown. Of these, 5,450 were strike sorties (2,824 flown by the US, 2,626 flown by Allied forces), 9,002 were combat support sorties (5,680 flown by the US, 3,322 flown by Allied forces), and 7,174 were Tanker/AWACS/UAV sorties flown by combined US and Allied forces. Over 14,200 bombs had been dropped by this date.

A further update on May 27 reported that to date, the US had flown 3,600 (52%) strike sorties and 14,150 (70%) support sorties. Allied forces had flown 3,350 strike sorties (48%) and 6,150 support sorties (30%), for a total of over 6,950 strike sorties and over 20,300 support sorties. At the same time, NATO expanded its basing and axes of attack so that it create an all-axis attack capability by early June. It could strike from Western Europe, carrier based forces in the Adriatic, bases to the north in Hungary, and bases to the east in Turkey (see Figure 4).

Between 600 and 800 sorties per day were flown from May 22 until June 8 (Day 74). The number of strike-attack sorties also increased from around 100 to between

Figure 4
The Shift to an All-Axis Attack

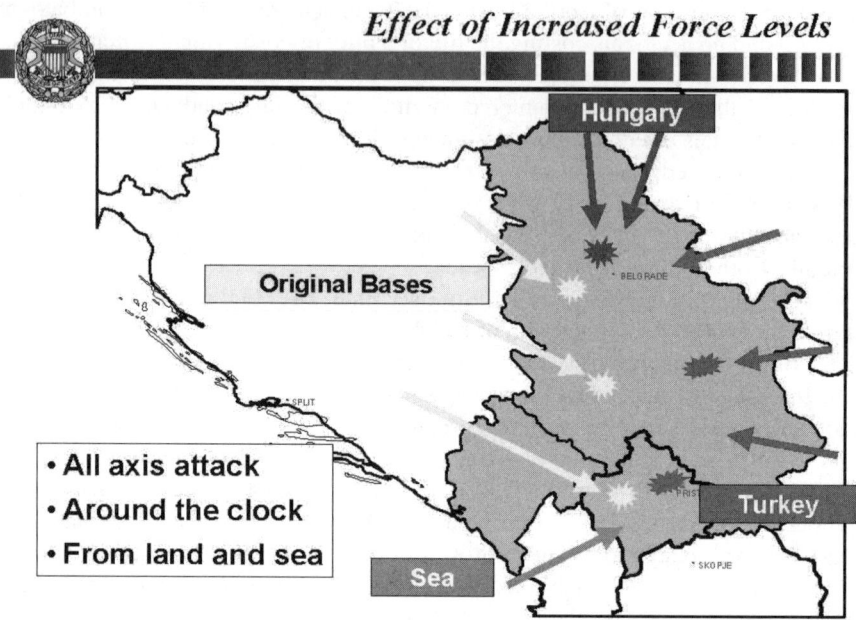

Source: Adapted from the Department of Defense press briefing for June 10, 1999.

300 and 350 per day. Air defense suppression sorties averaged between 74 and 93 per day. As of May 31 (Day 68), the total number of sorties flown was reported at 31,529. On June 8, the number of sorties fell to 500 and by June 10 (Day 76) only between 350 and 400 sorties were being flown for reconnaissance and air patrol to supervise Serb withdrawal. Postwar reporting indicates that NATO average 370 sorties per day during the first four weeks of the war. It averaged 522 sorties per day during the next four weeks, and 585 sorties per day during the last three weeks.[42]

Only limited detailed data are available on the exact number of shooter sorties that flew per day, the number of sorties that actually dropped ordinance, and the number of cruise missiles fired per day.[43] Sources also disagree about the sortie rates involved. For example, the French Ministry of Defense reports that NATO flew a total of 8,676 offensive missions by June 1, and 1,110 of these (12.8%) were flown by France. It reports that NATO flew 3,122 air operations sorties by that date and 337 of these (10.8%) were flown by France. It reports that NATO flew 1,371 reconnaissance sorties and 227 of these (20.2%) were flown by France.[44] It is obvious from these figures that France is using different mission defini-tions from the US.

Other French data indicate that the French Air Force flew nearly 2,000 missions, which included 851 attack missions, 476 air defense missions, 149 reconnaissance missions, 112 electronic warfare missions, and 320 in-flight refueling missions. The French naval air forces flew 412 more bombing missions, of which 88 had to be cancelled because of weather. The naval air forces were not equipped to use laser munitions at night and only flew day missions.[45]

Germany flew 394 sorties, largely suppression of enemy air defense or SEAD sorties. It fired 244 high speed anti-radiation or HARM missiles, and flew 46 additional reconnaissance missions.[46]

There are similar disagreements and definitional problems over how to count total sorties flown during the entire campaign. The US reported in mid-June that NATO had flown a total of around 33,000 sorties. SHAPE sources stated several days later that approximately 16,000 were shooter sorties, but the US said that only 12,600 were shooter sorties. NATO reported in early July, however, that it had flown a total 37,465 sorties, of which 14,006 were strike and suppression of air defense (SEAD) sorties, and 10,808 of which were dedicated strike-attack sorties.[47]

Secretary of Defense William S. Cohen testified to the US Armed Services Committee on July 20, 1999, that NATO had flown a total of 37,225 strike and support sorties.[48] Secretary Cohen reported later to the Senate Armed Services Committee that the US had flown "over 24,000 combat sorties."[49] The British report on the war states that a total of 38,004 sorties were flown, of which 10,484 were strike sorties. It reports that the United States contributed the major part of the effort, and that Britain flew a total of 1,618 sorties, of which 1,008 were strike sorties.[50]

The final Department of Defense report on the lessons of the war—issued in January 2000—refers to a total of 38,000 sorties, almost one third of which were strike and air defense suppression sorties. It says that the number of sorties flown per day varied from just over 200 day at the beginning of Operation Allied Force to over 1,000 per day by the end of the conflict, and that the total number of combat air patrol and other air defense sorties approached 3,600 by the end of the war. It also says that NATO forces conducted over 23,300 strike missions against an array of targets. These strikes were directed at roughly 7,600 target aimpoints associated with a variety of fixed targets as well as at just over 3,400 flex targets, 45 B-2 sorties delivered 656 JDAMs. These US estimates indicate that 14 of the 19 NATO nations contributed forces to the operation, and that allied (non-US) forces provided 327 manned and unmanned aircraft and flew over 15,000 sorties (about 39% of the total). There were extensive numbers of airlift, support, and refueling sorties. The US alone flew more than 500 sorties to aid refugees during Operation Sustain Hope.[51]

Some of the differences in these numbers reflect the uncertainties that are inevitable while an operation is in progress, and others are statistically unimportant. It is clear that the different counts normally reflect different definitions of what sorties should be counted as having contributed directly to the campaign in Kosovo, what sorties were combat versus support sorties, and how to count "shooter" or strike attack sorties. These differences do, however, make it difficult to estimate the contribution each NATO nation made with any precision—

although the US clearly flew over 60% of all sorties, and France, Britain, and Germany played a major role.

These various figures compare with a total of 109,870 sorties during the Gulf War. They also compare with a total of 3515 sorties in NATO's Operation Deliberate Force, which began against Bosnian Serb military targets in response to a Bosnian Serb mortar attack on civilians in Sarajevo on August 29, 1995 and lasted through September 14, 1995. Of the total of 3,515 sorties flown, approximately 2,470 were penetrating sorties, which included attacks on 48 target complexes, or 338 individual targets within the target complexes.[52] The statistics on other recent air operations are summarized in Table 3.

RELIANCE AND NON-RELIANCE ON PRECISION-GUIDED WEAPONS

The type of ordnance NATO used also changed over time. In the early days of the air and missile war, more than 90 percent of the bombs and missiles used were precision-guided munitions. Better weather and the steady attrition of Serbia's air defenses allowed NATO to use a steadily increasing number of unguided weapons. As a result, only 8,500 or 34–37% of the roughly 23,000–25,000 bombs and missiles used over the full course of the 78-day campaign, were precision guided—although these percentage is still more than four times higher than the 8% used in Desert Storm.[53] The rest were unguided weapons that were precisely dropped into small areas such as oil refineries, ammunition storage sites, and troop staging areas. By contrast, only eight percent of the bombs and missiles used in the Gulf War were precision guided.

Analysis by Farce: The Imprecise Nature of Precision Engagement

These are not facts that NATO emphasized during the war, and many briefings gave a false impression that NATO was relying almost solely on precision weapons. Similarly, the US report on the lessons of the war issued in January 2000 gives a similarly false impression by emphasizing "precision engagement" and the capability of the launch aircraft, and then ignoring the numbers of types of munitions actually used.[54]

During Operation Allied Force, NATO forces conducted over 23,300 strike missions against an array of targets. These strikes were directed at roughly 7,600 target aimpoints associated with a variety of fixed targets as well as at just over 3,400 flex targets. The weapons employed against these targets represent a full spectrum of capability, from unguided 500-pound bombs to sophisticated long-range cruise missiles.

... the significant discriminators among these weapons are their standoff range and guidance. Standoff allows the platform and aircrew to remain outside the threat area,

Table 3
The Statistics of Other Recent Air Operations

	Desert Storm *Gulf War* 1/16-2/28/91	Deliberate Force *Bosnia* 8/29-9/14/95	Desert Fox *Iraq* 12/16-12/20/98
Total Aircraft	2,400	300	213+
US	1,800	200+	201+
Total Munitions Used			
Cruise Missiles	333	23	425+ (90 CLCM) (425 SLCM)
Guided Smart Weapons	9,500	708	90%+
Unguided "Dumb" Weapons	162,000	1,026	600 pieces of ordnance?
Total Strikes	42,600	-	1,075-1,165
Air	42,000		300 night sorties
Targets/Strikes			
Weapons of Mass Destruction	32/9670	-	11/-
Command & Control	163/1,500	-	20/-
Leadership/Government	45/200	-	19/-
POL	28/540	-	1/-
Missiles	61/1,460	-	11/-
SAM/IADS	120/1,730	-	32/-
Military Industry	25/975	-	1/-

Source: Adapted from work by Dr. Elliot Cohen, and from the author's analysis of Desert Storm and Desert Fox.

thereby minimizing aircraft attrition. There are three categories of guidance: unguided, man-in-the-loop guidance, and Global Positioning System (GPS) guidance. Unguided weapons require the aircrew to deliver the weapon on a ballistic trajectory to the target. For man-in-the-loop guidance, there are several options, all involving specific aircrew input during the employment of the weapon. Crewmembers may identify the target via a seeker, steer the weapon during flight, point a laser at the target, or alter the aimpoint just prior to impact in order to maximize the weapon's effect on its target. Typically, man-in-the-loop systems require line of sight from the sensor to the target, and are degraded by adverse weather conditions. Global Positioning System guidance uses satellite input to track to specific target coordinates, which makes the weapon capable of all-weather employment.

Precision engagement was a cornerstone of Operation Allied Force. Over the 57 days of actual airstrikes, emphasis was placed on munitions that increased the probability of kill against a given target or that significantly improved survivability of weapon platforms or crew. For comparison, during Operation Desert Storm only 10 percent of U.S. strike aircraft were capable of delivering these types of weapons; this increased to 90 percent for Operation Allied Force.

The same false impression occurs elsewhere in the text, which invents the marvelous, if idiotic, term "legacy weapons" to describe unguided or "dumb" bombs.[55]

There are two notable aspects of the strike operations. First, there was a heavy use of standoff and Global Positioning System (GPS)-guided munitions to attack targets throughout the Federal Republic of Yugoslavia. Second, the operation was marked by the introduction of new weapons and systems, including B-2s equipped with Joint Direct Attack Munitions (JDAM), and new applications for the Standoff Land Attack Missiles (SLAM). Despite the heavy use of preferred munitions and newer technology weapon systems, legacy weapon systems played a significant role in successful strike operations.

. . . The majority of direct attack weapons employed during Operation Allied Force were laser-guided bombs. In addition, long-range, stand-off munitions such as the Tomahawk Land Attack Missile (TLAM) and the Conventional Air Launched Cruise Missile (CALCM) were employed extensively, especially during the initial stages of the operation and in periods of adverse weather. Strike packages received consistent support from air defense suppression platforms, including Navy and Marine Corps EA-6B radar jammers, HARM-equipped F/A-18s, and Air Force F-16C/J air-defense suppression aircraft. Onboard self-protection systems proved their value and once again demonstrated that suppressing hostile air defenses requires a comprehensive multi-platform, multi-system effort.

This set of illusions is compounded by a supporting table in the US report which lists ten categories of guided munitions compared to one category of unguided munitions, but which makes no mention of the number of munitions of each type that were actually used.[56] It is clear from many other portions of the text, however, that there were many cases where precision engagement and the use of precision weapons was simply not possible.[57]

The latest generation of air-delivered munitions was employed in substantial numbers for the first time during Operation Allied Force. Throughout the conflict, weapons fired at fixed sites hit intended targets producing the intended results, with limited collateral damage to civilians. In particular, the success achieved in delivering the new Joint Direct Attack Munition from altitudes above cloud cover demonstrated the wisdom of decisions made following the 1991 Gulf War. During that conflict, coalition forces had little choice but to allow the enemy a sanctuary from attack when target areas were obscured by adverse weather. In Kosovo, NATO forces operated under conditions in which there was at least 50 percent cloud cover more than 70 percent of the time, and yet were able to continue the operation.

. . . In some cases, only small inventories of the latest U.S. preferred munitions were available for operations. Several of these systems, such as JDAM and the Joint Standoff Weapon (JSOW), are in the early phases of production with plans for increasing these inventories over the next several years as a result of programs already funded by the Congress. Our success in using these systems in Kosovo validates these production plans. In addition to weapons used and proven during Operation Allied Force, other weapons under development will be available for employment later, including improved versions of the Tomahawk Land Attack Missile and the new Joint Air-to-Surface Standoff Missile (JASSM).[58] The Department has reviewed munition production and development programs carefully in constructing our annual defense program to ensure that munitions acquisition proceeds at an appropriate pace and scope in light of experience in Kosovo. DoD has also requested, and Congress has approved, use of $1.4 billion in FY 1999 supplemental funds to replenish stocks of the preferred munitions expended during Operation Allied Force.

... The requirement to maintain a mix of weapon capabilities and platforms was highlighted by Operation Allied Force. In the final stages of the campaign when the weather had improved and the air defense system had been degraded, the availability of a complete mix of weapons maximized the flexibility of strike options against the remaining priority targets. Because pilots could now employ direct attack weapons at less risk, less costly legacy weapons were, in many cases, as effective (and sometimes more) as more costly preferred weapons against such targets as fielded forces, large military storage complexes, and airfields.

Although we cannot predict every scenario that will require the employment of military force in the future, our flexibility and adaptability in providing precision engagement in Kosovo was certainly noteworthy. A balanced application of direct attack, standoff, and GPS-guided munitions will be the backbone of future air operations. Among the important tactical challenges encountered during Operation Allied Force were countering mobile surface-to-air missiles, employing all-weather precision and standoff weapons, and real-time targeting. To ensure that U.S. forces are adept at handling such challenges in any future campaign, they must be incorporated not only in individual unit training, but also more importantly, in joint training.

As is discussed shortly, NATO's problems were further compounded by the weather limitations of laser-guided weapons and the weather-visibility limits of most optical sensors, and by the fact that much of the target mix involved low cost–low value military equipment with limited strategic and tactical value. It simply does not make sense to fight a low-grade war with nothing but precision weapons.

British and French Use of Precision and Non-Precision Weapons

Most of the 329 cruise missiles that NATO ships and aircraft fired were fired during the first month of the campaign. There are no precise data available on the specific break out of munitions types, and the number of air to surface missiles used. One source reports that a total of 1,026 tons of bombs were dropped, including 708 precision munitions and 318 non-precision munitions. Another source reports that NATO aircraft dropped a total of 6,303 tons of munitions.[59]

The British Ministry of Defense reports that a total of 23,614 air munitions were dropped, and that Britain dropped 1,011 or 4.3%. The breakdown of the British munitions is 230 1,000 pound bombs, 226 Paveway II 1,000 pound general purpose bombs, 18 Paveway II 2,000 pound laser guided bombs, 532 BL755 cluster bombs, and six ALARM (Air-Launched Anti-Radar Missile) guided missiles. This reporting is a bit ambiguous since the Paveway II can be used as both a "dumb" and laser guided bomb. As a result, Britain fired a minimum of 250 smart weapons and a maximum of 476. This would mean that anywhere from 25% to 47% of these munitions were guided.[60]

The French air force reports that it flew 851 bombing missions of which 420, nearly half, ended in an effective strike. The air force dropped six laser-guided air-to-surface missiles, 314 laser-guided bombs, and 398 unguided bombs. This is 718 weapons, of which 45% were guided. The French naval air component was restricted to day-only missions using precision weapons, and dropped two laser-guided air-to-surface missiles, and 268 laser-guided bombs. This brings the total number of French weapons up to 988 weapons, of which 590 were guided (60%).[61]

The Limits of Precision Weapons and Precision Engagement

This analysis of the types of munitions used—and the later analysis of targeting, battle damage assessment, and mission effectiveness that follows—show that it is valid to describe NATO's air campaign in Kosovo as a "more precise engagement than the Gulf War or any previous war." However, calling the war in Kosovo "precision engagement" is an analytic and statistical farce. Furthermore, no data is available to show the extent to which improvements in avionics and targeting really did or did not allow more precise delivery of unguided ordnance. US and NATO claims imply that this was the case, but no specific data has yet been provided to validate such claims.

This experience is a lesson that it is dangerous to assume that an air and missile war can be fought solely with the precision made possible by guided weapons. This lesson is reinforced by the fact that the US faced growing constraints because it had only a limited number of advanced cruise missiles and GPS guided weapons, and allied air forces had even more restricted numbers of advanced guided weapons. Kosovo was not a major war by any means, but even it placed limitations on some aspects of US and NATO munitions stocks.

WEATHER

Weather was a major problem, although the weather patterns that NATO encountered were not unusual, either in the Balkans or much of Europe. Parts of Serbia have an unusually late spring. Belgrade, for example, has its highest annual rainfall during June. According to NATO figures issued on May 10, the weather for the first 47 days on the campaign was distributed as is shown in Table 4.

The impact of weather is illustrated by the fact that NATO could fly over 650 sorties per day on a day with excellent weather, as took place on May 13, the 50th day of the war. On a day with bad weather, however, NATO's strike/attack sortie rate was reduced by at least 30–50%, even when all-weather strike aircraft and suitable precision guided munitions were available. Weather was particularly important during the first month of the war. There were only seven "favorable" days of weather in the first 21 days of the air campaign, and 10 days in which at least 50% of the strike sorties had to be cancelled. Lt. General Michael C. Short,

Table 4
Weather Conditions During the Air and Missile Campaign

Weather	Days	Percentage
Favorable	6	13%
Marginal/Favorable	14	30%
Marginal	7	15%
Unfavorable/Marginal	14	30%
Unfavorable	6	13%

NATO's joint force air component commander for the Balkans operation, said later that the weather, "just kicked our butts for the first 45 days."[62]

This weather placed a heavy emphasis on Global Positioning Satellite (GPS) guided weapons like Joint Direct Attack Munition (JDAM), a $20,000-$25,000 add-on kit that can be strapped to 500–2,000 pound bombs to give them GPS guidance. It also showed the value of the Enhanced Paveway III LGB, and equipping UAVs like the Predator with laser illuminators so they could fly under the weather ceiling and illuminate targets.[63]

The overall patterns in weather are summarized in Figure 5, along with the rate of actual strike-attack sorties. It is clear that NATO averaged less than 0.5 sorties per strike-attack aircraft committed per day, largely because of weather problems. NATO operated under conditions in which there was at least 50% cloud cover more than 70 percent of the time. Weather forced NATO to cancel at least half of its total number of planned sorties on 39 days of the 78-day campaign, and allowed unimpeded air strikes on only 24 of 78 days.

Weather not only affected the target area, but also the airfields and tanker patterns. Furthermore, most movement of Serbian combat forces occurred during the night and/or under the cover of bad weather. This interaction between weather, night, and concealment was reinforced by the fact that the Serbs used small convoys and decoys and dispersed their forces among civilian traffic. The Serbs used camouflage extensively to hide both tactical targets, such as military vehicles, and fixed facilities, such as bridges. In addition, the Serbs used decoys.[64]

A similar interaction took place between weather and Serbian ground-based air defenses. There were many Serbian shorter-range antiaircraft artillery and man-portable air defense systems. Rather than shift the weight of effort that NATO aimed against destroying and suppressing these systems, NATO commanders chose to operate at altitudes beyond which most Serbian anti-aircraft systems could be employed effectively. The tradeoff of flying at higher altitudes to mitigate risk made weather conditions such as cloud layers and visibility more of a factor in daily execution.

These problems were made worse by collateral damage considerations and the absence of any land-component forward air controllers to assist in locating enemy forces. Engagement altitudes for both airborne forward air controllers and striking

Figure 5
Overall Patterns in Weather During the Air and Missile Campaign

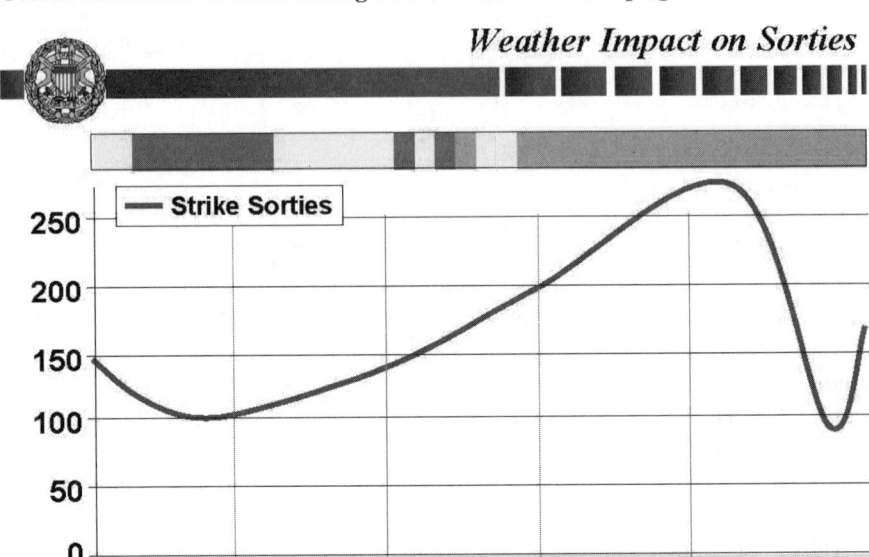

Source: Adapted from the Department of Defense press briefing for June 10, 1999.

assets were lowered as Operation Allied Force progressed, but weather and the threat posed by mobile anti-aircraft guns and man-portable missiles posed a problem throughout the conflict.

Accordingly, weather often limited the types of aircraft NATO could fly and affected the choice of munitions. The majority of direct attack weapons employed during Operation Allied Force were laser-guided bombs. However, long-range, stand-off munitions such as the Tomahawk Land Attack Missile (TLAM), the Conventional Air Launched Cruise Missile (CALCM), and GPS guided air-to-surface weapons were employed extensively in periods of adverse weather.

Secretary of Defense William S. Cohen described the impact of weather as follows in his speech to the International Institute of Strategic Studies on the lessons of the air and missile campaign:[65]

. . . Belgrade's battle strategy included a deliberate and manufactured humanitarian crisis. We were carrying out this air campaign, under circumstances in which the weather certainly was hardly cooperating. Again, I'd have to point out that out of the 78 days of this air campaign, roughly 20 days were actually clear enough to allow the uninhibited execution of that air campaign. So under extraordinary geographical limitations, environmental limitations, we also had to deal simultaneously with a humanitarian disaster. Our forces had to cope with helping to bring resources and relief to nearly a million refugees who had been expelled from that country. And we had to reassure the fragile nations on the front line to prevent them from imploding under the pressure, as Milosevic had intended.

The report on the lessons of the war that the US issued in January 2000 had the following summary comments on the impact of weather on NATO strike capabilities:[66]

Throughout the campaign, air operations and strike execution were impacted by the requirement for favorable weather in up to four geographically dispersed locations. These were (1) the target area, (2) the base from which the strike aircraft were operating, (3) the base used by any aircraft supporting the strike, and (4) the orbit location for the refueling tankers. This requirement complicated strike execution by allowing brief, localized periods of inclement weather to adversely affect overall operations. For example, on several occasions, morning fog at Aviano prevented strike-support aircraft from launching, which then caused missions to be cancelled even though strike aircraft from other bases were already airborne. On other occasions, thunderstorms or reduced visibility in the tanker pattern caused strike waves to be cancelled. Numerous other examples exist, making it clear why the capability to forecast weather conditions, which was greatly enhanced by space and weather forecasting tools in this conflict, is so valuable. Even if aircraft were able to get airborne, refueled, and matched up with supporting defensive and control aircraft, there was still no guarantee that the weather in the strike area would cooperate. As mentioned earlier, conditions in Kosovo were such that there was at least 50 percent cloud cover more than 70 percent of the time, hampering our ability to employ laser-guided munitions and putting a premium on other preferred weapons.

NATO's experience in Kosovo is a clear lesson that the "revolution in military affairs" has not solved the problem of weather and poor visibility, and that enemy forces will adapt to take maximum advantage of the cover provided by weather or other visibility problems.

NATO'S LIMITED LOSSES

Although Serbia claimed 71 kills of NATO aircraft by May 4, and eventually claimed a total of over 76 NATO losses, NATO only had had one confirmed combat loss (an F-117) by May 10 (Day 47). There were only two losses by mid-May. The second was an F-16 originally said to be lost to engine failure but which seems to have been hit by Serbian defenses. Both pilots were recovered. Two other aircraft—an F-117 and A-10—seem to have had some form of combat damage by May 5.

NATO only suffered combat losses of less than 0.02 percent per sortie as of May 13. Even if one includes an additional AV-8B and two AH-64s lost in accidents (killing two aircrew in one case), the total losses would only rise to 0.03 percent. These loss rates are about one-third of the Gulf War rate for similar periods of combat and well under 1/20th of the Vietnam War rate. They were also better that the expected accident rate in demanding peacetime training sorties.

No further losses took place through June 20, and in a campaign involving roughly 33,000 to over 38,000 sorties. The combat loss percentage for the entire campaign is statistically insignificant in percentage terms, although every loss still proved to be a source of major political and media concern.

CONFLICT TERMINATION

NATO's air and missile attacks were suspended at 10:00 PM EST on June 10, after roughly 11 weeks of air and missile war. This suspension came in response to FRY peace initiatives that had begun ten days earlier. Serbia did not accept all of NATO's initial terms, and the conflict only ended after a significant Russian diplomatic effort, agreement on a Russian role in the peacekeeping effort, and agreement that the UN rather than NATO would lead much of the peacekeeping effort.

These events had the following chronology:

- *June 1*: The FRY tell Germany that it has accepted the Group of Eight principles for peace and demanded an end to NATO bombing.

- *June 3*: The FRY accept terms brought to Belgrade by EU envoy Ahtisaari and Russian envoy Chernomyrdin.

- *June 6*: NATO Secretary-General Javier Solana announces it would be difficult to help rebuild Yugoslavia while Milosevic remains in power.

- *June 7*: NATO and Yugoslav commanders fail to agree to terms of pullout from Kosovo and suspend talks. NATO intensifies the bombing campaign. G8 Foreign Ministers in Bonn attempt to finalize a draft of a UN resolution. The FRY insists that a UN Security Council resolution must be in place before any foreign troops could enter Kosovo.

- *June 8*: The West and Russia reach a landmark agreement on a draft UN resolution at G8 talks in Cologne. NATO calls on Milosevic to resume military talks on troop withdrawal at once. Talks between senior NATO and FRY officers on a Serb pullout from Kosovo resume in Macedonia and continue into the night.

- *June 9*: Military talks continue with senior NATO and FRY officers. Late in the day, a Military Technical Agreement is signed between the two parties. The Serbian withdrawal from Kosovo that follows is in accordance with this Military-Technical Agreement concluded between NATO and the Federal Republic of Yugoslavia. It was signed by Lt. General Sir Michael Jackson, on behalf of NATO, and by Colonel General Svetozar Marjanovic of the Yugoslav Army and Lieutenant General Obrad Stevanovic of the Ministry of Internal Affairs, on behalf of the Governments of the Federal Republic of Yugoslavia and Republic of Serbia. The withdrawal was consistent with the agreement between the Federal Republic of Yugoslavia and the European Union and Russian special envoys, President Ahtisaari of Finland and Mr. Victor Chernomyrdin that had been reached on June 3.

- The Secretary General of NATO announces that he has written to the Secretary-General of the United Nations, Mr. Kofi Annan, and to the President of the United Nations Security Council, informing them of these developments. The Secretary-General of NATO urged all parties to the conflict to seize the opportunity for peace and called on

them to comply with their obligations under the agreements which have now been concluded and under all relevant UN Security Council resolutions. He states that NATO is ready to undertake its new mission to bring the people back to their homes and to build a lasting and just peace in Kosovo.

- *June 10*: The UN Security Council passes Resolution 1244. This Resolution welcomes the Federal Republic of Yugoslavia's acceptance of NATO's principles for a political solution to the Kosovo crisis. These include an immediate end to violence and a rapid withdrawal of its military, police and paramilitary forces. The resolution also announces the Security Council's decision to deploy international civil and security presences in Kosovo. Under United Nations auspices The Resolution is adopted by a vote of 14 in favor and none against, with one abstention (China).

Acting under Chapter VII of the UN Charter, the Security Council also decides that the political solution to the crisis will be based on the general principles adopted on May 6 by the Foreign Ministers of the Group of Seven industrialized countries and the Russian Federation—the Group of 8—and the principles contained in the paper presented in Belgrade by the President of Finland and the Special Representative of the Russian Federation which was accepted by the Government of the Federal Republic on June 3. Both documents were included as annexes to the Resolution.
The principles include

- An immediate and verifiable end to violence and repression in Kosovo;
- The withdrawal of the military, police and paramilitary forces of the Federal Republic; deployment of effective international and security presences, with substantial NATO participation in the security presence and unified command and control;
- Establishment of an interim administration; the safe and free return of all refugees; a political process providing for substantial self-government,
- The demilitarization of the Kosovo Liberation Army (KLA); and a
- Comprehensive approach to the economic development of the crisis region.

The Security Council authorizes Member States and relevant international organizations to establish the international security presence, and decides that its responsibilities will include deterring renewed hostilities, demilitarizing the KLA and establishing a secure environment for the return of refugees and in which the international civil presence could operate. The Security Council also authorizes the UN Secretary-General to establish the international civil presence and requests him to appoint a Special Representative to control its implementation.

After receiving definite evidence that Serb forces are withdrawing from northern Kosovo, NATO Secretary General Javier Solana announces that he has instructed General Wesley Clark, Supreme Allied Commander Europe, temporarily to suspend NATO's air operations against Yugoslavia. This decision is taken after consultations with the North Atlantic Council and confirmation from General Clark that the full withdrawal of Yugoslav forces from Kosovo had begun. The UN Security Council adopts Resolution 1244 on Kosovo. In Cologne, G8 ministers draft a plan to anchor the Balkans to Western Europe and rebuild Kosovo.

- *June 12*: Following the adoption of UNSCR 1244, the North Atlantic Council makes immediate preparations for the deployment of the security force (Operation Joint Guardian), mandated by the United Nations Security Council. The first elements enter

Kosovo on June 12. As agreed in the Military Technical Agreement, the deployment of the security force—KFOR—is synchronized with the departure of Serb security forces from Kosovo.

- *June 13*: UNHCR relief missions began.
- *June 20*: The bombing and missile campaign was formally halted at 10:50 EST. The Serb forces have completely withdrawn from Kosovo, leading NATO Secretary General Solana to officially end NATO's bombing campaign in the Federal Republic of Yugoslavia.

The peace process and the deployment of NATO forces into Kosovo did, however, not proceed quite as smoothly as this chronology suggests. Russian forces occupied the main airport in Kosovo without warning and created a crisis over the role of Russian the peacekeeping mission, as well as a lingering debate over whether Russia and Serbia had reached a secret agreement in which Russia agreed to force NATO to partition off part of Kosovo into a Russian zone that it would keep under Serbian control.[67]

There were other complications. NATO forces did not deploy as quickly as was needed and the relief effort was grindingly slow at a time when the Kosovar Albanians poured back into Kosovo. The Serbs could not withdraw as quickly as originally planned. The Albanian Kosovars began almost immediately to take revenge on the Serbs and Kosovar Gypsies. The UN was not organized to perform the police and internal security role and months elapsed before the UN could perform this role effectively.

Nevertheless, NATO won a major victory. By June 20, the Serb withdrawal was complete and KFOR was well established in Kosovo. Following confirmation by the Supreme Allied Commander Europe (SACEUR) that Serb security forces had vacated Kosovo, the Secretary-General of NATO announced on June 20 that, in accordance with the Military Technical Agreement, he had formally terminated the air campaign.

The air and missile war ended with Serbian agreement to withdraw all military and police forces from Kosovo according to the withdrawal schedule shown in Figure 6, and to allow NATO peace-keeping forces to occupy Kosovo as shown in Figure 7.

It is important to note, however, that the peace agreement did not fully define the future government of Kosovo, deal with the issue of independence, or describe the future role of the Kosovar Liberation Army (KLA) or of Serbian forces in Kosovo. Equally important, it did not describe the role of the UN in detail, or of other occupying powers like Russia, and created the ambiguity that NATO reached the agreement with a government it threatened to prosecute for war crimes.

As has been noted earlier, the cease-fire agreements also did not resolve Kosovo's future, or provide a broad basis for stability in the Balkans. The air and missile war has become a land war in which NATO may have to deploy over

Figure 6
The Serbian Withdrawal Plan

SERB FORCES
WITHDRAWAL TIMETABLE

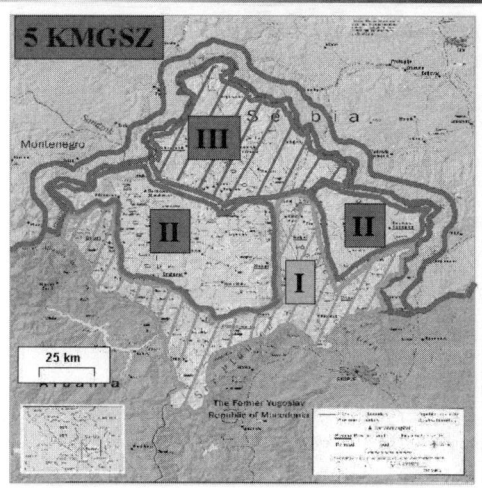

EIF + 1   10 Jun
Zone III (-) Withdrawal

EIF + 6   15 Jun
Zone I Withdrawal
EIF + 9   18 Jun
Zone II Withdrawal
EIF + 11   20 Jun
Zone III (+)
EIF + 11   20 Jun
Total Withdrawal from Kosovo

Source: Adapted from the Department of Defense press briefing for June 10, 1999.

50,000 men for at least half a decade, and where the air and missile war against Serbian forces may prove to be the prelude to low intensity combat between Serb and Kosovar Albanian.[68]

Like the Coalition's victory in Gulf War, there is no doubt about the scale of the immediate military victory but there was great doubt about the strategic consequences of that victory. Rather than "win" in absolute terms, NATO effectively exchanged an air and missile war for a ground-oriented peacemaking mission.

This highlights the lesson that detailed planning and preparation for conflict termination should occur as an integral part of war planning and before the use of force begins if at all possible. Events during a conflict can be counted upon to force constant changes in such planning and intelligent planners must count on the timing and nature of conflict termination to be unpredictable and often to come as a surprise. The failure to create comprehensive plans and preparations is, however, decisive proof of grand strategic incompetence, regardless of the military outcome. Furthermore, the cease-fire or peace treaty is only a small part of successful conflict termination. It is critical for lasting security that it lead to a desirable political, economic, and social outcome—which is the only meaningful standard of success.

Figure 7
The Initial Plan for the Ground Phase of Peacemaking

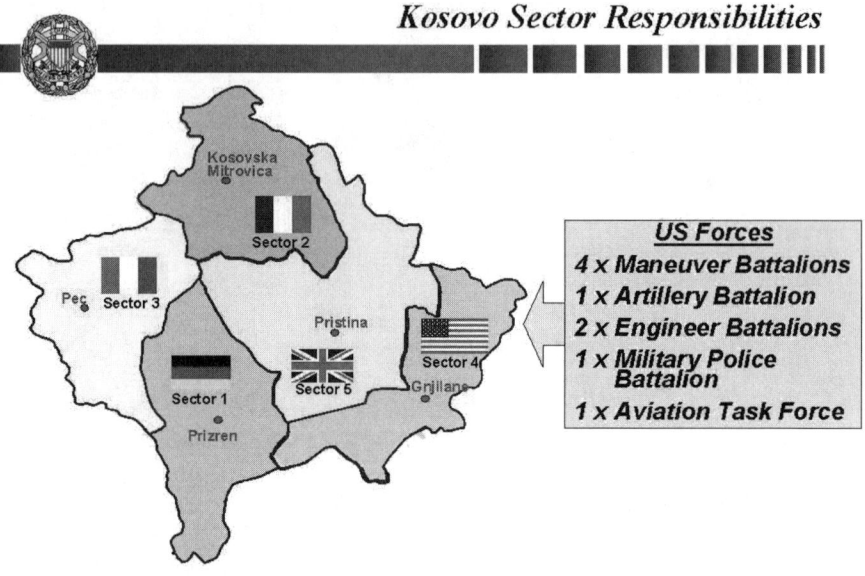

Source: Adapted from the Department of Defense press briefing for June 10, 1999.

3

The Grand Strategic Aspects of Kosovo: The "Whys" and "Hows" of the War and the Implications for Strategy and Force Planning

The air and missile campaign in Kosovo reinforced the several important long-standing questions about the "whys" and "hows" of how the West goes to war. It also raised important issues regarding NATO coalition warfare, and the ability of current US strategy, force planning, and defense spending to sustain America's present role as the West's only superpower.

Some of these issues have not received that attention they deserve because Kosovo was a "just war" in the sense that it was fought over highly visible, large scale violations of human rights, and because it ended in military victory against an opponent that did not succeed in inflicting casualties on NATO. Kosovo did, however, expose long-standing problems in the way that the US and the West go to war, and these problems will be of major importance in any future conflict that is less popular and less successful.

The issues Kosovo raised regarding the future of NATO, Coalition warfare, and Europe's role as independent power and a Transatlantic partner have received a great deal of attention. It is far from clear, however, that the West has found the right answers to either the grand strategic problems it faces or to the long serious of more detailed issues affecting NATO and Europe's military role that are discussed throughout this report.

THE "WHYS" OF GOING TO WAR

Kosovo presented one of the clearest moral imperatives for military action since World War II. Nearly two million people were threatened with ethnic cleansing, and there was no "night and fog" to conceal what was happening or the potential consequences. The West already had the experience of the Holocaust in Europe in World War II, and of the cost of ethnic cleansing in Bosnia. It had seen Serbia prepare for such operations in August 1998, and violate the terms of an October 1998 agreement in ways that provided strong evidence that Serbia would soon go to war with the people of Kosovo.

At the same time, the West still could not bring itself to call the war in Kosovo a "war." It had to use absurdist semantic evasions like "diplomacy using force" and "coercive diplomacy." Kosovo also again exposed the fact that the US and its allies had no clear doctrine for going to war. NATO and the US blundered into war through a series of diplomatic miscalculations that assumed that diplomacy would probably avoid the need for military action, and that demonstrative military action would be required only if diplomacy failed. At least at the political level, NATO and the US failed to properly asses the risks of war, and as a result, it lacked both a strategy and grand strategy for going to war until it was forced to act by the scale of Serbian ethnic cleansing.

A Lack of Criteria for Deciding on Military Action

There has been little debate in the West as a whole over what kinds of crises justify military action. Most European powers have tended in the past to deal with each new crisis on a case by case basis, and their parliamentary systems have limited the extent to which they have had to conduct open debates on these issues. NATO has not debated such issues, and the EU is now creating a crisis manage-ment force without defining what scenarios it should be used for.

Vietnam led the US into a much more focused debate on such issues, but this debate has not produced any clear doctrine or criteria for using military force, and the legal constraints set up after Vietnam in the War Powers Act have been honored largely by evading act test of the Act's provisions and constitutionality. The US has made an effort since the war to define a Clinton Doctrine for dealing with the commitment of military forces, but this "doctrine" so far consists of little more than moralistic statements such as these: "If the world community has the power to stop it, we ought to stop ethnic cleansing" (June 20) and "If somebody comes after innocent civilians and tries to kill them en masse because of their race, their ethnic background or their religion and it is within out power to stop it, we will stop it" (June 22).[69]

Vacuous catch phrases do not define real-world criteria for US or Western military action, regardless of whether or not they are moral or noble in character. It is far easier to use terms like "en masse" than define them. While a phrase like "their race, their ethnic background or their religion" may seem noble, one does have to wonder why the level of suffering in a case like Cambodia should be excluded.

It is equally vacuous, however, to use seemingly pragmatic terms like "vital strategic interest." The Weinberger Doctrine's emphasis on such criteria has proved to be no more meaningful than the Clinton morality play. The US simply cannot wait long enough to determine whether a crisis or problem does or does not involve a vital strategic interest, and one awkward corollary of being a global superpower is that anything anywhere in the world involves at least a tenuous tie to some strategic interest.

The fact is that American and Western military action tends to be event driven, and the use of force is often determined by whether the event affects US allies, there is major media concern, or those at hazard arouse political sympathy. As one ex-chief of staff of a US military service said after the Clinton speech on June 22, "We will use our power if they look like us." Senior European officers have similar feelings. They believe that they increasingly are being asked to use military force to make up for diplomatic failures in a context where civil political decisionmakers pay far too little attention to whether military force can be effective, the risks involved, the ability to withdraw if military action fails, and the endgame in translating military victory into lasting political success.

The US and NATO are not prepared for future crises and conflicts. They have no clear no doctrine or consensus for choosing between an involvement in a Bosnia, Burma, Cambodia, Chechnya, Congo, Iran-Iraq War, Kosovo, Lebanon, Liberia, Rwanda, Somalia, Sudan—or any of the other 1,200 or so conflicts that have taken place since World War II.

While many of these conflicts were small and relatively petty, many did involve significant civilian deaths and suffering. If one examines a recent analysis of the conflicts that occurred in the world after World War II and before 1994, one finds the results summarized in Table 5.[70]

It is important to note that well over 75% of these conflicts and deaths occurred before the end of the Cold War. It is also important to note that the idea that the number and intensity of third world, ethnic, racial, and religious conflicts has increased since the end of the Cold War is strategic rubbish for which there is no conceivable historical justification.[71] The patterns of global conflict are scarcely constant, but the levels since 1990 in no way depart from the levels between 1946–1989.

Other work by Adam Spiegel of the Center for Naval Analysis found that the US had overtly used military force more than 240 times before the end of the Cold War, excluding covert action and major military assistance efforts not involving an active combat presence. The real total would be well in excess of 300. These actions ranged from demonstrative actions to major wars, and they have very little in common. They are also almost impossible to categorize without getting into endless controversies over their context and definition.

It does seem fair to say, however, that the vast majority of US military interventions since the end of World War II did not involve any direct threat to vital American strategic interests, and that more than half had only a limited direct tie to the Cold War. Well over two-thirds did not involve significant strategic warning or occur under conditions where the US could credibly predict and put clear limits on the ultimate level of its military commitments. In passing, it seems equally fair to say that in well over 70% of the cases, it would be impossible to get any consensus

Table 5
Patterns in World Conflict: 1945–1994

	Number of Wars	Number of Wars Involving Over 10, 000 Dead	Number of Wars Involving US Military Action*	Total Dead
Caribbean and Latin America	19	6	8	477,000
Middle East and North Africa	19	11	9	993,000
Sub-Saharan Africa	26	15	5	4,177,000
Europe	6	0	0	186,000
Central and South Asia	10	6	1	2,857,000
East Asia	34	17	6	10,396,000
Total	114	55	29	19,086,000

Note: * Includes significant US military assistance, covert action, demonstrative action, occupation, humanitarian efforts, combat, and emergency evacuations.

from American foreign policy analysts over the level of "moral imperative" these crises created for US military action.

This situation has not eased since the end of the Cold War. Although the war in Kosovo was shaped largely by the projection of US air and naval forces, the land role has been just as important in other recent conflicts. The US Army, for example, has deployed ground troops 36 times since 1989—largely in peacekeeping missions. This compares with 10 times during the previous 40 years of the Cold War, including deployments for Korea and Vietnam.

These data are a clear historical warning that any broad grand strategic doctrine for defining the "whys" of American military involvement will collapse under the pressure of events, the uncertainties involved, and the unique character of a given contingency. As a result, the real lesson of Kosovo may be that the US and its allies need to develop far better and detailed criteria for characterizing a given contingency, carrying out risk analysis, and determining a range of military options, and to stop trying to reduce the whys of conflict to simplistic grand strategic catch phrases.

The Dilemmas in Deciding on Peacemaking

This conclusion is reinforced by the increasingly awkward Western inability to talk honestly about the word "war" and efforts to distinguish between "war," "police actions," "peacemaking," and "peace-keeping." If one looks at the patterns of major peacekeeping efforts between 1945 and 1998, which is shown in Table 6, it is clear that they tend to be open ended and expensive, and that Kosovo is scarcely unique in the fact that military action like the air and missile campaign can be the prelude to years of occupation and frequent low level military fighting on the ground.[72]

Table 6
Frequency, Duration, and Intensity of Recent Peacekeeping Operations

Peacekeeping Activity	Number of Activities	Duration in Years Over Two	Over Five	More than 10,000 Peacekeepers Involved	Some Combat Activity*	US Involvement
Current UN Operations	17	14	11	0	3	5
Past UN Operations	27	23	6	5	7	7
Current Non-UN Operations	6	5	1	1	3	2
Past Non-UN Operations	5	2	1	1	4	1
Total	55	44	19	7	17	15

Note: * Generally very low-level or indirect involvement during fighting between principals.

It is far from clear that Kosovo sets any precedents that will allow the US or NATO to resolve the increasingly awkward problem of defining the nature of military action, or when it should become involved in peace-keeping.

Even a cursory review of the NATO campaign in Kosovo and the trends in peace-keeping raises several issues that need close study:

- Only a small fraction of serious conflicts since World War II—well under 15%—have resulted in any meaningful peacekeeping activity,

- In the past, most peacekeeping efforts did not involve any form of serious combat, did not prevent conflict from reoccurring, did not end when any nation involved chose to go to war, US. Peacekeeping efforts rarely involved real "police" activity, and the US has not been the world's policeman,

- In most cases, the peacekeeping force could not engage in serious conflict, and the nations in the peacekeeping mission lacked the power projection capability to fight at any serious level,

- There is a post Cold War tendency to go from refereeing an established peace to peacemaking involving combat. In contrast to the past, the US has played an increasing role in such actions.

European nations must deal with these issues in a regional context. The US now faces the problem of seeking to redefine peace-keeping in a global context with no US consensus as to what policies and strategies to employ, and even less consensus among its allies and within the UN. Given the fact that there are roughly 20–30 conflicts going on in the world at any given time, the US cannot possibly carry out a doctrine or grand strategy involving more than a small number. At present, however, it has no clear basis for "strategic triage" other than ad hoc analysis of a given contingency, and no clear plan for shaping UN and world peacekeeping efforts that goes beyond the failed initiatives it took after Somalia.

If Kosovo provides any special lessons for the US as to the "whys" of war, it is that it is a warning that the US needs clearer criteria for involvement, that it must plan for repetitive sudden and unpredictable future deployments and size its forces and defense budget accordingly, and that it must resume its efforts to create more effective UN capabilities. Ironically, at least some Europeans resent the perceived US dominance of NATO, while nations outside NATO often see NATO as a symbol of western hegemonism in a broader sense. At the same time, it is important to note that much of the world and many members of the UN did not share the US self-image of a policeman forced to act to help the world. As the US considers what course of action to follow, it must understand that one nation's "policeman" will inevitably be other nations' "hegemon."

THE "HOWS" OF GOING TO WAR

Every Western nation faces individual problems in deciding how to reshape its political system to decide on the kind of military action that will be required in the post–Cold War era. These problems are especially severe in the case of the US, however, with its heritage of Vietnam.

Rightly or wrongly, the US government blundered into U.S. involvement in Kosovo, and into what became a significant regional war, without any declaration of war or meaningful consultation of Congress under the War Powers Act. In the process, it again became obvious that the US Executive Branch and the Congress have no clear way to decide whether to go to war, to provide legislative approval of the conflict, or to reach any formal consensus on the scale of military action.

Like its allies, the US could not call the war a "war," and the War Powers Act again proved a failure. Consultation between the Congress and Executive Branch was improvised after the fact, awkward, and often ineffective. Congressional action became an awkward melange of partisan criticism, failure to formally support military action, and over funding of the Executive Branch request for money to prosecute the conflict.

- *It may be that one of the lessons of modern war is that war can no longer be called war. It may also be that the US must muddle into war, muddle through it, and muddle out without any clear consensus or formal legal procedures to authorize a conflict.*

- *At the same time, this system of blundering in only works as long as everything goes relatively well. As Somalia warns if anything goes wrong, no one is firmly committed or responsible at the political level.*

- *Any consensus is also remarkably vulnerable to the media and one bad event.*

- *Given the current state of politics, partisanship, and leadership, there is little practical prospect of any legislative or procedural fix that will make things any better.*

COALITION WARFARE AND LEVELS OF COMMITMENT

It is dangerous to draw detailed conclusions about NATO, the role of Europe, and the future of coalition warfare without a full picture of the views and role of given countries in the decision-making process at each step of the conflict. At present, there is no reliable history of the command decisions made at the NATO and national level affecting the air campaign and ground option, and no detailed operational history of the relative role of US and allied forces. None of these data are as yet available in a detailed and reliable form—although enough data are available to make it clear that divisions within the alliance helped prevent NATO from exercising a ground option and severely limited the conduct of the air campaign.

Transatlantic "Euro"- and "Yank"-bashing may be the official sports of the NATO alliance, but they are rarely a good basis for strategic analysis. It is dangerous to talk about a "US view" when the US political leadership differed over many issues and senior US military officers held sharply different views about the best way in which to conduct the war. It is equally dangerous to generalize about the role of "Europe" as if it was an entity, and ignore the fact that NATO is an alliance of nineteen sovereign and often disparate nations. During Kosovo—as during virtually every other major post-war crisis since the founding of NATO—European nations often differed far more sharply within Europe than the US differed with key European partners like Britain. In at least some cases, there was no clear policy consensus within a given European country. In other cases, European political leaders took different public positions from the ones they took in shaping NATO military operations.

The Contributions of the US and Europe

One central fact is clear: the war was truly an allied operation. The US could not have begun serious air operations without access to European air bases and the support of all the NATO countries around Serbia. While NATO European air forces initially faced significant limits because of weather and their lack of advanced avionics and munitions, US and European air forces had flown roughly equal numbers of strike-attack sorties by the time the air campaign ended.[73] European nations like Britain, France, Germany, and Italy played a major role in the air campaign. (France alone budgeted up to $1.5 billion dollars for operations in Kosovo during 1999–2000.[74]) NATO also had the active support of Albania, Macedonia, and Bulgaria.

The number of sorties flown is a poor measure of alliance effort and solidarity. European air forces were limited more by weather and their equipment and not by any lack of willingness to flight. Those European nations that could fly sophisticated missions did so. Germany, for example, flew 394 Tornado sorties to suppress Serbian air defenses, and fired 244 High Speed Anti-Radiation Missile (HARMs); it also flew 46 reconnaissance missions. Furthermore, SHAPE took some time before it was willing to free "lower tech" aircraft like the A-10, GR-7, and

Etendard for missions against the Serbian forces in Kosovo, although the NATO air commander in the Balkans felt such aircraft could have been committed earlier.[75]

At the same time, Kosovo did expose serious imbalances in the ability to fight. The US did fly over 60% of all the sorties in the air and missile campaign. According to one report, it flew 53% of the strike-attack sorties, dropped over 80% of the strike-attack munitions. It flew 71% of the overall support sorties, carried out over 90% of the advanced intelligence and reconnaissance missions, and flew over 90% of the electronic warfare missions using dedicated aircraft. The US fired over 80% of the precision guided air weapons, and launched over 95% of the cruise missiles.[76]

This level of US commitment was a product of a series of military problems. Many allies lacked the advanced avionics, secure communications, and electronic warfare capabilities to fly strike-attack missions in poor weather, over a hostile environment, and with the precision needed to limit collateral damage. Many allied airforces lacked the training and stocks of precision attack munitions needed to engage in sustained precision strike operations. Some allied units had serious problems in participating in US air groups involving a mix of different aircraft with dedicated missions for communications and training reasons. Some allied air forces had national political leadership with little understanding of the strengths and weakness of airpower, or what was necessary to force the Serbs to concede.[77]

US Secretary of Defense William S. Cohen pointed out in testimony to Congress that[78]

... the operation did highlight that NATO would in the future have to give more attention to ensuring that our allies have the capability to operate effectively with US forces. We still need to work to ensure secure aircraft communications between alliance members. Above all, we must take full advantage of the technological advances that can keep NATO's decisive edge. For instance, our actions in Kosovo clearly demonstrate the necessity of having precision-guided munitions as a major component of the NATO arsenal. The majority of precision-guided munitions are in US stocks. NATO air forces do not, for the most part, have the ability to conduct sustained all-weather day and night operations.

Secretary of Defense Cohen also made the following points in his address on the lessons of Kosovo to the annual conference of the International Institute for Strategic Studies on September 9, 1999.[79]

Individually, all of the allies are making progress in transforming their militaries to meet the missions of the future. We're now seeing a largely European peacekeeping mission in Kosovo. But I must say that collectively there is much more that we have to do. We started talking about this at the NATO summit this spring. We talked about the Defense Capabilities Initiative, and very quickly I can summarize it. We have all agreed to develop forces that are more mobile, beginning with the reassessment of NATO's strategic lift requirements for planning purposes. We need forces, we've agreed, that can sustain themselves longer; that means having a logistics system that will ensure they have the supplies when and where they need them. [We need] forces that communicate more effectively, I just touched upon that. We have to have a common NATO command and control structure and communication architecture by the year 2002, so we are working to develop that as well. [We need] forces that can engage more effectively; that means having the new advanced technologies such as greater stocks of precision-guided munitions and forces that can survive better against chemical, biological or nuclear weapons, and also information warfare.

So we have had a political statement of agreement that this is what we have to do to become more effective for the future. What we now have to do is to measure up and to match the political commitment with actual deeds. There I would say the evidence is less encouraging.

As I look around at the budgets of the members of the NATO Alliance I certainly see restructuring taking place as far as the size of the forces, and one cannot criticize that. But I also see a corresponding reduction in a commitment as far as the budget is concerned. So while there is a great sense of enthusiasm for what we have to do for the future to modernize NATO, to make it as effective as it needs to be, there is not at this point the kind of political commitment to actually carry it out.

The Department of Defense report on the lessons of the war, which was issued in January 2000, reinforced these points:[80]

Notwithstanding the allied contributions, and overall success of the campaign, Operation Allied Force highlighted a number of disparities between U.S. capabilities and those of our allies, including precision strike, mobility, and command, control, and communications capabilities. The gaps in capability were real, and they had the effect of impeding our ability to operate at optimal effectiveness with our NATO allies. For example, because few NATO allies could employ precision munitions in sufficient numbers (or at all), the United States conducted the preponderance of the strike sorties during the early stages of the conflict. Problems regarding communication interoperability persisted throughout the campaign. Insufficient air mobility assets among our allies slowed deployment of Kosovo Force ground forces—beyond those already in the theater—once Milosevic agreed to NATO's terms to end the conflict. Disparities in capabilities will seriously affect NATO's ability to operate as an effective alliance over the long term.

If the alliance is to meet future military challenges effectively, it must successfully implement the Defense Capabilities Initiative (DCI). The Defense Capabilities Initiative seeks to enhance allied military capabilities in five key areas: deployability and mobility; sustainability and logistics; effective engagement; survivability of forces and infrastructure; and command, control, and information systems. The United States will continue to promote the Defense Capabilities Initiative and encourage experimentation by NATO's members with new and advanced warfighting concepts. Successful implementation of the Defense Capabilities Initiative must remain one of NATO's top priorities—a lesson strongly reinforced by the Kosovo experience. Within the alliance, efforts by the United States and its allies to implement the Defense Capabilities Initiative can be facilitated by close coordination through NATO's established structure, namely the Military Committee and High Level Steering Group. Review of alliance interoperability challenges highlighted by Kosovo operations could prove fruitful in addressing improved integration of forces.

NATO and Europe drew similar conclusions. George Robertson reached many of the same conclusions in a speech on September 8, 1999—at the time when he was phasing out his duties as Britain's Secretary of State for Defense, in preparation for becoming NATO's, next Secretary-General. He noted NATO's dependence on US air strength and intelligence assets, and shortfalls in signals, intelligence, and engineering. He cited the need for a new European approach to security that emphasized "deployability, sustainability, mobility, survivability, and interoperability," and illustrated the importance of sustainability by noting that the Russian paratroops that rushed into Pristina airport were forced to turn to the British troops in the area for food and force protection. Robertson summed up his remarks on the lessons of Kosovo by stating that, "The stark fact is that Europe now needs to face up to its security responsibilities."[81]

The NATO Defense Ministers agreed during their meeting in Ottawa on September 21–22, 1999. They endorsed the goals of a NATO Defense Capabilities Initiative that called for modernization in virtually all of the areas that Kosovo exposed as lacking, and which stressed interoperability at every level. Secretary General Javier Solana reinforced these points in his farewell appearance at the meeting. George Robertson set the stage for his new role by warning his fellow Europeans that they needed to implement NATO's Defense Capabilities Initiative to provide the capabilities missing in Kosovo, and that they could not send even two percent of their total forces to NATO and use them effectively, while Secretary Cohen stated that NATO countries spent nearly 60% of what the US did on defense, but only got about 10% of the same military capability.[82]

NATO's good intentions might have been more convincing, however, if nations like France had not announced simultaneously that its new defense budget for 2000 was cutting procurement funding by 3.5% and that it was favoring personnel funding over procurement. France was also scarcely alone. Many European countries voted one way in NATO meetings, and quite another when they were asked to vote with their budgets.[83]

Problems in Coalition Warfare: National Decision Making and the Air War

The most serious single problem in coalition warfare affecting the execution of the air and missile campaign was political and not a matter of resources and capabilities. NATO targeting and operations were so tightly constrained by individual European countries that they exerted a veto power over both the kind of targets that could be attacked, and even over individual missions. Lt. General Michael Short, NATO's joint force air component commander in the Balkans, stated in an interview after the fighting that one member of the North Atlantic Council (clearly France) consistently refused to allow NATO air planners to attack the targets they wished to target. He also said that one or two nations some times exercised their veto at the last minute, forcing airplanes that had already been launched to be recalled. This sometimes had to be relayed through a chain of AWACS and tankers, creating serious command and control pilots and risking aircraft in missions that could not be flown.[84]

These views were expressed in considerably more detail when General Short, General Wesley Clark, Admiral James Ellis, who led NATO's naval assets, testified to Senate Armed Services Committee on October 21, 1999. General Short stated that,[85]

I'd have gone for the head of the snake on the first night. I'd have turned the lights out, I'd have dropped the bridges across the Danube. I'd have hit five or six political-military headquarters in downtown Belgrade. Milosevic and his cronies would have woken up the first morning asking what the hell was going on.

Short stated that the way to stop ethnic cleansing would have been to put a dagger in the Serb leadership's heart "as rapidly and as decisively as possible. . . . If you hit that man hard—slapped him up side the head—he'd pay attention."

General Clark supported many aspects of Short's remarks, but noted that military strategy and operations had to reflect the political constraints imposed by an alliance operation.[86]

"Once the threshold is crossed and you are going to use force, that force has to be as decisive as possible in attaining your military objectives," he said. In the case of Kosovo, however, he said, the consensus of 19 nations was required to approve action, and many countries had preconceptions about how to apply force.

Every single nation had a domestic political constituency, and every single nation had a different set of political problems . . . . In some there were government coalitions. In others there were historic relationships. Some bore the agony of defeat in a previous conflict and the word 'war' couldn't be mentioned. Others were long-standing partners with American efforts elsewhere in the world.

The fundamental lesson of the campaign is that the alliance worked . . . . The procedures that were honed and developed over 50 years, the mechanism of consultation, the trust, the interoperability that we'd exercised time and again in preparation for missions, they all came together. "This operation had a remarkable effect in spurring European determination and resolve to pick up a greater burden within the alliance," he said. "They really want to strengthen the European pillar of NATO."

Press reports indicate that target selection often involved British and US attempts to expand the target base in the face of French resistance, and these reports were later confirmed in General Short's testimony to the Senate Armed Services Committee on October 21, 1999.[87] General Short referred to French "red carding" of many of the proposed strike plans, The red flag was played by France on many occasions. . . . we had differences of the center of gravity. . . . Targeting Belgrade was a problem."[88]

Press reports indicate that France's President Chirac was not fully aware of the scale of the NATO attacks until he saw live television coverage of their effects on April 3, and he then asked for the ability to review targets, including all strikes in Montenegro.[89] France resisted broadening the target base to include strategic targets like the Socialist Party headquarters in Belgrade on April 21, in part because NATO target analysis indicate that the worst-case outcome of cruise missile strikes on the building would produce 350 casualties, including 250 living in apartments near the headquarters. Chirac's concerns had a major impact because France contributed the second-largest air component to Operation Allied Force: sixty aircraft at the start of the campaign and 100 by its finish.[90]

It is important to note that the French side of this argument is that the US (and by implication Britain) often bypassed the NATO chain of command, that the US used the dual command role of SACEUR as both the NATO and US commander to enforce its own policies on NATO. The main French report on the lessons of the war is just as critical of the US as the US sometimes is of France. It states that "some military operations (in Kosovo) have been conducted by the US outside of the strict definition of NATO and its procedures. The commander in chief of the operation SACEUR is responsible not only to the Atlantic Council—but also to the national hierarchy (of the US) at the highest level." It also says that, "The political-military decision-making process of the Alliance has been marked by a strong American predominance founded on the double chain of command centered around SACEUR and a true superiority in terms of military capabilities."[91] It goes on to note that US used its cruise missiles, bombers, and stealth aircraft without integrating them into the NATO command chain and implies that some US strikes were carried out without consulting NATO or France.[92]

National sensitivities involving targeting affected missions like the NATO strike on the air base at Podgorica, which was in Montenegro. At the same time, mission planners were confronted by problems in managing the day-to-day issues in collateral damage that involved another set of national sensitivities. For example, the NATO attack on the two radio and television towers in Belgrade was originally scheduled for April 12. It had to be rescheduled because foreign journalists ignored a warning to leave the buildings, and then was delayed by French concerns over targeting journalists. As a result, it was not hit until April 23.

French concerns not only had a major impact on air operations, they altered key aspects of NATO's strike plans. For example, SHAPE had originally planned to knock out the Serbian power grid during the first week in the war. France opposed the strikes, and this eventually led to a joint discussion by US and French military planners in which the US first presented plans to knock out the power grid for several weeks with high explosives.

When France refused, the US presented plans to use a weapon called the CBU-94 that scattered conductive carbon fibers over key distribution nodes and knocked out the power grid for several hours without leaving permanent damage. (The CBU-94 disperses small tennis-ball sized canisters filled with spools of carbon-graphite thread that unravel into a web that falls on power lines and transformer centers.) France still resisted such strikes, and they were not launched until May 3, nearly a month after they were originally scheduled. They then knocked out power over 70% of the grid for roughly a day, rather than for several weeks. France did not agree to more severe strikes until three weeks later.[93]

A senior French officer later explained the French position as follows, "We . . . pointed out that some of the targets were not convenient (or) appropriate. . . . It was not a veto of any kind—it was a recommendation by the French President and President Clinton agreed." Another senior French officer stated that NATO, "still achieved what we wanted to achieve. . . . I don't think at any time the French military has kept NATO from conducting its mission. . . . Look at the Greeks, they didn't like the way NATO conducted the war."[94]

France was not the only nation seeking a veto power. Prime Minister Blair is reported to have asked for a veto on all B-52 strikes taking off from Britain. Although all 19 delegates to the North Atlantic Council had agreed to give their proxy to NATO's Secretary General Javier Solana during the first week of the war. However, French concerns, and added Italian and Greek concerns led to the creation of a de facto British, French, German, Italian, and US "management committee" in which Britain, Germany, and the US generally pressed for expand-ing the range and intensity of strikes in the face of French and Italian resistance.[95]

It should also be noted that the Geneva Convention prohibits air attacks on purely civilian buildings, and on dual military and civilian sites when this produces "incidental loss of civilian life" in excess of the military value of the target. This ambiguous guidance, which makes no allowance for the large civilian component in modern warfare or for the fact Serbia was involved in massive ethnic cleansing, reinforced the moral ambiguity surrounding NATO planning.

Although NATO steadily escalated its air campaign from late April through early May, new problems arose because of collateral damage—which came to a head when US B-2 bombers hit the Chinese Embassy in Belgrade on May 7. The resulting loss of Chinese lives forced NATO to adopt a new targeting process which involved even more review of the political sensitivity of each target, and which led to a near halt on attacks on targets in Belgrade—although most critical targets in the city had been hit by this time.

It is important to note, however, that US officers accepted this national role in NATO decision-making as one of the prices of alliance and coalition warfare. General Short, for example, recommended that US aircraft like the B-2, B-52, U-2, Tomahawk land attack missile (TLAM), and F-117 be included in future NATO air traffic orders, rather than reserved as US controlled strategic systems. Regard-less of any problems with European control, Short felt that this would lead to better mission planning and execution, and that the US was attempting to control assets that were often based in Europe and had to be taken account of in NATO; "we kind of go into our US-only defensive crouch and pretend they do not what we are doing, and we're not going to tell them."[96]

Problems in Coalition Warfare: National Decision Making and the Incident at Pristina

One other disturbing sign of divisions in the high command of NATO occurred at the end of the fighting when Russian paratroops rushed into Kosovo's main airport at Pristina and refused to allow NATO to use the airport until the Russian government was given a new role in the peacekeeping force. General Sir Michael Jackson, the commander of the NATO forces in Kosovo, refused an order to use tanks and armored fighting vehicles to evict the Russians from SACEUR General Wesley Clark, stating that, "No, I am not going to do that. It's not worth starting World War III." Reports of this incident, which first appeared in *Newsweek*, were confirmed by General Henry H. Shelton, the US Chief of Staff.[97]

The problem with General Jackson's action is twofold. First, Pristina was only part of the problem. The Russian talks with NATO had never firmly resolved the command structure to be used in the peace-making operation and had not assigned any areas to Russia. The Russian intervention in Pristina not only threatened to create facts on the ground at the airport, Russia was preparing to fly substantially larger forces into Kosovo and would almost certainly had done so if Hungary, Bulgaria, and Rumania had not denied it overflight rights. It might also have rushed in forces from Bosnia.

Second, some intelligence experts believe that either Russia or elements in the Russian military had promised Serbia that Russia would create a peacekeeping zone that would act as a de facto partitioning of Kosovo. Others believe that the Russian Foreign Ministry was acting in good faith, but elements of the Russian military were not. As a result, General Jackson may have been luck that the failure of Russian reinforcements to secure possession of Pristina did not turn a minor confrontation into a major crisis.

Certainly, his decision raises further questions about whether NATO is an alliance or a warfighting committee.[98] There are British and US intelligence analysts who feel that Russia deliberately was attempting to undercut the withdrawal agreement between NATO and Serbia, and would have moved substantially large numbers of troops into Kosovo if neighboring East European states had granted the transit and overflight rights. If such movements had taken place, Russia might have been able to confront NATO with a situation where it could demand its own peacekeeping zone, and could have created a de facto Serbian zone in Kosovo. The maze of conflicting Russian claims, actions, and denials makes it impossible to determine the exact truth, but Jackson's delay might have had much more serious consequences if Russia had strongly reinforced its presence in Kosovo while NATO delayed its ground movements and reaction to the occupation of the airport.

Unity of Command versus Unity of Coalition

These considerations which led Secretary of Defense William S. Cohen to make the following points in his address on the lessons of Kosovo to the annual conference of the International Institute for Strategic Studies on September 9, 1999.[99]

It was Winston Churchill who once remarked, "In working with allies it sometimes happens that they develop opinions of their own." Indeed, Allied Force reminded us that consensus is both the heart and, at the times, the hindrance of a coalition. It became clear quite quickly that NATO needed to retool its existing political machinery to be more effective for what I would call the staccato timing of a military contingency. In this instance we shifted more authority—over a relatively short period of time, given the history of the organization itself—to the military commanders in the field, allowing them greater flexibility.

You have read about this. We can talk about this. But indeed, it was quite a task for the military commanders to have to deal with the political aspects of this particular campaign. That there was to be political oversight, civilian oversight of any military operation is something inherent in our democracies. We do not simply turn to the military and say here is a campaign, carry it out, we are unconcerned with the consequences. We are unconcerned about how it will be carried out. So we'll always want to have some civilian oversight of a military campaign.

In this particular case it was particularly daunting because you had 19 democracies, all of whom wished to have some say or at least some oversight role. That made it quite a challenge for the military commanders. But in a relatively short period of time greater and greater authority and flexibility was granted to the commanders in the field, and you saw as the campaign went on much more intensification not only of the targets but the areas of operation, on not only an eight hour day but a 24 hour a day campaign.

Secretary Cohen and General Shelton provided an equally insightful summary in their testimony to the Senate Armed Services Committee on the lessons of the war. This testimony focused on the strengths of the alliance as well as its problems and broadened the discussion to note that the members of the Alliance had to consider Russia and other nations as well as their own debates. It is clear from this statement that Kosovo was a "transatlantic" validation of the NATO alliance, regardless of any problems in coalition warfare.[100]

Balancing NATO's response to the Kosovo conflict with the desire to maintain a positive and cooperative relationship with Russia, which strongly opposed NATO military actions against the FRY, was essential. Given the importance of maintaining a constructive relationship with Moscow, both the United States and NATO had to consider carefully how their actions in the Balkans would affect their long-term relationship with Russia. Reaffirming the Alliance. The North Atlantic Treaty Organization proved to be flexible, effective, and ultimately successful during a uniquely challenging time in its history. Despite domestic pressures in many NATO nations, an enormous humanitarian crisis, and isolated instances of inadvertent collateral damage, the nations of the alliance held firm and saw the operation through to a successful conclusion.

Some say that working within the NATO alliance unduly constrained U.S. military forces from getting the job done quickly and effectively. And certainly, it was no surprise to any of us as we entered this conflict that conducting a military campaign in the alliance would be challenging, as we will discuss in more detail later. Nevertheless, Operation Allied Force could not have been conducted without the NATO alliance and without the infrastructure, transit and basing access, host-nation force contributions, and most importantly, political and diplomatic support provided by the allies and other members of the coalition.

These immense contributions from our allies and partners-particularly those nations near the theater of conflict like Hungary, Macedonia, Bulgaria, Romania, Albania, and others-were in large part a dividend of sustained U.S. and NATO engagement with those nations over the last few years. This engagement-including vigorous participation in Partnership for Peace activities-helped to stabilize institutions in these nations so they were better able to withstand the tremendous burden inflicted upon them by the humanitarian crisis and the conduct of the operation itself.

Admittedly, gaining consensus among 19 democratic nations is not easy and can only be achieved through discussion and compromise. However, the NATO alliance is also our greatest strength. It is true that there were differences of opinion within the alliance. This is to be expected in an alliance of democracies, and building consensus generally leads to sounder decisions. If NATO as an institution had not responded to this crisis, it would have meant that the world's most powerful alliance was unwilling to act when confronted with serious threats to common interests on its own doorstep.

It is important to remember that the alliance had been addressing this crisis-through diplomatic activities and military planning-for some time before the onset of the military campaign itself. Because NATO had been engaged in trying to resolve this conflict before the operation commenced, because it had conducted planning for the operation itself, because of its member nations' respect for differences of opinion and the need for consensus, and, simply, because the alliance is the most effective means there is for addressing European security problems-as it demonstrated through perseverance and unwavering solidarity-it was both natural and inevitable that we would work through NATO. Without the direct support of our NATO allies and key coalition partners, the campaign would not have been possible.

Lessons for the NATO Alliance

Kosovo highlights several important lessons and issues regarding NATO and coalition warfare that clearly need further examination, but which need action and resources far more than institution-building, words and study:

- *Kosovo again raises major issues about the role of Europe and the need for a new Transatlantic bargain. Like Bosnia, Kosovo raises serious questions about the need for major US involvement in security activity in or near Europe. There is certainly a clear need for a US role in NATO per se, and in cementing a post–Cold War security structure. At the same time, the US serves Western interests by bearing most of the power projection burden in the Gulf, and helping to stabilize the military situation in Asia—which is now a vital part of Western economic interests. The issue is not why the US should participate in NATO or remain in Europe, it is why the US should have to lead and bear so large a portion of the burden. It is whether a new Transatlantic bargain is needed in which European states assume most of the responsibility for any action in the Baltic, Central and Southern Europe and North Africa.[101]*

- *Kosovo has again exposed the tendency of Europe to talk about European security concepts without creating meaningful war fighting capabilities or taking meaningful action to create serious military capabilities. Kosovo led many Europeans to bemoan the lack of a European capability to act in a unified way, dependence on the US, and US "hegemony." It has led to the usual efforts to find some new way to create a viable European security structure in NATO, the EC, or WEU; create an integrated European approach to examining the lessons of Kosovo; or rush the integration of the WEU into the EC.*

- *Unfortunately, such efforts seems likely to end by rounding up the usual suspects to discuss new European institutions and bureaucratic arrangements without actually funding more than token improvements in actual war fighting, deployment, and peace making capability. Germany, for example, cut its defense budget from 3% of its GDP in 1990 to 1.5% in 1998. Its procurement budget fell from 12 billion ($7.05 billion) in 1990 to DM5.3 billion in 1997, and dropped from 30% to 23.7% of the entire defense budget. In spite of Kosovo, the German government's budget for 2000 calls for cuts of DM 30 billion, with similar cuts in 2001 and 2002. This is a 3.7% cut relative to the budget proposed by the previous government.[102] At the risk of "Eurobashing," the issue is whether Europe will focus on creating more bureaucrats or better arm and equip its military forces and show any collective will to use them.[103]*

- *At the same time, Kosovo provided a further illustration of the military problems in coalition warfare and exploiting the revolution in military affairs. The political decision to rely on air and missile power meant that Europe could never exploit its potential advantage in land forces. Although many European aircraft like the Mirage 2000, Tornado, Jaguar, and Harrier proved effective in a variety of missions, the US flew around 80% of all demanding strike-attack missions, and many European air forces lacked the technology and training to carry out demanding attack missions in power weather, at night, and using precision-guided weapons.*

- *The war also exposed the lack of European power projection capability, C⁴I/battle management capability, advanced secure and digitized communications, sensors, target and intelligence assets, and battle damage assessment capability. Europe is lagging badly in the revolution in military affairs, and this is creating two major problems that badly need to be addressed (a) the need for a comprehensive force modernization program in key European states, and (b) the need for realistic US planning to integrate low to mid-level technology forces into an effective capability for coalition warfare—rather than creating US capabilities based on reliance on US forces for most key missions or segregating out partner forces and assigning them to less important missions.[104]*

- *There is a need to develop more effective command and consultation processes among the members of the alliance, particularly for wars outside the normal province of NATO. Secretary Cohen and General Shelton made this point in their testimony to Congress on the lessons of the war, "NATO's internal command relationships played an important role in the planning and execution of the operation. These relationships are well defined, but had not been used previously to plan and conduct sustained combat operations."*

- *Moreover, parallel US and NATO command and control structures and systems complicated operational planning and maintenance of unity of command. In the aftermath of the operation, we believe that we need to work with our allies to: Enhance NATO's contingency planning process for non-Article V operations; Develop an overarching command and control policy and agree on procedures for the policy's implementation; and Enhance procedures and conduct exercises strengthening NATO's political-military interfaces.[105]*

US STRATEGY, FORCE PLANNING, AND DEFENSE SPENDING

Kosovo validated many aspects of US strategy, force planning, particularly in terms of the effectiveness of air and missile power, improvements in technology, and the need for steady improvements in jointness. At the same time, it highlighted some of the basic problems in US strategy and several important lessons relating to US force planning and defense spending.

Major Theater War (MTW) Operation Plans

Secretary Cohen and General Shelton did not fully address the lessons of Kosovo for US strategy in their testimony to Congress on the lessons of the war. Secretary Cohen did, however, raise the issue of whether the US had the capability to engage in two near-simultaneous major regional contingencies or major theater wars—which has been the keystone of US strategy ever since the start of the Clinton Administration.[106]

We . . . need to consider the implications of this campaign for our overall defense strategy, including the foremost question in this regard: Did the operation jeopardize our ability to fight and win two nearly simultaneous major theater wars? To begin, we must be clear about our strategy and what this means for the nation. As a global power with worldwide interests, it is imperative that the United States, in concert with its allies, be able to deter and defeat large-scale cross-border aggression in two distant theaters in overlapping time frames. In short, we must be able to fight and win two major theater wars nearly simultaneously.

Without question, a situation in which the United States would have to prosecute two major theater wars nearly simultaneously would be extraordinarily demanding well beyond that required for Operations Desert Shield/Desert Storm in 1990 and 1991. It would involve our complete commitment as a nation and would entail all elements of our total force. We have always recognized that, if confronted with two major theater wars, we would need to withdraw U.S. forces from ongoing peacetime activities and smaller-scale contingency operations as quickly as possible, including, in this instance, from Operation Allied Force, prepare them for war.

Consistent with our defense strategy, U.S. forces could not have continued the intense campaign in Kosovo and, at the same time, been prepared to fight and win two major theater wars. We were clearly mindful of our strategy as we undertook the campaign in Kosovo, just as we do when we undertake all other contingency operations, and we continually assessed the impact of these operations on our ability to defend effectively in other potential warfighting theaters.

For example, we recognized that the air bridge supporting operations in Kosovo would have enhanced our ability to respond to the threat of theater war in Southwest Asia. (And we already believed our deterrent posture to be strong because of substantial military capabilities associated with Operations Northern Watch and Southern Watch, our naval presence in the Persian Gulf and routine ground force deployments.)

In the Pacific theater, we determined that it would be prudent to enhance our deterrent posture against North Korea through a variety of means, including repositioning of units and the placement of other selected units on a short-time response posture.

Our objective in both theaters was to maintain a very visible defense capability to discourage leaders in Baghdad and Pyongyang from believing that our focus on Kosovo would present an opportunity to threaten our allies and friends in those important regions. Should we have faced the actual threat of war, we have detailed plans for redeploying committed assets to these potential warfighting theaters. Ultimately, should we have faced the challenge of withdrawing U.S. forces to mount two major wars in defense of our vital interests elsewhere, we are confident that we would have been able to do so, albeit at higher levels of risk.

We were cognizant of these risks at the time and made various adjustments in our posture and plans to address them. We recognize, however, that managing these risks is a highly complicated endeavor that would benefit from a more structured and dynamic set of tools for assessing our ability to conduct major wars when we respond to contingencies.

The US report on the lessons of the war issued in January 2000 was somewhat more frank.[107]

. . . if the threat of major theater war had developed in another theater during Operation Allied Force, the United States would have taken all actions necessary to prevail. In order to provide the full array of combat capabilities necessary to meet our MTW (Major Theater War) objectives, we would have likely reduced the tempo of U.S. operations over Kosovo to make certain specialized air assets, particularly RC-135 aircraft and aerial refueling platforms, available for higher priority missions. The Department has always recognized that, if confronted with two major theater wars, we would need to withdraw U.S. forces from ongoing peacetime activities and smaller-scale contingency operations as quickly as possible, including, in this instance, from Operation Allied Force to prepare them for war. Consistent with our defense strategy, U.S. forces could not have continued the intense campaign in Kosovo and, at the same time, conducted two major theater wars.

Accordingly, the Department continuously assessed the impact of these operations on our ability to defend effectively in other theaters. As discussed previously, the Department initiated a number of actions to mitigate the risk in other theaters by enhancing our deterrent posture in those theaters. Ultimately, should we have faced the challenge of withdrawing U.S. forces to mount two major wars in defense of our vital interests elsewhere, we are confident that we would have been able to do so, albeit at higher levels of risk. We were cognizant of these risks at the time and made various adjustments in our posture and plans to address them. At the same time, we recognize that managing these risks is a highly complicated endeavor that would benefit from a more structured and dynamic set of tools for assessing our ability to conduct major wars when we respond to contingencies.

. . . Operation Allied Force represented an MTW's level of effort for some key air assets, particularly the so-called Low Density/High Demand (LD/HD) assets, as well as selected tactical aircraft, airlift aircraft, and refueling tankers. The high demand for these aircraft was met by deploying aircraft from the forces assigned to the Commanders in Chief of theaters outside Europe. To mitigate the risk to the affected commands, equivalent type aircraft stationed in the continental United States were placed on alert and issued orders to be prepared to deploy on short notice.

Risk analysis is important in judging force readiness where commitments are made to support important and necessary operations but do not involve our vital interests. Some smaller-scale contingencies may be in this category. Probable future commitments make it important to enhance the Department's process for providing timely assessment of the impact of smaller-scale contingencies on the ability to execute the overall defense strategy. The complexities of assessing risk and taking operational measures to reduce risk during Operation Allied Force provided insights as to refinements in our process that can be made. For example, some improvements can be gained by ensuring that theater CINCs and the Services fully utilize the deployment-order coordination process for risk analysis.

When coordinating deployment orders, CINCs can assess the impact of orders to deploy forces from their command to other theaters (i.e., to "swing" forces from one theater to another) on their ability to execute the defense strategy and, when possible, identify measures that can reduce risk. Another possible improvement is the Readiness Assessment System (RAS) currently in development by the Defense Information Systems Agency (DISA). This system holds promise to provide a user-friendly, Web-based tool that allows users to view time-phased force and deployment data that supports an operational plan. The Readiness Assessment System can assist theater CINCs, the Joint Staff, and the Services in performing risk analysis. The Department will continuously strive to refine our process for timely assessment of risk.

Problems in US Defense Spending and Readiness

These statements and lessons are true as far as they go, but they do not address the true scale of the strain that a relatively limited US involvement in Kosovo put on the total pool of US power projection capabilities, or the growing limitations on US ability to "fight and win two major theater wars." The US entered Kosovo having cut its major combat units forces by more than one-third since the end of the Cold War, and its active major weapons strength by more than 40%.

The US was spending an average of $40 billion a year on procurement to meet annual requirements that the Joint Staff estimated at $60–70 billion. The US Army alone had already cancelled over 100 modernization programs since the end of the Cold War. This "downsizing" of US forces often meant that 70% to nearly 100% of many specialized US power projection assets had to be deployed for a relatively limited contingency, and that forces had to be moved in from other regional hot spots like Northeast Asia and the Gulf.

Each of the chiefs of the US services had declared that his service had major readiness problems in testimony to the Senate Armed Services Committee on

September 29, 1998—shortly before the beginning of the action in Kosovo. While this testimony is now dated, it still represents the frankest testimony the Chiefs have ever given and much of it has been reinforced respects by the budget and readiness testimony the Chiefs gave during 1999 and 2000, and in their discussions of the lessons of Kosovo, and remains the most detailed single picture of the issues involved.

The key points raised by each Chief may be summarized as follows:[108]

Chairman of the Joint Chiefs of Staff, General Henry H. Shelton

- Far more military activity than anticipated during the Quadrennial Defense Review.
- Higher than anticipated wear on equipment.
- Significant increases in shortages of spare parts and maintenance backlogs.
- Growing problems in recruiting and retention.
- Pay gap for military pay relative to civilian pay of 8.5% to 13.5%.
- Different retirement system for most junior two-thirds of force because Congress cut retirement benefits in 1986.

Chief of Staff, US Army, General Dennis J. Reimer

- 40% cut in funding since end of Cold War, down 650,000 personnel and in 13th year of declining buying power.
- The Army is underfunded to adequately meet all competing demands. It is underfunded by $3 to $5 billion a year.
- There are too many undermanned and unmanned squads and crews, and shortages in officer and noncommissioned officer positions.
- Serious modernization problems. Fund only highest priority program and continue to mortgage our future.
- Could only fund base operations at 85% of need, and real property maintenance at 58% of need, in FY1999.
- Some divisions have had no battalion-level field training in last two years.
- The Army suffers from serious overdeployment. FOSCOM deployments have increased from an annual rate of 26% to 68% of last 12 years.
- Serious recruiting and retention problems.
- Satisfaction with retirement benefits down for officers from 61.8% to 39% since 1992, and from 44.8% to 28.1% for enlisted personnel.
- Value of retirement package has dropped by 25% since 1986.

Chief of Naval Operations, Admiral Jay L. Johnson

- One-third of navy forward deployed.
- Defer ordering of parts, maintenance, and training so that additional funds can be made available for deployers.
- Condition and readiness of non-deployed aircraft is on downward trend.

- Reversed long-term decline in aviation accidents: Rate increased by 82% in 1998.
- Unable to afford the reliability and capability upgrades required for our ships and aircraft, improvements that respond to evolving threats, enhance readiness, and reduced life-cycle support costs.
- Need to increase the shipbuilding rate from today's 6–7 ships per year to 8–10 ships per year. Construction backlog continuing to grow.
- Will not attain and acceptable aircraft procurement rate until FY2002. Have delayed funding of the Common support aircraft for two years, and have aging aircraft for anti-submarine warfare, airborne early warning, and carrier on-board delivery.
- We need to increase recapitalization and modernization now; we are at a critical juncture.
- Serious problems with the inventory level of critical munitions, particularly the Toma-hawk Block III missile.
- Waste on surplus bases because of Congress: Have reduced the number of ships, aircraft, and personnel by twice as much as infrastructure. Could save $3 billion a year with proper base closings.
- Grossly overdeployed. Surface warfare community is about to extend sea duty for department heads by 6–8 months, aviation and submarine community will fol-low in FY2000.
- Retention and recruiting short of goal. Short 7,000 sailors this year. Shortfalls in skilled E-1 to E-3s. Short about 5,200 general detail personnel at sea, and manning at sea is only 78% of requirement.

Commandant of the Marine Corps, Charles C. Krulak

- Present defense budget does not meet the needs of the Marine Corps. We are effectively mortgaging the readiness of tomorrow's Marine Corps.
- Over 23,000 Marines deployed overseas away from families. Average work hours approach 14 hours a day, six days a week.
- Cannot afford constant deployments: We continue to shortchange modernization, base infrastructure and quality of life. Spend more and more time maintaining aging equipment.
- Lack funding for modernization in 2000–2010 time frame.
- Spend money on maintenance and spares need for new equipment. Approaching end of planned service life for many items without new equipment coming into service. Has raised maintenance costs by $309 million. See 46% increase in the number of repairs required for some critical equipment.
- Major problems in maintaining aging ground equipment and aircraft. Have had to take $3.6 billion out of modernization for ground equipment over the last seven years and spend it on current readiness. Have an urgent requirement for $1.2 billion more in equipment spending. Need to double planned funding of $900 million a year and need at least $500–600 million.
- Overall reserve readiness down to 81% of requirement. And have only 70% of need engineer assets and 61% of motor transport assets. HMMWV numbers only 52% of need.
- CH-46Es about to reach end of service life, and CH-53Ds operating seven years beyond planned service life. Flying airframes 47 years old.

- Age increases aircraft maintenance costs. Up 49% in average cost of flight hours from FY96 to FY98—$2,341 to $3,481 per hour.
- Maintenance backlogs becoming critical. These had a cost of less than $200 million in FY1980 and were still below $400 million in FY1990. They are now in excess of $800 million with much smaller force and will reach $1 billion in FY2003.
- Maintenance funding is $125 million a year under requirement, and construction is $75 million. Meeting normal industry standards would require $275 million a year more. Have 12,000 family housing units needing urgent rebuilding,
- Training underfunded.
- Retention and recruiting efforts threatened.

Chief of Staff of the Air Force, General Michael E. Ryan

- Slow but steady decline in readiness and project continued decline in key areas.
- 90,000 uniformed personnel forward deployed.
- Mission capability rates have dropped 9% since 1991 and 2% since January 1998. Force has gone from 16% not-mission capable in FY1991 to 27% in FY1999.
- Overall major unit readiness has declined by 14% during the last two and one-half years, and stateside combat readiness by 49%, with half of the decline during the past seven months.
- Cost of spares outstrips funding. Cannibalization rate is up 50% since 1995.
- Average age of fighters is up from 8 years in FY1990 to 16 years now, and will reach 20 years in 2010.
- Average age of entire air fleet is up from 12 years in FY1990 to 20 years now, and will reach 30 years in 2010
- Recruiting becoming a major problem. Retention rate down in many critical specialties from nearly 90% in FY94 to well below minimum goal of 75%. Is about 52% for F-15 avionics specialists, 70% for F-15 and C-130 crew chiefs, and 52% for air traffic control experts.
- Pilot retention is in crisis state. Project 12,000 pilots for FY2002, short 2,000 of goal—shortfall of 15%. Retention rate well below goal of 50%.

The Force Drawdown Imposed by Kosovo

When the campaign in Kosovo escalated, it had a major impact on the global pool of US air power. Nearly half of the USAF was involved in the operation in Kosovo during the peak of the operation. This compares with 15% in Vietnam and 30% in Desert Storm. According to one estimate, the Air Force deployed 45% of high-demand command, control, communications and computers/intelligence, surveillance, and reconnaissance (C^4/ISR) assets. It deployed 22% of its bombers and 44% of its fighters, more than 40% of its tankers, and 80% of its tanker crews. It deployed virtually all of its F-16CJ air defense suppression aircraft.

As a result, President Clinton had to call up selected reserve components in late April.[109] While Kosovo did not imposed similar strains on the US Navy and

Marine Corps, they were forced to devote a large portion of their global assets of special purpose aircraft like the E-6A/B to a conflict that was scarcely a major regional contingency.

The Clinton Administration did request $6.05 billion for an emergency supplemental of April 19, 1999, and the US Congress eventually provided $14.9 billion in supplemental funds and $2.0 billion in offsetting revisions.[110] This appropriation more than offset the direct cost of Kosovo, although it involved a large amount of "pork" and items the military did not request.

As Brigadier General Richard E. Hawley, the head of the US Air Force Air Combat Command, pointed out in vast statistical depth, it also did not do anything to alter the fact that Kosovo put major new strains on an already over-deployed force.[111] It is also striking that the US Army declared that two of its active divisions—the 10th Mountain and 1st Infantry—had only C-4 readiness (the lowest category of readiness) in November 1999.[112]

Being the World's Only Superpower Without Paying for the Power

Furthermore, the supplement did not affect several major problems in the balance between US strategy and deployments and the funding available in recent defense budgets and projected in the current Future Year Defense Plan, and which Kosovo indicates are "lessons" that may come back to haunt the US:[113]

- *The US simply is not spending enough to create an active force structure large enough to meet its real-world deployment needs, maintain the level of readiness it needs, carry out sustained sudden deployments, and maintain and improve its technical edge. Part of the reason for the US Army's deployment problems is that it chose to fund force structure over readiness and deployment capability when it needed both. The US Navy and Air Force had to draw down on a large part of their inventory of advanced long-range strike assets. The Navy, Marine Corps, and Air Force are chronically over deployed, and all lack adequate deployment assets and funds for training and readiness. The US simply cannot sustain a force posture that costs some $25–40 billion dollars more a year than it is willing to pay for in its defense budget.*

- *The "two major theater war strategy" the US claims to fund is a hollow farce. The US has never really funded or planned to execute a strategy of being able to fight two near-simultaneous major regional contingencies. It now, however, must execute a strategy of three major regional containments whether it likes it or not while both being ready to take on new peace making commitments and preparing counterproliferation capabilities to meet new kinds of threats.[114] The Bottom Up Review and Quadrennial Defense Reviews are clearly exercises in political gamesmanship. The US needs to revise its strategy and force plans to suit its real-world strategic situation.*

- *The political vacuum created in US plans and doctrine created by the US military's failure to consider the political aspects of war in documents like Joint Vision 2010 and the denial of the need for continuing highly political peacemaking and low intensity conflicts threatens US military capabilities. As is discussed in some detail in the analysis of air and missile power, the US simply was not prepared for the political dimension of war. It talks about asymmetric conflicts without creating real world war fighting capabilities while its key doctrinal documents concentrate on fighting a large, exposed, conventional opponent like Iraq. The US military remains unprepared for the reality that war is an extension of politics.*

- *The US needs a Rapid Expeditionary Force Posture that is not tied to predictable contingencies. The US Army clearly lacked the rapid deployment and expeditionary capabilities it needed to make sudden and effective use of limited numbers of AH-64s and Multiple Launch Rocket Systems (MLRS). In fairness to the Army, this was partly a result of funding problems and a Congressional insistence on a total force concept involving the National Guard and Reserves that makes it difficult to create cost-effective US Army capabilities. The fact remains, however that the Army is something of a strategic dinosaur and it badly needs to restructure the "army right now" rather than waiting for the "Army after next." At the same time, The USAF often was forced to use over 90% of its total expeditionary assets in a war in which it could operate under sanctuary conditions from friendly and highly advanced air bases. The US needs to make a comprehensive review of its rapid deployment and expeditionary capabilities, and create the capabilities it needs.*

The FY2001 defense budget that President Clinton proposed to Congress in February 2000 makes some efforts to deal with these problems. It does solve some of the worst problems in the underfunding of US military manpower, and calls for broad rises in procurement spending. It also funds more than $3.5 billion in enhancements specifically designed to address the lessons learned from the Kosovo operation.

Of this amount, however, over $1.9 billion was provided by the Congress in the FY 2000 supplemental. The Department has added only $1.6 billion to react to the considerable lessons of Kosovo during the FY2001–2005 program.[115] Once one looks beyond rhetoric, much of the added money is consumed by inflation and cost escalation, and most of the readiness problems the Chiefs raised in their 1998 testimony remain. There are comparatively few new funds to deal with the broader lessons of Kosovo.

The Department of Defense recognizes these problems in other portions of its report on the lessons of the war, but only in passing and in a form that sharply understates the limitations the US would face in trying to fight two nearly simultaneous major theater wars regardless of whether it was involved a limited conflict like Kosovo.[116]

If the threat of major theater war had developed in another theater during Operation Allied Force, the United States would have taken all actions necessary to prevail. Our first course of action would have been to take additional steps to enhance our deterrent posture in the likely theater of conflict, as was the case during Allied Force. Had deterrence failed, we would have deployed those forces that would be required to halt the initial attack and then build our combat strength to conduct counteroffensive operations.

Without question, a situation in which the United States would have to prosecute two major theater wars nearly simultaneously would be extraordinarily demanding—well beyond that required for Operations Desert Shield and Desert Storm in 1990 and 1991. It would involve our complete commitment as a nation and would entail all elements of our total force. The Department recognizes that, if confronted with two major theater wars, we would need to withdraw U.S. forces from ongoing peacetime activities and smaller-scale contingency operations—including, in this instance, from Operation Allied Force—to prepare them for war. Consistent with our defense strategy, U.S. forces could not have continued the intense campaign in Kosovo and, at the same time, conducted two nearly simultaneous major theater wars.

Ultimately, if the decision was made to disengage from Kosovo in order to mount two major theater wars in defense of vital interests in other theaters, we would have been able to do so, albeit at higher levels of risk than would have been the case if U.S. forces had not been conducting operations in Kosovo. We were cognizant of these risks at the time and made various adjustments in our posture and plans to address those risks. Operation Allied Force heightened awareness to the fact that managing these risks is a highly complicated endeavor that would benefit from a more structured and dynamic set of tools for assessing our ability to conduct major wars when we respond to contingencies.

4

The Strategic Impact and Military Effectiveness of the Air and Missile Campaign

The success of the air and missile campaign in Kosovo has already led some advocates of air and missile power to talk about the war as evidence that air and missile power can win a victory without a ground campaign. It has led others to speculate that air and missile power is now so decisive that it should be given a larger share of military budgets and force postures relative to ground and naval forces.[117]

There is no doubt that the air and missile campaign in Kosovo demonstrated the steadily improving effectiveness and lethality of air and missile power. There is no doubt that steady and important advances are taking place in targeting and intelligence, battle management, all-weather offensive combat, weapons lethality, long-range attack capability, precision guided munitions, the precise launch of unguided ordnance, beyond-visual-range air combat, air defense suppression, and stealth and penetration capability. The air and missile war in Kosovo is clearly a validation of these trends, as well as of the importance of technology in reshaping the nature of war.

THE SPECIAL CONDITIONS OF THE WAR IN KOSOVO

At the same time, the growing importance of air and missile power has been characteristic of virtually every war since World War I, and it is far from clear that Kosovo says anything truly new or unique about the value of air and missile power per se. To begin with, it is important to consider the special conditions that shape the air and missile war in Kosovo:

- Serbia was a small power with limited air and surface to air missile assets, and had no resupply during the war.
- Serbia had no military allies, and was surrounded on all sides by nations friendly to NATO—although SHAPE sources reported on June 30 that 200 Russians were present in Serbia in some capacity, that at least two were killed by the KLA, and that some form of Russian presence existed in the Serbia forces used in the attack on Mount Pastrik.
- NATO fought a limited war that did not threaten the survival of the Serbian regime and military forces.

- NATO accepted a situation where Serbia could carry out massive ethnic cleansing—the key threat that NATO initiated the war to prevent.
- As has been noted earlier, NATO also did not really win through air and missile power alone, and could not prevent the need for a land phase involving the deployment of major peacekeeping forces with a risk of an extended presence of half a decade or more and a continuing risk of low intensity conflict.

MORE THAN AIR POWER LED TO NATO'S VICTORY

One must be careful about giving air and missile power more credit than it is really due. Jointness was critical to the operation in providing both land and sea-based air and missile power. Serbia was forced to withdraw from Kosovo for a variety of reasons other than the effectiveness of air and missile power:

- Serbia's acute economic weakness at the start of the war.
- Serbia alienated most of the world by its ethnic cleansing activities and lost all meaningful outside political support. Once Russia joined NATO in pressing for a peace settlement on terms that offered Serbia no hope of outside aid or that the world would tolerate ethnic cleansing.
- The total failure of Serbian forces to defeat the KLA in the planned 5–6 days, and Serbia's inability to defeat the ground operations of the Kosovo Liberation Army without exposing its forces to devastating air attack, and
- The presence of the substantial NATO ground force already in the region, which is shown in Figure 8, and the deployment of Task Force Hawk and the growing political debate in NATO over the need for a ground option created the growing possibility that NATO would pursue a ground option if NATO air and missile power did not achieve decisive results.

As is discussed later, there is also some evidence that the Serbian leadership was aware that NATO had secretly prepared a ground invasion option, and that it confronted a very real threat of a major NATO invasion in the fall of 1999.

THE RELEVANCE OF KOSOVO TO OTHER WARS

The "iron law" of military history is that no past war is ever a completely valid model of the next conflict. This may be particularly true of Kosovo. It is very

Figure 8
The Initial Plan for the Ground Phase of Peacemaking

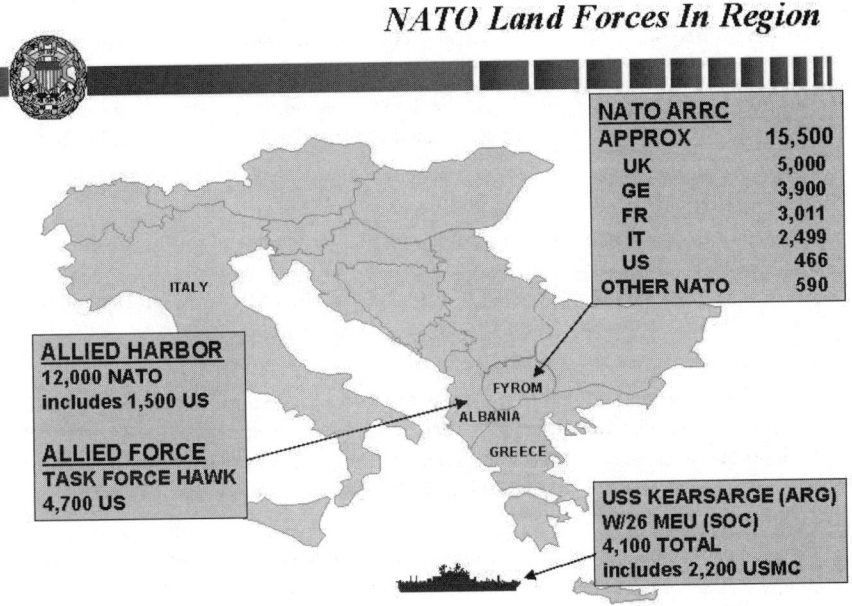

NATO Land Forces In Region

NATO ARRC	
APPROX	15,500
UK	5,000
GE	3,900
FR	3,011
IT	2,499
US	466
OTHER NATO	590

ALLIED HARBOR
12,000 NATO
includes 1,500 US

ALLIED FORCE
TASK FORCE HAWK
4,700 US

ITALY

FYROM
ALBANIA
GREECE

USS KEARSARGE (ARG)
W/26 MEU (SOC)
4,100 TOTAL
includes 2,200 USMC

Source: Adapted from the Department of Defense press briefing for June 3, 1999.

unlikely that the air and missile war in Kosovo will be a model for future wars, and the tactics and technologies used would not have decisively reversed or altered the outcome of many other wars fought since World War II.

The US alone has used military force well over 240 times since World War II. Without going through the list of cases, it is doubtful that the improvements in air and missile power reflected in Kosovo would materially have changed the outcome of most cases. The success of coalition air and missile power during the air phase of the Gulf War is almost certainly a far more important watershed in the role of air and missile power than Kosovo, and involved a far more serious enemy and set of tactical problems.

Consider the following cases—which involve both the kind of major regional contingencies which are the focus of US strategy and the kind of low intensity conflicts and peacemaking missions that seem to have become typical of post–Cold War military deployments:

- *Vietnam*: Improvements in air and missile power might have forced an earlier cease-fire and led to an earlier US withdrawal. Air power could not have altered the fact that South Vietnam was politically a "failed state."

- *Beirut and Lebanon After 1982*: A highly political and asymmetric war involving low intensity combat in which no combination of the US edge in land, air, and sea power could be decisive
- *The Liberation of Kuwait in 1991*: Air power made a massive contribution to victory, but could not have liberated Kuwait without a massive land component.
- *Somalia in 1992–1993*: A highly political and asymmetric war involving low intensity combat in which neither the US edge in land or air and missile power could be decisive.
- *Iraq Since 1991*: Air power has been used repeatedly to contain Saddam Hussein, and with considerable success, but the regime remains intact.
- *The Defense of Kuwait in 1999*: Air power might or might not be able to prevent a sudden Iraqi surprise attack on Kuwait, the seizure of Kuwait City, and holding the Kuwaitis for ransom. USCENTCOM experts seem to feel it could not halt an all-out Iraqi advance.
- *Korea in 1999*: Air power would have no chance of decisively defeating a North Korean advance without a massive land component.
- *Counterproliferation in 2000+*: Air power has a very uncertain capability to deter a threat with extensive missile forces and weapons of mass destruction unless it is armed with weapons of mass destruction. There are no current prospects that air and missile power can replace a land-oriented, on-the-scene body like UNSCOM in the counterproliferation mission.
- *Counterterrorism, Low Intensity Combat, and Peacemaking in 2000+*: The advances taking place in air and missile power are best suited to the defeat of exposed enemy forces in regular wars. Like other aspects of the "revolution in military affairs," they have uncertain advantage in highly political asymmetric wars.

As a minor historical aside, it is also worth pointing out that NATO's use of air and missile power in Kosovo was not the first victory of such power in war without a major land component. This is true even if one ignores the impact of Serbia's inability to defeat the ground operations of the Kosovo Liberation Army without exposing its forces to devastating air attack, and the fact that Serbia's decision to accept NATO's terms was probably influenced by the growing prospect that NATO would pursue a ground option if NATO air and missile power did not achieve decisive results.

The first decisive use of air and missile power to defeat a significant ground power without the use of extensive land forces was almost unquestionably the RAF's defeat of the advance of the Saudi Ikhwan on Transjordan in August 1922. If one objects to the presence of a few British armored cars in the conflict, it would then be the RAF's defeat of advance of the Saudi Ikhwan on Iraq at the "battle" of Busaiya in October 1927. If one picks the right war or battle, air and missile power has been "decisive" ever since the days of the biplane and for nearly eighty years.

ROB PETER TO PRAISE PAUL?

No analyst can deny that the outcome of the air and missile war in Kosovo is an important further argument to fund strong, combat ready air forces and to continue to fund major advances in the technology of air combat and the deployment of air combat systems. It is not, however, a reason for arguing for major trade-offs in the funding given air and missile power relative to other combat elements, or for redefining "jointness." Not only was airpower not decisive in Kosovo, trade-offs that weaken land and sea power put a steadily heavier burden on air and missile power, and create added pressures to use it in missions where air and missile power alone may not be able to do the job.

This is not a practical option for an America that is attempting to remain the "world's only super power" while spending some $20–30 billion less a year than is needed to maintain its current force structure, maintain its current rate of commitments, and modernize to maintain and reinforce its technical edge. "Military cannibalism" is not a solution to the problems of underfunding and overdeployment. It is interesting to note that both Secretary Cohen and General Shelton rejected the idea of air-oriented trade-offs during the same press conference given on June 10 to praise the performance of NATO air and missile power during the war.

Questioner: Mr. Secretary and Mr. Chairman, I'd like to ask you both, given the success of this air-war and the fact that there's extreme political reluctance in both this country and in Europe to bloody ground troops in combat any more, are ground troops in combat—is this going to be the way that the West fights wars in the future? Will ground combat troops become somewhat superfluous? And will Army budgets suffer to the Air Force because of this?

Secretary Cohen: Let me speak as Secretary of Defense, that we will continue to use ground forces wherever they are required in the best possible military campaign that can be devised, under the most optimum circumstances. We are not afraid to use, in any case, a ground component to a military campaign. We have ground forces that are currently deployed in South Korea. We have ground forces that are deployed in Southwest Asia. There's never any hesitancy on the part of this Department or this President to use those forces when the circumstances dictate.

As we've indicated so many times before, under this scenario, at least, we were constrained because we had to have consensus. We were not about to take unilateral action. We had to have a consensus of NATO. NATO had one consensus—which was for the application of air power. There was no consensus for the application of ground forces in a non-permissive environment. So ordinarily you would say you would always have a plan for both air and sea and ground. Under this particularly circumstance, the consensus was for the application of air power as the Chairman has laid out in a phased campaign. It ultimately proved to be successful.

You saw just a few weeks ago once the element of whether ground forces would go into a non-permissive environment, you certainly saw some question of division within the alliance itself. Had that taken place at the very beginning, we would have seen Milosevic carrying out his campaign of ethnic terror and purging at the same time that NATO countries would have been still debating the issue of who would participate and who would not. So we think, under the circumstances, this was the best of a series of bad options, but this was the best option under the circumstance, and ultimately has proved successful.

Questioner: . . .Chairman. Will the Army suffer and the Air Force benefit from what— smart weapons? I would ask the Chairman.

Secretary Cohen: The answer is no. The Army will not suffer as a result of this. The Army's in the process of reshaping itself, modernizing, acquiring the kind of equipment that will be necessary for the Army to function as a superior force in the 21st century. This is not a zero-sum game. This is not a situation where the Air Force with its superb performance will result in diminishing the Army's resources. We have one military and it's fully integrated and it is joint, and where the ground force is required the ground force will go. Where the Air Force is required, it will go as well. Presumably, we'll operate for the most part fully integrated and joint. This was a unique situation.

General Shelton: One of the great strengths of our armed forces are the complementary capabilities that are brought, that we have within the services that enable us to cover the entire spectrum of conflict. We've got the world's greatest Air Force, Army, Navy, Marine Corps, Coast Guard today, and we're able then to apply the forces that we need and do it in a joint environment to enable us to carry it out.

It would be a mistake to ever take any of those off the table. Depending on what you're asked to do to meet the political objectives, either of NATO or of the United States if we're acting unilaterally, requires you to have those types of capabilities if you're going to have global responsibilities, and you've got to have global power, and you've got to have the complementary capabilities of each of the services.

STRATEGIC LIMITS ON IMPACT OF AIR POWER IN KOSOVO: LESSONS FOR THE FUTURE?

There are other reasons to be cautious about generalizing the lessons of the air and missile war in Kosovo. The air and missile campaign in Kosovo involved constraints that made it impossible to use air and missile power with maximum effectiveness. NATO's air and missile campaign began with twelve major grand strategic, strategic, and tactical limitations that make much of the debate over the broader lessons of this air and missile campaign somewhat moot. The outcome of the air and missile campaign was heavily affected by these initial political and conceptual limits, and the resulting Rules of Engagement (ROE).

No one can now determine what would have happened if:

- *NATO and key NATO member-country political leaders had not repeatedly publicly ruled out a ground option and had not signaled Serbia that it had freedom of action in Kosovo.* Regardless of whether NATO would have used such an option, NATO failed to preserve an important political and strategic lever that might have contributed to an earlier termination of the conflict. While strategic ambiguity is not an ideal lesson for every conflict, it is often a powerful tool. In this case, NATO politics meant that NATO's leaders spent more time during much of the crisis trying to reassure their own peoples than they did in trying to influence the enemy, although it is possible that their secret efforts to prepare for a ground option did eventually help terminate the conflict.

- *Enough air and missile power had been assembled at the start of the campaign to approach "decisive force."* During the first 38 days of the Gulf War, allied air forces flew nearly 100,000 sorties, dropped around 226,000 munitions, and struck some 1,200 targets. In a similar period in Kosovo, they flew about 12,000 sorties and fired about 4,000 bombs and missiles at 230 sites.[118] At the end of the air and missile campaign in Kosovo, NATO had expended some 23,000 air munitions and 329 cruise missiles. The Coalition had claimed to have destroyed 40 percent of Iraq's tanks in the KTO, 32 percent of its armored personnel carriers, and 48 percent of its artillery. In contrast, NATO claimed to have hit less than 15 percent of the tanks and armored personnel carriers in Kosovo. The Coalition had also completed the deployment of some 700,000 troops for the liberation of Kuwait versus NATO's deployment of around 20,000 peacekeepers.

- *NATO entered the air and missile war having planned for an option other than the success of the initial negotiations or Serbian acceptance of these terms after a limited number of strikes.* NATO went to war without serious planning for key options or readiness for a major war.

- *NATO had planned from the start to deal with the risk of a dramatic increase in ethnic cleansing and ethnic warfare, rather than had had to adapt to the reality of these events once air strikes began.* NATO threatened war without having a clear contingency plan to deal with the very problem that led it to threaten air strikes in the first place.

- *NATO had immediately escalated to strategic bombing of Serbia when massive ethnic cleansing began,* and had been willing to attack targets vital to the functioning of civilian life. NATO's strategic bombing campaign did not reply to ethnic cleansing in kind.[119]

- *NATO had begun the war with a full targeting plan geared to all possible contingencies,* supported by the proper in-theater intelligence and reconnaissance assets, and taking the problems of collateral damage fully into account.[120]

- *NATO had been willing to take added casualties and losses in return for added effectiveness.*

- *NATO had given military effectiveness more priority relative to the risk of inflicting collateral damage.*

- *NATO had had a clear plan for a psyops and political warfare campaign when the campaign began,* and had struck to deprive Milosevic of his main propaganda instruments like radio and TV transmitters at the start, and had been prepared to beam in its own "truth" message. Serbia was able to maintain control over Serbia's media and the information available to most of its population throughout the war, and often out propagandized NATO in the world media. NATO never achieved information parity, much less "information dominance," in any political sense of the term.

- *If NATO had realistically planned for the technical limits of air and missile power in bad weather* and against a highly political target base like the mix of Serbian refugees and Kosovar refugees in Kosovo.

- *If the AH-64s and MLRS had been predeployed and combat ready,* or had been committed once they were combat ready, and/or

- *NATO had planned to deal with the refugee problem in humanitarian terms by creating military safe havens.*

This mix of limitations severely weakened the impact of the air and missile campaign during the initial weeks of the war, and several of these limitations continued to have a major impact throughout the campaign. Many of these limitations also reflect what seems to be a continuing US and Western inability to understand the risks inherent in threatening military action. It is easy to use terms like "peace making" but they are simply polite new ways of describing the 19th century concept of "just war." The result of threatening force can easily lead to worst case scenarios, and to wars that have to be fought to a grim conclusion.

Put differently, the need to avoid or minimize the kind of limitations placed on air power in Kosovo constitute one of the major lessons of the war. Major powers like the US and NATO cannot afford to plan for success under conditions that cripple military effectiveness. If they threaten to use force, they must be prepared to use it with the strength and decisiveness required, and they must plan for worst cases.

The mix of political and financial costs and risks inherent in deploying inadequate forces offset any savings in far too many cases to make this an acceptable policy. It may not be possible to avoid a wide range of political constraints in most contingencies, but the risk and probable military impact of such constraints needs far more explicit analysis, and any such trade-offs should be made only after very careful consideration.

"SHOCK AND AWE" OR "LIMITS AND RESTRAINT"

There is a strong case to be made for the use of decisive force even when moral and ethical factors are fully taken into account. The morality of war cannot be summarized in a sound bite or the kind of catch phrase that belongs in a fortune cookie. It also cannot be defined in terms of an effort to minimize short-term casualties, equipment losses, and collateral damage. Limiting military action in the short term can extend the overall length and intensity of war, increase casualties, and create conditions which make it more difficult to reach a stable outcome and a lasting peace. It can mean failing to protect an ally or to serve the humanitarian goal that is the purpose of fighting in the first place. Inadequate force is often as likely to produce the wrong strategic and moral outcome as excessive force.

NATO was not prepared to deal with these realities when it negotiated with the Serbs, or began the bombing campaign. It was not prepared to use decisive force in either political or military terms. The end result was thousands of dead and over 1.5 million refugees.

As Figures 9 and 10 show, this was not a casual issue. NATO did end the air and missile campaign with a military victory, but virtually all Serbian ethnic cleansing occurred during the course of the air and missile campaign. While some wartime estimates of mass killings and the hardships suffered by the Kosovar Albanians in Kosovo may be exaggerated, it still seems clear that ethnic cleansing reached the point by mid-May where it affected so much of the Kosovar Albanian population.

Figure 9
The Build-Up of the Refugee Crisis: The Human Cost of NATO Restraint and a NATO Victory

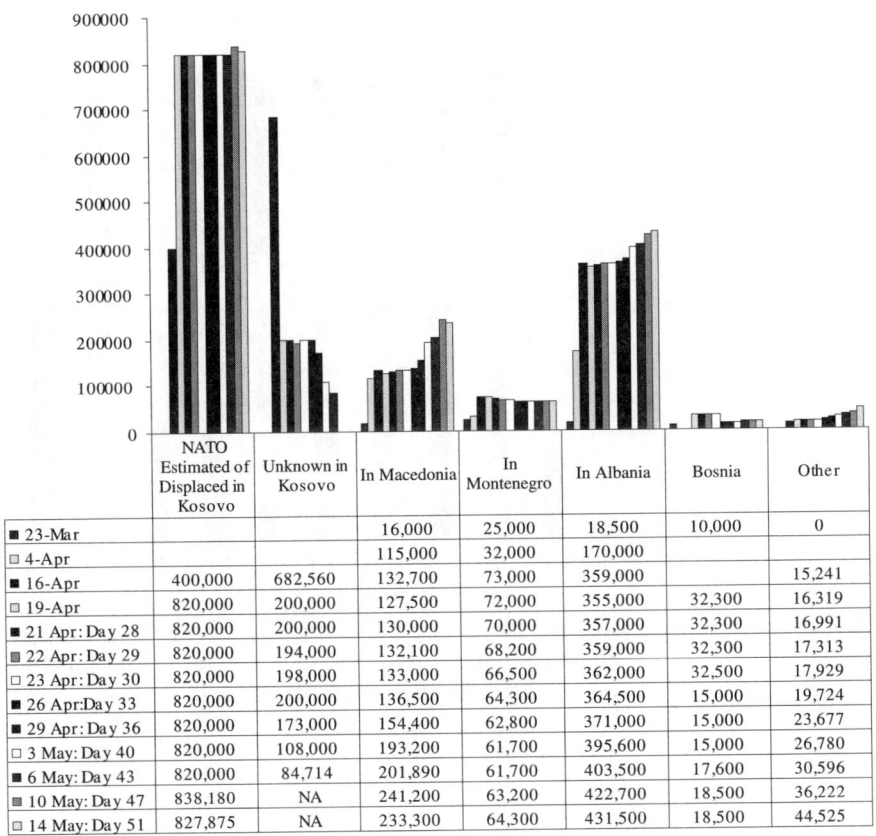

	NATO Estimated of Displaced in Kosovo	Unknown in Kosovo	In Macedonia	In Montenegro	In Albania	Bosnia	Other
■ 23-Mar			16,000	25,000	18,500	10,000	0
□ 4-Apr			115,000	32,000	170,000		
■ 16-Apr	400,000	682,560	132,700	73,000	359,000		15,241
□ 19-Apr	820,000	200,000	127,500	72,000	355,000	32,300	16,319
■ 21 Apr: Day 28	820,000	200,000	130,000	70,000	357,000	32,300	16,991
▨ 22 Apr: Day 29	820,000	194,000	132,100	68,200	359,000	32,300	17,313
□ 23 Apr: Day 30	820,000	198,000	133,000	66,500	362,000	32,500	17,929
■ 26 Apr:Day 33	820,000	200,000	136,500	64,300	364,500	15,000	19,724
■ 29 Apr: Day 36	820,000	173,000	154,400	62,800	371,000	15,000	23,677
□ 3 May: Day 40	820,000	108,000	193,200	61,700	395,600	15,000	26,780
■ 6 May: Day 43	820,000	84,714	201,890	61,700	403,500	17,600	30,596
▨ 10 May: Day 47	838,180	NA	241,200	63,200	422,700	18,500	36,222
□ 14 May: Day 51	827,875	NA	233,300	64,300	431,500	18,500	44,525

Source: UNHCR, NATO.

It also seems clear that at least 80% of the people NATO attempted to protect suffered grievously during the war. NATO totally failed to meet its initial goal of putting an "immediate end to ethnic cleansing" unless immediate is defined as 11 weeks.

NATO's restraint meant that it was not prepared to deal with the asymmetric nature of the war. It did not seek to use air and missile power decisively to force an end to ethnic cleansing. It gave the Serbs de facto strategic sanctuaries, and its slow pattern of escalation in some ways taught the Serbs to accept the damage done by air and missile power where a sudden, massive use of air and missile power might have led to far more immediate results. Gradual escalation tends to fail, or to make escalation the norm, where shock and decisive force can sometimes produce far

Figure 10

Ethnic Cleansing Reaches the 90th Percentile: The Human Cost of NATO Restraint and a NATO Victory

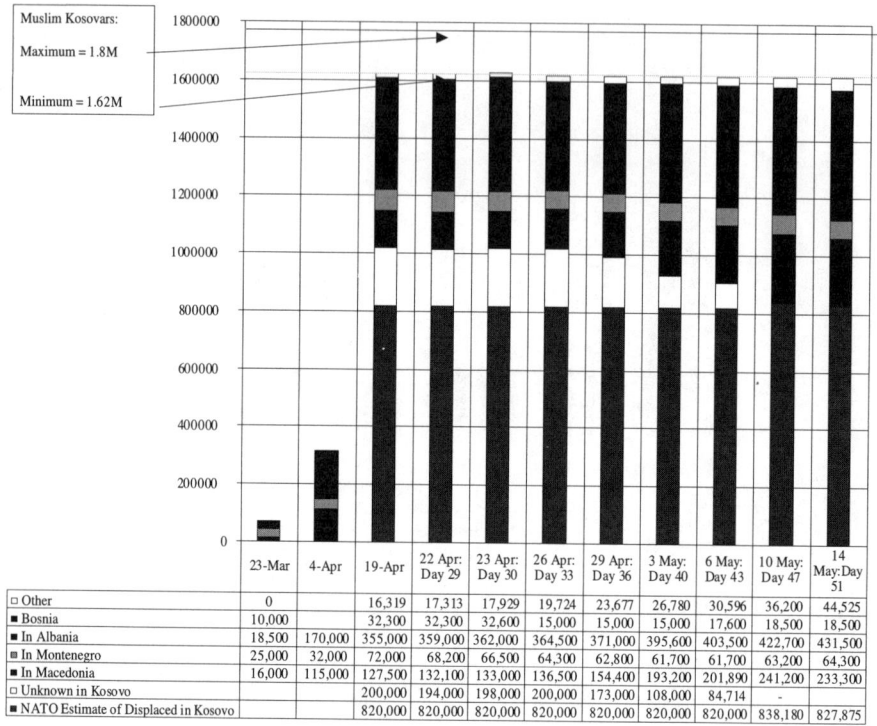

	23-Mar	4-Apr	19-Apr	22 Apr: Day 29	23 Apr: Day 30	26 Apr: Day 33	29 Apr: Day 36	3 May: Day 40	6 May: Day 43	10 May: Day 47	14 May: Day 51
□ Other	0		16,319	17,313	17,929	19,724	23,677	26,780	30,596	36,200	44,525
■ Bosnia	10,000		32,300	32,300	32,600	15,000	15,000	15,000	17,600	18,500	18,500
■ In Albania	18,500	170,000	355,000	359,000	362,000	364,500	371,000	395,600	403,500	422,700	431,500
▨ In Montenegro	25,000	32,000	72,000	68,200	66,500	64,300	62,800	61,700	61,700	63,200	64,300
■ In Macedonia	16,000	115,000	127,500	132,100	133,000	136,500	154,400	193,200	201,890	241,200	233,300
□ Unknown in Kosovo			200,000	194,000	198,000	200,000	173,000	108,000	84,714	-	
■ NATO Estimate of Displaced in Kosovo			820,000	820,000	820,000	820,000	820,000	820,000	820,000	838,180	827,875

Source: UNHCR, NATO.

more prompt results. There are no rules to history, but if force is worth using at all, the early use of decisive force is generally best.

It is also important to note that public opinion tended to shift against the war towards the end of the campaign, and that there were growing pressures to put an end to the fighting. Western public opinion had not be prepared for a long conflict or for a ground option because it was not politically convenient for NATO's political leaders to discuss these options in the short term. It is far from clear that the US, NATO, or other peacemakers are prepared for longer and more frustrating conflicts in the future, or ones with higher losses. The US withdrawals from Lebanon and Somalia are cases in point. Further the same factors which tend to limit US and NATO willingness to use force decisively are the same kind of factors that act to prolong conflicts and make their outcome uncertain.[121]

The practical problem for NATO, the US, and the West is whether it is possible for the West's political leaders to deal with these issues in ways that will permit the use of decisive force. If they do not, the kind of limitations NATO faced during the air and missile campaign in Kosovo are part of a pattern of growing political limitations on the ways in which Western democracies can wage war.

It may well be that the advances in war fighting capability that make up the revolution in military affairs have a self-canceling backlash by creating a steadily growing set of political limitations on the ways in which wars can be fought, and steadily growing demands to minimize friendly and hostile casualties and collateral damage. One of the ironies of the advances in modern air and missile power, and modern military technology of all kinds, is that it may be impossible to use it to achieve "shock and awe" in all but the most drastic contingencies, and that real-world military plans and doctrine must be based on "limits and restraint."

5

The Problem of "Perfect" and "Bloodless" War

Some of the problems that NATO, the US, and Western military forces now face in dealing with unrealistic expectations about the efficacy of force, and about the "perfect" and "bloodless" character of modern war, are a self-inflicted wound. NATO and the governments of member countries conducted major propaganda campaigns throughout the air and missile war design to create these illusions. Individual officers and spokesmen did stress the fact that equipment and weapons fail, that targeting and battle damage assessment are not perfect, and casualties and that collateral damage is unavoidable.[122] Most NATO and national briefings, however, sought to give the impression that NATO was fighting a nearly "perfect" or "bloodless" war.[123]

Far too often, NATO, US, and British briefings defended NATO actions on a day-to-day basis in ways that reinforced media and public expectations that there would be virtually no losses and minimal casualties and collateral damage. Airpower was shown almost exclusively in terms of perfect strikes with perfect weapons. The normal friction of combat was treated as mistakes. The briefings did not lie, but they were massive exercises in spin control, carefully tailored facts, and carefully chosen omissions.

THE ABSURDITY OF PERFECTION

The Department of Defense made particularly egregious claims in its briefing on June 2, seemingly hopelessly confusing the word "accuracy" with the absence of politically sensitive collateral damage. While this kind of reduction in absurdum was not always typical of NATO or US briefings it illustrates what happens when the military reinforces the illusion of "perfect" or "bloodless" war:

Questioner: Of all the bombs we've dropped, 99.6 percent have actually hit the target out of the 20,000 bombs. What percentage?

Major General Wald: 99.6 percent.

Questioner: Out of how many thousand?

Major General Wald: Nearly 20,000. Some military vehicles in central Kosovo, just north of Pristina. You see it's been attacked previously here. These vehicles here then will be attacked by this aircraft. It lands in the middle and more than likely destroys several and damages beyond repair the rest of them. His overall inventory of all types of equipment—SAMs, vehicles, are going down continuously.

Questioner: You made an astonishing claim here. You said that of the nearly 20,000 bombs dropped, 99.6 have hit their targets. Given the hype that happened after the Gulf War about one bomb/one target, can you walk us through a little bit where this fairly incredible statistic comes from?

Major General Wald: It comes from watching all the gun camera film, and I for one didn't give a lot of hype for one bomb/one target in the Gulf War. I think that was a media kind of myth.

But the fact of the matter is, I think from changes from Vietnam, for example, was probably the change that there was one bridge in North Vietnam called the Paul Dumoy [ph] bridge that we tried for years to attack, and at the end of the war they received laser-guided bombs, and in one day took the bridge out. So I think that was probably the exuberance at that time, if you will.

But there are some targets—where you saw the Straight Flush radar today, that's one bomb/one target. There are other targets like the barracks where it may take more than one bomb per target. It may take dozens of bombs per target. But I think all in all when you look at this, I, certainly, as much as I have been around air and missile power, would have never predicted that it would have been 99.6 percent of the bombs would hit the target. I think it's phenomenal.

On the other hand, I think there is probably a misunderstanding that you can take one bomb against any target out there on any day and attack it and be successful every time. That's not true. They're still being shot at all the time. There's weather. There still is some potential for mechanical problems on bombs, but I think the number is very, very impressive.

Questioner: The part that missed, those are collateral damage—People are going to say 99.6, but they've hit a lot of civilian targets they didn't mean to.

Major General Wald: We didn't hit a lot of civilian targets. There have been some targets that have been hit that were not intended to be hit, that in a case like this is to be expected. It's something that we said in the beginning is risk. We don't want to do that, but it's going to occur. But I think when you look at the other side of the coin, there are pilots, aircrews out there taking a lot of risks every night, doing a great job and hitting the targets. It's pretty impressive. That's the best I can say about that.

Questioner: The British defense minister briefer was asked about an estimate of Serb casualties of up to 2,000. He said he felt that was quite low and it was more like 10,000. Do you have a figure?

Major General Wald: I have no idea whether 2,000 or 10,000 is the number. I don't know the number. I haven't even read what the number is. I suspect there are some casualties on the ground. When they're around certain targets, you would expect that, but we don't know what the number is. We're not there.

Questioner: Two nit-picky questions. This 99.6 percent, is that actually bombs that the military has seen hit targets, or is that merely an extrapolation that we know 12 or 15 bombs went awry so all the rest of them were. . .

Major General Wald: They know after every drop where every bomb goes. They come back. They debrief it. An aircraft, say for example the B-52, may take overhead imagery of those bombs. So I imagine it could be a bomb or two off, but in 20,000 it's pretty good. So no, they watch every mission; they watch where every bomb goes; they make an account for that, and then after it's all said and done that's the number they come up with.

Questioner: And the second one is that every morning Major General Jertz gives his account of how many targets and what was struck, and they're always a little bit different. He said 32 artillery pieces; you say 29. The same on SAMs. But he said nine APCs, you said 16. Should I assume that yours are more accurate, since they're later in the day, and you have benefit of more BDA, or how do I. . .

Major General Wald: We're getting our numbers directly from European Command. So I just take the numbers they tell me they hit. If there's a disconnect between NATO and us, it may be the fact that they may be overlapping a little bit into what goes on today, possibly. I'm not sure. But the totals, after it's all said and done, are in consonance with each other.

Questioner: General, the 99.6% would then make this the most accurate air and missile campaign in the history of air and missile warfare, would it not?

Major General Wald: Yes.

This exchange exemplifies the kind of "spin" used to give the impression of perfect war. As NATO documented with brutal clarity in the assessment of its strikes in issued on September 16, 1999, such a figure had nothing to do with the real-world impact and accuracy of some 33,000 to 37,500 sorties, 12,600 to 16,000 strike sorties, and the "accuracy" of some 23,000 weapons—two-thirds of which were unguided. NATO found that it could only confirm about half of the some 1,955 target hits reported by its pilots—a figure representing outstanding performance by real-world standards but totaling only about half the 99.6% quoted by General Wald.[124] As is discussed later, even the revised the battle damage assessment data are so controversial that the real figure could be much lower.

NATO and its member nations have only been marginally more honest since the war. While NATO carried out the revised postwar battle damage assessment described later in this analysis, the results did not address the level of accuracy and precision NATO achieved, any aspect of the strategic strikes in Serbia, or any aspect of collateral damage.

The Department of Defense report on the lessons of the war dodged the issue of combat effectiveness at the direction of the Secretary of Defense. The Department was not able to resolve a bureaucratic battle between the US Air Force and the Office of the Secretary of Defense over these issues, and the services refused to release the details of their effectiveness analysis and postwar battle damage assessment for release to Congress. As a result, the report lagged months behind schedule, and the credibility of most of the US Air Force and US Navy claims in the report remain in doubt.

It is worth noting that this is the third time in recent history in which Department of Defense reporting on the lessons of combat has been deliberately dishonest or has omitted critical data. The official report on the Gulf War, the "Conduct of War" study issued to the Congress, used battle damage data dating back to the war, rather than the corrected estimates made after the war. It also deliberately suppressed large amounts of data on the problems in US systems that were disclosed in later studies by the US Air Force and General Accounting Office. The Department of Defense issued extremely controversial, if not deliberately misleading damage assessments during the Desert Fox strikes on Iraq in December 1998 and never issued a promised post-conflict assessment. Coupled to the suppression of data on the battle in Kosovo, this raises serious questions as to whether the Office of the Secretary of Defense and Office of the Joint Chiefs of Staff have the professional integrity to be entrusted with such damage assessments and lessons reports, or whether they must be turned over to an independent commission with direct oversight by Congress.

The practical question is whether the propaganda efforts surrounding modern wars have reached the point where it creates impossible expectations, and steadily reinforces political and media demands to avoid all casualties, losses, collateral damage, and mistakes. The answer seems to that the effort to create the image of "perfect" or "bloodless" war creates impossible expectations that are inherently self-defeating.

"BLOODLESS WAR": THE PROBLEM OF SUFFERING NO OR MINIMAL CASUALTIES

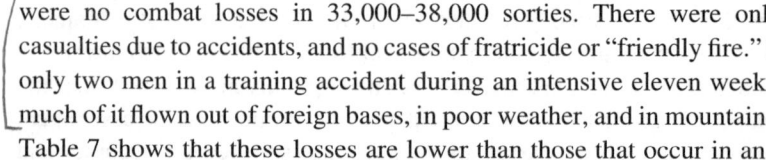

It is a major tribute to the US and other NATO air forces in Kosovo that there were no combat losses in 33,000–38,000 sorties. There were only minimal casualties due to accidents, and no cases of fratricide or "friendly fire." NATO lost only two men in a training accident during an intensive eleven week campaign, much of it flown out of foreign bases, in poor weather, and in mountainous terrain. Table 7 shows that these losses are lower than those that occur in an equivalent number of peacetime training sorties and are extraordinarily low in comparison with other recent wars and peacemaking actions.[125]

Table 7
US Casualties in Recent Wars

Conflict	Duration	US Casualties	
		In Hostilities	*Not by Hostile Fire*
Gulf War	1/91 to 9/91	148	235
Somalia	12/92 to 3/94	29	14
Haiti	9/94 to 4/96	0	4
Desert Fox	12/98	0	0
Kosovo	3/99 to 4/99	0	2

Casualties and Staying at Medium to High Altitudes

While NATO is sometimes criticized for flying at altitudes that were too high, it is also important to put this point in perspective. The British report on the lessons of the war draws the following conclusions:[126]

Some have criticized the fact that the majority of offensive missions were flown at medium level. It is true that offensive aircraft were initially restricted to operating above 15,000 feet (and some continued to do so throughout the campaign). Given the multitude of small arms, anti-aircraft artillery and shoulder launched missile systems, the decision not to fly at low level was entirely correct. However, as the Serbian air defense systems were degraded, operating height restrictions were eased and, for the latter half of the campaign, some aircraft operated down to 6,000 feet when target identification or weapons delivery profile required it. The near invulnerability of NATO aircraft operating at medium level was a major pressure point on Milosevic and any opportunity to exploit propaganda from capturing NATO aircrew was minimized.

In retrospect, this explanation seems valid. It is far from clear that lowering the altitude ceilings earlier and more broadly would have achieved any decisive tactical effects, and any losses might have had serious political effects. The British report seems equally valid in stressing the fact that any Western involvement in a conflict involves a battle for public opinion that is as important as what takes place on the battlefield.[127]

After action studies by the US air staff of the information available to pilots from electro-optical sensors in the cockpit, and from other sources such as the wing man and US/NATO intelligence, indicate that modern strike aircraft provide most of the situational awareness needed for even the most demanding strikes. Medium altitude flight profiles also give the pilot more overall situational awareness than low altitude flight, and the extended time over target also has advantages. This does not mean that "fast and low" does not have tactical advantages, but it does mean that "medium altitude, survival, and accurate" is generally sufficient unto the day.

There still, however, is a good case for reviewing operational constraints such as the 15,000–10,000-foot altitude ceilings imposed during much of the war. The practical question is what trade-offs can be established, if any, that are lessons as to the potential costs in effectiveness of seeking minimal casualties. Future wars may require very different thinking about risks and losses. Effective military planning and operations cannot simply accept some set of rules because the issue is controversial and the trade-offs are difficult to analyze. If "minimal casualties" is becoming a rule of modern war, then planning and operations must treat the issue honestly and explicitly.

Overall Sensitivity to Casualties

Many officers, officials, and politicians excuse their efforts to exaggerate the image of "perfect" or "bloodless" war on the grounds that they must deal with public opinion. It is far from clear, however, that the public really does demand that wars be fought with little or no casualties. Somewhat ironically, American politicians and the media seem to be more sensitive to casualties per se than the public. Public opinion polls strongly suggest that Americans will accept casualties if they believe in the war or peacekeeping mission, the quality of its leadership, and that American men and women are properly equipped and supplied.

Academic research into US reactions to casualties indicates, for example, that the Clinton Administration, Congress, and media were far more sensitive to the loss of 18 American lives in Kosovo than the American people as a whole. This work was summarized in an article in the *Washington Post* on November 7, 1999, by Peter D. Feaver and Christopher Gelpi:[128]

Studies by foreign policy experts Eric Larson, James Burk, Steven Kull and I.M. Destler, re-analyzing polls taken during the crisis, demonstrate that even after the television reports, there was a reservoir of public support for the operation. If the sight of dead American soldiers somewhat undermined it, it was because the Clinton administration made no effort to frame the casualties as anything other than a disaster in a mission that had drifted dreadfully off course. . . . Had the administration chosen instead to galvanize public opposition to Somali warlord Mohamed Farah Aideed, our research suggests that Americans would have tolerated an expanded effort to catch and punish him.

The authors reported on the results of a poll by the Triangle Institute for Security Studies (TISS) Project on the Gap Between the Military and Civilian Society that interviewed some 4,900 Americans. These included 623 military officers, 683 non-veterans selected from *Who's Who in America* and other directories of leading Americans, foreign policy opinion leaders, and civilians studying at professional military education institutions; the mass public; and 1,001 adults selected as a representative national sample by Princeton Research Associates.[129]

The poll asked those surveyed to evaluate how many American deaths in combat would be acceptable to complete three possible missions: defending Taiwan against China; preventing Iraq from acquiring weapons of mass destruction; and defending democracy in the Congo. It found a broad consensus among all three groups that this mission would be worth the sacrifice of a substantial number of American lives. The results were different for the missions in Iraq and the Congo. The general public was willing to accept thousands of casualties to accomplish these missions, and even higher numbers of casualties to curb Iraqi weapons than to defend Taiwan. The public's estimates of the casualties in a mission to restore democracy in Congo were significantly lower, but were still several times higher than "the actual casualties suffered by the U.S. military in all post-Cold War military actions combined."

The overall results suggested that a majority of the American people will accept combat deaths—so long as the mission has the potential to be successful and concluded that the public can clearly distinguish between suffering defeat and suffering casualties. In contrast, the lowest estimates of acceptable casualties came from the military. Military missions and elite military officers responded with estimates that were 25% to 50% of those of estimated elite civilians. These results seemed to be a function largely of the difficult military evaluation of the importance of the fighting rather than a fear of casualties per se. The sensitivity to casualties was not highest among officers whose roles are combat-related. The data showed no meaningful difference in casualty aversion among the combat, combat support and other sub-samples of elite military officers, and younger officers, who were most likely to take casualties in a conflict and were more willing to accept casualties.

These results highlight the fact that the search for casualty free war is more a failure of leadership than a condition dictated by public opinion. This is scarcely an argument for more casualties, but it is a strong argument for a Department of Defense effort to educate the public in the true risks of war, and public information campaigns that stress the real-world risk of casualties throughout any conflict. "Triumphalism" is an extraordinarily dangerous public relations strategy.

Wars like Kosovo may be training political leaders, military planners, the media, and the public to treat every casualty as a mistake and any significant number of casualties as failure. This can ultimately become a critical political and operational constraint on effective action, as well as lead policymakers to underestimate the risk of using force. The risks are obvious: Over-commitment because risks are minimized, rules of engagement that reduce losses but reduce military effectiveness even more, and political and strategic vulnerability to even minimal losses.

THE PROBLEM OF COLLATERAL DAMAGE

These points about the limits of perfect war are reinforced by the political and strategic impact of collateral damage on the air and missile campaign. NATO made a detailed effort to review the range of possible collateral damage for each target, and to plan its strikes so that the weapon used, the angle of approach, and the aim point would minimize collateral damage. This process was so exhaustive that

NATO often had more strike aircraft available than cleared targets, and many important targets were avoided or sent back for review again and again.

Nevertheless, collateral damage became significant as the war proceeded, and the globalization of communications and the near real time ability to report on collateral damage created public images that made each case of collateral damage steadily more politically sensitive. As a result, collateral damage became a political weapon that Serbia could exploit against the US and its allies.

Serbia made immediate efforts to take advantage of this situation, and collateral damage proved to be a major problem in terms of world political and media perceptions. It manipulated media coverage of collateral damage incidents. It provided carefully selected coverage on Serbian television that often failed to provide any evidence that the damage shown had been inflicted by NATO, or which mixed scenes of real collateral damage with scenes of what seem to have been Serbian artillery strikes.

Serbia carefully managed media interviews of "victims" and "witnesses." It removed military vehicles and casualties from the scene of attacks to give the impression that they were strikes only against civilians, arranged corpses for dramatic effect, and altered the amount of civilian debris in the scene of such damage to improve the media effect—possibly trucking in debris from the scene of Serbian ethnic cleansing. In a number of cases, Serbia set bodies on fire before media coverage was permitted. Serbian television showed a number of programs of still smoking bodies where there is no related incendiary damage to vehicles or the rest of the scene, and no source of any burning agent in the target area that explains why the bodies are burning.[130]

While a B-2 strike that was mistargeted against the Chinese embassy in Belgrade—and killed three Chinese diplomats and wounded 27—proved to be the case with the most serious political backlash, collateral damage was an issue long before this strike occurred. Serbia claimed that NATO had caused a total of 13 major incidents involving serious collateral damage in Serbia and Kosovo by Day 50 (May 14) of the air and missile campaign. Serbia also attempted to exploit the fact that one NATO missile had struck in Bulgaria—even though it caused no damage.

The Serbian claims regarding collateral damage that received the most political attention involved the following major incidents:

- April 5: A bomb hits civil targets in Aleksinac, killing 12. Serbia claims 17.
- April 9: A bomb hits a residential area. Casualties are unknown.
- April 12: A laser-guided bomb hits a train on a bridge near Leskova, killing at least 10 and injuring 55.
- April 14: Kosovar Muslim refugee convoys are hit near Djakovica. Serbia claims 75 killed.
- April 28: Civilian homes are hit in Surdicia, and Serbia claims at least 16 are killed.
- April 29: Bombs hit homes in Vracar, a suburb of Belgrade. Serbia claims 4 are killed.

- May 1: A stray missile hits a bus on a bridge north of Pristina. Serbia claims they are civilians and 40 are killed. (Still in question since no gun camera or other data indicate that it was a NATO strike and the damage is not typical of bomb damage.)
- May 3: A bomb hits a bus between Pec and the border of Montenegro. Serbia claims 20 are killed.
- May 6: NATO strikes a hospital and market place in Nis. Serbia claims 15 killed.
- May 7: NATO strikes the Chinese Embassy in Belgrade with four bombs launched from a B-2. Three are killed.
- May 12: Serbia claims NATO hits Serbian civilians.
- May 14: Serbian claims 50 Kosovar civilians are killed, and 50 more are wounded, by 8 cluster bombs dropped on a village called Korsia, about 40 miles southwest of Pristina, the capital of Kosovo.

While there is no way to compare the losses to NATO-caused collateral damage against Serbian military losses. Estimates of losses to NATO caused casualties from collateral damage range from around 150 to as high as 500–1,000, while Serbia admits to some 600 military and special police killed, and the total is unlikely to exceed 1,000–1,500.

The Chinese Embassy Bombing

No case of collateral damage created more difficulties for NATO than the tragic mistargeting of the Chinese embassy on May 7. It is now clear that this strike occurred as part of NATO's effort to strike at Yugoslav President Slobodan Milosevic by hitting targets of major value to the leadership. After over a month of debate within NATO over targeting Belgrade, NATO had approved eleven targets. These included three targets in central Belgrade—the Defense Ministry, the Army General Staff and the Federal Ministry of Interior (MUP) headquarters. They also included the Dobanovci underground bunker west of the international airport—which was seen as a target that might hit directly at the Serbian leadership—and the building in new Belgrade that supposedly housed the Federal Directorate for Supply and Procurement (FDSP). This Directorate was known in Yugoslavia as Yugoimport SDPR, and was government bureau responsible for coordinating the country's imports and exports. All of these targets were bombed as planned.

The CIA had targeted this building. Reporting by the *Washington Post* indicates that the CIA chose the FDSP as part of the CIA's Operation Matrix for several reasons. First, the FDSP had been on the US intelligence community's watch list for years, because of its role in export arms to countries like Libya and Iraq, and because of its involvement in building military bases and underground bunkers abroad. Second, the CIA believed that a subsidiary company of Yugoimport called Atera was one of the main sources of hard currency for Milosevic and his cronies. Under the United Nations' oil-for-food program for Iraq, Yugoimport had been granted numerous licenses to sell food and medicines to Baghdad, the latest contracts being approved in late 1998.[131]

A B-2 flying at around 40,000 feet dropped five Joint Direct Attack Munitions (JDAM) 2000-pound bombs on what NATO thought was the FDSP building at 23:46 local time. Unfortunately, the building the CIA had picked out was actually the Chinese Embassy. The B-2 strikes not only killed several Chinese and wounded many more, they hit the intelligence section of the embassy, convincing many Chinese that the strikes were deliberate. The end result was to poison US and Chinese relations at a time when there already were problems over other issues, and helped to push the Chinese towards siding with Serbia in the UN.

This mistake symbolizes the fact that the new expectations that have come out of the increased precision in air and missile strikes can lead a sophisticated nation to misinterpret collateral damage and see a horrible accident as a deliberate act. As is discussed shortly, targeting is an arcane and difficult procedure. As a result, many Chinese officials seem to have believed (and some may still believe) that the US had some covert motive in the strike in spite of the fact it did nothing but create political problems for NATO.

The Real-World Problems in Targeting in Wartime

The strike also shows that one mistake can sometimes offset a massive number of successes, and triggered a long series of US and NATO efforts to explain what had gone wrong and to convince the Chinese that the attack was not deliberate. A Department of Defense spokesman first made an attempt to put the attack into perspective in a May 8 briefing on the NATO strike on the Chinese embassy:

Answer: I'm not sure what the mistake was, but anybody can make mistakes. Once again, I don't know the reason for it, this mistake last night, but if you look through a scenario, there are many, many things that go into a mission. I think sometimes there's a tendency to think that we oversimplify it because we have, as Charlie kind of alluded to just a moment ago, we have a lot of success. I mean, 17,000 sorties, and I think there's in the neighborhood of seven or so collateral damage incidents that we've had. All regrettable. And nobody feels worse than the person that's involved in that. The planning process is synergistic. It goes from front to bottom whether it be targeting or the weapon or the weather or the aircraft's system itself. And that all is under review. And when the time comes, I think that will be clear to everyone.

Questioner: Can you give us a little more specific idea of the planning process for a target, particularly a building like that? How many people would look at it, how many people would approve it, the maps, sort of the process there?

Answer: Gosh, I don't even know the number of people. But it's very comprehensive. Some targets have been on the books for many years. Some come on the books later. As you know, there's some targets that may be targets of opportunity that could occur. We had a briefing yesterday from J-STARS and those type of targets are almost real-time fielded forces. But targets are reviewed routinely. There are various, different people that do review those, intelligence people as well as operators. They're reviewed early in the process. Some are archived type targets, but before they're attacked, people do review those targets. Of course, the pilots and air crews review those targets before they go as well as their local intelligence. And after 17,000 sorties, I think it's understandable that a mistake was made, as regrettable as this is.

Questioner: Are you talking in terms—you make it sound like (inaudible) misassignment of targets. This wasn't a misassignment of target, was it? The wrong target—the Chinese embassy wasn't ever assigned as a target. The arrow was . . .

Answer: First of all, I think as Mr. Bacon said, it would be unfair for me to even tell you what I think happened until the review is complete. But certainly, we're not attacking embassies intentionally. And the review will come out, and when that comes out, we'll . . .

Questioner: That's my point. You sat down, you talk about going through the planning process. The planning process never included that embassy as a target.

Answer: Once again, I can tell you this. The Chinese embassy was not a target. Anybody that would sit down and look at this and say this is a Chinese embassy would have said forget it, that's not a target. So there was never any intention to attack the Chinese embassy, and it's regrettable it happened.

Questioner: You knew where the Chinese embassy was on the planning data, so when you briefed that out, someone would know not to brief that as a target, right? A mistake.

Answer: Let me just put in perspective, not in this particular target, but a generic target. When you look at a target, and it says what that target is on the sheet, that's what you think you're attacking. There's no reason to question that. If it were to say it's a target you shouldn't hit, you wouldn't even get that target. So, obviously, a pilot or air crew would not attack something intentionally they shouldn't. We've gone through that before. So I think the best thing to do—there's all types of speculation you could make, what-ifs. And until the facts come out, we would let NATO speak to that. And I think that's the best way to go right now.

Questioner: Would they know what was next to the target? Would the pilot know here is my target, I have no idea what's around it or who are in these buildings?

Answer: The way targeting works, particularly high value targets or a target area that you're going to go in that has a high threat—the higher the threat, the more value the target, the more time you would study it. The more time you have to study it, the better. Of course, you would study all the terrain around it, anything else that would be included in that target area, of course—you'd want to avoid collateral damage. My feeling would be in an area like Belgrade that's probably the most highly defended area that US forces and NATO forces have flown in, similar to Baghdad in the last decade at least, that in an area like that, you're going to do a lot of study. You're going to study not only the target, but you're going to study the threat; you're going to study all the different things that may occur on that mission. I would suspect—I don't know— that a lot of study was put into that target. You would expect that, particularly in high value. So to answer your question, I don't know what happened. I frankly don't. And when the review comes out, I think everybody will find that out.

Questioner: In a similar vein, once or twice you've showed us pictures of a pilot thinking twice about something and deciding not to drop (inaudible) what the target was or if it was the right one (inaudible), however you want to characterize it. Was there that kind of fall back position here from your understanding? Could the pilot have said, "it doesn't look right"?

Answer: I don't know that. I will say this, that in certain areas under certain conditions, there are no back-up targets. So you don't out there in a case like this in Belgrade in an area that's highly defended and have a why don't you drive around until you find a target you like and drop it. So what happens is you study the target; you know what it is; you've studied the appearance of that target. And when you go strike that target, unless you're sure what you're attacking is the target, you don't do it. Now, once again, as Mr. Bacon in a very clear way made the analogy that mistakes happen. So I don't know why a mistake occurred, but I would suspect—just like I've said before, I know the discipline and the professionalism of the pilots and I've flown with many of the NATO pilots. And I've never seen once in my years of flying, and I've had ten years in Europe, one pilot drop a bomb on anything he thought he shouldn't have intentionally.

Questioner: General, Mr. Bacon mentioned some of the things that could go wrong with a laser-guided bomb. What are some of the other things that could effect the accuracy of a laser-guided bomb?

Answer: Well, I mean, I could probably give you several possible things that could happen. Some a little more likely than others, but once again, I think the most important thing is to understand that the reliability of these weapons is very good. But once again, anything can happen. It's the—kind of the one in a million kind of theory. It could have been a slight mechanical problem with a fin. It could have been something on an aircraft. It could have been many things, but once again, it may not have been a mechanical problem with the weapon at all. It may have been a number of things. So once that review comes out, I think it will be clear.

Jamie Shea made the following effort to put the bombing of the Chinese Embassy in perspective in the NATO briefing on May 10:

. . . I believe that we have been conducting this campaign in a professional as well as a deliberate way. We have so far struck at 1,900 aim points, that is the number of individual targets even if they may sometimes be on the same building, like an oil refinery, 1,900 aim points. We know that we have dropped around 9,000 pieces of ordnance, missiles and bombs. Only 12 have gone astray as a result of either mechanical error, or some other error, or the mistake that occurred yesterday. If you do a mathematical computation you are talking about a fraction of 1 percent, and so we continue to be accurate. Obviously I understand that sometimes international attention, or TV pictures, prefer to focus on the 12 that went astray, as opposed to the 8,988 that didn't go astray. But let's remember that if you look at the big picture, the overwhelming majority of these weapons are landing every day and every night accurately against legitimate military targets.

A US "senior defense official" provided more detail on the targeting process and the inevitable risk of collateral damage the same day:

A: To the best of our knowledge, the embassy moved in 1996. The map that was the principal map that most people have in the process was a 1997 map. I think the way the '92 map gets involved in this is the '92 map had the Chinese embassy in old Belgrade. And it had no building at the location of the new Chinese embassy. The 1997 map had a building unidentified at the location and had the Chinese embassy depicted in the same location in old Belgrade. But fundamentally, a map is out of date the day or the week after it's printed or produced. And what we rely on is databases, intelligence databases, which are all-source and automated, and regrettably in this case, the database not reflecting a move of the Chinese embassy did not help us uncover the original error in targeting the wrong building.

Questioner: [Sir], we were told that those databases, for instance, were not updated by people both from our State Department diplomats and people from Langley, be they diplomats or something else, who were actually in that complex in that building during the past three years. Is that true, and secondly, if so, why weren't they updated?

A: Well, I am sure there were people from our embassy in that building in the last three years. But what I am not sure of [is whether] any report got sent in [so] that a person who was working on the database was able to enter it. I also would stress this has been looked at for two and a half days now. It's a very large group of dedicated people who are working on these targeting issues, very long hours doing the best they can, and we need to go back and look all the raw material as well as all the databases. I mean databases sometimes are out of date because reports don't get sent in on new information. Sometimes they are out of date because they don't get entered as quickly as they should. The bottom line is: these that were used to do verifications of the targeting were not up to date, and we need to find out why.

Questioner: [Sir], there are two separate issues. One is how the wrong city block became to be identified on the map. And then, that's separate from the fact that the wrong city block you got happened to be the Chinese embassy. Could you go back to the initial identification of the wrong city block? Could you tell us rather than asking these scatter-shot questions? Could you walk us through the process by which you derive targeting information from looking at a mixture of addresses and city block photographs taken?

A: Let me say something about the generic targeting process. . . . Targets are nominated to a war-fighting commander from two directions. One is his components, who may nominate targets up to him—the air, ground or Navy component. And the other is National Agency or National Intelligence Committee nominations down to the JTF commander or the CINC. This was a nomination originally from an agency in Washington. And so, when the nominations are made, then they go through a process of validation and vetting and collateral damage analysis and things like that. And so, that's the generic process, and I will turn it over to my colleague to talk specifically about the initiation of this target.

There is an effort to, first of all, identify the target by its function and to evaluate whether or not it is a legitimate target for this purpose, and then secondly, to locate it geographically. In this instance, there was information as to what the appropriate street address was for the facility in question, and then the next step was to locate that on the base map, the 1997 base map that was just discussed. There are no street numbers on those maps; there are little street numbers on other available maps. There was a process that we went through to use what information we had on other facilities in this area as to their appropriate street addresses, to focus in on what was erroneously identified as the target facility. After that, there is a multi-stage check, both within the intelligence committee and DoD, to make sure that there is no— that this is the correct location. It's a multi-step process. None of those fail-safes worked.

. . . the map can be overstated. Maps are important to us. It's the data; it's the information that you need to try to run to ground to see if your targeting information is valid. Nobody is going out looking for the Chinese embassy. After the Chinese embassy was bombed on Friday night, my immediate assumption, when we looked at our targets that night, is that the nearest target to the Chinese embassy was the Minister of Defense headquarters in old Belgrade. There were several embassies closer to the Minister of Defense than where the Chinese was listed on the map and the databases. And so, we need to update the maps, and then bounce all of that information against every single target that we select. We have struck about 270 targets, I believe. We've struck many of them multiple times. There have been over 4,000 strike sorties. This is not an excuse, but this is the first time I have been aware of where there were inadvertent unintended casualties because of a target mistake at the wrong facility.

All embassies are not on a strike list. Hospitals, schools, mosques, churches, all those things are on a no-strike list. And we, you can imagine trying to keep a database on all of those things, not just embassies. Schools, churches, all of those things that are on the no-strike list. And, the people who work this do the best they can when a target is selected and validated as a good target for the function it performs, in the area or the building or whatever this located. And then we run that selection against multiple databases, which have other targets and no-strike list to see what shows up, as well as doing imagery analysis of the surrounding area to try to double check. So the words or the Chinese embassy did not show up in this validation of another target that was struck the same night that was very near by . . . It is early, but we have not—in trying to find any raw data, which in message searches of computer data files on messages—we have not found any which reported to the databases that the Chinese embassy had been moved.

. . . We are certainly looking at all processes. That—because this extrapolation is less than precise, that's why you have a system that has multiple checks, both with the CIA, within the intelligence community and within DoD. And as we said before, there's a two-part problem here. The first part was the initial identification was incorrect, and secondly, all the fail-safes failed to note that that was incorrect . . . The error was that the target development process got the wrong function at the wrong building, the wrong building, and that the checks and balances that we go through in trying to determine consequences of hitting the target that has now been incorrectly identified did not come up with the Chinese embassy being located nearby. I mean, it should have—if the databases had been completely up-to-date and correct—it should have said "the Chinese embassy is located nearby." We start looking at where is it at—oh my God, here's the target. So it was incorrectly identified. The target development incorrectly put this function at this building, and when we did the collateral damage assessments, the no-strike, you know, reviews and all that, there was nothing about—there were other targets; there were other facilities that came into our scope, our view there that we did not want to strike. And we looked at where they were, and we determined a successful strike on this target would not endanger those facilities. mean, but the Chinese embassy wasn't, regrettably, one of them.

The Results of the US Investigation into the Bombing

These comments reflect the difficulties in establishing the true causes of collateral damage and targeting errors in the midst of a crisis. A long investigation into the specific causes of the targeting of the Chinese embassy confirmed that the US had confused the embassy with the Yugoslav Directorate of Supply and

Procurement—a building located several blocks away with a somewhat similar shape as seen from satellite imagery. It also confirmed that the US had used maps that were not fully up to date.

The results of this investigation were briefed in detail in a formal statement by Under Secretary of State for Political Affairs Thomas R. Pickering to the Government of the People's Republic of China (PRC) on June 17, 1999. They seem to be totally accurate in content and they provide a real-world case study in both the causes of collateral damage and the kind of conspiracy theories that can arise in the aftermath of a major mistake that is, in itself, a major lesson of the air and missile campaign.[132]

The report shows that multiple factors and errors in several parts of the U.S. Government were responsible for the mistaken bombing. Beginning as early as 1997, mistakes in different parts of our government contributed to this tragic set of errors; and our operational procedures failed to catch these errors.

The CIA and Defense Department are continuing to interview individuals in the field who were involved in various aspects of the decisions that led to the bombing. Because the NATO air campaign has only just concluded, it has not been possible to debrief fully every person involved and to reach conclusions regarding responsibility for mistakes that led to the bombing. The Director of Central Intelligence, who is also Chief of the Intelligence Community, has directed the conduct of an accountability review which will go into the issue of responsibility, the appropriate results of which will be made available.

The bombing resulted from three basic failures. First, the technique used to locate the intended target—the headquarters of the Yugoslav Federal Directorate for Supply and Procurement (FDSP)—was severely flawed. Second, none of the military or intelligence databases used to verify target information contained the correct location of the Chinese Embassy. Third, nowhere in the target review process was either of the first two mistakes detected. No one who might have known that the targeted building was not the FDSP headquarters—but was in fact the Chinese Embassy—was ever consulted.

To help better understand the circumstances which led to the mistaken bombing, let me offer a chronology of events. . . . The first major error stemmed from mislocating the intended target.

In March of this year, officers at the Central Intelligence Agency began considering the Federal Directorate for Supply and Procurement (FDSP) as a potential target for NATO Allied Force strike operations. The FDSP, because of its role in military procurement, was a legitimate target.

We had a street address of the FDSP headquarters: "Bulevar Umetnosti 2" in New Belgrade. But military forces require precise geographic coordinates to conduct an attack with precision munitions. During a mid-April selection and designation of the target, three maps were used in an attempt to locate physically the address of the FDSP headquarters: two local commercial maps from 1996 and 1989, and the then most recent U.S. government map produced in 1997.

None of these maps had any reference to the FDSP building. And none accurately identified the current location of the Chinese Embassy . . . the 1997 U.S. Government city map shows the Embassy in Old Belgrade and depicts an unidentified building at the actual

Embassy site in New Belgrade. The 1996 commercial map made no reference to the Embassy at either location. The 1989 map predated the Embassy's move.[133]

Please keep in mind that the location of the Chinese Embassy was not a question that anyone would have asked when assembling this particular target package since it was not connected in any way to our intent to strike the FDSP headquarters.

In an effort to locate the FDSP building at Bulevar Umetnosti 2, an intelligence officer in Washington used land navigation techniques taught by the U.S. military to locate distant or inaccessible points and objects. These techniques—which involve the comparison of addresses from one street to another—can be used for general geographic location, but are totally inappropriate for precision targeting, and were used uniquely in this case. Using this process, the individual mistakenly determined that the building which we now know to be the Chinese Embassy was the FDSP headquarters. To use these techniques for targeting purposes was a serious mistake. The true location of the FDSP headquarters was some 300 meters away from the Chinese Embassy. This flaw in the address location process went undetected by all the others who evaluated the FDSP as a military target.

Because this first error was so fundamental, let me walk you through it. The method for determining the location of the intended target—the FDSP—was seriously flawed. It was not based on certain knowledge of the numbering sequence for addresses on the Bulevar Umetnosti. Rather, our attempts to determine the location of the building employed a method that is used in the field by the Army, but is not normally used for aerial targeting purposes. The system will provide an approximation of location, but cannot guarantee an accurate geographic fix.

A 1997 National Imaging and Mapping Agency (NIMA) map was first used to display the grid pattern of the streets in New Belgrade. Next, in order to identify locations to use as reference points, they identified and drew on the NIMA map to locate the Hyatt Hotel, the Intercontinental Hotel, and the Serbian Socialist Party Headquarters. Each of these buildings—which were clearly labeled on the maps being used—were approximately one mile east of Bulevar Umetnosti. Using these locations and their street addresses as reference points, parallel lines were drawn that intersected both the known addresses and Bulevar Umetnosti. In what proved to be a fundamental error, those same numbers were then applied to locations on Bulevar Umetnosti, assuming that streets were numbered in the same fashion along parallel streets. The effectiveness of this method depends on the numbering system being the same on parallel streets, that the numbers are odd and even on the same sides of the street and that the street numbers are used in the same parallel sequence even if the street names change. Unfortunately, a number of these assumptions were wrong.

Using this approximation method, your embassy building was designated as the target when in fact the Embassy was located on a small side street at some distance on Bulevar Umetnosti from where the intended target was actually located at number 2 Bulevar Umetnosti. Let me show you a satellite photograph and some maps to illustrate the method and the error it produced.

The identification of the building that actually was the Chinese Embassy as the FDSP building subsequently and in error took on the mantle of fact. It was not questioned nor reviewed up the chain of command. This was in part because everyone involved had, as a result of so many previously correct locations, assumed generally high confidence in our procedures to locate, check and verify such analytical facts. In this particular, and singular, case, our system clearly failed. In part it failed also because every established procedure in the review of this target was not followed.

Maps and satellite imagery were also analyzed to look for any possible collateral damage issues near the target. There was no indication that the targeted building was an embassy—no flags, no seals, no clear markings showed up. There were no collateral damage issues in the vicinity.

The second major error stemmed from flawed databases. . . . The incorrect location of the FDSP building was then fed into several U.S. databases to determine whether any diplomatic or other facilities off-limits to targeting were nearby. We do our best to avoid damage to sensitive facilities such as embassies, hospitals, schools and places of worship. Viewed from space, there was no indication that the office building being targeted was an embassy. On the satellite imagery available to U.S., there were no flags, seals, or other markings to indicate that the building was an embassy. And unfortunately, in this instance none of the database sources that were checked correctly identified the targeted building as the Chinese Embassy.

Multiple databases within the Intelligence Community and the Department of Defense all reflected the Embassy in its pre-1996 location in Old Belgrade. Despite the fact that U.S. officials had visited the Embassy on a number of occasions in recent years the new location was never entered into intelligence or military targeting databases. If the databases had accurately reflected the current location of the Embassy, the mistaken identification of the FDSP building would have been recognized and corrected.

Why was the Chinese Embassy not correctly located? It is important to understand that our ability to verify the location of fixed targets depends heavily on the accuracy of the databases, and the databases in this case were wrong. Further, it is difficult to keep current databases for cities around the globe. In general, diplomatic facilities have been given relatively little attention in our efforts to update our databases because such facilities are not targets. Military targets are the top priority in these databases because of the danger they pose to our own forces. Unfortunately, locations where strikes should be avoided had lower priority and our databases contained errors, notably in the failure to include the new location of the Embassy of China.

Now, this is an important point, so let me expand upon it. The databases which contained information about the physical location of organizations in Belgrade—including the so-called "no hit list" of buildings that should not be targeted—were faulty. Although database maintenance is one the basic elements of our intelligence efforts, it has been routinely accorded low priority.

The target and "no-hit" databases were not independently constructed. Outdated information that placed the Chinese Embassy in its former location in Old Belgrade was not updated when the Embassy moved. Because various databases were not independently constructed, this wrong information was duplicated. So when target information was checked against the no-hit list, the error was not detected.

Many U.S. and other NATO diplomats must have visited the new building. The address was in the phone book, the diplomatic list and perhaps other sources, including Yugoslav maps. Certainly, many citizens and officials of the United States were aware of the correct location of the Chinese Embassy in Belgrade. However, in error, their knowledge was not recorded in any of the military or intelligence databases used in the targeting process.

In addition, the correct location of the Chinese Embassy was not known to targeteers or NATO commanders because we were not, in fact, looking for it. Since your Embassy was not a target, and because we were unaware of any diplomatic or civilian facilities in the immediate vicinity of the presumed FDSP building, no effort was made to verify or precisely locate the whereabouts of your Embassy. We have subsequently found some maps which show the correct current location of the Chinese Embassy, although there are others, including some produced in recent years by the Yugoslav government, which do not.

Since the incident, the United States has updated its databases to show the best known location of diplomatic facilities. The databases will be updated as new information becomes available. Maps are out of date almost as soon as they are printed. Databases can and should be maintained to be effective.

The third problem was faulty checks. Once the target was proposed, the focus of the review was on the military value of the target, how best to attack it, and the issue of collateral damage. No one in any of the succeeding reviews questioned the accuracy of the location. The formal recommendation of the FDSP target was forwarded in late April to military staffs both in the U.S. and Europe, who were responsible for reviewing and identifying targets for Operation Allied Force. Maps and satellite imagery were analyzed to look for any possible collateral damage concerns near the target. We conducted a target review in Europe, and again, no significant risks to civilian or diplomatic facilities were uncovered.

Following submission by the European Command for approval, the target package mistakenly received no additional examination outside of the Defense Department. It did go through additional review at the Pentagon, but this review found nothing different from the review that took place in Europe. There were no known collateral damage concerns. From that point on the building incorrectly identified as an FDSP facility was included on a list of potential Allied Force strike targets.

Some of our employees knew the location of the new Chinese Embassy. But keep in mind that we were not looking for it, since the database with the old location was assumed to be correct. None of these individuals was consulted as the target was reviewed and, as a result, we lost any opportunity to learn that the building targeted was the new Chinese Embassy. We have also found one report from 1997 which gave the correct address of the Chinese Embassy, but unfortunately the correct address was not entered into the database.

. . . Once the wrong target was selected, the system of checks that NATO and U.S. command forces had in place to catch target errors did not reveal the mistake. The database reviews conducted by the European Command (EUCOM) were limited to validating the target data sheet coordinates with the information put into the database by NIMA analysts. Such a circular process could not uncover the original error and exposes our susceptibility to a single point of database failure.

There has been much press coverage of the fact that the U.S. and NATO relied on out-of-date maps to check targets. In fact, since any physical map can quickly become out of date, the key question is one of accurate databases. These were not properly maintained and did not catch the error. Furthermore, persons familiar with the layout of the city of Belgrade were not consulted in the construction of the target and no-hit databases. They were also not involved in a review of this target. This points up a flaw in our procedures.

The only question about the target information was raised by an intelligence officer who had doubts as to whether the building targeted was in fact the FDSP headquarters or might be some other unidentified building. At no time was there any suspicion that the building might be an embassy. This question was not raised to senior levels and the strike went ahead.

Let me explain further this attempt by an intelligence officer to question the reliability of the target information related to the FDSP. There was information that suggested a discrepancy between the selected target and the actual location of the FDSP. There was no information that the target location was the Chinese Embassy, only that it was perhaps the wrong building. However, there was a series of frustrating miscommunications—missed phone calls and lack of follow-up—which led to these doubts not being aired at a command level in time to stop the attack. (The officer had doubts early on in the process because of his own knowledge about the location of the FDSP building; attempted to check with working-level contacts; was continuing to check when the bombing happened; and was not able to communicate his suspicions to senior officers.)

The air strike then proceeded as planned on May 7 without any of the mistakes having been detected or doubts about the reliability of the target information having been addressed. At 2146 Zulu (about midnight local time in Belgrade) on 7 May 1999 one of the fleet of B-2 bombers from Whiteman Air Force Base (AFB) in Missouri dropped 5 Joint Direct Attack Munitions (JDAM) 2000 lb. GPS-guided bombs on the target designated as the FDSP building but which was, in fact, the Chinese Embassy in Belgrade. All B-2 strikes on Yugoslavia were flown from Whiteman AFB. The bombs were Global Positioning System (GPS) guided weapons and operate in all weather and at night using a satellite-based navigation system of a high order of accuracy.

The air crews carried out their mission as planned. They had no idea they were in fact bombing the Chinese Embassy. As a result, it is obvious that they bear no responsibility for this failure; the problem, as I have outlined, occurred earlier. They had no way of seeing any identifying markers that would show the building was an embassy. A flag in front of the building or any such features would not be discernible at night and at the speeds and altitudes at which our planes fly. No other buildings in the immediate vicinity were hit. Our weapons hit the target they were aimed at. Unfortunately, we did not realize the true nature of the target.

In summary, there were several crucial errors which led to the Chinese Embassy being struck. There was an error in locating the target. The approach used to attempt to locate the FDSP building was severely flawed. All sources of information used to prevent precisely this type of accident were either inaccurate or incomplete. The review process did not catch the locational error and did not consult any material or any person which could have provided correct information. The United States is, as I speak, continuing to conduct an in-depth review of this tragic accident. Based on our initial findings, it is clear that this terrible mistake occurred not because of just one organization, or because of any one individual.

There was in the immediate aftermath of the bombing some confusion as to what had happened and some of our early public statements were confused and contradictory. To summarize clearly and precisely: the attack on the PRC Embassy was the result of a series of errors that led to the destruction of the PRC Embassy instead of the Serb military target that was intended. The use of a map containing an error—the inaccurate location of the Chinese Embassy—contributed to the tragic mistake—but this was not due solely to a "map error."

. . . Our government has also undertaken corrective actions to prevent mistakes like this from happening in the future. New updated city maps have been published detailing locations of diplomatic sites and other "no-strike" facilities in and around Belgrade. Additionally, databases are being updated as changes occur. We rely on these databases for our most current information, because maps themselves are inevitably out of date the day or the week they are published.

Intelligence and Defense organizations have strengthened their internal mechanisms and procedures for selecting and verifying targets, and have placed new priority on keeping our databases current. All U.S. Government sources will be required to report whenever foreign embassies move or are established. This information will then be forwarded and incorporated into our intelligence and military databases. The U.S. Government will seek direct contact with other governments and interested organizations and persons to obtain their assistance in identifying and locating facilities and places of interest or concern. And as I noted earlier, we are continuing our internal reviews of the causes of the accident, and when these reviews are completed, we will determine whether any disciplinary action is called for.

I would like now to address various speculative theories that appear to be held by some people in China. We have heard that many people believe that our attack on your Embassy was intentional. Clearly the United States had absolutely no reason to want to attack your protected embassy facility. Any such decision to bomb an Embassy would have been contrary to U.S. doctrine and practice and against international standards of behavior and established international accords. No such decision was ever proposed or indeed made.

Bombing the Chinese Embassy also would have been completely antithetical to President Clinton's strong personal commitment to strengthening the relationship between the United States and China; he has defended this relationship and our engagement policy in the face of vociferous domestic criticism. It is not imaginable that President Clinton would make such a decision.

. . . Moreover, bombing the Chinese Embassy in Belgrade would have made absolutely no sense in terms of our policy objectives in Kosovo. The objective of the NATO bombing campaign was to diminish and degrade the capacity of the Yugoslav government and military for repression in Kosovo. The Embassy of China played no role in that set of activities. It had always been the intention of the U.S. and NATO to bring the Kosovo effort to conclusion through diplomatic efforts, including of the G-8 and in the UN Security Council.

The accidental bombing of your Embassy not only intensified international criticism of the NATO bombing campaign, it also had negative effects on our diplomatic efforts, and affected in a deeply negative fashion China's attitude and policies toward our effort in Yugoslavia. In particular, as Secretary Albright told Premier Zhu in April, we always expected that China, as a permanent member of the UN Security Council, would need to be a part of the resolution of the Kosovo crisis. We knew we would need China's support in this matter. Bombing your Embassy was hardly the way to persuade you to help. Thus, the bombing was contrary to two critically important U.S. foreign policy goals: the further development of U.S.-China relations and the resolution of the Kosovo situation.

I also have heard that some people in China subscribe to the theory that the bombing was caused by one or several individuals working in our government who conspired to subvert U.S.-China relations or who may have concluded that China was too friendly to Belgrade or that the Embassy was playing some role in assisting Belgrade.

We have found no evidence of an unauthorized conspiracy to attack the Chinese Embassy, for any reason whatsoever, or of any "rogue element" within the U.S. Government. The errors we have identified as producing the accident took place in three separate and independent areas. There was a series of three separate sets of events, some of which affecting the databases occurred as far back as 1997, when no one could have predicted this present set of circumstances. It is just not conceivable, given the circumstances and errors committed, that the attack could have been brought about by a conspiracy or by "rogue elements."

Science has taught us that a direct explanation, backed up by full knowledge of facts obtained through a careful investigation, is always preferable to speculation and far fetched, convoluted or contrived theories with little or no factual backing. In this tragic case, the facts show a series of errors: that the target was mislocated; the databases designed to catch mistakes were inaccurate and incomplete; and none of the reviews uncovered either of the first two errors.

The CIA Accepts the Blame

George J. Tenet, the Director of the CIA, took the unusual step of accepting CIA responsibility for the error in testimony to the US Congress on July 22, 1999. Tenet indicated that most of the 900-odd targets that NATO had struck during the war were chosen by NATO and the US European Command, but that US intelligence agencies had been asked to suggest targets as well. While the CIA had helped the military in other target selections, the choice of the Yugoslav Directorate of Supply and Procurement was the first and only target that was "unilaterally proposed and wholly assembled" by the CIA and its Combined Targeting Support Staff.

Tenet's comments both reinforce the lessons in Pickering's statement, and illustrate the kinds of problems that can occur within an intelligence organization that must now help fight a new kind of war.[134]

Mr. Chairman, the nature of warfare has changed. When cities were struck in past wars, none doubted that civilians, embassies, hospitals, and schools would be in harm's way. Today, our ability to strike precisely has created the impression that sensitive sites can be safe in the middle of a war zone. Our desire to protect innocents in the line of fire has added an enormous burden on all of us that we accept. It is our job to do our best to ensure that only appropriate targets be struck.

I think it is useful to note that this episode is unusual because the CIA does not normally assemble, on its own, target nomination packages containing the coordinates of specific installations or buildings. The targeting support typically provided by CIA is usually at the strategic and planning level, such as analytical judgments on the kinds of targets that are the most important, commentary or specific information concerning targets selected by the military or others, and information that assists the military in identifying future targets.

. . . The attack was a mistake. Let me emphasize, our investigation has determined that no one—I repeat no one—knowingly targeted the Chinese Embassy. Speculation to the contrary is simply unfounded. No one, at any stage in the process, realized that our bombs were aimed at the Chinese Embassy.

There were three basic failures. First, the technique used to locate the intended target—the headquarters of the Yugoslav Federal Directorate for Supply and Procurement (FDSP)—was severely flawed. Second, none of the military or intelligence databases used to validate targets contained the correct location of the Chinese Embassy. Third, nowhere in the target review process was either of the first two mistakes detected.

. . . To help understand the circumstances which led to the mistaken bombing, let me offer a brief chronology of events.

In March of this year, U.S. intelligence officers began considering the FDSP headquarters as a potential target for NATO ALLIED FORCE strike operations. The FDSP was a legitimate target given its role in support of the Yugoslav military effort. We had the street address of the FDSP headquarters as "Bulevar Umetnosti 2" in New Belgrade. But military forces require precise geographic coordinates to conduct an attack. During a mid-April work-up of the target, three maps were used in an attempt to physically locate the address of the FDSP headquarters: two local commercial maps from 1989 and 1996, and one U.S.

government map produced in 1997. None of these maps used had any reference to the FDSP building. None accurately identified the current location of the Chinese Embassy.

Please keep in mind that the location of the Chinese Embassy was not a question that anyone reasonably would have asked when assembling this particular target package. This package was intended to strike the FDSP headquarters and nowhere else.

In an effort to pinpoint the location of the FDSP building at Bulevar Umetnosti 2, an intelligence officer used land navigation techniques taught by the U.S. military to locate distant or inaccessible points or objects. These techniques are known as "intersection" and "resection." They can be used for general geolocation, but should not be used for aerial targeting because they provide only an approximate location. Using this process, the individual mistakenly determined that the building which we now know to be the Chinese Embassy was the FDSP headquarters. The true location of the FDSP headquarters was some 300 meters away from the Chinese Embassy. This flaw in the address location process went undetected by all the others who evaluated the FDSP headquarters as a military target.

A critical lesson that emerges from this event is that particularly when providing targeting nominations in urban areas, it is important to provide an accurate appreciation of our confidence in the location of a target, and the evidentiary basis for how that location was determined.

The incorrect location of the FDSP building was then fed into several U.S. databases to determine whether any diplomatic or other facilities off-limits to targeting were nearby. We try to avoid damage to sensitive facilities like embassies, hospitals, schools and places of worship and look to see what risk to them a nearby strike might pose. Moreover, satellite imagery of the target provided no indication that the building was an embassy—no flags, no seals, no clear markings.

Multiple databases within the Intelligence Community and the Department of Defense all reflected the Embassy in its pre-1996 location in Belgrade. Despite the fact that U.S. officials had visited the Embassy on a number of occasions in recent years, the new location was never entered into intelligence or military targeting databases. If the databases had accurately located the Chinese Embassy, the misidentification of the FDSP building would have been recognized and corrected.

Why wasn't the Chinese embassy correctly located? It is important to understand that our ability to locate fixed-targets is no better than the data bases, and the data bases in this case were wrong. Further, it is difficult—actually it is impossible—to keep current databases for cities around the globe. The data bases are constructed to catalog targets not non-targets. In general, diplomatic facilities—our own being an exception because of the need to plan for evacuation—are given relatively little attention in our data bases because such facilities are not targets. Military targets are the top priority because of the danger they pose to our own forces.

In this context I would add my belief that too much public emphasis has been given to the fact that the 1997 U.S. Government map did not reflect that the Chinese Embassy had moved. This criticism overstates the importance of the map itself in the analytic process. Maps of urban areas will be out of date the day after they are published. What is critical is having accurate data bases. We have subsequently found maps which show the correct current location of the Chinese Embassy although there are others, including some produced after 1996 by the Yugoslav government, which do not.

Some of our employees knew the location of the Chinese embassy. But keep in mind that we were not looking for it. None of these individuals was consulted as the target was selected and reviewed and, as a result, we lost the opportunity to learn that the building targeted was not the FDSP headquarters. We have also found one report from 1997 that gave the correct address of the Chinese Embassy but that information was ancillary to the focus of the report and unfortunately the address was not entered into the data base.

Very late in the process, questions were raised by an intelligence officer as to whether the building targeted was in fact the FDSP headquarters or might be some other unidentified building. At no time was there any suspicion that the building might be an Embassy. This officer had become aware of the nomination by chance, and remembered having seen information a few years earlier that the FDSP building was located a block away from the location identified. Although the matter had nothing to do with his usual responsibilities, this officer registered his concern and sought to clarify the facts by contacting, or attempting to contact, other working level officials who were involved in the preparation of the nomination package.

On Tuesday, 4 May—three days before the bombing occurred—this officer telephoned an officer responsible for the target at the Joint Task Force NOBLE ANVIL in Naples. He told him that he believed the FDSP headquarters building was a block away from the identified location and said that he was trying to resolve this discrepancy. That evening, he obtained information that tended to confirm his belief that the building had been mislocated. Due to a variety of circumstances, this officer was unable to relay this information before departing for training 6–7 May. At that time this officer was unaware that the FDSP headquarters was on the target list.

On his return to his office on Friday afternoon, 7 May, the officer learned to his surprise that the FDSP building was on the target list for bombing that night. He attempted without success to re-contact the officer in Naples with whom he had spoken earlier in the week concerning the "discrepancy." He raised his concerns with another officer at Naples and learned that the aircraft was already en route to the target. He tried to convey his concern that the building targeted may not have been the FDSP headquarters. Those in Europe state that they believed that he was trying to convey that while it might not be the FDSP headquarters, it was still a legitimate FDSP target. While recollections differ of exactly what was said and what was heard, there is no doubt that no one knew that the facility in question was an Embassy. The strike took place shortly thereafter. Throughout this series of missed opportunities, the problem of identification was not brought to the attention of the senior managers who may have been able to intervene in time to prevent the strike.

At this point, I would like to identify the principal shortcomings that caused this accident to take place. First, the approach used to determine the location of the FDSP headquarters was inappropriate for targeting. There were three meetings at CIA that reviewed the target nomination. The method of identification was not briefed, questioned, or reviewed. Therefore, the initial misidentification took on the mantle of fact. The absence of discussions on this matter resulted in a target package that contained no cautionary language on the location of the FDSP headquarters. Absent cautionary language, reviewers at EUCOM and the Joint Staff mistakenly assumed the location was accurate. This made it unlikely that they would focus on the need to re-validate the target's identification.

Second, within CIA there were no procedural guidelines for the officers involved in targeting to follow, and there was little senior management involvement in guiding the targeting process. Although our military support organization had been involved in targeting matters, they had not previously been involved in the approval of target nomination packages unilaterally proposed and wholly assembled at CIA. This occasion was precedent-setting. No institutional process existed within CIA for ensuring that all resources were brought to bear on the FDSP nomination.

Third, reviewing elements at EUCOM and in the Joint Staff did not uncover either the inaccurate location of the FDSP headquarters or the correct location of the Chinese Embassy was the result of both data base shortcomings and procedural errors. The data base reviews were limited to validating the target data sheet geographic coordinates with the information put into the data base by the NIMA analyst. Such a circular process did not uncover the original error and made us susceptible to a single point of data base failure. While collateral damage assessments were performed and indicated there were no sensitive facilities in the area, these assessments were based on incomplete data on the location of those sensitive facilities. Individuals in both CIA and the DoD who knew the correct location of the Chinese Embassy should have been consulted.

Fourth, the critical linchpin for both the error in identification of the building and the failure of the review mechanisms is the inadequacy of the supporting data bases and the mistaken assumption the information they contained would be necessarily accurate. The misidentification of the targeted building as the FDSP headquarters would not have occurred had the data bases had the correct location of the Chinese Embassy. All the data bases that contained information on the Chinese Embassy placed it at its original, pre-1996 location some four miles away. Thus, the question of possible damage to the Embassy was never a consideration.

U.S. officials who had served in Belgrade were aware that the Chinese Embassy had moved sometime in 1996. The information, however, was not entered into the data bases we rely on for our targeting and mapping. In this context I would add my belief that too much public emphasis has been given to the fact that the 1997 NIMA map did not reflect that the Chinese Embassy had moved. This criticism overstates the importance of the map itself in our analytic process. Maps of urban areas will be out of date the day after they are published. What is critical is having accurate data bases.

Data base maintenance is one of the basic elements of our intelligence effort, but it is also one that has suffered in recent years as our workforce has been spread thin. Some have suggested that this failure is the consequence of resource shortfalls. A more fundamental problem is not the absolute level of resources, but the application of resources at our disposal. We have diverted resources and attention away from basic intelligence and data base maintenance to support current operations for too long. Data base production and maintenance has been routinely accorded a low priority and often overlooked in production planning and scheduling. Data base production is often the first activity curtailed when resources are tight. Data base production is widely viewed as low visibility, unrewarding, and unappreciated. Leadership attention and emphasis on data base production is infrequent, episodic, and essentially reactive.

. . . Our goal is to ensure that such a mistake does not happen again. To this end, we are implementing corrections to prevent such mistakes in the future. In addition, the following near-term corrective actions are already being implemented:

- DIA and NIMA have established rapid response procedures for critical database updates.

- We are strengthening our internal mechanisms and procedures for selecting and validating targets and we are increasing the priority placed on keeping databases current.

- The Community and other government agencies will explicitly report whenever foreign embassies move or are built. This information will then be forwarded and incorporated into our intelligence and military databases.

- In future conflicts, we will contact other governments to help identify and locate their facilities.

Perhaps the greatest tragedy behind the strikes was that a CIA analyst had detected the possibility of such an error and had warned an officer in the US European Command targeting staff in Naples. The CIA analyst then went on a two-day training exercise, however, and although he again warned the US European Command targeting staff on May 7, the officer in Naples who took the call did not fully understand the warning, and neither the CIA analyst or US officer in Naples notified higher levels of command of the risk of a major mistargeting.[135]

The Imperfect Nature of Perfect War

There is no meaningful data to support reports that the US struck deliberately, or because the Embassy was transmitting intelligence, or transmitted Yugoslav army communications after Milosevic's residence. While all embassies have an intelligence function, it is clear from NATO signal intelligence that the embassy never acted as a major transmitting facility and it was clear at the time that the embassy had only limited access to the details of what was happening in Serbia and Kosovo. Hitting it was politically devastating, and it never had any military value.

Secretary of Defense Cohen summarized the broader problems involved in his speech to the IISS on the preliminary lessons of the war.[136]

We can't afford to have the kind of mistakes that were made as far as the accidental bombing, or mistaken bombing, I should say, of the Chinese Embassy. As good as we are, this vast intelligence system can create what I would call a haystack of data, but finding that one needle that will pinpoint a target in the right timeframe can be difficult. So even though we have this tremendous capacity, we also have to recognize it has some limitations, and also that the human factor involved can create some difficulty as it did with the bombing of the Chinese Embassy.

Given this background, it is fairly clear why problems with targeting and collateral damage can and must occur. There is no way to fully check out every target, or to ensure that the review process can avoid collateral damage. These problems were compounded by the compartmentation of the targeting effort between the US and NATO, and the fact so few US military and civilian intelligence officers have ever been on the ground in the area. The US, however, flew about 80% of all strike sorties and around 90% of all special purpose targeting, intelligence, and electronic sorties. It is the only nation capable of targeting the GPS guided weapons used in bad weather, the use of stealth aircraft, and demanding laser-guided bomb strikes in urban areas and areas where collateral damage is likely. For security reasons, many NATO officers cannot enter such US targeting cells.[137]

There is no question that the collateral damage was a major issue that placed very serious limits on NATO's targets during the first two weeks of the war. The incidents that occurred during the first half of the war then had a paralyzing impact on some NATO air operations towards the end of the war. Lt. General Michael Short, NATO's joint force air component commander in the Balkans, stated that, "Towards the end of the air effort, we were restricted by the enormous concern for collateral damage and unintended loss of life. During the last days of the campaign, that was the litmus we used to pick a target."[138]

NATO and Serbian Collateral Damage Claims: Hiding the Truth with a Liar's Contest

Collateral damage presents other problems, including the issue of how to count and assess collateral damage touched upon earlier, and how to treat the issue during and after a conflict. At present, there is no way to know how many cases occurred in which collateral damage of some kind took place by the time the war ended. The Department of Defense stated on May 4 that 99.93 percent of the bombs NATO had dropped "have not caused collateral damage."

By Day 50 (May 10), NATO had flown about 19,000 sorties, and around 6,000 strike sorties and 10,000 weapons. The figures on collateral damage it had released as of that date meant an incident rate of about 0.2 percent per sorties with total claimed losses of less than 300 killed due to collateral damage. The Department of Defense reported 20 incidents at the end of the air and missile war for 12,600 strike-attack sorties and 329 cruise missiles and a total of more than 23,000 bombs and missiles. NATO reported 17 incidents for 16,000 strike-attack sorties on June 30, 1999.

The Department of Defense was still self-congratulatory in its January 2000 report on the lessons of the war, although the number of incidents had now crept up to 38.[139]

Adverse weather greatly complicated efforts to acquire and identify targets, increased the risk to aircrews, and made it more difficult to restrict damage to only the targets we intended to strike. The rugged mountainous terrain also confounded NATO's ability to find targets and posed hazards of its own. Despite these difficulties, NATO conducted the most precise and lowest collateral damage air operation in history. We were able to do so largely because of our commitment to developing precision munitions, the platforms and systems to deliver them, and vigorously training forces under realistic conditions.

. . . Throughout the air operation against the Serbs, NATO made every effort to minimize collateral damage. Of the 38 sites visited after the war, only one had sustained any significant collateral damage from NATO weapons falling on areas other than their intended target. At the other 37 sites, collateral damage was limited to broken windows, blown off roof tiles, and detached ceiling tiles.

The Tragedy of Moral and Analytic Corruption

There is no doubt that NATO's overall performance was excellent, but these comments and statistics are still another example of spinning half-truths into "perfect war." The count of incidents and the definition of accuracy seem to be based solely on politically sensitive wartime incidents causing significant collateral damage with civilian losses.

Certainly, the US report on the lessons of the war quoted above is a travesty which deliberately fails to mention the human cost of collateral damage, provides no specifics, ignores the after action impact of weapons like cluster bombs, and only deals with the sites "visited after the war." Lying by omission is not unusual, but US government reporting is rarely so lacking in basic integrity and content, and neither NATO nor any European government has done better. To be blunt, reporting on collateral damage that does not examine key incidents, does not attempt to estimate human casualties, the economic and longer-term human costs of war, and then distinguish between avoidable mistakes and the inevitable price of war is honorless propaganda.

Sources in NATO and the US military indicate that the number of weapons causing some kind of damage to civilian facilities—but not killing embarrassing numbers of civilians—could have been at least an order of magnitude higher than the 38 incidents NATO and the US refer to. Some officials even speculate that the total of civilian casualties may be in excess of 1,000, although this seems far more likely to reflect the impact of Serbian propaganda than the truth.

The tragedy behind the moral and analytic corruption in the NATO and US estimates is that NATO did make every possible effort to minimize collateral damage and did succeed in achieving the lowest levels of collateral damage in the history of any similar level of conflict. Full and objective reporting would have done nothing to damage NATO. It would have prepared the West and the world for the reality of future wars, and would have exposed the utter dishonesty of most Serbian claims.

The Worthless Character of Serbian Claims

Serbian claims and figures are worthless. Serbia claimed far more casualties than NATO produced, and used each instance of collateral damage as a propaganda tool. The author examined Serbian television coverage of collateral damage at length during the war, and it often involved the blatant exaggeration of collateral damage. Medical scenes of injured being treated are obviously occurring hours after attacks and treatment and casualty movement occurs in ways that make no medical sense. Daylight and backgrounds change, as does the cloud cover and angle of the sun. The same doll is moved from location to location to add human interest.

Serbia clearly staged some incidents by removing military and paramilitary corpses and equipment. Serbian television often showed scenes of bodies that were moved and positioned for dramatic effect, and in ways that made no sense in relation to the physical damage around them. Bodies are shown burning hours after an attack, but with no nearby fuel source that could have made them burn even during the first moments after a strike. Bodies and physical damage are often shown without showing the cause of the damage. In many cases, there was no way to know if a bomb was ever involved, or the result of Serbian fire and human cleansing.

Outside Studies and Analyses: The Human Rights Watch and OSCE Reports

The efforts by some NGOs to make their own estimates have so far produced little more than informed guesstimates, and many have been little more than concealed attacks on the use of force per se, efforts to prove that NATO acted against international law, or indirect pro-Serbian propaganda.[140]

There is one major exception: A report by Human Rights Watch called "Civilian Deaths in the NATO Air Campaign."[141] This report produced the following summary conclusions:

Despite precautions, including the use of a higher percentage of precision-guided munitions than in any other major conflict in history, civilian casualties occurred. Human Rights Watch has conducted a thorough investigation of civilian deaths as a result of NATO action. On the basis of this investigation, Human Rights Watch has found that there were ninety separate incidents involving civilian deaths during the seventy-eight day bombing campaign. Some 500 Yugoslav civilians are known to have died in these incidents.

We determined the intended target in sixty-two of the ninety incidents. Military installations account for the greatest number, but nine incidents were a result of attacks on non-military targets that Human Rights Watch believes were illegitimate. (Human Rights Watch is currently preparing a separate report with a full analysis of our legal objections to the choice of certain targets.) These include the headquarters of Serb Radio and Television in Belgrade, the New Belgrade heating plant, and seven bridges that were neither on major transportation routes nor had other military functions.

Thirty-three incidents occurred as a result of attacks on targets in densely populated urban areas (including six in Belgrade). Despite the exclusive use of precision-guided weapons in attacks on the capital, Belgrade experienced as many incidents involving civilian deaths as any other city. In Nis, the use of cluster bombs was a decisive factor in civilian deaths in at least three incidents. Overall, cluster bomb use by the United States and Britain can be confirmed in seven incidents throughout Yugoslavia (another five are possible but unconfirmed); some ninety to 150 civilians died from the use of these weapons.

Thirty-two of the ninety incidents occurred in Kosovo, the majority on mobile targets or military forces in the field. Attacks in Kosovo overall were more deadly—a third of the incidents account for more than half of the deaths. Seven troubling incidents were as a result of attacks on convoys or transportation links. Because pilots' ability to properly identify these mobile targets was so important to avoid civilian casualties, these civilian deaths raise the question whether the fact that pilots were flying at high altitudes may have contributed to these civilian deaths by precluding proper target identification. But insufficient evidence exists to answer that question conclusively at this point.

Another factor in assessing the higher level of civilian deaths in Kosovo is the possible Yugoslav use of civilians for "human shields." There is some evidence that Yugoslav forces used internally displaced civilians as human shields in the village of Korisa on May 13, and may thus share the blame for the eighty-seven deaths there.

In an important development, sensitivity to civilian casualties led to significant changes in weapons use. Widespread reports of civilian casualties from the use of cluster bombs and international criticism of these weapons as potentially indiscriminate in effect led, according to senior U.S. Department of Defense officials interviewed by Human Rights Watch, to an unprecedented (and unannounced) U.S. executive order in the middle of May to cease their further use in the conflict. The White House issued the order only days after civilians were killed by NATO cluster bombs in the city of Nis on May 7. U.S. cluster bomb use did apparently stop at about that time, according to Human Rights Watch observations, although British cluster bomb use continued. Human Rights Watch released its own report on May 11 questioning the civilian effects of cluster bombs and calling for a moratorium on their use.

In its investigation Human Rights Watch has found no evidence of war crimes. The investigation did conclude that NATO violated international humanitarian law. Human Rights Watch calls on NATO governments to establish an independent and impartial commission, competent to receive confidential information, that would investigate violations of international humanitarian law and the extent of these violations, and would consider the need to alter targeting and bombing doctrine to ensure compliance with international humanitarian law. Such a commission should issue its findings publicly. Human Rights Watch also calls for NATO to alter its targeting and bombing doctrine in order to bring it into compliance with international humanitarian law.

With respect to NATO violations of international humanitarian law, Human Rights Watch was concerned about a number of cases in which NATO forces:

- conducted air attacks using cluster bombs near populated areas;
- attacked targets of questionable military legitimacy, including Serb Radio and Television, heating plants, and bridges;
- did not take adequate precautions in warning civilians of attacks;
- took insufficient precautions identifying the presence of civilians when attacking convoys and mobile targets; and
- caused excessive civilian casualties by not taking sufficient measures to verify that military targets did not have concentrations of civilians (such as at Korisa).

One disturbing aspect of the matter of civilian deaths is how starkly the number of incidents and deaths contrasts with official U.S. and Yugoslav statements. U.S. officials, including Secretary of Defense William Cohen, Deputy Secretary of Defense John Hamre, and Gen. Wesley Clark, have testified before Congress and stated publicly that there were only twenty to thirty incidents of "collateral damage" in the entire war. The number of incidents Human Rights Watch has been able to authenticate is three to four times this number. The seemingly cavalier U.S. statements regarding the civilian toll suggest a resistance to acknowledging the actual civilian effects and an indifference to evaluating their causes.

The confirmed number of deaths is considerably smaller than Yugoslav public estimates. The post-conflict casualty reports of the Yugoslav government vary but coincide in estimating a death toll of at least some 1,200 and as many as 5,000 civilians. At the lower end, this is more than twice the civilian death toll of around 500 that Human Rights Watch has been able to verify. In one major incident—Dubrava prison in Kosovo—the Yugoslav government attributed ninety-five civilian deaths to NATO bombing. Human Rights Watch research in Kosovo determined that an estimated nineteen prisoners were killed by NATO bombs on May 21 (three prisoners and a guard were killed in an earlier attack on May 19), but at least seventy-six prisoners were summarily executed by prison guards and security forces subsequent to the NATO attack. The countervailing claims about the civilian death toll underscore the need for full accountability by NATO for its military operations.

The Human Rights Watch report is as thorough, conscientious, and balanced a report as it is possible for a private organization to conduct. There are a number of US government analysts who privately admit that it is almost certainly more accurate in broad terms than NATO and US government reporting. It also tracks in broad terms with the results of two reports by the Organization for Security and Cooperation in Europe (OSCE) on human rights violations in Kosovo. These OSCE reports indicate that the NATO air campaign was considerably more costly than NATO and the US have reported, but that the collateral damage was minimal and unintentional, and that the Serbian violations of human rights were deliberate and massive.[142]

The conclusions of the report's analysis are that clear strategies lay behind the human rights violations committed by Serbian forces; that paramilitaries and armed civilians committed acts of extreme lawlessness with the tolerance and collusion of military and security forces whose own actions were generally highly organized and systematic; and that the violations inflicted on the Kosovo Albanian population on a massive scale after 20 March were a continuation of actions by Serbian forces that were well-rehearsed, insofar as they were taking place in many locations well before that date. While both parties to the conflict committed human rights violations, there was no balance or equivalence in the nature or scale of those violations—overwhelmingly it was the Kosovo Albanian population who suffered. The report also notes that persistent human rights violations lay behind the security breakdown which plunged Kosovo into armed conflict and a human rights and humanitarian catastrophe.

Human Rights Watch and the OSCE, however, did not have access to classified material, and the OSCE only examined the impact of NATO strikes in passing. As a result, it is impossible to determine exactly how much collateral damage occurred or the total number of civilian casualties from the data now available. It should also be stressed that even if Serbian claims were true, the resulting total collateral damage would still be small by the standards of weapons delivered against targets in populated areas in previous air and missile wars. It is also true that counting every bit of collateral damage as if it was important is pointless.

Lessons for the Future

One key lesson of Kosovo is that exaggerated or false claims regarding collateral damage may well come back to haunt the US and its allies, and should not be made during wartime or in after action reports. The quality and integrity of the reporting to date has done nothing other than undermine the credibility of a largely successful effort to minimize collateral damage and the moral position of the Western democracies.

Another lesson is that the assessment of collateral damage cannot stop with what has happened during the actual fighting. German and other NATO peacekeeping forces have found since the end of the air war that US cluster munitions again scattered large numbers of unexploded bomblets over the areas that NATO attacked. US cluster munitions have presented this problem since Vietnam, and anyone who visited the sites of air attacks during the Gulf War saw large numbers of cluster munitions scattered in large numbers.[143]

Modern war requires objectivity and integrity if it is to be fought in ways that preserve the moral position of those who fight to make peace, halt aggression, and to achieve humanitarian goals. The US and the West face a political and strategic climate in which independent wartime reporting on collateral damage can be expected to steadily improve, and in which any hostile power or movement will use collateral damage and targeting errors as a political weapon—often creating its own "myths" and false images of such damage when this is politically desirable. Like it or not, collateral damage has become a weapon of war.[144]

Economic Aftermaths and Environmental Effects

There is another side to the collateral damage story, and that is the issue of aftermaths. Like Iraq, Serbia made a deliberate effort to propagandize a region-wide environmental threat during the war. It claimed that the NATO attacks would produce major problems in terms of smoke, emissions, and pollution that would affect neighboring states.

Pekka Haavitso, a former Finish Minister of the environment, led the UN team on a ten-day mission of inspection, and the results of this investigation seem to be objective. In practice, a UN team inspecting Serbia after the war found little side of any broad environmental damage even within Serbia, and no evidence that deplete uranium rounds had produced any radioactive contamination. The UN team did find, however, that there were significant environmental "hot spots."[145] The inspectors found that three Serbian cities—Pancevo, Kragujevac, and Bor—had serious environmental problems, although the UN team could not distinguish the incremental impact of the NATO air and missile strikes from years of economic mismanagement and environmental neglect. In many cases, the NATO bombing may simply have been a catalyst triggering a problem that would inevitably have occurred at some point in the future.[146]

NATO repeatedly bombed a refinery, fertilizer plant, and petrochemical plant in Pancevo, and the UN team found large pools of mercury—potentially affecting water supplies and poisoning fish in the Danube and that air pollution had caused "black rain." The UN found that NATO strikes on the Zastava car factory in Kragujevac released high levels of polychlorinated biphenyls (PCBs). In Bor, the destruction of a copper factory led to sulfur dioxide emissions and helped caused acid rain.[147]

There were also more propagandistic reports that the NATO air strikes produced lasting psychological trauma in civilians in Serbia, particularly among children. There have also been reports of major environmental problems in towns like Pancevo, caused by the bombing of an oil refinery, petrochemical plant, and fertilizer factory. There were complaints of river pollution and "clouds of noxious gases that hovered for days over Pancevo," and that the "war's lingering, ghoulish touch could be affecting even the unborn."[148]

Economic impacts are another "aftermath effect" of target selection and collateral damage. Serbia has claimed that that its preliminary damage assessment indicates that NATO did $30 billion dollars worth of damage, although it says that a final figure will be developed by a special government commission. The end result may be open-ended claims that blame NATO for many of Serbia's internal economic problems, and which grossly exaggerate the damage, but which NATO has no way of refuting. Such claims allow a nation to both refight the political battles of a way long after it is over, and to seek aid.[149]

Serbia has also attempted what might be called "collateral damage extortion." The NATO attacks on the eight bridges over the Danube in Serbia limited or blocked barge traffic along the southern sector of the Rhine-Main-Danube waterway that eventually flows to the Black Sea. This traffic approached 100 million tons a year before the bombing. Preliminary estimates put the cost of clearing the waterway at $20 million and the cost of repairing the bridges at least $100 million. Serbia insisted that it would not allow the waterway to be rebuilt unless it received aid to rebuild its bridges although NATO had insisted that Serbia would get no aid until Milosevic had been deposed from power.[150]

No mix of NATO air and cruise missile strikes could avoid producing some serious environmental and economic effects. At the same time, serious questions arise as to the role environmental impacts will have in future wars—particularly in relatively low level and highly political conflicts. Similarly, economic and other "aftermath" effects may now have to be considered in ways that was never previously necessary.

Collateral damage is not simply a wartime issue. Careful consideration needs to be given to the impact after the war—in terms of human suffering, recovery costs, media and political problems, and long-term conflict resolution.

Another lesson is that accurate assessments of collateral damage will be essential in dealing with economic rebuilding, and aid claims and charges after a conflict, and in structuring conflict resolution. Collateral damage and targeting problems do not end with a war. Neither does the political struggle to shape perceptions of a war and its aftermath. It also is far harder to prove or disprove that bombing or missile strikes result in vaguely defined environmental impacts, psychological problems, and statistical increases in birth defects than that they did or did not produce direct physical damage and casualties.

THE PROBLEM OF TARGETING

The same issues that surround collateral damage affect targeting the NATO air and missile campaign against Serbia involved targeting problems that were very different from the situation in the Gulf War, where target planning and analysis could be carried out over a period of months after Iraq's invasion of Kuwait, and the air and missile war could concentrate on air defense targets and exposed Iraqi ground forces in the field.

While NATO had begun targeting activity in the summer of 1998, SHAPE sources state that serious, theater-wide targeting was only put on a true warfighting basis after air and missile campaign began.[151] The targets involved a mix of real-time targets, well-known surface facilities, surface facilities whose function was unknown or unclear, and a mix of underground bunkers, storage sites, and command bunkers. NATO had previously targeted Yugoslavia in depth during the Cold War because it assumed that Yugoslavia was likely to be the victim of a Soviet invasion, but it had not updated its targeting in nearly a decade and little of NATO's earlier efforts remained relevant. In spite of the use of NATO airpower in Bosnia, the US and NATO had never developed an updated target list to deal with the remaining Yugoslav Federal Republic, or which fully reflected the impact of the massive shifts in military forces and facilities, and in related civil facilities, which followed the ongoing break up of the former Yugoslavia.

Improvising a New Approach to Targeting

As a result, NATO had to suddenly shift from planning targets in a token campaign to targeting for true warfighting. Reports indicate that NATO went to war with a total of only 169 targets and 50 authorized targets for its initial campaign plan and ended the campaign with six volumes of detailed targeting data.[152]

The Combined Air Operations Center (CAOC) at the Fifth Allied Air Force headquarters in Vicenza, Italy was the key NATO facility coordinating pilots and controllers, and managing the tasking related to targeting. It grew from an improvised facility with less than 300 people to a full-scale war planning facility with over 1,000.[153] Sources in key US targeting facilities like the National Imagery and Mapping Agency (NIMA) indicate that the same was true in the US and that there were significant problems in organizing an effective all-source targeting effort.[154]

The US was aided, however, by new procedures it had developed as a result of the targeting problems that occurred as a result of the Gulf War, and by an improved integration of national and theater intelligence assets. The US made the first use of a new targeting system designed to integrated national satellite intelligence and airborne reconnaissance data with strike planning called the Joint Targeting Workstation. This workstation was a still-developmental system developed by Marconi Integrated Systems that was supposed to take data from the satellite systems operated by the National Reconnaissance Office (NRO) and surveillance aircraft, integrate them to provide precise targeting coordinates, and then model the impact of various precision guided munitions. It was supposed to provide near real-time sensor to shooter data to aircraft with on-board reception and processing capabilities like some F/A-18s and F-15Es.[155]

These targeting capabilities were supported by other developments. One US report on the lessons of the war notes both the role of other systems and some of the lessons involved:[156]

The capabilities available at the CAOC enabled C2ISR assets to successfully tighten timelines that had been problematic in the past. Real-time threat information provided by airborne signals-intelligence sensors were relayed to appropriate theater command-and-control assets, and, in some cases, even directly to strike aircraft entering airspace over the Federal Republic of Yugoslavia. U-2 imagery was exploited using the reachback capabilities described earlier.

Navy F-14 aircraft equipped with the Tactical Air Reconnaissance Pod System (TARPS) were also used effectively to identify targets during the conflict. Navy maritime patrol aircraft also made significant contributions to the ISR collection effort. The processing times achieved with these assets were well within the required timelines for the air tasking order, and in several cases allowed the CAOC to reassign aircraft to new targets rapidly (called "flex targeting"). Space assets also provided important capabilities. Improved weather forecasting capabilities, enabled by space-based sensors, made the application of aerospace power more effective throughout Operation Allied Force.

In addition, increased capability was provided both by enhancements to the CAOC itself, as well as by the application of specific reachback and distributed operations capabilities. These capabilities provided a major increase in capability and should be refined and standardized to ensure effective reachback in future conflicts. As much as possible, these capabilities should attempt to ensure 24-hours-a-day, 7-days-a-week operations. In normal joint task force operations, a representative of the land component commander (usually the commander of the battlefield coordination element) sits on the Joint Targeting Coordination Board (JTCB). As such, he acts as the land component commander's advocate for targets to be executed within the joint or combined air tasking.

General John Jumper, the Commander-in-Chief of US Air Forces Europe, provided the following description of the evolution of the targeting process, and the lessons that result, in his testimony to Congress on the Lessons of the War.[157]

Not only did we have to find and target surface-to-air missile sites that did not radiate, NATO air forces were tasked to go after Milosevic's fielded forces in Kosovo and other time-critical targets. Because there had been an early declaration that ground forces would not be used, fielded forces in Kosovo were free from the normal preparation activity we had seen in Desert Storm. Instead of preparing for a potential ground attack by digging into defensive positions and stockpiling supplies, activities that provide lucrative targets for airpower, enemy ground forces were free to simply hide from our airplanes.

The situation on the ground in Kosovo required significant modification to our tactics, techniques and procedures—we took full advantage of all available skills and technology to get inside the heads of enemy ground commanders and SAM operators. We invented new processes to integrate both air and space-borne Intelligence, Reconnaissance and Surveillance (ISR) platforms for collection along with advanced technology and procedures for analysis.

Our new processes took advantage of our ISR resources to identify "pop up" targets of opportunity. These assets then transmitted the data for analysis to the Combined Air Operations Center (CAOC) at Vicenza, Italy—the nerve center for NATO air operations—and to stateside locations. Planners at the CAOC rapidly translated the data into targeting information and relayed the target to strike aircraft for destruction. Throughout the campaign, we continually refined this process until we could process targeting information between our sensors and strike aircraft in a matter of hours.

. . . While rapid targeting worked, the process was not perfect. Aircrews faced a confusing barrage of verbal targeting instructions in the cockpit. Present aircraft are not capable of displaying target imagery or of receiving target coordinates digitally while in flight. Nevertheless, we achieved measurable success against mobile targets and Milosevic's fielded forces. These achievements benefited from the many precision weapons at our disposal.

. . . We must fully develop the technology and tactics to rapidly strike targets. To do this, we need equipment that will provide real-time imagery and target location directly to our fighter and bomber crews. This will allow us to reduce the barriers between the "sensor" and the "shooter" in the targeting cycle—what we call "attacking the seams." To make airpower as effective as possible against mobile targets, we must have complete integration between all available air and space sensors at our nation's disposal. Their targeting data also must quickly reach those commanding aerospace forces in the Air Operations Center (AOC). Ultimately, our goal is to reduce the time from target identification to target destruction from hours and days to minutes.

To avoid collateral damage in the future, the Air Force requires a continued investment in precision weapons and the bombers and fighters required to deliver them. We also need to work with other services to keep our aging ISR and EW systems effective, and to relieve the continuous pressure on them, we will seek additional aircraft and personnel. A fully developed CSAR capability must also be assembled within the European theater to locate and rescue anyone caught behind enemy lines—not only to protect our people but to deny an enemy the propaganda victory capture would bring.

National versus NATO Targeting

In spite of these improvements, NATO was incapable of doing most of its targeting on an alliance basis—in itself a major lesson about the limits of NATO and coalition warfare. Most of the detailed targeting activity took place at the US Joint Analysis Center in Molesworth, England. This center acted as the "fusion center" that integrated intelligence data—most of which came from US sources—and then transmitted the data over the secure US Sprint communications system to the US European Command (USCENTCOM) in Stuttgart. The data were also transmitted to the US targeting cells in Vicenza and Aviano, Italy.[158]

This workload over-tasked US and allied resources, and the need to obtain a British, French, German, Italian, and US consensus created further problems. So did the fact that each target required legal review and review for collateral damage. As a result, it often took nine or more people in different locations, working together over a secure communications system, to compete the review of a single target, and the procedures involved additional review in any case where 20 or more civilians might be killed. This part of the review process became even more complex after the strike on the Chinese embassy on May 7. It also involved considerable review and micro-management in capitals. For example, General Henry H. Shelton, is reported to have been at the Pentagon every night during the first 45 days of the war.[159]

Changes in the Targeting Effort over Time

Even so, the number of targets generated per day rose from five per day at the start of the war to 25 targets a day by May. Figures 11 and 12 show the steady rise in the number of target groups hit, and the steady build-up in the scale of the war in terms of the targets struck and restruck during the course of the conflict. It is important to note that these figures disguise the number of targets that NATO struck at in some ways because NATO often restruck given facilities and targets, but hit at multiple ground targets in any given target group for Serbian forces. As a result, the number of targets NATO reported are highly nominal.

Nevertheless, NATO more than doubled the total number of targets it struck between D-30 and D-45 (a 141% rise during weeks 5 and 6 over the first 30 days of the war. It had developed 802 target groups by Day 46. Figure 11 shows that only 25 percent of these target groups were Serbian military. Another 15 percent were air defense. Most of the remaining 60 percent were factories, infrastructure, oil and POL facilities, roads, bridges, railroads, and command and control facilities which tended to be dual-use civil-military facilities.

NATO had to carry out most of its strikes in a built up or urban environment. If one looks at the detailed targeting maps issued by NATO and the US, it is clear that about half of the strikes on Serbian VJ and MUP forces are near built-up areas and about 60 percent were in Serbia. NATO was not hitting targets isolated in a desert like Iraq, and it faced a completely different targeting environment than the Gulf War, and this had several important implications:

- The risk of civilian casualties and collateral damage was far more likely.
- About 37% of the targets were more civil than military: support, infrastructure (factories and utilities), oil refineries and POL facilities and storage, roads, rail roads, and bridges. They totaled about 287 target groups as of Day 46.
- About 70% of the command and control targets were facilities that are primarily civilian command and control facilities in peacetime. NATO has now struck a total of about 197 such target groups, and around 130 are dual-use and primarily civilian in peacetime.

These data and trends illustrate the need to fully prepare for what might be called a "surgical strategic" war where targets are chosen at least as often to try to alter Serbian political actions as degrade any military capability for ethnic cleansing.

The Department of Defense spokesman provided further insights into the problems and risks involved in targeting and minimizing collateral damage during an exchange in the Department of Defense briefing on June 24, 1999:

Questioner: Ken, the CIA IG report on the bombing of the Chinese Embassy says that, or reportedly says that a mid-level official at the CIA called mid-ranking military officers with the U.S. European Command in Europe and voiced his doubts that this building, in fact, was what they thought it was, the headquarters for that supply directorate. You've known about this from day one, apparently. One, why did you not make this public when you professed to be making a clean breast of everything that went wrong several days after the mistaken bombing? And two, what are you doing now to determine why those mid-level officers in Europe didn't do something when this guy voiced his doubts that this was the right target?

Mr. Bacon: First of all, I think you've given a somewhat sketchy, not totally accurate, and, I would say, somewhat weighted account of what in fact happened. So let me walk you through what we understand happened, and then I'll take more questions if you have more questions.

The issue here, of course, is the mistaken bombing of the Chinese Embassy in Belgrade that happened on May 7. A mid-level intelligence officer at the CIA, who was not involved in targeting, learned that the Yugoslav Federal Directorate Supply and Procurement Headquarters was on the target list. This was a building in Belgrade that was to be struck. He had an interest in this building, even though he was not involved directly in targeting, and he reviewed imagery of the building and decided that the building that was targeted did not appear to be at the location of the building he believed to be the Headquarters of the Federal Directorate of Supply and Procurement. He didn't know what the targeted building was, but he didn't think it was the correct building. He, in fact, thought that the building that was targeted was a valid military target, but he didn't think it was as high a value target or as lucrative a target as the Federal Directorate of Supply and Procurement.

On May 4 this mid-level officer called a mid-level officer in Europe and conveyed his concerns, and at the same time he attempted to arrange a meeting within the CIA to clarify his concerns. But he was not successful in arranging that meeting, a meeting with people in the CIA who were familiar with the targeting, and he didn't have a great sense of urgency about this, because he had no idea when the building was to be targeted. In fact he left the CIA for several days to participate in some pre-arranged training. He was out of the CIA on May 6 and 7. He returned in the afternoon of the 7th from his training to learn that the Headquarters of the Yugoslav Federal Directorate of Supply and Procurement was on the target list for the evening of May 7. So he called back to Europe in an effort to contact the officer he had spoken with before, and he was unsuccessful in contacting that officer, so he spoke to another mid-level officer in Europe and conveyed his concerns.

The concern he conveyed was not that they were going after an inappropriate target, but it wasn't perhaps the best target that they could be going after at the time. Although he thought they were going after a military target, he thought it probably was not the Headquarters of the Procurement and Supply Directorate. He was told when he called the second time and spoke to another officer—not the first officer with whom he'd spoken—that the planes were already in the air, and, in fact, the building was struck a short time later. He had no idea that the building that was struck was in fact the Chinese Embassy. So that's basically what happened in that case. This was known at the CIA and was part of their review from the very beginning, and the other side of it will be part of the Pentagon review as it continues to look into this.

Questioner: What are you doing in terms of investigating . . .

Mr. Bacon: Secretary Cohen has instructed Deputy Secretary Hamre and General Ralston, the Vice Chairman of the Joint Chiefs of Staff, to conduct an after-action review of Operation ALLIED FORCE that will look at all aspects of the operation and come up with an analysis of what went right, what went wrong, what could have happened better, what happened better than we anticipated. As part of that review, we will look into this aspect—that is what happened on our side in terms of targeting for the Chinese Embassy—but it will be in a broader context, not just the Chinese Embassy incident, but we'll look at targeting decisions generally, how they were made, how the information was gathered, how the intelligence information was fused with the operating information, the speed of the decision-making process, the accuracy of it, etc.

Questioner: Let me ask it a different way. If you're dropping 500- and 2,000-pound bombs and there's an element of doubt about what you're dropping it on, is that the right way to run a targeting operation?

Mr. Bacon: I think, again, one of the things that has to be reconstructed here—and has not—is the level of officials involved in this decision, what happened to the information, and exactly what the CIA official said to the military officials. Remember, he did not say, "You're about to hit an embassy." He said, "I believe you're going after an appropriate target, but maybe not the best target." That's our indication of what was said. But the entire chain has not yet been reconnected, so we know for sure how this worked out, and that's one of the things we'll be looking at.

Mr. Bacon: What we don't know, David, is what level this rose to, whether there was a review that led to a confirmation that turned out to be incorrect or there was no review. That's one of the things that's being determined.

Questioner: If you have a system where the doubts can't rise to the level. . .

Mr. Bacon: David, I'm not saying we have a system that allows that, or we don't. I'm saying we're looking into it, and the context for looking into it is a broader look at how targeting decisions were made, how the information was assembled, how it was conveyed, and how the types of doubts that were raised were processed—whether this was a one-time thing or whether it happened many times, and whether there was a process that worked or didn't work. That's all being done in the context of reviewing the entire operation and deciding how decisions were made over the course of the operation, not just in this one alone.

Questioner: When did the Secretary order that review?

Mr. Bacon: The Secretary ordered the after-action review after the operation was over. It was a week or so ago.

Questioner: When you came into the briefing room, didn't Cohen at that time—or am I remembering this incorrectly—did he not say that the Pentagon, the Defense Department, would be reviewing this matter at that time. Has there not been an ongoing Pentagon review of this?

Mr. Bacon: The review—we chose to concentrate on carrying out the military operation while the military operation was ongoing. The review was always going to be done after it was over. The initial—there was a review that was done on the intelligence side that had to do with databases. It had to do with how the intelligence was gathered that led to the initial targeting decision. That was done. It's been reported to the Chinese, and it's been reported to Congress.

There's another side of the review that has to do with the military side, and that was always going to be done in the context of a broader after-action review. That's what's being done by Secretary Hamre and General Ralston.

Questioner: I would like to just also follow up. You said that we want to look into this and see if this was a one-time event, or you said if this has happened many times. I'm not clear what you meant. What are you looking into to see if it happened many times?

Mr. Bacon: The question of how—the issue of how questions about targets were handled. In other words, were there other times when mid-level officials raised issues about targets, about specific targets, one. That's the first question. Two, if so, how were they handled?

So was this a one-time event where a mid-level official—who in fact was not involved, as I pointed out, in the targeting decision? He had another reason for being interested in this building, but it wasn't because he was part of the targeting team. Were there other incidents where an official called over, and for all we know he didn't call the right person, or it went to the wrong office? This is the type of thing that will have to be sorted out.

Questioner: Having raised the point, do you have any reason to believe there are other instances in which questions were raised about targeting?

Mr. Bacon: Absolutely not. I don't have any reason to believe that they were raised or they weren't. But that's one of the things that will be determined. The effectiveness of the targeting system is one of the aspects that will be considered in the after-action report.

Questioner: Ken, do you have any indication how far his concerns went?

Mr. Bacon: No.

Questioner: Pickering said the Chinese apparently said that the technique and the procedures used for choosing this target were "totally inappropriate for precision targeting for air attacks." Do you accept that as a valid judgment on the procedures that were used?

Mr. Bacon: I was not there, and I don't know what Pickering said, and I can't comment on it.

Questioner: Do you think the procedures used for targeting that building were appropriate for precision targeting of air attacks?

Mr. Bacon: I can't answer that question. All I can tell you is that during an extensive military operation most of the, I would say the overwhelming number of bombs landed where they were supposed to land on appropriate targets. There were several mistakes. This clearly was one of them. It's been the topic of considerable analysis, which is ongoing. When it's completed, we'll be able to give a more accurate assessment of what happened.

This kind of targeting, however, places a massive burden on targeteers. As a rough rule of thumb, interviews indicate that at least 10–20 targets had to be examined for each target struck, and the situation changed daily because of Serbian concealment, dispersion, and "work arounds."

Precision Targeting, Precision Engagement, and Precision Intelligence

Even during the war, many senior officers in the US Air Force felt that NATO failed to make a concerted effort to select the targets that would have a maximum impact on the perceptions and actions of the Serbian leadership, and concentrated on finding targets in broad pre-determined categories. Some US air planners felt that NATO repeated mistakes the Coalition had made during the Gulf War, and bombed "by the numbers," rather than by focusing on a much more limited set of politically sensitive targets. As will be discussed later, some other air planners felt that the bombing effort also wasted assets on tactical targets and focused much of its effort on "tank plinking" with limited military effect.

One of the most important lessons that the US has learned from this experience is that precision targeting can only take place if there is precision intelligence, and US postwar thinking on this subject is considerably more objective than some of the statements it made during the war.[160]

Precision engagement consists of the following sequence of events: (1) accurate target location and identification; (2) responsive command and control of strike forces; (3) achievement of desired engagement effects on the target; (4) assessment of the level of success of the engagement; and (5) reengagement of the target with precision when desired. In order to achieve precision engagement, precision intelligence is required. During Operation Allied Force, our precision-intelligence capability played a significant role in the employment of precision munitions to systematically degrade important Serbian military targets.

A number of systems currently in research and development would have been useful had they been available. In fact, if nothing else, Operation Allied Force emphasized that the Department needs to continue on the modernization path it has pursued with the help of Congress since Desert Storm. We need to field those systems that improve precision and timeliness with which we detect, identify, track, and assess potential targets, regardless of constraints imposed by adverse weather, nighttime, concealment and deception techniques, or rapid movement. Ongoing programs such as, Future Imagery Architecture, Global Hawk, Predator radar, and synergistic sensor pairing, offer an improved sensor mix. Likewise, those areas that contribute to precision intelligence, dynamic collection management, common battlespace awareness, and interoperable intelligence systems and architectures when fielded will all contribute to more effectiveness in conflicts such as this one.

In addition, improved policies, procedures, and tools are needed to further enhance the quality and responsiveness of precision intelligence support for military operations. Areas that warrant particular emphasis based on experiences in Operation Allied Force are as follows:[161]

- Preparation for crises and the transition-to-crisis by the Intelligence community

- Development of collection strategies that deconflict national policy and theater operational requirements when necessary

- Development of a mix of improved sensors with day and night, adverse weather capability to identify and track mobile targets with required timeliness and geo-location accuracy in the presence of sophisticated camouflage, concealment, and deception techniques

- Inclusion of UAV sensor data and cockpit video into the tasking, processing, exploitation, and dissemination processes
- Consideration of operational targeting needs when developing ISR system requirements
- Development of streamlined ways to exchange intelligence information exchange (to include Web-based collaborative tools) between the intelligence communities and supported forces of the United States and its coalition partners
- Continued development of capabilities to disseminate sensor data directly to in-theater tactical forces.

Targeting and C⁴: "Dynamic Battle Control"

The US Air Force has continued to rethink its targeting concepts since Kosovo, and has found other limitations in its targeting capabilities. The targeting system the US and NATO used in Kosovo, including the air traffic orders (ATOs)—the secure multi-service documents that assigned aircraft and strike packages to predetermined targets—failed to provide the level of flexibility commanders needed to address mobile and other time-sensitive targets. As a result, Serbian forces soon learned to quickly relocate forces, weapons, and key functions and equipment, and this created major problems for US and allied air operations. While the US is seeking to improve its targeting capabilities by developing techniques like foliage-penetrating radar, and adding much high resolution, all-weather radars to its UAVs, it is also examining possible changes to its methods of planning and controlling air operations.[162]

The US Air Force is seeking a new form of "dynamic battle control" that may lead it to restructure the ATO process, and leave a significant percentage of aircraft off of the daily ATO list of designated targets so they can be allocated to time urgent targets on a basis of need and opportunity. It is considering new ways to reallocate flight paths and re-task aircraft returning to their bases without expending their ordnance. It is examining possible changes in its Air Operation Centers (AOCs) to taking more advantage of emerging sensor, data management, and communications technologies to improve the center's situational awareness of the battlefield.

Some US Air Force experts believe that a new hybrid organization may be needed to exploit the steadily improving ability of aircraft to update their targeting information while still in flight, or to alter their mission to reflect new data on the overall course of the air campaign and threat air defenses. Some experts feel that this may be possible from command centers in the rear, rather than using forward-deployed AOCs.[163] One problem that needs to be addressed is the fact that the Combined Air Operations Center (CAOC) in Vincenza still operated on a 72-hour cycle in creating the air tasking order, although it increasingly adapted its operations to shift targets which strike aircraft while in flight, and experimented with real-time tasking based on U-2 and Predator data being relayed to the F-15E and the use of lasers on the Predator to illuminate targets.[164]

Accordingly, there are several lessons to be drawn from the conflict regarding targeting:

- *The need to create targeting staffs that maintain an on-going and constantly updated target base against any major potential opponent in peacetime, and a rapid reaction capability of personnel with dedicated skills and suitable reconnaissance and intelligence assets that can be deployed to deal with any sudden contingency.*

- *The need to develop targeting concepts and target lists designed to influence the behavior of the enemy leadership as surgically as possible, rather than bomb given categories by the numbers.*

- *The need for expeditionary targeting and intelligence assets that can deploy the proper combination of JSTARS, LAVS, radars, and targeting and battle damage assessment capabilities for a major regional conflict in less than 48 hours, and for a "sensitive target warning" survey for all nations where there is a serious risk of conflict. This is a major mission element of modern war.[165]*

- *The need for some system that can target paramilitaries and deal with the problems created by the use of civilians and civilian facilities as potential sanctuaries and human shields.*

- *At the same time, the need to understand the limits of what modern sensors, intelligence systems, reconnaissance systems and analysis can do. Once again, it is all too easy for US defense planners to talk blithely about "information dominance," but this is extremely difficult to achieve without a comprehensive target base that is geared to both military and political objectives. Improvising such efforts with partially experienced personnel operating under extreme pressure is not a proper answer to the real-world demands of modern war.*

THE NEW CONDITIONS OF WAR

Kosovo did not show that public opinion demands casualty-free or perfect war. In fact, it is a major warning that Western politicians and military planners are creating a false set of standards and constraints that may eventually become a self-fulfilling prophecy. What Kosovo does show is that military action requires leadership to both justify casualties and explain the real-world limitations of combat. Riding public opinion polls rather than leading, and stretching public relations-oriented reporting to the point of outright lies, are counter-productive forms of intellectual morale and political cowardice that will come back to haunt both political and military leaders the moment things go wrong. The problem is not the media and the "CNN effect"; it is having the courage and competence to both lead and explain and justify the truth.

In contrast, the *war in Kosovo did show that minimizing collateral damage has become a critical new aspect of modern war*. The mistargeting and bombing of the Chinese Embassy was a tragedy that caused the death of several residents. It also became an immediate cause celebre that had extremely negative political effects. As such is perhaps the best example of the new conditions that are shaping modern war, of why the political content of targeting has now become so critical, and the practical problems involved in responding to these new requirements.

NATO made minimizing collateral damage a major objective at the start of the war, and it was reacting to long standing lessons dating back at least as far as the

Gulf War. Nevertheless, this experience illustrates both the new limits on the use of air and missile power, and the risks of "perfect war." Few outside the military paid proper attention to warnings by senior military officers before and during the air and missile campaign that collateral damage was inevitable. In contrasts, the public, media, and politicians were deluged in "perfect war" briefings showing precision guided weapons precisely hitting their targets. This emphasis on image-building and perfection reinforced the later impact of high profile strikes that did involve collateral damage, like hitting a train or bus, a residential area, or a stray missile that hits in Bulgaria. It also helped ensure that the strike on the Chinese Embassy created a backlash because political leaders and the media expected "perfect" or "bloodless" war.

Such expectations are totally unrealistic in technical and military terms, and the situation has not been helped by talking about 99.6% "accuracy." They reinforce the growing gap between the image of "perfect" or "bloodless" war and the operational realities of actually having to fight. They also help ensure that neither NATO political leaders nor the Western media is really prepared to deal with the fact that even when bombing is "surgical" people still die on the operating table. They are equally unprepared for the reality that NATO probably cannot succeed by fighting a gentleman's war against a dictator involved in the ethnic cleansing of nearly two million people.

There are four lessons that can be drawn from this experience:

- *The first is that political and military leadership is needed to explain the necessity of using military force, and accepting proportionate levels of casualties and collateral damage. The goal is not perfect or casualty-free war; it is to justify the use of force and the inevitable losses that come with it.*

- *The second is that Western politicians and military leaders would almost certainly be far better off if their speeches, briefings, and public relations exercises stressed the true risks and uncertainties of war, stated that losses and collateral damage were inevitable, and educated the media, the public (and politicians) in the friction of war. It is far better to be self-critical and pessimistic, and create realistic expectations, than to treat war as an advertising campaign.*

- *The third is that minimizing collateral damage, military casualties and losses, civilian casualties, and even enemy casualties will still be a major part of virtually all Western military action short of all-out war no matter how well a war is justified and explained. At a minimum, this requires major improvements in targeting where a massive and comprehensive analysis is needed to create a target base tailored to minimize the risk of collateral damage—ideally before military action—and then constantly update and revise it. More generally, an equally massive revision is needed to the conceptual planning of strategy, doctrine, and tactics to reflect these political realities and give political limitations the real-world priority they will have in equal operations—equivalent in most cases to the defeat of the enemy.*

- *Finally, the need to treat targeting in its full political context and to give the risk of collateral damage the proper priority in intelligence analysis and operational planning. It is far easier for US military planners to talk about "information dominance" than it is to deal with the complex planning and targeting problems necessary to achieve it.*

6

NATO Reporting on the Effectiveness of the Air and Missile Campaign

Any detailed analysis of the effectiveness of an air and missile war requires careful caveats and an understanding of the limits to effectiveness data that NATO and the US have released to date. The data released had massive gaps and definitional problems and a history of the data that NATO, Britain, and the US released provides a strong warning regarding the risks in overemphasizing a propaganda-oriented approach to effectiveness reporting and a false image of "perfect war."

The lessons of war documents that NATO, Britain, France, and the US have issued since the war have been a little better. They have all been tailored as much for political and propaganda purposes as to provide any serious insights into what happened during the war. While many problems and shortfalls are discussed throughout the course of this analysis, one of the most striking aspects of these papers is that they draw conclusions regarding air and missile power that are unsupported by any of the detailed analysis the US Air Force made available after the Gulf War. They provide only generalized data on sortie rates, and there are no reliable data on the history of sorties by aircraft type and mission, on the use munitions by type and the resulting effectiveness against given targets, on the resulting damage assessment, and on the strategic and tactical effects of that damage.

EFFECTIVENESS REPORTING AS OF APRIL 13: THE FIRST THREE WEEKS

The initial NATO reporting on the effectiveness of the air and missile campaign had little value or credibility. Most of the data in the daily briefings meant far less than met the eye. NATO normally only showed numbers of strikes by target group.

The reporting on sortie rates was approximate and often contradictory. There was little reporting on how many strikes actually delivered munitions, what aircraft performed what missions, the number of weapons released by type, and their effectiveness. The end result was that NATO and member countries normally only reported the "inputs" to the campaign in terms of sortie groups attacked, and then made occasional broad judgments about effectiveness, many in percentage form that do not vary over time or where the definitions are obviously changing from day-to-day. Little attempt was made to define or validate NATO or national claims.

Nevertheless, NATO and member countries did provide enough data on effectiveness to provide some insights as to the probable effectiveness of the air and missile war. SACEUR, General Wesley Clark, provided the first meaningful effectiveness data on the on the air and missile campaign during a press briefing on April 13. The resulting statistics covered the first 20 days of the air and missile campaign and are as interesting for what they do not say as for what they do.

Figure 11 shows the results of the strikes as of April 13 (Day 20) by target category and by type of damage. If the data are taken literally, they imply that NATO has been most successful against oil production and supply route targets, has been moderately successful against command and control targets, and has had limited success against air defense targets and Serbian forces— the targets it has struck the most.

There are, however, severe problems with these data:

- There is no way to know the value of any target or group of targets.
- Many "strategic" targets, such as factories, are mysteriously omitted from the figures.
- No data are provided on the total number of targets to be hit in each category to give some indication of how much of the total number of targets has been hit.
- No failures are shown in terms of "no damage" and "light damage," and discussions with some US military officers indicate that "moderate" damage now includes any damage no matter how slight.

Figure 12 shows that NATO had flown just under 6,000 sorties in a period just short of three weeks. This was not particularly impressive by Gulf War standards, and was not yet an intense campaign. What is more striking, however, is that only 1,687 out of 5,926 sorties, or 28 percent, involved any kind of offensive mission. This worked out to about 80 sorties per day.

- Once again, the words NATO used meant less than met the eye. These figures counted bombing runs, not the number of sorties that actually delivered weapons or sorties that hit their targets. Some US sources indicate that actual strikes averaged under 45 sorties per day.
- Put differently, NATO flew 5,926 sorties to strike and restrike 102 target groups (the US says 200 targets), or 58 sorties per target group by Day 20. It flew 1,687 actual bombing runs or 17 sorties per target group hit. If one only counts target groups with severe

Figure 11
The Progress in the Air and Missile War in Kosovo by Type of Major Target: As of April 13, 1999

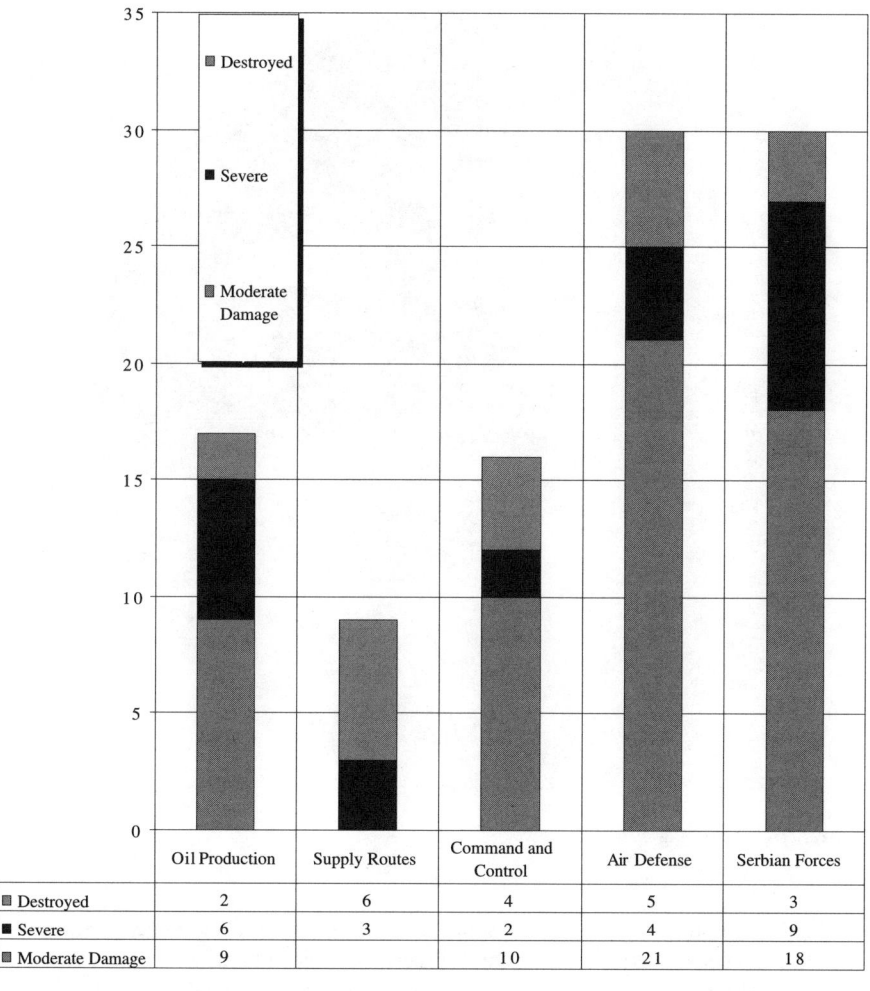

	Oil Production	Supply Routes	Command and Control	Air Defense	Serbian Forces
■ Destroyed	2	6	4	5	3
■ Severe	6	3	2	4	9
■ Moderate Damage	9		10	21	18

Source: NATO Briefing—April 13, 1999.

Figure 12
Total Sorties vs. Bombing Runs: As of April 13, 1999

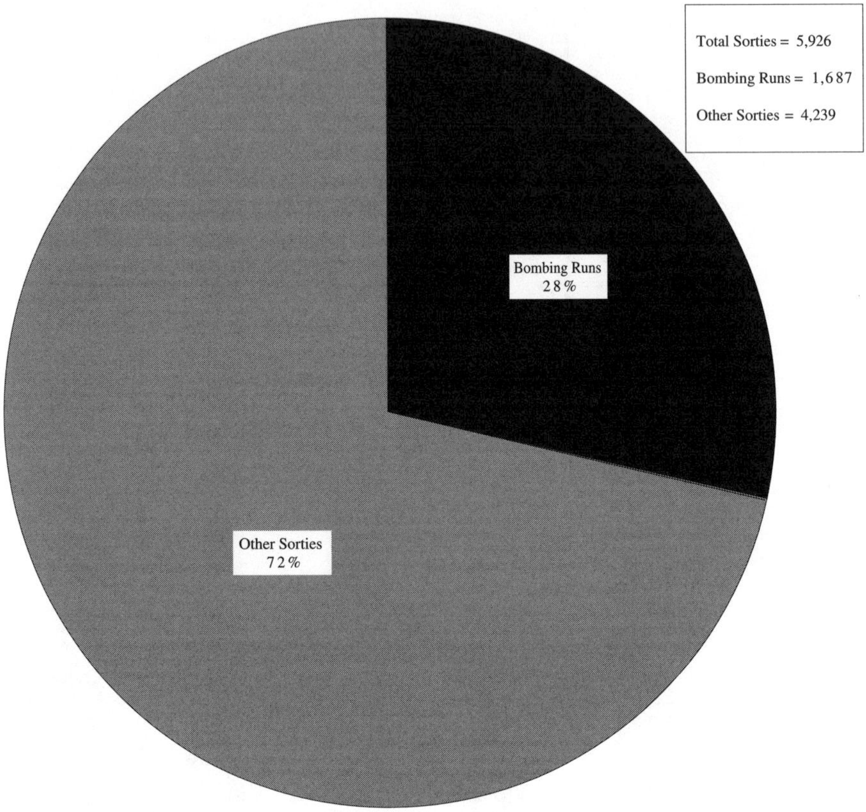

Total Sorties = 5,926

Bombing Runs = 1,687

Other Sorties = 4,239

Bombing Runs
28%

Other Sorties
72%

Source: NATO Briefing–April 13, 1999.

damage or destroyed, this is 5,926 sorties for 44 targets, or 135 sorties per target group, and 38 shooter sorties per target group with serve damage or destroyed. Note that NATO also fired several hundred cruise missiles not included in these totals.

- NATO averaged a strength of about 500 aircraft during the first 20 days of the air and missile campaign. It flew an average of 282 sorties per day, which means it has flown an average of 0.56 sorties per aircraft per day, and 0.16 shooter sorties per aircraft per day.

Figure 13 provides a summary picture of the air and missile campaign as of Day 20. After nearly three weeks of what was then called an "intensive" air and missile campaign, only 103 targets or target groups had been hit, and 60 were scattered air defense and Serbian force targets. Figure 13 also shows, however, that even where hits were reported, a total of 56% had only "moderate damage." Since "moderate

Figure 13
Overall Success of Air and Missile War As of April 13, 1999

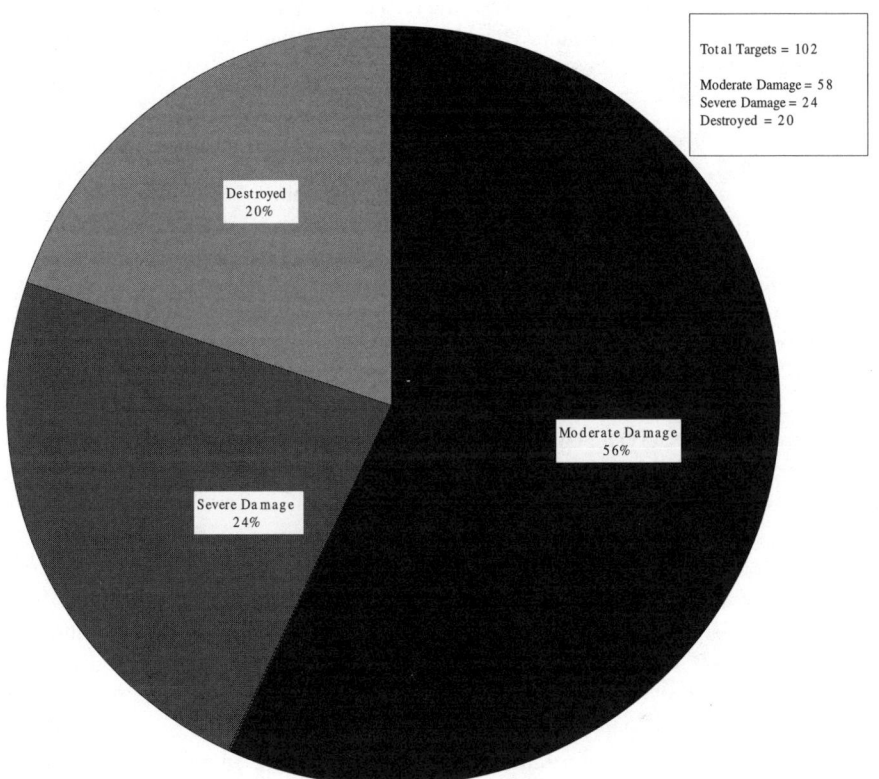

Source: NATO Briefing—April 13, 1999.

damage" seems to include any hit of any kind on any target, regardless of its importance, this does not qualify as high success. What these data do indicate is:

- The one area where NATO clearly had major success during the first 20 days was in striking refineries and POL facilities. At the time, NATO said that this could force Serbia into rationing fairly quickly and affect large-scale military operations. The problem with this appraisal was that the Serbs were already deployed in Kosovo and could seize all fuel stocks from the Kosovars, making the refugee problem even worse. They did not need fuel-intensive operations without a major ground opponent.

- The attacks on lines of communication, as of Day 20, had not affected low-level and largely infantry operations or the size of the Serbian forces already in Kosovo. Infantry and light supplies could bypass bridges after a day or two using boats. Once again, the key problem was that the Serbs in Kosovo could draw-down on the remnants of an economy that originally had 1.62–1.8 million Kosovar Muslims, and seize the remaining food and supplies of the refugees, letting them starve.

- Hitting command and control facilities largely meant hitting empty buildings. Serbia did not need the advanced communications facilities in these buildings for the kind of war it was fighting. Worse, destroying some facilities in Kosovo led the military and police to drive out even more Kosovars and use their facilities as headquarters.

- NATO hit many air defense targets and target groups as of Day 20—a total of 30. Only five, however, were destroyed, and only four had severe damage. The remaining 21 had "moderate" damage that normally means little or no operational effect. The bulk of land-based air defenses has survived intact, and can fire from dispersed sites. NATO had achieved a reasonable degree of air defense suppression and had badly damaged the central radar and command and control system. However, it had scarcely achieved secure freedom of action at low-to-medium altitudes since most Serbian surfaced-based air defense systems survived.

- As of April 13 (Day 20), the air and missile campaign claimed to have hit 33 army and police target groups. Of these, 21 had only moderate damage. Many of these targets were outside Kosovo. NATO hit only 13 targets in Kosovo proper—2 counted as destroyed, 3 with severe damage, and 8 with only "moderate" damage. These were scarcely impressive claims.

The punch-line is that NATO's wartime effectiveness reporting on the first three weeks of the air and missile campaign was about as credible as the body counts in Vietnam. It also showed few signs of reflecting the result of any "revolution in military affairs." NATO's figures indicate that the alliance flew a total of 135 sorties per target with serious damage, and 38 shooter sorties per target with serious damage. This was scarcely a sign of a successful "revolution in military affairs," particularly since virtually everything fired was then a "smart" or guided weapon. About 90% of the weapons used through April 15 were "smart" or guided weapons, versus only 9% during the Gulf War.

THE EFFECTIVENESS OF NATO AIRPOWER FROM DAY 20 TO DAY 24

The statistical data that NATO provided on total sorties flown during the middle of the air and missile campaign are shown in Figures 14 through 17. They clearly reflect a major increase in attack sorties after Day 20. At the same time, no data were provided on the number of strike sorties that actually released munitions, or which included severe damage. It should be noted that NATO had to restrike most targets, and that 80 percent of the strikes during the fist four weeks of the war were against target groups that had already been struck once.

After Day 20, NATO and member countries also provided improved day-to-day reporting on the number of target groups it strikes and restrikes. (The US reported the number of individual aim points as targets while NATO reported a cluster of related aim points in one area as a target.) The changes in the number of sorties

Figure 14
Combat Aircraft Involved in the Air and Missile War

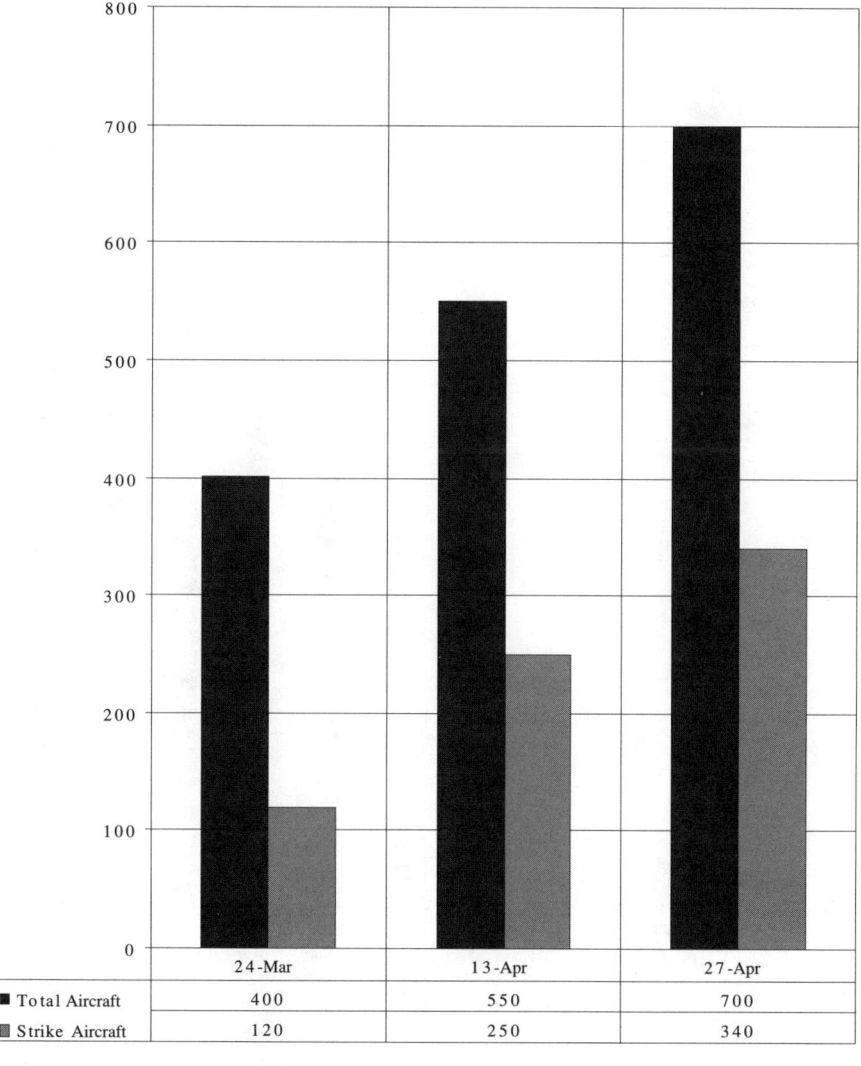

	24-Mar	13-Apr	27-Apr
■ Total Aircraft	400	550	700
▨ Strike Aircraft	120	250	340

Source: NATO Briefing.

Figure 15
Approximate Number of Sorties in the Air and Missile War in Kosovo: As of May 12, 1999

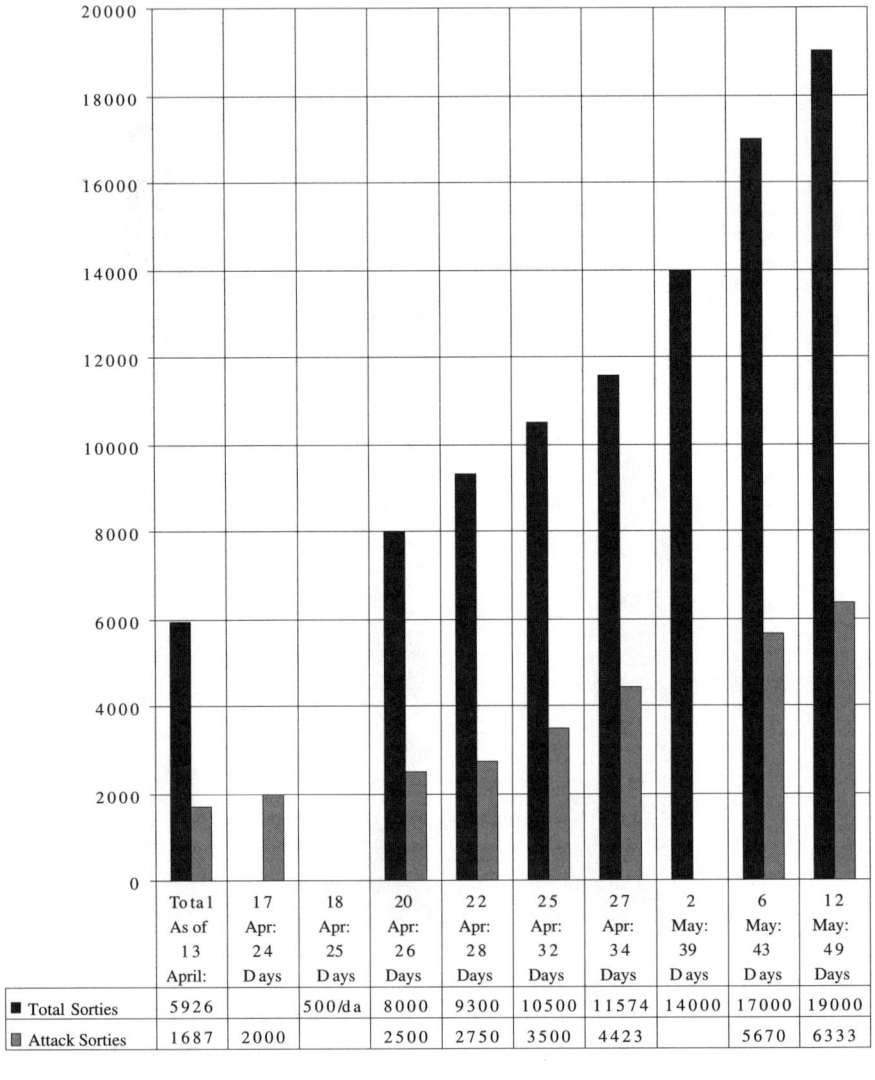

	Total As of 13 April:	17 Apr: 24 Days	18 Apr: 25 Days	20 Apr: 26 Days	22 Apr: 28 Days	25 Apr: 32 Days	27 Apr: 34 Days	2 May: 39 Days	6 May: 43 Days	12 May: 49 Days
■ Total Sorties	5926		500/da	8000	9300	10500	11574	14000	17000	19000
▨ Attack Sorties	1687	2000		2500	2750	3500	4423		5670	6333

Source: NATO Briefing.

146

Figure 16
Approximate Number of Strike/Attack Sorties in the Air and Missile War in Kosovo: As of May 12, 1999

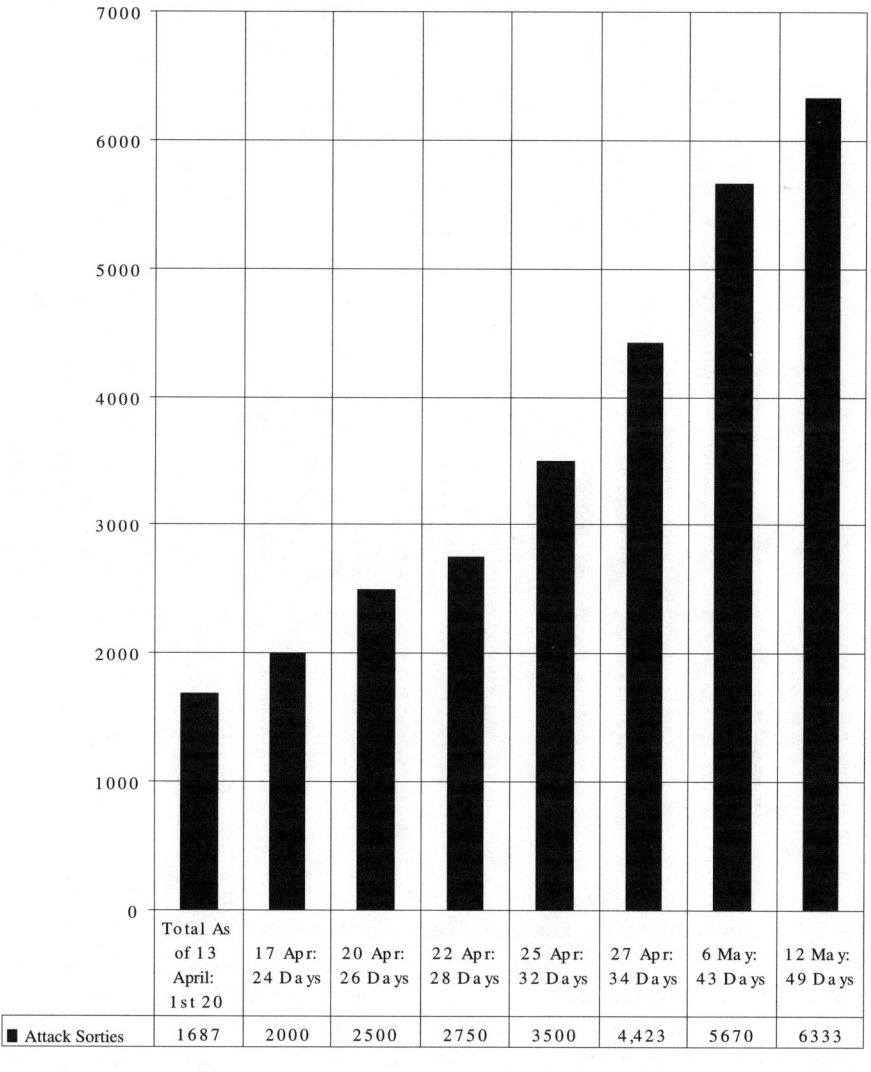

	Total As of 13 April: 1st 20	17 Apr: 24 Days	20 Apr: 26 Days	22 Apr: 28 Days	25 Apr: 32 Days	27 Apr: 34 Days	6 May: 43 Days	12 May: 49 Days
■ Attack Sorties	1687	2000	2500	2750	3500	4,423	5670	6333

Source: NATO Briefing.

Figure 17
The Air and Missile War in Kosovo: Strikes and Restrikes on Target Group Type per Day: As of May 13, 1999 (Day 50)

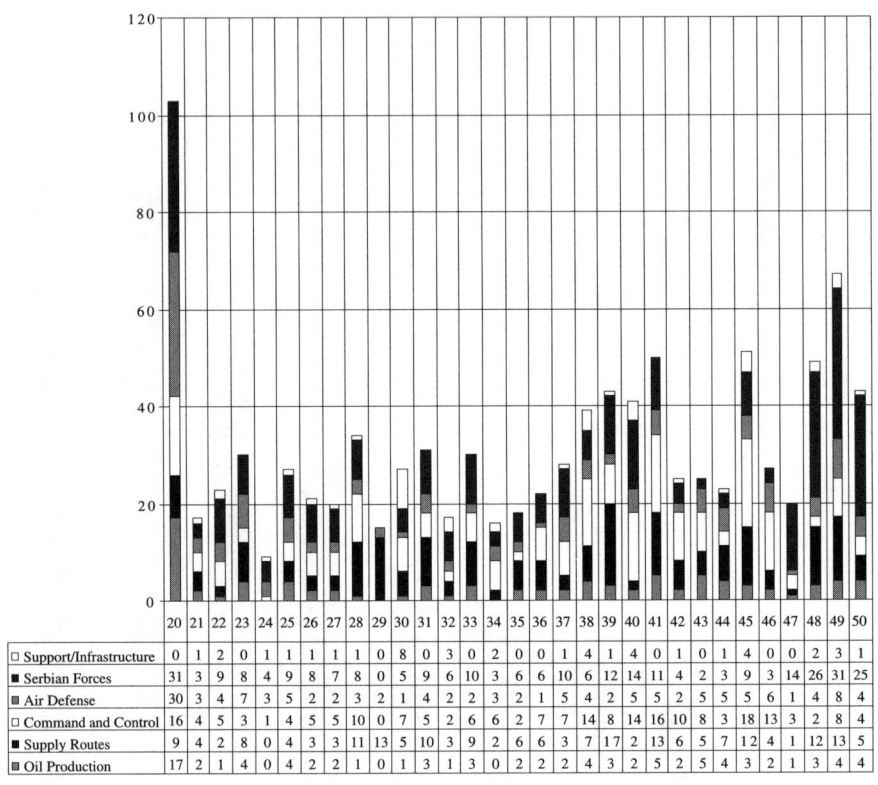

	20	21	22	23	24	25	26	27	28	29	30	31	32	33	34	35	36	37	38	39	40	41	42	43	44	45	46	47	48	49	50
□ Support/Infrastructure	0	1	2	0	1	1	1	1	1	0	8	0	3	0	2	0	0	1	4	1	4	0	1	0	1	4	0	0	2	3	1
■ Serbian Forces	31	3	9	8	4	9	8	7	8	0	5	9	6	10	3	6	6	10	6	12	14	11	4	2	3	9	3	14	26	31	25
▨ Air Defense	30	3	4	7	3	5	2	2	3	2	1	4	2	2	3	2	1	5	4	2	5	5	2	5	5	5	6	1	4	8	4
□ Command and Control	16	4	5	3	1	4	5	5	10	0	7	5	2	6	6	2	7	7	14	8	14	16	10	8	3	18	13	3	2	8	4
■ Supply Routes	9	4	2	8	0	4	3	3	11	13	5	10	3	9	2	6	6	3	7	17	2	13	6	5	7	12	4	1	12	13	5
▨ Oil Production	17	2	1	4	0	4	2	2	1	0	1	3	1	3	0	2	2	2	4	3	2	5	2	5	4	3	2	1	3	4	4

Source: NATO Briefing.

flown and target groups struck after April 13 (Day 20) are shown in Figures 15 to 17. These figures show the number of new target groups hit by type per day, the growth of the total number of target groups hit over time, and the growing impact that NATO had on Serbian ground forces and special police forces in the field.

These figures also show that NATO more than doubled the number of target groups it hit between April 13 (Day 20) and April 21 (Day 28), and did so in spite of poor weather. NATO had only seven days of "favorable weather" during the first three weeks of the campaign, and had to cancel more than half of its planned strike sorties on 21 days during the first 36 days of the air and missile campaign.

NATO announced on April 24 (Day 31) that it had achieved air superiority in the mid- to high-altitudes, significantly damaged the integrated air-defense system of Yugoslavia, destroyed 70 aircraft, and shot down 5 in direct air-to-air interceptions. NATO shot down another MiG-29 on May 4.[166] NATO claimed to have destroyed 40 percent of the SAM-3 facilities of Yugoslavia; 25 percent of the SAM-6 missile systems; and large percentages of petroleum, oil and lubricant stocks, 70 percent of them for military purposes and 25 percent of the fuel storage capabilities. Yugoslavia's capacity to refine crude oil had also been destroyed. NATO never explained the source of such percentage estimates at any point during the war, and there is no accepted method of calculating them. They are at best guesstimates.

NATO did provide a more detailed study of the overall status of the air and missile campaign on April 27 (Day 34) and more detailed summary targeting maps and assessments of effectiveness. It claimed that the Serbian integrated air defense system was ineffective, that it was destroyed when it tried to target NATO, and that Serbia was trying to conserve it by using it sparingly. NATO claimed it had destroyed roughly 70 aircraft, about 40% of Serbian SA-3 battalions, and 25% of the SA-6 batteries in spite of the fact it had flown some 400 strike sorties since its last report.

The NATO report was not optimistic when describing the attacks on command, control and communications targets. NATO reported that Serbia had a "very hardened and redundant command and control communications system." NATO said the systems used cable, commercial telephone, military cable, fiber optic cable, high frequency radio communication, and microwave communication and that the entire system was interconnected. It said there were more than 100 radio relay sites around the country, and that everything was wired in through dual use. Most of the commercial system served the military, and the military system could be put to use for the commercial system. There is no distinction between them other than a few private radio stations that were put up over the last decade.

Nevertheless, NATO claimed it had inflicted "moderate to severe damage" on the system. The Serbs were having trouble communicating, and were trying to pull together their information systems, but found this difficult. Television was a key instrument of the military command and control structure, and for propaganda and mobilizing resources. The TV system had been significantly degraded and disrupted across Yugoslavia through strikes against the radio relay network.

NATO made only limited claims regarding its attacks on military supply routes. It said that it was trying to interdict and cut off Kosovo and make it much more difficult for Serbia to sustain its military operations there. It said it was attempting to establish three bands of interdiction by carrying out strikes against railroads, roads, bridges and other means of transportation into Kosovo or out of Montenegro. It also said it was seeking to stop the flow of oil out of Montenegro and prevent any military supplies from going into Kosovo or elsewhere. It claimed that it was cutting off Serbia's ability to reinforce or to sustain its forces easily in Kosovo "step by step, bit by bit," but stated that Serbian forces could walk in through the gullies and the rivers and so forth and that such interdiction would never be complete.

NATO stated that it was seeking to degrade ground forces capabilities outside of Kosovo, that personnel and material losses were mounting, that a number of key facilities that Serbia valued highly had been destroyed and that it was seeing daily evidence of declining morale and increasingly widespread avoidance of the draft. It said it was using a variety of targeting means and a variety of weapons systems on Serbian forces in Kosovo; that personnel and material losses were mounting; that Serbia had lost the use of most of the key facilities there; and that NATO was seeing increasing numbers of desertions and declining morale among the troops. At the same time, it said that Serbian troop concentrations were still forcibly herding the refugees around, engaging in ethnic cleansing and continuing to fight against the UCK—although the UCK (KLA) had not been defeated in the field by the Serb forces. It also said that Serbian forces were trying to fortify defensive positions in anticipation of NATO ground operations.

NATO claimed that it had essentially destroyed Serbian production capability in petroleum, oil and lubricants and refinery capability, although it warned such facilities could be repaired. It claimed it had destroyed about one-third of the military fuel reserves, that the military was increasingly desperate for fuel, and there were at least three instances where operations had been shut down in an effort to conserve fuel or simply because they had run out of fuel. NATO said that its goal was the isolation of Yugoslavia because any air and missile campaign is a race of destruction against repair, reconstruction and resupply. NATO was using military means to destroy the FRY's oil refineries, and to ensure no oil flowed through pipelines from Croatia, Hungary and Romania. Once again, it never provided definitions or data to back up or support these estimates.

NATO noted that its efforts were being supported by Romania, who had an indigenous oil industry, but had cut off all commercial delivery of petroleum products to Yugoslavia. It stated that the major problem remaining was ongoing tanker shipments and this was the reason for the naval blockade. Before the air and missile campaign, only 2–3 ships per day went to Bar Harbor. By the fourth week of the war, there were 10 ships a day in port—almost exclusively tankers offloading 24 hours a day. NATO was also concerned that Serbia was trying to get supplies up the Danube, but said that it was going to use air and missile power to ensure it would not succeed.

NATO reported for the first time on its campaign attack on Serbia's military production and ammunition production. It said it had good success against ammunition stocks and had done serious damage to Serbia's ability to repair and maintain its aircraft, military vehicles, armaments and munitions.

NATO also stated that it was using precision munitions, and that its campaign was not directed against the people of Serbia, but rather against the regime, higher level command and control, the forces in the field, and their sustaining and supporting infrastructure. It stated that its overall assessment was that it was doing significant damage to every set of targets, and that it was conducting "a systematic, sustained and serious campaign (to) move methodically, systematically and progressively to attack, disrupt, degrade and ultimately destroy Serbia's forces, sustaining infrastructure, command and control and all of the other targets that are associated with Serbia's campaign of repression."

THE EFFECTIVENESS OF THE AIR AND MISSILE
CAMPAIGN: DAY 25 TO DAY 50

The NATO reporting on the number of target groups struck after Day 25 is summarized in Figures 18–21. It is important to note that the data on the number of strikes on given target groups became steadily less useful as time went by. The number of restrikes became so high that it became increasing difficult to tell what NATO was doing that was different and what was a restrike. Further, as the number of strikes increased against Serbian ground troops, the release of data on the number of target groups, as distinguished from numbers of actual targets, made it virtually impossible to determine the breadth and scope of the NATO air and missile war. NATO and the US did provide detailed strike maps during this period that were more useful than its statistics, but the data on target distribution and location in these maps cannot be summarized into statistical trends.

NATO claimed on May 7 that it had damaged 20% of the military equipment in Kosovo, over 300 individual items. It said this damage included all major road and rail lines into Kosovo, and all but two bridges over the Danube. It claimed that 60% of Serbia's MiG-29s were destroyed and the rest, including other aircraft, grounded. It claimed it destroyed 4 out of 7 of the major fuel storage sites in Kosovo, the two major oil refineries in Yugoslavia, nearly 40 of 52 radio-relay targets, 50% of ammunition storage sites, and 8 battalion-and-brigade field command posts in Kosovo. In addition, NATO claimed it had damaged strategic targets such as command posts, army headquarters, lines of communication and airfields and storage sites.

Nevertheless, NATO spokesman Jamie Shea made it clear on May 12 that the effectiveness of the air and missile campaign was still uncertain.

If you wish to judge us after 50 days, I would simply say that the game is not over yet quite frankly and I don't think we should start writing the history books until the final results are in. I wouldn't rush to any premature judgment here. We are starting to hit Milosevic very hard indeed in Kosovo and it is going to get harder, and harder in the days ahead. . . . we really are now turning our attention not simply to those who are being killed, but to those who are doing the killing, and we are going to continue to do this. And the fact that President Milosevic may not have agreed to the five conditions yet is no logical reason for saying that he won't agree to them tomorrow or the day after. He will and we are going to keep this up.

General Shelton, the Chairman of the US Joint Chiefs, gave a more optimistic picture on May 12.

Operation Allied Force is proceeding well, and the Serb army and security forces are being systematically and effectively attacked by NATO air and missile power. After seven full weeks of air strikes, we have significantly reduced the effectiveness and the capabilities of the Yugoslav army and its security infrastructure. Yugoslavia's integrated air defense system, though it remains a threat to our pilots and to our air crews, has been hit hard. And

Figure 18
Strikes and Restrikes on Total Target Groups in the Air and Missile War in Kosovo per Day by Type of Target: As of May 13, 1999 (Day 50)

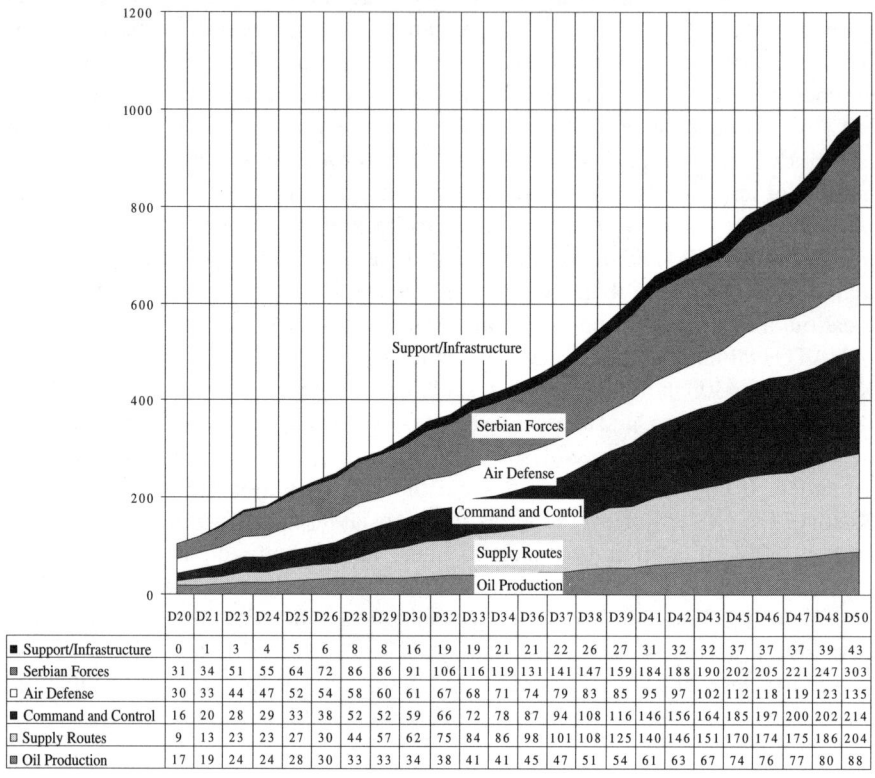

	D20	D21	D23	D24	D25	D26	D28	D29	D30	D32	D33	D34	D36	D37	D38	D39	D41	D42	D43	D45	D46	D47	D48	D50
■ Support/Infrastructure	0	1	3	4	5	6	8	8	16	19	19	21	21	22	26	27	31	32	32	37	37	37	39	43
▩ Serbian Forces	31	34	51	55	64	72	86	86	91	106	116	119	131	141	147	159	184	188	190	202	205	221	247	303
▢ Air Defense	30	33	44	47	52	54	58	60	61	67	68	71	74	79	83	85	95	97	102	112	118	119	123	135
■ Command and Control	16	20	28	29	33	38	52	52	59	66	72	78	87	94	108	116	146	156	164	185	197	200	202	214
▢ Supply Routes	9	13	23	23	27	30	44	57	62	75	84	86	98	101	108	125	140	146	151	170	174	175	186	204
▩ Oil Production	17	19	24	24	28	30	33	33	34	38	41	41	45	47	51	54	61	63	67	74	76	77	80	88

Source: NATO Briefing.

more than half of Milosevic's modern surface to air missile radars have been damaged or destroyed. As you know, he's lost nearly all of his front line MiG-29 fighters and nearly 20% of his ground attack aircraft.

Both of his oil refineries are shut down, and more than a third of his military reserve fuel storage is destroyed or severely damaged. Finally, and this is not an all-inclusive list, we have seriously damaged Milosevic's military industrial capacity, reducing his ability to repair and maintain his aircraft by 70% and his ammunition production capacity by two-thirds.

In Kosovo itself, Milosevic's army and his special police units continue to suffer damage from NATO air strikes. Nearly a quarter of his armored vehicles—that is tanks and armored personnel carriers—have been damaged or destroyed. And roughly 40% of the Serb artillery in Kosovo has been taken out. Most of the ammunition and fuel supplies of the Serb Third Army, which as you know by now, probably, is the unit that operates in Kosovo, has been destroyed along with more than half of the infrastructure that supports this force. Distribution networks into Kosovo for critical supplies such as fuel and ammunition have been

Figure 19
Total Strikes and Restrikes for All Target Groups in the Air and Missile War in Kosovo per Day: As of May 13 1999 (Day 50)

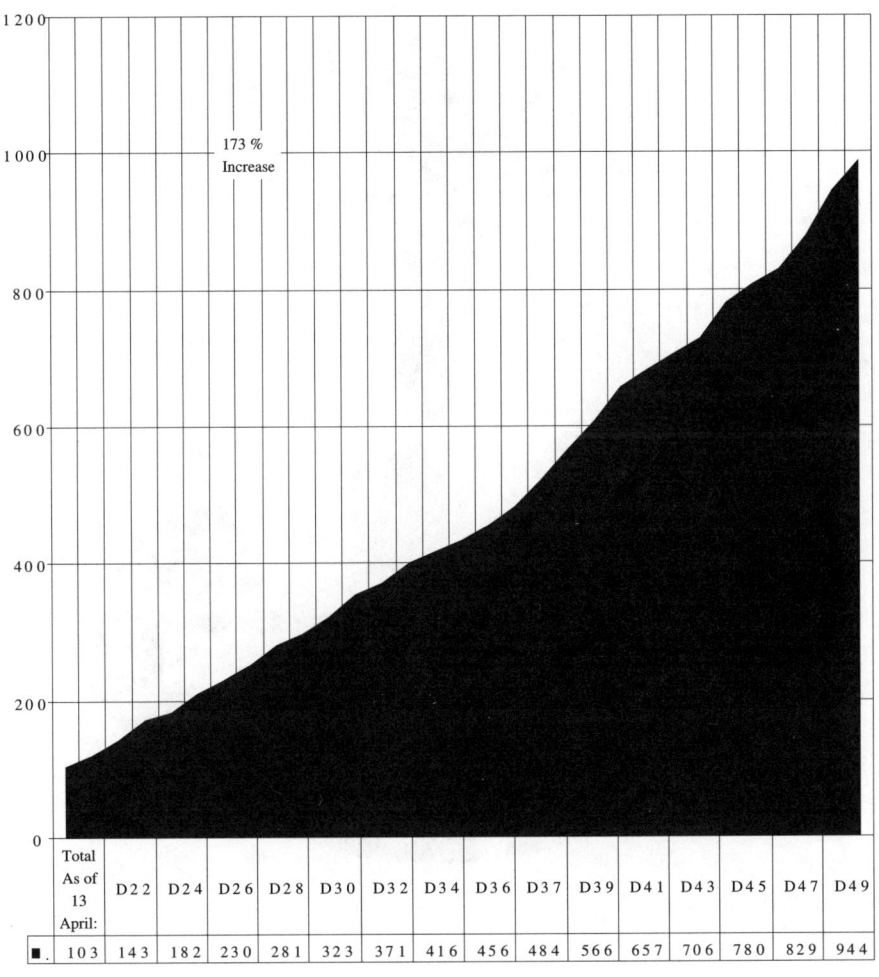

	Total As of 13 April:	D22	D24	D26	D28	D30	D32	D34	D36	D37	D39	D41	D43	D45	D47	D49
■.	103	143	182	230	281	323	371	416	456	484	566	657	706	780	829	944

Source: NATO Briefing.

severely disrupted. Rail lines into Kosovo are severed, and about half the roadways into Kosovo have been damaged as well.

We also continue to receive significant indications of growing unrest and discontent within the ranks of the Yugoslav army. Of course, these reports can hardly come as a surprise. You would expect that any military force that is first used against helpless civilians and then is subjected to tremendous pounding by NATO aircraft would have considerable doubts about its future and about the leadership that has gotten the military into this

Figure 20
The Progress in the Air and Missile War in Kosovo by Percentage of Total Strikes and Restrikes on Given Types of Major Target Group As of May 13 (Day 50)

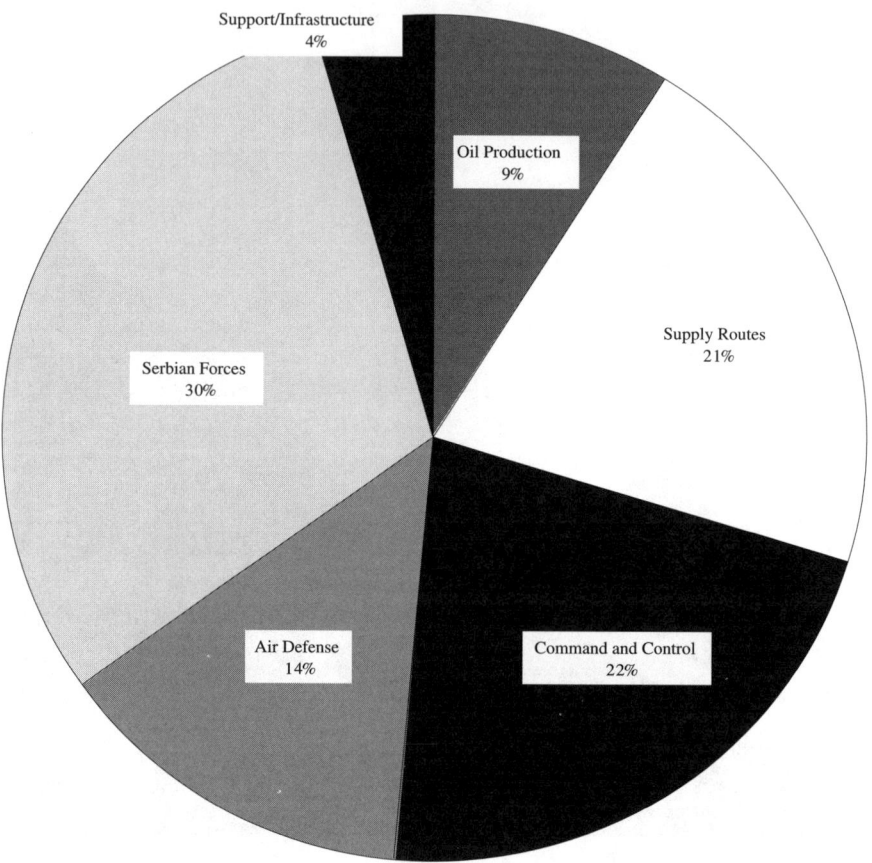

Source: NATO Briefing.

situation. I don't mean to paint too rosy a picture here. We are conservative in our estimates, and it is possible that a force like the one Milosevic is using for ethnic cleansing and terror in Kosovo could hold out for quite some time. But it is clear that NATO's air and missile campaign is exacting a significant toll on Serb forces in Kosovo and throughout the rest of Yugoslavia.

These statements reveal a number of contradictions, and NATO's summary statistics and damage estimates were scarcely consistent. Like the rest of NATO's statements during the war, they were designed more to shape public opinion than inform it, although some may have been designed to influence the Serbian people.

Figure 21
Growth in Strikes and Restrikes Against Serbian Army and Special Police Target Groups Hit in the Air and Missile War in Kosovo: As of May 13, 1999 (Day 50)

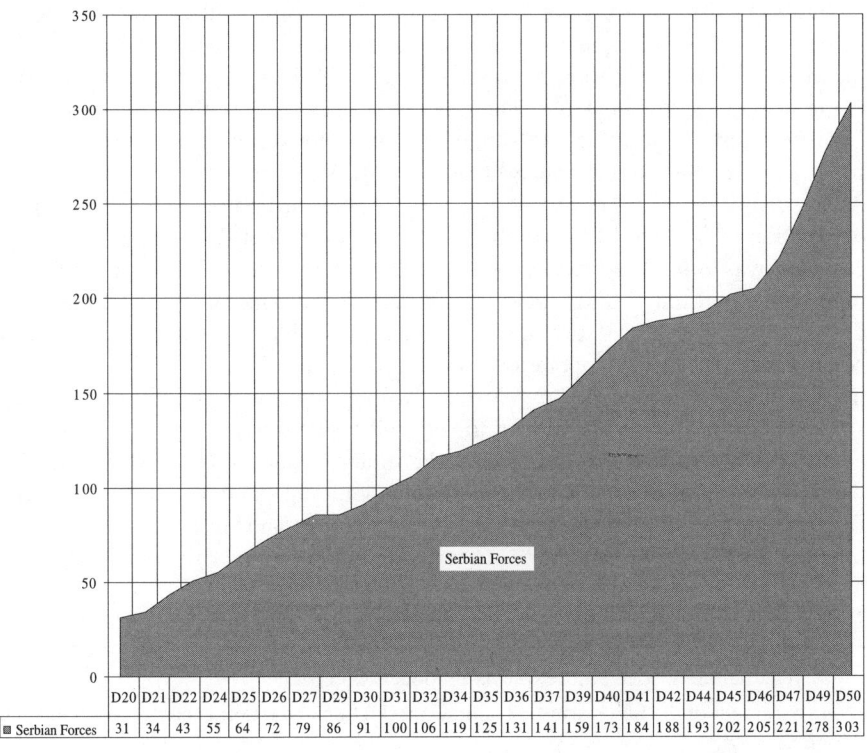

	D20	D21	D22	D24	D25	D26	D27	D29	D30	D31	D32	D34	D35	D36	D37	D39	D40	D41	D42	D44	D45	D46	D47	D49	D50
Serbian Forces	31	34	43	55	64	72	79	86	91	100	106	119	125	131	141	159	173	184	188	193	202	205	221	278	303

Source: NATO Briefing.

At the same time, they cannot be dismissed as propaganda alone. They do describe the broad trends in the NATO campaign and NATO's hopes—if not anything approaching a rigorous assessment of the tactical situation and meaningful battle damage assessment.

THE EFFECTIVENESS OF THE AIR AND MISSILE CAMPAIGN: DAY 50 TO THE END

NATO never tied its damage and effectiveness estimates specifically to the increase in its sortie rates or the type of aircraft and munitions it used. It is clear, however, that better weather, improved targeting, increases in aircraft numbers and sortie rates did shape NATO's steadily rising claims.

On May 19 (Day 56), NATO released a summary of the effect of NATO actions on Serbian capabilities. It estimated that 75% of fixed surface to air missile sites

(SAMs) had been destroyed, as well as 12% of the mobile SAMs. Sixty-nine percent of Serbian MiG-29s and 34% of all other combat aircraft had been destroyed. Thirty-one percent of all Serb heavy forces in Kosovo were destroyed, including 11 battalion/brigade command posts, 312 tank/artillery pieces/armored vehicles, and 244 other pieces of military equipment.

On May 27 (Day 64), Rear Admiral Thomas R. Wilson J-2 reported yet another battle damage assessment in a Department of Defense briefing. He stated that Serbia's ability to conduct and support air operations at nearly all airfields had been degraded and maintenance facilities, POL storage, and runways had been destroyed or damaged. The air-to-air threat had been virtually eliminated due to the destruction of 34 Serb MiG aircraft. He also reported that Radar air surveillance coverage was limited and ineffective. As to the status of the VJ/MUP, mobility was reported to be limited, the units were dispersed and concealed and morale was deteriorating. The VJ/MUP was not expected to be able to eliminate the UCK or conduct routine military operations without difficulty. The UCK was becoming more aggressive, especially in Western Kosovo, and their supply and military situations were improving thanks to the influx or seizure of weapons and the addition of professional and experienced military leaders and trained recruits.

NATO's key claims came at the end of the bombing campaign on June 10. The Department of Defense reported that the NATO air and missile campaign had inflicted the following damage to strategic and interdiction targets:

- NATO had destroyed 100% of the FRY's petroleum refining production capability.
- Sixty-five percent of Serbian ammunition production capacity was damaged or destroyed, including 50% of its explosive production capacity
- Forty percent of the Serbs armored vehicle production and repair capacity was damaged or destroyed.
- Seventy percent of aviation equipment assembly and repair capacity was damaged or destroyed.
- NATO had inflicted moderate damage to lines of communication throughout the country. Of the Danube bridges, 70% of road bridges and 50% of the rail bridges were reported destroyed, blocking river traffic between Belgrade and Croatia. In addition, rail capacity was totally interdicted and road throughput was degraded on routes to Montenegro, barring the Serbs ability to transport fuel from the Barr port facility into Kosovo over rail lines. Regarding the Kosovo corridors, 100% of the rail and over 50% of the road capacity had been interdicted.
- The Serbian national C3 operational capability was in a degraded status, with moderate functional damage to over 30% of military and civilian RADREL networks.
- The Serbian propaganda machine was severely degraded with 45% of TV broadcast capability non-functional and radio broadcasts limited to urban areas. Both the Serb Socialist Party Headquarters and the Presidential Residences, which were being used as alternate command posts, sustained severe damage.

The Department of Defense also estimated that NATO had done major damage to Serbia's military forces. It estimated that 85% of Yugoslavia's MiG-29s were destroyed or severely damaged beyond use, and 35% of its MiG-21s—24 of which were no longer available. It claimed that two of Serbia's three SA-2 battalions had been destroyed, 70% of its SA-3s, and three out of its 22 mobile SA-6 batteries.

The Department estimated that NATO had destroyed up to 450 artillery and mortar pieces, about 220 armored personnel carriers, and around 120 tanks. It had damaged or destroyed 35% of the facilities of the Serbian 1st Army. It claimed to have damaged or destroyed over 20% of the facilities of the 2nd Army, although this army was reported to still be able to reinforce Kosovo. It claimed to have damaged or destroyed 60% of the facilities of the 3rd Army and that their ability to sustain operation was significantly reduced. The US claimed the overall ability of Serbian land forces to sustain high tempo combat operations was reduced.

These claims, however, had all the gaps and uncertainties of previous claims. They were vague, poorly defined, and were not tied to any clear method of damage assessment. NATO did not provide supporting data on sorties, missiles, and munitions used, or the role of given types of aircraft. NATO also did a much better job of discussing physical destruction than the resulting military and political effects. These problems and potential lessons become much clearer when the effectiveness of the air campaign is analyzed by target category and when one considers the results of NATO's postwar efforts to fully assess its damage—an effort that was only concluded in the fall of 1999, and nearly six months after the war was over.

BATTLE DAMAGE ASSESSMENT, THE "FOG OF WAR," AND THE "FOG OF SELF-DECEPTION"

The problems in assessing NATO's overall effectiveness are discussed shortly by type of target, and it is important to note that the problems in targeting, carrying out strikes, and assessing damage varied sharply by target and munitions type, and according to weather, nearby defenses, and other factors. As a result, many of the sweeping generalizations made about the effectiveness of air and missile power after the war could not be true even if better data had been collected during the conflict. The illusion of "perfect analysis" is just as unreal as the illusion of "perfect war."

The Pentagon Lies to Congress and the American People

The report on the lessons of the war that the US Department of Defense sent to the Congress at the end of the war compounds many of these errors, and at best, lies by omission. While the US military services did carry out an independent assessment of battle damage, these assessments were not included in the report at the direction of the Secretary of Defense, and most politically embarrassing data were kept out of the report. All it provides is a cautiously worded overview of problems in measuring NATO's effectiveness that the Alliance did not address with any frankness during the war.[167]

Battle damage assessment and the evaluation of the effectiveness of allied attacks against the various targets in Serbia proper and Kosovo remained at the forefront of NATO and U.S. efforts and concerns. The ongoing assessments and analysis clearly show that while there were instances where collateral damage occurred, it was minimized by use of precise and accurate weapons. In addition, while wartime battle damage assessment did not always provide complete information, wartime assessments of damage to fixed targets in Kosovo were generally accurate. Allied strikes against fixed targets including bridges, airfields, tunnels, bunkers, petroleum and fuel facilities, and other above ground structures were highly successful and inflicted very limited collateral damage. However, Serbia's mobile Army and Interior forces presented a targeting and damage assessment challenge.

Analyses of the results of NATO attacks were conducted as the campaign proceeded based on the fullest available information. The Mission Analysis Tracking and Tabulation System (MATTS) was used to construct a primary target database as Operation Allied Force unfolded. The MATTS database began with the mission designations provided by the air tasking order; these designations were then correlated to mission reports filed by returning aircrews. The mission report data were loaded into the database to reflect weapons released and the Desired Mean Point of Impact (DMPI) for each weapon. Analysts used imagery and other sources to review the desired impact points to assess the damage done by each strike sortie. Time sequencing between strike sorties and reconnaissance of an impact point were critical. Typically, individual installations have multiple desired impact points — for example, a factory installation may have several buildings that must be struck individually, or an airfield may have multiple aircraft shelters, storage locations, and other targets within the complex. If reconnaissance resources could not be scheduled to review a particular installation until 2 or 3 days after air strikes had occurred; it was extremely difficult to determine properly the weapons and aircraft responsible for specific damage. In such cases, NATO was unable to confirm damage associated with a particular aircraft and weapons mix and therefore characterized the damage in the MATTS database as unconfirmed. After the conflict ended, NATO sent a team into Kosovo to assess the effects of air attacks. This assessment examined both fixed and mobile targets. The U.S. European Command has already made public an initial presentation of findings from this review. The results from the wartime analyses and the postwar assessment provide the basis for this study of lessons learned.

Further study is now underway within the Department to integrate the findings of all available data and to develop insights from this information on a variety of important topics. How good was our understanding of attack effectiveness as combat proceeded? What surveillance and reconnaissance systems proved most accurate and timely in delivering information critical to these assessments? What lessons can we draw from postwar examination of targets and target areas to modify or improve our battle damage assessment process? How should the inevitable uncertainty in the information be handled? For example, targets were often attacked by multiple systems, making an assessment of any single system's effectiveness against those targets nearly impossible. Further, judging the degree of impairment inflicted on a damaged, but not destroyed, target probably will always remain a source of uncertainty. New technologies, such as video imagery from munitions in the terminal attack phase or intrusive sensors at important pre-selected sites, will improve our capability to assess weapon performance.

On the other hand, munitions such as JDAM that do not incorporate a real-time imagery loop and will be used in much greater numbers in the future will complicate the damage-assessment process. Consequently, a substantial degree of uncertainty will continue to exist in any future war.

The reality behind these words is a further warning against efforts to create the illusion of perfect war, and the idea that collateral damage can be almost totally avoided. It is also a warning that even the most advanced military power in the world has no foreseeable prospect of achieving the level of "information dominance" called for in some versions of the writings on the "revolution in military affairs."

In fact, one of the reasons that the Department of Defense report on Kosovo is so empty of detail and the kind of data needed to give it credibility is that sources within the Pentagon indicate that the authors of the report from which these comments are taken could not come close to agreeing on the details of the damage assessments they were asked to make, or the real-world lethality of given munitions and strike systems. They found that battle damage assessment (BDA) is often at best an art form based on informed guess work, and that there is often limited correlation between even the most advanced forms of test and evaluation and real world effectiveness. In fact, it was so brutally clear that many of NATO's wartime claims regarding accuracy, lethality, and collateral damage could not be substantiated that the report on the lessons of the war had to gloss over many of the most critical issues involved.

A great deal of additional reporting and testimony is also beginning to emerge on individual aspects of the analytic effort that reinforces these points. For example, Brigadier General Robert M. Flanagan, the Deputy Commander, II Marine Expeditionary Force, provided the following comments on one of the operational problems in both targeting and BDA.[168]

The myriad Electronic Data Collection Agencies that exist today proved to be overwhelming and often confusing. The importance of real-time, accurate Electronic Battle Damage Assessment (EBDA) is vital to mission success, but is unavailable in a timely manner. The cumbersome, slow EBDA process made it difficult for Prowler aircrews to determine real time and accurate location of enemy air defense systems and inhibited crews from determining the success of HARM shots. The result was often redundancy in HARM attacks. We need to fund research for a common real time EBAA, DOD ELINT capability.

The Barry and Thomas Critique of the Pentagon Report

The most controversial critique of the Pentagon report is contained in an article in *Newsweek* by John Barry and Evan Thomas.[169] According to this report, the Secretary of Defense suppressed an Air Force report that showed that the number of targets verifiably destroyed was only a "tiny fraction" of the US claims: 14 tanks, not 120; 18 armored personnel carriers, not 220; 20 artillery pieces, not 450. The article states that Air Force investigators, spent weeks combing Kosovo by helicopter and by foot, only found evidence of just 58 successful strikes out of the 744 "confirmed" strikes by NATO pilots during the war.

The article states that General Clark was under constant pressure to produce positive bombing results, and that, "The surgical strike remains a mirage. Even with the best technology, pilots can destroy mobile targets on the ground only by flying low and slow, exposed to ground fire." It also says that the, "Pentagon essentially declared victory and hushed up any doubts about what the air war exactly had achieved."

According to Barry and Thomas, Clark doubted the resulting Air Force claims and initially tried to obtain accurate assessments. At the end of the war Clark publicly scoffed at claims by General Nobojsa Pavkovic, the Serbian ground commander, that Serbia had lost only 13 tanks. However, Clark's staff reported that Pavkovic might be right, and Clark dispatched a team into Kosovo in June to do an on-the-ground survey. It had 30 experts; some from NATO but most were from the Munitions Effectiveness Assessment Team, or MEAT. Barry and Thomas report that the NATO bombing was accurate against fixed targets, like bunkers and bridges, although it was able to use deception. For example, one bridge was protected from the high-flying NATO bombers by constructing a fake bridge 300 yards upstream, made of polyethylene sheeting stretched over the river. As a result, NATO "destroyed" the phony bridge many times.

The Serbian deception effort proved to be much more effective in protecting ground force targets. Mock artillery pieces were made of long black logs stuck on old truck wheels. A two-thirds scale SA-9 antiaircraft missile launcher was fabricated from the metal-lined paper used to make European milk cartons. They report that the MEAT team found dozens of burnt-out cars, buses and trucks—but few tanks.

According to Barry and Thomas, General Clark reacted by ordering the team to drive to the sites where Serbian weapons were supposed to be damage and to walk the terrain. In early August 1999, the MEAT team returned to Air Force headquarters at Ramstein air base in Germany with some 2,600 photographs of the sites. Both General Walter Begert, the Air Force deputy commander in Europe, and General Clark are reported to have rejected their conclusions, and Clark is said to have insisted that the Serbs had concealed their damaged equipment or that the MEAT team had failed to properly survey the sites. The MEAT team insisted, however, that it had conducted proper surveys and saw no physical evidence that heavy equipment had been lifted by cranes or dragged away.

Again according to Barry and Thomas, the USAF was ordered to prepare a new report. In September, Brigadier Gen. John Corley produced a survey that showed that NATO had successfully struck 93 tanks, close to the 120 claimed by General Shelton at the end of the war, and 153 armored personnel carriers, not far from the claim of 220. Corley's team did not do new field research, however but rather looked for indicators that would justify the pilots' claims. The article quotes "senior officer" at NATO headquarters who examined the data as stating that more than half of the hits the Corley report declared to be "validated kill" had only one piece of supporting evidence such as a blurred cockpit video or a flash detected by a spy satellite. The latter evidence is virtually meaningless since satellites usually can't discern whether a bomb hits anything when it explodes.

The *Newsweek* article also states that NATO sources reported that British Gen. Sir Rupert Smith—Clark's deputy—and his chief of staff, German Gen. Dieter Stockman, privately cautioned Clark not to accept Corley's numbers, and that the US intelligence community also questioned the Corley report. It states the CIA put far more credence in the results of meeting of US and British intelligence experts in November 1999, which determined that the Yugoslav Army after the war was only marginally smaller than before the conflict.

It is painfully clear from both the Barry and Thomas article, and from private interviews by the author with very high level US officers and defense officials, that Defense Secretary Cohen and General Shelton played a major role in ensuring that none of these issues were dealt with the report on the lessons of war that was sent to Congress. The report did provide a chart from the Corley report showing that NATO killed 93 tanks, but as Barry and Thomas note the text effectively disowns the chart without providing any alternative information; "the assessment provides no data on what proportion of total mobile targets were hit or the level of damage inflicted."

Off the record discussions with senior US Air Force officers also indicate, however, that they feel the Barry and Thomas article unfairly discounts a great deal of evidence obtained using intelligence sources, and that the MEAT team relied far too heavily on direct, after action inspection. They note with accuracy that such methods did not prove reliable in Vietnam, or in the Gulf War. The author also found that they did not prove accurate in the October War between Israel, Egypt, and Syria—a war where the author wrote the report that the Secretary of Defense sent to Congress and had to coordinate much of the US-Israeli analytic effort. On the basis of these discussions, the author believes that the NATO statistics are more likely to be correct than those of the MEAT team are, although any such conclusion is highly uncertain and most of the material evidence is classified and cannot be discussed.

The Fog of War, Surgical Bombing, and the Revolution in Military Affairs

It would take a major team effort with full access to classified material to resolve these uncertainties, however, and it is brutally clear that it would have to be independent of the Office of the Secretary of Defense and Joint Staff to have any credibility. As has been note earlier, Kosovo is the third consecutive major action in which the Office of the Secretary of Defense and Joint Staff have demonstrated they lack the professional integrity to be trusted in carrying out honest and objective studies of the effectiveness of US military forces in combat. The reporting and non-reporting by these groups on the Gulf War and Desert Fox was no better.

At one level, a key lesson seems to be that the assessment of war can no longer be trusted to the Office of the Secretary of Defense and Joint Staff. It is also unclear that it can be trusted to the services. For example, the US Army suppressed a self-critical report on the lessons of the Gulf War and then circulated a large book filled with self-praise to the Congress. The US Navy issued a preliminary report with considerable self-criticism, but classified its detailed report and did not circulate it outside the Navy. The only service to attempt an independent and objective analysis, to declassify the results, and give it broad circulation was the US Air Force, which reported in its *Gulf War Air Power Survey*. While the historical sections of all four services have since done excellent work, one lesson of the war in Kosovo is that the analysis of lessons must be done by an independent body, that it must report to Congress or some authority outside the Department of Defense, and that its results must be a public as possible—both to ensure that US military personnel and planners are properly informed and to establish checks and balances on the kind of public relations-oriented reporting that is now common place.

These issues also have grave policy implications. The "fog of war" remains the reality, and precision is not omniscience. Concealment, dispersion, deception, and the other aspects of asymmetric warfare adapt to defeat many of the advances in sensors. The uncertainties created by the real-world imperfections in targeting are compounded by the fact that advances in precision often lead to small visible damage areas that make observable damage far less apparent than the impact of area bombing. As Serbia showed during and after the war, the manipulation of the media and the physical phenomena left after an attack are also a key form of information warfare.

Unfortunately, this reality seems to go so deeply against the grain of the military and public information officers, that the end result is that the "fog of war" becomes a "fog of deception" in which self-deception plays little or no part. The end result is that policy makers, military officers, and strategic analysts are almost certainly being given a grossly exaggerated picture of the ability to target mobile forces in the field, to inflict damage with modern airpower, and to do so in ways that minimize losses and collateral damage. Both the current success of the "revolution in military affairs" and the ability to improve it are almost certainly being exaggerated, and so is the ability to achieve decisive results with limited force. As a result, the US and its allies cannot learn the right lesson from their military experience, and the cost of political posturing by of the Office of the Secretary of Defense and Joint Staff is almost certain to be paid for in blood.

7

Strategic Bombing

For some, it is as politically incorrect to refer to "strategic bombing" during the air and missile campaign in Kosovo as it is to refer to the air and missile campaign as a "war." There are equally important exercises in politically correct rhetoric in deciding who is a legitimate target. For at least some civilians and diplomats, it is, politically and morally, much easier to attack conscripts in uniform than the power base of the civilian leadership that sends them to war. It is more acceptable to conduct a slow and painful process of escalation that avoids overt references to the word "strategic" than to attempt a sudden and decisive campaign that attempts to openly force a sudden end to a war.

At the same time, one legacy of Vietnam is that it is politically incorrect to talk about casualties of any kind. "Body counts" are out. Wars no longer kill enemies and people. They destroy percentages of categories of physical objectives or military and industrial capabilities. In other cases, military effectiveness is measured in terms of inputs—total sorties flown, total munitions delivered, or percentages of precision strikes. There are no meaningful measurements of outputs in terms of either damage or casualties. War becomes bloodless by definition and omission, and analysts hide behind the uncertainties in counting the wounded and dead while accepting greater uncertainties in estimating the impact of strategic bombing by category.

These are problems that the US, Europe, and NATO were not prepared to deal with at the time of the conflict in Kosovo. They were still evolving post–Cold War and post–Gulf War approaches to combining strategic bombing and political forms of warfare—a point the Department of Defense makes clear in its report on the lessons of the war:[170]

Before and during Operation Allied Force, the National Security Council (NSC) oversaw a series of interagency planning efforts on Kosovo. These planning efforts were directed by the National Security Council's Deputies Committee and monitored by an interagency Kosovo Executive Committee. The first political-military plan on Kosovo, completed in the fall of 1998, focused on using the threat of NATO air strikes to achieve a political-military settlement. After this threat of force convinced Milosevic to garrison most Serb forces in October 1998, interagency planning efforts focused on deploying the Organization for Security and Cooperation in Europe's (OSCE's) Kosovo Verification Mission, facilitating humanitarian assistance, and responding to possible Serbian noncompliance.

As it was executed, the interagency planning process helped to mobilize and coordinate the activities of different agencies, identify issues for consideration by National Security Council Deputies, provide planning support for international organizations (e.g., OSCE and United Nations), and develop benchmarks for measuring progress. This political-military planning played an important role in ensuring that the United States achieved the objectives set forth by the NCA. At the same time, it is now possible to identify an important area for improvement.

Planning focused on air strikes and diplomacy as the primary tools to achieve U.S. and NATO objectives. As it became clear that Milosevic intended to outlast the alliance, more attention was paid to other ways of bringing pressure to bear, including economic sanctions and information operations. While ultimately these instruments were put to use with good effect, more advance planning might have made them more effective at an earlier date. Our experience in Operation Allied Force has shown that Presidential Decision Directive 56 (PDD-56), Managing Complex Contingency Operations, had not yet been fully institution-alized throughout the interagency. As a result of this experience, the interagency has applied the lessons learned to further institutionalizing PDD-56. The routine participation of senior officials in rehearsals, gaming, exercises, and simulations would strengthen awareness of the broad range of available policy tools.

Several senior US officers and officials privately go much further. They indicate that the US Air Force has not reached any internal consensus as to how to translate its doctrinal debates over how to use air power strategically into practical battle plans that could be translated into a detailed strategic bombing campaign. They indicate that the rest of the Department of Defense and the members of the US interagency process had not developed an effective doctrine for integrating strategic air power into the overall management of contingency operations. Finally, they indicate that little independent thinking about the issue had taken place in NATO and the major European powers that prepared the alliance for the kind of strategic bombing campaign it had to fight in Kosovo.

THE US POST-ACTION ASSESSMENT OF THE STRATEGIC CAMPAIGN

It is also important to preface any discussion of the claims made during the war, and of NATO's success by given target category, with the fact that the US Department of Defense report on the lessons of the war states that it was possible to confirm some of the material damage done to fixed and strategic targets after the war, but was not able to agree on details of such assessments or on an assessment of the strategic and tactical effects of most strikes.[171]

. . . Following the end of Operation Allied Force, NATO released an initial assessment of their attack effectiveness against a number of targets. These targets destroyed or significantly damaged include:

- Eleven railroad bridges
- Thirty-four highway bridges
- Twenty-nine percent of all Serbian ammunition storage
- Fifty-seven percent of petroleum reserves
- All Yugoslav oil refineries
- Fourteen command posts
- Over one hundred aircraft
- Ten military airfields

After the bombing campaign had ended, an assessment team visited a representative sample of such fixed targets as tunnels, bridges, bunkers, petroleum facilities, and above-ground facilities. At each site the team evaluated and recorded target characteristics, physical and functional target damage, weapon impact locations and effectiveness, and evidence of collateral damage. Based on these observations, the team assessed strike effectiveness against fixed targets:

. . . The assessment team examined damage to four tunnels in Kosovo that had been attacked by NATO aircraft: an underground aircraft storage and servicing facility, a military staging area, and two railroad tunnels. The team found that, in general, air attacks were very successful in closing tunnel adits (entrances). In addition, because of softer-than-estimated geological conditions, damage to tunnels was sometimes more significant than expected.

. . . For the most part, the bunkers encountered in Kosovo were constructed with reinforced concrete walls and ceilings. All had blast doors and some of the bunkers were hardened against nuclear, biological, and chemical (NBC) attacks, with independent manually operated electrical generators as well as an air filtration system. At every bunker site visited, the team found that NATO attacks were successful.

. . . NATO targeted bridges to hinder or stop enemy movement of troops and logistics along the major lines of communications. The air strikes effectively destroyed the targeted bridges and battle damage assessment of such strikes was reasonably accurate. d. Above-Ground Structures

Yugoslav Ministry of Interior Forces and Regular Army units had extensive garrisons and headquarters structures in nearly every major city in Kosovo. NATO airstrikes reduced a majority of these facilities to rubble. Once NATO airstrikes forced them from their traditional sites, the Interior Forces and Yugoslav Army fled to, and staged out of, several ad hoc garrisons, often at established industrial sites. Overall, NATO's effort against the majority of above-ground garrison structures and depots that were targeted and attacked was a complete success. NATO strikes severely damaged these structures with minimal collateral damage. No evidence of reconstitution was found.

As part of its look at above-ground structures, the team examined nine command, control, and communications facilities in Kosovo. These were part of the Serb communications network needed for command and control of Yugoslav Army and Interior Forces military system. In general, these targets fell into two categories: military specific targets (e.g., radio relay sites and air defense control and reporting posts) and dual-use facilities such as telephone systems and television and radio broadcast facilities. The military specific targets all had reinforced concrete bunkers to protect the mission critical equipment. The Serbs had removed electronic equipment from the sites and emptied the bunkers prior to the assessment team's arrival. The team could not determine when the Serbs removed the equipment. However, because they discovered little or no equipment in the destroyed above-ground support buildings, the team surmised the sites were not operational at the time of the attacks. It appeared that the inspected dual-use facilities (civilian and military) were operational at the time of attack causing the destruction of most of the equipment along with the destruction of the buildings.

. . . Throughout the air operation against the Serbs, NATO made every effort to minimize collateral damage. Of the 38 sites visited after the war, only one had sustained any significant collateral damage from NATO weapons falling on areas other than their intended target. At the other 37 sites, collateral damage was limited to broken windows, blown off roof tiles, and detached ceiling tiles.

This is a remarkably empty assessment of the strategic bombing effort, but the report the Department sent to Congress in January 2000 had to dodge around many critical issues relating to the effectiveness of NATO airpower. The most important of these obfuscations was that bureaucratic wrangling within the Department meant that it could only tie its BDA of strikes on given target groups to its resulting impact on Serbia's military and political behavior in ways that proved to rely on supposition and informed guesswork.

KOSOVO, NATO, AND STRATEGIC BOMBING

These basic problems in planning, doctrine, and assessing the impact of the strategic campaign were further complicated by deep divisions within the NATO country over what kinds of rear area targets could be attacked, and by a debate between the two most senior US officers in NATO that were directing the campaign over the relative weight of effort that should go to strategic bombing.

- SACEUR, General Wesley K. Clark, advocated a campaign that gave equal weight to attacks on key strategic and interdiction targets and Serbian forces in the field in Kosovo.
- Lt. General Michael Short, NATO's joint force air component commander in the Balkans, favored a campaign that focused on strategic bombing and an intensive campaign that would strike hard at the targets of most value to the Serbian leadership, halt its ability to communicate with its people, starve all military operations from the rear, and cripple the Serbian economy.[172]

Clark's view came to shape the course of the air and missile campaign, in part because much of the political leadership of NATO was totally unwilling to support the Short approach. Clark was constantly forced to negotiate with the political leadership of the alliance to escalate to new reader area targets which had a strategic content, and there was no practical chance that NATO's leadership would have accepted an air and missile campaign that did not visibly strike hard at the Serbian force in the field that were causing ethnic cleansing.

Nevertheless, the air and missile campaign did steadily escalate to the point where it had much of the targeting content Short advocated—although nothing approaching the intensity and focus he desired. It was also clear throughout the war that the traditional distinctions between strategic and tactical aircraft had little meaning. Bombers were often used against tactical targets, and strike fighters against strategic targets.

EVOLVING A COMMAND STRUCTURE IN MID-CRISIS

These issues were further complicated by the fact that NATO's command structure was compartmented along regional lines and key aspects of the strategic targeting and strike effort were left largely under US control. These problems were partially solved between August and December 1998, but the US and NATO chains of command remained separate. While the resulting problems affected tactical and theater operations as well, NATO faced its most serious problems in agreeing on and implementing the strategic aspects of the campaign.

The US Department of Defense report on the lessons of the war describes the resulting problems in depth and summarizes them as follows:[173]

... Joint Task Force Flexible Anvil and Joint Task Force Sky Anvil were activated, between August and December 1998. Under the new arrangement, the Commander in Chief, U.S. Air Forces in Europe, and the Commander in Chief, U.S. Naval Forces, Europe, were removed from the chain of operational control, and the Commanders, 16th Air Force and Sixth Fleet became joint task force commanders reporting directly to the U.S. Commander in Chief, Europe. The principal role of Joint Task Force Flexible Anvil was to execute a limited strike option using Tomahawk Land Attack Missiles, and that of Joint Task Force Sky Anvil was to execute a more extensive strike option if a limited strike did not achieve the desired end state. Targets were apportioned by matching target type to optimal weapon characteristics. The U.S. and NATO chains of command were still separated, and no other changes were made to the command and control structure.

... A new joint task force, Noble Anvil, subsumed Joint Task Force Flexible Anvil and Joint Task Force Sky Anvil during January-July 1999, and through an evolutionary process, U.S. and NATO organizations and command-and-control structures became linked. .... As previously discussed, NATO's political-military command structure played an important role in the planning and execution of the operation. NATO's command structure worked well, but parallel U.S. and NATO command-and-control structures complicated operational planning and unity of command. These structures are well defined, but had not been used previously to plan and conduct sustained combat operations. Despite the overall success of NATO's processes, we will work with our allies to:

• Enhance NATO's contingency planning process for operations outside the NATO area

• Develop an overarching command-and-control policy and agree on procedures for the policy's implementation

- Enhance procedures and conduct exercises strengthening NATO's political-military interfaces.

Put less politely, NATO's command structure was deeply divided and was not mission-oriented before July 1998. Improvements took place before the war in Kosovo, but it remained divided along US versus alliance lines. This was partially fixed during the fighting, but the control over a substantial number of US assets—including its cruise missiles and bombers—were still largely controlled by the US. Most importantly, NATO's senior political decision makers had no real exercise experience to prepare them to make decisions about strategic bombing, NATO has only limited contingency plans, and no detailed operation command and decision-making chain existed for integrating political and military decision-making on an alliance basis.

One lesson of Kosovo is that strategic bombing is strategic bombing, regardless of whether it is called by any other name. Another is that there are growing problems in distinguishing between strategic and tactical campaigns in a world where fighters can carry out deep strategic attacks and bombers can play a major role in striking ground forces, even in "close support" missions like attacks on the Serbian forces advancing on the KLA. Kosovo also raises a number of questions about the distinction between traditional strategic and interdiction targets, and as to whether such distinctions are meaningful. It is clear from NATO's reporting, however, that it engaged in a major strategic bombing campaign that expanded in scope and intensity throughout the war, and that it went far beyond interdiction bombing.[174]

Another lesson of Kosovo is that coalition or alliance warfare needs a clear decision-making and command chain to implement strategic bombing and that political decision makers need to be trained to play an effective wartime role in setting policy and making real-time decisions.

THE ECONOMIC AND INDUSTRIAL BASE THAT NATO ATTACKED

Another problem in assessing both NATO's claims during the war, and the impact of strategic/interdiction bombing after the war, stems from the fact the campaign never had the intensity and focus necessary to determine whether strategic bombing alone might have forced Serbia to concede. Furthermore, there is no way to determine the extent to which such strikes inhibited Serbian operations in the field.

The NATO campaign hit many rear area targets, although it generally tried to avoid hitting the Serbian population and most purely civil targets. NATO was also slow to escalate and rarely acted decisively. It only struck radio and TV transmitters for the first time on April 20–21, and one of Milosevic's residences on April

21. When it first struck at the power grid on May 3, it only deprived Serbia of 70 percent of its electric power for five hours.

The motives behind NATO's strike often involved guesswork about the political impact of such strikes. NATO's strikes on command and control facilities include an increasing number of political and leadership targets that had little to do with the current war, and factories said to be tied to the leadership at the political level. Many of the strikes on security forces in Serbia seem to have been directed at undermining the regime, and many of the attacks on military facilities and storage were instead directed at convincing Serbia it could become critically weak in a next war relative to its neighbors like Croatia.[175]

The Vulnerabilities of Serbia's Economy and Infrastructure

At the same time, NATO also hit many major area targets with a clear military value like production plants, military headquarters and depots, facilities at airfields, and major communications and supply targets like rail marshaling depots, transportation centers, multi-tank fuel depots, and Serbia's electrical power system.

Serbia had considerable economic vulnerability. The Yugoslav Republic had been in a steady state of economic decline since the early 1990s. Since 1993, it has had severe problems in financing its state budget, and its currency has been unstable and subject to hyperinflation. The CIA estimates that unemployment was around 30% before the bombing began.

The Yugoslav Republic had to feed and support a population of 11.2 million (10.5 million in Serbia and 679,900 in Montenegro) with an economy that now has virtually no trade, and which is relatively highly urbanized and dependent on the market sector of the economy. The GDP was roughly $24.3 billion in purchasing parity dollars before the start of the bombing campaign, and the average per capita income was around $2,300—although the economy has skewed by region and the per capita income of Kosovo was only about one-third that of Serbia. Yugoslavia also had serious foreign debt problems, and was importing three times the value of its exports.[176]

Serbian agriculture was heavily mechanized and dependent on fuel supplies, fertilizer deliveries, modern food processing, and market delivery. Serbia had had to introduce food rationing during the worst period of the Bosnia crisis for purely financial reasons. The cumulative impact of the bombing may severely reduce agricultural output in 1999, as well as efficient food processing and distribution.

It is important to note that agriculture accounted for only 5% of the labor force and 25% of the GDP. While the Yugoslav Republic did export food, it was also a net food importer. As a result, the near paralysis of the market and service economy affects 95% of the labor force and 75% of the GDP in an economy that already had very high unemployment—estimated at 27%. As a result, the economic impact of such bombing was potentially more severe than in a wealthy economy, and the political pressure of strategic bombing will be greater.

The Yugoslav economy was also highly dependent on electricity for an economy with this level of sophistication—3,009 kilowatt hours per capita—and its lignite-fueled power plants are very vulnerable. Knocking out both power and fuel would have potentially devastating results in terms basic aspects of life like agriculture, food distribution, water, and heating once winter sets in.

Jamie Shea of NATO made many of these points in the NATO briefing on May 4:

Serbian industrial production shrank by 50 percent between 1990 and 1998. National GDP in absolute terms in 1998 was estimated at £11.5/15 billion dollars, tiny for a country of the size and industrial importance of Yugoslavia. Per capita we calculate that the GDP income is $1400/1600 now. Unemployment, the official figure is 27 percent which is extremely high and more realistically it is probably double that. We know that salaries and pensions are paid late. In 1998, inflation was 45 percent. 45 percent of the population lives below or on the poverty line. 72 percent of the 1999 budget is planned for defense-related spending. By the way, these are World Bank and IMF figures, I haven't made them up.

What I want to say is that yes, it is true that after our attack of the night before and the short-circuits of the electricity supplies, the Serb people have suffered an inconvenience. But I think that inconvenience, which lasted a few hours and which had a severe effect on the military systems, is nothing compared with the day-to-day misery of that kind of economic melt-down which we have seen at the hands of Milosevic since he came to power in 1989.

Unrealistic NATO Claims versus Unrealistic Serbian Claims

These factors made Serbia vulnerable to the economic side effects of an air and missile campaign directed at military targets, and even more vulnerable as the campaign deliberately escalated to strategic levels. As Figure 23 shows, NATO struck a wide range of industrial, POL, and infrastructure targets. NATO claimed that it destroyed 100% of the FRY's petroleum refining production capability, that 65% of Serbian ammunition production capacity was damaged or destroyed, including 50% of its explosive production capacity, that 40% of the Serbs armored vehicle production and repair capacity was damaged or destroyed, and that 70% of aviation equipment assembly and repair capacity was damaged or destroyed. Serbia, in turn, reported that NATO damaged or destroyed 24 bridges, 12 railway stations, 36 factories, seven airports, 16 fuel plants and storage depots, 17 television transmitters, and several electrical facilities.[177]

It is clear that NATO generally sought to temporarily degrade capabilities that it could have destroyed, that it operated under severe political constraints relating to target choice, the risk of collateral damage, and the types of damage it could inflict. It also seems clear that NATO encountered a classic problem in strategic bombing. It could speculate on the importance of given targets to Serbia, but had no reliable way of knowing their importance. As a result, it tended to bomb by category and judge its success largely by perceived damage to physical facilities, rather than any clear insights into enemy perceptions and behavior.

Even as NATO escalated, however, it made continuing efforts to describe virtually all of its targeting as directed against the military capabilities of Serbian forces or the Serbian leadership. It was never comfortable in publicly announcing the fact it was engaged in a strategic bombing campaign that often went far beyond narrowly defined military targets, and was directed at intimidating the Serbian leadership and public and creating political pressure to end the war.

NATO has released only limited data on the strategic rationale behind these aspects of the air and missile campaign, its targeting plan, the number of sorties flown against given targets, the munitions used, the level of damage it sought, the resulting battle damage assessment, and the estimated impact on the behavior of the Serbian leadership and military forces. In spite of the leaks discussed earlier, it has never publicly discussed the political limits imposed on what it could and could not target, and its rules of engagement.

Serbia took the opposite tactic, and exaggerated NATO's strategic bombing effort. The Serbian Foreign Minister, Zivadin Jovanovic, claimed in September 1999 that the NATO bombing campaign had cost Serbia some $100 billion, versus the $30-$50 billion worst case estimates that came from other European sources. Serbia's estimate of the "strategic damage" that NATO inflicted was as just as exaggerated, however, as its estimates of the "tactical damage" NATO did to Serbian military forces were underestimated. Serbia also included the cost of the Serbian flight out of Kosovo after the air and missile campaign ended. As a result the Serbian estimate included some 50,000 Serbian houses and apartments in Kosovo. The Serbian Foreign Minister also claimed that some 250,000 Serbs had now fled Kosovo, and that 400 Serbians had been killed, 600 wounded, and 500 kidnapped.[178]

One of the key lessons of the war seems to be that NATO and US capabilities to inflict damage on strategic and rear area targets has steadily improved with time, but that the doctrine for strategic bombing remains relative crude, and success remains extremely difficult to measure. Like somewhat similar exercises during Desert Storm and Desert Fox, NATO planners made ambitious claims about their success in striking fixed facilities and urban targets but provided little evidence to validate them. This does not mean that strategic and interdiction bombing were not effective in many ways, but it is almost impossible to know how effective they were, whether a different mix of targets would have been more effective, and how much of the damage inflicted was actually justified by the results.

FUEL, PETROLEUM, OIL, AND LUBRICANTS (POL) TARGET GROUPS

Strikes on refineries and POL facilities are a good example of the strategic bombing effort that was a key part of the NATO campaign. They are also a good example of how difficult it is to tie the physical impact of strategic strikes to an assessment of their impact on warfighting and enemy political and strategic perceptions.

Wartime Gamesmanship with Damage Assessment

NATO increased the number of target groups hit by 65% from Day 20 to Day 29. By mid-April, it claimed to have destroyed 100% of Serbia's refinery capability and 25 percent of its military reserves and industrial fuel storage. NATO struck a wide range of industrial, POL, and infrastructure targets. The resulting effectiveness data are summarized in Figure 22. NATO claimed that it destroyed 100% of the FRY's petroleum refining production capability; that 65% of Serbian ammunition production capacity was damaged or destroyed, including 50% of its explosive production capacity; that 40% of the Serbs armored vehicle production and repair capacity was damaged or destroyed; and that 70% of aviation equipment assembly and repair capacity was damaged or destroyed.

The British Ministry of Defense claimed on April 23 that,

Fuel supplies have been a particular target and we have regularly attacked both production and storage facilities, in many instances we need to return to the same target area because facilities are spread over a large area or buried. Nevertheless, we've destroyed the Serbs' refining capabilities and have severely reduced their reserve stocks of fuel. This is having an effect on units in the field and will become increasingly apparent.

SACEUR, General Wesley Clark, stated on April 27 that,

We have essentially destroyed his production capability. He can't refine it. Now that doesn't mean it won't be repaired. We have taken about one-third of the military reserves, we know the military is increasingly desperate for fuel, we know of at least three instances where operations have been shut down in an effort to conserve fuel or simply because they have run out of fuel. Here is an attack from 22 April on a fuel facility in Pristina.

We were (had destroyed) 70 percent at one point of the refining capacity, we did not get the full 70 percent of the civilian reserves. What we believe we've got is 33 percent of the military reserves. I don't have the figure with me today on what the total reserves are that are available but like a lot of numbers in here I would encourage you not to do a sort of bean-counting-type BDA. I don't think anyone truly knows how much oil is present in Yugoslavia, probably the Serb regime doesn't either, it's probably squirreled away in many locations and so you will continually see us revise our figures. That's the reason why we try to give you a qualitative assessment rather than dwell on specific quantities or percentages.

NATO also provided detailed damage assessment and targeting maps on April 27. These maps provided a new way of summarizing damage assessment, based on a sliding scale from no damage to severe damage. The summary assessment approached the middle of moderate damage. The detailed target maps showed that 13 major storage tanks had been struck, and that four had little damage, five had moderate damage and four had severe damage. It also showed that NATO had struck 13 distribution capability targets, and that four had little damage, two had

Figure 22
NATO Damage Claims Relating to POL and Defense Industry

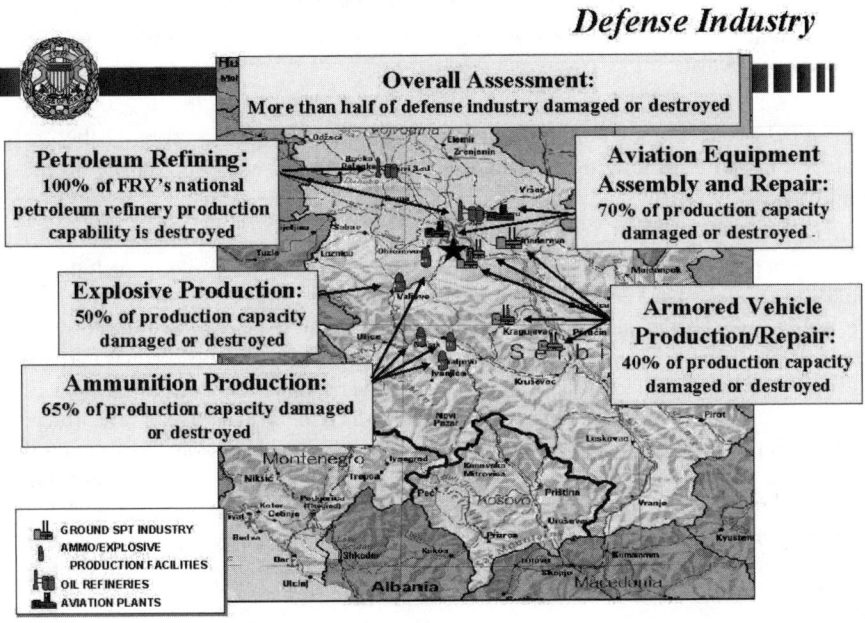

Source: Adapted from the Department of Defense press briefing for June 10, 1999.

moderate damage and seven had severe damage. The US reported somewhat different targeting figures that same day, showing the NATO had now hit two refineries and 14 fuel storage sites. It did not assess damage to these targets.

The US Department of Defense issued data on April 30 that showed that Yugoslavia now lacked the fuel to meet the strategic requirements of its civil, industrial, and military sectors. It concluded that the Army general and operational reserve was meeting requirements, but that the bombing had reduced the flow of fuel to the 3rd Army and Pristina to the "partially meeting requirements" level. It concluded that four of the seven brigades in Kosovo had adequate fuel, two could only partially meet requirements, and one could not meet requirements. At the same time, the data indicated that Yugoslavia had been able to import 40,000–45,000 metric tons, or around 300,000 barrels, of oil in the first month after the beginning of the air and missile campaign, and was importing oil in tanker trucks across its borders. A single commercial charter tanker delivered 65,000 barrels of oil products and gasoline to Montenegro on April 26, and a Russian tanker delivered more than 100,000 barrels. A total of 11 tankers delivered oil and products during the month of April.

The Department of Defense claimed in its press briefing on May 5.

Questioner: Can you summarize to date what percentage of Serbia's military fuel reserves has been hit? We've talked a lot about the POL refining capability. What's the best estimate of how many of the military stocks in the field have been hit or eliminated?

Major General Wald: I'm not sure exactly the number. I think it's in the 30–40 percentile, something like that.

NATO spokesperson Jamie Shea provided a broader perspective on the probable limits of the combined effects of air strikes and an oil embargo during his press conference on April 29.

We are not pretending that a visit and search regime is going to totally eliminate Belgrade's ability to acquire refined petroleum. As you know, there are always ways in which countries are able to get their hands on these products, particularly if they are willing to pay the price . . . So it is not a panacea, it is not something that we believe can be totally watertight, it is simply something that can help to reduce by several important percentage points the supply of refined oil and bring it down to a level at which the armed forces start hurting . . . But I think what we have done so far, quite frankly, is beginning to hit home. I saw today that Belgrade is now rationing each car on the streets of Yugoslavia to 20 liters a month, down from 40 liters a month, as the army has to raid if you like the petroleum piggy-bank of the country's citizens to continue to fuel its own activities. And you can't go very far, as you know, on 20 liters a month, so I think it is a sign that things are beginning to hit home.

NATO reported on May 6 that tanker ships still continued through Montenegro, but that:

We have totally destroyed oil refining capacity so that Milosevic has to rely on imported fuel—costing money. 70 percent of military stocks have gone, so has one-third of fuel storage capacity

General Shelton, the Chairman of the US Joint Chiefs, stated on May 12 that, "Both of his oil refineries are shut down, and more than a third of his military reserve fuel storage is destroyed or severely damaged."

The problem with all of these claims is that NATO's daily reporting on Serbian ground activity showed that these attacks did not affect most low-level, largely infantry operations, or further increases in the size of the Serbian forces in Kosovo discussed later. Infantry and light supplies can still bypass bridges after a day or two using boats. Once again, the key problem was that the Serbs in Kosovo could draw-down on the remnants of an economy that originally had 1.62 million Kosovar Muslims, and seize the remaining food and supplies of the refugees, letting them starve.

Furthermore, Serbia could import fuel and products from other sources, and NATO was not able to agree on an early and full embargo. As General Clark pointed out on April 27, the problem remained that the Serbs were already deployed in Kosovo and could seize all fuel stocks from the Kosovars, making the refugee problem even worse. The Serbs did not need fuel-intensive operations without a major ground opponent. Further, fuel was imported by land and by sea.

The US Department of Defense briefing on May 8 stated that:

Well, without getting into any specifics, I think it's very clear that NATO has established as one of its goals the interruption of petroleum supplies to the Yugoslav army and special police forces. And we have done that in a variety of ways. One is by attacking refinery capacity in Yugoslavia. Another is by attacking storage areas. And a third is by attacking routes or interdicting supply routes into Yugoslavia. We've done that aggressively over the last six weeks, and we will continue to work on those targets.

Questioner: Ken, a follow-on to the embargo. There's a report that Yugoslav navy ships are actually blockading that port. Is that an accurate report, making life a little easier for NATO personnel?

Answer: There is a Yugoslav blockade. I think it's semi-permeable. It has some judgment elements in it on the part of the Yugoslav navy. But there is a semi- permeable Yugoslav blockade of Bar.

Questioner: When you say you can get through it, permeable areas are which ships bringing oil or—

Answer: We're not aware that there's a ship that has brought oil to Bar for the last week or so. The oil flow or attempted oil flow has slowed to a trickle from what it used to be. I don't have numbers unfortunately, but there is very, very little traffic in and out of Bar now, I think, for obvious reasons. Shippers all have insurance, and their rates rise with the threat of conflict and in dangerous areas and there is sort of a self-policing element here even before you get to the fact that the European Union has imposed an embargo, and the U.S. has also tightened its regulations, its export regulations.

Guessing at the Impact from a Postwar Perspective

NATO's estimate of the effectiveness of this aspect of the air and missile campaign at the end of the war is shown in Figure 23. When the NATO attacks ended on June 10, the Department of Defense reported that it had destroyed 100% of the FRY's petroleum refining production capability.[179] Nevertheless, physical damage to facilities is not a measure of either industrial output or military impact, and by the end of the war, the NATO strikes on POL had scarcely achieved Serbian paralysis. While Serbian forces did experience growing operational problems in the field, they were able to maintain their wartime reserves and continue successful overall operations in ethnic cleansing and low-level operations against the KLA. They also proved able to conduct a relatively quick mass withdrawal from Kosovo, and the Serbian civilians in Kosovo had enough fuel to flee the area in large numbers.

It does not seem likely that a sustained major increase in VJ and MUP operations against the KLA would have led to POL problems that would have quickly forced Serbia to rapidly draw down heavily on wartime reserves, or that Serbia would

Figure 23
NATO Damage Claims Relating to Electric Power

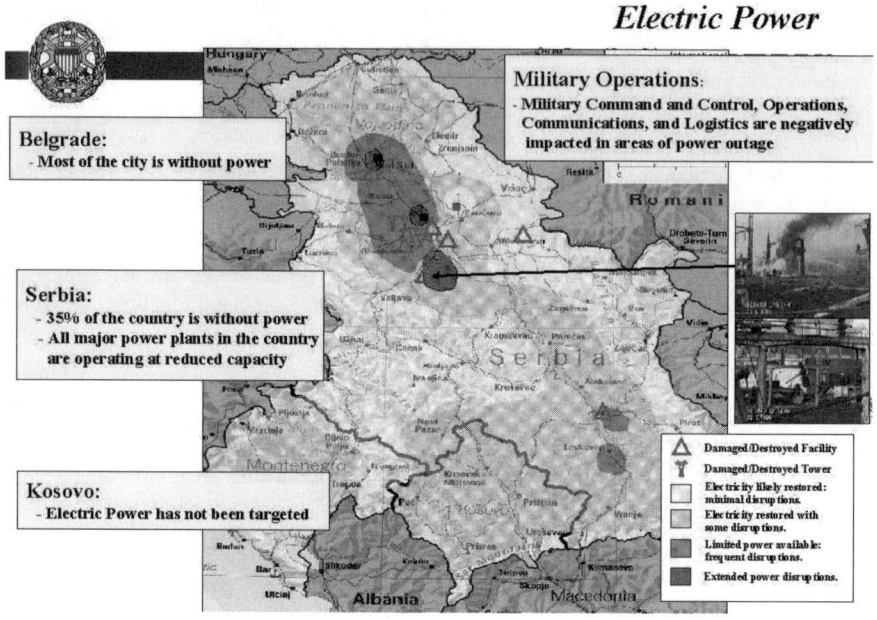

Source: Adapted from the Department of Defense press briefing for June 10, 1999.

have had critical distribution problems in supplying its armored and mechanized brigades in major deployments and the kind of combat operations needed to deal with the KLA—although the story might have been radically different if it had had to deal with a NATO ground option. Judging from Serbia's ability to rapidly withdraw from Kosovo after June 10, and the fact that there was a massive Serbian civilian exodus, Serbia does not seem to have faced critical near-term problems in its fuel supplies.

The impact of this aspect of the NATO air and missile campaign on the Serbian economy is equally uncertain. Serbia may have faced a future where energy shortages could have had a near-crippling impact. Once again, however, little evidence surfaced after the cease-fire that Serbia faced critical near-term problems that would have reduced its economy to a level that prevented continuing war fighting.

The situation might have been different if air and missile power had faced fewer constraints in attacking and permanently damaging POL-related facilities, if air and missile power could have been used to destroy loading and transit facilities in Montenegro, and/or if a total land-naval embargo had been imposed on POL shipments to Serbia from the start of the war. A full embargo and intense bombing campaign might have made the situation substantially worse over the period of a month to six weeks. Serbian forces would probably have experienced serious operational problems in the field, and in mobilizing and carrying out major deployments to defend against NATO. They might not have been able to maintain their wartime reserves and will have growing problems in ethnic cleansing and against the KLA. By some point in July to August, the Serbian economy might have reached the point of near collapse, and had serious problems in providing fuel for both military operations and agriculture.

The fact that the KLA was able to increase its activity in late May might also have created new strains on Serbian fuel supplies if the air and missile campaign had been extended beyond June, and an effective embargo had been established. The VJ and MUP operations might have forced Serbia to draw down heavily on its remaining wartime reserves. Serbia might have had critical distribution problems in supplying its armored and mechanized brigades in major deployments and for any kind of intense combat operations. It could also have had major problems in supplying its forces if they dispersed for defense in depth or retreated away from major surviving fuel distribution centers.

The fact remains that air attacks on POL were not decisive in limiting enemy capabilities during the air and missile war over Kosovo. Even if one assumes that all of the rough percentages shown in Figure 23 are accurate—and they seem to be more of an exercise in propaganda than the output of a serious analysis—they describe strategic bombing in a way that has no strategic meaning. The key lesson is the need for a far better way of assessing the impact of strategic strikes on POL facilities, the required targeting, and the proper method of battle damage—a lesson that applies to virtually every aspect of the strategic portion of the air and missile campaign in Kosovo.

Strikes Against Industry Support and Infrastructure Target Groups

As Figure 22 also shows, NATO hit a wide range of industrial complexes and facilities. They included car and military vehicle plants, aircraft plants, munitions plants, and other facilities relating to Serbia's ability to arm and repair its forces. Many were reported to be important to key political supporters of Milosevic. The full nature of these strikes was not made public in detail by either NATO or the United States. Both, however, released a series of photos that indicated that such strikes had a serious strategic and tactical effect and reported summary effectiveness data.

Admiral Wilson reported in his press briefing on April 22 that,

The degree of damage to the infrastructure and particularly on oil storage and refinement capability, the production of ammunition, the storage of ammunition, and even now some of the industrial targets is having a negative impact on not only the sustainment of the force, but also, I believe, the morale of the force and the morale of the people as this infrastructure is increasingly damaged and destroyed.

We talked before that 100 percent of the national refinery capability was not operating. Not only is it not operating, now we believe that 100 percent is not even operational because of continued strikes at Pancevo and Novi Sad. They may be out of commission for more or less periods of time, and there are more things we can do in those areas, but a near term restoration of refining capability is not on the horizon.

We believe that when you combine military reserve and industrial fuel storage capacity, about 25 percent of that has been damaged or destroyed in the country, which complicates their ability to A, store fuel, and also to move the fuel. I've said this before—I'd like to reemphasize—damaging the storage capacity is important, but when we do that we also attack in those installations the places where they transfer fuel—pumps and risers and things of that nature.

SACEUR, General Wesley Clark, stated on April 27 that, "We have had some very good success against ammunition stocks and we have done very serious damage to his ability to repair and maintain his aircraft, military vehicles, armaments and munitions." The US Department of Defense reported the same day that NATO had now hit five ammunition and weapons production facilities, four other industrial facilities, and 19–20 ammunition storage facilities.

NATO again provided detailed damage assessment and targeting maps on April 27. The summary assessment was low to moderate damage. The detailed target maps showed that 20 plants and industrial facilities had been hit, and that none had little damage, 6 had moderate damage and 14 had severe damage. The US reported somewhat different targeting figures that same day, showing that NATO had now struck 5 ammunition production facilities, 18 ammunition storage facilities, and five other industrial targets. It did not assess damage to these targets. It provided revised data on April 30, showing that NATO had now struck 5 ammunition production facilities, 18 ammunition storage facilities, and five other industrial targets. The strikes on ammunition storage facilities were largely in the center and south of Serbia and in Kosovo, and concentrated in the area of the Serbian 2nd and 3rd Armies.

The British Ministry of Defense reported on May 5 that, "We have attacked and significantly damaged a fifth of all major ammunition storage sites, 12 out of 57." General Shelton, the Chairman of the US Joint Chiefs, stated on May 12 that, " . . . we have seriously damaged Milosevic's military industrial capacity, reducing his ability to repair and maintain his aircraft by 70% and his ammunition production capacity by two-thirds. . . . Most of the ammunition and fuel supplies of the Serb Third Army, which as you know by now, probably, is the unit that operates in Kosovo, has been destroyed along with more than half of the infrastructure that supports this force. Distribution networks into Kosovo for critical supplies such as fuel and ammunition have been severely disrupted."

At the end of the air campaign on June 10, NATO reported that it had damaged or destroyed 65% of Serbian ammunition production capacity, including 50% of its explosive production capacity, 40% of the Serbs' armored vehicle production and repair capacity, and 70% of aviation equipment assembly and repair capacity. Once again, NATO did not explain how these percentages were calculated or if they went beyond a broad guesstimate. NATO also reported that it had inflicted enough damage on the Serbian electric power system to have had a major impact on the availability of power throughout Kosovo.

These latter estimates are summarized in Figure 24, but the problem with these claims is that there is an immense difference between "damaged" and "destroyed" and no clear way to determine the impact of such bombing on Serbian morale, actions, and military operations. It is logical that such strategic bombing had a major impact, but determining the nature of this impact is even harder to figure than the impact of the strategic attacks on POL facilities. As has been noted earlier, the US Department of Defense report on the lessons of the war provided no useful data on the effectiveness of such strikes. The British and French reports managed to provide even less.

It is uncertain whether the attacks on Serbian ammunition production capacity, explosive production capacity, and armored vehicle production and repair capacity had a major impact on Serbian operations up to June 10, although they might have had a major impact on Serbian capabilities in the face of a ground attack by NATO. Serbia had inherited the ammunition stocks of virtually all of the former Yugoslavia, and has long dispersed much of its ammunition and equipment in shelters. The slow initial pace of the air and missile campaign gave Serbia weeks in which to further disperse its weapons, munitions, and military material.

It is possible that NATO may have had an effect in striking at some dispersed storage facilities and equipment in the field, and eventually limited Serbia's capability to supply all its 2nd and 3rd Army units efficiently or reliably in the field. However, NATO's attacks do not seem to have had a major or lasting impact on the overall course of Serbian land operations in carrying out ethnic cleansing in dealing with the KLA.

The situation might have changed if the war had gone on. There had to be limits to how much ammunition and supplies Serbia could disperse without losing the ability to assemble and move large amounts of munitions in the timely and well-structured way necessary to support a major ground campaign. Serbia also seems to have lost much of its ability to produce munitions to fill in any gaps in supply and stocks and to manufacture, rebuild, and repair military equipment. However, past experience shows that many countries have found it possible to reconstitute a substantial part of their production and support capacity in dispersed and underground facilities, and that production rates are often surprisingly high—partly because of low peacetime production rates.

It does seems likely that Serbia would have had serious supply problems if it had had to defend Serbia proper and Kosovo at the same time. It might well not have the production capacity, supply stocks, and distribution and transport capacity to supply a 1st Army that would have to engage in intensive armored and artillery combat.

Figure 24
NATO Damage Claims Relating to Lines of Communication

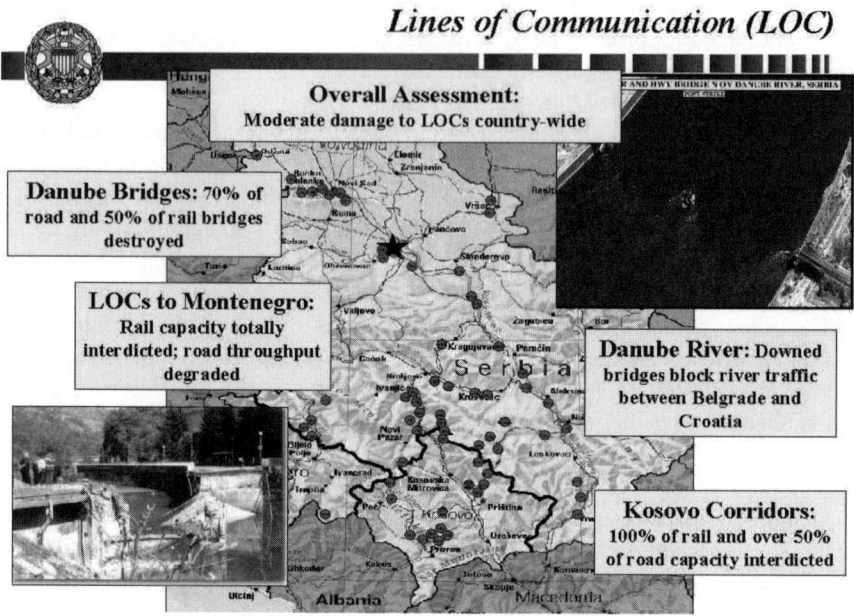

Source: Adapted from the Department of Defense press briefing for June 10, 1999.

The attacks on aviation equipment assembly and repair capacity had little operational meaning because of NATO's air superiority in other areas and because Serbia flew only very limited numbers of sorties. NATO's operational air superiority was also so great that the main impact of such strikes may have been to convince Serbia that it could not afford to keep losing facilities that might be vital in a future war with its neighbors.

If there is lesson here, it is that NATO again seemed to be bombing by category without a clear picture of the operational impact of its activities, and was using air and missile power in a broad effort to intimidate Serbia and achieve its political aims by degrading Serbia's capabilities in future war.

Even if one accepts the percentages that NATO reports, blowing things up is not a measure of impact on the enemy or of the impact of strategic bombing on war fighting outcomes, and even if one assumes that all of the rough percentages shown in Figures 23 and 24 are accurate—and they seem to be more of an exercise in propaganda than the output of a serious analysis. They describe strategic bombing in a way that has no strategic meaning. The lesson is the need for a far better way of assessing the impact of strategic strikes on military production and supply facilities, the required targeting, and the proper method of battle damage—a lesson that applies to virtually every aspect of the strategic portion of the air and missile campaign in Kosovo.

Strikes Against Electric Power Facilities

The kind of damage summarized in Figure 24 raises somewhat similar issues, but it includes targets and facilities that are much closer to NATO's attacks on POL facilities in their broad nationwide impact than its attacks on industry. It seems logical that the NATO attacks on power facilities must have had a political and economic impact, and an impact on public opinion. The problem is confirming that impact and measuring it, particularly because NATO temporarily interrupted power in most cases, rather than destroyed the end system and many military units had their own generator. This requires far more data on Serbian perceptions and the motive behind Serbian actions than is available to date.

The lessons here are threefold:

- First, there again is a clear need to go beyond the theory of strategic bombing and carry out a careful survey of all available data on the impact of given kinds of bombing and damage patterns to see what the impact really was. Anyone can assert the importance of such bombing, but there is a critical difference between blowing the roof off, or interrupting power for a period of hours, and winning the war.

- Second, it is almost impossible to determine from the data in Figures 22 and 23, or any of the figures that follow, whether NATO had any meaningful way to assess the levels of damage it claimed. The percentage data are so broad—and evidently so closely linked to physical damage as distinguished from an assessment of impact on operations, perceptions, and actions—that it is not clear what meaning they really have. There are strong indications that much more advanced forms of Battle Damage Assessment are required to validate strategic bombing.

- Third, all strategic bombing activity tends to be a race between destruction and construction. As is the case with the other strategic target sets, it is unclear how NATO's destructive capabilities were offset by Serbia's reconstruction capabilities.

LINES OF COMMUNICATION (LOCs) AND SUPPLY ROUTE TARGET GROUPS

NATO's attacks on lines of communication and supply route targets increased by nearly four times (480%) during Day 20 to Day 28. After that time, NATO, Britain, and the US reported that serious damage had been done to all four major supply routes into Kosovo, and that NATO continued to attack key brigades and road and rail links.

Rear Admiral Thomas Wilson, the J-2 of the US Joint Chiefs, reported on April 22 that:

We continue to work on the lines of communication, and it's having an impact down in the south. The last time we talked I believe three of the four main lines of communication into Kosovo had been interdicted to some degree or another. I would now say all four of the main lines into Kosovo have been interdicted, and more seriously than they were before. Probably close to 50 percent of the throughput capacity into Kosovo has now been denied to the Serbs, and we continue to work on bridges which, frankly, are difficult targets.

We also believe that up north the damage to the lines of communications as well as the psychological impact of seeing them destroyed is affecting not only the attitude of mobilization but even the movement and the ability to move reserves and reserve forces around the country.

I've already talked before—we are having, now have degraded the aircraft repair [capability] very, very severely. That really has been true since early in this overall bombing operation, and increasing damage to ammunition production is being, I think, seen in evidence we have of Yugoslavia reaching out to a number of sources to try to acquire more and different kinds of ammunition to be able to not only sustain their ability to fight, but also perhaps improve their ability to fight, and they're not having any success in that regard.

The British Ministry of Defense reported on April 23 that:

Some of our principal targets have been road and rail bridges. Both major rail routes into Kosovo have been cut and 2 of the 4 major roads. Both railways lines across the Danube have also been severed and we will continue to attack these types of targets to deny the VJ and the MUP the supplies they need to continue their operations and to restrict their freedom of movement in Kosovo.

The General Clark stated on April 27 that:

We have said before that what we are trying to do is interdict and cut off Kosovo and make it much more difficult for him to sustain his military operations down there. What you are seeing up here are three bands of interdiction. They represent essentially where we are taking action against railroads, roads, bridges and other means of transportation into Kosovo or out of Montenegro, because what we want to do is stop the flow of oil out of Montenegro, at the same time prevent any military supplies from going into Kosovo or elsewhere. Step by step, bit by bit, we are cutting off his ability to reinforce or to sustain his forces easily down in Kosovo. Of course he can still walk them in through the gullies and the rivers and so forth and it is never going to be complete, but it is certainly complicating their life down there.

NATO provided detailed damage assessment and targeting maps on April 27, but the summary assessment showed little to moderate damage. No detailed target group maps were provided. The US reported somewhat different targeting figures that same day, showing that NATO had now hit 37 bridges. It did not assess damage to these targets.

The US again reported in detail on April 30. It reported that it had destroyed or severely damaged 20 highway, eight railway, and two rail/highway bridges. Target maps showed these bridges were scattered over a wide area and affected the supply routes and lines of communication in all of Serbia, the Serbian-Montenegrin border area, and near Serbian centers in Kosovo. The US said that the NATO attacks had reduced the throughput of Serbian lines of communication, degraded the ability of the VJ to resupply units in Kosovo, had a significant impact on the sustainment of ground operations, and negatively affected mobilization, reinforcement, and long-term sustainment.

The British Ministry of Defense reported on May 5 that 32 road and rail bridges have been damaged or destroyed. NATO reported on May 6 that:

We have pretty much largely cut them off and are about to begin to take them out. We have achieved that by regularly and relentlessly harrying them in the field, as I shall go on to describe, to the point where far from moving with impunity, they can now move only furtively and with fear. Let me also summarize progress on the second of those goals, to cut them off, on which you have had several reports at these briefings in the recent days already. As of today, with the exception of the Danube Bridge in Belgrade, all but two Danube bridges are destroyed, and this is within a total of 31 bridges attacked throughout the area of operations. The two major rail routes into Kosovo have been closed. The two major road routes from Serbia into Kosovo have been closed also. The other two however more minor roads are severely damaged.

Similarly, General Shelton, the Chairman of the US Joint Chiefs, stated on May 12 that:

Distribution networks into Kosovo for critical supplies such as fuel and ammunition have been severely disrupted. Rail lines into Kosovo are severed, and about half the roadways into Kosovo have been damaged as well. . . . There are indications that some of the leadership is getting a little bit distraught over the loss of their military industrial complex, a lot of their infrastructure. They're seeing their capabilities degraded, reduced. They know what the impact is, and I mean, for a country that's got an $11 billion GNP—$11 to $12 billion GNP—they know that this is going to take a long time to ever get back to where started when it's over.

In spite of these claims, NATO's daily reporting on Serbian ground activity as of May 13 (Day 50) still showed that its attacks had scarcely halted Serbia's relatively low-level, largely infantry and artillery operations, or prevented further increases in the size of the Serbian forces in Kosovo. Infantry and light supplies could still bypass bridges using boats. Once again, a key problem was that the Serbs in Kosovo could draw-down on the remnants of an economy that originally had 1.62 million Kosovar Muslims, and seize the remaining food and supplies of the refugees.

On May 19 (Day 56), the US Department of Defense gave an airfield damage assessment, reporting that runways at Batajnica, Sjenica, Pristina, Obrva, and Ponikve were non-operational. The infrastructure at Batajnica, Pristina, and

Ponikve sustained moderate functional damage, while those at Sjenica and Obrva had been functionally destroyed. NATO claimed that Serbia's aircraft repair and assembly facilities at Batajnica and Pancevo had also been functionally destroyed.

At the end of the air campaign on June 10, the Department of Defense reported having inflicted "moderate damage" to lines of communication throughout the country. It estimated that 70% of road bridges and 50% of the rail bridges on the Danube were destroyed, blocking river traffic between Belgrade and Croatia. In addition, it claimed that rail capacity was totally interdicted, and road throughput was degraded on routes to Montenegro. This was said to "bar" Serbian ability to transport fuel from the Barr port facility into Kosovo over rail lines. It claimed that 100% of the rail and over 50% of the road capacity in the corridors to and in Kosovo had been interdicted. These estimates are summarized in Figure 25.

These percentage figures are impressive, but it again is far from clear what they really mean, or what their strategic and tactical impact was on Serbian operations. Serbia almost certainly did face growing problems in moving artillery and armor. Military and civil transport certainly faced growing movement constraints and there will probably be conflicts between maintaining a subsistence-level economy and meeting military requirements. The VJ and MUP seem to have lost much of their ability to rapidly reinforce across corps zone and from one part of the country to another, and resupply and sustainment will become problems if any major ground operations take place against NATO.

At the same time, military history is filled with over-ambitious claims by air planners, and no wartime estimate of the effect of bombing on supply and movement has yet proved to have been remotely correct in after-action studies. Figure 26 shows that Serbian forces were not prevented from a substantial build-up during the war, or from a relatively smooth and rapid withdrawal once it was over. Massive movements of Serbian civilians took place in Kosovo, as they fled the region and moved into Serbia proper. This aspect of the air and missile campaign also had little operational impact on Serbian operations in Kosovo. As the previous figures have shown, ethnic cleansing quickly came to affect at least 90% of the Muslim population in Kosovo, and NATO had to admit that its air strikes made some aspects of ethnic cleansing worse—at least in the near term.

One of the critical questions no one seems to have asked during the fighting is what impact the NATO effort to cut off fuel supplies and the major lines of communication from Serbia to Kosovo had on the plight of the refugees. It may simply have had the effect that the Serbs confiscated more of the supplies inside Kosovo and starved out more Muslims or deprived them of the fuel they needed. In short, the net impact of NATO operations during the first month of the air and missile war seems to have been to worsen the plight of the Kosovars, rather than paralyze Serbian operations.

The potential effects are clear from NATO's estimates of the size of the refugee problem as early as May 4.

Figure 25
The Rising Serbian Presence in Kosovo: As of April 27, 1999

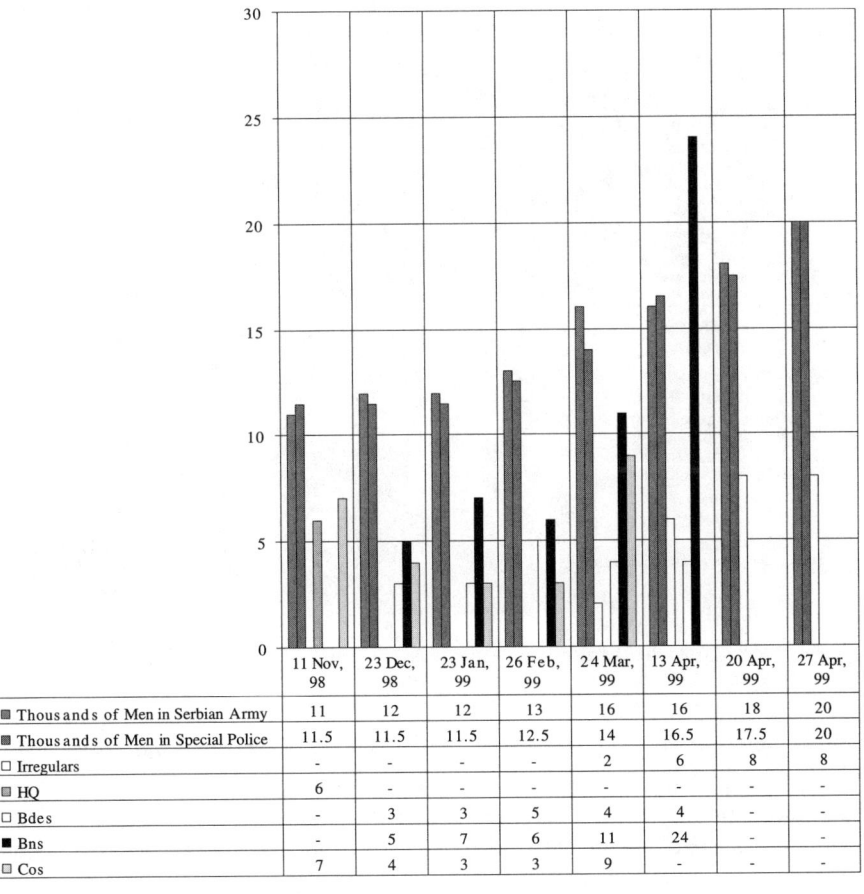

	11 Nov, 98	23 Dec, 98	23 Jan, 99	26 Feb, 99	24 Mar, 99	13 Apr, 99	20 Apr, 99	27 Apr, 99
▨ Thousands of Men in Serbian Army	11	12	12	13	16	16	18	20
▨ Thousands of Men in Special Police	11.5	11.5	11.5	12.5	14	16.5	17.5	20
□ Irregulars	-	-	-	-	2	6	8	8
▨ HQ	6	-	-	-	-	-	-	-
□ Bdes	-	3	3	5	4	4	-	-
■ Bns	-	5	7	6	11	24	-	-
□ Cos	7	4	3	3	9	-	-	-

Source: NATO Briefing—April 13, 1999 and NATO, April 21, 1999.

If you want the tally which we now have for the time being over the last twelve months, 800,000 Kosovar Albanians have fled Kosovo since March 1998, 650,000 are internally displaced, at least 100,000 men of military age are missing, at least 4,000 victims of summary executions are reported since the beginning of the year, nearly 1.5 million Kosovar Albanians—or 90% of the population—have been expelled from their homes. We have reports of mass executions in 65 towns and villages and mass graves in at least seven locations. So that is the macabre tally of this chamber of horrors thus far.

Like many claims about strikes on LOCs in previous air and missile wars— including the Gulf War—it again is far easier to use air and missile power to blow things up than it is to determine the consequences. As is the case with most of the

Figure 26
NATO Damage Claims Relating to Command, Control, and Communications

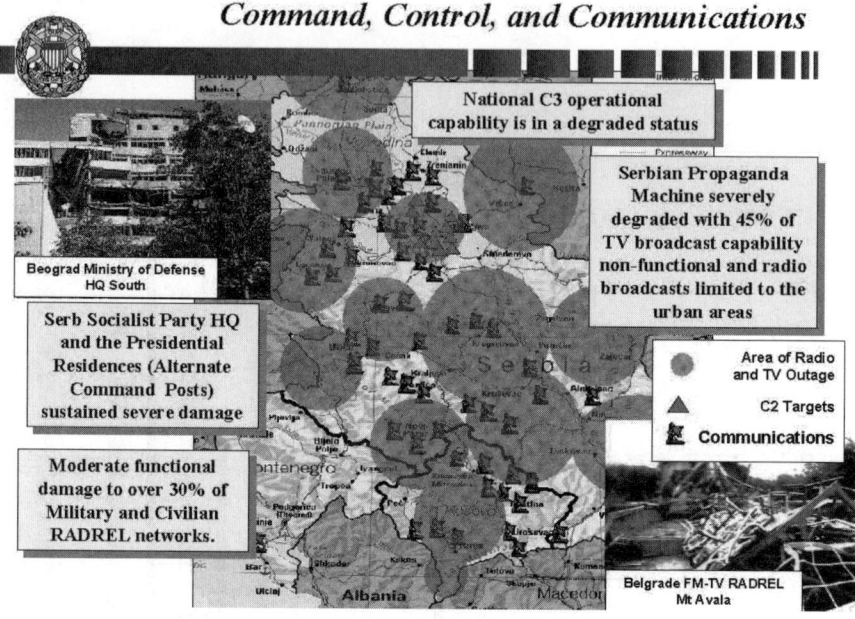

Source: Adapted from the Department of Defense press briefing for June 10, 1999.

other aspects of strategic and interdiction bombing, the lesson is that there simply does not seem to be an adequate analytic base to either validate individual targeting concepts or do battle damage assessment in the sense of producing a reliable chain of cause and effect. This does not mean that attacks on LOCs are not useful. It does seem to mean that this aspect of air and missile power remains an art form based on sophisticated guesswork.

COMMAND AND CONTROL TARGET GROUPS

NATO devoted a great deal of its air effort to destroying Serbian command and control capabilities. It reported that its strikes on command and control target groups increased by 124 percent between Day 20 to Day 28. The US reported on April 22 that this involved at least 27 major facilities, and severely degraded the national command and control system, special police and ministry of the interior targets, the facilities of the 1st, 2nd and 3rd armies, air defense headquarters and command posts, and airborne headquarters. Many of the strikes concentrated on the 3rd Army, the force operating in Kosovo, but the 2nd Army came under increasing attack after the third week of the war.

The "command and control" facilities NATO targeted expanded to include a residence of the president, key leadership targets, the socialist party headquarters (the 24-story USCE building), and major security forces facilities and headquarters. They also included "dual use" radio, TV, microwave, and telephone targets as well as military targets.

Rear Admiral Thomas Wilson, the J-2 of the US Joint Chiefs, reported on Defense reported on April 22 that,

We think we have both degraded the effectiveness and the efficiency of this overall command and control network, the national command authority, and in doing so have sent strong messages to certain elements, in fact all echelons of command that we will attack where and when we can to disrupt or degrade their ability to command these forces. So this is a very broad target set that ranges from functional headquarters to the technical or physical ability to move information to the field.

So for example, the Belgrade socialist party—that was the building that was destroyed the other night—not only was the party's propaganda organ, the building and the area where some of this information flows from the party, but also where they broadcast information on the television is from that particular source.

You know earlier about the Ministry of Interior, the MUP facilities in downtown Belgrade that were destroyed. Then you can see here key army level and corps level in the military command and control installations and headquarters that have been destroyed. The First Army, the Special Unit Corps, an airborne unit in Nis; Third Army headquarters, which is controlling operations in Kosovo; and, of course, the air defense headquarters and command posts have been attacked as well.

In addition to these, a key part of running the apparatus are their intelligence facilities and their communications facilities. We continue to attack those with fair, I think a good degree of effectiveness. We haven't destroyed all of them. They still have intelligence capability, clearly. They still have communications capability. But it is not as effective or as efficient as it once was, and we have reason to believe, based on multiple sources of information, that commanders and national command authority are having difficulty in rapidly and effectively commanding and controlling their forces.

So 27 communications facilities include broadcast facilities, radio relay facilities, telephone switching facilities, all of which are important to the long term sustainability of this system—they're important to the redundancy of it—and it is increasingly getting to where in various areas of the country we believe they are impaired and down to a smaller number of strands by which they can effectively command and control.

The radio and relay facilities which have been destroyed, by the way, in many cases are dual use. They include microwaves which communicate military command and control information; civilian microwaves which the military uses both as backup and sometimes primary to their communications; and on the same towers often radio and television relays where the stuff that may have been broadcast from the socialist party headquarters is relayed to various parts of the country, which we know now that some parts of the country don't have reliable television service, for example up in Novi Sad is one area in particular.

The British reported on April 23 that,

... the Yugoslav telecommunications network, supporting military operations, has been severely disrupted, degrading the command and control of operations in Kosovo. In some instances the same telecommunications sites serve both civilian as well as military networks and our attacks have therefore had some impact on civilian users. However, we are not targeting sites which are used solely for civilian purposes.

General Clark warned on April 27 that,

Essentially what we found is it is a very hardened and redundant command and control communications system. It starts with cable, it uses commercial telephone, it uses military cable, it uses fiber optic cable, it uses a high frequency radio communication, it uses microwave communication and everything can be interconnected. There are literally dozens, more than 100 radio relay sites around the country, and so everything is wired in through dual use. Most of the commercial system serves the military and the military system can be put to use for the commercial system, so there seems to be no distinction other than a few private radio stations which were put up over the last decade.

What we have found is that we have provided moderate to severe damage on this system, they are having trouble communicating, they are having trouble getting the message out. They are working through this and trying to pull together information systems, but it is difficult. The television of course has been a key instrument of his military command and control and his way of mobilizing resources has been significantly degraded and disrupted across Yugoslavia through strikes against the radio relay network.

NATO provided detailed damage assessment and targeting maps as part of this briefing on April 27. The summary damage assessment was low to moderate damage. The detailed target maps showed 35 radio relay centers, and that 5 had little damage, 16 had moderate damage and 14 had severe damage. It also showed that NATO had struck at 36 telecommunications relay targets, but did not provide a damage assessment. The US reported somewhat different targeting figures that same day, showing the NATO had now hit nine national command authority and 28 radio relay/radio communications stations targets. The US did not assess damage to these targets.

At the end of the campaign on June 10, the Department of Defense reported that Serbian national C^3 operational capability was in a degraded status, with moderate functional damage to over 30% of military and civilian RADREL networks. The Department also reported that the Serbian propaganda machine was severely degraded with 45% of TV broadcast capability non-functional and radio broadcasts limited to urban areas. Both the Serb Socialist Party Headquarters and the Presidential Residences, which were being used as alternate command posts, sustained severe damage. This assessment is summarized in Figure 27.

Once again, there is no way to measure what this aspect of the bombing campaign really did. The strikes on Serbian command, control, and communications have to have had a significant cumulative effect. Nevertheless, there were serious problems in attacking the Serbian command, control and communications systems. Many were relatively easy to repair. Many were highly redundant, and

Figure 27
NATO Damage Claims Relating to Serbian Air Force Capabilities

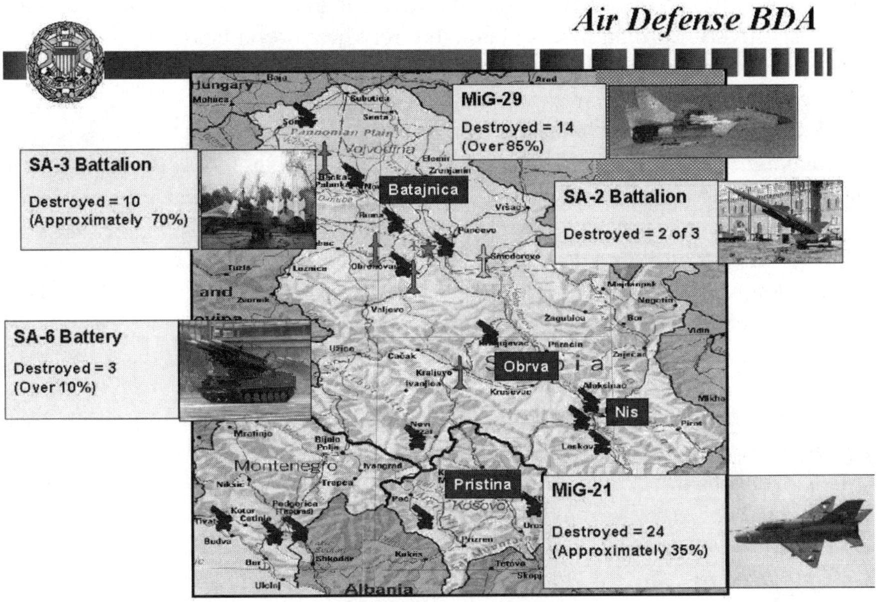
Air Defense BDA
MiG-29
Destroyed = 14
(Over 85%)
SA-3 Battalion
Destroyed = 10
(Approximately 70%)
Batajnica
SA-2 Battalion
Destroyed = 2 of 3
SA-6 Battery
Destroyed = 3
(Over 10%)
Obrva
Nis
Pristina
MiG-21
Destroyed = 24
(Approximately 35%)
Hungary
Vojvodina
Montenegro
Kosovo
Albania

Source: Adapted from the Department of Defense press briefing for June 10, 1999.

Serbia made extensive use of multiple cables and buried lines and optical fiber systems. Serbia seems to have found many rapid "work-arounds" which seem to have produced only highly uncertain results.

NATO's summary damage assessment as of May 6 was limited to a vague statement that, "NATO is progressively destroying Serb communications capabilities also." Many NATO strikes against fixed targets seem to have hit empty or nearly empty buildings, although Serbia does seem to have had key personnel and equipment in others. NATO said during its press briefing on April 17 and 18 that Serbia did not need the advanced communications facilities in its headquarters buildings for the kind of war it was fighting. Furthermore, the NATO and Department of Defense press briefings continued to confirm the fact that destroying some facilities in Kosovo has already led the military and police to drive out even more Kosovars and use their facilities as headquarters. None of the various postwar reports on the lessons of the conflict provide any discussion or insights into these issues.

NATO's air attacks certainly had to have had some effect in a ground war , but it might have been limited because of the other limitations on Serbian warfighting capabilities. Serbia would almost certainly have been unable to conduct joint land/ air and missile warfare or effectively use its integrated air defense system sensors and command and control system. This would have to have had an impact on Serbian war fighting but Yugoslav strategy and doctrine accepted the early loss of such capabilities in the event of a Soviet invasion and Serbia has continued such planning efforts. Serbian forces planned to rely heavily on land-lines and human intelligence, and any maneuvers and deployments would have had to be carefully planned to avoid NATO air attacks in any case.

Most military forces simply do not rely on the intensity and consistency of communications required by the US. There is also little tangible evidence that the near paranoiac desire for "control" exhibited by authoritarian regimes really requires efficient, dense, and continuous communications. Iraq and Serbia both seem to have found that discipline, delegation, and repression are more than adequate substitutes for communications in exerting internal control and low-level and asymmetric operations.

Once again, this aspect of the NATO bombing effort seems to be a case where a standard category of strategic bombing was selected, and NATO proceeded to work through the numbers. This bombing must have had an effect. It may have had an important one. The evidence released to date, however, indicates that NATO relied largely on the theory of air and missile power, and had only tenuous data on how much it degraded the physical structure of given Serbian capabilities, and no clear idea of the strategic, political, or military effect.

More broadly, the US and the West need to reassess the vulnerability of potential enemies to both attacks on C^3I/BM systems and to "information warfare." It was Serbia, after all, that initiated "information warfare" by hacker attacks on NATO's web pages. In contrast, NATO's massive air attacks may have been wasteful, inefficient, and unfocused in terms of this particular enemy in this war.

As is the case with similar operations against Iraq in Desert Fox in December 1998, Serbia seems to have adapted its operations to the level of communications available, and it seems likely that many future wars will be equally asymmetric. In contrast, it is the US and NATO which rely on progressively higher communications densities operating under near sanctuary or invulnerable conditions. It may well be that the US needs a "B-team" analysis to challenge the conventional assumptions regarding this aspect of attacks on "C3" facilities and information warfare as well as the growth of potential US and Western vulnerabilities.

8

The Air and Missile War and Serbian Air and Land Force Targets

NATO did not face a major air or land threat from Serbia at the beginning of the air and missile campaign. The Yugoslav Republic had become something of a political fiction by the time the air and missile campaign began, and the loss of many members of the former Yugoslavia had left Serbia without the funds to modernize its forces or maintain them at high readiness. Swedish sources report that Serbian forces had not carried out any major exercises in the seven years preceding the war and had cut back sharply on the other aspects of training.

Nevertheless, Serbia remained a significant military power—at least in terms of force numbers. The Department of Defense estimated at the start of the air and missile campaign that the Serbian Air Forces had 240 combat aircraft, including MiG-21s and MiG-29s, and 48 attack helicopters. It estimated that Serbian anti-aircraft forces included 100 surface-to-air missiles: a mix of SA-2, SA-3, SA-6, SA-7, SA-9, SA-13, SA-14, and SA-16s, and that all of these missiles posed a significant threat to NATO air and missile power. Yugoslavia also had 1,850 air defense artillery pieces. Although not as effective as the missiles, NATO estimated that these systems were dangerous to NATO planes.[180]

NATO also estimated that Serbian ground forces totaled 114,000 active-duty soldiers and 1,400 artillery pieces. It estimated that Serbian mechanized forces had 1,270 tanks, including T-72s, T-74s, T-55s and M-84s and 825 armored fighting vehicles. It estimated that there were approximately 40,000 Serb troops in and around Kosovo equipped with tanks and APCs. The Serb forces around the Kosovo border were divided into deployed forces, garrison forces, and reserve forces. The deployed forces had about 96 tanks, and the garrison forces had around 30 tanks in garrison. There was a concentration of Serb troops along the border between Kosovo and Macedonia, by the former Yugoslav Republic of Macedonia. These forces had been building up for several weeks.[181]

NATO has claimed that it did significant damage to these forces by the end of the air and missile campaign. NATO estimated at the end of the campaign that it had destroyed or severely damaged 85% of Yugoslavia's MiG-29s, and 35% of its MiG-21s—24 of which were no longer available. It claimed that two of Serbia's three SA-2 battalions had been destroyed, 70% of its SA-3s, and three out of its 22 mobile SA-6 batteries. It also estimated that the air and missile campaign had destroyed up to 450 artillery and mortar pieces, about 220 armored personnel carriers, and up to around 120 tanks. It had destroyed 35% of the facilities of the Serbian 1st Army. NATO estimated that over 20% of the facilities of the 2nd Army were damaged or destroyed, although NATO reported this army was still able to reinforce Kosovo. Sixty percent of the facilities of the 3rd Army were damaged or destroyed and NATO estimated that their ability to sustain operation was significantly reduced. The overall ability of Serbian land forces to sustain high tempo combat operations was "reduced."

There is good reason to question some aspects of these estimates, although considerably more supporting data are available than for the strategic/interdiction bombing campaigns. NATO unquestionably was able to attack Serbian forces with some success, but there were reasons to question the reliability of NATO's estimates even when they were first issued, and they have been cast into increasing doubt since the Serbian withdrawal from Kosovo. In practice, the lessons of the air and missile war seem to be that NATO was not as effective as it claimed, and that air and missile power still faces significant problems in attacking any force that it's not forced to mass and fight in ways that expose its target base. There are also significant uncertainties surrounding NATO's targeting capability and ability to carry out accurate battle damage assessment.

INTEGRATED AIR DEFENSE SYSTEM (IADS) TARGET GROUPS

NATO gave high priority to attacks on the Serbian air force and Serbia's land-based air defenses at the start of the war. There is little doubt that NATO had considerable success. At the same time, NATO did a far better job of suppressing Serbian forces than destroying them and most of Serbia's best land-based air defenses survived the war.

The Yugoslavian Air Force

Serbia was not a major air and missile power. Its forces had severe funding, training, and readiness problems. While it had 240 combat aircraft, including MiG-29s and 48 attack helicopters, only a limited number of its combat aircraft had significant air-to-air combat capabilities. Serbia had the following major types of combat aircraft when the war started:

- 17–19 MiG-29 FULCRUM. A relatively modern Russian fighter. (The most modern aircraft in the Yugoslav inventory.)

- 64 MiG-21 FISHBED and 18 MIG-21R. A air defense fighter. Old, but still capable. (The Air Force had about 64 of these aircraft at the start of the war, plus 18 MiG-21R reconnaissance fighters. They included some relatively modern MiG-21 Bis aircraft.)

- 30 J-22 Orao. An indigenously designed fighter, ground attack aircraft. Slow and relatively unmaneuverable. (66 at start of war; current strength unknown.)

- 25 G-4 Super Galeb (advanced trainer and light attack aircraft, similar to the British Aerospace Hawk) and 50 Galebs (an older and less capable light attack aircraft).

- SA-342L Gazelle. (44 armed helicopters at start of the war. Plus 3 Mi-14, 3 Ka-25 and 2 Ka-28 armed ASW helicopters.)

- SA-341 (14), SA-341H (63), Mi-8 Hip-C (90) and Mi-17 Hip-H utility helicopters.

- Liaison helicopters. 32 UTVA-66 and 14 Partisan.

NATO Attacks on the Serbian Air Force During the Campaign

Given the size and quality of this force, it is not surprising that NATO had early success in defeating and suppressing the Serbian Air Force and quickly established air supremacy. The US reported as early as April 22 that NATO had destroyed 50 percent of Serbia's 15–17 MiG-29 frontline fighters, had severely degraded Serbia's ability to sustain its aircraft and surface-to-air missiles, and had hit hard at its command and control and sensor system. It said that NATO had destroyed a total of 16 MiG fighters of all types, and a total of 35 aircraft—including a number of the light fighter attack aircraft still being used in Kosovo. It said that the capability of the light fighter-ground-attack (FGA) aircraft was down 50 percent, but did not define what that meant. It reported that Serbia now lacked the capability to service and maintain its aircraft, and had lost many hardened shelters and airfield maintenance and fuel facilities.

Admiral Wilson summarized the impact of NATO attacks as follows on April 22,

We . . . continue to attack key facilities, key aim points at the airfields. It may be the primary airfields from which he operates his fighter aircraft, or it may be dispersal airfields from which he operates fighter or attack aircraft on a given day. By further damaging and degrading and destroying facilities at these airfields—fuel supplies, fueling points, maintenance hangars, hardened aircraft shelters and things like that—we can deny the Serbs the ability to conduct successful operations with their declining inventory of fighter aircraft.

. . . We have not destroyed any MiGs recently . . . Neither have we seen very much flight activity by MiGs. We've destroyed more than half of the MiG-29s and several MiG-21s as well. So the first line fighter aircraft inventory as well as some of the older fighters have been seriously damaged.

We've destroyed more than 35 other aircraft, and the most important ones in this regard are the ground attack aircraft that he uses to conduct operations against fixed targets or even fielded forces on the ground. So by destroying these aircraft, many of which were done at

Podgorica, at Nis and other fields, we have reduced by probably around 50 percent his airborne ability to conduct ground attack operations, and we think that that along with the MiGs is a significant reduction of his air capability.

I've already talked before—we are having, now have degraded the aircraft repair [capability] very, very severely. That really has been true since early in this overall bombing operation, and increasing damage to ammunition production is being, I think, seen in evidence we have of Yugoslavia reaching out to a number of sources to try to acquire more and different kinds of ammunition to be able to not only sustain their ability to fight, but also perhaps improve their ability to fight, and they're not having any success in that regard.

The British Ministry of Defense provided a similar picture in its summary estimate on April 23.

The Serb Air Force made several attempts to engage NATO aircraft in the early days of the air and missile campaign, but were unsuccessful. Indeed several of his more capable fighters, such as the MiG-29s, were shot down. Since then we have attacked 5 major airfields destroying hangars and support facilities. We cannot be sure precisely how many aircraft we have hit on the ground because some were in hangars or under cover. However all our evidence suggests that we have destroyed at least 7 MiG-29s, which is 50 percent of his most capable fighter force, 12 MiG-21s, 10 Super Galebs, which he used to support ground forces, and 9 MI9 helicopters.

The Serb Air Force is still flying, but to a very small extent. We have seen helicopters and aircraft occasionally operating over Kosovo at low level, probably in support of ground forces. Refugees have reported being attacked by Serb aircraft, but the Serb Air Force's freedom to operate, unobserved, is severely curtailed by NATO's extensive airborne early warning coverage of the area.

General Clark stated on April 27 that,

Essentially this air defense system is ineffective. When it is turned on, when it attempts to target us, it is destroyed, so what he has tried to do is conserve it by using it sparingly and when he uses it we strike back and take it out. We reckon we are at 70+ aircraft destroyed, about 40 percent of his SA3 battalions, one-quarter of his SA 6 batteries. Whatever is coming up and engaging is taken out and increasingly we are finding these assets before they can engage us.

NATO provided detailed damage assessment and targeting maps on April 27. The summary assessment was low to moderate damage. The detailed target maps showed that 4 airfields had had significant strikes, but did not assess damage.

The British Ministry of Defense reported on May 5 that,

Over 80 Serb combat and other military aircraft have been destroyed out of an initial total of 450, they have lost a quarter of their critical aircraft types, the MiG-29s and MiG-21s; of the MiG-29 force, we believe we destroyed 50 percent. Nine of their 17 military airfields have been damaged, some severely; 32 road and rail bridges have been damaged or destroyed. We have attacked and significantly damaged a fifth of all major ammunition storage sites, 12 out of 57. The capability of Serbian military and paramilitary forces is gradually being weakened and the morale of the VJ and the MUP will have been affected by the seeming impunity with which NATO aircraft can operate over Serbia and Kosovo, the accuracy of their attacks and the intelligence base from which attacks are conducted. There have been more than 15,000 sorties flown, 5,000 of which have delivered ordnance, NATO has lost just two aircraft over Serbia.

NATO reported on May 6 and 7 that Serbia had now lost 50 percent of its 19 Mig-29s. General Shelton, the Chairman of the US Joint Chiefs, stated on May 12 that, "As you know, he's lost nearly all of his front line MiG-29 fighters and nearly 20% of his ground attack aircraft." He also reported that Serbia had lost one more MiG-29 and five more MiG-21s. The next day, NATO reported that it had destroyed five more aircraft in the open: one more MiG-21 and four more Super Galebs.

Major General Wald of the US reported the following Serbian losses on May 13 (Day 50):

I think they had 14 MiG-29s, and I think they had something like 70-something MiG-21s, and they had probably more than that of Galebs. I'm not sure of the number. He probably had a few hundred. But I think he's already had probably nearly 100 destroyed. Then his military capability to maintain his aircraft is obviously destroyed. He can't sustain, repair his aircraft. So he probably has a lot of aircraft that are sitting there no-flyable. And there are other aircraft that we haven't counted, because they've been under bunkers or in tunnels. So the number is very difficult. But over time as this goes on, the number eventually will end up being zero that are flyable, if that's what he wants.

Questioner: Do you think there are any MiG-29s left at this point?

Major General Wald: I think there are probably three or so left. What condition they're in, I don't know. They may not be flyable because he's probably used some of the parts for them. He could fly one, I don't know.

Questioner: Do you know how many MiG-21s?

Major General Wald: How many MiG-21s that he has left? I don't know the exact number. We've destroyed dozens of them. I think a couple of dozen, something like that.

NATO Claims at the End of the Campaign and Possible Lessons

At the end of the campaign on June 10, the Department of Defense reported that 85% of Serbian front-line fighters, MiG-29s, were destroyed or severely damaged beyond use. MiG-21 fighters had been reduced by 24 planes, nearly 35% of the total force. These results are summarized in Figure 28.

There is no question that NATO won air dominance, decisively defeated the MiG-29s in Serbian hands in air-to-air combat, and reduced any operations by

Figure 28
NATO Damage Claims Relating to Serbian Land-Based Air Defenses

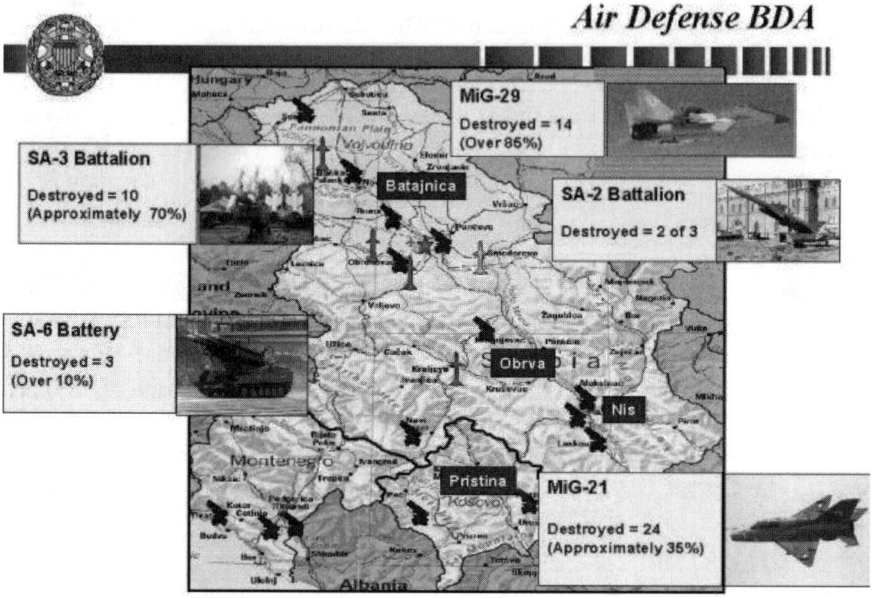
Air Defense BDA
MiG-29
Destroyed = 14
(Over 85%)
SA-3 Battalion
Destroyed = 10
(Approximately 70%)
Batajnica
SA-2 Battalion
Destroyed = 2 of 3
SA-6 Battery
Destroyed = 3
(Over 10%)
Obrva
Nis
Montenegro
Pristina
Kosovo
MiG-21
Destroyed = 24
(Approximately 35%)
Albania

Source: Adapted from the Department of Defense press briefing for June 10, 1999.

Serbian light attack aircraft to vestigial levels. They became more of an annoyance than an effective tool for ethnic cleansing. NATO did far less well in destroying Serbian attack helicopters and heliborne mobility, however, and in finding and destroying Serbia's light attack aircraft. Serbian did retain a substantial ride out capability and much of the Serbian air force survived.

The lesson seems to be that modern air and missile power can rapidly defeat an enemy in the air, suppress enemy air activity, and win a high degree of freedom of action. It cannot, however, locate and destroy a passive, well-dispersed, and well-sheltered, enemy air forces quickly and effectively. The decades old problem of attacking air bases, destroying runways, destroying hardened or soft shelters and facilities, and minimizing wasted strikes on decoys is as real as ever, and enemy forces can often exploit relatively simple asymmetric warfare techniques to limit the impact of improvements in targeting and strike power.

The US and NATO do, however, need to carefully examine two aspects of this campaign, the Gulf War, and attacks on Iraqi oil facilities since the Gulf War.

- *First, what are the trade-offs between attacks on enemy aircraft and air facilities designed to suppress versus destroy? Is there some way to improve the planning and doctrine for such bombing?*

- *Second, what improvements are needed in air power to rapidly and reliably destroy sheltered and dispersed air forces on the ground? Are such improvements credible?*

The Yugoslavian Land-Based Air Defense System

NATO was much less successful in dealing with the land-based air defense threat, and its problems raise more important lessons regarding future wars. It is not clear how well prepared NATO was to deal with Serbian land-based air defenses when the war began. Informal discussions with US, British, and NATO sources indicate that NATO had not prepared to launch the kind of air defense suppression campaign needed for full-scale war, and had counted on stealth, cruise missiles, and a limited number of suppression activities to allow it to fly the limited number of strikes it then felt would force Serbia to concede. NATO was not ready to perform the electronic warfare missions. The US was forced to pull in EA-6B electronic warfare aircraft from all over the world after the fighting began and then had to provide US and European aircraft with electronic warfare (EW) escorts for the rest of the war. As a result, it took several weeks to build-up the kind of attack and air defense suppression capabilities NATO needed to fight an efficient air and missile war.

The Size and Nature of Serbian Forces

These same sources indicate that NATO was not fully prepared for asymmetric warfare, and that air planners assumed that Serbia would aggressively employ its air defenses and use its radars at a high level of activity—making major land-based air defenses easy to target. The reasons behind this lack of preparation have already been touched upon, and NATO faced a difficult set of targets.

The former Yugoslavia had long practiced tactics based on wars of attrition and "riding out" a Soviet-Warsaw Pact attack by not actively employing air defense assets. Serbia had had ample time to learn the lessons of the Gulf War, and had good access to Iraq's experience during the post–Gulf War period—including the lessons of Desert Fox.

While Serbia did not have a modern air defense system, or extensive modern assets, it did have large numbers of assets that it could disperse efficiently and which were extremely difficult to target unless they emitted radar signals long enough to be targeted by anti radiation missiles. These assets included

- *Strategic Systems.* SA-2 (S-75 Dvina or Guideline), SA-3 (Perchora-M or Goa) and SA-6 (2K12 Kvadrat or Gainful) surface-to-air missiles (SAMs). The first two are old, but have a high ceiling. The latter is a very effective medium level missile. It has already been used in anger in Bosnia and was the weapon responsible for shooting down USAF Capt. Scott O'Grady's F-16 in 1995. (Yugoslavia had eight surface-to-air battalions at the start of the war with 24 SA-2 fire units, 16 SA-3 fire units, and 60–80 SA-6 tracked launch vehicles.)

- *Tactical Systems.* 113–130 SA-9 (9K31) on wheeled launchers and 17 SA-13s (Strela 10 Gopher) on tracked launchers. Essentially the same missile; the first is mounted on a wheeled chassis, the second on a tracked chassis. Both can be effective systems.

- *Man Portable Systems.* 850 systems, including 500 Strela 2M/ASA-7, 230 9K310 SA-16 and SA-18. These are single shot shoulder launched missiles similar to the US Stinger and the UK Blowpipe/Javelin. The SA-16s and 18s are the latest and most capable.

- *Air Defense Guns.* These guns are found in both the army and air force. The air force has 15 air defense artillery regiments. There were 1,850 guns when the air and missile war began. They include 20-mm towed and self-propelled guns, 266 ZSU-30–2 30 mm towed and self-propelled guns, and 54 ZSU-57–2 self-propelled guns. The numbers by type are unknown. One estimate includes 350 M53/59 30 mm; 60 M55 A2 Triple 20 mm, 75 X M55 A3 Triple 20 MM, 150 M55 A4 B1 Triple 20 mm; and 80 M75 20 mm.

Serbia's longer-range radars and central command and control facilities were seriously degraded and driven off-line during the war, but many of its air defense weapons remained intact, and systems like the SA-6 had an optical guidance system and self-homing missiles. As a result, most of the air defense assets Serbia had at the start of the war survived, with the possible exception.

NATO's Wartime Claims

The US reported on April 22 that it had destroyed 16 main radar units, 30% of the key communications nodes and main radars for the Serb SA-3 forces, and 10–15% of the tactical radars for its mobile, tracked SA-6 radars. Admiral Wilson said the same day that,

We've talked a lot about the integrated air defense system, the IADS. I don't think up until now I've shown a chart such as this for the IADS, but I wanted to make a few points about it.

You can see on the top there that we believe through the combination of attacks, destruction, and suppression that we have created a situation where we have air superiority over whatever part of the country we need to be operating in to conduct our strike operations.

We are also adding to the total, so to speak, in terms of the actual destruction of his air defense system. You always are asking about numbers and percentages. In this particular case, numbers and percentages are not the relevant factor. The relevant factor is can you create the condition that allows successful strike operations. We are doing that.

It's been a month now, and we continue to attack the kind of targets that we need to attack without suffering losses that would be of concern.

Now as we suppress and attack, we take the opportunity where we have it to also destroy. You can see in this chain of command chart right here shown in red the kind of facilities that we have not only suppressed, but have damaged or destroyed in the process of this campaign against the integrated air defense system.

They include, for example 16 early warning radars, a relatively small percentage of the total number of radars that the Serb air defense system has in its physical inventory, but we may be able to get on any given day or night an important radar node and attack it and destroy it because of the way it's being used and where it is being used in support of their air defense operations against our strikes.

So in addition to jamming the early warning radars, we believe that 16 have been severely damaged or destroyed and are no longer available for use.

We will continue this campaign of suppression, but also where we can to attack things like early warning radars that support their air defense systems.

Here you can see some percentages assigned to the SA-3 and the SA-6 force. We think we've physically destroyed key nodes of about 30 percent of his SA-3 batteries—the key node is normally the radar, the radar which is used to potentially guide, acquire the aircraft and guide the missile to a successful engagement—and 10 to 15 percent of the more mobile SA-6 force, which is a tactical surface-to-air missile, but serves a relatively strategic use in Yugoslavia and in Serbia.

Now the impact of the destruction of these is further leveraged by the significant damage which has been done to the surface-to-air missile support facilities, a number of which are shown on the map there. SAM support facilities are also shown with little missiles. Several of those have been struck and restruck and damaged to the point where we think the ability to repair and sustain the missile force for the long term is seriously degraded or severely degraded.

The British Ministry of Defense reported on April 23 that,

The air and missile campaign continues to have an incremental impact on the overall Serb military capability. We are degrading his integrated air defense system and we have had significant success against fixed air defense systems, damaging some 10 surface to air missile sites and their associated radars and 4 surface to air missile support facilities. Inevitably the mobile systems such as SA-3 and SA-6 have not suffered as much, but the need to move them frequently to avoid detection has severely reduced their effectiveness. Against NATO's suppression of air defense capability, the Serbs hesitate to use their radars. However, Air Forces operating over Serbia and Kosovo are conscious that there are many surface to air missiles which remain a threat, especially to aircraft operating at low level.

General Clark drew somewhat similar conclusions on April 27,

Essentially this air defense system is ineffective. When it is turned on, when it attempts to target us, it is destroyed, so what he has tried to do is conserve it by using it sparingly and when he uses it we strike back and take it out. We reckon we are at 70+ aircraft destroyed, about 40 percent of his SA3 battalions, one-quarter of his SA6 batteries. Whatever is coming up and engaging is taken out and increasingly we are finding these assets before they can engage us.

In practice, however, NATO often claimed to be destroying surface-based air defense assets it had only suppressed. This was reflected in the number of strikes and restrikes NATO continued to dedicated to air defense suppression. NATO nearly doubled the number of integrated air defense target groups it hit during the fourth week of the war, rising from 30 to 58. At its briefing on the 18, NATO again claimed that it had achieved a reasonable degree of damage to the integrated system, and that it had badly damaged the central radar and command and control system.

NATO provided detailed damage assessment and targeting maps on April 27. The summary assessment was low to moderate damage. The detailed target maps showed that 26 land-based air defense sites had been struck, and that 6 had little damage, 10 had moderate damage and 10 had severe damage. General Shelton, the Chairman of the US Joint Chiefs, stated on May 12 that, "After seven full weeks of air strikes . . . Yugoslavia's integrated air defense system, though it remains a threat to our pilots and to our air crews, has been hit hard. And more than half of Milosevic's modern surface to air missile radars have been damaged or destroyed."

Damage Assessments from May to the End of the Conflict

The problem with these damage assessments—as NATO fully admitted at the time—was that Serbia continued to fire anti-aircraft guns, manportable surface-to-air missiles, and optically-guided SA-6s against NATO aircraft. NATO briefings on April 29 made it clear that NATO strike aircraft had scarcely achieved secure freedom of action, particularly for the more vulnerable systems like the A-10 and AH-64.

General Wald reinforced these points in the Department of Defense briefing on May 6.

Questioner: General, we're getting reports of a lot of MANPADs being fired. Any more of our planes hit?

Major General Wald: I haven't heard of any aircraft over the last 24 hours being attacked, but yes, they are firing a lot of MANPADs, which is not unusual. And it's probably a good point, because a MANPAD can, as we know, probably from that A-10 the other day, got hit by it, we only talk about the larger SAMs. They're just as lethal in the right area, so they do fire a lot of MANPADs at us. Not at us. At them.

Questioner: I'm sorry if I missed this, but April 18th a Predator went down, (inaudible). Do you guys know what the cause of that was?

Major General Wald: I don't know if it was mechanical or not. I don't know.

At the end of the campaign on June 10, the Department of Defense reported that two Serbia's three SA-2 battalions had been destroyed, 70% of its SA-3s, and three out of its 22 mobile SA-6 batteries. These claims, however, are subject to all of the same problems in battle damage assessment described earlier, and are a further illustration of the fact that targeting and battle damage assessment data remain an art form that will require radical improvement to implement some of the more ambitious concepts of C⁴I/battle management/strategic reconnaissance used in setting goals for the "revolution in military affairs."

It simply is not clear how many major pieces of equipment Serbia had in inventory at the start of the war, how valid damage assessment claims are in any given case, and what it means to talk about percentages of damage. There seems to be considerable confusion between destroying radars and suppressing radar activity, and between destroying a major component of an air defense unit like a radar, launcher, or command vehicle and destroying the entire unit. It is also striking that NATO could not find and destroy most systems that were mobile and which did not actively use their radars and that the SA-6—the only quasi-modern and effective system in Serbian inventory—largely survived the war.

NATO was only able to increasingly suppress Serbian air defenses and not destroy them. Major General Chuck Wald, J-5, gave the following summary of Serbian air defense activity to date at the US Department of Defense briefing on June 2, which is summarized in Figure 28.

On this chart I'll show you the SAMs that we have observed, they have observed being fired at them over the last couple of months. Over 266 SA-6s, 175 SA-3s, 106 manned portables, they've observed, and a lot of times you don't see those, so these are all observed. 126 unidentified, for a total of almost 700. This is just a picture of the AAA over Belgrade. They continue to fire AAA all the time, so it hasn't stopped. I think last night they had five or six SAM shots that they observed, so they continue to shoot at the aircraft that are flying over both Kosovo and the FRY.

Major General Wald provided further insights about the survival of Serbia's equipment during the Department of Defense briefing on May 4, when he was asked how many land-based air defense systems might be in reserve, or were "riding out" the war:

That's a good point, because some of these missiles probably were in storage. We don't know. We know that he had a lot of SAMs, in the thousands. The problem is his SAM radars and control equipment [are] being destroyed, and a big chunk of his SA-3s and SA-6s have been hit. The SA-6s, he had more of those. SA-3s, not as many. That's being taken down significantly . . . So his ability to shoot is still there. As long as he's got something he can put it on, he can shoot it ballistically if he wants to, but his ability to have an integrated command and control capability to do that has been degraded, and that's why we'll continue to fly more and more sorties and different types of aircraft . . . I don't see him trying to conserve his missiles per se, but once again, I think if you go back and look over the last few days, there have been quite a few SAMs shot. There were some last night, not as many as the night before. But then again, last night he tried to get some aircraft airborne. When he doesn't shoot a lot of SAMs, in the past—at least the first couple of days he tried to fly with his aircraft, then he quit after about two or three days when he didn't have much success.

Damage Assessment after the War and the Impact of Serbian Air Defenses in Forcing NATO to Fly at Higher Altitudes

There was no agreement after the war among senior US air planners that NATO had inflicted critical damage on the Serbian system. US Navy Admiral James Ellis,

Figure 29
NATO Damage Claims Relating to Serbian Ground Forces

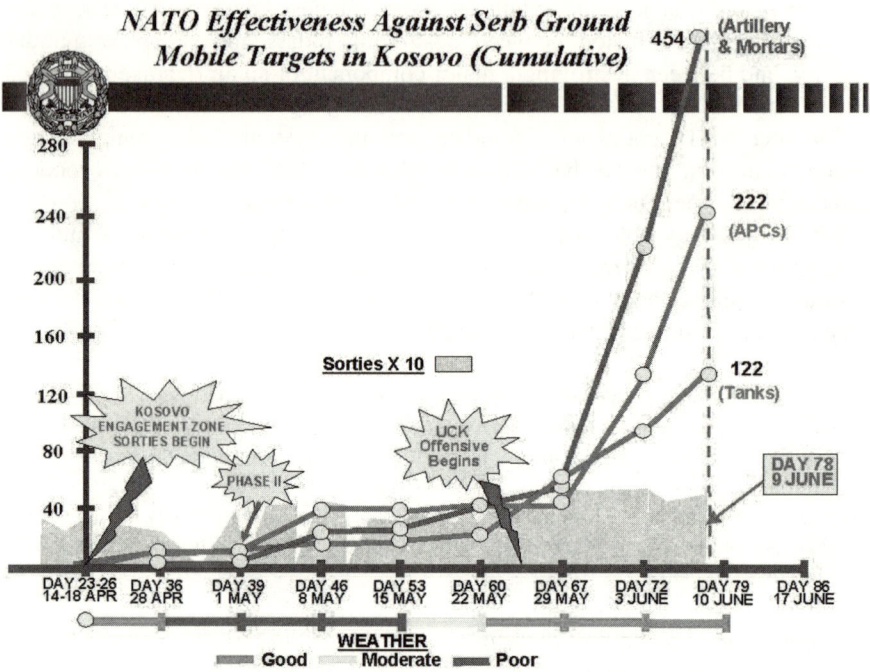

Source: Adapted from the Department of Defense press briefing for June 10, 1999.

the commander-in-chief of Allied Forces Southern Europe warned after the war that, "After 78 days of hard campaigning, we effected little degradation on a modern IADS system." US Air Force General John Jumper, the head of US Air Forces in Europe, disagreed and stated that, "We did take down a large percentage of the SA-6s (radars)." He also said, however, that, "That's not to say that Milosevic doesn't have missiles to shoot. He always has had a lot of missiles, but he has a lot fewer radars to use. In the end, the result was that we had enough air superiority to go anywhere in the country and drops bombs on any target we wanted to drop bombs on. To me, that's pretty effective."[182]

However, the US Department of Defense report issued on the lessons of the war in January 2000 draws a different conclusion. It notes that Serbia was able to force NATO to fly and strike at relatively high altitudes during most of the air and missile campaign, compounding the problems of target identification, weather, and collateral damage. It also makes it clear that being able to fly anywhere and drop bombs was not the same as being able to operate freely and effectively—although NATO steadily improved its air defense suppression campaign by the third week of the war, and caused Serbia substantial damage.[183]

While the threat posed by Serbia's offensive air capability was eliminated in the first few days of the conflict, reducing Serbian defensive capabilities did not proceed as quickly. Even before the campaign began, the Serbs began dispersing major elements of their integrated air defense system and then adeptly employed them throughout the conflict. While NATO plans called for the systematic degradation and destruction of these integrated air defenses, this proved problematic due to the tactics the Serbs adopted.

The Serbs chose to conserve their air defenses, while attempting to down NATO aircraft as targets of opportunity. Full effectiveness of an air defense suppression operation in future conflicts will depend on how the enemy chooses to employ its systems as well as on the capability of allied forces to attack across all aspects of the enemy's integrated air defense system.

One way to measure the severity of the Yugoslav air defense system that NATO encountered during Operation Allied Force is to compare it with the Iraqi air defenses that the Allied Coalition confronted during the 1991 Persian Gulf War. During Allied Force, NATO aircraft flew approximately one-third the number of combat sorties (21,000) that were flown by coalition aircraft during Operation Desert Storm (69,000). However, the number of radar-guided surface-to-air missiles launched by the Serbs during Allied Force was almost the same as the number launched by the Iraqis during Desert Storm. As a consequence, the average aircrew participating in Operation Allied Force experienced a missile-launch rate three times that encountered by the average coalition aircrew during Desert Storm. Despite the larger number of radar-guided surface-to-air missiles fired at NATO aircraft flying over Serbia and Kosovo, the Yugoslavs achieved a much lower success rate than did the Iraqis. Based on the ratio of combat losses to sorties, NATO aircrews participating in Operation Allied Force were six times less likely to be shot down than were coalition aircrews engaged in Operation Desert Storm. Overall, although Yugoslavia's integrated air defense system was very active against NATO aircraft during Operation Allied Force, NATO employment tactics rendered that system largely ineffective.

NATO forces rapidly achieved air supremacy in the theater by destroying Serb interceptor aircraft in the air and on the ground and by destroying or damaging their airbases. Rather than expend sorties prosecuting the large quantities of anti-aircraft artillery and man-portable missile threats, NATO commanders chose to operate their aircraft at altitudes above the effective reach of these systems. However, reducing the Serb defensive radar-guided surface-to-air missile systems that are effective against aircraft flying at higher altitudes proved more difficult than anticipated as a result of the tactics employed by the Serbs. By conserving their systems and attempting to down NATO aircraft as targets of opportunity, they gave up many of the advantages of a connected and continuously operating system in order to achieve tactical surprise in a few instances.

Within Kosovo, individual longer-range systems emerged to fire at our aircraft in an unpredictable fashion. Shorter-range Serbian antiaircraft artillery and man-portable air defense systems were plentiful, complicating NATO's efforts to defeat them. Rather than shift the weight of effort aimed against these systems, NATO commanders chose to operate at altitudes beyond which most Serbian anti-aircraft systems could be employed effectively. The tradeoff of flying at higher altitudes to mitigate risk made weather conditions such as cloud layers and visibility more of a factor in daily execution. Additional factors complicating these critical tasks were collateral damage considerations and the absence of any land-component forward air controllers to assist in locating enemy forces. Engagement altitudes for both airborne forward air controllers and striking assets were lowered as Operation

Allied Force progressed. However, mobile anti-aircraft guns and man-portable missiles posed a viable threat throughout the conflict.

Similarly, General Jumper provided a somewhat more frank description of the problem in later testimony to Congress on the Lessons of the War.[184]

Surface-to-air missiles (SAMs) posed the only credible threat—Yugoslav SAM operators fired over 700 radar guided SA-3 and SA-6 missiles at allied airmen. Our F-16CJ Wild Weasel pilots and joint U.S. Navy-Air Force EA-6B electronic jamming crews showed tremendous courage when attacking Serbian sites head-on, day after day. Our preliminary assessment is that we damaged or destroyed 40 percent of the sites. The difficulty in striking these missile sites was magnified by two Yugoslav actions. First, they frequently moved their missile batteries to stymie our attempts to bomb them. Second, they kept their tracking radars dormant and activated them only briefly when allied aircraft were nearby. Our tactics and equipment assume an aggressive enemy will engage us—we had to improvise new procedures to rapidly strike these elusive targets after identification. Our most successful innovation came in rapid targeting.

Suppression versus Destruction

One key lesson that was sometimes lost during the war, was also that it was the suppression of Serbian ground-based air defense activity that counted and not how much of Serbia's resources were destroyed. This point too is much clearer in the later reporting on the lessons of the war that it was during NATO's briefings on the daily "body count" of Serbian equipment that NATO had destroyed. The Department of Defense report after the war put considerably more emphasis on suppression than destruction.[185]

Several support assets were used to protect NATO strike aircraft during Operation Allied Force. These included air superiority aircraft supported by airborne warning and control (AWACS) to protect NATO strike aircraft from attacks by Serbian interceptors. These aircraft orbits also defended against air attacks by Serbian aircraft into neighboring countries friendly to the alliance effort. In addition, EA-6B and EC-130H electronic warfare aircraft and F-16CJ air-defense-suppression aircraft were used to protect NATO aircraft from attack by Serbian air defenses. Throughout the campaign, air defense and suppression aircraft flew thousands of sorties to ensure the safety of the strike assets.

EA-6B aircraft were absolutely important to the air operation. The EA-6B is the only U.S. electronic-attack aircraft able to use electronic jamming to suppress enemy air defenses Consequently, EA-6Bs are in high demand and are one of the Low Density/High Demand assets established in the Global Military Force Policy. At the same time that EA-6Bs were assigned to support Operation Allied Force, other EA-6Bswere providing support for Operations Southern Watch and Northern Watch over Iraq. To aid in the recovery of these important assets, an EA-6B reconstitution plan has been adopted in accordance with Global Military Force Policy. Our intent is to maximize EA-6B utility and effectiveness while returning these units to personnel and operating tempo guidelines.

While the initial plans developed by NATO for the suppression of enemy air defense had to evolve in response to Serbian actions, the results emphasize the importance holding the key nodes of the enemy's air defense system at risk and effectively employing those assets that are available. NATO used a combination of active support jamming and launch of High-Speed Anti-Radiation Missiles (HARMs) from a variety of aircraft to provide air-defense-suppression support for strike aircraft. In addition, NATO aggressively employed a variety of precision-guided munitions and bombs to destroy elements of the Yugoslav air defense system. Even though NATO forces had difficulty targeting the Serb defensive systems, the Serbs had minimal success downing NATO aircraft. Indeed, the allied air operation was sustained and, in fact, expanded greatly despite the presence of the remaining Serbian air-defense systems. NATO succeeded because we maintained pressure on their defenses, forcing the Serbs to keep their systems hidden under most circumstances and to use defensive tactics that limited their systems' effectiveness. We increased the tempo of operations in our air-defense suppression forces to provide the maximum protection to our forces. NATO also adapted its concepts of operation to sustain an increasing pace of strike operations without compromising our concern for minimizing casualties and collateral damage.

It is not clear just how many resources NATO devoted to this effort. The total number of sorties flown per day varied from just over 200 per day at the beginning of Operation Allied Force to over 1,000 per day by the end of the conflict, and NATO had to fly the largest percentage of air defense suppression when it most needed to by able to fly strike/attack sorties. The data NATO has made public, however, do not allow outside analysts to calculate just how much effort went into air suppression by day versus attacks on Serbian targets.

The US data on exactly how many air defense suppression sorties NATO flew are poorly reported and seemingly contradictory. The US reporting in the lessons of the war report issued in January 2000 states that NATO provided effective air protection for over 38,000 sorties throughout the course of the conflict. It also says that roughly 12,200 of these sorties were strike and air defense suppression sorties (a little under one third) that were flown over the area where Serbian air defenses were present. This total roughly agrees with the information in other sources, although a figure in the same report (Figure 14) indicates that NATO flew almost exactly 14,000 strike and air defense suppression sorties.

The US report then goes on to say that:

air superiority fighters continued to provide almost continuous combat air patrols over the course of the conflict to ensure that no Serbian interceptor aircraft could respond to allied attacks or take offensive action against allied bases or personnel. U.S. pilots shot down 5 of the 6 Serbian fighters that were destroyed in air combat operations; strike missions accounted for roughly 100 Serbian aircraft that were destroyed on the ground. the total number of combat air patrol and other air defense sorties approached 3,600 by the end of the war. The lack of an airborne threat to NATO forces provided a significant advantage to allied freedom of operation throughout the conflict.

The problem lies the fact that this total implies that about 30% of all actual combat sorties were flown in combat air patrol or CAP missions, but it does not indicate whether this total also includes land-based air defense suppression missions. As a result, it is impossible to estimate just how demanding the overall CAP and air defense suppression effort really was.[186]

The Problem of Survivability

It is difficult to predict how an even more sustained, intense NATO bombing campaign might have affected the survival of Serbian land-based air defense missiles and launchers. Much would have depended on whether Serbia quickly expended its assets or kept large amounts in reserve for a land campaign. During the air and missile campaign in Kosovo, Serbia fired its systems at relatively low rates and took only limited incremental losses. If Serbia persisted in this trend, it could probably have continued to harass NATO aircraft, and restrict their ability to fly at low altitudes and to take the time over target to deliver their munitions most effectively. It would, however, have had only limited impact on NATO aircraft with advanced avionics and long-range precision guided weapons delivery capability and steadily less impact as the weather cleared. The main effect would have been on low, slow fliers like the A-10 and AH-64 and even this effect would probably have been limited.

Serbia might also have pursued such a strategy in the event of a NATO ground attack. Such a strategy would have allowed VJ and MUP ground forces to conserve enough systems to provide limited low to medium altitude air defense of their movements and limit NATO interdiction and support operations in support of any NATO ground attack. However, if Serbia expended its assets more quickly to try to degrade an accelerating and steadily more effective NATO air and missile campaign, it would probably have rapidly lost many of its SA-6s and had had to expend many of its manportable missiles. It would have had little capability to defend any exposed or mass movements or limit NATO interdiction and support operations in support of NATO ground forces.

One key lesson is the continuing survivability of land-based air defenses, and the threat posed by "non-cooperative" air defenses that do not emit or deploy in ways that can be easily targeted. According to NATO figures, some 90% of Serbia's SA-6 assets survived the war, and could fire using pop-up radar and/or electro-optical techniques at the end of the war. Serbia retained substantial numbers of manned portable weapons, and had suffered only token losses of the its anti-aircraft assets. Another lesson, however, is that modern air and missile power can achieve very high levels of suppression, but cannot kill mobile systems or prevent land-based systems from riding out an extensive air and missile campaign.

At the same time, Kosovo showed that modern air and missile power cannot secure medium to low altitudes for air attacks even against a relatively weak force. It must rely heavily on stand-off attacks and unmanned intelligence, targeting, and damage assessment systems. As is discussed later, this raises serious questions as to how much Kosovo really says about an air war in which the opponent has more modern surface-to-air missiles, sensors, electronic warfare, and battle manage-ment systems. These are all questions that could be tested in the next conflict if an opponent has a larger and more modern airforce, surface-to-air missiles like the Russian S-300 and S-400 series, and matching combat electronics.

The US report on the lessons of the war does seem accurate in concluding the following:[187]

While NATO prevailed in delivering a punishing air offensive with virtually no loss to its forces, we must acknowledge some concerns for the future. Although among the most capable that the United States has faced in combat, the Yugoslav air defense systems do not represent the state of the art. Much more capable systems are currently available for sale in the international arms market. In the years ahead, the United States can expect to face adversaries armed with these state-of-the-art systems, and the Department of Defense needs to prepare for that possibility now. In particular, the Department needs to provide continuous, real-time, precision location of passive and active enemy systems to better enable U.S. forces to focus their efforts and achieve effective suppression and destruction of enemy weapon systems, allowing greater access over the target area for extended periods of time. Successful development of real-time sensor-to-shooter technology along with further enhancement of our offensive and defensive night vision systems would also improve effectiveness.

Operation Allied Force also served to re-emphasize the importance of a comprehensive air-defense suppression capability that is able to locate key defensive systems in real time and make use of limited assets in order to destroy them. While the combination of anti-radiation missiles and electronic attack did an effective job in suppressing enemy defenses in this case, our experience in Operation Allied Force indicated that how the enemy employs its air-defense systems will become increasingly important in the future. The effectiveness of U.S. air defense suppression efforts in future conflicts will depend on our ability to prosecute an unhindered, full-spectrum attack against an enemy's integrated air de-fense system.

As a result of Operation Allied Force, the Department will conduct a comprehensive study of joint capabilities to suppress enemy air defenses specifically to identify trade-offs in de facto versus destructive suppression. This study will examine improvements in destructive air defense suppression capabilities that will permit precision location of enemy systems even in a limited emissions environment as well as to identify systems and procedures allowing for time responsive attack against mobile or relocatable systems. Without such enhancements in capability and improvements in technology, the only other option is to increase that portion of the force structure capable of electronic combat operations to ensure continuous protection of all strike assets in future conflicts.

SERBIAN ARMY AND SPECIAL POLICE TARGET GROUPS

Halting the operations of Serbian land forces was the key tactical focus of the war. NATO had to minimize ethnic cleansing and create conditions where Serbia could not sustain the land occupation of Kosovo in order to win. While some US air planners felt this could be done by focused strategic strikes designed to put pressure on the Serbian leadership, NATO attempted to destroy Serbia's land forces in Kosovo in detail. The resulting campaign at best had mixed results.

The Size and Capability of Serbian Land Forces

The Serbian Army did not represent a massive force, but it did have three corps equivalents and a large amount of equipment. The Dayton agreement limited the number of active heavy weapons in the Armed Forces of Yugoslavia [VJ]. At the beginning of 1998, however, the land forces had at least 90,000 members and an active strength of at least 630 tanks (230 modern M-84s and the remaining 400 T-55s), 634 armored personnel carriers and infantry armored vehicles, 38 BPDM-2 armored reconnaissance vehicles, 474 105mm and 122mm guns and howitzers, 180 130mm guns, 75 122mm self-propelled howitzers, and 132 152mm and 155mm howitzers. Its total pool of equipment seems to have included 1,205 tanks, 656 other armored infantry fighting vehicles, 237 APCs, 83 self-propelled artillery weapons, 1,232 towed artillery weapons, and 267 multiple rocket launchers.[188]

The US Department of Defense estimated that Serbian ground forces totaled 114,000 active-duty soldiers and 1,400 artillery pieces. It estimated that Serbian mechanized forces had 1,270 tanks, including T-72s, T-74s, T-55s and M-84s and 825 armored fighting vehicles. It estimated that there were approximately 40,000 Serb troops in and around Kosovo equipped with tanks and APCs. The Serb forces around the Kosovo border were divided into deployed forces, garrison forces, and reserve forces. The deployed forces had about 96 tanks, and the garrison forces had around 30 tanks. There was a concentration of Serb troops along the border between Kosovo and Macedonia, by the former Yugoslav Republic of Macedonia. These forces had been building up for several weeks.[189]

The total inventory of equipment available to Serbia may have included the following major weapons that were available to Serbian forces before the NATO air and missile campaign began, and which might be involved in a ground option:[190]

- *M-84 tank.* An updated copy of the Russian T-72. An effective vehicle not normally deployed in Kosovo. (232–239 at start of war)

- *T-55 tank.* An old Russian tank that is the mainstay of the VJ armored forces. Late 1940's design but still reliable. (407–785 at start of war)

- *M-80 Armored Fighting Vehicle (AFV).* A copy of the Russian BMP-1 AFV. (517–568 at start of war)

- *BOV-M APC.* A wheeled reconnaissance vehicle. (50–237 at start of war)

- *MT-LB.* A tracked multi-purpose vehicle. (15 at start of war)

- *BTR-60 APC.* (6 at start of war) and M-60 APC. (6 at start of war)

- *BDRM-2 Recce Vehicle.* A wheeled reconnaissance vehicle. (40 at start of war)

- *BOV-3.* Self-propelled Anti-Aircraft Gun (SPAAG). A BOV-M chassis with a triple mounted 20mm cannon in a turret. Used in the ground role to good effect. (65–90 at start of war)

- *2SI.* A modern Soviet made 122mm self-propelled artillery weapon. (74–83 at start of war)

- *Towed artillery.* 60 76mm M48 mountain guns; 174–265 M-56, 15 M-18, and 54 M2A1 105 mm weapons; 90–168 M-38 and 310 D-30 122mm weapons; 132–206 M-46 and 132 D-20 130 mm weapons; 25 D-20 and 36–52 M-84 152 mm weapons; and 139 M-1 (60 M-59) and 6–24 M-65 155 mm weapons.

- *Multiple Rocket Launchers.* About 267 weapons before the war began. They include 107 mm , 72 (M-71) BM-21 122 mm, 48 Plamen 128 mm; 24 Oganj 128 mm 103 M-634 130 mm, 64 M-77 130 mm, and M-87 Orkan 262 mm weapons.

- *Mortars.* 1,665 82 mm; 1,303 120 mm.

- *Surface-to-Surface Missile Launchers.* 4–10 obsolete FROG rocket launchers.

- *Anti-Tank Guns.* 750 total. 24 M-42 76 mm; 94 M-48 76 mm; M-36B2 SP 90 mm; M-3 90 mm; 138 T-12 100 mm; MT-12 100mm.

- *Anti-Tank Guided Missiles.* 49–135 AT-3 (9M83) launchers, some on armored vehicles, 54 AT-4 (9K111) and 32 AT-5 (9P122) launchers.

- *Recoilless rifles.* 1,550 57 mm; 1,000 M-60P 82 mm; 650 M-65 105 mm.

- *PRAGA.* An armored truck with a twin mounted 30mm cannon. A SPAAG that has been used to great effect against houses and infantry. (total unknown at start of war)

- *Medium-Range Surface-to-Air Missile Systems.* SA-6 surface-to-air missiles which are effective medium level missiles. It has an electro-optical firing system so it does not have to use its radar. It has already been used in Bosnia and was the weapon responsible for shooting down USAF Capt. Scott O'Grady's F-16 in 1995. (Yugoslavia had eight surface-to-air battalions at the start of the war with 24 SA-2 fire units, 16 SA-3 fire units, and 40–60 SA-6 tracked launch vehicles.)

- *Tactical Surface-to-Air Missile Systems.* SA-9 and 13. Essentially the same missile; the first is mounted on a wheeled chassis, the second on a tracked chassis. Both are capable.

- *Manportable Surface-to-Air Missile Systems.* SA-7, 16 and 18. These are single shot shoulder launched missiles similar to the US Stinger and the UK Blowpipe/Javelin. The SA-16s and 18s are the latest and most capable.

- *Air Defense Guns.* These guns are held by both the army and air force. The air force has 15 air defense artillery regiments. There were 1,850 guns when the air and missile war began. They include 20mm towed and self-propelled guns, 30mm towed and self-propelled guns, and ZSU-57–2 self-propelled guns. The numbers by type are unknown.

- *J-22 Orao.* An indigenously designed fighter, ground attack aircraft. Slow and relatively unmaneuverable. (66 at start of war; current strength unknown)

- *G-4 Super Galeb.* Advanced trainer, similar to the British Aerospace Hawk. (50 Galebs and 25 Super Galebs at start of war; current strength unknown but Britain estimated 30% losses as of April 20.)

- *SA-342L Gazelle.* (44 armed helicopters at start of the war. Plus 3 Mi-14, 3 Ka-25, and 2 Ka-28 armed ASW helicopters.)

- *SA-341 (14), SA-341H (63), Mi-8 Hip-C (90) and Mi-17 Hip-H* utility helicopters.
- *Liaison helicopters.* 32 UTVA-66 and 14 Partisan.

NATO Attacks on Serbian Forces and Major Weapons

NATO air and missile power attacked Serbia army and paramilitary forces in several different ways. As has been discussed earlier, NATO struck at military facilities throughout Serbia, it struck at ammunition and equipment storage facilities, and it struck directly at Serbian ground units. While NATO struck at paramilitary forces as well as regular army forces, much of its strike planning concentrated on finding and destroying heavy military equipment—in part because this offered the highest probability of hitting true military targets and minimizing the risk of collateral damage.

NATO steadily increased its number of strikes on Serbian army and special police targets in the field once the air and missile campaign began on March 24, although it did not begin to have a major impact in terms of successful strikes until mid-May. The number of VJ and MUP target groups that NATO struck increased by 177 percent from Day 20 to Day 28 and from 31 to 86 army and police target groups. After that time, virtually every clear day over Kosovo led to 20–30 NATO strikes on groups of Serbian forces, while NATO struck regularly at other VJ and MUP target complexes in Serbia proper. These attacks had growing success, particularly as the KLA reinforced its presence in Kosovo and forced Serbian forces to expose themselves in concentrated attacks.

The data NATO provided on the results of its strikes against Serbian ground forces were often vague and often self-contradictory—reflecting both acute targeting problems and major problems in battle damage assessment. NATO first claimed in background briefings that it had destroyed 30–60 of 300 Serb tanks in Kosovo by April 22, and then that it had hit 10–15 percent of a strength of 400 tanks by April 23. US sources reported on May 4 that Serbia had lost 25 percent of it tanks, APCs, and trucks in Kosovo, but did not provide any figures and did not distinguish between holdings in Kosovo, total tanks in active units, or total tanks in inventory.

The US said on April 22 that NATO had hit particularly hard at the 3rd Army in Kosovo, striking hard at the facilities for the Pristina Corps and at 1 armored, 1 mechanized, and 2 infantry brigades within this force. It also did some damage to the Nis Corps (the lighter corps inside Kosovo). It claimed morale was declining, there were desertions, and that ammunition and fuel had been affected. Admiral Wilson reported that,

The Third Army . . . It hasn't changed much in terms of the amount of red from what you saw maybe ten days or two weeks ago . . . But we continue to pound away and work on forces in the field and the garrison locations in Kosovo as well as some of the supply networks that continue to feed them with POL, ammunition, and things like that.

There is increasing evidence both among forces in Kosovo and among the Serbian army in general, that this campaign is having an impact on their morale. They're concerned because of the inability of the air defense system to successfully engage NATO aircraft and prevent strikes. They're concerned about the destruction of the infrastructure that supports forces both in garrison and when they're in the field. All armies need a reliable supply and logistics network. And they're concerned about the desertion rates, which are on the climb, and concerned about, I think, the response to orders for additional mobilization or call-up of reserves which appears to be declining in terms of percentage response.

So this campaign down in the south and around Kosovo continues, I believe, to damage the capability of the military to conduct these operations and the will of the military to conduct these operations, although they are still responding to political guidance, and they are still conducting their operations. It's a matter of degradation, which has been our goal all along.

So we continue to work on the garrisons, to destroy the infrastructure and continue to attack the forces in the field where they're located, and are having increased success in actually engaging in engagement areas or in staging areas, tanks, APCs, and things like that. But, I believe, equally important is the engagement of ammunition and fuel and the lines of communications.

In spite of these claims, Serbia still operated with considerable efficiency in many areas. According to NATO estimates as of April 22, 1999, Serbian units operated against the Muslim Kosovars in over 250 scattered locations. Serbian elements were scattered in well over 100 locations. This kind of target base is almost impossible to attack without risking high levels of collateral damage, and the KLA lacked the strength to force the Serbians to concentrate heavy weapons in most areas or to maneuver along predictable routes in high concentrations.

NATO had already made it clear in its briefing on April 18 that the NATO air strikes on Serbian Army and Special Police forces had as yet done nothing to slow down the rate of atrocities and ethnic cleansing, to slow down Serbian movements in Kosovo, or affect command and control. NATO reported that the rate of atrocities seemed to have sharply increased during April 20–April 22, and the number of mass graves had increased by 4 to 10 times. NATO also reported on April 27 that Serbian Army and Special Police forces had again been reinforced from roughly 36,000 men on April 20 to 40,000 on April 27, in spite of the air and missile campaign.

The British Ministry of Defense said on April 23 that,

. . . our attacks against VJ and MUP forces in Kosovo pose the greatest difficulty since these units are relatively small and mobile and battle-damage assessment is difficult. Over the last week, we have had some successes and this process of attrition will continue. As you will understand, our attacks against tactical units such as tanks, artillery and vehicles have been less successful than against static targets but the U.S. Apache helicopters in Albania will greatly help in this respect and support operations in Kosovo including army and special police headquarters, storage depots and workshops. . . . The headquarters of the VJ First Army and Third Army at Nis in southern Serbia have been destroyed and the headquarters of the Second Army at Podgorica has also been attacked; 13 ammunition plants, depots and explosive stores have been hit as well as numerous tactical ammunition holdings stored at barracks or deployed in the field.

General Clark stated on April 27 that NATO was beginning to do serious damage to the operational capabilities of the 2nd as well as the 3rd Army and that,

Step by step, bit by bit, we are cutting off his ability to reinforce or to sustain his forces easily down in Kosovo. Of course he can still walk them in through the gullies and the rivers and so forth and it is never going to be complete, but it is certainly complicating their life down there. We are also working against ground forces outside of Kosovo. We know that his personnel and material losses are mounting, we know a number of key facilities that they value highly have been destroyed and we are seeing daily evidence of declining morale and increasingly widespread avoidance of the draft. . . . In Kosovo itself we are going after the forces as best we can, despite the adverse weather, and we are using a variety of targeting means and a variety of weapons systems on these forces. His personnel and material losses are mounting, he has lost the use of most of the key facilities there and we are picking up increasing numbers of desertions and declining morale among the troops. What you can see . . . are troop concentrations where they are still engaging in hurting the refugees around, ethnic cleansing and continuing to fight against the UCK who by the way have not been defeated in the field by the Serb forces. And they are also trying to fortify defensive positions in anticipation of NATO ground operations.

NATO provided broad damage assessment maps as part of General Clark's briefing on April 27. These maps did not go into great detail, but their summary assessment was that NATO had only inflicted light damage on Serbian 1st, 2nd, and 3rd Corps forces outside of Kosovo, and only slightly more damage on the 3rd Corps forces inside Kosovo. The US reported somewhat different targeting figures that same day, showing that NATO now had 21 regular army (VJ) and 13 Special Police (MUP) targets. It did not assess damage to these targets.

As has been discussed earlier, NATO also reported, however, that the air and missile campaign had failed to prevent a major Serbian build-up. The total for military and special police rose by 32 percent after December 23, and about 8 percent between March 24 and April 13. They rose by around 51 percent after December 23 by April 22, and about 36 percent between March 24 and April 22. There were at least 36,000 Serbian military and special police in Kosovo as of April 22, with roughly 1,800–2,500 armored vehicles and heavy weapons scattered all over Kosovo. There were 27 identifiable military units, and there were probably another 7,000–8,000 irregulars.

The Problems of Operational Effectiveness

NATO provided a good overview of the operational problems it faced during its May 6 briefing:

There is significant progress in attacking strategic targets that allows us to move on to our ultimate goal of taking out the Serb fielded forces in Kosovo. First, let me say a word about the environment. Our pilots are operating under very difficult conditions, as you can see on this slide, both of weather and of terrain. As an airman myself, I want to pay a tribute to their professionalism to do the work they are doing in such a good manner.

At the beginning of our operation, as you all are aware, Allied forces had to fight with bad weather, it was so poor that we could operate against fielded forces only about 15 percent of the time—15 percent of the time. This sketch draws a little attention on what I am saying, clouds hiding the top of mountains. It has subsequently improved, allowing us to inflict greater damage on Serb forces on the ground.

Since those early days we have been able to adapt our tactics to take maximum advantage of our comprehensive array of intelligence gathering capabilities and now we are able to collect and distribute information efficiently so that our aircrews are able to react quickly to targets, also of opportunity. We have also adjusted our flying patterns to ensure a continuous presence of combat air and missile power that is able to operate in the directed attacks against these ground forces. We have planes circling, awaiting the call to strike from other aircraft flying forward air control or what we call spotter missions.

So Serb fielded forces that we confront are arrayed throughout Kosovo, as portrayed on this map. To attack these forces we have employed a mix of NATO aircraft that are available for use in direct attacks. The versatility of these aircraft allows us to use a type of weapon that provides maximum effectiveness against a target and minimize damage to civilians and to civilian property. Our arsenal ranges from guns to precision guided weapons and munitions, and to specialized weapons employing the very latest technology.

Remember what we have been going against—a sophisticated network of command posts, anti-aircraft missiles and guns, tanks, artillery pieces, armored personnel carriers, supply convoys, ammunition and petroleum stockage points and Serb Army and special police units.

Serb fielded forces are very keenly aware of the need for camouflage, concealment and deception to protect themselves from our aircrews. Serb forces have proven particularly adept at using tunnels, natural camouflage and buildings in villages to make it difficult to locate and attack, sometimes even impossible, because they might be in houses where we do not know if persons are still living there. However, this limits also their own mobility. Additionally the uneven nature of their operational tempo appears to be grinding down morale. There are several reasons for that: long field duty and arduous living conditions; poor food; low pay, particularly in comparison to special police force rates; a lack of sleep caused by sporadic movement in the few quiet moments they can find; and not least a continual fear of attack from NATO aircraft. This makes individuals more fatigued, less alert, more irritable, less likely to work effectively together, and hence less of a threat to Kosovars on the ground or NATO Air Forces in the air. When combined with the predictable fear of being struck by determined NATO air crews there is evidence that the whole of the fielded forces are experiencing declines in morale and efficiency.

General Shelton noted on May 12 that destroying Serbian major weapons like tanks did not necessarily help the refugees: "I think that the effective tools that Milosevic's forces have used have been rifles and pistols that they're shot people through the head with, which gets down to the individual thug that—otherwise known as a VJ or a MUP—that is, in fact, doing the ethnic cleansing, taking the revenge, if you will, against the Kosovar Albanians. And I think that those can be effective until such time as he calls them off or until such time as the UCK—as VJ and MUP forces are reduced to the level that the Kosovar Albanians, UCK or KLA, are able to then to drive them out of Kosovo, leveling the balance of power between the two forces."

At the same time, other NATO briefings were more optimistic about the impact that NATO air and missile power was having on Serbian ground troops, and NATO's ability to solve its operational problems. NATO stated on May 6 that,

So what have we achieved so far? You will note that we generally speak in terms of targets struck. There is a simple reason for this. We have no direct access to the individual target sites, so even so we conduct battle damage assessments after each attack, we cannot be absolutely certain that these targets we have struck have been totally destroyed, or just only damaged, or only temporarily put out of action.

NATO air crews fly regularly against fielded forces targets, often in marginal weather. And in case weather or other circumstances prevent a strike against its primary target, every time an aircraft flies out on a mission it has a pick-up target to engage also.

So let me turn to the damage done. It is considerable, it is having a powerful impact on the ability of Serb forces to carry out their policy of ethnic cleansing, both now and also in the long term. I have already spoken about the earlier priorities of the air and missile campaign: to pin Serb forces down and cut them off from their resupply routes and their political and also military masters in Belgrade. And I have described the impact that poor weather has had on air operations. Our increasing success in achieving our early priorities, and better weather, means that we are now making good progress in taking out Serb fielded forces.

I can report to you that to date we have struck 8 important battalion brigade command posts, I am talking Kosovo. We estimate that some 50 percent of ammunition storage in Kosovo has been destroyed and we have struck more than 300 individual pieces of equipment including tanks, artillery pieces, armored personnel carriers and trucks. Some 200 of those, which is about 20 percent of the entire estimated Serb . . . Kosovo, Serb heavy forces, talking tanks and artillery.

And an important indicator, we have achieved the vast majority of those strikes in the past 2–3 weeks, I have to admit I did tell you the reason, bad weather in the beginning.

Past military campaigns have shown that combat effectiveness of formed units is to all intents and purposes eliminated at levels of damage of course less than 100 percent, perhaps at around 50 percent losses or even a little lower. At that stage the forces concerned focus on survival rather than fighting, they are no longer that effective and we all hope that Milosevic will see reason well before we reach those levels of damage and agree to meet NATO's five conditions. But if he does not and if we have to prosecute this campaign until we break the will to fight of Serb forces in Kosovo, we are prepared to take them all out.

What do all these statistics mean where it matters—on the ground? Milosevic's forces in the field are being taken apart bit by bit, faster and faster. Their ability to operate effectively, let alone carry out acts of brutality, is further reduced with each day that passes. We have already achieved significant benefits from our campaign against fielded forces, first by relentlessly pursuing fielded forces we have all but entirely pinned them down, they can no longer move with impunity. Beyond that, our intelligence has detected that the fielded forces are dispersing into even smaller units, and recent intelligence reports indicate that they now have little option but to dig in and to protect their equipment. They can only move furtively and with great fear. Of course that makes it even more difficult to find and to destroy them, I have to admit. But it also makes it much more difficult for them to carry out their attacks against the Kosovar people.

In fact a review of the activities of both the fielded forces and the UCK reveals an interesting trend. This map from April shows the activity areas of both the fielded forces and the UCK. This map, from yesterday, portrays a different situation. It would seem that as we have been able to increase our strikes in Kosovo our intelligence assets have identified fewer and more centralized areas of fielded forces operations.

Unfortunately this does not mean that all Serb military actions against the Kosovar people have stopped. But this trend would suggest that the opportunities for persecution on a large scale are diminishing as the fielded forces lose their mobility. As a consequence, it appears that refugees may be finding it easier to move around dispersed Serbian forces and to seek refuge across the border.

This combination of relentless pursuit in the field and strategic attacks to isolate them enables us to achieve our ultimate goal—to really take them out. When they dare to move they are exposed and vulnerable as targets of opportunity.

The impact of our campaign is reflected in the recent reports of low morale and in desertions from forces operating in Kosovo. Perhaps that should not surprise you. Imagine what it must be like in one of those units, having already lost 20 percent of their heavy forces, and presumably the military comrades who manned them, or even more persons, their fuel stocks have been destroyed, half their ammunition supplies have been destroyed, they know that bridges into the theatre have been struck and the major road and railroads are closed, so they are receiving resupplies of food, fuel and ammunition only sporadically. They are in only irregular and unreliable contact with super (?) headquarters in the field and in Serbia because we have struck at command and communication sites and they know that power could go out at any time.

They are able only to scurry from cover to cover and always in fear of being struck. They are increasingly exhausted from lack of sleep and for Commanders they are left with the growing knowledge that they are on the losing side and that looming over the horizon is accountability to the international community for the atrocities that they and their men, under their command, have committed. And always there is a nagging fear of attack from NATO aircraft, now operating around the clock when the weather allows.

The most striking evidence of this, and of the scale of our success, is demonstrated by the most recent intelligence reports that when they hear the approach of NATO aircraft, Milosevic's forces leap from their vehicles and run away seeking cover.

Jamie Shea struck similar optimistic themes in the NATO daily briefing on Day 50 (May 13) of the air and missile campaign.

Milosevic's main army units are suffering increasing problems, four in particular; the 243rd Brigade, the 125th, the 252nd and the 211th have been damaged by NATO air strikes and there we see signs of slowing down, of dispersion to avoid NATO air strikes and morale problems and the rest but Milosevic as you know, has never relied purely on his army, he has spent a lot of money in recent years on his MUP, his special police forces as well, and as the army forces suffer enormous problems so he relies more and more on those special police forces and on paramilitary units as well but of course, to the extent that the army is not able to provide protection for those paramilitary forces in terms of artillery and tank support, they are going to have a harder and harder time against the Kosovo Liberation Army and sustained losses and they also of course will be targeted by NATO as well so I see this as a progressive thing.

We have begun with the army forces and as I say, the fact that Milosevic is now calling on his MUP or special police, I think clearly shows that the army is less and less up to the job here of keeping control in Kosovo and then we will move on to those special police forces and to those paramilitary forces. The moment we can oblige the main army to leave Kosovo, then of course the other forces, particularly paramilitaries, will have no logistic base of support any longer, they will be forced to leave as well. But it is the easiest thing in the world for somebody with a gun to go along, knock on the house of a family that don't have any guns and order them out and that is again the reason why all of these Serb forces have to leave and they will. As General Jertz says, if the people are fleeing from Kosovo it is also because they have seen what the Serb forces can do and of course they want to try to protect themselves as best they can by seeing refuge in other countries.

General Shelton, the Chairman of the US Joint Chiefs, said on the same day that,

In Kosovo itself, Milosevic's army and his special police units continue to suffer damage from NATO air strikes. Nearly a quarter of his armored vehicles—that is tanks and armored personnel carriers—have been damaged or destroyed. And roughly 40% of the Serb artillery in Kosovo has been taken out. . . . The tank threat has been diminished, I think, by a couple of ways. Number one is the numbers that have been damaged or destroyed. But just as importantly, I think, is the fact that they know now that we're looking for them. They're having to disperse; they're having to hide. And, of course, a tank that is being hidden in a village or kept well out of the area is out of the immediate area where they need it to operate is not of much use. And so, it's a combination of trying to destroy or damage the tank, which we've done, combined with the dispersal and hiding. They've been forced into that has significantly reduced his armor threat down in that area, and, I think from all indications, has allowed the UCK to obtain some degree of success in some of the areas that they've attacked.

Most of the ammunition and fuel supplies of the Serb Third Army, which as you know by now, probably, is the unit that operates in Kosovo, has been destroyed along with more than half of the infrastructure that supports this force . . . We also continue to receive significant indications of growing unrest and discontent within the ranks of the Yugoslav army. Of course, these reports can hardly come as a surprise. You would expect that any military force that is first used against helpless civilians and then is subjected to tremendous pounding by NATO aircraft would have considerable doubts about its future and about the leadership that has gotten the military into this situation. I don't mean to paint too rosy a picture here. We are conservative in our estimates, and it is possible that a force like the one Milosevic is using for ethnic cleansing and terror in Kosovo could hold out for quite some time. But it is clear that NATO's air and missile campaign is exacting a significant toll on Serb forces in Kosovo and throughout the rest of Yugoslavia.

It may be months or years, if ever, before an accurate historical picture emerges of what NATO did and did not do to affect Serbian land operations. This very uncertainty, however, poses potential lessons of the war:

- *There is a need to improve the understanding of the impact of air power on land force operations and to do so in near real time to improve targeting, tactics, and the assessment of effectiveness. Asserting effectiveness is not the same as achieving effectiveness.*

- *Vehicle counts are no more meaningful than body counts, even if they could be made accurate. Physical damage is not a measure of operational effectiveness.*

- *As the analysis of recent wars and peacekeeping incidents discussed earlier indicates, asymmetric warfare is a well established reality that is the norm, rather than the exception. The kind of effort to destroy a massed enemy engaged in intense joint combat on a theater level emphasized in Joint Vision 2010, the "Revolution in Military Affairs," the Bottom Up Review, Quadrennial Defense Review, and a great deal of US plans and doctrine represents a real threat, but it is only one form of war and not the most likely form.*

The Impact of Problems in Reporting on the Strikes on Serbian Land Forces and Battle Damage Assessment

There are other lessons that seem to emerge from the data that NATO, the US, and UK have provided on the detailed impact of NATO's strikes on Serbian land forces. It is important to note that NATO and the US made many statements warning about the uncertainties in battle damage assessment during this period.

Major General Wald made the following points in the Department of Defense briefing on May 4:

Questioner: General, as you go along now with looking for targets of opportunity and increased tempo, can you give us a little better idea, especially in the coming days, how you're doing on taking out tanks, artillery, APCs, armored vehicles?

Major General Wald: I just did. We're about 25. . .

Questioner: You said about 25 percent.

Major General Wald: Right.

Questioner: But we had a 25 percent figure almost 10 days ago.

Major General Wald: It was about 20 percent 10 days ago.

Questioner: So you're doing about five percent. . .

Major General Wald: That's the problem with numbers. Everybody keeps saying don't say numbers because you'll go down a path of numbers. But the fact of the matter is it may be more than that, it may be less, it may be 22.5 percent, it may be 31 percent; it may be something. But it's in a category that a big chunk of his tanks are gone.

Questioner: So if we can get a running count on it so we know on a daily basis. . .

Major General Wald: I'll tell you what. I've tried every day to call Milosevic and ask him, and he won't tell me. (Laughter)

Questioner: No, but I mean your BDA.

Major General Wald: Like I say, our BDA, I'm telling you every day. If you'd kept track since the beginning you'd probably have about as good a count as I do. But the fact of the matter is, just like these two. We hit them yesterday. What we'll do is we'll go back, and we'll look at a photograph. If they're gone, we don't know if they pulled them off, if they drove them off. If they're still there and it doesn't look like the turrets on it anymore, we'll probably call it destroyed.

So we go down this path. Our concern is we're going to tell you something that's wrong. And the last thing we want to do is give you bad information, because our credibility means everything. So suffice it to say when we show you a picture up here—I've never shown a film twice. As a matter of fact today I showed maybe 20 films. There were 80 attacks last night. So there are another 60 of those out there someplace that I haven't shown, and that's about the number each day. So you can imagine if I showed two here, there were—from what I understand last night there were 16 tanks and APCs totaled, APCs and tanks destroyed.

Similarly, General Jertz, the NATO briefer, was very careful to qualify the limits in NATO's estimates and numbers during the question and answer session that followed the NATO briefing on May 12:

Questioner: General Jertz, some of this is just asking you to repeat what you said so I understand it more clearly but you said, if my notes are correct, that more than 300 tanks, artillery pieces, APCs and trucks had been struck and that 200 of these were representing 20 percent of the total of that category of stuff. Would this be about a quarter of all such heavy equipment that has been put out of action or destroyed as a briefer in the Pentagon suggested two days ago?

You then went on to say something about 50 percent losses meant the forces weren't effective and I didn't understand what you were saying there. If you could repeat that or make it clearer, I'd appreciate it.

General Jertz: When I was talking about the 20 percent, keep in mind that I always quote SACEUR—a tank is not a tank is not a tank—a tank, even if it is not destroyed, if it is hiding somewhere and it doesn't have a fuel and it doesn't have ammunition, it just does not have any combat effectiveness so even though you were asking for numbers of the last few days, numbers always have to be related to the kind of operations we are in so if a tank cannot move there is no difference if it is destroyed or if it is out of order or if it has no ammunition, the effectiveness is exactly the same.

Craig: Can you clarify the numbers of 20 percent of 300?

General Jertz: As I said, we hit 300 pieces, 200 of them were heavy pieces and saying "heavy pieces" I am talking of artillery and tanks.

Craig: Is that 20 percent in Kosovo or 20 percent of the total?

General Jertz: I am talking of Kosovo forces.

Jamie Shea: The rest are military vehicles?

Major General Jertz: You mean the other armor?

Craig: Yes.

Major General Jertz: Military trucks.

Craig: You made it about 50 percent, what was that, that if it reached 50 percent the forces wouldn't be effective?

Major General Jertz: Here I would say I was talking in theory. Our experience in combat is that if the forces are worn down to round about 50 percent or less, they are no longer combat-effective—that is what I was saying—that you don't need to really wear them out 100 percent. I mean pieces, equipment, assets.

Jamie Shea: We are talking about equipment, vehicles, armored military vehicles.

NATO's Damage Claims in Mid-May

There were serious consistency problems in many of NATO's claims during mid-May. NATO quoted totals of both 300 and 400 heavy weapons for Serbian forces. NATO sometimes said that the 300 or 400 figure only included main battle tanks. It sometimes said it included both tanks and other major armored vehicles. On May 6, for example, it stated that the figure was 300, but now included tanks, other armored vehicles, and artillery—and possibly trucks. Serbian formations are small by the standards of NATO armies, but they would normally have 600–800 major weapons, including artillery for a formation this size, plus a mix of some 1,400 military and civilian trucks, cars, and engineering systems.

The implied contradictions between the NATO damage estimates in percentages and the reports on the Serbian forces engaged cannot be reconciled from the information made available. It seems unlikely that NATO had actually hit even 15–20% of active tanks and heavy armor in Kosovo by early May, and it is clear NATO could not cannot calculate the percentages for other categories.

NATO issued new figures as part of the NATO briefing on May 13, although they scarcely resolved all of the uncertainties involved. Major General Walter Jertz stated that

Coming now to a very short up-date on numbers, however please bear in mind what I have said over and over again, numbers as such are not a very precise indication of combat capability of a unit. The shortages of food, fuel, ammunition, the latter leading to a decrease and reduction of morale of the soldiers must also be taken into consideration. Since my presentation last week concerning the Serbian ground forces in Kosovo, we told you we had destroyed 306 pieces of heavy equipment. We have now raised this figure up to 432. We have now struck over 20% of his critical inventory. Additionally we have in the meantime destroyed two-thirds of the Serbian ammunition production capacity. In fact, this image shows a post-strike assessment of the Kacak ammunition production plant. You will notice significant damage as indicated by the circles. In particular, please note the absolute destruction of the building in the upper right of the picture. Our bombs hit the building but the massive destruction you see is a result of the secondary explosion of ammunition stocks within the building . . . Out of the 432 pieces of Serb heavy equipment, when I say "heavy equipment" I am talking artillery and tanks and these are the ones which we really are planning to attack which we want to destroy because they are the most important and the most dangerous ones because they give shelter and make sure that the military police and also the paramilitaries are able to carry on and that is why we do have to continue to attack those too. Tanks and very heavy stuff. You know, there is also some very heavy stuff like personnel carriers which look pretty much like tanks and they can shoot, they do have a cannon unfortunately.

Let me re-emphasize again that the numbers we have already mentioned are more than 25 percent critical heavy inventory hits so far, thus they have lost, including the latest update of aircraft today, almost about 40 percent of their air assets; they have lost two-thirds of their munitions products and capability; they have lost half of all their ammunition storage sites and that means that the destruction is really very heavy on them.

NATO's Damage Claims on June 10

NATO's final damage claims were made at the Department of Defense briefing on June 10. They are summarized in Figures 30 and 31, and Major General Wald provided the following summary of the data in Figure 30:

This is a somewhat complicated chart, so I'll spend just a few moments. You don't have to have a degree in calculus, but I will walk you through it slowly. We'll start over here on day number 23, around the 14th of April. Across the bottom you can see in the background—these are the numbers of sorties multiplied by ten. You can see that they start fairly low over here, [then] they build up. Bad weather comes in. The weather is reflected across the bottom. Bad weather comes in, the sorties go down, etc. But then we start building up the aircraft, which happened around the 11th of May.

At the same time, these are the fielded forces. These are the tanks, the artillery and the mortars along with the armored personnel carriers shown in the three various colors. So as you move across you can see that the numbers as we bring the air defense down, as the weather starts to get better, as the number of assets in the area increase, the numbers of kills of fielded forces start to increase also. Then when we get the really good weather, down in this area, you can see almost exponentially it starts to go up to the point that when we suspended we were up to 450 artillery and mortar pieces, approximately, about 220 armored personnel carriers, and we were up to around 120 tanks at that time.

Senior sources at NATO provided similar estimates on June 30. They claimed that Serbia had lost 110 tanks, 200+ APCs and other armored vehicles, and 454 artillery weapons and mortars. It soon became clear, however, that these claims presented major problems.

NATO announced on June 22 that it estimated that that the Yugoslav army and special police forces had departed Kosovo with about 47,000 Serb troops and nearly 800 tanks, armored personnel carriers, and artillery pieces. This withdrawal proceeded smoothly over 11 days—creating growing uncertainties about NATO's claims in terms of damage to POL facilities, lines of communication, and infrastructure. It also created serious questions about the credibility of NATO reporting on damage to the Serbian ground forces in Kosovo. Not only did the withdrawal confirm the Serbian build-up that had taken place during the war, it indicated that NATO might well have over estimated the numbers of Serbian weapons it had destroyed.

Serbia's False Damage Claims and Deception Efforts

These uncertainties were compounded by Serbian claims that Serbia had only lost about one-third of the equipment NATO reported, and that Serbia had successfully made massive use of decoys that NATO did not detect in the targeting, operational attack, and battle damage assessment phase. Serbian sources

Figure 30
NATO Damage Claims Relating to Serbia Army Military Infrastructure

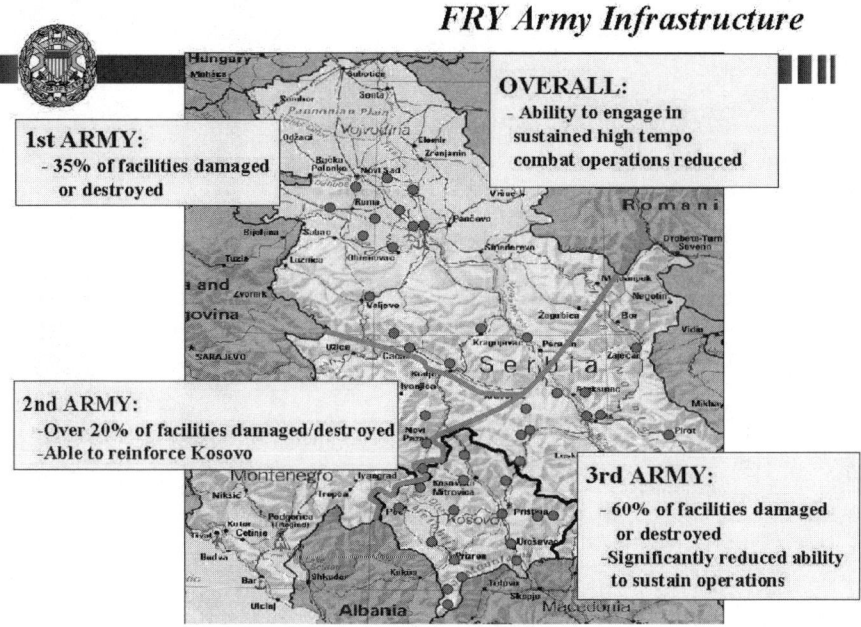

Source: Adapted from the Department of Defense press briefing for June 10, 1999.

stated that NATO had hit nearly 500 decoys, but only 50 tanks, in using what other sources estimated were 3,000 guided weapons.[191] Lt. General Nchojsa Pavkovic, the Serbian 3rd Army commander, went further. He claimed that NATO only destroyed 13 tanks, six armored personnel carriers, and 27 artillery pieces. Also his other claims that that Yugoslav air defense units had shot down 47 NATO planes, four helicopters, and 21 drones scarcely did much to enhance his credibility.

Even so, such claims led to articles that attacked the NATO claims by like those of Michael Evans, the Defense Editor of the *London Times*, who took the Serbian claims seriously. Evans reported from Pristina on June 24 that NATO had only destroyed 13 out of 200 Serbian tanks in Kosovo, and a small fraction of Serbian other armored vehicles, and artillery. The *Times* claimed that only three destroyed tanks had been found in Kosovo. The *Times* reported that NATO had wasted much of its ordnance on Serbian decoys, and that Serbia succeeded in withdrawing at least 250 tanks, 450 other armored vehicles, and 600 artillery weapons and medium-heavy mortars from Kosovo.[192]

Similar reports were made in Berlin's *Die Welt* on June 28, Rome's *La Republica* on June 15, London's *Sunday Telegraph* on June 27, Paris's *La Point* on June 29, and the *New York Times* on June 28.[193] It is hard to avoid the conclusion

Figure 31
Revised NATO Estimate of Serbian Ground Force Losses in Kosovo as of
September 16, 1999

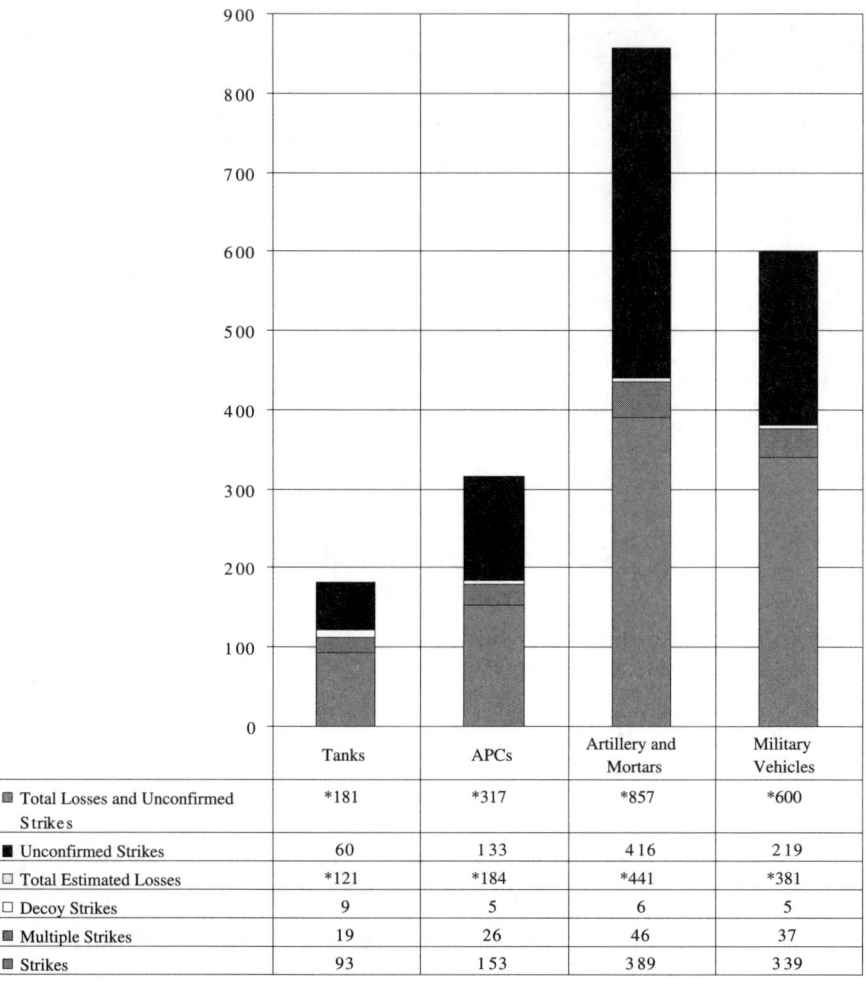

	Tanks	APCs	Artillery and Mortars	Military Vehicles
▨ Total Losses and Unconfirmed Strikes	*181	*317	*857	*600
■ Unconfirmed Strikes	60	133	416	219
▢ Total Estimated Losses	*121	*184	*441	*381
▢ Decoy Strikes	9	5	6	5
▨ Multiple Strikes	19	26	46	37
▨ Strikes	93	153	389	339

Source: Adapted by Anthony H. Cordesman from data provided in the NATO Briefing by SACEUR, General Wesley Clark, on September 16, 1999.

that the same media that was uncritical of NATO claims during the war was equally credulous in accepting Serbian claims once the war was over.

Serbia made so many false claims that they lead to the following exchange at the Department of Defense briefing on June 24:

Questioner: General Clark said recently that the Yugoslav forces skillfully deployed a lot of decoys in Kosovo during the air and missile campaign—inflatable tanks, artillery pieces, and so forth. Meanwhile, we're starting to get reports coming out that only three destroyed tanks have been found so far. The KFOR forces are telling people that no where near 100 tanks were destroyed. Sometimes, people are saying only 13 tanks were destroyed.

How extensive was the decoying by the Yugoslavs? And have we found anything on the ground to substantiate what we thought we had actually destroyed in terms of numbers?

Mr. Bacon: I don't know how extensive the decoys were. You'll recall, I'm sure, that General Wald referred to decoys several times when he briefed up here, so we do know that they used decoys. It's a standard operating procedure to use decoys in situations like this.

I can't answer your question about—we've done no census on the ground of tank carcasses at this stage, but in general numbers we believe that before this began, there were approximately 1,500 tanks, armored personnel carriers, and artillery pieces in Kosovo. We destroyed approximately 700 of those, and approximately 800 exited during the 11 days when the Serb troops left. That's in round numbers what we think happened.

Now we tried to be pretty careful throughout this, not to get into the precise bean-counting business, because we were operating on a lot of estimates and precision's—there's no such thing as a precise estimate. But this is our best guess as to the size of the force, the damage that was done, and the number that exited.

Questioner: You don't believe that the number of decoys being struck was way out of proportion where we were really throwing away millions of dollars of. . .

Mr. Bacon: I think the only conclusion that matters here is that we struck enough targets to win.

Questioner: Did the films that you folks were watching every day, the gun-camera footage, show any substantial number of targets that after the bombs struck it was obviously a decoy? Or after. . .

Mr. Bacon: Well, there were some. There was—I mean, General Wald showed several decoys being hit. Other times he said that was no decoy.

Questioner:. . .in his mind, and we didn't bring it up to him. That's why I wonder if he or other people saw a large number of these.

Mr. Bacon: As I said, I don't have a figure on the number of decoys that were hit. Clearly, we did hit decoys. There were, clearly, decoys put up, and we also hit many real tanks. I think you saw pictures of tanks blowing up. You wouldn't fill a decoy with oil or ammo just so you'd get a pretty picture on the Pentagon gun-camera footage. At least I assume the Serbs didn't do that.

NATO's Post-Conflict Damage Assessment Efforts

NATO made a major effort to reexamine its estimate during the following months. It conducted an exhaustive analysis of the physical destruction found in the field, aircrew mission reports, forward air controller interviews, cockpit video, human intelligence, member country intelligence, witnesses at the scene of strikes, and pre- and post-strike imagery from the U-2, Predator, UAVs, tactical reconnaissance aircraft, satellites, and national intelligence sources.[194] This intelligence and damage assessment efforts were a major NATO team effort that was not completed until early September, and was not briefed publicly until September 16. The team was coordinated by Supreme Headquarters Allied Powers (SHAPE), and included members from the NATO Combined Air Operations Center (CAOC), the NATO force in Kosovo (KSFOR), the US European Command (USEUCOM), the NATO intelligence community, NATO aerial reconnaissance units, and representatives of NATO wings and squadrons.

The team developed a comprehensive evaluation and record of all target characteristics, the physical and functional damage to each target, the location and effectiveness of weapons impacts, and the accuracy of the battle damage assessments made during Operation Allied Force. It then used a building block method based on reviewing each mission—for example, the 181 mission reports the claimed successful strikes against tanks. It then assessed the results of ground mobile targeting of Serbian field forces, and the effectiveness of NATO's air-to-ground weapons against fixed targets. It carefully analyzed the level of damage, the reliability of the source, the impact of single versus multiple strikes, the damage done to decoys, and the number of cases where insufficient evidence existed to confirm a strike, but where further Serbian losses were a significant probability.[195]

The end result was to assess the number of strikes where a weapon impacted on a valid target. For example, NATO found 26 Serbian tanks that had been destroyed by catastrophic kills still on the ground in Kosovo. It found 57 more tanks where there was convincing evidence from other sources that a tank had been destroyed on the day where a kill was claimed, and 19 more where an assessment of reports of strikes and various intelligence sources over a period of days added to the total. It found 9 cases where the strikes hit decoys and there were 60 more cases where a claimed kill could not be confirmed because there was not enough evidence beyond the mission report to support a successful strike assessment.

The revised NATO assessment is shown in Figure 32. While it is scarcely based on certainty, which is impossible in war, it has considerable credibility and far greater credibility that any of the reports that came out of the Serbian disinformation campaign. It also provides a quantified estimate of the number of cases where mission claims could not be confirmed. These unconfirmed strikes totaled 60 claims for tanks, 133 claims for APCs, 416 claims for artillery weapons and mortars, and 219 claims for other military vehicles. It is likely that a number of these unconfirmed strikes were successful, given the fact that Serbia routinely recovered damaged vehicles and weapons, and sent them to the rear for repair or the salvage of spare parts.

Figure 32
Revised NATO Estimate of Serbian Ground Force Losses in Kosovo as of
September 16, 1999 versus Initial NATO Battle Damage Assessment as of June 10,
1999

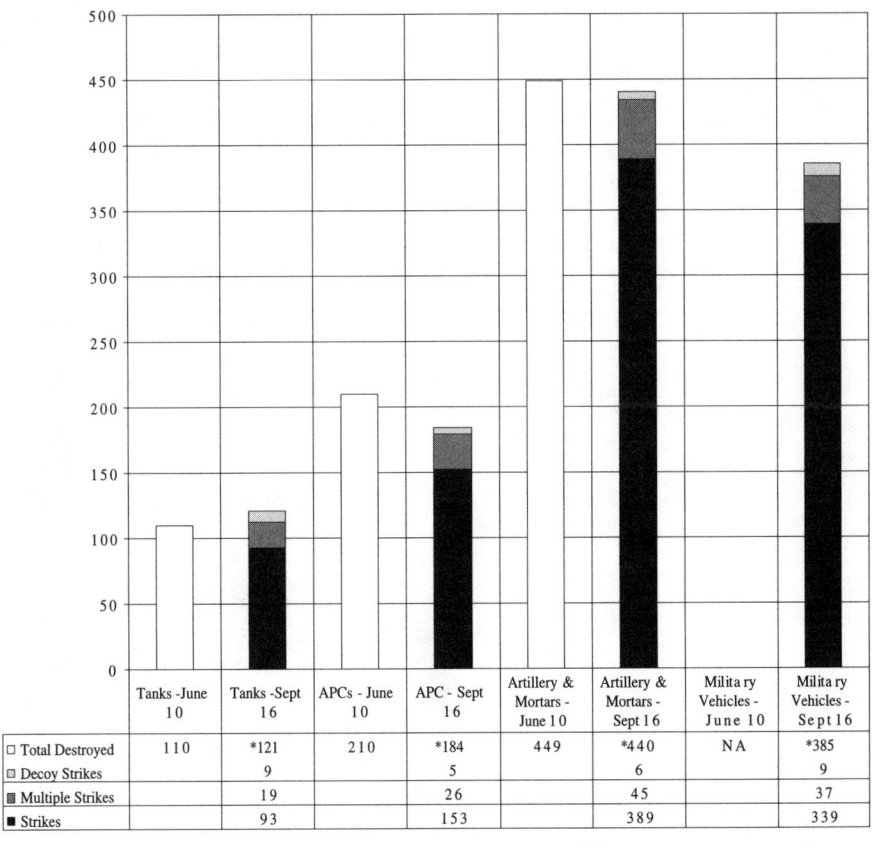

	Tanks -June 10	Tanks -Sept 16	APCs - June 10	APC - Sept 16	Artillery & Mortars - June 10	Artillery & Mortars - Sept 16	Military Vehicles - June 10	Military Vehicles - Sept 16
□ Total Destroyed	110	*121	210	*184	449	*440	NA	*385
□ Decoy Strikes		9		5		6		9
■ Multiple Strikes		19		26		45		37
■ Strikes		93		153		389		339

Source: Adapted by Anthony H. Cordesman from data provided in the NATO Briefing by SACEUR,
General Wesley Clark, on September 16, 1999.

It is clear from Figure 33, which compares the NATO battle damage assessment
of September 16 against NATO's initial damage estimates right after the war, that
NATO did exaggerate its initial claims, and counted some decoys in its initial
estimates. It is certainly clear from the number of unconfirmed strikes that some of
NATO's more absurd claims about success, like the 96.6% accuracy figure
discussed earlier, were nothing more than military rubbish. At the same time, the
NATO revised claims are not strikingly different from the claims NATO made
immediately after the war, and NATO added impressive new claims regarding
major Serbian losses of other military vehicles.

Figure 33
Revised NATO Estimate of Serbian Ground Force Losses in Kosovo as of September 16, 1999 versus NATO Estimate of Total Serbian Holdings on June 10, 1999

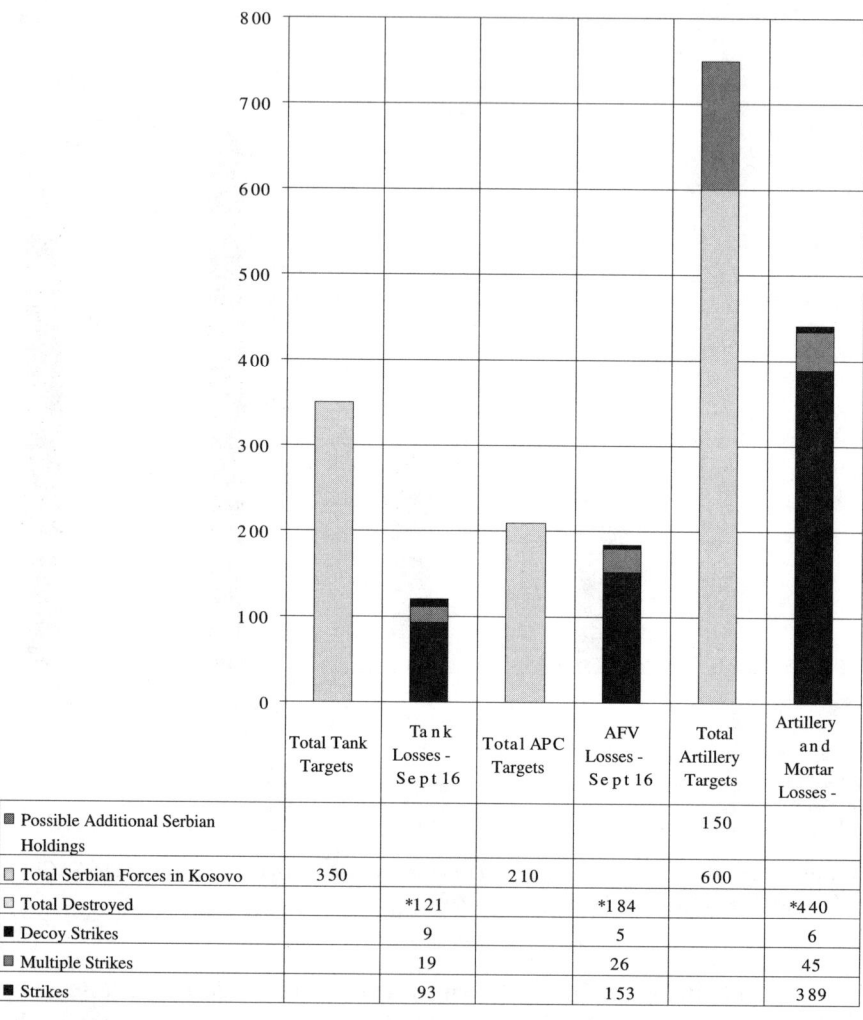

	Total Tank Targets	Tank Losses - Sept 16	Total APC Targets	AFV Losses - Sept 16	Total Artillery Targets	Artillery and Mortar Losses -
▨ Possible Additional Serbian Holdings					150	
▢ Total Serbian Forces in Kosovo	350		210		600	
▢ Total Destroyed		*121		*184		*440
■ Decoy Strikes		9		5		6
▨ Multiple Strikes		19		26		45
■ Strikes		93		153		389

Source: Adapted by Anthony H. Cordesman from data provided in the NATO Briefing by SACEUR, General Wesley Clark, on September 16, 1999.

British Post-Conflict Damage Assessment Claims

The British Ministry of Defense summed up the situation as follows in its October 1999 report upon the lessons of the war:[196]

Overall, the air campaign was singularly effective. Well over 400 static targets were attacked. More than three-quarters suffered moderate to severe damage. There is also clear evidence that air strikes against Milosevic's field forces in Kosovo were successful in restricting their operations. The Supreme Allied Commander has published his battle damage assessment. Figures however cannot show the extent to which Yugoslav tanks and other assets had to remain immobile to avoid the onslaught. As they were immobile, they couldn't be used. If they broke cover, they could be attacked. And in the final analysis a successful military campaign is not just about material destruction or a numbers game. It is about the impact on the psychology of an aggressor. How much damage did we do? The answer has to be "enough". Milosevic ultimately signed up to the international community's conditions for ending the bombing. The conflict ended on NATO's terms. The air campaign contributed materially to the achievement of the international community's objectives. It was a success.

US Post-Conflict Damage Assessment Efforts

Battle damage assessment remains a time consuming and uncertain art, but the balance of evidence is heavily in favor of NATO's revised damage claims. Similarly, the comparison of NATO estimates of total Serbian holdings with the revised NATO estimate of Serbian losses shown in Figure 34 supports the thesis that NATO strikes against Serbian land forces had considerable effectiveness. This is particularly true since no infantry or other casualty figures are included and NATO often struck at exposed Serbian forces, and because the disruptive and shock effects of air power cannot be quantified or included in either Figure 32 or Figure 34.

At the same time, this experience is a further indication that major improvements still need to be made in both targeting and battle damage assessment capability. This point is made quire clearly in some of the US testimony on the lessons of the war, along with the equally important statement that no advances in tactics and technology can eliminate a high degree of uncertainty.[197]

NATO's air attacks clearly had an impact on military operations in the FRY. Air attacks on military forces in the field forced Serbian forces to remain largely hidden from view, traveling only under limited circumstances, and made them ineffective as a tactical maneuver force. Air attacks on selected infrastructure targets, such as bridges and electric power systems, degraded the ability of the FRY military to perform command and control and to resupply and reconstitute its forces. Together, these effects created political pressure on Milosevic to yield to NATO demands. Intensive analyses of the results of our attacks

Figure 34
US Estimate of Serbian Ground Force Losses in Kosovo in the US Lessons of the War Study of January 2000

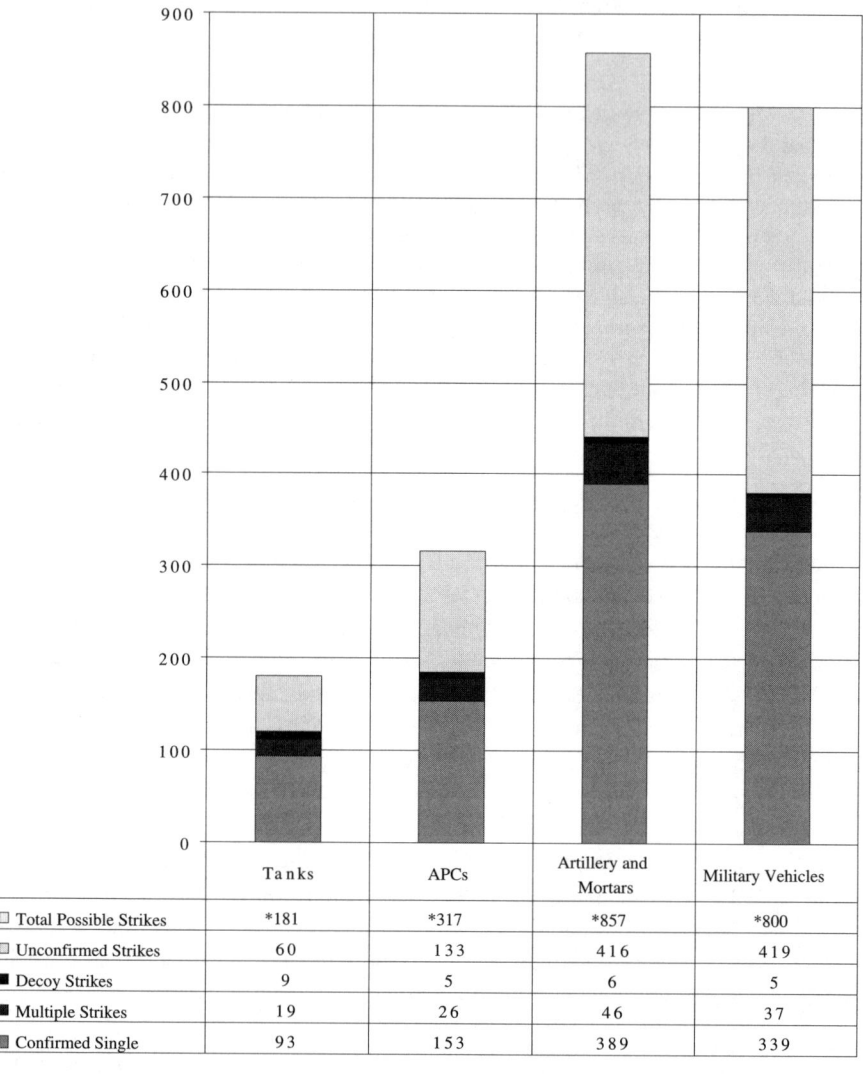

	Tanks	APCs	Artillery and Mortars	Military Vehicles
☐ Total Possible Strikes	*181	*317	*857	*800
☐ Unconfirmed Strikes	60	133	416	419
■ Decoy Strikes	9	5	6	5
■ Multiple Strikes	19	26	46	37
▨ Confirmed Single	93	153	389	339

Source: Adapted by Anthony H. Cordesman from data provided in Department of Defense, *Report to Congress: Kosovo/Operation Allied Forces After Action Report*, Washington, Department of Defense, January 31, 2000, pp. 85–86.

were conducted as the campaign proceeded, based on the fullest available information. These analyses were essential to the formulation of campaign plans on a day-by-day basis.

Subsequently, after the war's end, NATO conducted a new analysis of air attack effects, including visits to selected locations throughout Kosovo. This analysis, the Allied Force Munitions Effectiveness Assessment or "AF-MEA" report, addressed both fixed and mobile target attacks. An initial presentation of findings from the review of attacks on mobile targets already has been made public by the U.S. European Command. These two data bases, the wartime assessment and the postwar analysis, are the starting point for our subsequent analysis.

This further analysis is underway now to integrate the findings of all available data and to develop insights from those data on a variety of important topics. How good was our understanding of attack effectiveness as combat proceeded? What surveillance and reconnaissance systems proved most accurate and timely in delivering information critical to these assessments? What lessons can we draw from postwar examination of targets and target areas to modify or improve our battle damage assessment process? How should the inevitable uncertainty in the information be handled?

For example, often targets were attacked by multiple systems, making an assessment of any single system's effectiveness nearly impossible. Further, judging the degree of impairment inflicted on a damaged, but not destroyed, target probably will always remain a source of uncertainty. New technologies, such as video imagery from munitions in the terminal attack phase, will likely help improve our assessment performance in the future, but a substantial degree of uncertainty will continue to exist in any future war.

Given this background, it is not surprising that the US report on the lessons of the war that was issued in January 2000 provided only a limited amount of additional data. As Figure 35 and Figure 36 show, the results of the US lessons of the war study presented reformatted versions of the data NATO had issued in September 1999. The US study did not provide any detailed data on the munitions used, their individual effectiveness, or the overall effectiveness of NATO's strikes on mobile targets. The US study did, however, provide additional data on the way in which the NATO damage assessment analysis was carried out, and the summary results of the damage assessment effort:[198]

To assess the number of mobile targets struck during operations in the Kosovo, a team conducted a comprehensive day-by-day, mission-report-by-mission report reconstruction of the operation to determine the actual number of mobile targets struck with high confidence. This assessment covered all 78 days of Operation Allied Force, focused exclusively on mobile targets, *and covered only strikes in the area of Kosovo and the Presevo Valley.* The assessment team was comprised of 67 personnel from all Services and intelligence agencies, and included air and air defense analysts, ground analysts, Balkans analysts, imagery analysts, signal intelligence analysts, collection managers, targeteers, battle damage assessment analysts, and systems operators. The team gathered data and other pertinent information related to the following essential elements of information:

- Indications of destruction or damage of tanks, armored personnel carriers, artillery, mortars, and military vehicles

Figure 35

Comparison of the Results of the Initial NATO Battle Damage Assessment of June 10, 1999, the Revised NATO Estimate of Serbian Ground Force Losses in Kosovo as of September 16, 1999 and the US Lessons of the War Study of January 2000

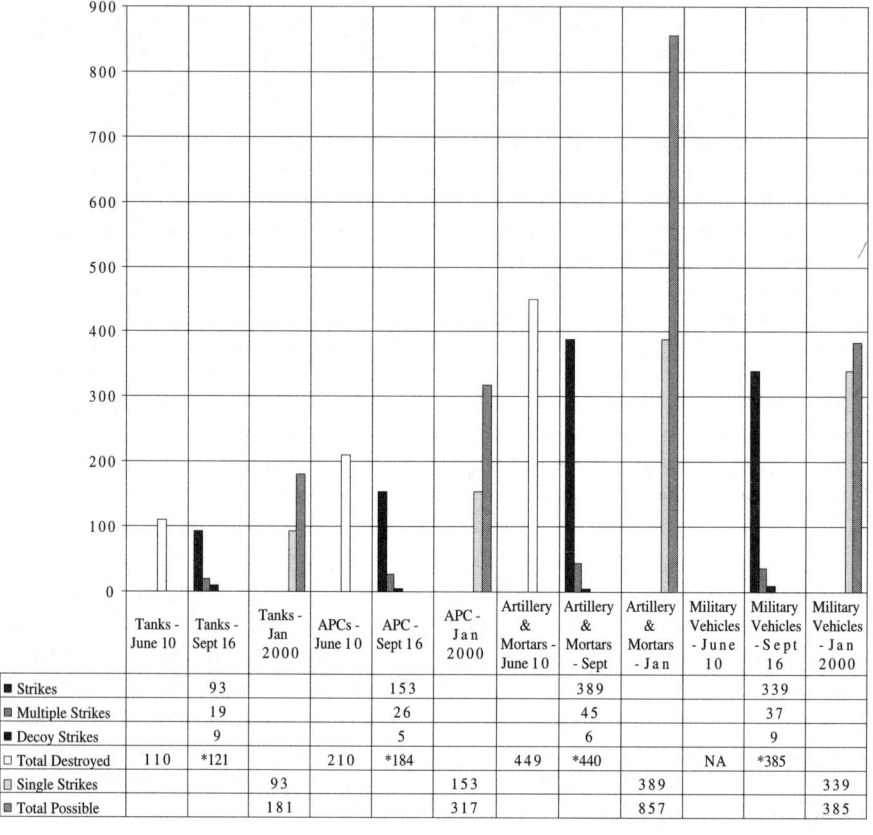

	Tanks - June 10	Tanks - Sept 16	Tanks - Jan 2000	APCs - June 10	APC - Sept 16	APC - Jan 2000	Artillery & Mortars - June 10	Artillery & Mortars - Sept	Artillery & Mortars - Jan	Military Vehicles - June 10	Military Vehicles - Sept 16	Military Vehicles - Jan 2000
■ Strikes		93			153			389			339	
■ Multiple Strikes		19			26			45			37	
■ Decoy Strikes		9			5			6			9	
□ Total Destroyed	110	*121		210	*184		449	*440		NA	*385	
▨ Single Strikes			93			153			389			339
▨ Total Possible			181			317			857			385

Source: Adapted by Anthony H. Cordesman from data provided in the NATO Briefing by SACEUR, General Wesley Clark, on September 16, 1999, and Department of Defense, *Report to Congress: Kosovo/Operation Allied Forces After Action Report*, Washington, Department of Defense, January 31, 2000, pp. 85–86.

- Indications of the use of camouflage, concealment, and deception campaign by the Yugoslav military
- Indications that some NATO strikes missed specific targets (tanks, armored personnel carriers, artillery, mortars, and military vehicles)
- Indications of evidence that Yugoslav military forces cleaned the battlefield
- Indications that the Kosovo Liberation Army destroyed or damaged tanks, armored personnel carriers, artillery, mortars, and military vehicles
- Indications that some NATO missions struck the same targets on multiple occasions.

Figure 36
The Rising Serbian Presence in Kosovo: As of April 29, 1999

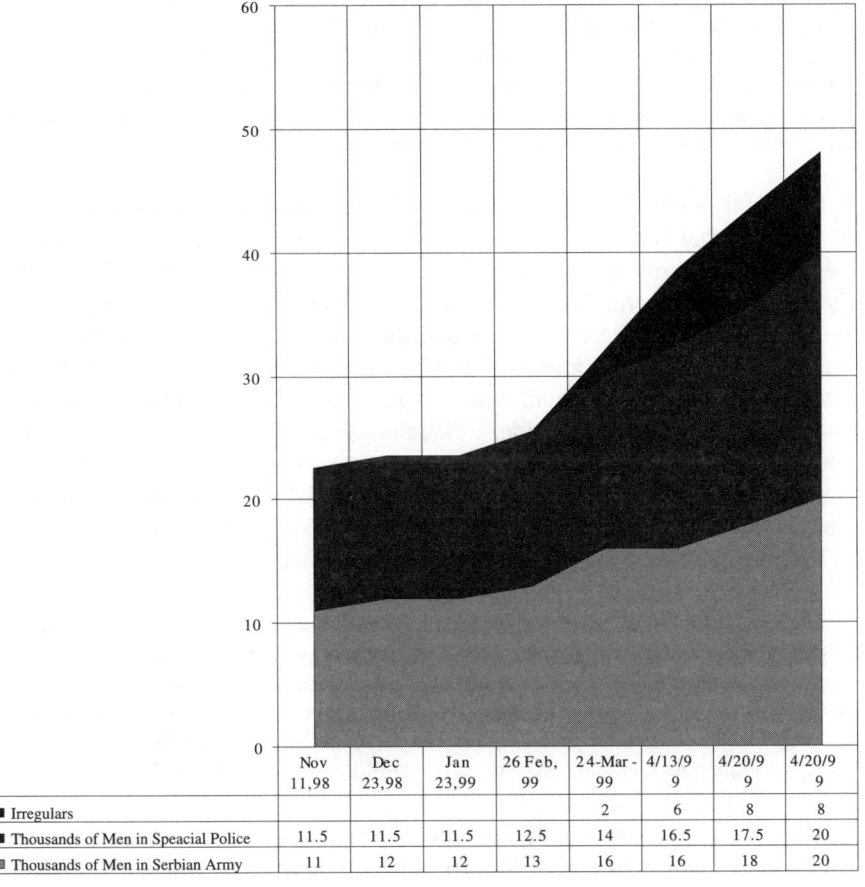

	Nov 11,98	Dec 23,98	Jan 23,99	26 Feb, 99	24-Mar - 99	4/13/9 9	4/20/9 9	4/20/9 9
■ Irregulars					2	6	8	8
■ Thousands of Men in Speacial Police	11.5	11.5	11.5	12.5	14	16.5	17.5	20
▨ Thousands of Men in Serbian Army	11	12	12	13	16	16	18	20

Source: NATO Briefing—April 13, 1999; NATO, April 21, 1999.

Assessments of these indications were made using cockpit video from actual strikes, image intelligence, measurements and signatures intelligence, signals intelligence, human intelligence, interviews with forward air controllers and on-scene witnesses, and through on-site observations by the team. Figure 34 shows the results of the assessment. *The assessment provides no data on what proportion of total mobile targets were hit or the level of damage inflicted on the targets that were struck. Instead, the number of target hits were collected.* Thus, the first segment of each bar represents the final number of strikes that were determined to have achieved successful hits against mobile targets as confirmed by the assessment team. The last segment on each bar represents those mission reports that provided sufficient evidence of a hit based on the methodology to support a successful strike assessment. Thus, the targets in this category represent possible hits that cannot be confirmed. The team also determined that a small number of targets had been hit and reported by more than one strike mission (49 probable across all target classes and shown in the second segment) and that a more limited number of decoy targets had been attacked (25 across all target classes and shown in the third segment).

As is apparent from the figure, roughly 60 percent of the target-hit claims made during Operation Allied Force could be confirmed by the assessment team. However, the on-site visits did not occur until more than a month after the conflict had ended, allowing time for the Serbs to remove damaged vehicles from the battlefield.

It is mildly amusing to compare this modest assessment to the incredible claims of accuracy that NATO, the British Ministry of Defense, and the Department of Defense made during the war. It is also important to read the italicized portions of the US text with care. *The results are not a damage assessment.* They are an assessment of hits, regardless of the damage inflicted. They are not related to the total number of strikes or munitions fired, and are not related to any estimate of the total force engaged. The unconfirmed category also consists of pilot or crew claims without any filtering or validation, although such claims are notoriously inaccurate and exaggerated. The end result is to undercut the earlier NATO claims because it is now clear that they included all hits, rather than "kills," and that the unconfirmed category is very unlikely to include a significant number of additional hits.

It is also important to note that the same report states,[199]

As expected, attacks on mobile targets proved more problematic than attacks against fixed targets. The Serbs hid many of their mobile ground force systems, making them difficult to locate and attack. NATO's desire to limit collateral damage also constrained us in some circumstances from attacking possible ground force targets. On the other hand, by forcing the Yugoslavs to hide their ground maneuver forces and not operate them as units in the open, we limited their combat effectiveness, therefore achieving the desired effect.

More broadly, these results that speak volumes about the value of wartime claims and briefings, the ability to carry out wartime and after action battle damage assessment, the real world accuracy of air strikes against mobile targets, and the current real world ability to achieve the absurd level of "information dominance" called for in some versions of the revolution in military affairs.

The Lessons of Attacks on Serbian Ground Forces

Given this background—and the detailed statistics in Figure 29 relating the nature of the NATO build-up, weather, and the impact of the KLA—there are other important lessons that need careful consideration. NATO lacked the forces it needed early in the war to carry out the number of strike sorties needed to have a decisive early impact on Serbian forces, even if the weather had been suitable. Weather clearly had a major impact on NATO's capabilities at any time, particularly on NATO European strike-attack aircraft, which normally lacked advanced avionics and poor weather-night vision systems equal to those of US aircraft. It is also clear that NATO encountered very serious problems in targeting Serb forces until the KLA (UCK) begin to launch an offensive in mid-May, and that there was a "ground phase" to the air and missile war.

The data available are so weak that it is difficult to generalize with any certainty. Nevertheless, this analysis indicates that it may be possible to draw the following lessons from the air and missile campaign (or at least to raise them as rhetorical questions):

- *The targeting of ground forces remains a major problem, and the difficulties posed by weather, the need to operate at stand-off ranges, decoys, Serbian ability to shelter in civilian areas or disperse and hide in rough terrain, are likely to be far more typical of most air operations that the static, exposed target arrays that Iraq presented during the Gulf War.*

- *The battle damage assessment of strikes against individual ground weapons remains as much an uncertain art form as during the Gulf War in spite of advances in UAVs, reconnaissance and intelligence systems, and analysis. NATO and the US lack the capability to "close the loop" in terms of reliable, real-time battle damage assessment that can be used for effective tactical decision making. (This lesson is reinforced by the extraordinary vagueness of US and NATO battle damage claims regarding the effectiveness of the unguided ordnance used in the war.)*

- *Weather remains a major enemy of air and missile power, in spite of new avionics and sensors. The use of advanced radars, other sensors, GPS-guided weapons, and smart terminal guidance may eventually change this situation. It did not succeed in doing so in this campaign, and the US and NATO may have over-relied on laser guided bombs and weapons with limited electro-optical capabilities.*

- *Even relative low-grade air defenses, with weapons technology dating back to the 1970s, can seriously degrade the effectiveness of air attacks by forcing aircraft to attack at relative high altitudes and long ranges. This problem is compounded by a reluctance to take losses, the inability to predict where air defenses are present, and a seeming lack of any way to reliably alert aircraft that they are under attack in time to risk more dangerous attack profiles.*

- *Air power can force an enemy to rely on dispersal and concealment. Dispersal and concealment does not, however, paralyze an enemy involved in low intensity operations or that can use civilians and civilian facilities to shelter in.*

- *It still takes a ground threat to force enemy ground forces to expose themselves and to create predictable and vulnerable target arrays. In other cases, air and missile power still confront the same problem that the Israeli Air Force encountered in 1973. Most ground force movements occur too quickly and too unpredictably, and in too small a set of concentrations, to ensure that air and missile power can successfully attack.*

- *This, in turn, raises serious questions about the loiter—and time-over-exposed-target capability—of bombers like the B-1 and B-2. Far too much of the public analysis of plans to use such aircraft seems to rely on the ability to arrive over exposed massed mixes of armor at precisely the right moment.*

- *It also raises questions about the value of using modern air power for "tank plinking," and search and destroy missions against heavy enemy land weapons that substitute a "weapons count" for a "body count" in a war of attrition rather than destroy concentrations of enemy forces to achieve a tactical purpose. There is always an argument for missions that destroy large amounts of enemy weaponry with great efficiency, but it is unclear that search and destroy missions truly serve a tactical and strategic purpose unless they can have this effect and air confirmed by battle damage assessment that has great reliability.*

- *More generally, this kind of concealment, dispersal, use of decoys, and use of air defenses to degrade air attack can be counted on to be a feature of asymmetric warfare in threat forces. The same is true of a focus on politicizing wars, the use of hostages and human shields, and other measures to limit the impact of the "revolution in military affairs."*

It is important to reiterate the fact that NATO won, that these lessons and limitations are anything but crippling, and that technological solutions exist for many of these problems and some are nearing deployment. Certainly, these problems are a powerful endorsement of the need for the JSF and the strike features of the F-22, advanced sensors and targeting systems, GPS-guided weapons, and other smart munitions.

The other side of this particular coin is that low and moderate technology air and missile power is now probably obsolete for Western democracies. Forces that cannot take maximum advantage of avionics, sensors, smart weapons, and advanced targeting and BDA systems are not capable of dealing with such problems under demanding tactical conditions and risk unacceptable losses and/or levels of effectiveness. In many cases, they will become coalition liabilities rather than coalition partners.

THE SERBIAN BUILD-UP, SERBIAN OPERATIONS, AND THE CHALLENGE OF ASYMMETRIC WARFARE

Many of the previous lessons about the air and missile campaign are reinforced by an examination of the history of the Serbian build-up in Kosovo. Serbian land forces fought precisely the kind of asymmetric warfare that experts have warned is a critical potential weakness in the so-called "revolution in military affairs."

In such cases, air and missile power cannot be used against a well-defined enemy that can be separated from civilians and engaged in the field. Instead, it must be used against a Serbian force that consists largely of relatively lightly armed forces, which is co-located with the civilians NATO is seeking to protect, and which has both regular military and major paramilitary elements.

Serbian and NATO Actions in 1998

At the same time, the history of the Serbian build-up supports NATO's thesis that ethnic cleansing of some kind would have occurred if NATO had never launched its air and missile campaign. NATO had ample experience with Serbian attitudes and actions in Bosnia. NATO was confronted by violent Serbian repression in Kosovo in the spring of 1998, and began to debate what action it should take in May 1998. On June 15, it conducted a four-hour air exercise over Albania and Macedonia called Determined Falcon. This exercise involved 80 aircraft from 13 NATO nations that flew from 15 bases in five different countries. It included 27 US aircraft from land and carrier bases.[200]

This demonstrative action did not halt Serbian action, nor did NATO diplomacy. NATO intelligence detected the first cases of Serbian "village busting" in July 1998. It also saw indications that Serbia was planning a major Kosovo-wide campaign designed to defeat the KLA. During the summer of 1998, a quarter of a million Kosovar Albanians were forced from their homes as their houses, villages and crops were destroyed. This led to new discussions in NATO and on September 24, 1998, NATO ministers of defense authorized an "activation order" placing the necessary forces under NATO command to force Serbia to halt. The following day, Milosevic and US Negotiator Richard Holbrooke announced an agreement that postponed the threat of NATO air strikes if Serbia (a) reduced its troops and security forces in Kosovo, (b) permitted unarmed NATO reconnaissance flights over Kosovo, (c) allowed in 2,000 unarmed civilian monitors to oversee a cease-fire, and (d) began meaningful negotiations with the Kosovars over autonomy. The UN Security Council passed a resolution calling for the immediate withdrawal of Serbian security forces from Kosovo on September 23, 1998.

The September 1998 agreement did not bring meaningful negotiations or put an end to violence, and the civilian monitors faced steadily growing problems with the Serbian government. NATO and US intelligence also found evidence that Serbia was planning a major campaign by December 1998, and that the Serbian general staff had assured Milosevic that an all out campaign could defeat the KLA in 5–6 days and achieve the equivalent of pacification in several weeks.[201] In January 1999, evidence was discovered, by a United Nations humanitarian team, of the massacre of over 40 people in the village of Racak. As a result, NATO Ministers met on January 30, 1999, and authorized the Secretary General Solana to carry out air strikes anywhere in Yugoslavia if some form of peace settlement had not been reached by February 20, 1999. NATO estimates that over 2000 people were killed as a result of the Serb government's policies in Kosovo between March 1998 and March 1999.

A "Contact Group" on the Balkans composed of informal representatives from Britain, France, Germany, Italy, Russia, and the US attempted to negotiate a settlement and propose a possible framework. Serbia rejected this framework. It also began to systematically build up the capability to carry out its campaign against the Kosovar opposition. US experts estimate that the total VJ strength in Kosovo was approximately 15–16,000 in early 1999, with some reinforcements from other VJ formations outside Kosovo.

The FRY/Serbian Build-Up in 1999

In March, Yugoslav army and paramilitary forces from the Ministry of the Interior moved out of their garrisons in Kosovo, and 20,000 additional troops moved to the border of Kosovo. One armored mechanized brigade was located in Pristina, and another in Urosevac. One motorized brigade was located in Kosovska,

Mitrovica and in Pec, and another in Djakovica and Prizren. These units were deployed in two main locations: garrisons in Leposavic, Kosovska Mitrovica, Vucitrn, Pristina, and Urosevac and garrisons in Pec, Djakovica, and Prizren, which dealt with KLA forces entering from Albania

The Serbs also had border security facilities including the watchtowers in the Morina, Gorozup, Pastrik, Kosare, Koznjar and other sectors. The Army of Yugoslavia had extended the depth of the border control zone to five or six kilometers, significantly impeding movement between Kosovo and Albania. Soldiers have mined the area along the border with Albania. The violence in Kosovo escalated steadily in March, which led NATO to begin Operation Allied Force on March 24, 1999.

The Serbian Build-Up During the War

NATO issued only limited data on the Serbian mobilization after the air and missile campaign began and on the number of reservists being organized into added combat units. The data it has issued, however, indicate that the total manning of the Serbian military and special police rose by 32% after December 23, and about 8% between March 24 and April 13. They rose by around 51% after December 23 by April 22, and about 36% between March 24 and April 22. It is important to note that these figures do strongly argue that Serbia was preparing for ethnic cleansing before NATO began its air and missile campaign. The air and missile campaign, however, clearly did not prevent a major Serbian build-up.

There were at least 36,000 Serbian military and special police in Kosovo as of April 22, with roughly 1,800–2,500 armored vehicles and heavy weapons scattered all over Kosovo. There were 27 identifiable military units, and probably another 7,000–8,000 irregulars. By late April, NATO estimated that there were a total of 40,000 army and MUP forces in Kosovo, plus up to another 8,000 irregulars, police, fire, emergency and other paramilitary elements. US estimates put the total of Serbian forces at 48,000 on April 30, and Milosevic claimed the same day there were 100,000 Special Police in Kosovo. These estimates illustrate the fact that it is almost impossible to estimate the precise number of men Serbia has, or can deploy, in Kosovo or other parts of the FRY. Modern intelligence systems do not include any sensors capable of detecting and tracking manpower on this basis.

NATO's estimates of the build-up of Serbian forces though April 27 are shown in Table 8. The US reported that there were at least seven active brigades in the Kosovo area on April 30, 1999. NATO reported on May 6 that the Serbs had two armored and seven mechanized "units" in Kosovo, which seem to have meant a total of nine brigades, plus an artillery regiment. The definitions involved were so different that there is no way to compare this reporting to the previous reporting.

The trends in the Serbian build-up are summarized in Figure 37, and it is again important to note that NATO and the US repeatedly stated during their briefings that NATO air operations had only had a limited impact on Serb operations in

Table 8
The Serbian Build-Up in Kosovo

	11/11/98	12/23/98	1/23/99	2/26/99	3/24/99	4/13/99	4/20/99	4/27/99
Thousands of Men in Serbian Army	11	12	12	13	16	16	18	20
Thousands of Men in Special Police	11.5	11.5	11.5	12.5	14	16.5	17.5	20
Irregulars	-	-	-	-	2	6	8	8
HQ	6	-	-	-	-	-	-	-
Brigades	-	3	3	5	4	4	-	-
Battalions	-	5	7	6	11	24	-	-
Companies	7	4	3	3	9	-	-	-

Kosovo until late May. Further, they have made it clear that Serbian army and MOP forces are displacing civilians to use their homes and facilities and seizing their supplies. General Clark stated on April 27 that,

The Yugoslav military now . . . number along with the police at least 40,000, they have been reinforced in the last three or four days by an influx of newly-mobilized reservists to replace combat casualties and they've also been reinforced by the continuing assistance and movement of elements from the Yugoslav Second Army which is based in Montenegro, they are fighting over the border.

They are principally engaged in three things: First in working against the elements of the UCK who are still present in many locations in Kosovo and still offering resistance; secondly, in conjunction with the special police and with the paramilitaries, trying to maneuver and otherwise manipulate the large numbers of internally-displaced people. It is not clear to us at this point precisely what the aim of this activity is but we know they're engaged in it. And third, they're attempting to build and strengthen defensive positions along the borders in anticipation of NATO attacks or to block infiltration from the UCK. But I might tell you what they're also doing is whenever the weather is good, whenever there are NATO aircraft, they are stationary and hidden; they are knocking down the walls of houses, backing into the forests, getting under haystacks and generally ceasing all action whenever we're in the area because they very much fear what NATO air is doing to them and we are doing something to them there and so the pace of their activities has been apprecia-bly affected.

Milosevic claimed in an interview on April 30 that Serbia had 100,000 men in Kosovo—a figure he later repeated when he claimed that Serbia would withdraw half of its forces from Kosovo at a rate of 100–150 a day. A US spokesman replied on May 1, however, that,

We have no reason to believe that. None of our information is even close to that. Now obviously, counting troops is difficult and we've always given ranges of the number of troops in and around Kosovo, and they don't come anywhere near 100,000. When this began we were estimating about 40,000 troops in the area. That is still pretty much our estimate in Kosovo—in or very close to Kosovo. We have not seen huge numbers of troops streaming into Kosovo. So I would say that this is either a sign of this lack of information about his own military force disposition or it's a sign of desperation to create some sort of propaganda force that doesn't exist on the ground.

The entire Yugoslav army is a little over 100,000—the active army. If you were to mobilize everybody, it would be about 400,000. So to go back to the original answer, we see no indication that there are 100,000 people there now. That would be adding up the VJ or the army and the MUP or special police.

It is clear, however, that he does—that he seems to think that he is going to be attacked by ground forces because he's been lining up defensive positions along the Macedonian border and the Albanian border. He's been digging in with artillery and armor, and other types of forces. This is not bad from our standpoint because they're static and we know where they are, and although they're dug in, they're much easier to attack than forces that might be dispersed or on the move. So we have taken account of that, obviously, in our operations. But we have nothing to confirm this number of 100,000.

The British Ministry of Defense estimated on May 2 that the Serbian presence in Kosovo included approximately 20,000 men in the 52 (Pristina) Corps, with some reinforcements from other VJ formations outside Kosovo. The Pristina Corps was headquartered in Pristina and is subordinate to the 3rd Army. It had elements in Pristina, Pec, Prizren, Kosovska Mitrovica, Urosevac, Djakovica, and Gnjilane. The Ministry of Interior Police (MUP) in Kosovo had risen from a peacetime strength of around 6,000 to at least 16,000 men. These forces were concentrated in two sub-organizations, the SAJ (specialist anti-terrorist police) and the PJP (combat police forces). They were largely co-located with the VJ in their barracks. They manned all the check-points on the main roads.

NATO's next major report on the Serbian build-up occurred during the press briefing on May 11, when Jamie Shea reacted to Milosevic's announcement that he would withdraw 50% of the Serbian forces in Kosovo—which Milosevic still estimated at 100,000 men. Shea's statement denied there was any evidence of a meaningful withdrawal and warned at just how difficult any peace settlement could be to enforce:

. . . we have to be very cautious in the Alliance on this because President Milosevic's record on partial troop withdrawals is not very encouraging. You recall our experience of last October when President Milosevic agreed with NATO to a partial withdrawal of his forces and to observe a cease-fire in Kosovo. At that time President Milosevic said that he would retain in the province after 27 October 1998 approximately 11,500 troops. But the verifiers of the Kosovo Verification Mission confirmed that this number gradually increased over a four month period by at least 1,000 personnel. In addition, President Milosevic never withdrew all of the units which were not part of his 52nd Corps normally based in Pristina. This was also in contravention of the agreement that he signed. In fact beginning in February 1999 he began deploying entire units and elements of other battalions and brigades into the province in the guise of border defense and winter training operations. As of April 1999 there were at least 20,000 Yugoslav Army troops in Kosovo.

And if we look at the figures for the Ministry of Interior and regular police forces, we see that President Milosevic provided a peace-time personnel authorization for the province of about 10,000 personnel. This number incidentally reflects one of the highest police-to-citizen ratios in all of Europe. However, at the beginning of October there were at least 2,000 more police in the province than President Milosevic claimed were on leave status, and in addition to the 2,000 police personnel on leave status in Kosovo, the verifiers of the Kosovo Verification Mission assessed a number of police in excess of the agreed limit of 10,000, probably fluctuating anywhere between 1,000–2,000 more. After that period, police forces from outside Kosovo began to arrive in truly significant numbers by bus and train convoys. By March 1999 there were as many as 15,000 special police and regular police forces in Kosovo. The total Serb security forces in Kosovo, a country which has a population of about 800,000 at the moment, now exceeds 40,000, or around 40,000 personnel. Again, one of the highest ratios that you will find anywhere.

Serbian Use of Human Shields and Manipulation of the Media

The US and NATO did not discuss Serbian reinforcements in detail during the following briefings on the war, but they did make it clear that Serbia was able to reinforce to some extent by infiltrating in limited numbers of men as reinforcements or replacements. It also was able to move units, men, and supplies in small unit operations with only erratic NATO targeting and air and missile attacks except in those cases where it was forced to concentrate to deal with significant KLA forces.

Serbia learned to exploit the use of Kosovar civilian facilities and populations as shields, to disperse its movements of heavy military equipment and concentrate only when needed, to mix military movements with civilian movements, to use civilian vehicles or vehicles that looked like civilian vehicles, and to alter deployment patterns to reduce NATO's ability to characterize military targets.

There is also considerable evidence that Serbia stage managed some "collateral damage" incidents by either removing military and paramilitary casualties and equipment, or by arranging the victims of ethnic cleansing to make them appear to be the victims of airpower. A detailed review of Serbian video coverage of "collateral damage" reveals many cases where casualties are shown without any indication of the source of the damage, casualties are removed or treated only after TV cameras arrive, and bodies are burning hours after the attack without any nearby fuel source.

A Serbian View of the Build-Up

While there is no way to confirm his figures, Colonel General Nebojsa Pavkovic—the Serbian commander in Kosovo—claimed after the war that he had some 150,000 soldiers and other security forces at his disposal when the war ended. He also claimed that they knew the terrain well and that it would have taken a NATO force of 300,000 to defeat them in a ground war, rather than the 170,000 that NATO estimated in its preliminary plans. Pavkovic said that, "our willingness to defend Kosovo at any price (deterred NATO from a war) with close conflict where air strikes in support would not be that effective . . . I estimated that the losses would have been very high and that NATO forces simply could not accept that."[202]

Pavkovic also made several other observations about the war that are of interest, although their credibility is again uncertain. He explained the Serbian military view of the war by saying,

The police and the army in the last few years, and especially in the last year, were under constant attack from terrorist units, and a lot of soldiers and police were killed. By March 1998, the security of our forces was in danger and the territory of Kosovo was in danger. And the state, like all states in the world, took measures to prevent terrorism in our country. The Albanians were trying to make a state within a state.

Pavkovic denied that there were "paramilitary or special volunteer units (operating independently). All the units and relatively specialized police were practically under the command of the police and the volunteer units that were about 1,000 people in Kosovo were dispersed and placed in regular army units and didn't operate in special units." He states that the police were responsible for most actions against the Kosovars, "most were actions of the police . . . police made special police actions and we in the army had the battle against organized terrorism in Kosovo (the KLA)."

Lessons from the Serbian Build-Up

It is impossible to determine the true nature and impact of the Serbian build-up during the war, or the exact state of Serbian forces in Kosovo at the end of the NATO campaign. It is clear, however, that Serbian forces continued to fight and were able to move, concentrate, and step up their activity in the border area in the closing week of the war. It is also important to note that while Serbia could not afford to pay the 8,000 reservists it called up for the war, it was able to retain enough manpower, fuel, and C^3I capability in Kosovo so that it had relatively little trouble in withdrawing after June 10, although some delays had to be made in the original withdrawal schedule.[203]

There are several possible lessons that can be drawn from this experience:

- *Asymmetric warfare is likely to involve an enemy attempt to cloak military operations in a political context that limits military action in the build-up phase, and to exploit dialogue and diplomacy to limit the ability of the US and NATO to use air and missile power to prevent both the preparatory phase and actual operations—particularly if these efforts can be restricted to security operations or termed defensive. Enemies will exploit every apparent political weakness or fault line both in terms of US politics and within a coalition. Diplomacy will be made an extension of war by other means.*

- *Civilian populations and facilities will be used as weapons of war to defend against air and missile power, and create shields or sanctuaries.*

- *Enemies will systematically exploit "collateral damage" to enhance their ability to use civilians and civilian facilities as sanctuaries or shields, and "stage manage" either false incidents or the character or actual incidents.*

- *Build-ups, reinforcements, and operations will be conducted in ways that minimize the concentration of force wherever possible. They will be tailored to maximize the shielding effect of civilian populations and facilities, and given political "cover" where possible.*

- *Future enemies will probably learn from the Serbian experience that overt mass military and paramilitary operations against civilian populations create a risk of US or Western military intervention that can be avoided by slower, less intense paramilitary operations.*

- *At the same time, Kosovo provides an important lesson that refugee populations and movements can be used as a weapon of war to shield against the use of air power and deep strike operations. This is not a new lesson—it was certainly exploited with great success in World War II, Korea and Vietnam. It is, however, a lesson that the West tends to forget.*

- *All of these lessons interact to reinforce the political character of asymmetric warfare, and challenge the assumption that military doctrine and planning can concentrate on the physical destruction of the enemy.*

9

The "Ground Option": The Possible Impact of NATO Planning for an Invasion

Many of the details surrounding NATO's effort to plan a ground option remain unknown. So do the exact political circumstances surrounding NATO's political announcements, like the statements that it had rejected a ground option at the beginning of the air and missile campaign. One of the great unknowns surrounding the air and missile campaign in Kosovo is the level of intelligence Serbia had on NATO plans, and the extent to which Serbia's knowledge that it might face a NATO invasion led Serbia to terminate the conflict. NATO denied throughout the air and missile campaign that it was planning an invasion and this remained a serious option.[204]

The most public rejection of a ground option came when US President Clinton gave a television address on April 24, the first day of the campaign, and said, "I do not intend to put our troops in Kosovo to fight a war." At the same time, it is unclear that any NATO nation argued for a major ground option at the start of the air and missile campaign, or even for preserving the option as a means of putting political pressure on Serbia. Certainly, Greece and Italy actively opposed such an option at the start of the fighting, and France and Germany did not support it.

THE QUIET SHIFT TOWARDS A GROUND OPTION

By mid-April, however, SACEUR General Wesley K. Clark had brought together British and US officers at the Supreme Headquarters Allied Powers in Europe (SHAPE) headquarters in Mons, Belgium, to reexamine the options for a ground invasion. Although the political leaders of the North Atlantic Council had not authorized such planning, the US Security Advisor Sandy Berger had persuaded Javier Solana, the Secretary General of NATO, to authorize such secret discussions. The large scale of ethnic cleansing, and the slow pace of the air and missile campaign, was forcing NATO to change its plans.

The are reports that President Clinton secretly decided to send in ground troops if the air and missile campaign failed shortly before NATO's 50th anniversary summit meeting in Washington on April 25, 1999. While the senior US generals in the US command structure—including US Defense Secretary William Cohen and Chairman of the Joint Chiefs of Staff General Henry H. Shelton—do not seem to have endorsed a ground option, the NATO military staff does seem to have agreed that ground forces would be necessary and this judgment seems to have led both President Clinton and British Prime Minister Blair to agree that a ground option might well be necessary.

This led to the formation of a secret invasion planning staff that included several dozen officers at Mons, and some 60 US personnel at the US Central Command (USCENTCOM) Headquarters in Stuttgart. At the same time, President Clinton persuaded Prime Minister Blair to drop public support for a ground option on the grounds that premature debate might divide the alliance and lead the Russians to end any diplomatic support of a peace initiative that favored NATO.

By mid-May, SHAPE seems to have come up with an option involving some 175,000 men, most of which would have to advance up the single road through Kukes to Kosovo. These were to be supported by helicopter attacks from Italy and a possible feint through Hungary. NATO evidently rejected a full-scale invasion of Belgrade and chose an option that would protect the Kosovars in Kosovo.

This planning effort seems to have had enough German and Italian support so that US, German, and Italian military engineers cooperated in a contingency effort to strengthen the road through Kukes to take armored traffic, using the cover of improving the road to allow more rapid aid to the Kosovar refugees. This effort was essential because the road could not support M-1A1 tank traffic without such improvement. The planning for the ground option also seems to have led the US to step up its Special Forces support to the KLA.

Proceeding with the ground option did not win immediate support from Secretary Cohen and all the Joint Chiefs when it was briefed to them on May 19. US support came largely from Sandy Berger and the civilians in President Clinton's security team. It was clear, however, that some of the chiefs did support Clark, and that President Clinton was tilting towards the ground option. It was also clear that a final decision would have to be taken by June 10 if the US was to have the 90 days of preparation time that it felt was essential to launch the ground option before winter. Even this schedule was ambitious, since Britain felt that at least 120 days of preparation time was required.

PUTTING ALL THE OPTIONS ON THE TABLE

President Clinton very publicly announced on May 18 that, "all options are on the table," openly ended the flat rejection of the ground option he had made on

March 24. He also approved the positioning of up to 45,000 troops in Macedonia, including 7,500 US troops, that could either be used to support a ground option or occupy Kosovo if Milosevic conceded.

On May 23, President Clinton and Prime Minister Blair held a secret phone conversation in which they agreed to allow Solana to formulate a detailed plan for operations. British Defense Secretary George Robertson then organized a secret meeting in Bonn on May 27 that lasted from 10:00 to 16:30, and which included Cohen, Robertson, other senior allied defense officials and senior military officers from Germany, France, and Italy. Robertson also evidently pledged some 50,000 British troops to support a 150,000-man ground option—although this total implied that Britain would deploy half of its standing army and it is far from clear that Britain could have supported such a power projection effort without major US aid.[205]

There does not seem to have been a clear consensus at the meeting on May 27. The German and Italian defense ministers did, however, show more support for a ground option than in the past, and France did not openly oppose it—although the French minister argued that there was insufficient time to prepare and execute an invasion before winter. Secretary Cohen seems to have argued that it was safer to rely on the air and missile campaign at the risk of dividing the alliance: "It was clear at that meeting that a consensus for ground forces was not going to materialize. I argued for intensifying the air war and for broadening and streamlining the target selection process."[206]

There still was no unified mandate for action. Nevertheless, the meeting does seem to have produced an agreement by British, France, Germany, Italy, and the US that NATO could not afford to lose a war, that progress in the air and missile campaign was less successful than NATO's public briefings implied, and that ground action would be required if the air and missile campaign did not succeed. This possibility became a real issue in late May when a KLA offensive that began on May 27 led to a KLA defeat, and diplomatic negotiations failed to produce any clear signs of Serbian concessions.

LATE MAY: ON THE EDGE OF GOING TO A GROUND OPTION

President Clinton decided to delay action, hoping that the increasing intensity of NATO's air strikes might still force Serbia to withdraw. At the same time, the decision was taken to reexamine the ground option ten days later, and to deploy another engineering battalion to strengthen the road though Kukes to take tanks and heavy self-propelled artillery as well as lighter armored fighting vehicles. Preparations are also reported to have been serious enough so that German and British forces were standing by with pontoons and bridging tanks to allow NATO to use navigable waterways to bring in heavy equipment.

According to press reports, General Clark went to Washington on June 1 to try to persuade President Clinton to authorize the beginning of ground invasion on

September 1. The timing was growing steadily more urgent, and by this time the US build-up and deployment included up to 120,000 men and women. Britain too faced an urgent deadline, since its plans called for the call up of 30,000 reserves in early June.

At the same time, the growing political frustration over NATO's failure to win a quick victory led Berger to meet with outside security experts who supported a ground invasion on June 2. The meeting included critics like Jeanne Kirkpatrick, the former ambassador to the UN; Robert Hunter and William Taft (former ambassadors to NATO); General George A. Joulwan, a former SACEUR; Helmut Sonnenfeldt, a former state Department official; Steve Larrabee of the Rand Corporation; and Ivo Daalder and Jeremy Rosner, who were former members of the staff of the National Security Council. He made it clear at this meeting that the Administration was closer to supporting a ground option than had previously been announced, and that it would do anything necessary to win, including a ground invasion.[207] Berger is quoted as saying that the Clinton Administration still believed that the air campaign was working, but that the Administration was determined to win, and that the President had not ruled out the ground option.[208]

President Clinton was scheduled to meet again with the Joint Chiefs on June 3, and this was close to the deadline that Clark has set for announcing that the US was preparing for a ground option and mobilizing the necessary reserves in time to have 90 days in which to prepare the ground attack and still begin the operation before winter.

Ironically, however, June 3 proved to be the day that Milosevic told the EU envoy Finish President Martii Ahtissari, and the former Russian Prime Minister Victor Chernomyrdin, that he would accept their proposed peace agreement. The US did not trust Milosevic's initiative, however, and President Clinton met with the Joint Chiefs that same afternoon to discuss the invasion. Clark also reacted skeptically, and called for continued bombing and preparation for an invasion

As a result, the bombing continued down to the last day, and so did preparations for an invasion. This was one reason that NATO launched B-52 strikes to support the KLA on June 7. NATO both wanted to avoid any further major defeat of its principle potential ally in an invasion, and to keep the border with Albania open for a later NATO invasion. General Clark is quoted as saying, "That mountain is not going to get lost. I'm not going to have Serbs on that mountain. We'll pay for that hill with American blood if we don't help (the KLA) hold it."[209]

This planning for the ground option would be an interesting historical footnote if it were not for the possibility that Serbian intelligence knew of the NATO effort, possibly with assistance from Russian intelligence. There are some indications that Serbia did know a great deal about the NATO effort, and that the knowledge that Serbia could not simply ride out the air and missile campaign without having to deal with a ground invasion was a key reason for Milosevic's concession. It is interesting to note, for example, that Major General Vladimir Lazarevic, the commander of the Serbian Pristina Corps, stated on May 26 that the KLA effort to open up a secure supply line to Kosovo from the round through Kukes and the area around Mount Pastrik was " . . . the beginning of a new phase of operation, the so-called land invasion."

At the same time, Serbia may not have known the details of the NATO planning effort, and the Serbian commentary on an invasion may have referred only to the support Albania and others were giving the KLA. Alternatively, the Serbian leadership may have reacted to the many press reports indicating that NATO would eventually pursue a ground option if the air and missile campaign failed. It scarcely needed access to intelligence data to know this was a possibility. Furthermore, there is no way to rank Serbia's perception of this risk relative to the impact of the fact the air campaign was becoming more successful, and Serbia had failed to defeat the KLA.

Barring access to the highest levels of Serbian decision-making, it may never be possible to determine how much the NATO "ground option" contributed to the end of the war—or whether a NATO decision not to reject a ground option at the start of the war would have brought a quicker end to the fighting.

10

The "Ground Option": The Role of the KLA

The same uncertainties regarding the impact of a ground option surround the role of the KLA. As has been touched upon earlier, one of the major factors that led to the Serbian move into Kosovo, and the ethnic cleanings that followed, was the Serbian calculation that decisive military action could destroy the KLA in as little as 3–5 days and in no more than a few weeks.

In practice, the Serbian forces soon found they could defeat any fixed concentration of KLA forces, but could not surround or eliminate KLA guerrilla forces and that they could not identify KLA sympathizers and part-time militias. Like many other guerilla wars, including Vietnam, the ability to win battles against fixed formations of light, easily dispersible forces did not win wars. At the same time, ethnic cleansing created massive new numbers of KLA supporters and volunteers, and led to a flood of new funds and weapons, and a major increase in Albanian support for the KLA.

THE REAL-WORLD GROUND OPTION THAT NATO DID NOT DISCUSS

The end result was to create a very tangible "ground option" based on the KLA's resistance and Serbian inability to win a quick military victory and secure the province. While there is no way to know the exact views of the Serbian leadership, the fact that the KLA resistance continued on into June without diminishing, and that "ethnic cleansing" created new military problems, may have been a major factor that eventually led Serbia to end the war. The threat posed by the KLA almost certainly interacted with the growing threat that NATO would invade if

See next page ...

Serbia did not accept NATO's terms, as did the fact that NATO increasingly came to both use the KLA to provide help in targeting its air strikes and used increasing amounts of airpower in support of the KLA. KLA representatives evidently met with US officials and officers at the US Embassy in Tirana, including an officer from Task Force Hawk. The center for the US intelligence and military assistance effort seems to have been Kukes.[210]

The full details of the covert support the KLA received from NATO countries are still unclear, but at least the US and Britain seem to have provided the KLA with training, aid, and equipment to both blow up Serbian targets in the field and to provide NATO aircraft with targeting data. US and British intelligence and special forces seem to have operated out of Albania, and other countries may have provided covert support as well. One source indicates that that NATO began such covert support almost immediately after the start of the air and missile campaign, that the CIA had a major support mission based in Tirana, Albanian; and that 24 US Army Special Forces provided the KLA with training assistance at the KLA bases in Kukes and Durres in Albania.

It is also clear that NATO tailored its air campaign to help ensure that the KLA would not be defeated. NATO began to claim on May 6 that the air and missile campaign had begun to have a significant impact on Serbian day-to-day operations and ethnic cleansing, although it noted that the Serbs could also use the remaining Kosovar Muslims in Kosovo as de facto human shields simply by intermingling with a helpless population or manipulating flows of refugees to shield their military movements in ways that confront NATO with either being ineffective, or repeating the kind of collateral damage to Kosovar Muslims that occurred in the attack on a Kosovar refugee column on April 14.

NATO described the role that the combination of the air and missile operation and the KLA were having on Serbian operations for the first time during its press briefing on May 6.

On the question about the VJ versus MUP, we have evidence that of course MUP obviously has a higher morale than the VJ, by nature. On the other hand, straight numbers are pretty hard to get at the present time, but we have enough intelligence gathering on that so that we know that morale is really going down, but I wouldn't be able to give you numbers, that can come towards that later on. On the paramilitaries, they are convinced that what they are doing is correct because they have nothing to deal with when the war is over. We have seen the same in Bosnia Herzegovina you know and I am afraid that their morale is pretty high because they have no future.

Jamie Shea: And if I can just add to what General Jertz said, that is the problem of the paramilitaries, the VJs being forced to disperse. It hasn't been particularly successful by the way at engaging the UCK in recent weeks for a number of different reasons, and therefore Milosevic is relying both on special forces, what he has, in other words throwing all of the forces that he can find because the VJ is no longer performing as it was able to in the past and of course is relying too on Arkan and the Black Hand and these other rather notorious units.

But as I have often said, their presence in Kosovo depends upon the existence of the VJ to provide the area protection, to provide the heavy artillery which first of all shells and intimidates and destroys villages, and creates the kind of climate of mass fear and terror in which these paramilitary forces with their Kalashnikovs can operate more freely. So it is very important to drive away the VJ because once the heavy equipment goes then that environment of permissiveness for the paramilitaries begins to change rather radically and they will find it much more difficult to operate as well.

It is quite remarkable that despite a very intensive VJ effort for the last couple of weeks to try to close off a UCK supply corridor up in the north into Albania, around the village of Kosari, that supply corridor remains open and that does suggest, particularly when you take the enormous force disparity between the UCK and what they have, they have got enthusiasm, they have got people but they are lightly armed, and you have got a very heavy force, but if that very heavy force is still not able to close off that corridor after two weeks I think it does suggest that they are experiencing internal problems.

The US briefers made similar points about the growing strength and effectiveness of the KLA during the Department of Defense briefing on the same day. They indicated that the bombing might well be creating a "ground option" for the KLA that will aid NATO during the air and missile campaign, but they also warned it could present a growing problem if any peace settlement was reached:

Mr. Bacon: The KLA has increased in size. I believe that the number of KLA fighters has risen perhaps to as much as 8,000 or 10,000 since this began. That would be an increase of several thousand. The number of supporters has also risen fairly dramatically to about 20,000. They are receiving recruits, obviously, from the refugee population, in Albania primarily. They continue to fight in the country. They also continue to take losses. They are out-manned and out-gunned by the Serb forces. That remains the case. But it also remains the case that Milosevic's estimate that he could wipe out the KLA, the Kosovar Liberation Army, in five to seven days was just wrong. And if anything, we know that the army is stronger today, the rebel force is stronger today than it was on March 24 when this began.

Questioner: How much of a factor are they in Kosovo right now? They've never been said to really hold the territory.

Mr. Bacon: First of all, they have, from time to time, held blocks of territory. There's always been an ebb and flow, and that's been the dynamic of this fight. If they achieve an area, then the Yugoslav army or the special police will come in and counterattack and try to drive them out through counterinsurgency operations. That's still going on. But the fact is they are attacking; they are blowing up vehicles, and they are inflicting fatalities on the VJ and the MUP, the special police, and they're doing that with increasing regularity. Now, it's hard to quantify this, because all the reports come from the KLA; they are one-sided reports. But clearly they are in there; they are fighting, and it's also clear to us that they are continuing to buy weapons on the international market; they're continuing to raise money, and they're continuing to look for ways to strengthen themselves.

Questioner: In what ways are they stronger now, Ken?

Mr. Bacon: They have more people. They are training aggressively. They, I think, have a broader base of support than they had before. And they continue to acquire or gather weapons. Some of these, of course, they gather from the Serb forces at the point of the engagements they have, if they win the engagements and if the Serb forces abandon their weapons.

Questioner: So are they better armed now?

Mr. Bacon: I'd say they're slightly better armed, but they're still overwhelmed in that they're a light force, basically an insurgency force, lightly armed, facing a force that has tanks and APCs and artillery. And they do not have that type of weaponry.

Questioner: Are they able to move freely?

Mr. Bacon: In some places they can move, but generally they can't move as freely as they'd like. They do not control vast amounts of territory. They operate more in terms of attacking bands going after targets of opportunity. They're insurgents, and they operate as all insurgents do. They're best at attacking established forces. They're not as good at maintaining territory. Their ability to maintain territory is also reduced somewhat by the fact that the Serbs have successfully depopulated Kosovo of large numbers of Kosovar Albanians, which would be their natural support base.

Questioner: Back to the KLA. When the KLA crosses the border into Kosovo, have they been drawing concentrations of Serbia MUPs and VJ? Have they basically been presenting a situation that NATO could take advantage of in further reducing the KLA and MUP?

Mr. Bacon: There are concentrations of the Serb army border patrol and special police along the border. General Wald showed some attacks against some of the border, the patrol posts a couple of days ago. Where we find concentrations of troops, NATO aircraft are attacking those concentrations, whether they're on the border or elsewhere.

To answer your question I guess more directly, the KLA is out on its own looking for concentrations of troops that they can attack, but I want to point out that they are a very lightly armed, mobile insurgency operation, and they do not have much ability to attack an armored, much more heavily defended, organized military force, so they have to pick targets of opportunity when they arise.

Questioner: When you said they were stronger, stronger than when? Than when this started on the 21st [*sic*] of March?

Mr. Bacon: I think what happened is that they took very heavy hits, starting actually before March 21st, because it was clear that Milosevic sent his army and special police forces out to try to wipe out the Kosovar Liberation Army starting before the NATO attacks. And so they were reduced starting probably around March 20th or before that, and reduced into the early days of the NATO bombing. They were not eliminated, as Milosevic had hoped or projected. And in recent weeks they've been coming back. And the main reason they're stronger is they have begun to recruit more people, and they have a stronger base of support.

Questioner: Is NATO helping them recruit people, Ken? Are they showing, helping people in the camps meet KLA representatives?

Mr. Bacon: I don't think that NATO has to help displaced Kosovar Albanian refugees find the one group they think has been working on their behalf. The Kosovar Albanians are very able to find the KLA representatives.

The problem with such comments is that they implied that NATO air and missile power should be given almost exclusive credit for the success of the KLA and the

Kosovar resistance. In fact, NATO was only one factor involved. It soon became obvious that Serbian ethnic cleansing was having a massive backlash effect, had created a vast new pool of manpower for the KLA to draw upon, and was giving the elements of the KLA a large amount of money. Albania allowed the free import of arms for the KLA and their transit over the border. In addition, well over 800,000 Muslim Kosovars stayed in Kosovo throughout the conflict, and many men had nowhere else to go because they could not leave safely with their women and children. As a result, the Serbs probably did as much to strengthen their own enemy as the NATO air and missile campaign.

This conclusion is supported by the NATO briefing on May 11. Jamie Shea was careful to stress that NATO was not the air force of the KLA. At the same time, he stated that,

I don't have the exact figures on the KLA, they claim themselves to have anywhere between 10–15,000 fighters available and they don't seem to have a recruitment problem. Every time President Milosevic massacres a village, the UCK can swell their ranks with another 1,000 or 2,000 volunteers. That is the tragedy of this, that President Milosevic is better than General Kitchener was in the First World War as a recruiting sergeant. But they are taking heavy losses, clearly it is a very difficult struggle with the light arms that they have against a much better armed adversary and they are taking heavy losses. But on the other hand they show no sign of losing morale or wanting to give up and we know that in Kosare in particular they have been able to form a pocket which once again the Serb forces don't seem to be able to break down; and secondly, as I often mention, up in Junik they keep open their resupply corridor into Albania, but I understand that the losses are fairly heavy on their side.

The Serb forces are using more of their special police and more of their special units against the UCK because the conventional army, the VJ, has proven ineffective and has also suffered heavy damage. Three brigades in particular have suffered heavy damage at the hands of NATO and we know now that they have supply problems, morale problems, that could be a reason for this partial withdrawal. I am speculating, but it could be a reason that Milosevic simply needs to pull them out so that they can try to rest or reconstitute, so that is why it is happening. One of the reasons why the VJ units have proven to be ineffective is that they can only operate with extensive artillery fire and NATO air strikes have succeeded significantly in reducing that artillery fire. So I think there is the explanation there. And in any case with 40,000 he still has a large numerical advantage over the UCK but it is a nut that he doesn't seem to be able to crack, despite his best efforts.

Like many other powers that felt they could quickly win low intensive combat against a weak but politically motivated enemy, Serbia learned that it not only could not defeat the KLA in the "5–6 days" the Serbian high command had promised Milosevic, it learned that it could not defeat it at all. The Serbs made a major effort to create better defenses, barriers, and mine fields along the Albanian and Macedonian borders. These often raised KLA and Kosovar casualties and had some effectiveness, but they did not come close to being decisive. If anything, cross border infiltration increased steadily while each Serbian effort that forced Serbian forces to concentrate or deploy into isolated and clearly military facilities or areas created new targets for NATO air and missile power.

A day by day review of the maps that the US Department of Defense and NATO issued on KLA activity reveals a relatively broad pattern of KLA activity throughout the war that began to intensify by mid-May. Descriptions of the enemy also reveal a classic pattern in guerrilla warfare where (a) Serbia could win every "battle," but found few static concentrations of men and equipment to attack, (b) the Serbian forces were reluctant to carry out detailed infantry search and destroy operations and engage in close infantry combat because of the resulting casualties, and (c) Serbian reliance on artillery and armor produced KLA casualties and allowed Serbia to occupy territory but did not defeat the KLA. Like the US in Vietnam, Serbia won most of its battles but not only did it not defeat the KLA, it could not prevent it from growing steadily stronger.

SYNERGY? GUESSING AT THE IMPACT OF AIRPOWER ON THE KLA GROUND OPTION AND VICE VERSA

As has been touched upon earlier, the synergy between NATO air and missile power and the KLA grew steadily in late May, and gave NATO even more of a de facto ground option. This synergy was reinforced as the KLA (as possible elements of NATO special forces) became forward air controllers that helped to provide targeting data to NATO and as NATO exploited good weather and its improving targeting capabilities and freedom of action to attack Serbian forces that concentrated against the KLA.

There was also synergy with the preparations for a NATO ground option. Even if Serbia had no knowledge of NATO's secret preparations for a ground option, it cannot have ignore the risk that the KLA might receive direct support from NATO ground troops. The media discussion of a NATO ground option continued, as did statements by senior politicians that undercut NATO's earlier denial that it would ever carry out a ground option. This had to have partially corrected the negative impact of NATO's early and categorical rejection of a ground invasion. This risk was also reinforced by the build-up of European land forces in Albania and Macedonia for protection and humanitarian missions, and to prepare for peace making. It was also reinforced by the deployment of the US Army's Task Force Hawk, although it never used its AH-64s, MLRS, and artillery weapons in combat.

NATO never officially admitted to this synergy between its air and missile campaign, or to the fact that it had become involved in de facto coalition warfare. It is also important to note that this synergy had its costs. It almost certainly led to more rapes, killing, and cruelty, and more Serbian use of civilians and civilian facilities as shields. Its benefits are clearly reflected in Figures 29–35, however, and in the NATO and US briefings after mid-May. On May 27 (Day 64), for example, Rear Admiral Thomas R. Wilson discussed the KLA forces in an intelligence briefing.

I think the big change for the last time I briefed you in this room and now really is what's happening in the KLA or the UCK. They appear to be a resurgent group, which has taken advantage of NATO air strikes, general Western sympathy, and a groundswell of volunteer fighters who have gotten to Albania from other parts of the world as well as in the camps to increasingly resume in some parts of Kosovo offensive harassment operations against the Serb military. This is a force which numbered, as late as I think the March timeframe, around 5,000 in Kosovo and another 1,000 or 2,000 in Albania, to a force which we now estimate between 15,000 and 17,000 with as many as 5,000 currently in Kosovo who can be undergoing training in camps there in northern Albania, which have been drawing some attention from Serb artillery. Their improved situation is a result of the air strikes, which has reduced the mobility of the VJ or army operations. They are now led by more experienced military officers. In face, the new commander is a former commander in the Croatian army, before that a member of the Yugoslav army. And they have a somewhat improved supply situation. In fact, we have evidence of a significant operation occurring in southwestern Kosovo now. And the number of UCK participants in this may actually be as large as their total strength was as recently as a year ago. So they've, I think, dramatically increased their ability to operate in the country as a result of the NATO air strikes. In fact sometimes the reduced number of IDPs, displaced persons, works to their advantage. And, as I say, their supply situation is improving. More weapons coming in from their traditional sources outside of Kosovo and Albania, and in fact, we have evidence that they managed to capture some important Serb weapons in the southwest.

As has been mentioned earlier, it is also clear that NATO flew missions directly in support of the KLA by late May or early June, both to keep the KLA's supply lines open to Albania and to ensure that the Serbian ground troops could not create effective barrier defenses against a NATO invasion. The KLA had attempted to attack through the passes in Mount Pastrik area beginning on May 27. The KLA only had about 250 poorly trained and equipped troops, however, to some 700–1,000 Serbian forces, and they were close to defeat by May 30. It is not clear how many missions NATO flew directly in support of the KLA, but it is clear that at least two B-52 strikes were flown in support of the KLA and against the Serbian troops massing on the Serbian side of Mount Pastrik on June 7.

LESSONS FROM THE KLA GROUND OPTION

NATO and US sources reported shortly after the war end that NATO air power was particularly effective in carrying out these strikes, and that the B-52s dropped cluster bombs on some 800–1,000 exposed Serbian troops, killing as many as 200 Serbians and triggering secondary explosions by Serbian munitions.[211] These reports have since proven to be extremely controversial, however, and little material evidence has emerged that the B-52 strikes produced high levels of Serbian casualties.[212] As a result, it may have been the very fact that NATO had shifted to providing direct support missions that led Serbia to concede, and not the effectiveness of the strikes per se.

NATO's overall claims regarding Serbian weapons and equipment losses also seem to be considerably more valid, however, and the accelerating trend in such losses is summarized in Figure 29.[213] NATO reported in mid-June that its estimates showed that NATO had only destroyed 20 Serbian tanks, 40 other armored vehicles, and 40 mortars and artillery pieces as of Day 60, versus 122 tanks, 222 other armored vehicles, and 454 artillery weapons and mortars by the end of the war, and that the massive rise in equipment "kills" began on Day 63 when the KLA began attacking Serbian forces across the Albanian border.[214] Other sources report that 80% of Serbia's armored losses occurred after May 25, in the last 2.5 weeks of the 11-week war, as a result of having to mass against the KLA.[215] As has been discussed earlier, NATO's review of its damage assessment claims after the war largely validated these figures, as has been shown in Figures 31–35.

It is also apparent that Serbia never came close to destroying the KLA. SHAPE sources reported on June 30 that the KLA forces in Kosovo had built up to roughly 20,000, plus another 4,000 men in holding positions in Albania. They also reported that the KLA increasingly acted as the equivalent of forward air controllers, greatly aiding in supplementing the targeting data provided by UAVs and the JSTARS. The size of the surviving KLA force is also indicated by the fact that the KLA troops in Western Kosovo alone eventually turned 2,500 rifles, 215 machine guns, 150 mortars, 1,000 mines, 4.5 million rounds of ammunition, 100 antitank weapons, and thousands of hand grenades over to the Italian forces in the NATO headquarters in Pec. Although the KLA may well have held some weapons back and this was only part of the total the KLA turned over to NATO, it was twice the total the KLA had originally agreed to.[216]

There are several lessons that can be drawn from this experience:

- *Exploiting de facto coalitions can be as important—and as difficult—as exploiting formal ones.*

- *Asymmetric warfare can work in two directions—for the US and the West, as well as against it.*

- *Low intensity combat remains a military nightmare. If the US or NATO had had to use air and missile power against the KLA, it might well have been no better off than the Serbs.*

- *"Jointness" works even when no one calls it jointness, and/or when there is only the tacit threat of jointness.*

- *De facto coalitions can create problems in peace or in the aftermath of a conflict that are serious threats to future stability—reinforcing a lesson learned in Angola and Afghanistan.*

- *The effectiveness of the NATO air attacks on Serbian forces in the field must be judged in terms of the impact in strengthening the credibility of the KLA (and the prospective NATO ground option), and not simply in terms of how much of the Serbian land force was destroyed and whether this halted ethnic cleansing.*

11

Detailed Lessons and Issues of the Air and Missile Campaign

In many cases, an effort to draw detailed lessons from the war has to be speculative. It is difficult to make accurate judgments even when a substantial amount of unclassified data are available. The effectiveness reporting immediately after the Gulf War demonstrates just how dangerous it is to rush into detailed judgments about the relative effectiveness of given tactics, weapons, and technology. The *Conduct of the War* study that the Department of Defense sent to the Congress on the lessons of the Gulf War has become the reference point for one report on lessons after another. This report, however, turned out to be filled with erroneous data and "facts," to praise technological failures more stridently than the many real-world successes, and to include a long series of half truths and distortions of military history. Many of these problems only became apparent several years later in the US Air Force *Gulf War Air Power Survey*, and it is one of the ironies of lessons of the war analyses that most studies ignore this report and still use the discredited data and conclusions in the *Conduct of the War* study.

It is clear from the reporting of the US Department of Defense that a similar process is taking place in reaction to the lessons of Kosovo. Much of the wartime reporting described earlier deliberately or inadvertently disguised the seriousness of many of the problems NATO faced. The first lessons of war efforts that followed the end of the conflict made claims almost as ambitious as those made after the Gulf War, and also dodged around the details of key issues like collateral damage, weapons effectiveness, and NATO's internal political and command problems. The more comprehensive effort the US Department of Defense made in its full January 2000 report on the lessons of the war was still unable to address many of these issues with any frankness.[217]

There are, however, enough disparate reports of "lessons" from the air and missile campaign that have enough credibility to raise important lessons or issues. It is impossible to prioritize such lessons, to clearly separate such lessons from issues or to categorize them as "political," "strategic," "tactical," and "technical." The following points are made in rough alphabetical order.

AIR SUPERIORITY

NATO's extraordinary success in air-to-air combat, in suppressing the Serbian air force, and halting the operations at Serbian air bases was so great that it now receives little attention. NATO was only able to succeed to this degree, however, because it had an overwhelming superiority in air combat capability, air combat aircraft, sensors and battle management systems, and the strike capabilities needed for air base suppression. These are dangerous advantages to take for granted, and many air forces are considerably more sophisticated than Serbia.

Lt. Gen. Michael Short noted that parts of the battle for air superiority were unexpectedly easy in his October 21, 1999, testimony to the Senate Armed Services Committee "We expected them to come up and fight; they did not," he said. "Their MiG-29 drivers turned out to be incompetent at best. And their surface-to-air missile system operators chose to survive as opposed to fight."[218]

General John Jumper, the Commander of the US Air Force in Europe, cautioned in separate testimony to the House, however, that if the Serbs had had modern fighters and surface-to-air missiles, "this would have changed our strategy considerably. I can guarantee you that it would not have been without loss."[219]

The value of air superiority in air combat and air suppression is one of the major lessons of the war, and it is important to consider what would have happened if NATO had taken significant losses or faced the political risk of doing so. This is an important issue to consider in evaluating the future of aircraft like the F-22.

THE A-10

The A-10 shifted from the high altitude and spotter and observer role to low altitude missions in the last week of April. There have been no public effectiveness data on the role of the aircraft in combat, and it should be noted that the USAF study of the Gulf War found that the A-10 provided 75% of the false hit claims made during the war, and that damage assessment experts routinely discounted all A-10 claims by 50%. This makes the A-10's effectiveness and mission limits to ensure its survivability in the war in Kosovo is an area of considerable concern.

There is no question that the A-10 can be effective. The question is how effective. This needs independent "B-team" review.

THE AH-64

The AH-64 never flew in combat during the air and missile campaign, and two aircraft and two crew members were lost to training accidents. The reasons for not employing the AH-64 and the detailed results of its training experience in Kosovo are a subject of considerable concern since the AH-64 is potentially a key US rapid deployment asset.

Tactical and Technical Problems

The Department of Defense provided the following largely technical explanation for the failure to use the AH-64s in its early testimony to Congress on the lessons of the war:[220]

This deployment presented numerous challenges: Basing the task force in Albania required accompanying ground forces to protect against a cross-border attack by Serbian ground forces. Conditions at the airport were poor, as was the weather. Therefore, constructing the improvements to the local infrastructure needed to permit wartime operations was particularly difficult, as was conducting needed training.

Transporting the task force and its supporting elements competed directly with establishing and sustaining Joint Task Force Shining Hope, which provided humanitarian assistance to the Kosovo refugees. Although deployed independently, the units assigned to Task Force Hawk were organized, equipped, and trained to operate as an integral part of a larger land force, providing direct support to its operations and under the control of its commander. These units previously had trained for operations in regions with significantly different terrain and environmental conditions than those encountered in Albania and Kosovo.

Apache aircrew training had been oriented toward areas that are predominantly open desert and have relatively flat terrain. Albania and Kosovo, however, are over 75 percent mountainous and have terrain with a 14 degree or greater slope. Apache pilots therefore had to develop navigation and piloting skills that were different from those previously emphasized.

The same air defense system, including man-portable air defenses, that posed a threat to relatively high-altitude operations by fixed-wing aircraft posed a more substantial threat to low-altitude helicopter operations. Overcoming these challenges required extensive training in theater, as well as development of a plan for integrating the Apaches into an air campaign not directly supporting a ground force. Operation Allied Force ended just as the needed training was completed and plans were developed.

It should be remembered that the decision to deploy Task Force Hawk was made at a time when persistent poor weather had been hampering air operations and NATO's tactics for attacking mobile targets in Kosovo were in the early stages of development. Under these circumstances, the contributions that the Apaches might make to prosecuting mobile targets in Kosovo were considered potentially worth the risks associated with their use. As the campaign progressed and the weather improved, the effectiveness of higher-flying fixed-wing aircraft improved and the benefits of Apache operations at low altitude were no longer judged to outweigh the risk of their vulnerability to shorter-range air defenses.

As we reflect on the challenges associated with Task Force Hawk, we recognize the need to regularly experiment with the innovative, independent use of key elements of all of our forces in the absence of their usual supporting and supported command elements.

Readiness and Training Problems and Detailed Technical Issues

This statement, however, glossed over both the political constraints placed on the use of the AH-64, and many serious problems in the readiness and equipment of the AH-64 forces the US sent to Kosovo. The US commander of Task Force Hawk made a preliminary assessment of the AH-64's performance, which revealed the following problems:

- Over 65% of the assigned aviators had less than 500 flight hours; none were qualified to use night vision goggles in the CPG position. Both units were short of warrant officers and 11 crews had to be brought in from other units.

- The junior officers and enlisted men that deployed lacked experience as forward air controllers.

- The advanced course for junior officers the AH-64 at Flight School did not produce officers with the required expertise and experience, and Battalion and Bridge Commanders needed more training in balancing the leadership, training, maintenance, and other duties in aviation units.

- Mission planning and mission training was too narrow in scope and too limited in intensity and failed to prepare units for a wide range of demanding missions.

- The sensor-shooter links between the AH-64, MLRS, and UAV-equipped military intelligence units had to be improvised and were not digitized. The US Army TRADOC schools need to develop an advanced "decided-detect-track-deliver" decision cycle and provide the proper training and equipment.

- The radios in the AH-64 and UH-60 do not have the range for nap of the earth and long-range attacks, and two satellite communications nets had to be improvised—one for the AH-64/UH-60s and one for artillery. There were problems in monitoring the AWACS, ABCCC and DOCC Strike Net.

- Forward-looking infrared (FLIR) is not adequate for demanding night missions and must be combined with the use of the ANVIS-6 night vision goggle. Task Force Hawk had to improvise a suitable training program after its deployment, as well as develop suitable mission profiles to use the equipment. Even with such systems, a second-generation FLIR system is badly needed.

- The AH-64 had to use 230 gallon auxiliary wing tanks designed only for ferry flights and the tank is non-ballistic tolerant, wing heavy, and uses up two weapons points on the wing. This problem emerged during Desert Storm, and there is a long-standing need for a 150 gallon auxiliary tanks that can be mounted directly on the belly of the AH-64 and which is compatible with the main fuel system, crashworthy, and nitrogen inerting. Such a tank seems to be available from Robertson Aviation and has been tested by the National Guard.

- The electronic warfare suite does not function properly. Pilots have lost confidence in the APR-39 and ALQ-136 radar jammers, and are unsure of the capabilities of the ALQ-144 jammers. The current electronic warfare suite displays random ghost acquisitions and trackings. In spite of attempted fixes, pilots ignored the system altogether, and had not warning and jamming capability against the ZSU-23–4—a primary threat. Major improvements are need for the entire AH-64, UH-60, and CH-47 fleets.

- Adequate training and mission planning aids were not available to map out and game missions in mountainous areas. "Sandbox" and computer simulation systems are needed.

- The downlink from the Hunter UAV needs to be transmitted directly to AH-64s in flight and MLRS units.

- The Army had not organized or equipped itself for rapid ad hoc deployments of over 30 days although this had happen several times before during the past six years. The Aviation Force Structure was not large enough to support such deployments without taking men and assets away from other units.

Command Problems and Failure to Prepare for Independent Operations

The Department of Defense report on the lessons of the war issued in January 2000 largely supports these latter points and comments:[221]

The threat to Task Force Hawk's helicopters from Serbian anti-aircraft artillery and shoulder-fired air defense weapons posed significant risks. Task Force Hawk's capability to detect and track ground targets in Kosovo was constrained—both by the enemy's employment of defensive tactics (Serbian ground forces were widely dispersed, well camouflaged, and employed decoys) and by the lack of friendly ground forces into Kosovo. Although Task Force Hawk achieved some visibility over the battlespace in Kosovo from overflights by manned and unmanned reconnaissance systems, the Task Force's lack of ground forces and low-altitude forward air control capability increased the level of difficulty they would have experienced had they been required to locate and track mobile, well concealed Serbian ground forces in hostile territory.

Current attack helicopter training primarily involves division and corps level operations. In some scenarios, a land component commander uses his attack aviation assets to shape the battle and provide fire support to the advancing friendly ground forces. In these situations, the land commander is able to employ organic surface-to-surface missiles to suppress enemy air defenses as the attack helicopters reach deep into enemy territory.

The attack helicopters and other land component assets were integrated with tactical aircraft assets through the air tasking order. Coordinating rotary-wing aircraft operations into the Air Tasking Order proved problematic because this is not a traditional mission defined in Army doctrine nor is it exercised on a regular basis in joint training. As a result, the Services had to work through numerous complexities associated with the evolution of new missions and employment concepts in the middle of a major conflict. Integrating Army helicopters, radars, artillery, and other assets through the Air Tasking Order requires significant refinement. In short, the tactics, techniques, or procedures required for this mission had not yet been developed when Operation Allied Force took place.

While the Apaches engaged in rigorous mission rehearsals in preparation for combat, the conflict terminated without their being committed to combat operations. As Operation

Allied Force progressed and the effectiveness of the ongoing campaign became evident, it was decided not to add Task Force Hawk's firepower to the ongoing air operation. Task Force Hawk's Army Tactical Missile Systems (ATACMS), deployed with Task Force Hawk to engage deep targets and suppress enemy air defenses, were never used due to collateral damage concerns. Ultimately, while Task Force Hawk represented a threat to Milosevic's ground forces and was likely a factor in his decision to capitulate, attack elements of Task Force Hawk were not used. Additional training and integration issues arose as Task Force Hawk was incorporated into support of the operations. In the future, the concept of Joint Deep Operations in which Army tactical missiles and attack helicopters are employed as part of a supporting operation must be reinforced in joint training. Integration of Army tactical missile employment into Joint and Combined operations also requires more emphasis on the development and practice of standard tactics, techniques, and procedures.

Moreover, the report notes that Task Force Hawk was deployed without adequate command and control and intelligence assets, and without the resources needed to target enemy forces.[222]

The Army units assigned to Task Force Hawk were organized and equipped to form part of a larger land force under the assumption that certain additional command-and-control and support elements would be present as part of this larger force. After Task Force Hawk arrived, a Deep Operations Coordination Cell and an Air Coordination Element were added. This finally provided elements that had been missing in developing the ground intelligence preparation of the battlefield and nominating targets to the air tasking order. An important lesson was learned from this experience: extraordinary methods are needed to focus collection and analysis efforts on enemy ground forces in operations where ground forces are not integrated from the beginning, and a ground commander is not present.

Mobility and Deployability

It is also important to note that some of the problems that Task Force Hawk encountered were the product of the size of the overall force and the difficulties of deploying in an area that was not ready to support sophisticated military operations:[223]

Task Force Hawk was originally directed to deploy to Macedonia and to use the existing facilities and local experience provided by U.S. Army units based at Camp Able Sentry. The expectation that this infrastructure would be available drove the early deployment planning. Unfortunately, based on availability of space, the Macedonian government determined they could not allow helicopters to be based there and the deployment had to be shifted to Albania, where the government had agreed to accept them. The change in deployment site to Albania necessitated the deployment of additional force protection assets and infrastructure support. Consequently, the material required to deploy this force grew by a factor of three.

Exacerbating the dramatic increase in the lift requirement was the fact that Task Force Hawk was in competition with the humanitarian Joint Task Force Shining Hope for scarce airbase resources in Tirana, Albania. The airport remained a bottleneck despite heroic efforts by Air Force Red Horse Engineers to expand its capacity. 2. Deployment Execution

Given the changes in the scope and specifics of Task Force Hawk's deployment, a different means of moving the task force might have been chosen. It is a misimpression that the Task Force Hawk deployment merely involved 24 Apache helicopters. In fact, Task Force Hawk was an Army Aviation Brigade Combat Team.

This unit included a corps aviation brigade headquarters, a corps artillery brigade headquarters with a Multiple-Launch Rocket System (MLRS) battalion, an attack helicopter regiment (Apache), a ground maneuver brigade combat team, a corps support group, a signal battalion, a headquarters troop battalion, a military police detachment, a psychological operations detachment, and a special operations command-and-control element. Had time permitted, it might have been advantageous to ferry Task Force Hawk from Italy to Albania by ship. Indeed, much of the logistics support was moved by ship.

Politics versus Technical and Tactical Problems

In spite of these technical and tactical problems, many US military officers and officials feel that the US would have committed the AH-64 to combat in spite of all of these problems if the political situation had been more favorable. A German analyst sees the following mix of political and military factors as having led to the decision not to use the aircraft:[224]

- It would have been seen as the start of a ground war.
- Any use would have led to the risk of Serbian retaliation against Albania and Macedonia.
- There was no target-rich environment suitable to a system designed largely to kill heavy armor.
- It required deep attacks of 80–100 kilometers at night across difficult terrain filled with unpredictable objects like wires.
- Attacks would have had to be flown through two predictable access valleys.
- Serbian ground troops at the border area had had their air defense weaponry reinforced and had some 200 SA-7s.

Lessons and Non-Lessons

There simply is not enough unclassified evidence to know how much the political debates over escalation and the ground options affected the employment or non-employment of the AH-64. The US Army did, however, ground much of its AH-64 fleet in November 1999 to replace a faulty component in its tail rotor system, and Israel too has experienced major problems in making the aircraft ready for new missions.[225] It seems likely that substantial changes are needed in the readiness, training, equipment and organization of the AH-64 and Army aviation if it is to function effectively as a rapid deployment and expeditionary force. There also is a need for more operations research into the range of different types of conflict weapons systems may have to be used in and into the "micro-climes" that can impose new requirements in terms of weather, terrain, and other operating conditions.

It should be noted, however, that some of the crews of the AH-64s deployed to Task Force Hawk disputed the idea they were not combat ready. They stated that they only trained to use night vision goggles as back-up safety devices and relied on the aircraft's FLIR systems, that they had flown repeated deep penetration missions in Bosnia before Kosovo, and that the only new mission was search and rescue cooperation with the US Air Force. They also stated that they successfully flew 11 scale missile rehearsal exercises, that they were tasked at one point to carry out attacks eight kilometers deep into Kosovo using Hellfires against targets designated by F-15Es, and that they had a full campaign plan to attack Serbian forces across the border. According to these sources the AH-64s were not used in combat because General Wesley Clark's repeated requests to use them were never authorized at the political level.[226]

Furthermore, it is interesting to note that the AH-64 also had considerable success in supporting the NATO KFOR peacekeeping mission after the end of the air and missile campaign. The US Army based a Task Force 12 at Petrovac airport and Macedonia, with 12 Apaches, 11 Sikorsky UH-60 Black Hawks, and four Boeing CH-47D Chinooks. The Apaches provided security and reconnaissance throughout Kosovo. Their missions included halting Albanian attacks on Serbs, halting looting and armed groups traveling on roads, and halting mortar attacks by Serb paramilitaries on NATO bases. The aircraft flew in teams during both day and night missions. They were used primarily at night, however, and were one of NATO's few assets that could patrol the entire region at night and under poor visibility conditions. They could be supported by UH-60s when troops had to be flown in and deployed on the ground.[227]

It is also interesting to note that the US Department of Defense did conclude after the war that the lack of organization, planning, and training to employ the AH-64s was a major lesson of the war.[228]

The Department will develop Joint Deep Operations concepts to guide the employment of Army attack helicopters and tactical missiles in support of overall operations. The concepts will include procedures for including Army assets on the Air Tasking Order, when appropriate. In addition, the Department will continue to evolve standard tactics, techniques, and procedures for integrating Army Tactical Missiles into Joint and Combined operations. We will then reinforce these concepts and procedures through appropriate joint training exercises. Finally, the Department will explore technological innovations (e.g., using unmanned aerial vehicles or other airborne platforms to find and designate targets for attack helicopters) and attendant equipment upgrades that will improve our ability to integrate air operations.

More broadly, the campaign in Kosovo also *indicates that the US and NATO still need to conduct extensive exercises to determine the proper mixture of jointness between fixed and rotary wing assets and long-range artillery systems like the MLRS.* The lack of support from land forces in Kosovo seems to have create many cases where fixed-wing aircraft were over-tasked or tasked against relatively low value target opportunities, but where radars like the Guardrail, Q-36, and Q-37 Firefinder would have allowed the AH-64 or MLRS to hit Serbian mortars, artillery, and small formations with great efficiency. *One key approach might be to simulate what Task Force Hawk might have contributed to the operation if it had been allowed to operate under optimal conditions both to establish the role of "ground power" and what could have been done to allocate air power more effectively.*

ASYMMETRIC WEAPONS AND WARFARE

The war in Kosovo demonstrated that an intelligence opponent will not attempt to fight a superior power with advanced conventional weapons on its own terms and will respond by turning to asymmetric warfare. The Department of Defense makes this point in some depth in its report on the lessons of the war:[229]

The campaign over Kosovo was not a traditional military conflict. There was no direct clash of massed military ground forces in Operation Allied Force. Milosevic was unable to challenge superior allied military capabilities directly. His fielded forces were compelled to hide throughout most of the campaign, staying in caves and tunnels and under the cover of forest, village, or weather. He was forced to husband his antiaircraft missile defenses to sustain his challenge to our air campaign. Therefore, he chose to fight chiefly through asymmetric means: terror tactics and repression directed against Kosovar civilians; attempts to exploit the premium the alliance placed on minimizing civilian casualties and collateral damage; creation of enormous refugee flows to create a humanitarian crisis, including in neighboring countries; and the conduct of disinformation and propaganda campaigns.

These tactics created several serious challenges for our forces, all of which we were able to overcome thanks to excellent training, leadership, equipment and motivation. Nevertheless, these challenges underscored the continued need to develop new operational concepts and capabilities to anticipate and counter similar asymmetric challenges in the future. Simply put, adversaries will use unconventional approaches to circumvent or undermine U.S. and allied strengths and exploit vulnerabilities. Milosevic illustrated very clearly his propensity for pursuing asymmetric approaches. He chose his tactics in the hope of exploiting the NATO nations' legitimate political concerns about target selection, collateral damage, and conducting military operations against enemy forces that are intentionally intermingled with civilian refugees.

In the case of refugee flow, the time-scale was so rapid and the numbers so great that it initially overwhelmed the neighboring countries, particularly the Former Yugoslav Republic of Macedonia (FYROM) and Albania. The humanitarian crisis created by Milosevic appeared to be an attempt to end NATO's operation by "cleansing" Kosovo of ethnic Albanians, overtaxing bordering nations' infrastructures, and fracturing alliance cohesion. He failed, despite all these efforts, principally because NATO adapted to the changing circumstances. One general lesson learned is that similar attempts at asymmetric challenges should be anticipated in future conflicts as well.

Asymmetric warfare is not a one-way street. The US use of carbon fiber weapons against power grids further illustrates the fact that the US can introduce new asymmetric warfare techniques as well as its enemies. *It might be useful to conduct a "what if" analysis of Kosovo to see how the introduction of other asymmetric weapons now under development might have changed the course of the fighting.*[230]

More broadly, however, NATO and the US need to examine Serbia's use of asymmetric warfare in more depth to determine the merit of relative techniques, and to examine worst cases in which Serbia made maximum use of such techniques to defeat NATO. The fact NATO won did not mean NATO had to win.

For example, Serbia might have been able to ride out the war without provoking a decisive NATO reaction if it had used a more subtle form of ethnic cleansing. It might have been able to create much deeper divisions in the UN Security Council; it might have been able to exploit the differences between the NATO allies or create and then exploit a bombing pause. The threat of the use of chemical weapons might have had a major political impact. Serbia might have made even more use of its disinformation campaign regarding the ineffectiveness of NATO strikes and the nature and scale of NATO's collateral damage. Accidents and media reaction might have placed critical limitations on NATO targeting.

It is one of the clichés of military planning that the victors in any war plan to repeat their past victory. NATO might learn a great deal by reversing the direction of this cliché, and examining how it might have lost. Certainly, neither the US nor NATO should plan to fight a weaker mirror image. If enemies did not learn from the Gulf War, they will learn from Kosovo. The "revolution in military affairs" will be decisive in straight conventional wars where one side can exploit the revolution and the other cannot. The key question is how much of a counter that asymmetric warfare ultimately be to such "conventional" superiority.

AV-8B HARRIER

Kosovo involved new types of operations for the US Marine Corps Harrier. Brigadier General Robert M. Flanagan, the Deputy Commander, II Marine Expeditionary Force, provided the following comments these operations in testimony to Congress.[231]

The introduction of Marine Corps AV-8Bs was marked by several firsts: it was the first-ever pre-planned combat employment of MEU(SOC) embarked AV-8s, and was the first time AV-8Bs used Laser Guided Bombs (LGBs) in combat, although the capability has been resident in the airframe since its introduction. Laser designation for AV-8B LGBs was provided by U.S. Air Force F-16s, marking the first time that "buddy lasing" by another fixed wing aircraft was employed for AV-8s. Operation Allied Force also marked the first combat use of CBU-99, cluster advanced munitions by the AV-8B aircraft. Additionally, the AV-8Bs embarked with the 24 MEU(SOC) and 26 MEU(SOC) were able to equal any of the other allied strike aircraft's "time on station." These aircraft were embarked aboard amphibious shipping in close proximity to Kosovo and did not require airborne refuelers to strike pre-planned targets—again, validating the merits of forward deployed Naval forces and Operational Maneuver from the Sea.

Due to the organic expeditionary maintenance and supply capabilities provided aboard amphibious shipping, the 24 MEU(SOC) AV-8Bs lost no sorties for maintenance availability; had no weapons release failures; no Defensive Electronic Countermeasures (DECM) failures, and no failures of its expendable countermeasures systems. During the 6-month deployment, 24 MEU(SOC) AV-8B aircraft readiness rates averaged 91.8% mission capable (MC), and 88% full mission capable (FMC), well above established DON standards.

The need for Laser Self-designation Capability (a "Targeting Pod") on the AV-8B was a recognized "lesson learned" following Desert Storm. Yet, the AV-8B remains the only TACAIR asset in the U.S. inventory without such a capability. The lack of this capability contributed to the delayed entry of the AV-8B into Operation Allied Force—strike assets within minutes of Kosovo airspace but unable to participate because of Air Tasking Order (ATO) Special Instructions (SPIN) requirements for a self-designation capability. The Kosovo Supplemental Appropriation has provided limited funding for an initial buy ($16M for nine LITENING Pods), but additional funding is needed to field a capability sufficient for training and deployment across the entire fleet, $76M for an additional 47 systems.

At the onset of OAF, the Amphibious Ready Group supporting 24 MEU(SOC) held only 27 LGBs. In a high intensity conflict, the total numbers of PGMs available were insufficient to sustain combat operations. Although the AV-8B was one of only two platforms in the operation allowed to drop "iron" bombs on GPS coordinates, integration of the next generation PGMs, the Joint Direct Attack Munitions (JDAM) needs to be incorporated in the AV-8. This weapon provides precision accuracy in virtually all weather conditions, and will preclude many of the weather cancellations that were a factor during combat operations in Kosovo. Additionally, this operation only reinforced sensitivities to collateral damage—damage that is far more likely in urban environments, particularly when aircraft are primarily dropping large munitions from high altitude. We feel there is a requirement to invest in smaller precision and non-precision weapons (250–500 pound class) that have dual utility in both battlefield and urban environments, with less probability of collateral damage.

Our experience during OAF was that strike capability against time-critical or fleeting targets in a dynamic environment remains modest. We only scratched the surface of the sensor-to-shooter equation. As the military forges ahead to expand this capability, all USMC strike aircraft must have communications and datalink capabilities in order to be fully interoperable with Joint and Combined operations.

BOMBERS: THE B-2, B-1, AND B-52 AND GLOBAL FORCE INTEGRATION

Long-range US bombers played a major role in Kosovo and served as a major demonstration of US global power projection capabilities. The US has made the use of bombers and precision munitions a key part of its strategy, but it has not provide any public data that convincingly demonstrate their cost-effectiveness in any detail.

Global Force Integration

NATO made use of the B-2 and B-52 from the first days of the war, and came to seem them as core weapons systems for what it calls "global force integration."[232]

Operation Allied Force exercised our military as a global force; forces were not only deployed from locations around the globe to support the theater, but forces were also employed from the continental United States and other distant bases to provide support in order to accomplish assigned tasks via reachback. Attack planning for cruise missiles, B-2 missions originating in the United States, and space operations highlight the widely dispersed nature and global capabilities of the U.S. military. Multiple federated agencies throughout Europe and the continental United States provided direct support to the Joint Force Commander in the execution of the operation. The full spectrum of maritime operations, to include sustained forward presence, extensive participation in the air operation, air and sea support operations, protection of the allied western flank, and putting Marines ashore, was significant to the success of the campaign. As noted previously, the ability to perform all-weather precision strike was limited during Operation Allied Force. However, the B-2 bomber combined with the Joint Direct Attack Munition became an effective counter to these limitations. Over the course of Operation Allied Force, 45 B-2 sorties delivered 656 JDAMs on critical targets in the Federal Republic of Yugoslavia.

Extensive tanker support was needed to refuel B-2s flying global attack sorties. As indicated previously, each plane had to be refueled multiple times during its sortie. While such capability is essential for rapid employment in any scenario, forward basing would substantially reduce tanker requirements, reduce sortie length (simplifying everything from mission preparation to crew fatigue), and allow these assets to be utilized at a greater rate. Forward basing remains the optimum employment scheme for all our long-range platforms. Accordingly, the Air Force is examining ways to enhance its forward bomber-base infrastructure enhancement.

Another global force initiative was the employment of the B-1B bomber from bases in the United Kingdom. The B-1B's Block-D modification performed flawlessly during Operation Allied Force.

Cruise missile employment also benefited from global capabilities, with mission planning being done in the United States and then forwarded to launch platforms in theater. In fact, Allied Force saw the successful realization of TLAM as a tactical weapon. New capabilities were also implement for air-delivered cruise missiles. The Department is now investigating ways to expand these capabilities further. The complexities associated with an emerging global force that will employ with distributed operations and federated systems support via reachback must be captured in our training scenarios. As we learned in Operation Allied Force, even with a theater focus, using the global force is the best way to achieve the desired result. Given the probability that the United States will continue to be involved in small scale contingencies, with precision requirements and high knowledge demands that may again exceed the capacity of in-place theater forces, the Department needs to plan now to utilize the advantages offered by our global force capabilities. Because the United States might face a myriad of unpredictable scenarios, the Department needs to develop new levels of adaptability and flexibility in the interoperability and integration of this force.

This suggests that we develop a global focus in our organization and training. We must continue to improve doctrine and training, and to organize and equip our forces to meet the demands of global engagement. Key to the success of future operations will be the concept of a joint operational architecture that clearly defines the relationships between elements of the global force in a contingency or major theater war. Given an appropriate joint operational architecture, the Department can then develop the technical architectures to support warfighter needs, prioritize our resources and training requirements against the spectrum of global threats, and describe the organizations necessary to support our National Military Strategy. The Joint Staff is in the process of evolving such a joint operational architecture based on the tenants of Joint Vision 2010

Global Attack

Interestingly enough, the USAF did far less to emphasize joint operations and global integration in its testimony on the lessons of the war, and stressed the term "global attack." Lt. General Marvin R. Esmond, the Deputy Chief of Air and Space Operations, described the role of the bomber as follows in his testimony to the House Armed Services Committee on the lessons of the war.[233]

Nothing so well represented the Air Force capability to conduct global attack in the air war over Serbia as our B-2s delivering precision-guided munitions via 29-hour missions from Missouri to Yugoslavia and back. As with any global attack sortie, superb tanker support facilitated these operations. The combination of on-board systems and GPS guidance on the B-2 proved even more accurate than planners had expected. This meant the B-2 could precisely engage multiple targets per sortie, destroying a disproportionate share of total targets in some of the most heavily defended areas of the conflict.

Other global attack assets like the B-1B Lancer and B-52 Stratofortress deployed forward and conducted extensive operations from Fairford Air Base, England. The heavy payload capability of the B-52 and B-1 brought massive firepower to bear against the Serbs in the form of inexpensive unguided bombs. These two platforms delivered over 70% of the non-precision munitions dropped by U.S. assets in ALLIED FORCE. The B-52's precision-guided Conventional Air Launch Cruise Missiles also provided a much needed stand-off strike capability, which was especially crucial in the opening days of the conflict.

Continued near-term modernization will provide several types of GPS precision weapons to the B-52, B-1, and B-2 giving them even greater employment flexibility. Additionally, use of the Multiple Source Tactical System (MSTS) provided real-time intelligence in the B-1 cockpit. This was a near real-time flex targeting prototype capability. A more permanent, rapid information classification solution should be pursued for all bomber platforms.

The Air Force also demonstrated its Global Attack capability by rapidly augmenting in-theater attack aircraft with CONUS stationed forces. The Air Force's ongoing expeditionary force structure realignment will further enhance this rapid-response expeditionary capability.

Esmond not only made no mention of jointness, he provided no meaningful details on effectiveness, and simply summarized the volume of munitions delivered— a measurement of effectiveness that have proved meaningless in every war where airpower has every been used and which was thoroughly discredited by the Strategic Bombing Survey in World War II.

Levels of Bomber Action

The US began to use substantial numbers of B-52s to deliver area ordnance on May 4—delivering 54 500-pound dumb bombs on a single airfield. The US Air Force has said that the B-52s used in Kosovo were far more accurate than the aircraft used in Vietnam. In Vietnam, the US would normally fly a flight of three B-52s to hit an area target and they would lay a string of 330 bombs over an area longer than a mile. The avionics, GPS, and computer release systems on modern B-52s allowed them to drop a string of 54 500- to 750-pound bombs over a maximum area of 1,000 feet with fairly good accuracy. This allows individual B-52s to hit a normal area target with considerable precision.

The US and NATO made claims late in the fighting that two B-52s had surprised some 700–1,000 exposed Serbian soldiers deployed against the KLA near Mount Pastrik on June 7, and have killed hundreds of Serbs. No evidence has since surfaced to support such claims.[234]

The B-2 "stealth" bomber had flown some 42 sorties by May 4, and 49–50 by the end of the air and missile campaign.[235] Each aircraft could drop as many as 16 GPS-guided 2,000 pound bombs or eight 5,000 pound bunker busters regardless of weather or visibility conditions.[236] The flights were non-stop missions of nearly 30 hours from Whiteman Air Force Base in Missouri. The B-2s were normally supported by jamming aircraft and other support aircraft, and did not rely purely on their stealth capabilities.

The B-2 dropped fired more than 650 Joint Direct Attack Munitions (JDAMs), usually GBU-31s and firing an average of six per flight. The USAF claimed that the B-2s hit 89% of their targets.[237] At 2,000 pounds a bomb, that would equal over a million pounds of precision munitions. Some sources indicate that the B-2 dropped 1.4 million pound of ordnance, or 11% of all the munitions dropped between March 24 and June 30—although the B-2 flew no more than 50 of the 33,000–37,500 sorties NATO flew during the campaign.

Uncertain Bomber Effectiveness, Certain Bomber Politics

The USAF stated in background briefings that the B-2 was the first US aircraft with the ability to transmit target information into the cockpit of an aircraft, and program the GPS guided bombs in the wing of the B-2 from the cockpit while the aircraft is in flight.[238] It also claimed that all B-2s flew without any degradation to their stealth coatings, and participated in 34 of the 53 air tasking orders prepared for Operation Allied Force. Some were refueled, rearmed, and turned around in intervals as short as four hours.

Claims but No Evidence Regarding the Details of Effectiveness

These are all interesting claims, but many claims have been made regarding the lethality and effectiveness of bombers in the past which have not been supported by either detailed battle damage assessment or after action interviews with enemy POWs. The report that the Department of Defense issued in January 2000 also did nothing to validate these claims or provide any specifics on the effectiveness of bomber dropped ordnance.

The previous analysis of targeting and battle damage assessment also makes it plain that it is far from clear that the USAF has any battle damage data and methodology which allow it to make meaningful cost per kill estimates from bombers, or even accurately estimate the physical damage inflicted on mobile targets with anything approaching useful results. *Serious questions arise as to whether bombers are being assigned to missions for publicity and force justification purposes or because this mission allocation is truly cost-effectiveness.*

It also is not clear what the availability, deployabilty, and payload capability of the B-1 and B-2 were, and what the criteria were for using bombers in given missions. According to Congressional reports, spare parts shortages for the B-1 were so high that the cannibalization rate, and percentage of aircraft that had to be repaired with parts from other aircraft rose to 99%. One of the five B-1Bs that were deployed to Operation Allied Force was deployed to provide spare parts.[239]

Similar broad issues arise over the cost-effectiveness of investments in various types of bombers and strike aircraft. The resource constraints imposed by the US defense budget may force Congress to make painful trade-offs in down-sizing its overall force of such aircraft, or to trade or maintain the bomber force for future force modernization.

Lessons or Air Force Propaganda

Normally pro-defense Congressmen, like Jerry Lewis and Jack Murtha, the chairman and the ranking members of the House Defense Appropriations Subcommittee, have raised basic questions about the affordability of American airpower, and the future role of the bomber. In arguing for a hold on spending $40 billion to purchase 339 new F-22 fighters, they note this one development will cost $65 billion when all RDT&E costs are included, and that the US also has a $47 billion program to buy 548 F/A-18E/Fs and a $223 billion program to buy 2,850 Joint Strike Fighters. As a result, the US went into the war in Kosovo with tactical modernization programs with a cost of well over $340 billion over the next few decades.[240]

The long-term cost effectiveness of the B-2 is of concern because of reports that it (a) needed improvements in the maintainability of its stealth coating material, (b) the air force has only half the trained crews needed to sustain long—range missions from the US at maximum sortie rates, (c) the aircraft needs improved active countermeasures and in-flight intelligence links to provide real time data on enemy electronic orders of battle to help avoid surface-to-air missiles, and (d) needs similar improvements in real time targeting data to improve its capability against mobile ground targets. Some sources indicate that the lessons of Kosovo raise serious questions about past USAF studies showing the effectiveness of idealize arrays of enemy ground troops because such arrays rarely occur, and are unlikely to be located during the "window" in which the B-2 can be over the target. Others raise questions about an over-dependence on US-based missions.[241]

The role of the B-1B needs similar mission analysis. Careful examination is needed of the extent to which the war did or did not validate the upgrade of the ECM on the B-1 and the ALQ-161. Similar analysis is needed of its mission effectiveness relative to the B-52, B-2, and future strike-attack fighters.[242]

CLUSTER BOMBS AND MINES

Kosovo again demonstrates the problems created in dealing with mines and unexploded ordnance, and the "aftermath effect" of collateral damage. The US Department of Defense report on the lessons of the war issued in January 2000 totally ignores the role of such munitions in causing collateral damage, but it does state later that[243]

Our experience in Operation Allied Force also demonstrated the importance of Combined Effects Munitions (CEM). These munitions are soda-can-sized bomblet submunitions, designated BLU-97 or cluster bombs, that are dispensed in large numbers (approximately 150–200 bomblets per weapon) to attack "soft" area targets. These submunitions are dispensed by several different weapon airframes—the TLAM-D from long range, the JSOW from medium-standoff range, and the CBU-87 tactical munitions dispenser for direct attack. CEM is an effective weapon against such targets as air defense radars, armor, artillery, and personnel. However, because the bomblets are dispensed over a relatively large area and a small percentage of them typically fail to detonate, there is an unexploded-ordnance hazard associated with this weapon. These submunitions are not mines, are acceptable under the laws of armed conflict, and are not timed to go off as anti-personnel devices. However, if the submunitions are disturbed or disassembled, they may explode, thus, the need for early and aggressive unexploded-ordnance clearing efforts. Combined effects munitions remain an appropriate and militarily effective weapon when properly targeted and employed. However, the risk of collateral damage, as with any weapon, must be considered when employing these weapons.

Saying that such weapons cause collateral damage but ignoring them in the assessment of collateral damage is just one more way in which NATO and the US failed to address the issue of collateral damage in realistic terms and with analytic integrity. It also begs a long-standing issue in US weapons development.

The problem of unexploded bombs is as old as air power, but has been greatly complicated by submunitions and cluster bombs. Kosovo may indicate that there is a need for some kind of autodestruct system—although random autodestructs present risks of their own. The problem of large numbers of unexploded cluster munitions dates back to the Vietnam War and represents a continuing design flaw that the USAF has failed to correct over a period of nearly four decades.

According to some press estimates up to 170 people were killed or injured by mines and unexploded air weapons in Kosovo and Serbia during July 1999 alone—figures which would radically change NATO's estimates of wartime collateral damage. Cluster bombs (CBUs) present a special problem because over 1,100 were dropped in Kosovo. Each carried an average of 202 bomblets and scattered hundreds of anti-armor and anti-personnel weapons in canisters over a wide area. According to some estimates, more than 200,000 bomblets were dropped during the air campaign.

While any such estimates of post war collateral damage have proved to be notoriously inaccurate in the case of past wars, Human Rights Watch estimates that up to 5% failed to explode and that 11,110 unexploded anti-armor and anti-personnel weapons could have been left in Kosovo and Serbia. (The same organization estimates that 24–30 million bomblets were dropped in the Gulf War, and that 1.2–1.5 million failed to explode. It estimates that 1,200 Kuwaitis and 400 Iraqis were killed by such weapons after the war.)[244]

US cluster munitions still need significant improvement to reduce the number of unexploded bomblets and possibly to include a self-destruct mechanism. More generally, a broad technology review is need to determine the best way of minimizing the "aftermath" effect of unexploded weapons in causing collateral damage. One basic question for research is whether there are better ways of disarming such munitions in a secure environment where the issue is rapid, mass clearance under conditions where there is no military threat.

COALITION/NATO TECHNOLOGY AND INTEROPERABILITY

The fact there were so few losses by any NATO nation, and no instances of friendly fire, shows that NATO can achieve a high degree of interoperability in intense air operations. Nevertheless, Kosovo demonstrated the need for a comprehensive review of current planned NATO capabilities for integrated coalition air and missile warfare.[245] It became clear in Kosovo that the US was setting a technological, tactical, and training standard that other NATO nations have to meet. Most European powers, however, were not ready to meet this standard.

European Problems and Weaknesses

Many European airforces only had aircraft without the sensors and avionics to locate targets at night or in poor weather, or find dispersed Serbian forces in the field and target them. They lacked the sensors to track precision-guided weapons to their target under demanding mission conditions.[246] There were incompatible secure communications links that often forced air controllers to call out guidance in the clear which Serbian forces could—and did—intercept. The lack of advanced identification of friend and foe (IFF) systems created significant additional problems for NATO air controllers.[247]

Many NATO aircraft lacked the equipped to detect which surface-to-air missile systems were targeting them, and whether they threatening to launch. Most NATO European air forces could not designate targets for laser guided bombs from the air, and this sometimes required a complex buddy system with an additional target-designating aircraft.

General Klaus Nauman—the Chairman of NATO's Military Committee during most of the air and missile campaign—raised many of these issues. He also noted a lack of advanced training, a lack of interoperable field equipment, and poor English language skills. (English is used as NATO's language for alliance air operations.) He pointed out that, "We now have three generations of equipment in the field. In some cases the gaps can be bridged. But in others they cannot." Nauman referred to "national egoism" as a major barrier to interoperable modernization, and stated that European nations were "very generous in giving themselves a peace dividend. That has to stop. I believe that we are at a turning point."[248] Nauman was referring to so-called "stove pipe" systems that are designed for one-service and one-country operations.

Admiral Guido Venturoni, the new Chairman of NATO's Military Committee raised technology and interoperability as key priorities for NATO planning. He stated that the US provided more that 70% of all the air assets used in Operation Allied Force, and the "lion's share" of advanced weapons and aircraft.[249]

Indeed, without the United States's assets, the European Alliance members and Canada could never have mounted a successful air campaign such as this. Quite frankly, they simply do not have the capacity. Unless there exists a real European resolve to acquire the necessary military resources, the European Defense and Security Initiative will remain nothing but a noble concept.

Venturoni also noted NATO's lack of any intelligence assets of its own, and that it must now solicit its members for considerably more than was previously the case if it wished to remain inside the decision-cycle of any potential adversary. He noted the need for additional intelligence-gathering platforms such as the Airborne Ground Surveillance program and for intelligence systems that could deal with political issues and the political sensitivities of targeting and damage assessment.

European Views on the Lessons for Force Upgrades and Interoperability

There is no great transatlantic debate about these lessons. The British Secretary of State for Defense, George Robertson, touched on some of the same issues in an article in the Royal United Services Institute Journal in September 1999.[250] Robertson, who is now Secretary General of NATO, drew the following summary lessons in his report on the war:[251]

From the international perspective, the first lesson for the Alliance is the value of unity of purpose. To ensure this unity NATO required clear objectives and a determination to achieve them. It had both.

Second, in co-operation with our Allies, we need to examine ways in which member states can increase their qualitative and quantitative military contribution to NATO's overall capabilities. The priority lies in such areas as precision attack weapons, secure communications and strategic movement assets. Interoperability of systems will, of course, be a key component of this.

Third, there is a particular need to boost European capabilities. In order to strengthen our ability to use force effectively, we Europeans need to improve the readiness, deployabilty and sustainability of our armed forces and their ability to engage in both high intensity operations and those of an expeditionary nature. This would strengthen our contribution to NATO, which remains the sole instrument for collective defense. NATO will still be the natural choice for the conduct of non-Article 5 crisis management operations which North American and European Allies might choose to undertake in the future. A strengthened European capability would allow us to undertake European-led crisis management operations, in circumstances in which the whole Alliance is not engaged. We strongly support the focus of the European defense debate on these key capabilities and the more effective targeting of defense resources. We will pursue these aims through NATO's Defense Capabilities Initiative, and the Western European Union's audit of European capability. The work on performance criteria which we launched with the Italians in July will help to achieve this.

Fourth, our experiences have vindicated the analysis that underpinned the Strategic Defense Review. While full implementation of the Review's recommendations has not yet been completed, the requirements on deployabilty, mobility and sustainability have been firmly underlined.

The fifth lesson reflects the importance of efficient military and political consultation and decision making machinery in the Alliance. Throughout the conflict, Allies kept in constant touch, both in NATO and through bilateral and multilateral contacts at Ministerial, Head of Government and senior military and diplomatic staff level. This network of information sharing helped to maintain Alliance unity throughout the campaign, a significant achievement and one crucial to the Alliance's success. Milosevic did not expect the Allies to hold together, and the realization that he had failed to divide us undoubtedly contributed to his decision to back down. What was seen as possibly the Alliance's sternest political test, the NATO Summit in Washington on 23–25 April, turned out to be a resounding success. Allies reaffirmed their resolve to see NATO's objectives achieved and received the support of all Partnership for Peace partners with the exception of Russia and Belarus. We need to ensure that the cohesion is maintained and, where necessary, improved upon.

On a national level we will be looking at the UK's capability for air and stand-off attack of a range of targets in varying weather conditions. Detailed examination of what was achieved, as well as operational analysis of future options, will be required. A range of issues in the very fast-moving communications and information systems areas need continuing scrutiny to ensure that we can gather and pass information securely and quickly at a number of levels. These range from Headquarters to, perhaps, individual aircraft, tanks and ships. We need to take forward work already outlined in the Strategic Defense Review on deploying and supporting our Services on expeditionary operations.

Secretary Cohen's Summary Comments on Interoperability

Secretary of Defense William S. Cohen discussed these interoperability problems in depth in his address to the annual conference of the International Institute for Strategic Studies on September 9, 1999. He made the following comments about the lessons of the war:[252]

I'd like to say that like Bosnia, before Kosovo, we also had a reminder that NATO's transformation from a force ready to repel an armor-heavy invasion to one that could mount a more flexible and mobile defense is still incomplete. We could not, we the United States, could not have carried out this operation alone. A great deal of this operation, however, rested on American capabilities. The United States conducted virtually two-thirds of all the support sorties that were flown and half of all the combat missions. And because we were the only country with precision-guided munitions that can operate in all weather, heavy cloud cover in the initial stages of this campaign made it almost an exclusively American operation.

Moreover, I'd point out that not all of our allies possess the kind of communications gear that's required to maintain total security. As a result, there were times when our pilots had to communicate over unsecured lines and that allowed the Serbs to perhaps intercept and make use of this source of information to compromise the effectiveness of the air campaign itself and put our pilot's lives unnecessarily at risk.

Individually, all of the allies are making progress in transforming their militaries to meet the missions of the future. We're now seeing a largely European peacekeeping mission in Kosovo. But I must say that collectively there is much more that we have to do. We started talking about this at the NATO summit this spring. We talked about the Defense Capabilities Initiative, and very quickly I can summarize it. We have all agreed to develop forces that are more mobile, beginning with the reassessment of NATO's strategic lift requirements for planning purposes. We need forces, we've agreed, that can sustain themselves longer; that means having a logistics system that will ensure they have the supplies when and where they need them. [We need] forces that communicate more effectively, I just touched upon that. We have to have a common NATO command and control structure and communication architecture by the year 2002, so we are working to develop that as well. [We need] forces that can engage more effectively; that means having the new advanced technologies such as greater stocks of precision-guided munitions and forces that can survive better against chemical, biological or nuclear weapons, and also information warfare.

. . . What we now have to do is to measure up and to match the political commitment with actual deeds. There I would say the evidence is less encouraging. As I look around at the budgets of the members of the NATO Alliance I certainly see restructuring taking place as far as the size of the forces, and one cannot criticize that. But I also see a corresponding reduction in a commitment as far as the budget is concerned. So while there is a great sense of enthusiasm for what we have to do for the future to modernize NATO, to make it as effective as it needs to be, there is not at this point the kind of political commitment to actually carry it out.

. . . this is something that we must continue to point to otherwise the gap that you have been reading and hearing about—the technological gap between the United States and the other NATO Allies—will continue to grow. If that disparity becomes deeper and more prolonged, that will carry political implications for the NATO Alliance itself.

NATO's Defense Capabilities Initiative

These lessons reinforce the findings of NATO's Defense Capabilities Initiative (NDI or DCI), reported at the NATO summit in April 1999. The report found five major shortcomings in the alliance's capabilities for Coalition Warfare:[253]

- The inability to rapidly deploy forces and equipment.

- The inability to provide and sustain logistic support, including the rotation of forces at regular intervals.

- A lack of interoperability between national military capabilities, including disparities in equipment.

- A lack of interoperable command, control, and communications, including real-time satellite intelligence—such as the potential need for the NATO JSTARS force that Europe has not funded.

- Insufficient survivability of forces and infrastructure, particularly regarding the risks posed by weapons of mass destruction.

NATO Defense Ministers agreed to act upon the broad recommendations of NATO's Defense Capabilities Initiative at their meeting on September 21, 1999. NATO did not issue any details of how it would act to implement these recommendations, however, other than to indicate it would focus its efforts on strategic lift; intelligence, surveillance and reconnaissance (ISR), and command, control, and communications (C^3).[254]

NATO and European Action or Inaction?

Secretary General Solona did warn that, "Countries have to think seriously about the level of capabilities of their armed forces if they want to continue to have the possibility of participating in a constructive manner in the alliance."[255] Once again, however, it was Secretary Cohen who provided the most detailed review of what NATO Ministers had "learned" from Kosovo in a press conference with General Shelton after the Ministerial meeting,[256]

At the Washington Summit, our heads of state agreed to a Defense Capabilities Initiative— the so-called DCI—and focused on the need to improve five core capabilities: mobility, sustainability, effective engagement, command, control and communications, and force survivability. Kosovo showed the need for progress in these areas, and there is a clear agreement at this conference that we have to move forward on all fronts.

In some cases, countries will have to spend more money. But in many cases, we can achieve improvements by working together and spending our defense budgets more intelligently. For instance, Germany has proposed a European mobility command that promises to lead to greater coordination in the movement of troops and equipment.

And there are other examples. The Alliance is studying ways to increase the use of commercial sea and airlift to improve military mobility. Italy and the United Kingdom are working together to create performance standards or benchmarks for measuring improvements in capabilities. NATO is developing a Multinational Joint Logistics Center to help the Alliance manage and deploy its assets more efficiently. NATO is developing a new architecture for a unified, modern communications capability.

Ministers hope to achieve progress in many of these areas at our December meeting, and I'd like to take this occasion to stress that the United States learned of shortfalls in its forces during Kosovo and we are working to correct them. For example, we are buying more C-17 transport planes and additional ships for carrying heavy equipment. We are developing new precision guided munitions and increasing supplies of others that are already in our inventory. We are looking at the increased use of commercial off the shelf technology to improve our ability to detect chemical and biological attacks.

General Shelton also stated that "One of the most important lessons that we take away from Operation Allied Force is that the strength of NATO can only be harnessed through our interoperability. And the key to interoperability is found in the common capabilities in the DCI, or the Defense Capabilities Initiative. If all NATO nations, regardless of the size of their defense budgets, are guided by this shared vision, NATO will remain a preeminent force for peace and stability in Europe."[257]

One lesson of Kosovo is that validated NATO and the need for a Transatlantic alliance. Neither the US nor any European power can afford to plan for air war on a "fight alone" basis. Kosovo revealed a host of technical and training problems, short comings in the equipment of given allies, and inability to create the kind of fusion of command, control, communications, computers, intelligence, battle management, and strategic reconnaissance ($C^4I/BM/SR$) systems needed to fight with maximum effectiveness and interoperability. The fact that the US spend some $36 billion a year on research and development while European nations spend another $10 billion on largely uncoordinated and often parallel efforts is only one case in point.[258]

Another key lesson, however, is that military effectiveness costs far more money than many NATO countries have spent in the past, and probably much more than they are willing to spend on the future—particularly on true interoperability. Many of the key problems revealed by Kosovo were exactly the same problems revealed by the Gulf War nearly ten years earlier. As a result, one lesson of modern war may be that it is far easier to determine what the lessons and priorities are than it is to find the money to pay for them.

COMMAND, CONTROL, COMMUNICATIONS, AND COMPUTERS (C^4)

The lessons Kosovo poses in terms of C^4 cannot be separated from the lessons regarding coalition warfare, technology, and interoperability that have just been discussed, or from the lessons regarding intelligence discussed later. The US report on the lessons of the war does, however, provide a good overview of how rapidly C^4 is changing.[259]

The European Theater's unprecedented reliance on organizations and personnel in the United States and elsewhere was enabled by advances in information technology. High-capacity communications made possible the exchange of large amounts of data such as high-resolution imagery and secure video teleconferencing. In addition, extensive growth and availability in defense data and communications networks enabled unprecedented coordination by staff members in European commands and supporting commands outside Europe by secure e-mail. Secure high-capacity networks using Web-based technology permitted personnel engaged in theater to access up-to-date information posted for their use on military Web sites around the world. Space support was instrumental to our success. Satellite communications provided a significant portion of the communications capacity and were a major enabler of the global integration of our forces. Global Positioning System (GPS) satellites provided highly accurate navigation necessary for synchronization of complex operations, conduct of precision strikes, and input to GPS-guided weapons. Increased use of recently available GPS-guided weapons signals even greater reliance on satellite navigation. Weather satellites provided detailed and timely information necessary to exploit locally favorable environmental conditions for strikes. Reliance on space continues to grow in our military operations. Space operations during Allied Force illustrate our dependence on widely dispersed global capabilities that were effectively integrated.

Key Lessons from the War

The US report also describes a number of specific problems that every European expert interviewed in drafting this study seems to agree with.[260]

Although successful in some areas, NATO C4 capability was limited by the lack of C4 agreements and the need for more stringent enforcement and implementation of existing agreements. Problem areas included (1) sharing of bandwidth and C4 assets, (2) C4 network integration training standards at the combined and joint task force level, (3) spectrum management within combined and joint task forces, (4) network security, (5) lack of timely compliance with NATO standardization

... Information interoperability was sometimes a major problem. This was true during both U.S. joint operations and combined NATO operations. Interoperability concerns were noted in how information is disseminated (the supporting C4 infrastructure) and how to disseminate it securely (releasability of various levels of classification). Dissemination networking and procedures were ad hoc, and it was never possible to present a common operational picture to joint and allied commanders. 1. Interoperability Between U.S. and NATO Data Networks Interoperability between U.S. and NATO data networks was complicated because a single, integrated data network to support dissemination of coalition information was never established. Existing data networks were not adequate to support the flow of tactical, operational, and theater-level data among key nodes of the NATO information grid. The problem was further compounded by a lack of interoperability between U.S. and NATO databases and by the use of different security classifications to protect information.

The inability to pass high fidelity digital data was a shortfall in every phase of Operation Allied Force. Successful strikes against time-sensitive targets require a rapid exchange of precision target data and continuous precision updates from sensor-to-shooter until the target is destroyed. However, during Operation Allied Force strike reaction times were often slow, and diminished our ability to engage time-sensitive targets throughout the conflict. Data sometimes could not be transmitted to the required location at all. A joint data network was established within the theater, but it was composed of disparate tactical digital systems with multiple transmission systems and message formats. Information had to be passed through "stovepipe" systems with liaison personnel fulfilling the functions that should be done through automated interfaces. This ad hoc system increased the operations tempo, workload, and potential for error at the joint task force headquarters.

A joint, secure, tactical data link capability such as Link 16 is needed across all strike platforms to allow real-time data exchange and precision target processing between sensor and shooter, and to establish a robust common tactical picture. The Single Integrated Air Picture is planned to represent the air track portion of the common tactical picture and should improve battle management if it evolves successfully. The Joint Requirements Oversight Council has supported the designation of a lead organization to be responsible for Single Integrated Air Picture systems engineering, focusing on the joint data network/Link-16 component. Per the Joint Requirements Oversight Council's request, U.S. Joint Forces Command will recommend the lead organization by January 2000.

Because of the ad-hoc framework, the first organization in theater was left to set up the joint data network and to solve the most immediate problems. Given the complexity of the operation, the lack of joint and multinational doctrine, and the number of different tactical networks, no one was able to successfully integrate all these systems and maintain an overarching tactical network. As Operation Allied Force became more complicated, it was obvious that a Joint Interface Control Officer (JICO) element was needed. The JICO is the only activity that is trained to integrate tactical data systems at a joint level, but CINCs are not authorized this organization within their headquarters. Consequently, the JICO school at U.S. Army Forces Command dispatched its joint training team to support the operation. The JICO school has now been reestablished at Joint Forces Command, but it will need to be strongly supported with automated tools and the right people. The joint requirements process, working through the Joint Requirements Board (JRB), will be used to formally establish authorized Joint Interface Control Officer positions on each CINC's staff.

In addition, U.S. sensitivity to releasing certain types of information greatly inhibited combined planning and operations in some areas. Battle damage assessment products generated by the Joint Task Force Noble Anvil J2 were classified at a level that limited their use by allied forces. The same kinds of concerns precluded any integration of deception planning between U.S. and NATO information operations planners. Much of the U.S. information in question should be classified at the SECRET collateral level releasable to the coalition operation so that it can be effectively used by both U.S. and coalition warfighters. To the extent possible, imagery and signals intelligence data should classified "SECRET/ NOFORN Releasable to NATO," and sources and methods should be protected "by exception," rather than the other way around.

To address interoperability deficiencies in the near term, combatant CINCs need joint and coalition warfare concepts of operations that identify interoperability shortfalls and define contingency plans. For the long term, the Department is pursuing an end-to-end joint operational architecture as directed in Defense Planning Guidance 98–3 in order to provide a roadmap for U.S. acquisition strategies. This joint operational architecture will also aid our allies and coalition partners in their acquisitions, organization, and training to ensure compatibility with U.S. forces. Accordingly, the Department will develop a joint operational architecture with appropriate functional lines to facilitate and interface with the analogous structure in NATO and other coalition partners. We will clearly articulate system requirements for information systems interoperability and network architectures. Once these requirements are laid out, and materiel solutions identified, we can proceed with decisions on funding our efforts. Additionally we need to implement, where operationally viable, commercially accepted standards and specifications in ways that enhance interoperability between our NATO and coalition partners. By employing a common, high-level system engineering approach to solve interoperability challenges and ensuring that the end result supports the established Joint Operational Architecture, we believe we will accomplish a high degree of interoperability as part of Joint Vision 2010.

In summary, we see that interoperability will be the cornerstone for future alliance participation. With the pace of U.S. modernization, it becomes imperative to ease the modernization burden on our allies to the maximum extent possible. The United States must carefully review its policy regarding licensing requirements for our allies and ensure, where appropriate, these requirements are eliminated and do not unnecessarily allied modernization.

Reiterating the Need for Capability and Interoperability

The same US reporting on the lessons of the war includes a list of measures that NATO needs to take that are important lessons for both alliance and coalition warfare:[261]

The command, control, communications, and computer (C^4) support to Operation Allied Force was highly successful. Several important communications capabilities saw their first significant combat application: use of Web-based technologies for coordination and information sharing; video teleconferencing for command, control, and coordination; and e-mail for coordination and tasking. As the United States and NATO fielded these capabilities, some policy differences emerged that highlighted the need for increased emphasis and coordination in the alliance. The Defense Capabilities Initiative and NATO's Strategic Concept provide mechanisms to assist in formalizing C^4 policies. Intensive efforts in this vital area of alliance command, control, communications, and computers will contribute to improved interoperability and reduction in the imbalance in capabilities. In particular, the United States must work with our NATO allies to develop an overarching command-and-control policy and a detailed agreement on procedures for the policy's implementation. Additional policy and agreements, or implementation and enforcement of existing agreements, are essential in the following key areas as part of the development of a comprehensive and overarching NATO C^4 policy:

- Collaboration on allocation of limited bandwidth and communications assets to alliance members

- Establishment of network integration training standards for Commander Joint Task Force (CJTF) command, control, communications, and computers

- Management of the electromagnetic spectrum to optimize operations and to avoid mutual interference in support of the Joint Task Force

- Implementation and enforcement of coalition agreements on network security

- Improvements in timely compliance with NATO Standardization Agreements

- Improvements in interoperability by focusing on overarching standards and architectures rather than hardware

- Refinements in the policy and process of releasing information
- Acceleration of Host Nation Agreement processes affecting extensive networks of command, control, communications, and computers for Commanders of Joint Task Forces.

Lessons for High Level and Political Decision Makers

It is equally important that high level decision makers know how to exercise the new tools at their command, and to know when to intervene directly, and when to delegate. As the US report on the lessons of the war also indicates, the growth in real time communications and situational awareness is creating tools and information systems that are fundamentally changing the nature of combat leadership and crisis management.[262]

NATO commanders used video teleconferencing for the first time as a major instrument for exercising command and control. Daily commanders' video teleconferences were held to review progress of operations, coordinate future operations, and promulgate intentions. These conferences spanned the chain of command from the Supreme Allied Commander Europe to the Commander Joint Task Force and onward to component commanders. In other words, these commanders' video teleconferences spanned the strategic, operational, and tactical levels of command, thus greatly compressing normal command-and-control processes. As a result, strategic and operational commanders were able to directly influence tactical operations. Joint Vision 2010 anticipates these phenomena—from use of technologies such as video teleconferencing—by observing " . . . higher echelons will use these technologies to reduce the friction of war and to apply precise centralized control when and where appropriate. Real time information will likely drive parallel, not sequential planning and real time, not prearranged, decision-making. The optimal balance between centralized and decentralized command and control will have to be carefully developed as systems are brought into the inventories."

The ability of high-level commanders to influence tactical operations directly had positive as well as challenging aspects. Among the positive developments was the speed with which commanders and key staff officers could perform essential coordination. One of the challenges remains timely documentation and promulgation of the most essential substance of the proceedings, such as the commander's intentions, to those key personnel who did not attend the video teleconference. The Department is continuing to review the Kosovo experience in search of improvements that can be made in the use of video teleconferencing as a major tool for exercising command and control. Where appropriate, revisions to doctrine will be incorporated. The compression of time to exercise command and control made possible by video teleconferencing and other technologies is already a topic for Joint experimentation.

. . . It was very apparent that there is still a need for written documentation and dissemination of decisions, however. As already expressed in Joint Vision 2010: "Accelerated operational tempo and greater integration requirements will likely create a more stressful, faster moving decision environment. Real-time information will likely drive parallel, not sequential, planning and real-time, not prearranged, decision making." In order to optimize their application and accustom operational commanders to their effect on operations, such systems should be included regularly in future large-scale joint and combined training exercises. Likewise, doctrine, tactics, techniques, and procedures must be developed to adapt the optimum combinations of technologies to corresponding warfighting scenarios.

Combined Air Operations Center

There are a number of more detailed lessons regarding command and control. One is the critical importance of having adequate air operations command and control facilities. These were not present at the start of the war, in spite of the importance that NATO and the US planning and doctrine supposedly gives such capabilities. The US report on the lessons of the war notes that,

The Combined Air Operations Center (CAOC) was the nerve center that connected pilots and airborne controllers and directed air operations. It had been in place at 5th Allied Tactical Air Force in Vicenza, Italy, since the Bosnia operations, and grew from a hodgepodge of unique systems to an integrated operation. For Operation Allied Force, its staff swelled from 400 personnel to more than 1,300. Because the number of aircraft available in theater was large relative to the number of approved targets, the CAOC was able to schedule assets some time in advance. However, the target approval process often resulted in targets being assigned on the same day that they were to be attacked, thereby compressing the mission planning time available to aircrews. A variety of intelligence, surveillance, and reconnaissance sources were downlinked into the CAOC where operators analyzed information, integrated the target lists, and provided strike approval. Airborne elements of the theater air control system (AETACS) such as the airborne battlefield command-and-control center (ABCCC), airborne warning and control system (AWACS), and the joint surveillance and targeting radar system (JSTARS) provided inputs and enabled strike aircraft to flex from pre-planned targets to time critical targets (TCTs). This entire process reinforced the dictum that centralized control and decentralized execution of air and space forces are critical to force effectiveness.

Future conflicts will continue to require appropriate command-and-control centers to effectively execute and manage the joint force commander's strategy and execution plans. To be most effective, such centers cannot be set up from scratch. The development of established expeditionary air operations centers with supporting resources and manpower will allow the military to create CAOCs that can be tailored to the crisis at hand and deployed quickly. This faster deployment will help shrink the strategic decision loop while the greater cohesion and training of an expeditionary CAOC will enable it to tighten the operational decision loop. Such units will be able to develop and standardize tactics, techniques and procedures and be more effective as a highly value-added weapon system.

Secure Communications and Operational Security

Another key set of lessons is the need for common secure communications and proper operational security procedures. The US report on the lessons of the war indicates that,[263]

During Operation Allied Force, shortcomings were evident in both operations security (OPSEC) and communications security (COMSEC); and there is some evidence that these were exploited by the Serbs. Poor operations and communications security procedures reduced the effectiveness of NATO air strikes and increased the risk to NATO forces.

. . . Some allied aircraft were not equipped with either the cryptograph devices or keying material needed to conduct secure communications with other elements of the force. As a result, airborne command-and-control aircraft and other allied aircraft had to pass information in the clear, severely compromising operations security. This situation can only be corrected by ensuring all allied forces have the kinds of technologies, equipment, communications, planning, and training that will make them fully secure and interoperable.

In addition to the shortage of compatible, secure communications, NATO vulnerabilities were also linked to the use of predictable operating patterns and poor understanding of operations security. The Serbs capitalized on these shortcomings, in conjunction with a variety of other techniques, to help ensure the survival of deployed Serb forces.

Other security problems were caused by multiple security levels, which at times acted as a barrier in disseminating operational intelligence to warfighters. A review commissioned immediately after the conflict found that "the electronic flow of NATO data through US systems precluded effective US exploitation of . . . NATO databases." To resolve this problem, the review recommended that intelligence and other information be classified at the lowest reasonable level to enable its being used most effectively by warfighters and coalition partners.

In future operations, NATO must vary the operating patterns that it employs so as to degrade the accuracy with which any future adversary can predict routes and during operations. It is imperative that the well being and legal rights of the individual returnee be the overriding factors when planning and executing repatriation operations.

. . . Some of the operations security concerns were caused by disparities in the communications security equipment available to U.S. forces and their NATO allies. The major differences were in the numbers and types of secure telephones at the various timing associated with an air operation. Security procedure awareness training at all levels and locations, particularly at sites with augmentees, is essential. Computer-network details useful to hackers must be made more restricted. System administrators must train effectively and enable available security features in hardware and software.

NATO will continue to be among the highest-value targets for intelligence organizations of our potential adversaries. There should be no misunderstanding that our effort to achieve and maintain information superiority will also invite resourceful enemy attacks on our information systems.

These comments may explain why some US officers felt that NATO leaked key data to Serbia. They also indicate that this aspect of information warfare is not reserved to high technology powers.

Joint Operational Architecture, Network, and Information Management

More broadly, the US note the need for new forms of network integration and information management which will be critical if any power is ever to translate the theory behind the "revolution in military affairs" into practice. The US found that it had not really trained and organized its forces to carry out the following functions:[264]

- Rapidly improvise and deploy a joint operational C^4 architecture tailored to the needs of a given operation.
- Deal with task of creating effective joint networks to disseminate information.
- Deployment management tools to dynamically allocate bandwidth on demand.
- Create effective tools to provide real-time management and assessment of the effectiveness of joint networks.
- Handle the new data intensive burden imposed by extensive use of graphics, video, and imagery.
- Provide the user friendly interfaces and ergonomics necessary to reduce the workload on military personnel and support high tempo operations.
- Allow rapid, immediate, and focused access to real-time information.
- Break down the compartmentation between operations, intelligence, and planning.
- Take advantage of the new capabilities provided by the Internet.

These are all lessons that will be as important to any European and coalition operations as they are to NATO and US operations.

CONSCRIPTS VERSUS PROFESSIONALS; WELL-TRAINED RESERVES VERSUS A LARGE MOBILIZATION BASE

Kosovo seems to have reinforced the lessons that many military experts drew about the value of conscripts versus professionals after the Gulf War, and about the need for small, well-trained reserves that can provide immediate support to active forces versus a large mobilization base that can take months to bring up to combat readiness. The level of technology and the tactical demands of Kosovo clearly required highly trained and proficient soldiers, regardless of whether they were actives or reservists.

This experience helps validate the decision to phase out conscription to many French officers. It also raised growing concerns among German officers over their government's insistence that conscription was necessary to ensure a democratic force. Some senior German officers feel that the net result is to alienate German conscripts while wasting scarce resources on useless low-grade manpower.

A number of British and American officers express different concerns about reserves, although it should be noted that US air reserve units played a critical role in the airlift and air refueling missions, and reserves played a value in augumenting intelligence and a number of specialized tasks. The US reserve component provided personnel augmentation for staff functions through the Individual Mobilization Augmentee (IMA) program. The utility of this program was demonstrated by the fact that roughly 5,600 Reserve component personnel were mobilized. Nearly 4,000 served in the European theater.[265]

The made up 40% of KC-135 tanker aircraft crews and 25% of the A-10 attack aircraft crews in theater, and roughly 10 percent of the total number of US military personnel deployed there. While most of the Reserve personnel were committed following a Presidential Selected Reserve Call-up, thousands of Reservists and National Guardsmen voluntarily supported Operation Allied Force. Fifteen of the 19 Air National Guard tanker units that supported Allied Force, for example, had volunteered and deployed aircraft and personnel before the Call-up was announced.

Some British professionals feel that Kosovo is yet another lesson that reserves like the Territorial Army are only useful to the extent they are nearly combat ready and can be called up in crises like Kosovo. American officers feel that reserves play a critical role and note the role reserves have played in other recent US military actions. These figures are shown in Table 9.

At the same time, they feel that lobbying by the National Guard and reserves has created a total force concept that integrates the reserves too fully into US expeditionary forces and makes them difficult to deploy while maintaining large numbers of reserves that are only useful in a scenario where there are months to bring them up to readiness and the US Army needs a massive force rather than rapidly deployable expeditionary forces. They see the reserves and Congress as creating at least some of the problems in expeditionary capability for which the US Army is criticized.

CRUISE MISSILES

Kosovo was yet another crisis in which the US may a great many general claims were made about the "accuracy" and effectiveness of the TLAM and ALCM cruise missiles but provided few meaningful details. The performance of the TLAM and ALCM generally seems to have been good, and the British now plan to equip all 12 of the Royal Navy's attack submarines with TLAMs as a result of the successful use of such systems by the HMS Splendid.[266]

Speaking in Glittering Generalities

The US report on the lessons of the war issued in January 2000 describes the role of cruise missiles as follows:[267]

Cruise missiles were used extensively in the first few days of Operation Allied Force and during periods of adverse weather. These weapons were selected to match NATO's campaign strategy. In particular, the desire to limit the exposure of manned aircraft in the threat area, as well as the need to minimize collateral damage, made cruise missile employment a logical choice.

. . . The Tomahawk Land Attack Missile (TLAM) is a conventionally armed, long range, land attack cruise missile that can be launched from surface ships or submarines. All TLAMs expended during Operation Allied Force were the Block III configuration. Tomahawk missiles utilize a solid propellant rocket motor to accelerate the missile through

Table 9
Total US Active and Reserve Manpower in Crises and Conflicts Since the Gulf War

Operation	Type of Mission	Manpower		
		Active	Reserve	Total
Bosnia	Peacemaking	118,152	33,081	151,233
Central America	Humanitarian (Hurricane Mitch)	150	24,130	24,280
Iraq *	Combat/monitoring	193,884	19,169	213,053
Kosovo	Peacemaking	46,160	10,016	56,176
Haiti	Peacekeeping	23,400	8,100	31,500
Venezuela	Humanitarian (mudslides)	73	84	157
East Timor	Humanitarian	458	37	495

Note: *Combined operations from various bases including monitoring the Iraqi no-flight zone.
Source: Department of Defense and the *New York Times*, March 5, 2000, p. A-20.

the initial boost phase of flight until the turbofan engine takes over for the cruise and terminal phases.

Two versions of TLAM were used in this operation. The TLAM-C has a conventional unitary warhead, while the TLAM-D carries conventional submunitions. TLAMs were continuously present in the theater, and could be used to execute timely attack. This gave the joint force commander the ability to utilize the principles of surprise, initiative, and massed firepower on key enemy targets. Six ships and three submarines from two U.S. Navy battle groups and one UK submarine launched 218 missiles in preplanned and quick-reaction strikes. Target types ranged from traditional headquarter buildings and other infrastructure targets to relocatable targets such as aircraft and surface-to-air missile launchers. Tomahawk was often a weapon of choice for targets with the potential for high collateral damage, and was used to attack numerous targets in Belgrade.

. . . The Conventional Air Launched Cruise Missile (CALCM), designated AGM–86C, is a guided, air-to-ground missile armed with a conventional blast fragmentation warhead. The missile has been designed specifically to provide accurate attacks against long range, strategic "soft" targets. During Operation Allied Force, CALCMs were delivered by B-52s operating from forward bases in England.

It is striking, however, that this report provides absolutely no data on the reliability, accuracy, and damage effects of either type of cruise missile. Similarly, Vice Admiral Conrad C. Lautenbacher, the Deputy Chief of Naval Operations for Resources, Warfare Requirements, and Assessments provide little more than generalities regarding the importance of the cruise missile in his testimony to the House Armed Services Committee on the Lessons of the War.[268]

. . . we learned a great deal about the Tomahawk cruise missile. The fact that the Tomahawk is a weapon of choice is not new. In fact, more than 600 of these weapons have been employed by our ships and submarines since August of 1998. What is new is how responsive this weapon is becoming. A true 24 hour a day, all weather weapon, Tomahawk accounted for a disproportionate number of key targets attacked and destroyed. Not long ago, the timeline from planning and transmitting a mission to a firing platform, to actually launching the missile was measured in days. During ALLIED FORCE, the process was condensed to as little as a few hours. Still, timeliness is essential in striking mobile targets and we know we must continue to improve.

We have a number of initiatives underway to enhance the land attack capability of our ships and submarines. Several of you have expressed concern about the numbers of Tomahawks in our inventory. The Kosovo Emergency Supplemental provides funds to remanufacture a total of 624 Tomahawk missiles. I believe this represents the most cost-effective measure to fulfill our requirements until the Tactical Tomahawk enters service in 2003. As far as the Tactical Tomahawk is concerned, it promises to be even more capable and responsive. The Tactical Tomahawk will provide, among other features, in-flight retargeting capability, longer range, and greater lethality. In addition, we are developing the Land Attack Standard Missile as a near term, affordable weapon to complement Tactical Tomahawk and address the Marine Corps' requirement for accurate, high speed fire support. Farther downstream, we envision the DD-21 Land Attack Destroyer employing the Advanced Land Attack Missile and the Advanced Gun System, which will provide an even greater capability.

Growing Effectiveness?

There are precedents for not reporting any details on the performance of cruise missiles. The US Navy claimed during the Gulf War that 50% of its TLAMs "hit in the area of the target." This claim ignored failures to launch and misfires, and provided no meaningful data on damage. It claimed far higher levels of perform-ance in Desert Fox, but never provided any details.

As is clear from the above statements, no detailed official claims have been made in the case of Kosovo. Some US officers have stated on background, however, that the TLAM has become steadily more reliable and accurate since the Gulf War. They have stated that the accuracy of the TLAM has improved strikingly since the US cruise missile strikes on Iraq in the mid-1990s. They claim that the missiles had an 85% accuracy rate in both the strikes on Osama Bin Laden's bases in Afghanistan in 1998, and during Kosovo.[269] Other officers in the Navy have claimed that the TLAM proved to be more effective than manned aircraft in striking aircraft shelters and cratering runways—normally very diffi-cult missions.

Some US experts indicate that the ALCM achieved about an 85–90% launch rate and a successful significant damage hit near target rate of more than 50% per round fired. This is much better than its performance during the Gulf War, but it is still not clear how many missiles actually created the level of damage they were supposed to and what a "hit" means even when data are reported. There are also questions as to whether a range of roughly 600 miles is adequate for the kind of missions involved, and the adequacy of the USAF inventory of CALCMs.[270]

As is the case with the ALCM, it is still not clear how many TLAMs actually created the level of damage they were supposed to, and what a "hit" means even when data are reported.[271] These issues are particularly urgent given the tendency of the US to rely on the cruise missile early in attacks and/or to use it in the 20th century equivalent of gun boating. (The US fired 291 TLAMs during the Gulf War, 99 more against Iraq during 1993–1996, 13 against Bosnia in 1995, 79 against Afghanistan and the Sudan in August 1998, and more against Iraq during Desert Fox.)

Present US Navy plans to rush procurement of the Block III and the remanufacture older missiles are another reason for detailed validation of the program. So are plans to improve the warhead, GPS guidance, and use of the Digital Scene Matching Area Correlation (DSMAC) system and the interface between the Block III upgrade program and procurement of the Tactical Tomahawk in 2002–2003.[272]

DECOYS

Both sides used decoys. The discussion of NATO attacks on Serbian ground forces has shown that Serbia had some success in using decoys to divert NATO attacks and mislead NATO reconnaissance and intelligence. It is important to note that many of these decoys were relatively crude, and still managed to deceive NATO sensors.

A Russian analysis of the lessons of the war points out that, "the Yugoslavian side . . . failed to create in good time a network of dummy airfields, dummy air defense positions, and alternative command posts. Nor, did it resort in adequate measures to other types of operational camouflage, concealment, and deception."[273]

Nevertheless, the US Department of Defense reported in some of its testimony on the lessons of the war that,[274]

. . . the FRY employed concealment and deception tactics extensively. While reliance on cover and concealment protected much of the FRY force, it also precluded conventional maneuver operations in the field. Given that the United States may confront the use of similar tactics in the future, our limitations in being able to locate enemy forces under cover are being assessed, with emphasis on understanding how we can quickly develop and implement approaches to counter such tactics.

The ability to search and attack despite the cover of weather is one potential area for improvement. Technologies exist to provide high-fidelity radar penetration of cloud cover, for example.

Similarly, the length of time needed to move from target location to target attack could be shortened. Capabilities exist to pass large targeting data files up the chain of command via digital data links. Unfortunately, some of these capabilities currently aren't sufficiently mature, in terms of both technical readiness and cost, to field across our forces. Until we are convinced they can be made affordable, we need to explore a mix of procedural as well as material improvements to enhance our capabilities in a way that will not force reductions in other essential parts of the defense program.

The report on the lessons of the war that the Department of Defense issued in January 2000 also states the following:

Serbian forces in Kosovo employed camouflage, concealment, and deception tactics extensively. While reliance on camouflage and concealment protected much of the Serbian force, it also precluded conventional maneuver operations and limited their fighting effectiveness. Air defenses also moved and hid a significant amount of time—a tactic that increased their survivability, but greatly reduced their ability to hit NATO aircraft.[275]

Throughout Operation Allied Force, the Serbian forces conducted an extensive strategic, tactical, and operational-level denial and deception campaign against NATO forces. The objectives of this campaign were to degrade the effectiveness of NATO air strikes, ensure survival of Serb forces, discredit the NATO bombing campaign, retain key foreign support by hiding and discrediting evidence of atrocities, and exert pressure on NATO determination and resolve. However, the Serbs were largely unsuccessful in preventing the destruction of their fixed-wing aircraft; key fixed installations such as bridges, television and radio stations, petroleum and oil facilities; and some underground command and control bunkers. However, as NATO forces increasingly learned how to deal with Serbian deception tactics, the impact on allied operations became much more limited.

The Serbs employed a wide variety of tactics to deceive NATO forces. For example, most barracks were emptied prior to hostilities and troops and equipment were dispersed and hidden throughout the countryside. The Serbs also used natural cover such as woods, tunnels and caves, civilian homes and barns, and schools, factories, monasteries, and other large buildings to hide their personnel and weapons. Most movement of Serbian combat forces occurred during the night, or under the cover of bad weather. In addition, the Serbs used small convoys and decoys and dispersed their forces among civilian traffic. The Serbs used camouflage extensively to hide both tactical targets, such as military vehicles, and fixed facilities, such as bridges. In addition, the Serbs used decoys. . . to create a variety of false targets.

. . . Overall, NATO's recognition of the broad scale of Serbian denial and deception activities somewhat limited their success. However, because future adversaries are likely to study Serbian denial and deception tactics and could present more advanced threats to future operations, the Department is working on a variety of techniques to further improve our capability to counter an adversary's use of camouflage, concealment, and deception.

For reasons that have been discussed earlier, there is no way to know how effective such decoys really were. The fact that the same Department of Defense report that failed to discuss the effectiveness of airpower mentions these problems, however, is a warning about some of the limits to even the most advanced air power, given the fact that mass produced decoys are easy to move, can be rapidly assembled, and are far cheaper than aircraft or precision-guided munitions. It also raises questions about the ability of even advanced sensors to distinguish between more realistic and advanced forms of decoys and real targets—particularly if a threat force simultaneously intermingles its military weapons with civilians and civilian facilities and equipment.

NATO too made use of decoys. These included the Raytheon AN/ALE-50 fiber optic, towed, repeater jammer. Many of these decoys were shot down by Serbian forces, who confused them with NATO aircraft. This may account for some of Serbia's exaggerated claims to shooting down NATO aircraft and cruise missiles.

The other side of the hill is that advanced technology forces can make better use of sophisticated decoys and "phantom" electronic decoys than low technology forces.[276]

ELECTRONIC WARFARE AND THE EA-6B

One lesson of Kosovo was that NATO lacked the electronic warfare capability it needed to fight a small and relatively unsophisticated opponent, and that even the US lacked sufficient electronic warfare aircraft for more than one regional contingency. As General Michael E. Ryan, the Chief of Staff of the US Air Force, put it, "We don't have enough suppression of enemy air defense (SEAD) capability. We used almost every one of our block 50 F-16CJ capability (the Block 50 F-16CJ has high speed anti-radiation missile targeting capability). . . . we had to cease training in the States." The USAF had phased out all of its F-4G Wild Weasels with HARM after the Gulf War, and is seeking 30 more F-16CJs.[277]

Over-Reliance on the EA-6B and Insufficient Electronic Warfare Assets

The US Navy and Marine Corps had equal problems in obtaining enough EA-6B Prowlers, and the USAF had no independent electronic warfare aircraft because it had also phased out the 24 EF-111 Ravens it had used during the Gulf War by 1997. This presented problems because the EA-6B was slower than the EF-111 and was a stand-off jammer rather than a plane that escorted strike aircraft into defended areas, and because the Air Force had not trained in depth to use the EA-6B. The USAF had phased out the EF-111s because of its overall budget squeeze, their high flight costs, and the fact that some $1 billion worth of improvements were programmed to keep them combat effective.[278]

Lt. General John R. Rhodes, the Commanding General of the Marine Corps Combat Development Command, described the problems in deploying the EA-6B as follows in his testimony to the Congress on the lessons of the war.[279]

Navy and Marine Corps EA-6B Prowlers, the only standoff jamming aircraft available in theater, were vital to the success of air operations and the overall campaign. The high usage rate of these LDHD assets severely strained both aircrew and airframes. Of the four Marine EA-6B squadrons, three were deployed in theater and the remaining squadron was in the United States prepared to deploy within 96 hours. Critical as they were to the success of this and any other operation, our Prowlers need upgrades that will enhance their situational awareness. Specifically, data-link upgrades (Link 16 upgrades) and Night Vision Devices (NVDs) for the Marine EA-6Bs should be procured at the earliest opportunity. These upgrades will enable the Prowler to maintain its current edge on the modern battlefield. There is also a demonstrated need for more integrated joint training of aircrews to maximize the potential of this most important system across the services. Even with these enhancements, however, the fact remains that our Prowlers are simply old and over-committed. Both the aircraft and their crews are showing the stress of heavy use over many operations. In order to reduce the stress on Prowler personnel and equipment, we have suspended normal EA-6B rotations to Iwakuni, Japan. We will reinstate the normal deployment cycle in the spring of next year.

Another Marine Corps officer, Brigadier General Robert M. Flanagan, the Deputy Commander, II Marine Expeditionary Force, provided further insights into the problems involved and the limits of the role the EA-6B could play in active air defense suppression.[280]

Aircrew survivability, in the event of a shoot-down, was also a concern for our Prowler crews. VMAQ-2 aircrews were not issued the latest survival radios (PRC-112) prior to arriving in theater due to a DOD wide shortage. The PRC-112 is a GPS equipped radio that can be directly attributed to the successful rescue of two downed aircrew during OAF. VMAQ-2 arranged for a temporary loan and the required training on these radios to ensure that aircrew were prepared for this contingency. We need to accelerate the fielding of the PRC-112 throughout DOD. We are working hard to overcome this shortfall and hope to have an adequate supply of the PRC-112 survival radio in the near future.

Aviation parts and re-supply were also issues from OAF. Marine Prowlers flew 464 combat missions, taking a toll on an already strained EA-6B airframe. During the 78-day air campaign, each Marine airframe averaged 95 hours per month with one aircraft flying 123 hours in one month. These numbers become significant when you consider that planned aircraft utilization rates during sustained operations are 36 hours per month and a much higher, wartime surge rate. This increase in aircraft flight hours directly impacts future EA-6B utilization, maintenance schedules, spare parts, and overall life cycle. Despite this high utilization rate, Marine Prowlers maintained a remarkable 100% mission completion rate.

To achieve this success, our parts supply system was drawn down to critically low levels. In addition to struggling for parts in Aviano, the lone Marine Corps CONUS based Prowler squadron was brought to a virtual standstill. The lack of spare parts dramatically reduced their ability to train and maintain aircrew proficiency. The supply system does not currently possess the necessary aviation parts nor manpower to support full time contingency operations and simultaneously support CONUS based units at normal rates. This affects our ability to execute simultaneous operations in two theaters.

. . . High Speed Anti-Radiation Missiles (HARM) were employed by the EA-6B, primarily in pre-emptive strikes against known targets at known locations, supporting airborne strike packages. The locations of targets were determined from available intelligence sources. A total of 57 HARMs were expended from Marine EA-6Bs. Bomb damage assessment for HARM was difficult to accurately determine, and a "soft kill" from a "hard kill" could not be substantiated with certainty. The target sets ranged from SA-6 and SA-3 surface to air missiles to TPS-63 and TPS-70 type surveillance radars. Enemy radar was not routinely active, but would radiate during strikes by U.S. aircraft.

Lessons Regarding the EA-6B

The US was forced to devote 30 of its 90 EA-6Bs to the air and missile campaign in Kosovo in order to make up for the lack of EF-111s, and then had to fly them at rates which involved eight hour sorties in which the aircraft had to refuel in mid-air to escort several strike packages. Quite aside from the strain on aircrews, the strain on the EA-6B fleet now raises questions about whether the aircraft can fly to the end of its projected life span, which is 2015. This may force the US Navy to accelerate development of a variant of the new F-18G to replace the EA-6B, although it is also considering an increased number of overhauls to extend aircraft life. The Navy is also considering bringing four-six stored EA-6B aircraft, and 20–30 pilots, into a new squadron to make up for the shortfall in total forces. It potentially would create a force of 104 EA-6Bs, with 19 more in training squadrons or maintenance, This would create a deployable force of 104 aircraft.[281]

The Department took other short-term measures in its FY2000 supplemental and FY2001 budgets. The FY2000 supplement funded a number of EA-6B upgrades at a cost of $158 million, along with the procurement of 7,600 additional ALE-50 towed decoys. The FY 2001–2005 budget and program invests an additional $389 million to accelerate improvements to the EA-6B electronic warfare aircraft, to add another Navy expeditionary squadron (the fifth) to support joint missions and ease the deployment strain on that important element of the force. It also funded the initiation of a jointly-conducted Analysis of Alternatives to determine what capabilities will be required to replace the EA-6B beginning in about 2010 to 2015.[282]

There are many detailed lessons regarding the EA-6B. Kosovo demonstrated the need to upgrade the EA-6B to give it night vision equipment and to reduce its vulnerability to nighttime attacks by surface-to-air missiles. This upgrade has already been funded. Other questions exist about the ability of the EA-6B to fly close enough to heavily defended areas to provide jamming support for the F-117 and other stealth systems. This may or may not be addressed by the Improved Capability (ICAP-3) upgrade to make the EA-6B more responsive to frequency hopping radars.[283] There is also a need to improve the AN/ASQ-213 High Speed Anti-Radiation Missile (HARM) targeting system to allow it to pass targeting information to the Raytheon AGM-154 Joint Stand-Off Weapon.[284]

The are also questions about the EA-6B's capability to deal with more sophisticated threats. The Band 9/10 jammer to counter the Russian S-300 and S-400 (SA-10 and SA-12) is not yet deployed or proven in combat. It is not clear that the US has programmed the advanced jamming equipment it needs to deal with modern threats. The US Congress did, however, appropriate supplemental FY1999 funds for an improved version of the ALQ-99 and VAQ-137 jammers, and accelerated procurement of the Tracor high-band jammer pod which operates in Bands 9 and 10 (10–20 GHz.). The EA-6B will also be modernized with the ICAP-3 modification to its jammer suite and improved color and tactical displays, plus new electronic support measures and improved geolocation capabilities to target the HARM missile. Study is underway of how to give the EA-6B night vision capability, collision avoidance, and improved chaff.[285]

The US is expanding its fleet of EA-6Bs to 123 aircraft by upgrading earlier variants to the Block 89 standard, but no clear program seems to exist to phase in variants of the F/A-18 or JSF as replacements to the EA-6B, and the past history of efforts to replace the EA-6B has been filled with false claims about the cost, performance, and test results of projected replacements. The unfortunate fact is that neither the officers and civilians managing such programs, or the defense industry, has a good track record in developing new electronic warfare systems.[286]

The Navy's efforts to replace the EA-6B with an electronic warfare version of the F/A-18F require careful program validation, given the Navy's long history of mismanaging its tactical aviation developments. The F/A18-G "Growler" radar and communications jamming aircraft is a possible replacement to the EA-6B after 2015, but some experts believe that a JSF-like platform is essential to ensure the survival of such an aircraft even though one could not be deployed before 2020. Others believe that a large stand-off jammer platform based on an airframe like the B-757 or B-767 is the solution.[287]

Lessons Regarding the Overall Need to Improve US Electronic Warfare Capabilities

Concepts like using bombers, the F-22, or JSF as electronic warfare platforms raise equally serious questions. An ongoing Rand study of the USAF management of its electronic warfare programs during and after the phase out of the EF-111 is expected to raise major questions about the quality of the Air Force's program management and its failure to bring aircraft survivability, stealth, speed, and structures into balance with electronic warfighting capability.[288]

Another issue that has been raised as a result of Kosovo is the fact that US and European electronic warfare efforts are now focused largely on air defense, rather than information warfare directed at communications. Jacques Gansler, the head of Pentagon acquisition, has cautioned that, "In future conflicts, the enemy is much more likely to jam our communications and interfere with out computing systems and use camouflage and deception . . . we are focusing on better ways to gather intelligence."[289]

The war in Kosovo raises serious questions about the adequacy of the US air fleet dedicated to active electronic suppression of surface-to-air missile defenses now that the EF-111 Raven has been phased out of the USAF. The US used approximately 50 of its total of 95 EA-6Bs in the Balkans during the height of Operation Allied Force, and 26 in direct support of operations in Kosovo. It had to take EA-6Bs off carrier forces to support land missions, and still could not supply the needs of forces like the US Marine Corps.[290]

These problems have led the US Air Force to reexamine both its future upgrade plans for the F-16 and the kind of electronic warfare protection its new Joint Strike Fighter would need in spite of its stealth features. It is leading some planners to advocate more reliance on unmanned aerial vehicles as a partial substitute for electronic warfare, and new trade-offs between electronic warfare and stealth.

Lessons Regarding NATO and Alliance Electronic Warfare Capabilities

The US and Europe need to reassess electronic warfare in a broader sense, and particularly the balance of assets it needs for intelligence, information warfare, and electronic warfare. There seems to be a tendency to compartment such efforts, particularly at the tactical level. There also seems to be a tendency to focus on the offensive aspects of information warfare, although the increasingly sophisticated and demanding netting of US tactical assets raises serious questions about US counter-vulnerability and the problems Europe might face if it copied the current US approach.

Kosovo creates even more serious questions about NATO and European electronic warfare capabilities. At present, Europe simply lacks effective electronic warfare capabilities. Given the fact that European aircraft had to rely on US electronic warfare protection to fly against a threat limited to SA-6s, this indicates that European air forces would take high levels of casualties against any threat with more advanced fighter and/or surface-to-air missile defenses

EXPEDITIONARY CAPABILITY AND POWER PROJECTION OF US AND NATO FORCES

Kosovo demonstrated that the US and its NATO allies have very different levels of expeditionary capability and strategic lift. The US provided almost all of the dedicated military air and sealift used during the air and missile campaign. The scale of the US effort is indicated by the fact that the US European Command (USEUCOM) conducted 1,751 airlift missions at a cost of $99 million, and 75 sealift missions at a cost of $18 million. (Although the US also made use of 93 trains at a cost of $6.8 million.)[291]

The US had a distinct advantage in many areas of expeditionary capability, although some of its services proved more capable than others. Kosovo again demonstrated the importance of US carrier forces and the mobility of the US Marine Corps. It also demonstrated the value of USAF planning of expeditionary packages for rapid deployment. At the same time, the USAF operated largely out of highly advanced allied bases, and serious questions exist about the adequacy of its current and planned inventory of expeditionary assets. Senior US Air Force officers feel that the USAF needs significantly more forces and equipment to properly perform an expeditionary mission outside Europe.

Deployment Planning and Management

The US has significantly improved its ability to plan and manage deployments since the Gulf War, when the US system virtually collapsed under the burden of conflicting demands and the US was often forced to "flood" shipments forward almost regardless of priority and the validity of the requirement or theater request.

Nevertheless, Kosovo again illustrated how difficult it is to bring supplies, lift, priorities, and in-theater requests into balance:[292]

One of the linchpins of a successful military deployment is detailed planning. In the case of force deployments, this planning takes the form of an accurate description of what units need to be moved, their points of origin, their destinations, their size (e.g., weight, volume, and number of personnel), and when they are required to arrive. This basic information comprises the backbone of the Time-Phased Force and Deployment Data (TPFDD) that drives the allocation of transportation assets to the units that must be moved. As the deployment data is developed, additional information is incorporated (e.g., preferred mode of transportation) to ensure that scarce mobility assets are used in the most efficient fashion.

Given the great level of detail required to coordinate a large deployment, the rapid generation of the deployment data to support a quick reaction operation such as Allied Force is a monumental task. The quite substantial force and deployment data for Operation Allied Force had to be developed in weeks. Further complicating deployment planning is the fact that the TPFDD is a living document that must be continuously modified in response to changes in the operational situation. As the Commander's plans change, so must the deployment data. This inherent aspect of deployment data development was graphically illustrated in the Task Force Hawk deployment when political and operational imperatives required a significant shift in basing from the Former Yugoslav Republic of Macedonia to Albania. A large portion of the deployment data had to be rapidly reworked in response to this change. Of course, the ideal of a stable, pre-planned TPFDD is never achievable. The deployment data and its planning process must be flexible and responsive to the inevitable shifts in the commander's operational priorities.

We have identified two major factors in Operation Allied Force that contributed to avoidable delays in TPFDD development: inadequate planning systems and poor planning discipline.

1. Deployment Data Planning Systems

Automated planning systems are essential for rapid and accurate TPFDD development. Today, many different planning systems contribute to the deployment data. These systems range from unit-level tools up to the often-mentioned Joint Operation Planning and Execution System (JOPES), a high-level system that is the primary driver for strategic deployments. This hierarchy of lower-level systems feeding data to progressively higher-level systems culminates with the global TPFDD. Unfortunately, the limited interoperability of today's systems creates friction at all levels of the deployment planning process. Among the specific problems are inconsistent data requirements and electronic data formats that cannot be easily shared between systems. This lack of "user friendliness" slows data development and places an unnecessary premium on the relatively few individuals with the experience to work through an ad hoc end-to-end TPFDD generation process. Unfortunately, the pressure of crisis action planning can significantly strain such an ad hoc system. To improve TPFDD generation, the Department is reviewing the suite of tools used for TPFDD generation with the goal of providing a more seamless system for planners at every level. Much has already been accomplished in this direction. For example, the Transportation Coordinators' Automated Information for Movement System (TC-AIMS II) now under development, will integrate the functionality of the Services' existing movement planning systems into a single tool. Taking this integration another step, the Department is considering integrating TC-AIMS II with the Joint Forces Resource Generation II (JFRG II) system to further speed unit data into the deployment data.

A related shortcoming of deployment planning was the difficulty assessing the impact of Allied Force deployments on major theater war plans. Many assets deployed to Operation Allied Force are simultaneously tasked for the major theater wars. Should a major theater war erupt, this engagement in another contingency would be expected to delay deployment to the larger conflict. From the more general perspective of deployment planning tools, the capability to track the status and location of major theater war forces would be valuable. This would help planners avoid adverse impacts to major theater war plans and allow them to identify any decrements to our senior leadership.

2. TPFDD-Generation Process Discipline

Improving the automated planning systems is only part of the solution to delays in the TPFDD-generation process. Deployment policies, process procedures, and trained personnel are as integral to the JOPES as are the hardware and software described above. Additional emphasis is required to ensure all participants follow the established deployment data development procedures and policies in a disciplined manner. Failure to follow proper procedures can result in conflicts and other delays as the system tries to incorporate inadequate or incomplete movement requests into the deployment data. The problem with poor discipline in the execution of established planning procedures was at least partially an outgrowth of the planning system shortcomings described above. With multiple planning systems and their associated procedures in use at any given time, there were few policies and procedures that could be consistently followed across the spectrum of data development activities. Individuals encountering an unfamiliar aspect of the process were forced to improvise solutions. Although this might get a specific job done, other aspects of the deployment could be adversely impacted. The integration of planning systems recommended above will go a long way toward solving this problem by providing a more unified set of procedures and policies across the full range of TPFDD-development activities. By ensuring all participants are able to collaborate in a real-time environment, we can increase the efficiency of strategic lift planning.

Even with improved planning systems in place, a better understanding of the TPFDD-development process is needed at all levels. For example, specific information is required if deployment requests are to be included in the data in a timely manner. Without the necessary data, requests cannot be processed, and the time consuming task of asking for clarification will ensue. During Operation Allied Force, delays resulted from errors as simple as failure to specify the desired delivery locations for deploying units. It was like placing a catalog order without specifying a mailing address. Since individuals can only follow procedures if they know what the procedures are, deployment-oriented continuation training should be provided from the highest staff levels down to the lowest. As a proponent of the Joint Deployment process, U.S. Joint Forces Command intends to pursue end-to-end solutions, including process, training, and technology, in an effort to identify the best long-term solutions to this aspect of the deployment process.

. . . . In-transit visibility also gives a commander a better idea of when forces will arrive in theater. Especially important is accurate knowledge of when the unit will be ready for employment. Some current tracking systems list a unit as in theater when the first ship or transport aircraft arrives. In reality, it might be several more days before the entire unit has arrived. By solving problems such as these, in-transit visibility gives a commander a much clearer picture of the status of the deployment. Asset visibility continues to mature within the military transportation system. However, there is still room for significant improvement. A major impediment to achieving in-transit visibility is the inability to capture data accurately at the source. Without this data, the best of systems would remain functionally useless. Even if the necessary data were available, there is currently a lack of adequate feeder systems and the associated communications support needed to collect and fuse the data into a coherent picture on the Global Transportation Network (GTN). At a higher level, there remains a lack of theater in-transit visibility doctrine and supporting policies. This necessitates ad hoc planning in critical times, and results at best in fragmented theater in-transit visibility.

To help overcome these problems, the Department is continuing to place emphasis on improving end-to-end asset visibility. The Unified Commanders will continue to develop internal in-transit visibility plans that leverage the technical in-transit visibility capabilities that are developed and deployed by the Services and other agencies. As the in-transit visibility functional lead, the U.S. Transportation Command will evaluate the need for additional joint doctrine and procedures to link strategic and theater in-transit visibility into an integrated process. Furthermore, the current Joint Staff study on Information Technology for Deployment, Force Tracking, and Sustainment will consider technical solutions to the problem of multi-point collection of in-transit visibility data.

While these lessons may seem to fall into the category of technical trivia to some observers, it is important to understand what is really involved. Military forces with scarce resources and lift cannot afford to over-use or over-deploy. Commanders without the right resources cannot fight. The use of modern information systems to manage deployments is just as much of a force multiplier as advanced precision munitions, and forces with limited financial resources can only be effective if they give deployment management the proper priority.

The Role of US Strategic Lift

Senior US military planners also feel that Kosovo demonstrated the need for more US airlift and sealift. General Charles T. Robinson, the Commander in Chief of the US Transportation Command, provided the following overview of US airlift and sealift activity in testimony to Congress on the lessons of the war.[293]

The importance of our C-5 fleet was highlighted again during Kosovo operations. Although C-5s flew only 20 percent of our overall strategic airlift missions, they were critical in moving outsize equipment along the "long leg" of the deployment—from CONUS to Europe. In his testimony, General Shelton, Chairman of the Joint Chiefs of Staff, testified that Allied Force prosecuted " . . . the most precise and lowest-collateral-damage air campaign in history-with no U.S. or allied combat casualties in 78 days of around-the-clock operations and over 38,000 combat sorties." A portion of that success belongs to the C-5's responsive movement of precision munitions from CONUS into the AOR.

Successes aside, the C-5's readiness remains a significant concern as its MC rate continues to decline from the 61 percent I reported to you earlier this year, to about 58 percent today. This aircraft, important to every peacetime deployment we undertake today, is even more critical in an MTW scenario where we would be required to move significantly more unit equipment from CONUS. As stated earlier, to meet the MRS BURU "two MTW" requirement, we need a 75 percent MC rate for the C-5. We are putting a C-5 modernization program in place in an effort to raise the C-5's reliability to the required level, but even if we succeed, based on the length of time required to complete the associated research, development, testing and subsequent modifications, we will not see MC rates rise significantly until 2005 nor, assuming full funding for the current program, and assuming the modifications are successful in reversing the C-5's declining reliability rates, will we begin to approach the required 75 percent MC rate until 2014. As we move in this direction, Air Mobility Command's "Oversize and Outsized Analysis of Alternatives", using MRS-05 scenarios, is currently examining these future combat power projection deficiencies alongside the MRS-05 requirements. We are hopeful that the recommendations from that analysis will suggest operationally effective, best value force mixes of C-5 and C-17 aircraft to meet today's and tomorrow's Oversize/Outsize requirements.

The use of the C-17 in the *intra*theater role was a genuine success story, validating once again its critical importance as an instrument of national strategy. Twelve C-17s, placed under the tactical control of USEUCOM's air component, flew 430 intratheater airlift missions, mostly in support of TF Hawk's deployment. With its large cargo capacity and superb ground maneuverability, the C-17 gave the supported commander the maximum flexibility possible to deploy his forces into Albania. As successful as it was though, we have to be very cautious as we come to depend on future use of the aircraft in this role. Only because of the minimal demand for strategic airlift were we able to dedicate C-17s for *intra*theater use. As you know, we are replacing 270 C-141s with just 134 C-17s . . . being procured primarily to replace the C-141 in support of its MRS BURU strategic, *inter*theater role. In addition, even though tonnage capabilities remain close to the same, we lose tremendous flexibility with so many fewer "tails." In other words, 134 C-17s can only be in half as many places as 270 C-141s . . . a tremendous capability shortfall in peacetime. And, if the demand for strategic airlift is higher in future conflicts, and we know it will be in an MTW, we will probably *not* be able to take C-17s out of the strategic flow for *intra*theater support at the currently planned force structure numbers. A separate Intratheater Lift Analysis is in progress to determine the force structure necessary to support worldwide intratheater aircraft lift requirements.

. . . Our MSC organic and chartered ships deployed everything from humanitarian supplies to ammunition to unit equipment. Before the conflict ended, ALLIED FORCE was supported by 34 strategic sealift ships, moving 7,594,674 barrels of fuel, 245,280 square feet of ammunition, 1,225,849 square feet of vehicles and equipment, and 1,533 twenty foot equivalent containers. To put this in perspective, this is enough fuel for 20 million minivans, and enough cargo to fill the floor space of 13 Super Walmarts.

Three of our prepositioning program ships, as part of MSC's force, also provided direct support: one tanker with JP5 fuel and two ammunition ships with munitions for the air campaign. Again, the value of prepositioned afloat stocks and our partnering with the commercial sealift industry proved vital. We saved considerable time and effort by calling these ships forward instead of activating or contracting shipping, loading in CONUS, and waiting on transit time to the theater.

Lessons Regarding the C-17

Virtually all US planners feel the lift capabilities of the C-17 proved to be of great value throughout the campaign. Secretary Cohen made this point in his testimony to Congress on the lessons of the war.[294]

In conducting this rapid buildup of forces, we made extensive use of existing plans and capabilities for conducting major wars. For example, the C-17 was the workhorse of the airlift force, providing for the rapid deployment of critical warfighting and humanitarian materiel. Our aerial-refueling fleet overcame extended sortie durations and high usage rates to deploy and support a multinational air force. And our sea mobility assets resupplied preferred munitions in addition to providing transportation for key deployment forces.

Throughout Operation Allied Force, U.S. forces had to overcome many limitations in transportation infrastructure. Poor airport surface conditions in Tirana, Albania, for example, slowed aircraft turnaround times, limited throughput, and slowed the onward movement of forces and humanitarian supplies. Our transportation and other logistic assets proved to be flexible, effective, and efficient in responding to these limitations.

In particular, the C-17 made the concept of direct delivery—the strategic air movement of cargo from an aerial port of embarkation to an airfield as close as practicable to the final destination-a reality. And, as discussed later in more detail, the deployment to Europe of aircraft based across the world, coupled with the wide range of bases used by combat aircraft in the theater, made aerial refueling a challenge.

The US made similar points in its final report on the lessons of the war.[295]

The performance of the C-17 in Operation Allied Force demonstrated the great utility of the demanding requirements originally established for that aircraft. The C-17 flew half of the strategic airlift missions required by the operation. Because of its small-field capability, the C-17 made the concept of direct delivery (strategic movement from port of embarkation to airfield closest to final destination) a reality. It was no longer necessary to transfer cargo from an inter-theater airlifter to an intra-theater airlifter for the final leg of deployment. In addition to being able to use small airfields, the C-17's average ground time was significantly less than the published planning factor times. Rapid turnaround such as this is critical at airfields that can only accommodate small numbers of aircraft on the ground, and is testimony to the design of the aircraft as well as the efforts of aerial port personnel supporting the off-load operations.

Almost all of the Air Force's 50 C-17s were involved in the Balkan operation, partly because 39 C-17s had been delivered ahead of schedule. The US Air Force reports that C-17s from Charleston Air Force Base, S.C., had flown 1,092 missions into the theater as of June 29, 1999, with a departure reliability rate of 96 percent. As many as 20 C-17 missions were flown into Albania each day. The C-17's

missions included, "the initial deployment of warfighters and equipment; deployment of Apache attack helicopters and their support units to Albania; providing
supplies to Kosovar refugees in Albania; deployment of peacekeepers to Kosovo,
and the ongoing re-deployment of forces from allied bases in Europe."[296]

Col. Ted Bowlds, the director of the C-17 System Program Office, stated that
three factors account for the aircraft's success in Allied Force and related
operations in the Balkans: high payload capacity; ability to land on short, austere
airfields; and ground maneuverability. "The C-17 can carry four times the payload
of a much smaller C-130, yet land in the same area, airfields as short as 3,000 feet,"
the colonel explained. It also has the ability to move in confined areas. Unlike any
other large transport aircraft, the Globemaster III can back up and turn around,
much like an automobile. The C-17 also had the advantage that it did not have to be
reconfigured to off-load different types of cargo. All cargo and equipment could be
rolled directly off the aircraft. This meant that C-17s had about three times the
"through-put" of similar heavy-lift aircraft, and a single C-17 could carry almost
three times as many tons per day as other similarly sized transport aircraft. All of
the C-17 aircraft flying into the area were equipped with protective crew armor
developed when the Air Force first began operations in Bosnia in December 1995.

The Air Force reports that these features made the C-17 uniquely suited for
operating in Albania's Rinas Airport, where the aircraft delivered weapons and
equipment for the Army as part of Task Force Hawk, the colonel said. The runway
there is small, and taxi and parking areas are extremely limited. These are
potentially important points about future strategic and tactical airlift missions,
since the C-17 is the only aircraft in any NATO force with these capabilities. Even
the US, however, faces problems with its long-range airlift force. It now has only
51 aircraft in service out of a total procurement of 120. Moreover, the USAF is still
dependent on a large force of aging C-151s and C-5s.

The demands placed on the C-17 force during Kosovo indicate that the US may
need a considerably larger C-17 force than is now planned. This has led both the
Clinton Administration and the Congress to consider buying 60 more aircraft,
bringing the total buy to 180, rather than 120 aircraft.[297] If this buy is fully funded,
upgrades to the C-17 will make it even more useful. The Block 10 version of the
aircraft was introduced after the air campaign in Kosovo, and incorporates a new
composite/metal tail 20% lighter than its predecessor. It has a dual rail internal
cabin that increases air drop capacity by 266%, and an extended range fuel tank
that increases its range by 600 nautical miles. New communications and navigation systems allow the aircraft to fly with more precision and sharply reduce the
internal required between aircraft in flight.[298]

The Impact of US Air Refueling Capabilities

The USAF also had a massive advantage because of its airborne tanker and
refueling capability. While this capability is sometimes ignored in analyzing the

lessons of Kosovo, it was a major point in the Department of Defense's testimony on the lessons of the war.[299]

... active and reserve component tankers provided multiple air bridges for aircraft transiting to the theater, while also supporting over 24,000 combat air sorties. Other logistics successes include timely intertheater movement of stocks of preferred munitions, including prepositioned munitions ships, and effective and efficient management of theater fuel distribution, including the use of prepositioned fuel ships.

One of the most challenging aspects of Operation Allied Force was providing tanker support for transport aircraft delivering forces to the theater and for combat aircraft deploying to the theater and conducting strike operations. Aerial-refueling missions were particularly demanding because tankers operated, in many cases, from bases on the periphery of the theater.

There were not enough air bases in the area immediately around Kosovo to support all the aircraft committed to Operation Allied Force. Strike aircraft were placed on bases closest to Kosovo, and longer-range tankers were based at locales farther away. Because of the basing arrangements, tanker missions were longer than would typically be the case in a major theater war. Extensive tanker support was also needed for the global attack sorties flown from the continental United States by B-2 bombers.

As a result of the longer missions, crew ratios for tankers participating in Operation Allied Force were higher than what we would typically plan. We met aerial-refueling demands by using reserve crews and by drawing on active crews assigned to aircraft that were in depot for modifications. While the demands for tanker crews were high, we were able to meet them with the forces planned for major theater wars.

Although we succeeded in providing the tanker support needed to sustain the air campaign, we are reviewing our tanker forces and crew ratios to determine whether they are sufficient to meet future needs in either major theater wars or other contingencies. We also found that our ability to plan in theater, in real time, for the most effective use of our tanker fleet was limited. The Department is reviewing options for improving this key planning capability.

It is also important to note that refueling presented interoperability problems with important implications for NATO and coalition warfare. General John Jumper noted in testimony to the Congress on the less of the war that,[300]

With the great flight distances from many bases to Yugoslav airspace, air refueling was a critically needed capability. By the end of the conflict, we had assembled a force of nearly 200 NATO tanker aircraft to provide the lifeblood of the air campaign. However, pilots from several allies lacked adequate training for in-flight refueling, which diminished their participation.

The Expeditionary Capability of the US Air Force

The US Air Force experienced other problems in power projection which are worth noting. The Department of Defense report on the lessons of the war found that it needed to develop plans to preposition critical munitions, and that it needed more mobility readiness spares packages:[301]

Prepositioned munitions are stored on the ground or on ships located near the supported theater. However, because munitions stockpiles must be divided among several overseas theaters, theater inventories of preferred munitions tend to lag requirements. In the event of a contingency like Operation Allied Force, these inventories can become strained very quickly. During Allied Force, rapid resupply from the United States was required early in the operation.

Airlift of preferred munitions from the United States adds a significant burden to an airlift fleet already tasked with deploying units. In light of the high demand for preferred munitions, the Department plans to reexamine the allocation of preferred munitions to the different theaters. This assessment will try to reconcile the demands of smaller-scale contingencies with the operational plans for major theater wars in an effort to minimize the overall risk to our military posture as a whole. In a similar vein, the Department will examine the mix of preferred to non-preferred munitions in prepositioned stocks.

. . . Present day U.S. Air Force Mobility Readiness Spares Package (MRSP) levels reflect the projected demands for a scenario involving two nearly simultaneous major theater wars and rely heavily on the availability of deployed aircraft that can be cannibalized for spare parts to offset MRSP shortfalls. Cannibalization is the primary source of many parts not carried in present fighter MRSPs. When these MRSPs are used to support a partial squadron deployment (split-based operations), stay behind (home station) aircraft must be cannibalized to fill spares shortfalls of the deployed element, since there are not enough aircraft deployed to meet spares (cannibalization) requirements. The lower than planned aircraft loss rates and higher aircraft availability rates experienced in OAF exacerbated this problem by increasing the demand for spares while further limiting the availability of cannibalization aircraft. Our experience in Operation Allied Force provided indication that current Air Force Mobility Readiness Spares Packages may be insufficient to achieve aircraft availability targets under the Air Force's Air Expeditionary Force (AEF) concept. For AEF commitments, the Air Force may not deploy entire squadrons, creating split-based operating conditions not unlike those experienced during Allied Force.

These issues reinforce the lesson that the kind of readiness problems discussed earlier can play a critical role in power projection, and that the US is not spending enough on such capabilities. More generally, they illustrate the fact that moving the force is one thing, and sustaining it is another. This may be a lesson that Europe needed to learn as much as the US.

The Expeditionary Capability of the US Army

Kosovo raised more serious questions about the expeditionary capabilities of the US Army. The US Army does have considerable expeditionary capabilities, including the XVIIIth Airborne Corps, with four light infantry divisions, 590 M-1 tanks and M-2 Bradleys, 230 combat helicopters, and a number of special formations. Its 3rd Mechanized Division provides rapidly deployable armor. The 82nd and 101st Airborne Divisions are designed for rapid deployment, and the 25th

Infantry Division is design for rapid deployment in the Pacific theater. The basic reason the US Army was not deployed to Kosovo was not that it had no expeditionary capability, but rather that NATO and the US did not support a ground option.[302]

Nevertheless, the US Army seems to have chosen force size over rapid deployment capability. Senior US Army officers admit that the Army's heavy forces are top heavy and its light forces are often too light and lack lethality, sufficient mobility, and advanced protection.

Other officers feel the Army is still wedded to slow-moving heavy forces, and will keeps its light forces too light and lacking in lethality and sustainability. Even though the Army's six heavy divisions are down from an average size of around 18,000 men to 15,000, they are still very heavy and require long-movement preparation time and extensive sealift. In contrast, the four light active divisions do not have modern light armored vehicles, and lack long-range firepower.[303]

Other major problems include the fact that the Army has trouble breaking key elements out of its normal formations and rapidly tailoring the proper mix of forces for expeditionary deployment. The army's logistics are bloated and its light forces lack integral staying power and take too much time to resupply and support. Finally, the Army's problems in creating a rapid reaction force have been compounded by Congressional pressures that have forced the Army to rely on the reserves and National Guard in a total force concept. A number of senior Army officers in the field feel that the Army has been afraid to take on politically difficult trade-offs like reducing dependence on the National Guard and reserves.

Senior US Army officers like General Reimer and General Eric Shinseki seem to have recognized that the Army faces serious problems in creating new rapid deployment packages with heavier firepower and the ability to use helicopters and long-range artillery systems like the MLRS. General Shinseki announced in mid-October 1999 that the Army would create new light and heavy brigades in which the heavy bridges had more mobility and the light brigades had more firepower. The 3rd Brigade of the 2nd Infantry Division and the 1st Brigade of the 25th Infantry Division (light) are to serve as a the test beds for these concepts. General Shinseki announced that the Army would solicit bids for the development of light and less logistics intensive weapons, including wheeled light armored vehicles, a lighter armored gun, and more mobile artillery. He talked about a largely wheeled force some 50% to 70% lighter than today force, the ability to put a brigade anywhere in the world in 96 hours, a division on the ground in 120 hours, and deploying five divisions in 30 days.[304]

Some aspects of the US Army's efforts to design the "army after next" will help.[305] The US Army is already taking measures to reduce its logistic require-ments and modify key weapons like the M-1, Paladin, and AH-64 to reduce their logistic burden and employ fewer systems in power projection. It is trying to accelerate its development of the Future Scout Cavalry System, the Crusader, and Land Warrior program to acquire lighter systems that are easier to deploy and sustain, and improve its support and battle management systems to allow it to use smaller forces. It is also seeking to modify its training and doctrine to improve its mobility and rapid deployment capability, and to introduce fully digital warfighting concepts in its division and corps formations that would make them leaner and faster-reacting.[306]

The fact remains, however, that the Army did not react adequately to similar lessons from the Gulf War over a nearly decade-long period, and some of its "solutions"—like the Paladin—are so heavy that they do not meet conventional airlift requirements.[307] Deputy Secretary of Defense John Hamre made this point quite clearly in a speech to the University of Chicago Law School on August 4, 1999. It was clear that he was referring to the lessons of Kosovo, and he stated that, "If the Army holds on to nostalgic versions of its grand past, it is going to atrophy and die . . . It cannot simply be what it was, and think it is going to be relevant for this new, complex world that is emerging."[308] It is also uncertain whether the Army will get the money it needs to properly implement a conversion to more rapid power projection plans even if it makes the right changes in its plans, force structure, and doctrine.

Moreover, the Department of Defense found that Kosovo showed that the US had inadequate mobile engineering assets, had failed to preposition adequate assets, and has limited air-transportable capability:[309]

Had ground forces been deployed into Kosovo, the requirements for engineering support would have been substantial. Engineers would have had to make necessary improvements to airfields, seaports, and the road and rail network so that the transportation network could adequately support the movement of refugees as well as the ground-combat forces involved in offensive operations. These demands may have exceeded the capability of in-theater engineering assets. Moving engineering units form the United States to fulfill this requirement would have adversely affected the CINC's concept of operations owing to the strategic lift required to move these engineering units.

The large volume of airlift required for equipment-heavy engineer units makes airlift impractical and uneconomical. Sealift, on the other hand, is very slow; its use would have delayed the arrival of engineer assets in theater, thereby postponing the completion of needed improvements in the region's transportation network and slowing the movement of forces into Kosovo. After the Military Technical Agreement was signed, EUCOM was able to substantially reduce its requirement for CONUS-based engineers. However, even these smaller forces had to deploy by sealift so as not to impact higher priority elements of the Kosovo Force which were being moved by airlift.

. . . The shortage of an initial level of engineer response capability that is air transportable may lead to ineffective engineering support in some circumstances. Even though most engineer units are deployable by air or sea, they are so heavy that there is insufficient engineer capability that can be quickly brought to a crisis situation given the competing demands for strategic lift assets. In support of the initial phase of contingency operations in Kosovo, Air Force Red Horse teams and a Navy Seabee Air Detachment (both are air deployable and much lighter than other engineering units) provided engineering capability in Albania. These units made road and airfield repairs to help support the overwhelming flood of refugees leaving Kosovo. Both of these units are air deployable and light compared with other engineering units, yet they provide a substantial level of engineer capability.

Depending on the type and size of unit being deployed into an expeditionary theater, temporary facilities may be required for base camps, electrical power, water supply, vehicle and equipment maintenance and storage, administrative space, and command-and-control centers. Engineers are responsible for preparing suitable sites for all of these facilities as well as providing important force-protection support. In many cases, units have very specific requirements that impose unique demands on engineering units. As a result, engineers are called upon to accommodate the storage of ammunition and petroleum products, as well as improve ports, airfields, road networks, railroads, waterways, and pipelines. The current automated planning system used by engineers to sort through the myriad of issues attendant to a major deployment is designated the Joint Engineer Planning and Execution System (JEPES). It became evident during Operation Allied Force that this tool cannot adequately support facility requirements planning for deploying forces in a fast-moving crisis situation. Moreover, no other automated system is available that enables engineer planners to rapidly identify facility requirements and to effectively assess and execute required engineer support in acquiring the needed facilities for deploying forces. Consequently, JEPES will have to be modernized or replaced.

Once again, the lessons relating to combat and service support, and logistics, often receive less attention than those that apply to combat arms. These comments indicate, however, that they could easily be just as important to both European and US power projection.

US Sealift and Logistics over the Shore

The Marine Corps and US Navy long deployed expeditionary forces with considerable success. Kosovo did, however, demonstrate that their overall force structures are too small to support their current rates of deployment, and this has already led both services to speed up efforts to merge their support forces, streamline their administrative services, and consider personnel exchanges like pilot exchanges.[310] Both services currently face unacceptable trade-offs between force size, readiness, and modernization. This provides strong evidence that the current US Future Year Defense Plan and spending program is incapable of meeting the real-world needs of US forces, and of reacting to the real-world nature of US commitments and deployments.

Certainly, the US found that it needed to improve both the quality and quantity of its sealift capabilities:[311]

Logistics over-the-shore is the process of discharging cargo from vessels offshore, transporting it to the shore or a pier, and marshalling it for movement inland. These operations range in scope from bare beach operations to operations supplementing fixed-port facilities. Joint Logistics Over-the-Shore (JLOTS) operations occur when both Army and Navy LOTS elements conduct operations together under a Joint Force Commander. The scope of JLOTS operations extends from acceptance of ships for offload through the arrival of equipment and cargo at inland staging areas. Executing JLOTS requires a great deal of

large specialized equipment. The Navy's Cargo Offload and Discharge System or the Army's Modular Causeway System form the primary structures spanning the distance from the sealift ship to the shore. Landing craft and warping tugs are also used to assemble causeways and move other equipment. Prior to assembly, unloading the causeway systems requires heavy lift capability such as Navy amphibious construction battalions or Army floating craft companies. Additional systems may be needed to provide logistics support across a broader range of major theater wars and smaller-scale contingencies.

The Department of Defense has standing plans for moving forces to major theater wars. As we have seen, however, it did not have such plans for Operation Allied Force. The rapidly evolving requirements of Allied Force strained our ability to quickly develop plans for deploying our forces that utilized our lift assets efficiently. We relied heavily on strategic airlift to deploy forces to the theater, while the sealift component of the strategic mobility triad lay essentially idle. This was due to the understandable desire of the commanders in the field to have needed equipment and personnel transported as quickly as possible; air transport was not, however, mandatory in all cases. The impact on operations was that it overburdened limited strategic airlift assets and was costly. The proper use of all means of strategic lift, supported by earlier assessment of ground and sea infrastructure, might result in faster force closure in future deployments.

Since Desert Storm, the Department has spent over $6 billion to augment the capability to move U.S. forces in a contingency. We have purchased 19 large, medium-speed, roll-on/roll-off ships (LMSRs); 10 have been delivered. When delivery is completed, these ships will add 5 million square feet to the total strategic sealift capacity. Additionally, 14 roll-on/roll-off ships were added to the Ready Reserve Force, increasing its capacity by an additional 2.2 million square feet. Additionally, the readiness level of the Ready Reserve Force has been increased to ensure its reliability, readiness, and speed when needed. When possible, increased use of sealift assets should be considered in future conflicts and contingencies. The improvements that the Department is making to its automated capabilities for real-time transportation planning will enable better use of these improved sealift assets to support the rapidly evolving needs of a contingency such as Operation Allied Force.

US Strategic Lift and Jointness

As the Department of Defense has pointed out in its studies of Kosovo, there are additional areas that need improvement.[312]

Operation Allied Force highlighted some aspects of the planning process that could be improved. For example, the Department's systems for planning and executing transportation of its forces were strained by the rapidly evolving requirements of Operation Allied Force. The operation also required rapid augmentation of the capabilities and joint staff at Headquarters, European Command.

The pool of personnel available to perform certain key functions, such as language translation, targeting, and intelligence analysis, was limited. While some individual reserve personnel were assigned quickly to perform such functions, some shortages occurred because reserve units had not been activated.

Prior development of a detailed crisis augmentation plan for the European Command would have facilitated more rapid assignment of personnel to the theater. Consistent with

this experience, the Department is improving its ongoing programs to provide automated, rapid-response transportation planning. In addition, the Joint Staff, services, and commanders-in-chief will develop crisis augmentation plans, and the Department will develop options for earlier and more efficient use of the capabilities resident in its reserve forces.

. . . The Department has standing plans for moving forces to major theater wars. It did not have such plans for Operation Allied Force, however. The rapidly evolving requirements of Allied Force strained our ability to quickly develop plans for deploying our forces that utilized our lift assets efficiently. We relied heavily on strategic airlift to deploy forces to the theater, while using strategic sealift sparingly. This was due to the understandable desire of the commanders in the field to have needed equipment and personnel transported as quickly as possible; air transport was, however, not mandatory in all cases.

Improvements have been made in sealift capability to increase the readiness level of the Ready Reserve Force (RRF) to ensure its reliability and speed. When possible, increased use of sealift assets should be considered in future conflicts and contingencies. And the improvements that the Department is making to its automated capabilities for real-time transportation planning will enable better use of these improved sealift assets to support the rapidly evolving needs of a contingency such as Operation Allied Force.

The US is also stressing efforts to make US power projection forces more interoperable with those of its allies. New Department of Defense Directives that went into effect on October 1, 1999 made interoperability a "key performance factor" for the first time, and called for a "plug and fight" capability with allied forces. US officials stressed common interfaces like the Link 16 system, but noted that interoperability had to become a broader goal of the Joint Forces Command and efforts of the Joint Requirements Oversight Committee.[313]

"Eurolift": Requirement or Unaffordable Luxury?

At the same time, the power projection capabilities of NATO European land forces need equal study. The European forces involved in creating the peacekeeping forces in Albania, Macedonia, and Kosovo experienced some serious movement and logistics problems.[314] The US noted in one of its reports on the lessons of the war that, "Insufficient air mobility assets among our allies slowed deployment of KFOR ground forces—beyond those already in the theater, who led the KFOR entry—once Milosevic agreed to NATO's terms to end the conflict. Such disparities in capabilities will seriously affect our ability to operate as an effective alliance over the long term."[315]

Equally important, "Eurolift" has become a politically correct part of the European effort to create added European self-sufficiency as part of a European defense initiative. There has, however, been little study of the practical costs and trade-offs involved. It is easy to say that Europe should have strategic lift, but if European military expenditures are to remain constant or decline, purchasing strategic lift would have to come at the cost of other and potentially more important

force improvements. Is long-range lift really a higher priority than other force improvements like precision strike capability and electronic warfare if painful trade-offs have to be made?

There is also a real question about how much European strategic lift will be needed and for what contingencies. What level of airlift and refueling capability would be needed? Is the lift needed for "Eurocentric" local conflicts or long-range out-of-area operations? It's the lift to be adequate for sustained combat or only for force deployment in "crisis management" and "peacekeeping" missions. Like many aspects of the European self defense initiative, "Europe" seems more interested in symbols and validating institution building than in serious efforts to plan real warfighting capabilities and a serious security architecture.

More broadly, many European countries have only limited movement and power projection experience, and serious questions arises as to whether movements and logistics should be purely national responsibilities in this kind of effort, or whether economies and scale and improved efficiency could be obtained from a more integrated approach. A number of European experts also believe that added lift will be meaningless without extensive new cross-regional training, and organizing forces trained to fight in a wide range of tactical "micro-climes ranging from the Baltic in winter to the coast of North Africa.

An Alliance Approach to Strategic Lift?

In short, Kosovo showed that expeditionary capability, power projection, lift, and sustainability are a problem for both the US and its NATO European allies. Secretary Cohen made this point during the press conference following the NATO ministerial meeting on September 21, 1999:[316]

The Alliance is studying ways to increase the use of commercial sea and airlift to improve military mobility. Italy and the United Kingdom are working together to create performance standards or benchmarks for measuring improvements in capabilities. NATO is developing a Multinational Joint Logistics Center to help the Alliance manage and deploy its assets more efficiently. NATO is developing a new architecture for a unified, modern communications capability.

. . . the United States learned of shortfalls in its forces during Kosovo and we are working to correct them. For example, we are buying more C-17 transport planes and additional ships for carrying heavy equipment. We are developing new precision guided munitions and increasing supplies of others that are already in our inventory. We are looking at the increased use of commercial off the shelf technology to improve our ability to detect chemical and biological attacks.

. . . I think all countries have to look to that (the use of the commercial sea and airlift) as one way to deal with the strategic lift requirements. What we've indicated is that a number of countries already have legislation in their countries that will allow them to turn to commercial aircraft and vessels, commercial vessels. Not everyone has that. We did not

identify which countries have that legislative—the laws on the books that allow them to do that. But it was a suggestion that, certainly, I and others made as a way to achieve what we need in the way of strategic airlift and sealift by calling upon the commercial sector to make available their aircraft and vessels in time of crisis.

There is no doubt that these are valid lessons. Once again, however, history provides great reason to doubt whether the US and NATO will spend enough money to act upon them. There is a need for a broad review of both US expeditionary force capabilities and force improvement plans, and of capabilities for coalition warfare.

The Humanitarian Side of Power Projection

Finally, Kosovo involved more than military power projection. Operation Sustain Hope had to be conducted at the same time to prevent mass starvation and homelessness among the estimated 850,000 Kosovars who fled to Albania and Macedonia. This required more than 500 airlift sorties and extensive sealift to provide bulk food, humanitarian daily rations, tents and other shelters, bedding, medical supplies, and a variety of support equipment and vehicles. It also required NATO to evacuate refugees from Macedonia and Albania to third countries and to construct refugee camps.

The humanitarian and nation building aspects of military operations were scarcely unique to Kosovo. They were important in Lebanon, Somalia, and Bosnia, and they illustrate the fact that modern combat operations must pay far more attention to humanitarian considerations that was the case in World War II, Korea, and Vietnam.

The US found in its analysis of the lessons of the war that it needed to develop tighter coordination of humanitarian operations both within the US and with its NATO allies (and Partnership for Peace members). Coordinated assessments of needs and response efforts were felt to be particularly important to provide input to many critical logistics issues such as road conditions and existence of suitable housing for refugees. Effective assessments are critical because of their impact on the allocation of humanitarian relief supplies.[317]

The US government found that it failed to properly coordinate its humanitarian operations.[318]

The effective assessment of humanitarian needs is a critical element of any relief effort. By evaluating road conditions and establishing the existence of suitable housing for refugees, such assessments help determine the priority of engineering projects and the need to build refugee camps. During the Kosovo operation, the CINC designated the JTF commander, who in turn designated the deployed Marine Air Ground Task Force (MAGTF) to act as a Humanitarian Assessment Team and provide an assessment of the humanitarian conditions

in Albania and Macedonia. As a result, the team had little familiarity with embassy personnel, the CINC staff, or the Disaster Assistance Response Team (DART) that had been provided by the interagency process.

Moreover, the U.S. ambassador in Albania did not have a good understanding of the assessment team's role. The consequent lack of coordination and cooperation resulted in the departure of the assessment team before it had completed its mission. A humanitarian assessment team provided by the CINC staff, rather than a deployed unit, would have had better ties with embassy staffs and would have been more familiar with theater conditions. To avoid such problems in the future, in-theater personnel who are familiar with the area and the embassy staffs in neighboring nations should be used to conduct humanitarian assessments. These assessment teams should also develop effective liaison with other interagency humanitarian efforts such as Disaster Assistance Response Teams.

The was the same need for an integrated "joint command" in carrying out the deployment and operations of humanitarian relief as for military deployment and operations. The establishment of an Emergency Management Group in Albania played a critical role in coordinating the resources of international organizations, non-governmental organizations, and donor countries, while preserving overall host nation sovereignty.

Coordinating humanitarian action and military support were equally important. A NATO cell was established at the Emergency Management Group to coordinate military resources effectively. For its part, the US Department of Defense established a Civil Military Operations Center at Rinas Airport in Albania. This Center worked effectively with the United Nations High Commissioner for Refugees and with non-governmental organizations. To foster such superb humanitarian assistance relationships and logistics interactions for future operations, we are examining the use of activities such as liaison officer exchanges or conducting humanitarian assistance exercises.

One specific problem that is likely to prove a lesson in all future large-scale peace keeping operations is the need to prepare the same kind of planning and deployment capabilities for refugee camps as for military deployments.[319]

A lack of standard procedures for establishing refugee camps either within or outside the continental United States caused some confusion and prevented full unity of effort among the various U.S. Government agencies involved. The interagency participants did not anticipate an executive policy directing development of refugee camps and processing centers in the United States. After discussion of several; alternatives, it was determined that refugees would be brought to the United States, and the U.S. Department of Health and Human Services (HHS) would act as the overall lead agent for support within the continental United States. Overseas, because the presence of thousands of refugees fleeing Kosovo could have hindered ongoing NATO military operations and presented a target for cross-border operations by Serb forces, the U.S. concept for easing the refugee crisis was to have the Department of Defense undertake refugee relief efforts, including the establishment of refugee camps in the region. The interagency employed ad hoc solutions when executive policy dictated a need for refugee camps and processing centers to accommodate up to 20,000 refugees for resettlement within the continental United States.

EUROPEAN VERSUS NATO DEFENSE INITIATIVES

Kosovo has raised broad lessons about both Europe's capability to play an independent role in its own defense and its military capabilities. It has led Europe to speed up absorption of the West European Union's defense structure into the European Community, and a new emphasis on European security initiatives. This emphasis ranges from a search for a limited European options like "crisis management" to the creation of a true independent European war fighting capability.

Kosovo has also led to an examination of Europe's role and capabilities in every military mission from air wars to emergency relief. It has raised major questions about the quality of Europe's level of training and technology, and many other areas of warfighting At a July 19–20 summit meeting in Britain, the British and Italian Prime Ministers called for a "road map" for more effective European defense procurement, including the harmonization of military requirements, collaboration in arms procurement, and the restructuring of defense industry.

European Institution-Building versus Real-World Military Capabilities

The present consensus in Europe seems to be that Europe should have a limited "crisis management" force that is capable of fully independent action under the leadership of the European Union, and should make major improvements in its military capabilities as part of the European Security and Defense Initiative (ESDI). This force would include a 40,000 man, largely Anglo-French corps, although the force would not be a standing force, but would rather consist of the command and control and logistics to deploy such a force backed by European air forces. It would have capability for power projection, but would supplement, rather than replace, NATO and would have only limited warfighting capability.[320]

A number of Europeans feel such an effort will complement NATO. Lord Robertson, the new Secretary General of NATO, felt that there was no prospect that such a force would be large or effective enough to act on its own even in the case of another Kosovo.[321] Prime Minister Tony Blair has said that "It is not an attempt in any shape or form to supplant or compete with NATO. NATO for Britain remains the cornerstone of our defense. But it is necessary for us, in circumstances where the alliance as a whole is not engaged, that we are able to act in circumstances where it is in our interest to do so." President Jacques Chirac of France has said that, "The Anglo-French defense proposals have absolutely no negative consequences for NATO. They reinforce NATO in reality."[322]

Other strong supporters of NATO like General Klaus Nauman, the former head of NATO's Military Committee, stated that, "With no corrective action taken as a matter of urgency, there will be increasing difficulties to ensure interoperability of allied forces and operational security could be compromised . . . I am ashamed that we had to ask for American help in such a tiny region as Kosovo. That is something intolerable for a Europe in the future."[323]

Some Europeans, however, clearly feel that such a European force must be an independent counterbalance to the US. While France has officially denied that a European force would have this objective, the French report on the lessons of the war in Kosovo is in many ways as critical of the US as the US has sometimes been critical of France. It states that Europe needs a unified defense capability in part because, "some military operations (in Kosovo) have been conducted by the US outside of the strict definition of NATO and its procedures. The commander in chief of the operation—SACEUR—is responsible not only to the Atlantic Council—but also to the national hierarchy (of the US) at the highest level." It also says such an option is needed to offset the fact that, "The political-military decision-making process of the Alliance has been marked by a strong American predominance founded on the double chain of command centered around SACEUR and a true superiority in terms of military capabilities."[324]

It is too early to know where Europe is really headed. It is clear that the majority of Europe does not feel that ESDI means independence from NATO, but does feel it needs some form of European force both to provide independence of action and to create a more effective combined force than European states can create independently.

At the same time, European efforts to create the equivalent of a European defense community have been going on ever since the 1950s, however, and so far have had little substantive impact. Europe has focused on institution-building rather than capabilities. As a result, Europe has been strong on rhetoric and creating new bureaucracies, but has done little to create new real-world war fighting capabilities or to go beyond paper changes in command structures and orders of battle, and create effective capabilities to perform key military missions. The West European Union existed for decades without accomplishing much of anything, and thrusting it into the EC may not accomplish more.

While Europe has tentatively agreed on plans to place the new "crisis management" force under the EU, and a new EU headquarters for military planning and command, similar efforts in the past have proved to be little more than Pan-European political cosmetics. NATO plans to create a European rapid reaction force did little more than rearrange orders of battle as European nations downsized their forces. Earlier plans to create a Franco-German corps at Strasbourg—with Belgian, Luxembourg, and Spanish participation—proved to be little more than a further exercise in improving Franco-German political relations. Similar problems have emerged in the past efforts to try to create a European surface-to-air missile belt in the Central Region and efforts to create integrated European naval forces.

The problems in buying air and sealift are also minor in comparison with developing out of area power projection forces than can actually fight without access to foreign bases. The teething problems of the new Charles de Gaulle— which have involved a major refit of the 40,000-ton carrier after initial sea and air trials—are only a minor indication of the difficulties of creating carrier task forces, and the US has found that major dedicated expeditionary assets are needed to convert foreign air bases even when these are made available.[325]

The European Force Improvement or Non-Force Improvement Effort

The European effort to improve military capabilities has also not been particularly productive. Both France and Germany cut their defense expenditures, including procurement, in the summer of 1999 at virtually the same time they were talking about new modernization efforts and defense cooperation.[326] Many of the NATO European powers found it difficult to carry out their post-Kosovo commitments to deploy peacekeeping forces at anything like the time-scale required.[327]

It is interesting to note in this regard that Secretary Cohen was remarkably cautious about the progress Europe was likely to make during the question and answer session in the press conference that followed the September 21 Ministerial.[328]

Questioner: Secretary Cohen, you say that in some cases they'll have to spend more money. But in some cases of European countries—I'm thinking specifically of Germany—there have been severe economic issues. Do you have some new plan to raise this apparent budgetary cap?

Cohen: Well, what we did discuss today is ways in which money can be spent more efficiently. For example, if we can reduce the amount of revenues devoted to operations and maintenance and devote it procurement, that is one way to stay within existing—and perhaps in this particular case, somewhat declining—budgets. But there are ways in which budgets can be restructured in order to eliminate some of the perhaps older systems— getting rid of some of those systems designed to combat a Soviet thrust across a central front, and to take those resources and apply it to kind of capabilities that we have outlined in the Washington Summit. So in some cases, nations will not be able to increase their defense budgets—they may even face some budget reductions. But devising ways and learning from what is being done in other countries, to reshape their militaries can produce some efficiencies.

Questioner: Mr. Secretary, did any countries—any European countries—say that they would increase their defense budgets?

Cohen: There were, in fact—yes. There were, in fact, some starting at a fairly low level in terms of where they have to come from, but most of them indicated that they needed to address these issues, and some indicated that they would be looking to get increases, yes.

Questioner: Which countries are looking to get increases?

Cohen: I will let them speak for themselves.

Questioner: What kind of timeframe are we talking about? When will you be able to sit back and say "We've found the shortcomings, and we're ready to roll"? Is this a very long term thing, or . . .

Cohen: Some of it short term, and some of it's long term. There are things that can be done in the short term . . . But there are long term goals. It's not going to happen overnight. These capabilities have been identified that we need to identify. It may take a number of years to finally fully fund and acquire [them].

Questioner: The future of the European Self-Defense Initiative?

Cohen: Oh, I'm sorry, on the ESDI? We are supportive of the concept of ESDI. What we would insist upon, and there is no disagreement on this, is that the Transatlantic link remain strong, that the European Security and Defense Identity is not something that is a separate bureaucratic institution, but something constructed under the umbrella of NATO itself, that whatever developments take place under ESDI, there must be a transparency between NATO and EU, that there should be a sharing of information representatives from EU to NATO so that as ESDI is developed the capabilities remain constant with those identified in the Defense Capabilities Initiative so we don't have one set of requirements developing in Europe and a separate set for NATO which would lead to certainly a disassociation of those kind of requirements and capabilities. So with that as a caveat and I think that everyone agrees with that principle, that ESDI is something that will be valuable for the Europeans to start developing capabilities they currently do not have and they must be compatible and consistent with the NATO objectives.

Questioner: Two brief questions. One, what should the relationship between DCI (the NATO Defense Capabilities Initiative) and the normal NATO forces planning process be, my understanding was the DCI was something that was supposed to speed that up a little bit. The second questions is what do you think of the British Italian Benchmarking Initiative and specifically do you think it would be useful for those benchmarks to be quantitative rather than qualitative in nature?

Cohen: With respect to DCI, the purpose behind the initiative was in fact to identify those areas where we saw weaknesses and deficiencies and that was the initiative we talked about in Vilamoura last year. A year ago, as a matter of fact we raised the issue of DCI, we finally adopted it—developed it and then adopted it—at the Washington Summit. So it really is part of the NATO planning process, but to specifically identify those things that we all should commit to improving. With respect to the British and Italian initiative we are basically supportive of it. I can't give you an answer in terms of whether it should be quantitative or qualitative since I don't have enough information about the details on it yet, but we generally are supportive of what both United Kingdom and Italy are seeking to do.

The report of the French Minister of Defense on the lessons of Kosovo also raises a long list of real-world force improvements that Europe must make, regardless of whether it is seeking to work within NATO or act independently. The major priorities include:[329]

- Modern command and control systems.

- All-weather reconnaissance.
- GPS systems.
- Tactical and strategic lift and support.
- Real-time communications and liaison.
- Damage assessment (and targeting) systems.
- Cruise missiles.
- Offensive and suppressive electronic warfare and anti-air defense systems.
- Creation of an integrated UAV and satellite intelligence system.
- Adequate supplies of advanced munitions.
- All-weather strike systems.
- Autonomous identification of friend or foe systems.
- Improved support systems, and
- A permanently deployable aeronaval group.

A similar list of priorities from a leading German analyst is very similar, but adds:[330]

- Pilot rescue.
- Airborne refueling.
- Secure communications.
- Logistics, and
- Strategic reconnaissance.

The Right Kind of European Initiative and the Right Kind of Alliance

This is an impressive list of force improvement priorities, and various British, French, German, and Dutch working reports would add substantially to this list. It also, however, may well be a list that is unaffordable for a Europe attempting to move forward on its own, just as the US faces major problems in paying for its force plans and force improvement plans. Dividing the NATO alliance not only is unlikely to make it stronger, it is likely to create the wrong force improvement priorities, and make effective defense even more unaffordable.

These problems do not mean that a European defense initiative is counterproductive or will necessarily divide the alliance. If anything, the US faces such severe resource pressures in dealing with Asia and the Middle East that increased European self-reliance in "Eurocentric" crises and contingencies would relieve the strain on the US in lesser contingencies and be a natural way to increase burden sharing and create a new "Transatlantic bargain." These problems do, however, mean that any European action must involve the development of a realistic and affordable security structure and force improvement plan. It also means that the US and Europe cannot afford to compete, even if this was politically and strategically desirable.

The problems in NATO's command structure and warfighting efforts described throughout this report need to be solved, not simply segregated into a separate but not equal European component. It is clear than the divisions within Europe over how to deal with Kosovo were at least as serious as the differences between the US and some individual European powers. It is also clear that any major escalation of a conflict could place a major strain on European capabilities, and either force Europe to turn to the US (under the worst conditions in terms of US preparation and NATO interoperability) or confront Europe with defeat.

It is also virtually inevitable that any EU military planning and command structure will become a rival of NATO, regardless of what is said about its functions, as well as the center of efforts by European countries and politicians to find a way of excluding the US from security decisions. No matter what the intent, bureaucracies behave in no other way, and national rivalries inevitably purse targets of opportunity. This makes creating formal arrangements to coordinate and sequence European and US action critical, and the devil will lie in the day-to-day details of how things actually work and not in the letter of any broad agreements.

This reinforces the need to train US and European leaders in exercises that make them understand how to cooperate in NATO military action and crisis management. The problem is not only the US versus Europe, but Europe versus Europe under conditions where most senior civilian military leaders have no military experience of any kind, only limited national experience in crisis management, and virtually no experience in working together to manage conflict contingency planning, actual crises and conflicts, and conflict termination. The military axiom that you cannot execute what you do not practice applies doubly to civil-military cooperation, and triply to such cooperation in an alliance or coalition context.

A Common Operational Vision

Moreover, there is a clear need for a common operational vision that will allow European forces to work with other European forces, as well as improve the capability of European and US military forces to work together efficiently in combat. The lack of such a concept is one of the most important lessons the US drew in its report on the lessons of the war—although the US did not discuss the problems of developing a common operational concept within Europe per se:[331]

The term Common Operational Vision . . . is not used by NATO; it is a U.S. construct to evaluate current NATO capabilities and efforts to meet NATO's 21st century challenges.

NATO capabilities will have their own unique characteristics, and they will not necessarily mirror those of the United States. However, the more nearly parallel U.S. and NATO processes are for development of future capabilities, the more likely it is that we will achieve the desired level of interoperability.

. . . Operation Allied Force provided a real-world laboratory for gaining insights into the capabilities envisioned by Joint Vision 2010. Operation Allied Force confirmed the need for the goal of Joint Vision 2010 to develop force capabilities that can handle unexpected circumstances and threats across the full range of military operations. The Allied Force experience demonstrated the need for forces that are able to adapt and transition across diverse operations calling for combat, peace enforcement, peacekeeping, and humanitarian assistance. This experience also provides a potential framework for assessing the approach to projecting future requirements—by focusing on capabilities and the effects they can deliver—across the spectrum of warfare.

Operation Allied Force confirmed the importance of Allied Joint Doctrine to improving the interoperability of NATO forces. Consistent allied joint tactics, techniques, and procedures will improve integration of NATO's sea, air, and land forces involved in activities across the range of military operations. Allied Joint Doctrine should enable future NATO operations to be more effective and to achieve higher operational tempo, and should increase the probability of mission success while reducing the risk to forces.

To enhance our ability to support development of Allied Joint Doctrine, the Department is currently reviewing U.S. procedures for participating in the formulation of Allied Joint Doctrine. We believe NATO also needs to streamline its procedures for doctrine development and approval. Accordingly, the Department will engage NATO in the Military Committee and High Level Steering Committee to facilitate these improvements.

The last thing the alliance needs is a US and "European" approach to the lessons of Kosovo. The US, for example, may have a great deal to learn from European experience with the CL-289 UAV, and BL-775 cluster bomb. The US also needs to work closely with its allies to examine how the lessons drawn from USAF use of the F-16 interact with those drawn by the European use of the F-16AM and Mid-Life Update Programs, and how US lessons from other aircraft and munitions compare with the European experience.[332]

F-16 AND THE JSF

Some articles have appeared questioning the stress that ground-attack operations in Kosovo have put on the F-16 fleet, and claiming that major structural upgrades have been needed at 4,000 flight hours and questioning the ability of the aircraft to meet its 8,000-hour life. The validity of such claims seems uncertain, but deserves investigation.[333]

What is clear is that Kosovo demonstrates the value of efforts to upgrade the F-16 in strike missions and the possible need for improved on-board data links for targeting and battle damage assessments, and better avionics for targeting at altitudes above 12,000 feet and in poor weather. It also highlights the need to realistically match the MSIP program and projected fleet size for the F-16 against the real-world availability of JSF. Stretching the life of the F-16 seems practical, but it must be based on a realistic assessment of when the JSF will be available and in what numbers.

Kosovo may also provide further evidence of the need to deploy the JSF as soon as possible to maintain the US edge in technology. *Threat nations can be expected to learn from Kosovo as well as the US, and Kosovo is a strong argument for acquiring systems like the S-300 and S-400, as well as more advanced fighters and air-to-air missiles.*

F-14, F-18, AND ATARS

Kosovo seems to have validated the ability to use the F-14 in attack missions. At the same time, it showed the need to improve the interface between the Lantirn, GPS navigation, and GPS ordnance delivery capability. It also showed the need for better avionics to acquire and share targeting data, and the value of the Fast Tactical Imagery (FTI) system for the F-14.[334]

F-18 officers serving in Kosovo note the need for improved expeditionary support for the Marine Corps to enable units using allied bases with limited capabilities to have the C4I/battlemanagement assets they need. The F-18s used in the attack mission also had problems with night vision and their FLIR systems and needed added support from the ground to find dispersed Serbian forces. Officers noted the need for more realistic peacetime training, IR flares, and an embedded GPS system. They also noted the need for more training in operating in urban and built up areas.[335]

Kosovo also validated the need for the Advanced Tactical Airborne Reconnaissance System (ATARS) for the F/A-18 to improve target acquisition and battle damage assessment capability.[336] The Atars provides major improvements in imagery data links, medium and low altitude sensors, and infrared line-scanning for night and poor weather operations at altitudes between 200 and 25,000 feet. One US report on the lessons of the war notes that,[337]

The Advanced Tactical Aerial Reconnaissance System (ATARS) was employed aboard USMC F/A-18D aircraft in the latter stages of Operation Allied Force. Although operational evaluation of ATARS is still ongoing, the system was cleared for use in theater. In several weeks of strike operations, ATARS produced numerous digital, multi-spectral images using primarily synthetic aperture radar (SAR) and medium-altitude electro-optical (MAEO) imagery to augment the imagery and information available to commanders from other ISR systems. These images were used for targeting, battle damage assessments, and tactical reconnaissance while maintaining the aircraft's complete weapons capability.

One of the key issues that needs to be analyzed, however, is the trade-off between an investment in platforms like bombers and an investment in strike aircraft. A senior US aerospace official was quoted after the war as saying,[338]

If you have a lot of distributed or hard-to-find targets, you are probably better off with small aircraft that can make lots of sorties If you have massed targets you can make use of what a heavy bomber brings to the table. Since no one can predict the target in the next conflict, you need a mix of both.

At the same time, it is clear that the US Navy and Marine Corps have the same need as the USAF to reexamine their overall modernization plans, and to develop a real-world plan for modernizing the F-14 and F-18, deploying the F-18E/F, and acquiring the JSF.

F-117, JSF, AND F-22 AND THE FUTURE OF STEALTH

As of September 1999, there still was no firm indication of the precise reasons the F-117 had been shot down. Serbian military sources had claimed that the shoot-down was a result of spies within NATO that provided the details of NATO's daily air traffic orders to the Russian GRU or military intelligence service which passed the data to Belgrade. The information supposedly included the intended target (the defense research facility at Budjanovic, north of Belgrade) and the projected flight path. The Serbians claimed this allowed them to use three P-12 "Spoon Rest" early warning radars, modified to reduce the normal level of radar clutter, to detect an F-117 moving along a known track.

This kind of claim is typical of Serbian disinformation efforts, however, and NATO sources claimed that the F-117 and other US strategic assets were never included in the detailed ATOs generated by NATO. Other GRU sources claim that they were able to visit the crash site soon after the attack and had access to the F-117, but there is no confirmation of such reports.[339]

The loss of a single F-117 scarcely means that the F-117 has outlived its usefulness. The US committed 24 F-117s to Kosovo and they flew successfully throughout the campaign. It does, however, raise questions about the F-117's vulnerability in more sophisticated air defense environments. Such threats might use existing surface-to-air missiles with more advanced passive tracking systems and homing systems, or more advanced radars and missiles.

At the same time, the F-22 has escalated to a cost of nearly $200 million per airplane and the cost and stealth characteristics of the JSF are uncertain. This raises serious questions about the future of "stealth" in the US mix of tactical aircraft.

While the F-117 seems to preserve a high degree of stealth, the lessons of Kosovo should be examined to see if they validate the need for the strike-attack capability of the F-22 and JSF, and their ability to supplement or replace the F-117 in this role.[340]

More broadly, the US may need to comprehensively reassess all of its air modernization programs in terms of both the lessons of Kosovo and their rising cost. There is a major and growing affordability issue that surrounds any of the previous "lessons" relating to individual aircraft. Normally pro-defense Congressmen, like Jerry Lewis and Jack Murtha, the chairman and the ranking members of the House Defense Appropriations Subcommittee, have raised basic questions about the affordability of American airpower, and the future role of the bomber.

They have argued that the US should not spend $40 billion to purchase 339 new F-22 fighters, they note this one development will cost $65 billion when all RDT&E costs are included, and that the US also has a $47 billion program to buy 548 F/A-18E/Fs and a $223 billion program to buy 2,850 Joint Strike Fighters.

The US went into the war in Kosovo with tactical modernization programs with a cost of well over $340 billion over the next few decades.[341] This may well prove unaffordable. Nevertheless, canceling the F-22 would mean the US would have now strike or air defense fighter with advanced stealth features until the deployment of the Joint Tactical Fighter—if this aircraft is deployed and deployed with such features. This helps explain why the F-22 was fully funded in the FY2001 defense budget, but it still leaves major questions about the overall affordability of US airpower.[342]

GLOBAL FORCE INTEGRATION

The US "discovery" in some of its reporting on the lessons of Kosovo that it needs to integration its world-wide power projection capabilities on a global basis borders on translating the self-evident into the painfully obvious. It is the kind of "milspeak" and "buzzword" approach to planning and strategy that is generally more irritating than insightful. At the same time, the basic validity of the point remains, and US reporting on it as one of the lessons of the war deserves at least passing attention.[343]

Our ability to reach-back and use capabilities in the continental United States to perform functions formerly accomplished only in the theater of military operations is one of the highlights of Operation Allied Force. Such capability improves responsiveness to urgent requirements in a conflict and reduces the amount of equipment and the number of personnel that must be transported to the theater. In short, the capability to integrate our force globally yields significant improvements in our ability to respond to crises, particularly during their initial stages

. . . Extensive growth in communications capacity enabled an unprecedented degree of reliance on U.S.-based forces to provide direct support for in-theater tasks. Targets in Kosovo and the Federal Republic of Yugoslavia were developed through the concerted effort of numerous agencies in the United States cooperating closely with commands in Europe. Planning and integration of cruise missile attacks by bombers operating from the continental United States and the United Kingdom and by ships and submarines operating in the Mediterranean were closely coordinated by commanders and planners who were widely separated geographically. Bomb damage assessments of strikes made against targets in theater were conducted by agencies and commands located in the United States in close support with efforts by commands in the European theater. This system of using geographically dispersed activities to perform and integrate bomb damage assessment (BDA) became known as federated BDA. Expert personnel located in the United States and Europe performed detailed planning of information operations. Kosovo operations continued a trend of increasing global integration of U.S. forces and commands to support operations in a distant theater.

. . . Integration of global forces during Kosovo operations provides insight to the design of future exercises and training required for increasing our proficiency in the complex actions necessary for integrating a global force. While our focus is on theater operations, the Department must exercise the global capabilities required in support of theater operations. Additionally, the Department must recognize the need to deploy forces in a myriad of unpredictable scenarios requiring new levels of adaptability and flexibility in global interoperability and integration.

. . . our experience in integrating worldwide capabilities during Operation Allied Force highlights the importance of the joint operational architecture concept. This architecture would define the relationships between forces and commands involved in complex operations. A joint operational architecture would also serve as the basis for developing technical architectures to support warfighters' needs, and for prioritizing resources and training requirements. These technical architectures would be defined for the spectrum of global threats and would identify any organizational changes required to support the National Military Strategy.

HARDENED TARGETS: DAMAGE ASSESSMENT "INSIDE THE BOX"

It is not clear how many hardened targets NATO attacked, or how it distinguished levels of hardness in the targets it struck. NATO also did not have to attack most hardened Serbian targets like caves and tunnels—as it would have if it had fought a land campaign on Serbian soil. It does seem clear, however, that NATO had only very limited hard target kill capability and that it would have had to attack most targets by shutting the entrance, blowing up access routes and cutting off water and power. This, at best, would have been suppression rather than destruction.

Further, NATO lacked any clear way to know exactly what was in even unhardened buildings and the level of survivability of fixed equipment assets. It could neither target reliably inside the box or perform damage assessment to know what it had done to facilities and equipment. At best, it had to rely on pattern analysis over days or weeks to determine the extent to which it had or had not affected a given activity.

It is not clear that there are easy technical solutions to these problems, but attacking "closed" targets and hardened targets presents major challenges in terms of targeting, munitions, and damage assessment. Threat forces can be expected to learn that access and support must be hardened as well as facilities, that they will begin to use modular and rapidly mobile equipment that can be easily moved and dispersed to new facilities, and that systems must be redundant and degradable. Much of the thinking behind the "revolution in military affairs" seems to assume a relatively static enemy and a solution to both knowing what is in the box and the ability to destroy both large fixed and hardened facilities. It is far from clear that future enemies will behave in this manner or that the US or its allies actually have the capability to kill hardened targets and know what goes on "inside the box."

HARM AND ANTI-RADIATION MISSILE SYSTEMS AND PASSIVE TRACKING

Serbia demonstrated that it could use passive electro-optical tracking to avoid using radar and making its surface-based air defense systems vulnerable to systems like the High Speed Anti-Radiation Missile (HARM). Although its surface-to-air defense systems were not lethal at altitudes above 10,000 feet, they could still significantly degrade NATO air attack capabilities, force NATO to fly at higher altitudes, and maintain a high degree of survivability even for comparatively large tracked systems like the SA-6. As has been discussed earlier, there were a number of other problems in using HARM effectively in the EA-6B.

This experience raises serious questions about the value of anti-radiation missiles unless targeting systems, reaction times, and area lethality can be greatly improved. It also raises the issue that new targeting systems may be needed that do not rely on a radar signature. The DARPA Advanced Targeting Technology system may produce improvements in targeting that allow HARM missiles to target even short "pop-up" bursts of radar. Similarly, the R7 enhancement of the HARM targeting systems may provide enough accuracy to allow the use of an area attack weapon like the AGM-154A Joint Stand-off Weapon (JSOW) against a SAM, or air defense radar/command and control site. Nevertheless, Kosovo raises broad questions about the future of air defense suppression mission, whether anti-radiation missiles can be counted on the play their past role, and the need for systems that can target and destroy land-based air defense systems rather than simply suppress them.

INFORMATION WARFARE: TRADITIONAL AND NEW

Both sides used information warfare during the campaign. Some of this warfare involved traditional use of propaganda and the media. The NATO briefing effort and Serbian disinformation campaign have already been discussed in depth. The US stressed the importance of this aspect of information warfare in some of its reporting on the lessons of the campaign.[344]

The first political-military plan on Kosovo, completed in the fall of 1998, focused on using the threat of NATO air strikes to achieve a political-military settlement. After this threat of force convinced Milosevic to garrison most Serb forces in October 1998, interagency planning efforts focused on deploying the OSCE's Kosovo Verification Mission, facilitating humanitarian assistance, and responding to possible Serbian noncompliance. During Operation Allied Force, two interagency planning efforts occurred simultaneously. The first involved the development of a strategic campaign plan designed to ensure that wider U.S. and allied diplomatic, economic, and information efforts were integrated with our military operations.

As it became clear that Milosevic hoped to outlast the alliance, more attention was paid to other ways of bringing pressure to bear. The second effort involved planning for a NATO-led peace implementation force in Kosovo and an international civilian presence for the UN Mission in Kosovo (UNMIK) after NATO's military campaign had achieved its objectives.

This experience has taught us that our planning must better reflect the full range of instruments at our disposal, including the use of economic sanctions, public diplomacy, and other information efforts. Our initial planning focused on air strikes and diplomacy as the tools to achieve U.S. and NATO objectives. To ensure comprehensive planning and high-level awareness of the range of instruments available to decision-makers, we believe it is important that senior officials participate routinely in rehearsals, gaming, exercises, and simulations.

Successfully conducting operations to disrupt or confuse an enemy's ability to collect, process, and disseminate information is becoming increasingly important in this "information age" of warfare. The importance of such capabilities was recognized fully during Operation Allied Force, but the conduct of an integrated information operations campaign was delayed by the lack of both advance planning and strategic guidance defining key objectives. The Department will address this problem by developing the needed plans and testing them in exercises.

There is good reason to "address the problem." One of the most striking aspects of any review of the propaganda campaign conducted by both sides is how inept many portions of the campaign was, how unconvincing many media and propaganda statements were, and how often the content lacked the depth to be convincing. In many cases, the statements also seemed to ignore the different values and perspective of the other side, and may have done more to reassure those issuing the statements than influence either the enemy or world opinion. While NATO certainly did a better job than Serbia, it had far more means and a far better case. It also did not avoid over-selling in shallow ways that alienated a considerable amount of the media, and created a major credibility problem.

NATO was slow to attack Serbian TV and radio and deny Serbia its propaganda machine. It also followed the examples of Desert Storm and Desert Fox in giving foreign journalists a de facto sanctuary in broadcasting from enemy territory although this was done with much of the same censorship and manipulation used by Iraq in previous conflicts. There are obvious drawbacks to attacking enemy media, and risking casualties among foreign journalists. There also, however, are strong advantages to taking a more aggressive stance and announcing before a conflict that foreign journalists cannot expect to be safe from attacks on enemy information warfare facilities. Serious war requires serious action.

Serbia's Role in Information Warfare

Both sides also made extensive efforts to intercept the other side's communications, jam or deceive sensors, and conduct other forms of electronic warfare. In both cases, the campaign in Kosovo reinforced the critical role that information warfare can play in the broadest sense of the term.[345] One interesting aspect of the campaign was that the Internet became a new global propaganda tool for both sides, and that Serbia launched a computer attack on the NATO web page—perhaps the first attack of its kind.

Serbia also made extensive use of another new tool in information warfare—the cellular phone. NATO experts feel that Serbians regularly observed NATO air bases and facilities, and would "phone home" to warn of NATO take-offs and probable attacks.[346] Ironically, NATO struck constantly at military relay stations, but only damaged three out of about 20 telephone nodes and none of the three network control stations that supported Serbian cell phones. This left most communications and Internet access intact.[347]

Some US officers, like General John Jumper, the commander of the US Air Forces in Europe (USAFE), feel that the Serbs may also have been able to exploit leaks within the NATO targeting and command structure: "We were concerned about the compromise of target lists and even the air tasking order in some cases. I could not tell you if that was the result of the target process (which included non-US NATO officers) or the result of leaks somewhere else in the operational and tactical system. But, yes, it was a significant concern to all of us, and in some cases I was convinced that (the Serbs) had that information (target data) ahead of time."[348]

Vice Admiral Daniel Murphy, the commander of the US Sixth Fleet, also noted in testimony to Congress that, "We took special care with respect to the Tomahawk and CALCM cruise missiles and our stealth technology so those missions were never made available (to NATO) in terms of precise timing or ingress and egress. We know that they weren't compromised. This was a reflection of a very real concern that senior commanders had that we didn't have airtight security within NATO."[349]

NATO's Role in Information Warfare

NATO, Serbian, and KLA units made use of the GPS system—another system open to civilian use. As a result, the distinction between civilian and military information systems was increasingly blurred—a pattern that is likely to be equally true in future conflicts.

Both also attacked the other's information and computer systems. The Serbian attacks seem to have been limited and rather crude. The most visible sign were Serbian efforts to block access to the NATO web page on the Internet, and to corrupt some of the graphics on that page. Serbia does not seem to have had significant success in penetrating any major NATO communications and computer system.

NATO and the US have kept most of their efforts classified, but it seems that NATO was able to penetrate some Serbian systems and either overload them with extraneous information and other "brute force" methods, or manipulate and alter data to protect some of NATO's attacking aircraft. This situation differed from the Gulf War, where the US developed the ability to read Iraqi E-mail systems, but did not actively attack the system. While the US Air Force planned such attacks in depth, they were blocked by the US intelligence community that felt that they would do more to corrupt the quality of intelligence collection than damage Iraqi operations. The CIA and National Security Agency both raised key issues about the trade-offs between information warfare and a loss of intelligence and targeting data.

The US Air Force does seem to have been able insert false targets into the Serbian air defense system—although there is no precise way to determine how much of the attempted penetration actually appeared on Serbia radars and data read outs. Although the details remain classified, the primary method of attack seems to have been the use of false radar images supported by false communications and emissions designed to deceive Serbian electronic intelligence. It seems, however, that these attacks were delayed because Kosovo had not been seen as presenting a serious risk of a large-scale air conflict, and that this delay contributed to the loss of one F-117 and damage to another.[350]

There are indications that the US Air Force is modifying its EC-130 fleet and UAVs to allow them to intercept microwave beams and side lobes and penetrate enemy communications systems. The US Army is considering adding similar capabilities to its RC-7 airborne reconnaissance systems, RC-12 Guardrails, tactical UAV, and future Airborne Common Sensor. It is also possible that the US Milstar and Defense Satellite Communications System (DSCS) satellites are being modified to support computer intercept and penetration.[351]

Is Western Information Warfare Legal and Worth Its Costs?

The problem with these developments is that US information warriors must find some way to overcome the long-standing objections by the CIA and National Security Agency to direct attacks on enemy computer systems that are prime sources of intelligence Furthermore, the Department of Defense encountered major legal objections during Kosovo to attacks using international links that might affect public and financial systems. Lawyers raised strong "law of war" arguments that information warfare can only be used against dedicated military systems, and the General Counsel's office of the Department of Defense ended up issuing some 50 pages of complex guidelines on the legal issues involved.[352]

This raises serious questions abut a potential new form of collateral damage, the conflict between information warfare. intelligence gathering, and prohibitions on "indiscriminate attacks on civilian facilities—and how to solve the resulting organizational problems on both a national and alliance basis.

INTELLIGENCE, SURVEILLANCE, AND RECONNAISSANCE (ISR), AND BATTLE MANAGEMENT

Kosovo again demonstrated the need for a theater-level expeditionary capability to rapidly deploy the intelligence, reconnaissance, targeting, and battle damage assessment assets needed to get maximum benefit from both air power and long-range land artillery systems. The combination of JSTARS, the ABCCC, U-2, unmanned aerial vehicles (UAVs), and better satellite and reconnaissance coverage—plus target analysis—proved critical in giving NATO strike-attack sorties more lethality.

US Lessons and Non-Lessons

Some of the Department of Defense reporting on this aspect of the war has been more than a bit self-congratulatory.[353]

Ground-based communications capabilities in Europe are among the most robust and flexible available to the United States in any theater of operations. Nonetheless, these capabilities were used to their full capacity, and there was a need to augment them during the operation to facilitate rapid dissemination of the large volumes of data needed by commanders to prosecute the air war.

One of the most useful communications capabilities was provided by the wide-band dissemination system, an advanced concept technology demonstration used extensively throughout the conflict for rapidly transmitting high-priority imagery of emerging targets. Because the need for this and related capabilities is likely to grow in the future, the Department is studying the improvements that ought to be made to our ground-based communications systems in all theaters.

Allied Force was an extremely complex operation requiring real-time coordination of a large military force comprising many sophisticated elements. In order to attack targets in the FRY, NATO forces had to transit regions in which everyday civilian activities, including commercial air traffic, continued unabated, further complicating command and control. In addition to providing carrier-based combat aircraft, U.S. naval forces in the Adriatic Sea provided capabilities for command and control, including interfaces with civilian air traffic control systems, that were invaluable.

US reporting on the intelligence aspects of Kosovo has become progressively more frank with time, however, and the US report on the lessons of the war issued in January 2000 raises a number of lessons which are surprisingly close to many of the lessons of the Gulf War—some 10 years earlier:[354]

In general, a well-managed, multi-source intelligence collection system is necessary to support all military operations. In Operation Allied Force, two specific operational requirements made effective and robust collection management a high priority: (1) the need to create a comprehensive picture of the battlespace, and (2) the need to simultaneously detect and track elusive mobile targets. Because this system did not provide all of the support desired, the Department is reviewing the need for improvements in our capabilities, employment, and collection-management processes to ensure that we can handle future contingencies. In particular, we are focusing on achieving time-sensitive operational objectives using an integrated multi-mode collection systems-of-systems approach.

. . . . For the most part, intelligence systems and architecture shortfalls that surfaced in Operation Allied Force had been recognized prior to the crisis and remedies had been programmed. However, the Department needs to further develop and refine tactics, techniques, and procedures for federated intelligence efforts and to reassess and size long-haul communications needs accordingly. Planning for intelligence communications needs must include deployable systems and technicians. Additionally, the Department needs a clear policy and implementation plan to explain when and how coalition partners can be connected to U.S. networks and, when and how data can be shared with those partners.

. . . The overall quality and level of intelligence support provided during Operation Allied Force was far superior to that provided during the Gulf War. Because the Serbs frequently dispersed their air defenses and fielded forces from one location to another, it was difficult for NATO to find, fix, and destroy them.

- *Dynamic Targeting:* The Department needs to meet the difficult challenge of rapidly targeting enemy forces and systems that can move and hide frequently. In addition, the Department also need to place emphasis on rapidly collecting and disseminating no-strike target information to avoid collateral damage.

- *Foliage and Weather Penetrating Sensors:* Detecting and tracking mobile targets on the ground in poor weather can be extremely difficult. Further, we should expect that future adversaries will use concealment and deception to hide their forces. Thus, the Department needs to develop and acquire sensors for use in all weather and in foliage-covered terrain.

- *Geolocation Accuracy and Timeliness:* The Department needs to improve our ISR sensors and streamline the targeting process to be able to employ precision munitions against fixed and mobile targets and to re-target those weapons dynamically.

- *Numbers of Intelligence, Surveillance, and Reconnaissance (ISR) Assets:* Based upon the shortfalls in targeting capability evident during Operation Allied Force, and the stresses placed on U.S. ISR assets, initiatives are underway to optimize coordination between theater and national assets . . . Intelligence, surveillance, and reconnaissance assets such as the U-2, Iron Clad, RC-135 Rivet Joint, and special-mission aircraft were in extremely high demand during the Kosovo operations. The U-2 is a single-pilot, multi-role collection platform that can take photographic or radar images, as well as monitor enemy communications and locate the sources of electronic signals. The RC-135 can also monitor enemy communications and signals. Maritime patrol aircraft also provided a number of important capabilities to support commanders' ISR needs. These platforms are especially critical since they also support multiple intelligence collection activities in other areas around the world. The limited availability of these critical ISR assets will require careful force management in the future.

- *Reachback:* Operation Allied Force saw the first extensive use of sensor platforms deploying forward while their data reduction and analysis components remained at the home base. This "reachback" technique was also used as part of the federated intelligence process to perform timely battle damage assessment as discussed earlier, thus reducing the number of scarce imagery analysts required in theater.[355]

It is also important to note that the US found that there was an important lesson in terms of human intelligence resources and the role of reserves. Complex power projection operations almost always create sudden new needs for linguistic skills and area expertise that military forces cannot anticipate or afford to create in peacetime. Peacemaking operations compound these issues because of the high political content of every aspect of military operations. As a result, the human dimension of intelligence is as important a lesson as any lesson relating to technology and intelligence methods and organization:[356]

Augmentation planning is a necessary component of crisis intelligence operations. Given this fact, the Intelligence Community needs to develop a rapid reaction capability that enables the various intelligence agencies to better anticipate requirements, prepare their workforces, and streamline procedures for individual or organizational augmentation. Moreover, the Department can hedge against possible future need for specific low density/ high demand skills by better anticipating requirements and building them into the Reserve Forces. Investments must be geared toward developing a rapid reaction capability, comprised of both active and reserve personnel. Linguist shortfalls are the subject of several ongoing studies. Currently, the Assistant Secretary of Defense (C3I) is developing a strategy, policies, plans, and resource programs to meet the Department's language requirements.

The shortfall in linguists is also being reviewed by the Joint Staff, with help from Service language program offices. In a complementary initiative, the National Security Agency has convened a task force to look at all aspects of the linguist issue to ensure that the United States is better prepared to deal efficiently with the full range of potential crisis scenarios. Among the topics of major interest are the development of an overall linguist requirements strategy and the use of contracted services.

The Joint Reserve Intelligence Centers (JRICs) are one example of a new capability that allows Reserve component members of the Intelligence Community to surge and focus resources without deploying to the mission location. Virtual augmentation through online collaboration, federated burdensharing, and reach back have already proved their potential. The Department needs to accelerate similar developments to improve accessibility to the entire pool of intelligence professionals.

The report the Department issued on the lessons of the war in January 2000, and other sources, listed the following additional lessons:[357]

- The performance of the ABCCC, RC-135V/W Rivet Joint, RC-135U Combat Sent, and U-2 need examination in terms of the ability to provide a near real-time synthesis of all the required data.

- The J-8 JSTARS seems to have made significant progress since the Gulf War, but serious questions remained as to its ability to characterize small military movements and adequately distinguish armor and artillery from other vehicles. Questions also exist regarding the size of the currently planned J-8 fleet (13 aircraft now versus an original requirement of 13) and whether it will be adequate for more than one major regional contingency.

Preliminary examination of the performance of JSTARS indicates that:[358]

- It needs improved data links to transmit data directly to attack aircraft,

- "Fusion" of JSTARS radar data and imagery will often be required to confirm the true nature of a target and avoid collateral damage.

- The Radar Technology Insertion Program (RTIP) must be accelerated to provide new sensor and software technology to better track and identify military targets, and distinguish between given types of targets more reliably.

- Systems are needed to respond to JSTARS targeting in near real-time, possibly by providing targeting data to use stand-off munitions with smart area kill capabilities or eventually to allow fighters like the F-16 to target using direct JSTARS downlinks.

- At least some experts feel that national intelligence assets do not adequately support theater commanders in terms of information, reaction times, fusion of information from different agencies, adequate dissemination of classified material, and responsiveness to theater-level tasking. These problems were major lessons of the Gulf War and need review.[359]

- As part of this review, the US needs to study information flow to coalition allies, and the ability to maximize the fusion of data provided to facilities like NATO's Combined Air Operations Center (CAOC).[360]

- Some officials in the Department of Defense believe that the need to suddenly improvise a new integrated approach to communications and information to fight the air and missile campaign in Kosovo illustrates the need for a broader Global Information Grid (CIG). This system would cover the entire world, and link all of the service and intelligence systems together and which is tied to both operators and support elements. It will give them command computing and communications links, as part of the Defense Information Infrastructure (DOI) and Common Operating Environment (COE) effort led by the Defense Information Systems Agency. This effort would incorporate service elements like the Navy/Marine Corps Intranet. It is unclear how quickly such a system can be created, but it conceptually would change much of the US approach to warfare.[361]

The importance of these lessons is reflected in the fact that the US Department of Defense was forced to fund immediate improvements in its ISR budget. Its description of these improvements in its final report on the lessons of Kosovo was considerably less optimistic than some of its immediate postwar reporting, and illustrates the fact that even NATO's best-funded ISR effort had serious limitations:[362]

The (FY2000) supplemental provided $37 million to replace and enhance UAVs, $111 million for additional EP-3 aircraft and enhancements, and $30 million for other ISR-related investments. These investments reflect, among other lessons, the fact that the operations in Kosovo saw an unprecedented use of unmanned aerial vehicles. Funding is being used to replace Predator UAV losses, to repair Hunter UAVs and maintenance facilities, and to add a laser designator capability to Predator. The FY01–05 budget and program invests an additional $918 million for: a new JSTARS aircraft ($260 million), accelerated acquisition and early deployment of the Global Hawk program ($390 million), and additional EP-3 and other ISR enhancements. Finally, . . . the Department's FY01–05 program adds $1.5 billion to address the need for increased investments in the tasking, production, exploitation, and dissemination (TPED) of intelligence assets. Although plans to make these enhancements were well under way prior to the Kosovo conflict, these investments address many of the shortcomings in ISR integration that were identified in the Kosovo lessons learned review.

There are two additional lessons drawn that several senior US Air Force officers feel emerged from the US experience in Kosovo:

- The need to develop integrated targeting and reconnaissance systems that can pass targeting data on to aircraft in flight, strike aircraft with the avionics and secure communications to use such data to conduct precision strikes, and mission planning and air control systems that allow the mission of strike aircraft to be changed in real time, regardless of the number of allied aircraft in the theater of operations, and

- The need for UAVs or other systems that can gather targeting and intelligence data at low altitudes, under poor weather conditions, and at night and feed the targeting and reconnaissance system with the information that space-based and higher altitude sensor systems cannot gather or cannot provide with sufficient real-time flexibility and resolution to minimize the risk of collateral damage. Officers like General John Jumper, the commander of Allied Air Forces in Europe, have made these points and have effectively called for a new level of real-time situational awareness, mission flexibility, targeting, and strike capability.[363]

NATO Lessons and Non-Lessons

Many of these lessons regarding the need for information superiority apply equally to NATO. General Marvin R. Esmond, the Deputy Chief of Air and Space Operations, made the following point in his testimony to the House Armed Services Committee on the lessons of the war:[364]

In future operations, information warfare planners should contribute to the establishment of a comprehensive, theater-wide, joint and combined Information Warfare (IW) architecture that supports the joint commander's objectives and effects desired at the tactical, operational, and strategic levels. The USAF operated a first-ever distributed ISR architecture, providing actionable information to the decision makers. Employing distributed operations, targeting and intelligence support was accomplished between units located at Beale (CA), Omaha (NE), Washington, Ramstein, HQ SHAPE, and several other sites located overseas and CONUS supporting real-time operations. To successfully support the expeditionary nature of our forces, we must continue to invest in systems and the architecture to support these type of distributed real-time operations.

The basic systems NATO needs to use air and missile power seem to be in place, but serious questions exist as to the adequacy of the current number of assets, and the ability to integrate national intelligence assets to supporting theater operations. There were many problems that arose in Kosovo and which NATO and Europe allies clearly need to address. A number of these problems are closely related to the C⁴, interoperability, and European force improvement issues discussed earlier:

- The US Link-16 secure data-sharing system worked well, but was not disseminated widely enough, and the US military services were not prepared to use it to pass on real-time command and targeting data efficiently. The system needs to be expanded in coverage, and designed to allow rapid retargeting and shifts in tactical command and control. It also is not clear that the Army has the same level of integration as the Navy and Air Force.[365]

  More generally, the US found it difficult to cooperate effectively with allies that did not have an equal level of secure communications, and major questions arise about interoperability as the US shifts increasingly to integrated, near-real time, and automated reliance on a system than many allies do not share.

- The US Air Force was not allowed to use the Joint Tactical Information Distribution Systems (JTIDS) to provide automated situational awareness data, and had to rely on voice to provide situational data to allied aircraft. The Serbs were sometimes able to monitor these communications. This is another case where interoperability was a problem.[366]

- Both the US and Europe need to study the lessons of Europe's experience and ways to improve fusion and interoperability for NATO. This includes European experience with UAVs, and with more sophisticated systems like the Helios 1 and Mirage IVP, F1CR, and Etendard IVP. Lessons should not be drawn in a "fight alone" context.[367]

- NATO and US failed to anticipate the need for improved communications density, and for the near real time fusion of operational and intelligence information—just as they did during the Gulf War. It is unclear that the US as yet has the proper architecture for the C⁴I/BM/SR systems needed to achieve its goals as part of the revolution in military affairs.

- Both targeting and battle damage assessment seem to have created major problems during Kosovo which severely challenge the credibility of many US plans for "information dominance" and to execute the revolution in military affairs. These problems have been discussed in detail in the previous analysis, and strongly indicate that much of the present US effort to substitute force quality for force numbers may be little more than high technology wishful thinking. The lesson of Kosovo seems to be that the US cannot eliminate the "fog of war" or enemy ability to exploit asymmetric warfare and needs significant improvements in *both* technology and force numbers.

European forces can only be interoperable and effective if they acquire C⁴ capabilities similar to those of the US or tailor their forces to use US systems.[368] For example, SACEUR Wesley Clark told the press that, "We had a lack of ability in some cases to transfer information, some cases voice, some digital, beyond visual range, and identification of friend or foe."[369] General Klaus Nauman, the former head of NATO's Military Committee, stated that, "Kosovo taught us that

NATO's force structure is in contrast to NATO's integrated command structure and is not longer flexible enough to react quickly and decisively to unforeseen effects . . . The lesson we have learned is that we have to be increasingly prepared for asymmetric responses. To cope with these threats will be necessary and hence it is critical for NATO's future successes to enhance mobility, flexibility, and deployability of its forces These capabilities are inadequate at this time."[370]

Secretary Cohen drew a broader conclusion during the question and answer session in his press conference after the NATO Ministerial in September.[371]

Cohen: . . . There are things that can be done in the short term by looking at command, control and communications, for example. We found out during the Kosovo conflict that a number of countries did not have as secure communications as we want to have. And therefore, Milosevic's forces were either trying to or were successful in intercepting some of the communications, putting our pilots at risk. So there can be some rather short term goals achieved there, and also in the form of greater logistical support activities. But there are long term goals. It's not going to happen overnight. These capabilities have been identified that we need to identify. It may take a number of years to finally fully fund and acquire [them].

Questioner: Mr. Secretary, there's been a great deal of discussion about strains on intelligence capabilities. Only France has a intel satellite of its own. Are the Europeans going to have to begin to invest in these very expensive, highly technical pieces of equipment?

Cohen: Well, there has to be a commitment to acquire aircraft which are intelligence, surveillance and reconnaissance aircraft—the so-called ISR. We had a shortage of that capability and when you have a shortage of that capability, it also impacts on your ability to deliver precision guided munitions. So the two act in concert. So the short answer is that there has to be a greater acquisition of these aircraft whether they're developed in Europe or acquired from the United States. The requirement remains.

Questioner: And satellites, as well?

Cohen: Well, to the extent that we share satellite capability, what we've tried to point out is in this particular campaign, we had an example of intelligence from a variety of sources—including satellites—that are communicated directly to the shooter. And that allowed those aircraft to acquire that information from the satellites to the United States over our European commanders out to the pilots within a matter of seconds, allowing them to change targets while on the mission itself. And that's the kind of sharing of technology that we'll have to continue to have in the future.

"KILL BOX" SYSTEM, "TANK PLINKING," THE "EQUIPMENT COUNT," AND THE REAL VALUE OF JOINTNESS

Some of the most senior officers in the US Air Force officers feel that Kosovo demonstrates that a comprehensive review is needed of the best ways to use strike fighters in anti-armored and heavy weapons operations. These officers include the Lt. General Michael Short, NATO's air commander in the Balkans, and NATO's new SACEUR, General Joseph Ralston (then the Vice Chairman of the US Joint Chiefs of Staff). These officers strongly favor quick and decisive air campaigns focused on strategic targets. They feel it is wasteful to use aircraft like the F-15 and F-16 in "equipment count" campaigns to find and kill enemy armor, artillery, and vehicles for the sake of numbers rather than tactical effectiveness, and that there is pressure on battle damage assessment to maximize the count.

Vice Admiral Daniel J. Murphy, commander of the NATO naval forces opposing Serbia, is quoted as saying that, "There was a fundamental difference of opinion at the outset between General Clark, who was applying a ground commander's perspective . . . and General Short as to the value of going after fielded forces."[372] Short is quoted as saying that, "Body bags coming home from Kosovo didn't bother Milosevic, and it didn't bother the leadership elite." He is also quoted as saying that, I never felt the 3rd Army was a center of gravity."[373] General Ralston is quoted as saying, "The tank, which was an irrelevant item in the context of ethnic cleansing, became the symbol of Serbian ground forces. . . . How many tanks did you kill today? All of a sudden, this became the measure of merit although it had nothing to do with reality."[374]

At the previous analysis has shown, the data so far available on Kosovo do not support either position. NATO's air strikes on both strategic and interdiction targets, and tactical targets in the field, produced considerable losses and casualties. At the same time, both had to be conducted under serious political constraints, and it is impossible to determine both the exact level of physical damage inflicted and the ultimate impact on Serbian perceptions and actions. The same, for different reasons, might be said of strategic and tactical strike efforts during the Gulf War.[375]

There are no hard data to validate claims that NATO could have succeeded through strategic bombing alone, or that support a clear assessment of the relative merits of strategic and tactical campaigns, but these issues need detailed examination. Certainly, risking aircraft costing over $60 million dollars in sorties with costs in excess of $100,000 each (including all necessary support) to fire munitions costing well over $40,000 to hit targets that may be decoys or cheap military vehicles has to have great tactical effectiveness to be justified. But for that matter, so does blowing up a "strategic" communications tower or similar target in the rear.

At the same time, there are other ways to fly tactical missions. Some planners point to the high survivability achieved by the much leaner mission packages flown by the Marine Corps, US Navy, and several allied air forces. At least some air planners outside the US Air Force feel that it over-protected many of its missions with complex fighter and electronic warfare escorts. The US Navy reports that it was able to fly many missions in areas like ground support and with much simpler and more flexible air tasking orders (ATOs). This debate over sophistication versus simplification is a long-standing one in NATO, and any decisions about the cost-effectiveness of attacking tactical targets must include a careful examination of ways to reduce the cost as well as ways to measure and justify the effectiveness.

MAPS AND MAPPING

Kosovo raised a number of issues regarding maps and mapping. *The most politically sensitive was the need for up-to-date and accurate maps of all key politically important facilities where collateral damage was a problem.* This is much easier to ask force than provide. Ironically, China found it very difficult to understand how NATO and the US could have used data maps that contributed to the strike on the Chinese embassy in Belgrade, but have virtually no fully up-to-date maps of their own cities, or of state and state-owned facilities.[376]

More generally, Kosovo reinforced the need for a comprehensive US effort to create a detailed topographic map of the entire earth for military purposes. This is the goal of the Shuttle Topographical Reconnaissance Mission (SRTM) which is a joint effort by NASA and the Department of Defense. It is intended to create a topographic mosaic map of about 60% of the earth's surface with 30-meter resolution. It will cover the area between the latitudes of 60° north and 56° south.[377]

The mission will use two C-Band and X-Band radar systems developed by NASA and the German and Italian space agencies and will produce elevation data that will greatly enhance the ability to use low flying missiles and aircraft, and terrain-mapping guidance systems. The current US military mapping system only has 100-meter resolution, and this did not provide good enough for precision targeting and strike guidance. The new 30-meter resolution mapping will support far more accurate strikes, and ensure coverage of all potentially hostile regimes without any delay if a crisis begins.

MUNITIONS AND MISSILE STOCKS

The data on US and allied inventories of smart weapons and cruise missiles are somewhat uncertain, but post-conflict reports indicate that the US had to draw on munitions stocks from throughout the world. They also indicate that the total US inventory of AGM-86 conventional Air Launched Cruise Missiles, and the GBU-30 and GBU-31 Joint Direct Attack Munitions (JDAMs), dropped below 100. There also were evidently severe supply problems with the AGM-130 television-guided air-to-surface missile, and the GBU-10 and GBU-12 versions of the laser-guided bomb.[378]

This reporting raises serious questions about whether the US has the munitions inventories needed for more than one major regional contingency—if that. It also raise questions about the risk inherent in US munitions development and procure-ment plans. The US, for example, was only building 200 JDAM kits a month when the air campaign began. The number will be raised to 500 a month in August 1999, and the goal is now 700–1,500 per month (although the Boeing plant in St. Louis seems to have been designed for a maximum rate of 1,200 per month).[379]

The report the US Department of Defense issued on the lessons of the war noted the need to reassess US stockpile planning and the procurement of precision weapons, and provided a clear warning that the growing emphasis on precision weapons requires both much larger stockpiles that the US had previously planned and an industrial base capable of surging production to meet wartime needs.[380]

Because of the character of Allied Force operations, heavy reliance on preferred munitions throughout the conflict resulted in a high expenditure rate. These rates reduced weapon stockpiles, especially for cruise missiles—the inventories of which had already been reduced by Operation Desert Fox, which was executed just months before Operation Allied Force began—and JDAM, a weapon that is still in low-rate production.

... There were several acquisition-related actions taken during and shortly after Operation Allied Force to improve our military readiness. 1) Emergency Supplemental Appropriations Request for Weapons. Before Operation Allied Force began, there was concern about our cruise missile inventory due to the high expenditure rate during Operation Desert Fox. The TLAM and CALCM cruise missile replenishment was considered necessary since developmental missiles, slated to supplement and eventually replacement these fielded cruise missiles, were several years from production. After Operation Allied Force began and cruise missile use continued at a steady pace, it became even more apparent that replenishment was essential. Other precision guided weapons were also used more than anticipated and usage of several weapons that are in the early phases of production (most notably JDAM) caused inventory shortages.

The decision to include funding for weapons in the Emergency Supplemental Appropriations Request was made early in Operation Allied Force. Some specific weapon systems were requested by name for Congressional consideration. Since weapon use for the remainder of the operation could not be forecast adequately, the Department also requested a contingency fund to provide flexibility in funding weapons that might be depleted. Congress approved the Emergency Supplemental Appropriations Request, and the funds were distributed to replenish the weapons that had been most significantly impacted by the military operations.

... As a near-term solution during the operation, the Department investigated the possibility of accelerating weapons with active production lines. JDAM was one of the programs that could be accelerated, and the Department worked with the contractor to speed delivery. In addition to early deliveries of the JDAMs already ordered, a follow-on contract was expeditiously awarded to acquire the next production lot. As part of normal business practices to reduce excess capacity and reduce production costs, some prime contractors were already consolidating and physically relocating weapon system production lines. These geographical moves had been planned well in advance, but proved untimely nonetheless.

... While exploring the possibilities of accelerating production and the execution of the emergency supplemental appropriations, concerns arose regarding competition for common components. Since some weapons have common components or suppliers, it was expected that the acceleration could pose allocation problems with the supplier's existing contractual commitments. A task force was established to help guide reallocation of industrial resources where necessary by prioritizing weapon systems. In these cases, the Department asked the Department of Commerce to intervene and provide legal direction to the suppliers, ensuring priority to key DoD programs. The task force relied on the Joint Requirement Oversight Council as the decision authority to establish priorities among weapon systems competing for common components. While only a few Commerce directives were ultimately issued, the task force proved beneficial and would have been even more valuable had the conflict continued for a longer period of time. b. Fuse Settings ... The lessons learned in the area of precision engagement lead to the following observations:

- Continue Service initiatives to replenish inventories of preferred munitions. Continue to assess development of weapons that fill gaps and shortfalls in current capabilities and their subsequent certification on launch platforms.

- Assess methods to determine wartime planning factors affecting expenditure rates.

- Assess future weapon inventories to achieve the right balance of capabilities for future requirements.

At the same time, plans to push ahead both the purchase of additional Block IIIC TLAMs, and increase the buy of some 1,353 Tactical Tomahawk missiles the Navy had planned to start buying in 2003, require careful validation of the postulated requirement. The successful test and completion of a hard target warhead for the Tactical Tomahawk is particularly important. The same is true of plans to convert 322 additional ALCMs to CALCMs and the need for a new and longer-range air-launched cruise missile.[381]

Little detailed information is available on the munitions stocks of NATO European forces. The comments of NATO ministers have made it clear, however, that European air forces had far more serious problems in terms of their stocks of precision-guided weapons and were not equipped to sustain more than a few days of combat.[382]

Major questions exist as to whether a major fund-driven gap exists between the level of precision guided and advanced munitions on-hand and ordered and real-world requirements for war fighting. At the same time, both the US and NATO must find an affordable balance between high-cost, high technology weapons and the ability to maintain large weapons inventories and fund suitable numbers of launch platforms.

PRECISION STRIKE: ADVANCED GPS, STEALTH AND STAND-OFF "ALL-WEATHER" AIR ORDNANCE

The US and its allies have failed to provide meaningful unclassified data on the effectiveness of precision-guided weapons during Kosovo. Unlike the Gulf War, no information has been made available to assess the strengths and weaknesses of given munitions and tactics, and sources within the Department of Defense indicate that this is partially the result of a bitter internal debate over what numbers of use and the deliberate efforts to exaggerate the effectiveness of given aircraft and munitions.

This seems to reflect the same self-destructive emphasis on "perfect war" described earlier, and the previous analysis has shown that senior officers repeated made false claims about accuracy during the war that cannot possible be true. At the same time, Kosovo did involve a new level of precision strike capability. General Marvin R. Esmond, the Deputy Chief of Air and Space Operations, summarized the situation as follows in his testimony to the House Armed Services Committee on the lessons of the war:[383]

... this was the most precise conflict of this size ever fought. Over 70% of the weapon aim points (Desired Mean Points of Impact or DMPIs) were attacked with preferred munitions. Major General Charles Wald, Vice Director for Strategic Plans and Policy on the Joint Staff, vividly described and displayed the effectiveness of NATO's precision engagement capabilities against fixed targets in the Serbian theater in his daily Department of Defense briefings. The extraordinary pinpoint accuracy of the NATO air forces' delivery of precision-guided munitions was impressive. Close to 50% of all the precision munitions employed by U.S. assets were laser guided munitions delivered by F15Es and F16CGs. These weapons plus conventional air-launched cruise missiles and Maverick air-to-surface missiles again proved their value. GPS-guided Joint Direct Attack Munitions added significantly to our all-weather precision strike potential. Continued acquisition of this highly successful munition combined with efforts to integrate it on more of our strike assets promises even more capability in the near future. The U.S. Air Force is well along a modernization path which will ensure the vast majority of our strike assets are capable of delivering precision munitions in good weather or bad and at day or in darkness.

While quantity of munitions delivered is an even worse measure of military effectiveness than "body counts," few dispute the fact that precision strike is a lesson of modern war. Regardless of the debates over accuracy and battle damage assessment, the officers and analysts working on these issues do agree that US and some allied precision strike capabilities were superior to those engaged in the Gulf War in spite of the fact they often had to be used under far more difficult conditions.

The US Reaction

Certainly, the US has treated the need for improved precision strike capabilities as one of the key lessons of the war. It has also translated this lesson into immediate efforts to improve its capabilities. Its final report on the lessons of the war notes that,[384]

Using the emergency supplemental funds provided by the Congress, the Department's current program incorporates $1.2 billion in fiscal year 2000 to procure additional precision munitions. This includes $431 million to convert 624 additional Tomahawk missiles to the latest land-attack configuration, $306 million to procure approximately 11,000 additional Joint Direct Attack Munition (JDAM) kits, and $178 million to convert 322 additional air-launched cruise missiles to a conventional configuration. Other investments include substantial additional numbers of expanded response standoff land attack missiles (SLAM-ER), high-speed anti-radiation missiles (HARM), Maverick air-to-surface missiles, laser-guided bombs, and general-purpose bombs. In addition to the $1.2 billion provided by the FY2000 supplemental, the Department's FY01–05 program includes an additional $234 million for various precision strike investments, including a substantial investment ($158M) for targeting pods.[385]

The Value of Systems Using GPS Guidance and Stand-Off Systems with "All-Weather" Capability

Money and short-term force improvements, however, are only part of the story. Kosovo validates the value of systems using GPS guidance and of stand-off systems with "all-weather" capability. Secretary of Defense Cohen described this lesson as follows in the his speech to the IISS on the preliminary lessons of the war.[386]

. . . what we were able to achieve through this campaign reminds all of us that the revolution of military affairs is fundamentally changing the way in which we fight. In the past, by way of example, we needed multiple bombers to hit a single target. In Kosovo, a single bomber could destroy multiple targets. In Operation Desert Storm, which is rightly celebrated for its technological progress and prowess, there were only a handful of sophisticated aircraft that could carry precision-guided munitions, and only nine percent of all munitions expended during that campaign were precision-guided. In Kosovo, nearly all of our fighters could deliver these devastating weapons, and in the opening days, as I mentioned, of Allied Force, one-hundred percent of the U.S. ordnance was in fact precision-guided.

In the revolution of military affairs, it's also important that we take advantage of the kind of technology that has been developed to give us what we call the sensor-to-shooter capability. In Kosovo we had a vast number of intelligence, surveillance, and reconnaissance systems. We had analysts in Washington and across Europe, we had space-based satellites, and for the first time we had a fairly significant use of unmanned aerial vehicles or UAVs, all of which allowed for a fairly rapid collection of information, a collating into a single system of the battlefield intelligence that we then sent to our shooters.

Taken together, all of these innovations allowed pilots to hit virtually any target any time, day or night, in any kind of weather to within a few feet of accuracy. I'll give you one example. During one mission we were able to strike a radio transmitter in downtown Belgrade with little, if any, damage to surrounding buildings. Of the thousands of bombs that were dropped and the missiles that were fired, nearly all of them hit their intended target. Of all those thousands of weapons that were dropped and expended, approximately 20 had unintended consequences or were not on target. So that is unprecedented. The fact that we were able to carry out a campaign of this size and this magnitude with no casualties and only two aircraft lost is something that is unprecedented and really overwhelming in concept.

Similarly, the Department of Defense strongly endorsed the need for more stand-off, all-weather precision weapons in its testimony on the lessons of the war.[387]

The latest generation of air-delivered munitions was employed in substantial number for the first time in this conflict. We are gratified that weapons fired at fixed sites succeeded very well in hitting their intended targets and in producing the intended results, with limited collateral damage to civilians.

In particular, the success achieved in delivering the new Joint Direct Attack Munition (JDAM) from altitudes above cloud cover demonstrated the wisdom of decisions taken after the 1991 Gulf War. Then, we faced similar constraints that allowed the enemy a sanctuary from attack when target areas were obscured in poor weather. In Kosovo, we operated under conditions in which there was at least 50 percent cloud cover more than 70 percent of the time, and yet we continued the campaign.

As expected, attacks on mobile targets proved more problematic than attacks against fixed targets. As with its air defenses, the FRY hid many of its mobile ground force systems, making them difficult to locate and attack. Concerns for limiting collateral damage also constrained us in some circumstances from attacks on possible ground force targets. On the other hand, by forcing the FRY to hide its ground maneuver forces and not operate them as units in the open, we greatly limited the Serb ground forces' combat effectiveness.

In some cases, only small inventories of the latest U.S. precision munitions were available for operations. Several of these systems, including JDAM and the Joint Standoff Weapon (JSOW), are in the early phases of production. Inventories of many of these weapons will be increasing dramatically over the next several years as a result of programs already funded by the Congress. Our success using these systems in Kosovo validates these production plans.

In addition to weapons used and proven during Operation Allied Force, we have other precision weapons under development that will be coming to fruition later, including improved versions of the Tomahawk long-range cruise missile and the new Joint Air-to-Surface Standoff Missile (JASSM). We have been reviewing munition production and development programs carefully as we develop the FY 2001 defense program to ensure that they proceed at an appropriate pace and scope in light of experience in Kosovo. We have also requested that about $1.4 billion of the supplemental funds available in FY 1999 be used to replenish stocks of preferred munitions used during Operation Allied Force.[388]

Investments in More Advanced Precision Strike Capabilities

General John Jumper, the commander of the US Air Forces in Europe (USAFE), and Vice Admiral Daniel Murphy, the commander of the US Sixth Fleet, stressed the value of precision-guided stand-off ordnance in reducing the risk posed by Serbian air defenses and in overcoming the much greater risks that will be posed by more modern surface-to-air missiles. Admiral Murphy noted that value of such munitions in reducing the need for support by electronic warfare aircraft like the EA-6B, and stated that the US should do "whatever it takes to rapidly equip all tactical aircraft for the use of precision guided munitions to remove the sanctuary provided by modern long-range air defense weapons."[389]

The US Department of Defense report on the lessons of the war issued in January 2000 noted that,[390]

Sea-launched and air-launched cruise missiles (TLAM and CALCM), JDAM, and JSOW provided the capability to penetrate enemy air defenses and attack a wide spectrum of targets throughout the battlespace. Attacking day or night in any weather, GPS-guided weapons placed all target sets at risk, denying the enemy sanctuaries created by weather or the use of heavily concentrated defenses.

As was the case with cruise missiles, the report did not provide any data on the number of munitions fired, their reliability and accuracy, or their damage effect. According to Pentagon services, this was the result of both a serious of bureaucratic fights over what data to release, and of the fact that operational precision did not approach the levels of accuracy and lethality NATO either reported or implied during the war. Nevertheless, precision weapons were more reliable, accurate, and lethal than the ordnance used in any previous conflict—including the Gulf War—and the report did single out several types of munitions as having been particularly effective.[391]

. . . The Joint Direct Attack Munition is designated GBU-31, a 2,000-pound class munition guided by an $18,000 tail kit. (The GBU-37, which is similar to JDAM, includes a 5,000-lb class warhead and is also guided by a GPS tail kit.) During Operation Allied Force, the JDAM, which is still in low-rate production was employed at nearly the same rate that it is being manufactured. The B-2 was the only operational aircraft used to deliver JDAMs; the combination of its all-weather precision capability and the B-2's ability to penetrate lethal defenses put high-value fixed targets at risk. Several additional aircraft are pending JDAM operational status in conformance with the JDAM acquisition plan.

To deliver JDAMs, the B-2s had to fly from Whiteman Air Force Base, Missouri, requiring multiple air-refueling hook-ups per mission. Using rotary launchers in their internal weapons bays, each B-2 was able to carry and deliver up to 16 JDAMs. A selectable fuse on each JDAM was set before the munition was loaded, and allowed for a variety of time delays—before or after impact—for the weapon's explosion..

. . . The Joint Standoff Weapon (JSOW), designated AGM-154, is a 1,000-pound class air-to-ground weapon. It is unpowered, but has a kinematically efficient airframe that provides standoff outside point defenses. The "A" variant, which is the only configuration currently operational, dispenses combined effects bomblets against area soft targets such as air defense radars, armor, artillery, and personnel. During Operation Allied Force, JSOWs were employed from Navy F/A-18 aircraft.

The AGM-130 is an air-to-ground, rocket-motor-powered missile with a television (TV) or infrared (IR)-guidance system. The AGM-130 was designed for stand off outside point defense attack missions using the remote control capability provided by a data link system. Under control of a crewmember, the missile flies toward the pre-selected target through midcourse, transition, and terminal phases. Through the data-link system, the crewmember can acquire the target or target area, issue steering commands as necessary, and lock-on or manually track the target to impact. The AGM-130 also contains an inertial navigation system that can be updated with location data obtained from the Global Positioning System to point the seeker and navigate to the target without operator input if required. However, with a crewmember monitoring the video display, man-in–the-loop control can be provided at any time. During Operation Allied Force, AGM-130s were employed from Air Force F-15E aircraft.

. . . Another success story from Operation Allied Force was the development of techniques for employing Standoff Land Attack Missile (SLAM) from Navy aircraft.

SLAM provided the Joint Task Force and the Joint Force Air Component Commander with new flexibility to strike mobile targets on short notice.

The AGM-142 HAVE NAP is a self-powered munition with inertial midcourse guidance and an 800-pound fragmentation or penetrator warhead that is launched from the B-52. Only two HAVE NAP munitions were launched during Operation Allied Force.

The reporting on these munitions also reinforce the need to link improvements in targeting to the increasing use of precision weapons and added comments on the need for improved fusing:[392]

A long-standing military requirement, again validated during Operation Allied Force, is the need to provide rapid targeting and re-targeting of aircraft and preferred munitions against known and emerging targets. A rapid targeting system that included reachback, distributed operations, and real-time collection, intelligence, surveillance, and reconnaissance assets was successful in shortening timelines from sensor to shooter. Real-time threat information detected by various systems was relayed to the Combined Air Operations Center, passed directly to strike assets, and exploited at national intelligence centers.

. . . Preliminary and follow-up ground battle damage assessments show that fuse setting can be a critical factor in the amount of damage inflicted. Effective real-time targeting may require that aircraft have the capability to change weapon fuse settings while airborne. This would allow the aircrew to maximize target destruction while adjusting for specific collateral damage restrictions.

. . . The lessons learned in the area of precision engagement lead to the following observations:

- Continue to assess technologies that will ensure flexibility and enable all-weather precision strikes, including on-board and off-board accurate targeting capability against fixed and mobile targets, that can be executed within minutes of target assignment.

- Incorporate real-time targeting training in individual unit training; perform joint training exercises and practice the use of national, theater, and tactical collection assets in support of reduced timeline employment tactics.

- Continue to pursue technologies that will process, exploit, and disseminate target information in a timely manner to support precision engagement; review Intelligence Community procedures and capability to enhance the level of detail and quality of intelligence to support theater-wide GPS-targeting requirements, especially in real time or near real time.

The US Air Force seems to have concluded that smart or advanced area munitions are the only way to conduct cost-effective missions in a high threat environment; it does not make sense to risk a pilot and aircraft to deliver unguided or dumb weapons when there are serious risks or weather problems. At the same time, US air planners feel they tended to become over-reliant on laser guided weapons after the Gulf War, and were too slow in taking advantage of additional guidance systems like GPS. General Michael E. Ryan, the Chief of Staff of the Air Force, stated that, "The service can't and shouldn't rely . . . on one class of munition or class of sensor or range. You have to have a full spectrum capability, depending on the situation that's presented to you."[393]

The JDAM, JSOW, JASSM, Sensor-Fused Weapon, and BAT

The key munitions the US Air Force is procuring in the near term to improve its capability to execute this aspect of the "revolution in military affairs" include as the Joint Direct Attack Munition (JDAM), Joint Standoff Weapon (JSOW), Joint Air to Surface Standoff Missile (JASSM), and smart self-homing submunitions like the Sensor-Fused Weapon and Brilliant Anti-Tank Munition (BAT). The US Air Force evidently will not order additional AGM-130s, in spite of their extensive use in Kosovo, because they do not have sufficient all-weather capability.[394]

The Air Force is examining low cost improvements and fixes to its stand-off weapons like adding pop-out wings to the JDAM to extend its range to 30 miles, and equipping it with a single warhead to eliminate the problems of selecting and mounting the warhead in the field. It is also upgrading its AGM-65G Mavericks to fix a problem in hitting armor at low altitudes and short ranges. The scale of this problem is illustrated by the fact that the Air Force can only afford to fix 1,800 of the 3,800 missiles it intends to keep in inventory. The campaign in Kosovo has again demonstrated that test and evaluation are no substitute for the real thing.[395]

The Navy has drawn similar lessons about cruise missiles and naval precision guided systems. It now plans to deploy the EX-171 ERGM Extended Range Guidance Munition (a precision guided system that can be fired by a naval gun), the Land-Attack Standard Missile, and the Tactical Tomahawk cruise missile by 2004, and is examining an Advanced Land Attack Missile (ALAM) for its destroyers with GPS guidance and a 450 kilometer range. The Tactical Tomahawk is due to be operational by 2003 and has a range of up to 2,250 kilometers.[396]

At the same time, Kosovo has not made it easy for the US to rush ahead in reshaping its air munitions, partly because of weapons development problems and costs. Such problems have delayed deployment of the JASSM to at least FY2002, partly because of problems in the test program and integrating the air data system with the autopilot and flight control. Desirable as smarter weapons may be, they have to be extraordinarily effective to justify costs of at least $400,000 a round and the US plans to buy 2,400 such weapons.[397]

The three variants of the JSOW include the AGM-154B for attacking targets like armor and surface-to-air missiles and the AGM-154C with a unitary warhead for greater accuracy. Both warheads have so far proved to have significantly less combat capability than was called for in their design. The AGM-154A, which is designed to kill wide-area, fixed targets is in full production. All the variants of the JSOW, however, may now have to be reconfigured to take outside targeting data, rather than rely on self-targeting, and to allow new target data to be fed directly into the missile.[398] This requirement illustrates the growing interaction between weapons design and new battle control and targeting methods.

This helps explain why the US is also looking at the use of conversion kits for its laser guided bombs that would give them GPS guidance. GPS guidance has the defect that it is not possible to control the precise point and angle of attack, but it does offer all-weather and advanced night attack capability, and GPS and laser guidance can be combined in the same bomb. This Paveway III program has already made experimental conversions of GBU-24, GBU-27, and GBU-28 laser guided bombs, and offers the cheapest potential solution to all-weather warfare.[399]

The Sensor Fused Weapons (CBU-97) is a critical aspect of US plans to improve the lethality of air power against armor. A detailed appraisal is needed of the success of this system in Kosovo and of its BLU-108 submunition and SKEET sensor.[400]

The European View of Such Lessons

Britain, France, and Italy seem to have drawn similar lessons about the need to expedite development and deployment of weapons like the Matra BAe Dynamics Storm Shadow, SCALP EG (Black Shaheen) and the Alenia Marconi Systems Brimstone. European forces faced significantly greater problems in using such weapons than the US. The RAF, French Air Force, and Italian Air Forces were restricted to laser-guided weapons during Kosovo, and encountered weather problems and difficulties in attacking at long ranges.[401] France was forced to make significant upgrades to both its air force and naval aircraft to improve their precision guided munitions and all-weather operations capability during the course of the campaign.[402]

These problems led both European nations and the US to make the lack of such European capabilities a major lesson of the war.[403]

. . . the operation highlighted a number of disparities between U.S. capabilities and those of our allies, including precision strike, mobility, and command, control, and communications capabilities. The gaps in capability that we confronted were real, and they had the effect of impeding our ability to operate at optimal effectiveness with our NATO allies. For example, because few NATO allies could employ precision munitions in sufficient numbers (or at all), the United States conducted the preponderance of the strike sorties during the early stages of the conflict. The lack of interoperable secure communications forced reliance on non-secure methods that compromised operational security. These problems persisted throughout the campaign.

British and French reports on the lessons of the war made similar points, as did staff studies in SHAPE, the Netherlands, and Germany.[404] The problem for Europe is affordability, although there are European weapons developments that could change this situation. the Storm Shadow has an integrated Terrain Reference Navigation (TRN) and inertial global positioning satellite (GPS) navigation suite, plus an integrated imaging infrared terminal seeking with automatic target recognition. It can be programmed to divert to a predetermined alternative target if recognition fails to minimize collateral damage. It can also be programmed to fly in ways that minimize vulnerability to known enemy land-based air defenses. The

SACLP EG is largely identical to the Storm Shadow but is designed to mount on different aircraft. It is scheduled to enter service in 2002–2003. Alenia Marconi is examining possible production of the system for Italy. The Alenia Marconi Systems Brimstone is a shorter-range armor killing system with a fully autonomous millimeter wave seeker. It is designed for fire and forget attacks in all kinds of weather.[405]

The Limits of GPS and Stand-Off Weapons

Past experience has shown, however, that it is easy to exaggerate the success of such systems based on wartime estimates and promised technical specifications. It is also unclear whether the nominal 13 meter accuracy of GPS guided weapons was either adequate or achieved under operational conditions.[406] Stand-off and GPS weapons can also present major problems in terms of targeting and collateral damage against mobile targets. There are still major problems in acquiring and validating mobile targets, particularly if they are disperse in civilian areas, mixed with civilian movements and equipment, and/or mixed with decoys.

One senior US aerospace official was quoted after the war as saying,[407]

You want to hit with great accuracy while making sure it's a missile launcher and not a school bus. That means you are talking about a sophisticated sensor and logic package. That's hard to keep affordable Penetrating aircraft can use much cheaper weapons.

The success of both air-delivered weapons and cruise missiles needs detailed post-war examination and validation, and development and procurement plans need to be changed accordingly.[408] Such analysis is equally important for NATO allied forces—such as Britain and France—which had no plans for the early purchase of GPS-guided munitions before the campaign in Kosovo.[409]

US Secretary of Defense Secretary Cohen made similar points during the question and answer session in the press conference that followed the NATO Ministerial in September 1999.[410]

Questioner: In the war in Kosovo, much of the fighting was done, many of the air missions were done on the frontlines, by American planes using very advanced technology—technology which is not now in the hands and is not possessed by the other Allies. Do you think that the other Allies—particularly the larger countries—will have to get into the business of either buying or developing that very expensive, high technology? Or is that not what you envision? Do you envision that to continue to be the American role and that other people do other stuff?

Cohen: No. We envision the NATO countries acquiring what we call precision guided munitions. This was demonstrated during the Kosovo conflict, compared for example to Desert Storm, where most of the munitions that were dropped were not precision guided. Where most of those that were dropped during this campaign—certainly during the initial phases—were all precision guided. So we think that other NATO countries will have to acquire those; those that have them in short supply will have to replenish them and increase their inventories; those that do not have them, we hope that they will turn to them as well for the future.

The second point I would make, however, is you say they are very expensive, perhaps implying they're behind the range of acquisition by a number of countries. What we have found is that a number of the new precision guided munitions are actually quite inexpensive compared to existing stocks, and so as a result of our research and development activities, developing lower cost precision guided munitions which we think can be available to those who wish to acquire it or they can develop it on their own—either way.

Questioner: The munitions may be affordable, but they can't be delivered by a Mack truck, they have to be delivered by a fairly sophisticated airplanes with fairly sophisticated electronics and communications. You guys fight a very high-tech war. It's all part of it—the intelligence has to be there, the ability to communicate with satellites and everything—it all has to work together. Are you saying they also have to purchase all the stuff that goes along with precision munitions?

Cohen: No. And the point we tried to make is that not every country has to have exactly the same thing that every other country has. One of the reasons we are devoting so much time to developing this Defense Capabilities Initiative is to have an allocation of resources to fit the countries and what they can do and what would be best suited for their capabilities to be fully integrated into a future type of campaign. So we don't expect every country from small to medium to large to have the identical equipment that the United States or Great Britain or France or Germany or Italy might have. So it's really a question of balancing it and integrating it, but those countries that do have the capability of delivering it, I believe, will focus on delivering precision guided munitions. There was unanimity on that point.

PROLIFERATION: THE "DOG THAT DIDN'T BARK"

One of the key "what ifs" affecting the lessons of Kosovo is what would have happened if Serbia had used the threat of weapons of mass destruction to threaten its neighbors. US experts indicate that Serbia may well have inherited the capability to build chemical weapons from the former Yugoslavia and may even have had some stocks of chemical weapons.

There are some reports that Serbia did use chemical weapons selectively against the KLA, shelling KLA forces with a disorienting agent like BZ. The KLA claims that 20 of its soldiers had to be sent to other European countries for treatment, and that the Serbs have used nerve gas on up to 4,000 civilians since the early 1990s.[411] It is clear, however, that Serbia neither made open threats to use such weapons, nor used enough gas to have a major psychological or military effect.

Serbia did inherit the stockpile of chemical weapons held by the former Yugoslavia, and moved the country's major chemical and biological warfare research facility from Mostar to Serbia following the Bosnian war.[412] At the same time, such reports are not confirmed. Further, Serbian stocks of chemical weapons seem to be highly limited and Serbia lacked any delivery system that could strike at NATO bases because of NATO's vast superiority in air defenses.

The more urgent question is what NATO would have done if Serbia did have missiles that could reach most targets in Europe and had advanced to more lethal weapons like biological weapons. The answers range from arguments that NATO would never have developed and sustained a consensus to launch air and missile strikes in the face of a threat to European territory to arguments that an otherwise weak and vulnerable Serbia would not risk challenging NATO and facing NATO conventional escalation and retaliation.[413]

There is no way to resolve these "what ifs." It is clear, however, that at some point interventions like Kosovo will encounter a major proliferator and/or a proliferator willing to take major risks. The ability to rapidly deploy effective "counterproliferation" forces will then become a major operational reality.

REFUELING

Refueling has become so basic a part of US military operations that the US tends to take its importance for granted. Nevertheless, the US still drew lessons from the war:[414]

Aerial refueling missions were particularly demanding because tankers operated, in many cases, from bases on the periphery of the theater. There were not enough air bases in the area immediately around Kosovo to support all the aircraft committed to Operation Allied Force. Strike aircraft were placed on bases closest to Kosovo, and longer-range tankers were based at locales farther away, often at distances that exceeded those expected for a major theater of war operation. Because of the multiple locations and long distances, planners had to overcome a host of coordination and support issues including providing support for global attack sorties flown from the continental United States by B-2 bombers. Another key factor that increased tanker demand was the need to provide refueling support for at least four combat air patrol stations that were filled continuously, 24 hours per day, from the beginning until the end of the war. Consequently crew ratios for tankers participating in Operation Allied Force were higher than typically planned. Many of the considerations mandating increased crews could be confronted in an intensive air-refueling scenario in the future.

Although U.S. forces succeeded in providing the tanker support needed to sustain the air operation, the Department is reviewing the tanker forces and crew ratios to determine whether existing and planned forces are sufficient to meet the two MTW requirement or other future contingencies. The Department is also investigating our ability to plan in theater, in real time, for the most effective use of our tanker fleet and is reviewing options for improving this key planning capability.

. . . Operation Allied Force represented an MTW's level of effort for some key air assets, particularly the so-called Low Density/High Demand (LD/HD) assets, as well as selected tactical aircraft, airlift aircraft, and refueling tankers. The high demand for these aircraft was met by deploying aircraft from the forces assigned to the Commanders in Chief of theaters outside Europe. To mitigate the risk to the affected commands, equivalent type aircraft stationed in the continental United States were placed on alert and issued orders to be prepared to deploy on short notice . . . . Risk analysis is important in judging force readiness where commitments are made to support important and necessary operations but do not involve our vital interests. Some smaller-scale contingencies may be in this category. Probable future commitments make it important to enhance the Department's process for providing timely assessment of the impact of smaller-scale contingencies on the ability to execute the overall defense strategy.

These lessons may be even more important to powers that lack major refueling and long-range strike, airlift, deployment, and reinforcement capability.

RESTRIKES

NATO has not published detailed figures on the number of restrikes that it conducted during the air and missile war in Kosovo, but some US experts indicate that numbers are very high. An unofficial histogram of the number of restrikes indicates that they averaged at least 40 a day, and peaked towards the end of the war, when they reached nearly 160 restrikes on day 68. The figures for that period show three others days in which there were nearly 100 restrikes, and there were a total of nine days with more than 60 restrikes.[415]

While some targets do require multiple strikes, the number of restrikes during the air campaign raises further questions about the lethality of air and missile power, even with precision weapons, and the ability to target maximum points of vulnerability. It also reinforces the problems raised by the use of decoys and deception, and questions about the true meaning of the battle damage assessment data available to US and NATO planners.

The fact that most targets required multiple restrikes may be inevitable, but reducing the restrike rate would greatly reduce the risk of losses and increase the effectiveness of air power. Examining this aspect of the lessons of Kosovo should have a highly priority.[416]

SURFACE-TO-AIR MISSILES

NATO scarcely faced advanced air defenses in Kosovo, and was able to do an excellent job of rapidly suppressing these defenses with virtually no losses even though it achieved only a limited number of outright kills. In practice, this suppression was adequate to meet virtually all mission needs, although it did place some altitude and penetration constraints on NATO aircraft. The Department of Defense provides a good summary of this aspect of NATO operations in Secretary Cohen's testimony to Congress on the lessons of the war.[417]

The threat posed by Serbia's offensive air capability was eliminated rapidly. Reducing Serbian defensive capabilities did not proceed as quickly, however, because the Serbs possessed a capable integrated air defense system that was very difficult to eliminate. NATO plans called for the systematic degradation of these integrated air defenses. This proved problematic because of our concerns regarding target selection and collateral damage, and because of the tactics the Serbs adopted.

⌜The Serbs chose to conserve their air defenses, while attempting to down NATO aircraft as targets of opportunity. Individual longer-range systems emerged to fire at our aircraft in an unpredictable fashion. Shorter-range Serbian antiaircraft artillery and man-portable air defense systems were plentiful, and their locations were difficult to predict. And the command and control system supporting the Serb air defenses was redundant, flexible, and adaptable, further complicating its defeat. Rather than expend sorties attempting to attack these threats, commanders chose to operate at altitudes beyond which most Serbian antiaircraft systems could effectively be employed.⌝

Although NATO forces had difficulty targeting the Serb defensive systems, the Serbs had minimal success downing NATO forces. Indeed, the allied air offensive was sustained and, in fact, expanded greatly despite the remaining Serbian air defense systems. We succeeded because we maintained pressure on their defenses, forcing the Serbians to keep their systems hidden under most circumstances and to use defensive tactics that limited the systems' effectiveness. For example, the Serbs had to limit greatly the time they could keep radars operating, and on occasion they fired missiles without ground-launch guidance signals rather than expose their air defense systems to immediate counterattack.

We increased the tempo of operations in our air defense suppression forces to help make this possible. We also adapted our concepts of operation to sustain an increasing pace of strike operations without compromising our concern for minimal casualties and collateral damage.

While we prevailed in delivering a punishing air offensive with virtually no loss to NATO forces, we must acknowledge some concerns for the future. Although among the most capable that the United States has faced in combat, the FRY air defense systems did not represent the state of the art. Much more capable systems are available for sale in the international arms market. In the years ahead, we may face an adversary armed with state-of-the-art systems, and we need to prepare for that possibility now.

NATO's air defense suppression forces were committed heavily to this campaign. U.S. systems such as RC-135 Rivet Joint electronic intelligence aircraft and EA-6B tactical airborne electronic warfare aircraft were employed in numbers roughly equivalent to those anticipated for a major theater war, and even then were heavily tasked. We need to find innovative and affordable ways to exploit our technological skills in electronic combat to bring greater pressure to bear on a future enemy's air defense system.

It is the latter part of this statement that requires close attention. Kosovo is a warning that obsolete systems like the SA-2 and SA-3, and obsolescent systems like the SA-6 can still have a major impact on air operations. A rough assessment from pilot reports indicates that Serbia may still have fired up to 700 missiles. This includes 266 SA-6s, 174 SA-3s, 106 from man-portable systems, and 126 from unidentified systems. According to one report, the crews in the B-1 bomber counted at least 20 surface-to-air missiles fired against them during their first 50 missions. The ALE-50 electronic countermeasure system on the B-1 protected it from most attacks, and diverted 10 missiles than had locked up to B-1s. One missile (probably an SA-3) did shoot down an F-117 on March 27, however, and one came close enough to an A-10 to cause mechanical damage and force it to return to base.[418]

Most Serbian surface-to-air missiles and air defenses also survived. The various claims have been discussed earlier, but NATO did major damage to a maximum of two out three SA-2 units, 10 of 12 SA-3 units, and only three out of 22 SA-6s.

Variations of the far more modern Russian/Ukrainian S-300 (SA-10 and SA-12) are now available for export with slant ranges of up to 80–140 miles and significant anti-tactical missile defense capabilities. China, for example, has purchased the older S-300PMU1. The new S-400 is nearing the point where it will be available for export with a claimed maximum slant range of up to 250 miles.

One indication of the importance of this lesson are reports that Serbia bought at least 6–10 S-300PM surface-to-air missile systems before the campaign began on March 24, 1999, and that they and 20 missiles were delivered—but could not be used because the Clam Shell radar units associated with the missile had not yet be delivered. There have also been reports that missiles were smuggled in on a Russian Humanitarian convoy. Russia has denied all of these reports, but Serbia would almost certainly have posed a significantly more serious threat if it had been able to deploy operational S-300PMU1s before the campaign began.[419]

Threat powers can also be expected to improve their shorter range air defense systems. For example, Russia is now marketing a conversion of the ZSU-4–23 radar guided anti-aircraft gun that has greatly improved optical sighting with a day/night tracker and a launch rack of two pods of two SA-16 or SA-18 radar/IR guided surface-to-air missiles to improve its range.[420]

General John Jumper, the commander of the US Air Forces in Europe (USAFE), expressed this concern in his testimony to Congress: "We would have had to fight our way in with brute force because we don't have the techniques to adequately defense ourselves against the capabilities of those missiles. The SA-10 is good enough that it can actually see the HARM (High Speed Anti-Radiation Missile being short at it and shoot the HARM down. We're just not prepared . . . it would have altered our strategy considerably. I can guarantee you that it would not have been without loss."[421]

Kosovo needs to be studied carefully, as well as the Gulf War, to determine how US and NATO air and missile operations would have had to change if more modern surface-to-air defenses had been available to the Serbs. [422]

TRAINING AND PERSONNEL QUALITY

The value of training and high quality personnel is such a cliché in the lessons of war that it is sometimes ignored. There are constants in military operations, however, and the conclusions drawn in the US Department of Defense report regarding these issues are as valid for Kosovo as they would be for virtually every military operation in history.[423]

Not surprisingly, nearly every issue addressed within this report has direct or indirect training readiness implications. One of the most significant readiness lessons learned, and one which has been repeatedly revealed in the analyses conducted post-Operation Allied Force, is the criticality of and need for Service, joint, and coalition interoperability training.

1. Service Doctrine and Training

Operation Allied Force presented a unique operational and strategic environment for our forces. In some cases, however, Service doctrine and training had not fully prepared us for the missions and conditions that were encountered. As discussed earlier in this report, Apache pilots assigned to Task Force Hawk were not fully prepared, upon their arrival in theater, to fly the full spectrum of combat missions required to support the Joint Force Air Component Commander, and in the existing conditions of poor weather, mountainous terrain, and unmapped flight obstacles to be found in the region. Though professional, motivated, and highly skilled, these pilots required extensive training with night vision goggles. Similarly, Navy pilots had not been fully trained for the mission of providing close-air-support type missions (i.e., locating targets, while minimizing collateral damage) under the unique operational conditions of Allied Force.

. . . Operation Allied Force also validated the need for joint, integrated training among the Services to enhance their ability to execute both joint and coalition air operations such as those encountered in Kosovo. Working as a joint team, the capabilities of each Service's aircraft and supporting systems can complement each other to enhance both force survivability and combat effectiveness, and permit the full exploitation of capabilities in contingencies, as well as in major theater wars. The importance of integrated training was also evident in the need for interoperability between the deep-strike assets assigned to Task Force Hawk (Apache attack helicopters and multiple-launch rocket systems) and other deep-strike assets such as fixed-wing aircraft and their command-and-control network. Operation Allied Force underscores the criticality of joint doctrine, interoperability training, and supporting Service doctrine, tactics, techniques, and procedures. Greater emphasis must be placed on interoperability training among our own forces, with those of our allies, other nations, and partners; as well as on interagency training within our Government.

. . . The ability to plan, conduct, and sustain complex integrated operations of this kind demonstrated both a very high level of professional skill and the availability of material resources that were adequate for the task at hand. Losses due to accidents were few; indeed, they were even below levels typically anticipated in peacetime operations. The capability of U.S. forces to achieve this degree of success is reassuring, but must be tempered by an understanding of the indirect costs in terms of reduced readiness in U.S.-based forces and the post-conflict "reconstitution" expenses necessary to restore the deployed forces to a satisfactory steady-state operational tempo. Further, as discussed elsewhere, certain key force elements were deployed to this conflict as a very high proportion of their total inventory. Recognizing the challenges presented by the Kosovo operation, the Department is reviewing its planning for both peacetime and wartime readiness. Previous sections of this report have discussed how our troops quickly solved the problems associated with the limited transportation infrastructure in Albania; how our engineers and other support personnel quickly constructed refugee facilities and distributed supplies, thereby providing critically needed shelter and preventing starvation; and how our pilots and their commanders quickly developed and implemented tactics and techniques to successfully attack Milosevic's elusive forces in Kosovo. These and their many other accomplishments make it clear that our people made Operation Allied Force a success. They were well trained, disciplined, and creative. Their ability to overcome the many challenges they faced through initiative and innovation is unrivaled among the world's military forces. The paramount lesson learned from Operation Allied Force is that the well being of our people must remain our first priority.

UNMANNED AERIAL VEHICLES (UAVs)

US reports on the lessons of Kosovo have stressed the importance of unmanned aerial vehicles (UAVs). For example, Secretary Cohen made the following statement in testimony to Congress.[424]

Unmanned aerial vehicles (UAVs) were used to an unprecedented degree in Operation Allied Force. The Army, Navy, and Air Force each employed UAV systems in the theater to conduct important reconnaissance operations, reducing the need to send manned aircraft into hostile airspace. These systems—the Army Hunter, Navy Pioneer, and Air Force Predator—reflect the state of the art in ground control and mission planning capabilities, airworthiness, and mission payloads. Other NATO members also contributed UAVs to the operation. German Droner UAVs were used to conduct battle damage assessments and to detect emerging targets in Kosovo. French and British UAV systems took part in the operation as well.

U.S. development of enhanced UAV capabilities is being pursued in programs such as Global Hawk. Lessons learned in operations over Kosovo will help in refining our plans for such longer-term UAV programs. Improved mission planning, improved processes for interaction between UAV operators and manned aircraft, frequent and realistic training opportunities, and equipment upgrades for individual UAVs all would benefit future force effectiveness.

While a significant number of UAVs were lost, their ability to loiter over hostile territory enabled them to provide surveillance information unavailable otherwise and avoided the risk of losing aircrews. Moreover, UAVs are designed deliberately to be expendable, with acceptable cost a higher priority than survivability. UAV losses during Operation Allied Force totaled 15 air vehicles, most of which are believed to have been lost to hostile action. Analysis of UAV operations is ongoing.

US UAV Programs

The Predator, an unmanned aerial vehicle, logged 2,000 flight hours in Kosovo and the Hunter logged about 900. UAVs were a key tool in ensuring low altitude and poor weather reconnaissance and intelligence coverage. The Predator, or Medium Altitude Endurance Unmanned Aerial Vehicle, is a good example of the emerging role of UAVs. It was first deployed to support US forces when they entered Bosnia before it had finished its demonstration phase—less than 19 months after the program started in 1996.

The Predator has a wingspan of 48 feet, a length of 26 feet, and weighs about 1,500 pounds when fully fueled. It flies around 90 miles per hour, and costs about $3.2 million. It can stay in the air for 40 hours, loiter over dangerous areas, and transmit real-time video images of what it is observing. These images can be relayed to ground stations anywhere in the world, and the USAF is developing methods to transmit the Predator information to manned attack aircraft. The aircraft is flown by rate pilots using the kind of controls found in normal cockpits to remotely control the aircraft. Targeting lasers have been fitted to three Predators on an experimental basis, and they seem to have been successful in targeting laser-guided bombs.[425]

General John Jumper described the importance of the Predator as follows in his testimony on the lessons of the war.[426]

Planners were aided by one of the most successful innovations of the air campaign. For the first time, we used the Predator Unmanned Aerial Vehicle (UAV) in a targeting role. Before Allied Force, the Predator could transmit targeting imagery to its operator on the ground as part of the intelligence collection network. During the air campaign, we reviewed Predator video in real-time and immediately provided pilots with the location of mobile Serb targets. Toward the end of the war, we equipped the Predator with a laser so that it could place a beam on a target—this identified it so a loitering strike aircraft could destroy it. We were able to successfully employ the Predator with laser only once before Allied Force ended, but in doing so, we developed a capability with great potential for rapid targeting.

The success of UAVs during Kosovo led Secretary of Defense William S. Cohen to issue a directive calling for a "strong renewed commitment" to UAVs on July 6, 1999. The directive stated that, "We are at a critical juncture in airborne reconnaissance . . . Technology, especially in the areas of sensors and processing, has moved forward at an amazing pace, and correspondingly, the demand for information has increase even more quickly. The opportunity is here to develop, acquire, and integrate unmanned reconnaissance capabilities into the force structure at a rapid, but prudent pace."[427]

The Cohen memo called for bringing the Predator into full production and providing the resources to ensure that Predator and Pioneer units would be fully supported and properly crewed. It called for the development of common, cross-service exploitation and dissemination systems in a netted, long-distance environment, and for discussions with allies of interoperability and common mission requirements.[428]

The memo also called for the eventual fielding of the USAF high altitude endurance UAV, the Global Hawk, which will be bigger than the Predator and have a higher speed and operating altitude. It is supposed to be able to fly for 40 hours, and have a 3,000-mile range and 65,000-foot ceiling The US is now considering buying more Global Hawk unmanned, long-endurance reconnaissance aircraft than it originally planned. Kosovo put continued stress on the USAF U-2 force, and has a total force of around 35, of which 20 are combat available at any given time. Recent deployments like Kosovo have shown that the Air Force needs either 10 more U-2s, or a larger force of the $15 million Global Hawks, which can fly for 30–40 hours versus 10–12 for the U-2. The Global Hawk is not electronically silenced to carry advanced signals intelligence (SIGINT) packages, but it can carry out advanced electro-optical and radar imaging missions, and can potentially be modified for SIGINT missions.[429]

The report on the lessons of the war that the US issued in January 2000 notes that,[430]

During Operation Allied Force, unmanned aerial vehicles were used extensively for surveillance and reconnaissance in much the same way they had been used earlier in Bosnia. In addition to using UAVs in these traditional roles, we developed innovative employment tactics whereby UAVs helped locate and target Serbian military forces in Kosovo. By providing target-location data back to the Combined Air Operations Center, the UAVs helped cueing fighter attacks against Serbian forces in the field. When employed in this way, UAVs were being used as a component of the forward-air-control system.

UAVs were also used to perform near-real-time battle damage assessment to allow timely re-strike and to cross-cue other ISR assets. The Navy used UAVs extensively to conduct surveillance of surface ships and coastal areas, where they successfully identified Yugoslav naval vessels, surveyed potential landing areas for the U.S. Marines, and targeted coastal defense radar sites. Despite problems, the successful application of UAVs in Kosovo clearly demonstrates their potential to become a highly flexible and effective ISR asset on the future battlefield. b. Needed Improvements

Although UAVs were used effectively during Operation Allied Force, a number of technical improvements are still needed to attain the full promise of these systems. In addition, the Department needs to improve the tactics, techniques, and procedures that guide UAV employment to better integrate their operations into overall campaign plans.

European UAV Programs

Britain, France, and Germany seem to have drawn similar lessons, and made good use of UAVs in the Balkans.[431] The British flew the Phoenix for 20 flights before the air campaign ended, beginning on June 6. The Marconi Phoenix had been developed to locate and designate targets for the British multiple launch rocket system and AS90 self-propelled howitzer, and to be integrated into the Ptarmigan command control system and Battlefield Artillery Targeting Engagement System. Unlike the other UAVs, it was being adapted from land-support to air support missions, and to provide targeting data for the Harrier GR7 and Britain continued to use the Phoenix to support the KFOR peacekeeping mission after the air and missile campaign ended. Press reports indicate that Britain is now considering the purchase of additional UAVs like the Sender and Spector, and will work with the US to develop more advanced and longer-range UAVs.[432]

France and Germany flew some 180 CL-289 flights over Serbia and 220 over Bosnia, and found their use of UAVs to be equally successful. The CL-289 has a maximum speed of more than 700 kilometers per hour, a range of around 200 kilometers, a flight time of 40 minutes, and can operate at altitudes as low as 300 meters. It is equipped with optical and infrared cameras and a radio down-link to base. France also used drone called the Crecerelle that has a 50-kilometer range, can loiter for up to five hours, and is equipped with optical and infrared cameras.[433]

New Uses for UAVs and the Issue of Vulnerability

A number of experts note that it is now possible to equip UAVs with far more advanced high resolution ground surveillance radars than were available in Kosovo, including developmental systems like the 150 pound tactical synthetic aperture radar made by Northrop-Grumman, and a 115 pound system developed by Sandia. These developments potentially allow UAVs to perform for more sophisticated surveillance and targeting functions. Other developments allow UAVs to be armed in ways that would allow them to take on roles similar to low cost cruise missiles at attack land and enemy air defense targets. One example of such concepts is the Raptor program designed to develop a long-loiter UAV that could be used to attack surface-to-air missiles at their launch site. More advanced concepts involve UAVs carrying hypervelocity missiles with kinetic kill capabilities.[434]

Vulnerability, however, is an issue. The US lost three Predators and four Pioneers to hostile air defenses. It lost six Hunters—two for mechanical reasons, three to infrared guided missiles, and one to a radar guided missile. This raises serious questions about whether the US and NATO can afford to lose the required number of high cost UAVs in future wars, or whether the sensors in UAVs need to be improved to allow their use at something closer to stand-off ranges. There are also questions about the need for systems to directly feed UAV data and imagery to strike systems, about IFF functions and capability under poor visibility conditions, and how to integrate the data from UAVs with data from other systems and with the information from the UAVs operated by other countries.[435]

Officers like General John Jumper, the commander of Allied Air Forces Central Europe, however, feel that some of these issues are actually an incentive for using UAVs.[436] The counter-argument to the vulnerability and battle management of UAVs is that any losses of UAVs are far cheaper than losses of manned aircraft, and such losses are much more likely in any conflict involving advanced surface-to-air missile systems like the S-300 series. UAVs require far less electronic warfare support, and do not need support from mission packages. UAVs also are cheap enough so that European countries can afford them, and they can be used to bridge the growing gap between the level of tactical technology used by the US and Europe.

The success of UAVs in Kosovo, even in fog and haze, highlights the need to develop more advanced and less vulnerable UAVs, to provide them in greater numbers with better secure real time data links, and to consider rapid procurement of larger numbers of systems. [437] It again raises long-standing questions about the slow overall progress of the UAV effort and the adequacy of the existing US and European inventory to support intense, joint, theater-level operations.[438]

URBAN WARFARE AND MILITARY OPERATIONS IN BUILT-UP AREAS (MOBA); HUMAN SHIELDS

Reports indicate that US Army urban training for the peace keeping mission in Kosovo revealed a broader need for more training in urban warfare and built-up areas, and dedicated manportable and squad-level equipment to give US forces an edge in such fighting.[439] The US Army, for example, completed a major new Mounted Urban Warfare Training Site at Fort Knox in Kentucky in September 1999. While the facility had been planned for nearly ten years, the problems raised in Kosovo helped rush its completion, and it will be used in cooperation with the US Army Aviation and Missile Command in Huntsville. The facility is designed for armored, heliborne, and light infantry operations and can be used to simulate different cities, languages, sounds, and civilian conditions.[440]

Kosovo also revealed a broader problem in dealing with urban warfare and built-up areas. Episodes like the strike on the Chinese embassy reveal a need for fully up-to-date maps of urban and built-up areas that reliably show the location of all sensitive collateral damage targets. It was equally clear that NATO intelligence and targeteers have major problems in learning enough about Serbian cities and the facilities in these cities to know what targets were really important, to plan strikes to produce the right level of damage, and then to assess battle damage. NATO found that such target is extremely difficult to improvise, particularly when minimizing collateral damage is at an absolute premium. *New kinds of imagery and maps are also required to support the most effective use of precision-guided weapons.*

The problem of urban warfare is even more difficult when friendly civilians, and civilian facilities and equipment, are used as shields by enemy forces, and enemies disperse in friendly built-up or urban areas. Most NATO reconnaissance systems did not have the resolution to easily distinguish military targets from civilian targets, and the problems were far worse under poor weather conditions or when time urgent movements were involved.

The need to minimize collateral damage and protecting friendly civilians is likely to force any advanced technology force that is sensitive to the political issues involved to redefine its reconnaissance and targeting systems. Put differently, human shields are now an effective, low-cost form of asymmetric warfare. The development of improved attack systems to deal with this situation is a major priority for the US Air Force Research Laboratory, and the US is considering modifying airborne sensor systems, developing advanced UAVs, and modifying JDAM to allow it to strike hostile targets in urban environments.[441]

12

Beyond Air and Missile Power: The Ground Phase of Kosovo, Nation-Building, and Continuing Instability in the Balkans

Any analysis of the NATO air and missile campaign in Kosovo must recognize that NATO did not "win" in the sense that the air campaign produced anything approaching a grand strategic outcome. NATO ended the air and missile campaign in an environment where it had to deal with the reality of up to 1.4 million refugees and an unknown number of Kosovar dead. It must also deal with much broader issues in shaping regional stability and the future of Kosovo.

THE STRATEGIC CONSEQUENCES OF A "PEACE"

Hopefully, the world will have learned enough from Dayton and Somalia to understand that negotiations do not change human nature and the current agreement between the UN and NATO and Serbia will simply be a prelude to continuing problems in Kosovo and the Balkans. In Kosovo, however, peace may also become an extension of war by other means. It will also involve far more than a settlement between Serbia and the Muslim-Albanian Kosovars.

Any peace that truly results in conflict resolution and regional stability must deal with the following regional issues:

- *A united Bosnia remains a dangerous fiction*: The Serbian part of Bosnia is still effectively a different country—allied with Serbia proper. With a few exceptions, Croats and Muslims find it difficult to live and work together. The US had to suspend military assistance to Bosnia during the current crisis because of the refusal of the Croats to work together with the Muslims. The hatreds and resentments in Bosnia could combine with those in Kosovo and Serbia to create another Balkan war.

This means that any peacekeeping effort affecting Kosovo interacts with the peacekeeping effort in Bosnia. The US still has a heavy brigade in Bosnia and there is still a massive peace keeping force. This presence now seems likely to continue for the next half decade. Even so, there is a serious risk that the slow drift towards ethnic partition will end in violent Serbian and/or Croatian separatism.

- *Croatian ambitions*: Croatia has been the quiet beneficiary of the NATO air and missile campaign. It is watching Serbia decline sharply as a military power, and it may act on Serbian weakness. Regional stability will require a continuing NATO effort to ensure that Croatia does not act upon its ambitions.

- *Montenegro*: The Kosovo crisis has made Montenegro even more critical to Serbia, and Serbia even more threatening to Montenegro. Serbian may respond by attempting a quiet coup, while Montenegro may wish to move towards independence and ties to the West. The fact that Montenegro is Serbia's only access to the sea, and is now the only real remnant of "Yugoslavia" and "greater Serbia." This makes any such Montenegrin actions a potential source of future tensions and conflicts. NATO and/or the UN will have to decide whether to try to deal with these issues, or ignore them in the same way that the Dayton Agreement ignored the Kosovars.

- *Macedonia*: Macedonia has no real military forces, and will either need continuing peace keeping support to secure its borders or military aid and assistance. It will have to deal with both a hostile Serbia and potentially hostile Muslim Kosovars who remember Macedonia's treatment of refugees. Macedonia may also experience internal instability because of pro-Serbian and pro-Kosovar factions. If NATO and/or the UN do not provide a peacekeeping force to secure the border between Macedonia and Kosovo/Serbia, there is a good change of future low-level conflict and/or that Macedonia will be used as a route to smuggle arms and men into Kosovo.

- *Albania*: Albania is also militarily weak and divided. At the same time, it is likely to find any compromised peace inadequate and to support the KLA or some similar Kosovar Muslim effort to win independence. It has reason to see Kosovar independence as the prelude to the creation of a greater Albania, and to encourage Montenegrin separatism. At the same time, growing ethnic separatism in Bosnia could lead to a religious alliance between the Bosnia Muslims and Albania. If NATO and/or the UN do not provide a long-term peacekeeping force to secure the border between Albanian and Kosovo/Serbia/Montenegro, Albania is almost certain to be used as a route to smuggle arms and men into Kosovo.

- *Hungary, Romania, and Bulgaria*: A compromised peace settlement is almost certain to lead to continuing tension between Serbia and its northern and eastern neighbors. This will inevitably interact with the future of NATO expansion and tensions with Russia. There is a serious risk that NATO-Hungary-Romania-Bulgaria will become one bloc and Serbia and Russia another.

- *Russia and China versus Containment*: Unless a peace agreement is linked to a rigid arms control agreement, there is a good chance that Russia and China will become major suppliers for Serbian rearmament and actively resist any Western efforts to contain Serbia. Peace will effectively create a new Iraq on the edge of Europe. This, in turn, will exacerbate the arms race in the nations surrounding Serbia. It seems highly questionable whether a "peace" can work that does not include something approaching a regional arms control plan. It seems equally questionable that there can be a regional arms control plan.

- *Locking in NATO, US and European Power Projection Forces*: One potential implication of the previous problems is that NATO countries will find themselves projecting 20,000–60,000 troops into the Balkans under a UN and international management indefinitely into the future. The end result will be to tie up military manpower and resources, and a good part of the limited power projection capability of the major members of the Alliance, in a frustrating and unpopular mission. It is also likely to limit future Western contributions to peacekeeping in other regions.

Previous peacemaking efforts have tended to concentrate on the issues of the moment and ignore the need for lasting regional strategic stability. The divisions and pressures surrounding this crisis lend themselves to similar opportunism. If so, the end result will almost certainly fail to meet the needs of the people in the Balkans. The range of problems in the region means an enduring NATO commitment to the region. It also means that the US must look beyond a strategy committed primarily to dealing with major regional contingencies in Korea and the Gulf, and adopt a de facto strategy of three major regional containments—the Gulf, Korea, and the Balkans.

THE ECONOMIC AND MILITARY CONSEQUENCES OF A "PEACE": THE PROBLEMS IN KOSOVO AND SERBIA

It is already clear that the "peace" in Kosovo is faltering and may well fail. There is nothing inherently wrong or naïve about the principles the G8 agreed to on May 6, the terms NATO set forth for a peace settlement during the Washington summit, or the much more vague agreement that the UN and NATO finally reached with Serbia. There is, however, much that is dangerous about assuming that a settlement can be made to work without a far greater consensus than now exists, a massive peacekeeping effort lasting half a decade, arms control, and mass economic aid.[442]

Each of the major aspects of the settlement NATO and Serbia agreed to and which were approved in the UN Security Council resolution raises major problems for the future. The terms of this settlement are shown in italics and the problems in regular text below.[443]

Demands in particular that the Federal Republic of Yugoslavia put an immediate and verifiable end to violence and repression in Kosovo, and begin to complete verifiable phased withdrawal from Kosovo of all military, police and paramilitary forces according to a rapid timetable, with which the deployment of the international security presence in Kosovo will be synchronized; Confirms that after the withdrawal an agreed number of Yugoslav and Serb military and police personnel will be permitted to return to Kosovo; Decides on the deployment in Kosovo, under United Nations auspices, of international civil and security presences, with appropriate equipment and personnel as required, and welcomes the agreement of the Federal Republic of Yugoslavia to such presences; Requests the Secretary-General to appoint, in consultation with the Security Council, a Special Representative to control the implementation of the international civil presence, and further requests the Secretary-General to instruct his Special Representative to coordinate closely with the international security presence to ensure that both presences operate towards the same goals and in a mutually supportive manner; Authorizes Member States and relevant international organizations to establish the international security presence in Kosovo as set out in point 4 of annex 2 with all necessary means to fulfill its responsibilities; Affirms the need for the rapid early deployment of effective international civil and security presences to Kosovo, and demands that the parties cooperate fully in their deployment.

It may prove impossible to achieve internal security without de facto partition of Kosovo along ethnic lines. The Albanian Kosovars have bitter memories of discrimination and ethnic cleansing. Some 11,334 Kosovars have been reported as missing and presumed dead, and while the UN prosecutors had only exhumed 195 of 529 suspected grave sites in Kosovo by mid-November, they had already found 2,108 bodies.[444]

By early August 1999, Kosovar reprisals had already killed at least 200 Serbs in Kosovo. While nearly 90% of the roughly 800,000 Kosovar Albanians that had fled the country had returned to the province, there had been a massive Serbian exodus. For example, the Serbian population of Pristina had fallen from 40,000 to 1,000. Much of the Serbian population had fled the rest of the province or concentrated in largely Serbian areas, and the same was true of the Kosovar gypsies—which had back the Serbs before and during the war.[445]

In mid-September 1999, three months after the NATO peacekeeping force had enter Kosovo, Albanian Kosovar attacks on the Serbs had reduced the Serbian population in Kosovo from around 200,000 to anywhere from 30,000 to 99,000. (The Red Cross estimate supported the lower figure, based on 173,000 Serbian refugees registered in Serbia; the UNHCR estimated that 97,000 Serbs and some 73,000 other ethnic minorities still remained in Kosovo.)

During the fall and winter there were continuing clashes in several regions in Kosovo, including Mitrovica in the north and Gniljane in the east, and Mitrovica had been partitioned along ethnic lines. Serbian forces were reinfiltrating into Kosovo, and the KLA had officially transformed, but was shifting much of its personnel into a civil defense corps while attempting to became the center of both political action and the native police force in Kosovo.[446]

An analysis in February 2000 found there were 190,000 Serbia refugees from Kosovo in Serbia. These had joined 300,000 earlier refugees from Croatia, 200,000 from Bosnia, and 4,500 from Slovenia and Macedonia.[447] NATO peacekeeping forces were having serious problems in separating warring Kosovar and Serbian populations, in the Mitrovica area, Kosovars were leaving Serbia proper, and the KLA was organizing forces in Serbia to "protect" Kosovars there.[448]

Partition, however, means finding some acceptable dividing line. This might logically mean giving Serbia control of the key Lignite and economic resources in the north, but this would impoverish the Muslim Kosovars, who had an average per capita income only one-third that of Serbia before the crisis began. There are also a significant number of Muslim Kosovars who live in Serbia proper. At the same time, Serbian monasteries and cultural/historical areas are scattered throughout much of Kosovo, including in the mountains in the south.

Partition, however, would also mean (a) creating a new economic structure to allow the Muslim Kosovars to live without dependence on Serbia and this means economic links to Albania, (b) relocating Serbs to partitioned and secure areas, (c) relocating any Muslim Kosovars outside the Serbian area, and (d) finding some way to divide up and secure key urban areas and infrastructure.[449]

NATO and the UN have found that it is extraordinarily difficult to suddenly fill the kind of power vacuum that emerges once a civil war ends in the defeat of the former government. One lesson of Kosovo may prove to be that effective peace keeping requires the creation of new kinds of peace enforcing units with rapid deployment capability. More tragically, another may be that a peace based on the illusion that the king's men can rebuild an ethnic Humpty Dumpty is only a prelude to future problems.

The responsibilities of the international security presence to be deployed and acting in Kosovo will include: a. Deterring renewed hostilities, maintaining and where necessary enforcing a cease-fire, and ensuring the withdrawal and preventing the return into Kosovo of Federal and Republic military, police and paramilitary forces . . . ; b. Demilitarizing the Kosovo Liberation Army (KLA) and other armed Kosovo Albanian groups as required . . . ; c. Establishing a secure environment in which refugees and displaced persons can return home in safety, the international civil presence can operate, a transitional administration can be established, and humanitarian aid can be delivered; d. Ensuring public safety and order until the international civil presence can take responsibility for this task; e. Supervising demining until the international civil presence can, as appropriate, take over responsibility for this task; f. Supporting, as appropriate, and coordinating closely with the work of the international civil presence; g. Conducting border monitoring duties as required; h. Ensuring the protection and freedom of. . . .

One test of this part of the agreement is whether Serbia can eventually deploy border guards for Kosovo in ways the Kosovars can live with. If not, Serbia cannot maintain sovereignty. If so, it may lead to low-level conflict with the KLA and possibly Albania as well. A significant number of Serbians did return to Kosovo in the fall of 1999, but they were only safe where KFOR troops could provide them with security and vengeance killings were routine incidents.[450]

Another problem is trying to truly disarm the KLA. The KLA signed an agreement with KFOR on June 21, 1999 that stipulated that it would disband as of September 20, 1999. This Undertaking of Demilitarization, however, created a "Kosovo Corps" of 3,000 regulars with 2,000 reserves, and the idea it would have 10% "minority (i.e. Serbian) membership seems unrealistic. The KLA did transfer more arms to the NATO peacekeeping force than it originally promised (more than 9,000 rifles, 800 machine guns, 300 anti-tank weapons, 178 mortars 27,000 hand grenades, 1,200 mortar bombs, over a ton of explosives and 5.5 million rounds of ammunition as of September 1999).[451] The new force, however, has 200 weapons to guard bases and headquarters and 1,800 rifles in trust, and the KLA received so many weapons towards the end of the war that it almost certainly has major stockpiles hidden in both Kosovo and Albania.

Many experts feel the KLA is still seeking to remain a covert army rather than become a civil defense group.[452] Given the hatreds involved, it may well be that the peacekeeping force will have to secure the entire mix of Serbian-Montenegrin-Albanian-Macedonian borders, provide a police force for the entire area in the Muslim-Kosovar and mixed areas of Kosovo, and try to train a neutral police and security force of native residents. If not, any remaining elements—Serbian or Kosovar—are likely to be violently irredentist and trigger low-intensity conflict that the peacekeepers will have to suppress.[453]

If is far too soon to compare the problems raised by KLA in any way to the problems raised by the Afghan Mujahideen, but it is clear that there is a serious risk that one war's ally of convenience can become the enemy of a successful peace. The US and the West may well be entering an era of informal and ad hoc coalitions. There have already been Kosovar massacres of Serbians in Kosovo, and there is clearly a power struggle to seize control of the instruments of government, key economic positions, and to punish the Serbs and drive them out of the country.[454] In retrospect, Kosovo is somewhat similar to Iraq after the Gulf War. The US and NATO needed to prepare to deal with their wartime allies and failed to do so.

Decides on the deployment in Kosovo, under United Nations auspices, of international civil and security presences, with appropriate equipment and personnel as required, and welcomes the agreement of the Federal Republic of Yugoslavia to such presences.

The words imply a force that can aid and secure 1.8 to 2.0 million Serbs and Muslim Kosovars for at least several years. (The Chief of Staff of the US Army has already estimated a minimum of four years.) They also imply securing the borders of Kosovo, and raise all of the same problems discussed earlier in terms of creating native security forces. NATO is already planning to deploy around 50,000 men to implement the operation. If the low level fighting that started between the Serbs and Albanian Kosovars after the peacekeeping force was deployed intensifies, things could be a great deal worse, and Russia may prove to be a "wild card."

The UN has found it extremely difficult to recruit civil security and aid personnel, and to get nations to pay from them. NATO has found it equally difficult to get money, that members do not agree to deploy added men in a crisis, and that serious differences exist over how to best perform the role of peace making. Some deal with treatment of the population and peace-keeping issues, but others are an awkward version of the US versus European differences in military standards and capabilities.[455]

The US deployment at Camp Bondsteel, for example, created semi-permanent facilities that appeared to be needless luxury to many Europeans and which made a sharp contrast to the plight of local Kosovars. The Camp also put some 4,860 US troops (77% of the force) behind dozens of earthen berms, concrete barriers, 11 guard towers, and some 10 miles of barbed wire.[456] The experience of the Marine Corps Barracks in Lebanon and Al Khobar Towers in Saudi Arabia justify some of this isolation and construction, but no other force has similar facilities, and it is clear that no one is really welcoming Serbians into any form of security force.

Authorizes the Secretary-General, with the assistance of relevant international organizations, to establish an international civil presence in Kosovo in order to provide an interim administration for Kosovo under which the people of Kosovo can enjoy substantial autonomy within the Federal Republic of Yugoslavia, and which will provide transitional administration while establishing and overseeing the development of provisional democratic self-governing institutions to ensure conditions for a peaceful and normal life for all inhabitants of Kosovo:

This vague agreement has already raised the issue of independence versus the return of the Serbian government, and created major questions about the future political and military status of the KLA. Without partition, it is almost certain to exacerbate the fault lines in the nations supporting the UN resolution and contributing to the peacemaking force and UN (e.g., NATO versus Russia and China).

With ethnic partition, it is an almost certain road to near independence or independence and will provoke acute Serbian resistance. The practical problems will be compounded by the need to simultaneously create a Kosovo-wide peace and police force and an entity to both deal with repatriation and economic aid. One key question is who will pay for such a body.

The safe and free return of all refugees and displaced persons and unimpeded access to Kosovo by humanitarian aid organizations:

A key question is who will really provide the scale of aid required, and what tensions will arise from the effort to exclude Serbia from such aid until Milosevic is gone. Even if one ignores Serbia, there is no way that the economy of Kosovo can handle full repatriation without massive outside aid. The displaced population and the loss of so many houses and businesses has already presented a massive human management problem with all kinds of legal and practical problems. It also requires the ability to adjudicate every property dispute that arises. Once again, it also means restructuring an economy that will have lost one agricultural season, and where the average per capita income was one-third that in Serbia, will raise major practical problems.

Promoting the establishment, pending a final settlement, of substantial auton-omy and self-government in Kosovo, taking full account of annex 2 and of the Rambouillet accords (S/1999/648); Performing basic civilian administrative functions where and as long as required), organizing and overseeing the develop-ment of provisional institutions for democratic and autonomous self-government pending a political settlement, including the holding of elections; transferring, as these institutions are established, its administrative responsibilities while oversee-ing and supporting the consolidation of Kosovo's local provisional institutions and other peace-building activities; facilitating a political process designed to determine Kosovo's future status, taking into account the Rambouillet accords (S/ 1999/648); In a final stage, overseeing the transfer of authority from Kosovo's provisional institutions to institutions established under a political settlement:

This provision goes far beyond forging swords into plowshares and calls for forging hatred into love. It does not deal with any aspect of men as they are, and only with hopes for what they should be. In effect, everyone gets everything and everyone gets nothing. The practical impact has been to leave virtually every security issue unaddressed, but still active as incentives for civil war between Serbia and the KLA at whatever level either side can get away with in spite of the peacekeeping force.

Supporting the reconstruction of key infrastructure and other economic re-construction:

This provision may prove to be a noble promise that no one is prepared to pay for, even if the region is defined simply as Kosovo-Serbia-Montenegro. The UN and NATO have already failed by narrow definition of this clause. As winter settled in Kosovo, there was virtually no water and power for some two million residents and almost none of the 125,000 homes damaged in the fighting had been rebuilt. Some 300,000 people were without heated shelters, and the backlog of trucks waiting to bring relief was so great that it took an average of four days from loading a relief truck to the time it reached Kosovo.[457]

If the definition is made broader, it potentially means simultaneously indulging in nation-building in every part of the former Yugoslavia. At a more practical level, this could mean providing economic incentives to both Serb and Muslim Kosovars to accept a peace settlement. This latter option is far more practical, but it still leaves the question open of who will give Serbia any aid with its current government and how to decide on building a Kosovar economy that can meet Kosovar Muslim expectations.

Such provisions also raises the much broader problem of how outside powers can "rebuild" economies that suffer as much from years of past mismanagement and state control as from war.[458] Serbia had severely weakened the economy of Kosovo for nearly a decade before the war began, establishing a pattern of massive ethnic discrimination against Kosovo that gave it a far lower average per capita income than Serbia proper and forced many ethnic Kosovar Albanians out of important and high paying jobs. This discrimination now compounds the cost of aid to Kosovo and the backlash effect of Kosovar control of the province and reaction to the Serbs. At the same time, Milosevic horribly mismanaged the economy of his own country for virtually the same period. Moreover, both states are surrounded by weak economies and Bosnia still presents major and related problems. The reconstruction of wartime damage must not be confused with success in rebuilding failed economies. At the same time, conflict resolution may ultimately depend on regional economic success of a kind that involves precisely this kind of broad national (and regional) economic restructuring.

The European Union and World Bank summit on aid to Kosovo and the region that took place on July 30, 1999, only began to address these issues, although the IMF did address the need for broader aid commitments to Montenegro, Albania, Macedonia, Romania, and Bulgaria, and costed them at $1.25 billion to $2.25 billion a year.[459]

Kofi Annan, the Secretary General of the United Nations, warned of many of these problems in a report to the General Assembly on September 20, 1999. His report cautioned that the UN Interim Administration in Kosovo (UNMIK) face three pressing challenges. First, to firmly establish the rule of law, show extremists that ethnically motivated murders and violence will not be tolerated, and provide security for all communities, especially for vulnerable minorities. Second, to ensure temporary winterized accommodation for at least 350,000 people in need.

Such efforts, however, could only be a stop gap solution, and the restoration of public utilities, including electricity generation, must be addressed on an emergency basis along with long-term efforts at reconstruction. Finally, the future stability of the territory depended on successful demobilization of the Kosovo Liberation Army and other armed elements. Somewhat ironically, the headlines in US papers announced some four days later that the US now considered independence for Kosovo to be the best policy option and that it was strengthening Kosovar institutions to prepare for that option.[460]

Most "peaces" in history have involved unsatisfactory compromises whose main rationale is that they are better than war. As a result, almost all successful peace agreements are based to some extent on false promises, the deliberate neglect of many issues, and are inherently unstable. It is at least possible that the peace keeping phase of Kosovo can lead to outcomes no worse than most peace settlements since the end of World War II.

There is a real danger, however, that the peacekeeping phase in Kosovo will prove to be so bitter, and conducted between such hostile parties, that it will degenerate into a low intensity ground war or simply be the prelude to future crises. About the only thing that is clear is that Kosovo is far from over and the Balkans are far from stable. *Once again, there is a clear need to consider the broader aspects of conflict resolution and to carefully consider what can be done to create post-conflict national and regional stability. This is as much a lesson of Kosovo as it is of past wars.*

As a result, Kosovo is likely to continue to be a test bed for international peacekeeping and nation-building exercises long after the end of a "victorious" air and missile campaign. It is also a symbol of a pattern of global diplomatic and military activity filled with similar internal contradictions. There is no doubt that the world is still a violent place.

One recent estimate indicates that some 35 million individuals are involved in some 22 regional conflicts and humanitarian emergencies.[461] The number of UN peacekeeping missions has also increased since the end of the Cold War. There were 13 such operations during 1945–1988, and 36 have been mounted since that time. A total of 17 were active in late 1999, including East Timor. While UN peacekeeping efforts peaked in the early 1990s, with some 80,000 personnel and an annual cost of around $3 billion, there were still 11,000 peace keepers active in 1999—not counting the unassigned NATO and Russian military forces in Kosovo.[462]

The practical problems raised in Kosovo apply to virtually all current peacekeeping efforts. There is no "good" or "bad" side, simply a stronger side that makes the weaker side(s) suffer. There is at best a fragile UN consensus for limited humanitarian and military action, and often the action must take place outside or parallel to the UN and be regional. There is no consensus as to what should trigger a peace making mission, what levels of force are justified, how to link military action to full conflict resolution, and how to link military action to the economic and political "nation-building" necessary to create a lasting peace. Efforts to transform the UN into an organization capable of organizing and fighting a peacemaking mission have largely failed, and massive ambiguities exist regarding the UN's role in enforcing civil rights and dealing with potential war crimes— which are still often defined in de facto terms as the most heinous acts of the strongest side.

It is probably axiomatic that diplomacy cannot save most failed nations, and neither can military force. It is equally clear that the world cannot stand by and do nothing. As a result, many of the grand strategic, strategic, and military lessons of Kosovo are likely to be only one case study in what will be decades of painful efforts to learn how the world can fight limited wars in the name of humanitarian causes and nation-building. Many of these conflicts are likely to expose the same inherent contradictions as Kosovo when war is waged in the name of peace.

These lessons are reflected in the ambiguities in the address President Clinton gave to the opening of the UN General Assembly on September 21, 1999 and in

Secretary General Annan's annual report to the General Assembly on September 20. President Clinton's speech did not build on the lessons of Kosovo to clarify a well-defined "Clinton Doctrine." It instead summarized the very real challenges and problems the US and the world face in going from specific cases like Kosovo to any broader approach to peacemaking.[463]

The . . . resolution I hope we will make today is to strengthen the capacity of the international community to prevent and, whenever possible, to stop outbreaks of mass killing and displacement. This requires, as we all know, shared responsibility—like the one West African nations accepted when they acted to restore peace in Sierra Leone; the one 19 democracies in NATO embraced to stop ethnic cleansing in Bosnia and Kosovo; the one Asian and Pacific nations have now assumed in East Timor, with the strong support from the entire United Nations, including the United States.

Secretary General Annan spoke for all of us during the Kosovo conflict, and more recently in regard to East Timor, when he said that ethnic cleansers and mass murderers can find no refuge in the United Nations, no source of comfort or justification in its charter. We must do more to make these words real. Of course, we must approach this challenge with some considerable degree of humility. It is easy to say, never again; but much harder to make it so. Promising too much can be as cruel as caring too little.

But difficulties, dangers and costs are not an argument for doing nothing. When we are faced with deliberate, organized campaigns to murder whole peoples, or expel them from their land, the care of victims is important, but not enough. We should work to end the violence.

Our response in every case cannot or should not be the same. Sometimes collective military forces is both appropriate and feasible. Sometimes concerted economic and political pressure, combined with diplomacy, is a better answer, as it was in making possible the introduction of forces in East Timor.

Of course, the way the international community responds will depend upon the capacity of countries to act, and on their perception of their national interests. NATO acted in Kosovo, for example, to stop a vicious campaign of ethnic cleansing in a place where we had important interests at stake, and the ability to act collectively. The same considerations brought Nigerian troops and their partners to Sierra Leone, and Australians and others to East Timor. That is proper—so long as we work together, support each other, and do not abdicate our collective responsibility.

I know that some are troubled that the United States and others cannot respond to every humanitarian catastrophe in the world. We cannot do everything everywhere. But simply because we have different interests in different parts of the world does not mean we can be indifferent to the destruction of innocents in any part of the world.

That is why we have supported the efforts of Africans to resolve the deadly conflicts that have raged through parts of their continent; why we are working with friends in Africa to build the Africa Crisis Response Initiative, which has now trained more than 4,000 peacekeepers from six countries; why we are helping to establish an international coalition against genocide, to bring nations together to stop the flow of money and arms to those who commit crimes against humanity.

There is also critical need for countries emerging from conflict to build police institutions, accountable to people and the law—often with the help of civilian police from other nations. We need international forces with the training to fill the gap between local police and military peacekeepers, as French, Argentine, Italian and other military police have done in Haiti and Bosnia. We will work with our partners in the UN to continue to ensure such forces can deploy when they're needed.

What is the role of the UN in preventing mass slaughter and dislocation? Very large. Even in Kosovo, NATO's actions followed a clear consensus, expressed in several Security Council resolutions that the atrocities committed by Serb forces were unacceptable; that the international community had a compelling interest in seeing them end. Had we chosen to do nothing in the face of this brutality, I do not believe we would have strengthened the United Nations. Instead, we would have risked discrediting everything it stands for.

By acting as we did, we helped to vindicate the principles and purposes of the UN Charter, to give the UN the opportunity it now has to play the central role in shaping Kosovo's future. In the real world, principles often collide, and tough choices must be made. The outcome in Kosovo is hopeful.

During that same session, Secretary General Annan warned the UN that the world faced a long list of issues in moving beyond Kosovo to a global approach to dealing with humanitarian crises and ethnic wars.[464]

State sovereignty, in its most basic sense, is being redefined by the forces of globalization and international cooperation. The State is now widely understood to be the servant of its people, and not vice versa. At the same time, individual sovereignty—and by this I mean the human rights and fundamental freedoms of each and every individual as enshrined in our Charter—has been enhanced by a renewed consciousness of the right of every individual to control his or her own destiny.

These parallel developments—remarkable and, in many ways, welcome—do not lend themselves to easy interpretations or simple conclusions. They do, however, demand of us a willingness to think anew—about how the United Nations responds to the political, human rights and humanitarian crises affecting so much of the world; about the means employed by the international community in situations of need; and about our willingness to act in some areas of conflict, while limiting ourselves to humanitarian palliatives in many other crises whose daily toll of death and suffering ought to shame us into action.

. . . From Sierra Leone to the Sudan to Angola to the Balkans to Cambodia and to Afghanistan, there are a great number of peoples who need more than just words of sympathy from the international community. They need a real and sustained commitment to help end their cycles of violence, and launch them on a safe passage to prosperity.

While the genocide in Rwanda will define for our generation the consequences of inaction in the face of mass murder, the more recent conflict in Kosovo has prompted important questions about the consequences of action in the absence of complete unity on the part of the international community. It has cast in stark relief the dilemma of what has been called humanitarian intervention: on one side, the question of the legitimacy of an action taken by a regional organization without a United Nations mandate; on the other, the universally recognized imperative of effectively halting gross and systematic violations of human rights with grave humanitarian consequences.

The inability of the international community in the case of Kosovo to reconcile these two equally compelling interests—universal legitimacy and effectiveness in defense of human rights—can only be viewed as a tragedy. It has revealed the core challenge to the Security Council and to the United Nations as a whole in the next century, to forge unity behind the principle that massive and systematic violations of human rights—wherever they may take place—should not be allowed to stand.

The Kosovo conflict and its outcome have prompted a wide debate of profound importance to the resolution of conflicts from the Balkans to Central Africa to East Asia. And to each side in this critical debate, difficult questions can be posed.

To those for whom the greatest threat to the future of international order is the use of force in the absence of a Security Council mandate, one might ask—not in the context of Kosovo—but in the context of Rwanda: If, in those dark days and hours leading up to the genocide, a coalition of States had been prepared to act in defense of the Tutsi population, but did not receive prompt Council authorization, should such a coalition have stood aside and allowed the horror to unfold?

To those for whom the Kosovo action heralded a new era when States and groups of States can take military action outside the established mechanisms for enforcing international law, one might ask: Is there not a danger of such interventions undermining the imperfect, yet resilient, security system created after the Second World War, and of setting dangerous precedents for future interventions without a clear criterion to decide who might invoke these precedents, and in what circumstances?

In response to this turbulent era of crises and interventions, there are those who have suggested that the Charter itself—with its roots in the aftermath of global inter-State war—is ill-suited to guide us in a world of ethnic wars and intra-State violence. I believe they are wrong.

The Charter is a living document, whose high principles still define the aspirations of peoples everywhere for lives of peace, dignity and development. Nothing in the Charter precludes a recognition that there are rights beyond borders. Indeed, its very letter and spirit are the affirmation of those fundamental human rights. In short, it is not the deficiencies of the Charter which have brought us to this juncture, but our difficulties in applying its principles to a new era; an era when strictly traditional notions of sovereignty can no longer do justice to the aspirations of peoples everywhere to attain their fundamental freedoms.

The sovereign States who drafted the Charter over half a century ago were dedicated to peace, but experienced in war. They knew the terror of conflict, but knew equally that there are times when the use of force may be legitimate in the pursuit of peace. That is why the Charter's own words declare that "armed force shall not be used, save in the common interest". But what is that common interest? Who shall define it? Who will defend it? Under whose authority? And with what means of intervention? These are the monumental questions facing us as we enter the new century. While I will not propose specific answers or criteria, I shall identify four aspects of intervention which I believe hold important lessons for resolving future conflicts.

First, it is important to define intervention as broadly as possible, to include actions along a wide continuum from the most pacific to the most coercive. A tragic irony of many of the crises that continue to go unnoticed and unchallenged today is that they could be dealt with by far less perilous acts of intervention than the one we witnessed recently in Yugoslavia. And yet, the commitment of the international community to peacekeeping, to humanitarian assistance, to rehabilitation and reconstruction varies greatly from region to region, and crisis to crisis.

If the new commitment to intervention in the face of extreme suffering is to retain the support of the world's peoples, it must be—and must be seen to be—fairly and consistently applied, irrespective of region or nation. Humanity, after all, is indivisible. It is also necessary to recognize that any armed intervention is itself a result of the failure of prevention. As we consider the future of intervention, we must redouble our efforts to enhance our preventive capabilities—including early warning, preventive diplomacy, preventive deployment and preventive disarmament.

A recent powerful tool of deterrence has been the actions of the Tribunals for Rwanda and the former Yugoslavia. In their battle against impunity lies a key to deterring crimes against humanity. With these concerns in mind, I have dedicated the introductory essay of my annual report to exploring ways of moving from a culture of reaction to a culture of prevention. Even the costliest policy of prevention is far cheaper, in lives and in resources, than the least expensive use of armed force.

Second, it is clear that sovereignty alone is not the only obstacle to effective action in human rights or humanitarian crises. No less significant are the ways in which the Member States of the United Nations define their national interest in any given crisis.

Of course, the traditional pursuit of national interest is a permanent feature of international relations and of the life and work of the Security Council. But as the world has changed in profound ways since the end of the cold war, I believe our conceptions of national interest have failed to follow suit.

A new, more broadly defined, more widely conceived definition of national interest in the new century would, I am convinced, induce States to find far greater unity in the pursuit of such basic Charter values as democracy, pluralism, human rights, and the rule of law.

A global era requires global engagement. Indeed, in a growing number of challenges facing humanity, the collective interest is the national interest. Third, in the event that forceful intervention becomes necessary, we must ensure that the Security Council, the body charged with authorizing force under international law—is able to rise to the challenge.

The choice, as I said during the Kosovo conflict, must not be between Council unity and inaction in the face of genocide—as in the case of Rwanda, on the one hand; and Council division, and regional action, as in the case of Kosovo, on the other. In both cases, the Member States of the United Nations should have been able to find common ground in upholding the principles of the Charter, and acting in defense of our common humanity.

As important as the Council's enforcement power is its deterrent power. Unless it is able to assert itself collectively where the cause is just and where the means are available, its credibility in the eyes of the world may well suffer. If States bent on criminal behavior know that frontiers are not the absolute defense; if they know that the Security Council will take action to halt crimes against humanity, then they will not embark on such a course of action in expectation of sovereign impunity.

The Charter requires the Council to be the defender of the common interest, and unless it is seen to be so—in an era of human rights, interdependence, and globalization—there is a danger that others could seek to take its place.

. . . consistency is essential. Just as our commitment to humanitarian action must be universal if it is to be legitimate, so our commitment to peace cannot end with the cessation of hostilities. The aftermath of war requires no less skill, no less sacrifice, no fewer resources in order to forge a lasting peace and avoid a return to violence.

Kosovo—and other United Nations missions currently deployed or looming over the horizon—presents us with just such a challenge. Unless the United Nations is given the means and support to succeed, not only the peace, but the war, too, will be lost. From civil administration to policing to the creation of a civil society capable of sustaining a tolerant, pluralist, prosperous society, the challenges facing our peacekeeping, peacemaking and peace-building missions are immense.

But if we are given the means—in Kosovo and in Sierra Leone, in East Timor—we have a real opportunity to break the cycles of violence, once and for all.

Just as we have learned that the world cannot stand aside when gross and systematic violations of human rights are taking place, so we have also learned that intervention must be based on legitimate and universal principles if it is to enjoy the sustained support of the world's peoples.

This developing international norm in favor of intervention to protect civilians from wholesale slaughter will no doubt continue to pose profound challenges to the international community. Any such evolution in our understanding of State sovereignty and individual sovereignty will, in some quarters, be met with distrust, skepticism, even hostility. But it is an evolution that we should welcome.

Why? Because, despite its limitations and imperfections, it is testimony to a humanity that cares more, not less, for the suffering in its midst, and a humanity that will do more, and not less, to end it.

It is a hopeful sign at the end of the twentieth century.

It is tempting to try to go beyond the Secretary General's remarks and draw specific lessons about how the US, the West, the world, and the UN should deal with each of the issues raised by President Clinton and Secretary General Annan.[465] The fact is, however, that Kosovo is only one case study in what is going to be a long and painful set of experimental efforts to change the international system and learn empirically how to carry out effective peacekeeping. Like Korea, the Gulf War, Bosnia, Somalia, and the host of other "wars" that have recently been fought in the name of "peace," Kosovo is both a warning of the consequences of failing to act and a warning that action is extremely difficult. The broader lessons are ones that are going to have to be learned through further interventions and further fighting. They can only be learned the hard way.

Annex One:
Supporting Charts and Figures

The Role of British Forces in the NATO Air and Missile Campaign in Kosovo

UK Contribution to Operation Allied Force by Type of Sorties

Strike	1,008
Combat Air Patrol (CAP)	102
Airborne Early Warning (AEW)	184
Air-to-Air Refuelling (AAR)	324
Total	1,618

UK Aircraft Contributing to Operation Allied Force

Aircraft Type	Number
Harrier GR7	16
Sea Harrier FA2	7
Tornado GR1	12
E3D	3
Nimrod	1
Tristar	4
VC10	5
Total	48*

Sorties Flown

NATO	
Total Sorties	38,004
Total Strike Sorties	10,484
UK	
Total Sorties	1,618
Total Strike Sorties	1,008

UK Aircraft Munitions Released

Type of Munition	Number Released
1000 LB Bomb	230
Paveway II	226
Paveway III	18
RBL 755	532
Alarm	6
Total	1,012

Air Munitions Released

NATO Total	23,614
UK Total	1,011

Note: Excludes Helicopter force of 8 Chinook, 6 Puma and 4 Lynx (source: PJHQ).

Source: Lord Robertson of Port Ellen, Secretary of State for Defense, "Kosovo: An Account of the Crisis," London, Ministry of Defense, October 1999, http://www.mod.uk/news/kosovo/account.

The Role of French Forces in the NATO Air and Missile Campaign in Kosovo
(all prices in millions of French francs)

Air and Naval Air Force Deployments and Build-Up

	March 24	April 1	May 1	May 17	Flight Hours
Jaguar Strike/Attack	4	8	8	12	668
Mirage 2000D/Attack	5	7	12	15	332
Mirage F!-CT/Attack	-	-	-	10	-
Mirage 2000C Air Defense	8	8	8	8	2,222
Mirage F-1CR Recce	0	3	4	8	-
Mirage IVP Recce	0	2	3	3	-
Transall Gabriel Recce	0	1	1	1	-
Puma CSAR Support	4	4	4	4	-
E-3F AWACS	0	1	1	1	132
CS-135	0	3	3	6	1,040
Total Air Force	21	37	44	68	-
Super Etendard Naval Attack	16	16	16	16	-
Etendard IVP Recce	4	4	4	4	-
Total	41	57	64	88	-

Munitions Used

	Air Force			Naval Air Units		
Type	Quantity	Cost per Unit	Total Cost	Quantity	Cost per Unit	Total Cost
AS-30 laser missiles	6	2	12	2	2.7	5.4
1,000 kg. laser guided bombs	127	0.9	114.3	-	-	-
250 kg. laser guided bombs	187	0.165	30.8	268	0.28	75
250 kg. Mark 82 unguided bombs	128	0.022	2.8	-	-	-
250 kg. SAMPT 25 unguided bombs	270	0.036	9.7	-	-	-

Missions Flown

	Air Force Total	Air Force Effective	Naval Total	Naval Effective
Strike/Attack	851	420	412	324
Air Defense	476	-	-	-
Reconnaissance	149	-	-	-
Electronic Warfare	112	-	-	-
In-flight Refueling	320	-	-	-

Note: The naval air units left on June 1, 1999. Weather and other factors caused a number of missions not to be effective.

Source: Assemblee Nationale, Rapport d'Information, "Le cout de la participation de la France aux operations menees en vue du reglement de la crise au Kosovo," presente par Jean-Michel Boucheron, No. 1775, July 1, 1999.

Notes

1. Department of Defense, *Report to Congress: Kosovo/Operation Allied Forces After Action Report*, Washington, Department of Defense, January 31, 2000.

2. John Barry and Evan Thomas, "The Kosovo Cover-Up," *Newsweek*, May 15, 2000, on-line edition.

3. Department of Defense, *Report to Congress: Kosovo/Operation Allied Forces After Action Report*, Washington, Department of Defense, January 31, 2000, p. 1.

4. Some of the historical summary of the diplomatic politics of the campaign is adapted from the history NATO made available on its web site during the campaign. (See www.nato.int.) While there are many excellent histories of ethnic conflict in the Balkans, and studies of the recent problems of Serbia and the Kosovars, a good summary is provided in an article by William W. Hagen, "The Balkan's Lethal Nationalism," *Foreign Affairs*, July/August, 1999, pp. 52–64.

5. Much of the following historical summary is adapted from Lord Robertson of Port Ellen, Secretary of State for Defense, "Kosovo: An Account of the Crisis," London, Ministry of Defense, October 1999, http://www.mod.uk/news/kosovo/account.

6. Much of the negotiating chronology is adapted from Annex A-1 to Department of Defense, *Report to Congress: Kosovo/Operation Allied Forces After Action Report*, Washington, Department of Defense, January 31, 2000.

7. The use of Serbian throughout the rest of this text refers to the leadership and dominant ethnic group of the Federal Republic of Yugoslavia. The use of Kosovar refers to Albanian Kosovars. While such descriptions are not legally correct, they provide a much clearer picture of the forces at work during the fighting.

8. The author reviewed such statements in the FBIS, and in various Serbian web pages, and reviewed tapes and translated transcripts of Serbian television broadcasts during the war while acting as a military analyst for ABC News.

9. Prepared joint statement on the Kosovo After Action Review presented by Secretary of Defense William S. Cohen and Gen. Henry H. Shelton, Chairman of the Joint Chiefs of Staff, before the Senate Armed Services Committee, October 14, 1999. Also see Department of Defense, *Report to Congress: Kosovo/Operation Allied Forces After Action Report*, Washington, Department of Defense, January 31, 2000, pp. 3–4.

10. Department of Defense, *Report to Congress: Kosovo/Operation Allied Forces After Action Report*, Washington, Department of Defense, January 31, 2000, pp. 7–8 and 21, 23.

11. These failures have been confirmed in off-the-record statements by some of NATO's most senior officers. For an on-the-record description of some of the problems involved, see John A. Tirpak, "Short's View of the Air Campaign," *Air Force Magazine*, September 1999, pp. 43–47.

12. Rebecca Grant, "The Kosovo Campaign: Aerospace Power Made it Work," Arlington, Air Force Association, September 1999, p. 6.

13. Steven Erlanger, "NATO Was Closer to Ground War in Kosovo Than Is Widely Believed," *New York Times*, November 7, 1999, p. A-6.

14. Department of Defense, *Report to Congress: Kosovo/Operation Allied Forces After Action Report*, Washington, Department of Defense, January 31, 2000, pp. 23–24.

15. Department of Defense, *Report to Congress: Kosovo/Operation Allied Forces After Action Report*, Washington, Department of Defense, January 31, 2000, pp. 23–24.

16. Rebecca Grant, "The Kosovo Campaign: Aerospace Power Made it Work," Arlington, Air Force Association, September 1999, p. 6.

17. American Forces Information Service, Linda D. Kozaryn, "Cohen Previews Kosovo Lessons Learned," Defenselink, September 14, 1999.

18. Rebecca Grant, "The Kosovo Campaign: Aerospace Power Made it Work," Arlington, Air Force Association, September 1999, p. 6.

19. Department of Defense, *Report to Congress: Kosovo/Operation Allied Forces After Action Report*, Washington, Department of Defense, January 31, 2000, pp. 7–8.

20. Prepared joint statement on the Kosovo After Action Review presented by Secretary of Defense William S. Cohen and Gen. Henry H. Shelton, Chairman of the Joint Chiefs of Staff, before the Senate Armed Services Committee, October 14, 1999.

21. Dana Priest, "Tension Grew With Divide Over Strategy," *Washington Post*, September 21, 1999, p. A-1.

22. John A. Tirpak, "Short's View of the Air Campaign," *Air Force Magazine*, September 1999, pp. 47; Dana Priest, "Tension Grew With Divide Over Strategy," *Washington Post*, September 21, 1999, p. A-1.

23. This discussion relies heavily on Dana Priest, "Tension Grew With Divide Over Strategy," *Washington Post*, September 21, 1999, p. A-1.

24. Rebecca Grant, "The Kosovo Campaign: Aerospace Power Made it Work," Arlington, Air Force Association, September 1999, p. 11.

25. Department of Defense, *Report to Congress: Kosovo/Operation Allied Forces After Action Report*, Washington, Department of Defense, January 31, 2000, pp. 7–8.

26. Rebecca Grant, "The Kosovo Campaign: Aerospace Power Made it Work," Arlington, Air Force Association, September 1999, p. 21.

27. Lord Robertson of Port Ellen, Secretary of State for Defense, "Kosovo: An Account of the Crisis," London, Ministry of Defense, October 1999, http://www.mod.uk/news/kosovo/account.

28. Prepared joint statement on the Kosovo After Action Review presented by Secretary of Defense William S. Cohen and Gen. Henry H. Shelton, Chairman of the Joint Chiefs of Staff, before the Senate Armed Services Committee, October 14, 1999.

29. Department of Defense, *Report to Congress: Kosovo/Operation Allied Forces After Action Report*, Washington, Department of Defense, January 31, 2000, pp. 10–12.

30. Kent Kresa, "Investment in the Future, Kosovo Unveiled Fruits of Smart Research," *Defense News*, August 30, 1999, p. 30; General Merrill A. McPeak, "The Kosovo Result," *Armed Forces Journal International*, September, 1999, pp. 62–64.

31. Department of Defense, *Report to Congress: Kosovo/Operation Allied Forces After Action Report*, Washington, Department of Defense, January 31, 2000, pp. 8–87.

32. Dana Priest, "Tension Grew With Divide Over Strategy," *Washington Post*, September 21, 1999, p. A-1.

33. Department of Defense, *Report to Congress: Kosovo/Operation Allied Forces After Action Report*, Washington, Department of Defense, January 31, 2000, pp. 82–83.

34. Assemblee Nationale, Rapport d'Information, "Le cout de la participation de la France aux operations menees en vue du reglement de la crise au Kosovo," presente par Jean-Michel Boucheron, No. 1775, July 1, 1999, pp. 8–9. Also see Alain Richard, *Les Enseignements du Kosovo*, Paris Ministry of Defense, November, 1999, www.washington/actu/kossovo/actualities/dossier/d36.

35. NATO statistics refer to 400 aircraft on day one. The lower figure comes from Department of Defense, *Report to Congress: Kosovo/Operation Allied Forces After Action Report*, Washington, Department of Defense, January 31, 2000, p. 31.

36. Department of Defense, *Report to Congress: Kosovo/Operation Allied Forces After Action Report*, Washington, Department of Defense, January 31, 2000, p. 32.

37. Department of Defense, *Report to Congress: Kosovo/Operation Allied Forces After Action Report*, Washington, Department of Defense, January 31, 2000, p. 32

38. Assemblee Nationale, Rapport d'Information, "Le cout de la participation de la France aux operations menees en vue du reglement de la crise au Kosovo," presente par Jean-Michel Boucheron, No. 1775, July 1, 1999, pp. 14–16. Also see Alain Richard, *Les Enseignements du Kosovo*, Paris Ministry of Defense, November, 1999, www.washington/actu/kossovo/actualities/dossier/d36.

39. Lord Robertson of Port Ellen, Secretary of State for Defense, "Kosovo: An Account of the Crisis," London, Ministry of Defense, October 1999, http://www.mod.uk/news/kosovo/account.

40. Lord Robertson of Port Ellen, Secretary of State for Defense, "Kosovo: An Account of the Crisis," London, Ministry of Defense, October 1999, http://www.mod.uk/news/kosovo/account.

41. *Jane's Defense Weekly*, July 7, 1999, p. 21

42. Dana Priest, "Tension Grew With Divide Over Strategy," *Washington Post*, September 21, 1999, p. A-1.

43. Some useful unofficial data and histograms are available in *Air Force Magazine*, August 1999, p. 59.

44. *www.defense.gouv.fr/ema/operations/ex-yougolavie/kosovo,* accessed on October 15, 1999.

45. Assemblee Nationale, Rapport d'Information, "Le cout de la participation de la France aux operations menees en vue du reglement de la crise au Kosovo," presente par Jean-Michel Boucheron, No. 1775, July 1, 1999, pp. 14–15. Also see Alain Richard, *Les Enseignements du Kosovo*, Paris Ministry of Defense, November, 1999, www.washington/

actu/kossovo/actualities/dossier/d36. The latter document claims that France flew 10% of all missions, 12% of all offensive missions, 21% of all reconnaissance missions, and 12% of all support and transport missions.

46. Dr. H. C. Uwe Nerlich, "Lessons from Operation Allied Force," IABG, Trier, Germany, November 12, 1999.

47. *Jane's Defense Weekly*, July 7, 1999, p. 21.

48. Prepared statement to the Senate Army Service Committee, July 20, 1999, p. 4.

49. Prepared joint statement on the Kosovo After Action Review presented by Secretary of Defense William S. Cohen and Gen. Henry H. Shelton, Chairman of the Joint Chiefs of Staff, before the Senate Armed Services Committee, October 14, 1999.

50. Lord Robertson of Port Ellen, Secretary of State for Defense, "Kosovo: An Account of the Crisis," London, Ministry of Defense, October 1999, http://www.mod.uk/news/kosovo/account.

51. Department of Defense, *Report to Congress: Kosovo/Operation Allied Forces After Action Report*, Washington, Department of Defense, January 31, 2000, pp. 67–69, 87–88, 104.

52. Prepared statement to the Senate Army Service Committee, July 20, 1999, p. 4; Dana Priest, "Tension Grew With Divide Over Strategy," *Washington Post*, September 21, 1999, p. A-1.

53. Kent Kresa, "Investment in the Future, Kosovo Unveiled Fruits of Smart Research," *Defense News*, August 30, 1999, p. 30; *Jane's Defense Weekly*, October 6, 1999, p. 3.

54. Department of Defense, *Report to Congress: Kosovo/Operation Allied Forces After Action Report*, Washington, Department of Defense, January 31, 2000, p. 79.

55. Department of Defense, *Report to Congress: Kosovo/Operation Allied Forces After Action Report*, Washington, Department of Defense, January 31, 2000, p. 79.

56. Department of Defense, *Report to Congress: Kosovo/Operation Allied Forces After Action Report*, Washington, Department of Defense, January 31, 2000, p. 89.

57. Department of Defense, *Report to Congress: Kosovo/Operation Allied Forces After Action Report*, Washington, Department of Defense, January 31, 2000, pp. 86–87, 90.

58. For further data on this system, see *Jane's Defense Weekly*, December 1, 1999, p. 6.

59. Prepared statement to the Senate Army Service Committee, July 20, 1999, p. 4; Dana Priest, "Tension Grew With Divide Over Strategy," *Washington Post*, September 21, 1999, p. A-1.

60. Lord Robertson of Port Ellen, Secretary of State for Defense, "Kosovo: An Account of the Crisis," London, Ministry of Defense, October 1999, http://www.mod.uk/news/kosovo/account.

61. Assemblee Nationale, Rapport d'Information, "Le cout de la participation de la France aux operations menees en vue du reglement de la crise au Kosovo," presente par Jean-Michel Boucheron, No. 1775, July 1, 1999, pp. 12–15.

62. See John A. Tirpak, "Short's View of the Air Campaign, *Air Force Magazine*, September 1999, p. 47.

63. The "enhanced" Paveway allowed the GPS guidance to achieve theoretical accuracies of 13 meters using GPS is the laser lock should be broken. *Jane's Defense Weekly*, July 7, 1999, p. 21

64. Prepared joint statement on the Kosovo After Action Review presented by Secretary of Defense William S. Cohen and Gen. Henry H. Shelton, Chairman of the Joint Chiefs of Staff, before the Senate Armed Services Committee, October 14, 1999. Department of Defense, *Report to Congress: Kosovo/Operation Allied Forces After Action Report*, Washington, Department of Defense, January 31, 2000, p. 60.

65. The text is excerpted from Secretary Cohen's speech to the International Institute of Strategic Studies at San Diego, California, on September 9, 1999 as reported in www.defenselink.mil/speeches/1999.

66. Department of Defense, *Report to Congress: Kosovo/Operation Allied Forces After Action Report*, Washington, Department of Defense, January 31, 2000, p. 98.

67. For a detailed argument that Russia actively sought to disrupt NATO operations and supported Serbia, see Zbigniew Brzezinski and Chris Swift, "Russia and the Kosovo Crisis," CSIS, Washington, 1999.

68. NATO's initial plans called 45,000 to 48,000 troops. When NATO called for KFOR peacekeepers, the 19-member alliance got more than it asked for. Member and non-member nations offered to contribute a total of about 55,000. About 3,600 Russian soldiers are also slated to take part in Operation Joint Guard. The United States planned to deploy 7,000 service members to the peacekeeping operation. KFOR first entered Kosovo June 11. As of June 27, 30,000 troops had been deployed into the southern Yugoslav province. NATO has asked contributing nations to speed up deployments. Tension exists between Serbs in the region and returning Kosovar Albanians. Pentagon officials estimate more than 285,000 refugees have returned to Kosovo despite the risk of land mines and lack of shelter.

69. For an interesting discussion of the issues involved, see Andrew J. Bacevich, "Policing Utopia," *The National Interest*, Summer 1999, pp. 5–13.

70. IISS, *The 1998 Chart of Armed Conflict*, London, IISS, 1998.

71. The historical survey work of Herbert J. Tillema, *International Conflict Since 1945*, Boulder, Westview, 1991.

72. IISS, *The 1998 Chart of Armed Conflict*, London, IISS, 1998.

73. Secretary of Defense William S. Cohen, Prepared Testimony to the Senate Armed Services Committee, July 20, 1999, pp. 5–6.

74. The exact totals are controversial. France formally budgeted 714 million francs for operations in 1999. *Jane's Defense Weekly*, September 1, 1999, p. 11.

75. John A. Tirpak, "Short's View of the Air Campaign," *Air Force Magazine*, September 1999, p. 45.

76. Secretary of Defense William S. Cohen, Prepared Testimony to the Senate Armed Services Committee, July 20, 1999, pp. 5–6.

77. Interviews and report on the comments of Lt. General Michael C. Short in the *New York Times*, June 18, 1999, p. A-16.

78. Secretary of Defense William S. Cohen, Prepared Testimony to the Senate Armed Services Committee, July 20, 1999, p. 7. Cohen reinforced these points in his speech on the preliminary lessons of the war in Kosovo to the conference of the International Institute of Strategic Studies (IISS) in San Diego or September 9, 1999. (Text drawn from www. defenselink.mil/speeches.)

79. The text is excerpted from Secretary Cohen's speech to the International Institute of Strategic Studies at San Diego, California, on September 9, 1999 as reported in www.defenselink.mil/speeches/1999.

80. Department of Defense, *Report to Congress: Kosovo/Operation Allied Forces After Action Report*, Washington, Department of Defense, January 31, 2000.

81. Reuters, September 8, 1999, 0813.

82. *New York Times*, September 22, 1999, p. A-13; Associated Press, September 22, 1999, 0649; Reuters, September 21, 1999, 2020.

83. *Defense News*, September 27, 1999, pp. 1 and 4.

84. *Aviation Week and Space Technology*, August 23, 1999, p. 27; *Air Force Magazine*, September 1999, p. 47.

85. Linda D. Kozaryn, "Air Chief's Kosovo Lesson: Go for Snake's Head First," American Forces Information Service Updated: 26 Oct. 1999.

86. Linda D. Kozaryn, "Air Chief's Kosovo Lesson: Go for Snake's Head First," American Forces Information Service Updated: 26 Oct. 1999.

87. Department of Defense News Briefing, October 21, 1999, 1330, *www.defenselink.mil/news.*

88. *Jane's Defense Week*, October 27, 1999, p. 3; Linda D. Kozaryn, "Air Chief's Kosovo Lesson: Go for Snake's Head First," American Forces Information Service Updated: 26 Oct. 1999; Department of Defense News Briefing, October 21, 1999, 1330, *www.defenselink.mil/news.*

89. The French view of these issues is laid out in some detail in Alain Richard, *Les Enseignements du Kosovo*, Paris Ministry of Defense, November 1999, www.washington/ actu/kossovo/actualities/dossier/d36.

90. This analysis is based largely on Dana Priest's reporting in "A Decisive Battle That Never Was," in the *Washington Post*, September 20, 1999, pp. A-1, A-10.

91. Also see Alain Richard, *Les Enseignements du Kosovo*, Paris Ministry of Defense, November, 1999, www.washington/actu/kossovo/actualities/dossier/d36.

92. *International Herald Tribune*, November 11, 1999, p. 4.

93. Dana Priest, "A Decisive Battle That Never Was," *Washington Post*, September 20, 1999, p. A-1.

94. *Jane's Defense Week*, October 27, 1999, p.3.

95. *Washington Post*, September 20, 1999, p. A-1.

96. *Air Force Magazine*, September 1999, pp. 46–47.

97. For a good summary, see *New York Times*, September 10, 1999, p. A-6. This description of events was confirmed by later interviews.

98. The diplomatic history of the crises is not the subject of this book, For an interesting view of Russia's conduct, however, seem Dr. Erik Yesson, "NATO and Russia in Kosovo," *Royal United Services Institute Journal*, September, 1999, pp. 20–26

99. The text is excerpted from Secretary Cohen's speech to the International Institute of Strategic Studies at San Diego, California, on September 9, 1999 as reported in www.defenselink.mil/speeches/1999.

100. Prepared joint statement on the Kosovo After Action Review presented by Secretary of Defense William S. Cohen and Gen. Henry H. Shelton, Chairman of the Joint Chiefs of Staff, before the Senate Armed Services Committee, October 14, 1999.

101. These issues are explored in depth in David C. Gompert, Richard L. Kugler, and Martin C. Lubbock, *Mind the Gap: Promoting a Transatlantic Revolution in Military Affairs*, Washington, National Defense University, 1999.

102. *Jane's Defense Weekly*, July 7, 1999, p. 26.

103. A good summary of post-Kosovo European discussions is provided in Nicholas Florins, "Identity Crisis: Kosovo Experience Prompts European Soul-Searching," *Armed Forces Journal International*, September 1999, pp. 66–70.

104. Interestingly enough, Colonel A. B. Krasnov draws similar conclusions in an Russian analysis of the lessons of the war. See Col. A. B. Krasnov, "Aviation in the Yugoslavian Conflict," *Soviet Military Thought*, MTR-No,005, September 1, 1999.

105. Prepared joint statement on the Kosovo After Action Review presented by Secretary of Defense William S. Cohen and Gen. Henry H. Shelton, Chairman of the Joint Chiefs of Staff, before the Senate Armed Services Committee, October 14, 1999.

106. Prepared joint statement on the Kosovo After Action Review presented by Secretary of Defense William S. Cohen and Gen. Henry H. Shelton, Chairman of the Joint Chiefs of Staff, before the Senate Armed Services Committee, October 14, 1999.

107. Department of Defense, *Report to Congress: Kosovo/Operation Allied Forces After Action Report*, Washington, Department of Defense, January 31, 2000, pp. 121–122.

108. This summary is prepared from the prepared text of each officer. It does not include points raised in their additional comments made during the actual testimony.

109. Rebecca Grant, "The Kosovo Campaign: Aerospace Power Made It Work," Arlington, Air Force Association, September 1999, p. 15.

110. Stephen Daggett, "Kosovo Military Operations: Costs and Congressional Action on Funding," Congressional Research Service, RS20161, June 3, 1999,

111. The trends and statistics involved are shown in depth in Otto Crasher, "Haley's Warning" *Air Force Magazine*, July 1999, pp. 51–57.

112. Ironically, this was partly the result that elements of the divisions were deployed as peacekeepers in Kosovo, which meant the divisions were not combat ready for deployment in the major regional contingencies which were their primary missions. See *Washington Post*, November 15, 1999, p A-21; Department of Defense Background Briefing, "Army Readiness," November 10, 1999.

113. See the list of continuing US military problems in US Senate Committee on Armed Services, "Senate and House Complete Conference on National Defense Authorization Bill for Fiscal Year 2000," August 6, 1999; House Armed Services Committee, "Summary of Major Provisions S.1059: National Defense Authorization Act for FY2000," Conference Report, August 5, 1999.

114. General Eric K. Shinseki stated in an interview in June 1999, that, "We could be there at least four years if our experience in Bosnia is any lesson." *New York Times*, June 24, 1999, p. A15.

115. Department of Defense, *Report to Congress: Kosovo/Operation Allied Forces After Action Report*, Washington, Department of Defense, January 31, 2000, Introduction.

116. Department of Defense, *Report to Congress: Kosovo/Operation Allied Forces After Action Report*, Washington, Department of Defense, January 31, 2000, p. 12.

117. These speculators did not include the Chief of the Staff of the US Air Force or senior officers in the Air Staff, who stressed the need for joint operations. For a balanced view of Kosovo pro-air enthusiast, see Air Marshall Sir John Walker, "Air Power for Coercion," *Royal United Services Institute Journal*, September 1999, pp. 13–19. Good descriptions of how the US Air Force is approaching the future development of air power, and of its emphasis on joint operations, can be found in Bryan Bender, "USAF: The Strategic Vision," *Jane's Defense Weekly*, September 8, 1999, pp. 8–36, and Major General Bruce Carlson, "Juggling Air Dominance," *Armed Forces Journal International*, September 1999, pp. 50–56.

118. See the comments on these problems by Lt. General Michael Short, NATO's joint force air component commander in the Balkans, in John A. Tirpak, "Short's View of the Air Campaign," *Air Force Magazine*, September 1999, pp. 43–47. The impact of the rapid assembly and deployment of forces is also raised in a Russian analysis of the lessons of the war. See Col. A. B. Krasnov, "Aviation in the Yugoslavian Conflict," *Soviet Military Thought*, MTR-No,005, September 1, 1999.

119. John A. Tirpak, "Short's View of the Air Campaign," *Air Force Magazine*, September 1999, pp. 43–47.

120. The problems in targeting are also raised by Colonel A. B. Krasnov in a Russian analysis of the lessons of the war. See Col. A. B. Krasnov, "Aviation in the Yugoslavian Conflict," *Soviet Military Thought*, MTR-No,005, September 1, 1999.

121. Edward N. Luttwak raises a number of these issues in "Give War a Chance," *Foreign Affairs*, July/August 1999, pp. 36–44.

122. For discussions of these issues by some of those involved, see the post-war articles by Alastair Campbell, "Communications Lessons for NATO, the Military, and the Media, *Royal United Services Institute Journal*, September, 1999, pp. 31–36, and Oona Muirhead, "May Job: At the Sharp End of the Media Operation," *Royal United Services Institute Journal*, September, 1999, pp. 37–42.

123. For an interesting discussion of these issues, see Dr. Michael Evens, "Dark Victory," *Proceedings*, September 1999, pp. 33–37, and Dr. Scot MacDonald, "The Mission Must Be Worth the Risk," *Proceedings*, September 1999, pp. 36–37.

124. *New York Times*, September 17, 1999, p. A-10; *Washington Post*, September 17, 1999, p. A-22; NATO press conference by SACEUR, General Wesley K. Clark, September 16, 1999.

125. *Washington Post*, June 29, 1999, p. A-12.

126. Lord Robertson of Port Ellen, Secretary of State for Defense, "Kosovo: An Account of the Crisis," London, Ministry of Defense, October 1999, http://www.mod.uk/news/kosovo/account.

127. Lord Robertson of Port Ellen, Secretary of State for Defense, "Kosovo: An Account of the Crisis," London, Ministry of Defense, October 1999, http://www.mod.uk/news/kosovo/account.

128. Peter D. Feaver and Christopher Gelpi, "A Look at . . . Casualty Aversion. How Many Deaths Are Acceptable? A Surprising Answer." *Washington Post*, November 7, 1999; Page B-3. Peter Feaver is an associate professor of political science at Duke University, and co-principal investigator of the TISS Project on the Gap Between the Military and Civilian Society. Christopher Gelpi is an assistant professor of political science at Duke.

129. For the full details of this survey, see the authors' web site at www.poli.duke.edu/civmil.

130. The author examined uncut tapes of Serbian television coverage in detail while covering the war for ABC News. Many of the tapes involved faked or manipulated scenes tailored for propaganda purposes.

131. See William Arkin, "Chinese Embassy Continues to Smolder," *Washington Post*, November 8, 1999, Internet edition.

132. State Department press release, July 6, 1999, Internet edition.

133. A reporter familiar with the maps of Belgrade made the following report on this issue, "In its post-war investigation of the incident, the CIA now says three maps were used in an attempt to locate the FDSP, the intended target: two local commercial maps from 1989 and 1996, and a U.S. government map produced in 1997. None accurately identified the current location of the Chinese Embassy. When I was in Belgrade this summer, I picked up four different maps of the city, two from 1998. Only one—a 1:25,000 scale 'Magic Map'—places the Chinese Embassy in its proper location. William Arkin, "Chinese Embassy Continues to Smolder," *Washington Post*, November 8, 1999, Internet edition.

134. Statement by Director of Central Intelligence, George Tenet, on the Belgrade Chinese Embassy Bombing, House Permanent Select Committee on Intelligence Open Hearing, July 22, 1999, Public Affairs Page, CIA Homepage.

135. *Washington Post*, July 23, 1999, p. A-16.

136. Secretary Cohen's speech to the International Institute of Strategic Studies at San Diego, California, on September 9, 1999 as reported in www.defenselink.mil/speeches/1999.

137. There is a good history of problems in moving a CIA analyst's warning forward to the targeting center in the *New York Times*, June 24, 1999, pp. A-1 to A-15.

138. John A. Tirpak, "Short's View of the Air Campaign," *Air Force Magazine*, September 1999, p. 45.

139. Department of Defense, *Report to Congress: Kosovo/Operation Allied Forces After Action Report*, Washington, Department of Defense, January 31, 2000, pp. xiv, 82.

140. These have included efforts to prosecute the leaders of the NATO alliance at the war crimes tribunal in the Hague. *Washington Post*, January 20, 2000, p. A-15.

141. Volume 12, Number 1, February 2000, www.hrw.org.report/2000/nato.

142. Organization for Security and Co-operation in Europe, Background Paper—Human Rights in Kosovo, Reports: Human Rights in Kosovo: As Seen, As Told; Part I—October 1998 to June 1999; Part II—14 June 1999 to 31 October 1999 www.osce.org/kosovo/reports/hr/index.htm.

143. *Washington Post*, July 19, 1999, p. A-15.

144. See the comments on these problems by Lt. General Michael Short, NATO's joint force air component commander in the Balkans, in John A. Tirpak, "Short's View of the Air Campaign," *Air Force Magazine*, September 1999, pp. 43–47.

145. *New York Times*, July 28, 1999, p. A-6.

146. *New York Times*, July 28, 1999, p. A-6.

147. *New York Times*, July 28, 1999, p. A-6.

148. *New York Times*, July 14, 1999, p. A-1, A-10; *Washington Post*, July 21, 1999, p. A-15.

149. Reuters, July 15, 1999, 1129.

150. *Washington Post*, July 29, 1999, p. A-23, February 6, 2000, p. A-21: *New York Times*, July 31, 1999, p. A-3; *Economist*, July 31, 1999, p. 53.

151. See the comments by Lt. General Michael Short, NATO's joint force air component commander in the Balkans, in John A. Tirpak, "Short's View of the Air Campaign," *Air Force Magazine*, September 1999, pp. 43–47.

152. *Washington Post*, September 20, 1999, p. A-11.

153. Rebecca Grant, "The Kosovo Campaign: Aerospace Power Made It Work," Arlington, Air Force Association, September 1999, p. 18.

154. *Washington Post*, July 10, 1999, p. A-3.

155. *Jane's Defense Weekly*, July 14, 1999, p. 3.

156. Department of Defense, *Report to Congress: Kosovo/Operation Allied Forces After Action Report*, Washington, Department of Defense, January 31, 2000, pp. 58–59.

157. Military Procurement Subcommittee hearing on lessons learned from the Kosovo conflict—the effect of the operation on both deployed/non-deployed forces and on future modernization plans, October 19, 1999.

158. *Washington Post*, September 20, 1999, p. A-11.

159. *Washington Post*, September 20, 1999, p. A-11

160. Department of Defense, *Report to Congress: Kosovo/Operation Allied Forces After Action Report*, Washington, Department of Defense, January 31, 2000, pp. 59–60.

161. Department of Defense, *Report to Congress: Kosovo/Operation Allied Forces After Action Report*, Washington, Department of Defense, January 31, 2000, pp. 59–60.

162. *Defense News*, September 20, 1999, p. 20; *Jane's Defense Weekly*, September 8, 1999, p. 13.

163. *Jane's Defense Weekly*, September 8, 1999, p. 13.

164. Rebecca Grant, "The Kosovo Campaign: Aerospace Power Made It Work," Arlington, Air Force Association, September 1999, pp. 18–19.

165. The US is beginning to address some aspects of this issue by improving the battle damage assessment capabilities of the LANTIRN pod it puts on its attack aircraft. It is clear, however, that many of the problems encountered in Kosovo can only be solved with more advanced targeting and damage assessment pods and systems. *Jane's International Defense Review*, 1/2000, p. 3.

166. A HARM carrying F-16CJ was flying combat air patrol, in conjunction with EA-6 type aircraft for jamming. They were protecting a strike package that was going into the middle of Serbia around Batajnica airfield on a target. During egress the F-16 detected an aircraft in the vicinity of the strike package as it was exiting. It determined that it was a hostile aircraft, identified it, and then shot it down by firing two AMRAAMs, both of which hit. After that, all NATO aircraft left area safely. This was the first air-to-air engagement since the third day of the war—on 27 April.

167. Department of Defense, *Report to Congress: Kosovo/Operation Allied Forces After Action Report*, Washington, Department of Defense, January 31, 2000, pp. 80–81.

168. Military Procurement Subcommittee hearing on lessons learned from the Kosovo conflict—the effect of the operation on both deployed/non-deployed forces and on future modernization plans, October 19, 1999.

169. John Barry and Evan Thomas, "The Kosovo Cover Up," *Newsweek*, May 15, 2000, on-line edition.

170. Department of Defense, *Report to Congress: Kosovo/Operation Allied Forces After Action Report*, Washington, Department of Defense, January 31, 2000, pp. 1–16.

171. Department of Defense, *Report to Congress: Kosovo/Operation Allied Forces After Action Report*, Washington, Department of Defense, January 31, 2000, pp. 82–84.

172. Dana Priest, "Tension Grew With Divide Over Strategy," *Washington Post*, September 21, 1999, p. A-1.

173. Department of Defense, *Report to Congress: Kosovo/Operation Allied Forces After Action Report*, Washington, Department of Defense, January 31, 2000, pp. 17–24.

174. For a good summary overview of many of these issues see Earl H. Tillford, Jr., "Operation Allied Force and the Role of Air Power," *Parameters*, Vol. XXIX, No. 4, Winter 1999–2000, pp. 24–39.

175. For unofficial commentary on this aspect of the bombing, see *New York Times*, May 1, 1999, p. A-6.

176. Other estimates indicate that the per capita income of Serbia was $3,000 in 1989, before sanctions, and dropped to $1,650 in 1997. Unemployment was estimated at 27 percent in 1998, before the bombing began.

177. Dana Priest, *Washington Post*, September 21, 1999, p. A-1.

178. *New York Times*, September 29, 1999, p. A-10; Reuters, September 28, 1999.

179. Dana Priest, *Washington Post*, September 21, 1999, p. A-1.

180. This estimate was provided by the Department of Defense on May 13, 1999. Other estimates often used significantly different numbers.

181. This estimate was provided by the Department of Defense on May 13, 1999. Other estimates often used significantly different numbers.

182. *Defense News*, September 27, 1999, p. 18.

183. Department of Defense, *Report to Congress: Kosovo/Operation Allied Forces After Action Report*, Washington, Department of Defense, January 31, 2000, pp. 64–66.

184. Military Procurement Subcommittee hearing on lessons learned from the Kosovo conflict—the effect of the operation on both deployed/non-deployed forces and on future modernization plans, October 19, 1999.

185. Department of Defense, *Report to Congress: Kosovo/Operation Allied Forces After Action Report*, Washington, Department of Defense, January 31, 2000, pp. 66–68.

186. This section of the report is extraordinarily badly written, and Figures 13 and 14 on sortie rates have extreme credibility problems. They not only do not track with any prior US and NATO reporting, the smooth orderly rise in sorties rates does not seem to track with any of the histories of operations. See Department of Defense, *Report to Congress: Kosovo/Operation Allied Forces After Action Report*, Washington, Department of Defense, January 31, 2000, pp. 67–71.

187. Department of Defense, *Report to Congress: Kosovo/Operation Allied Forces After Action Report*, Washington, Department of Defense, January 31, 2000, pp. 70–71.

188. There are sharp differences between the Dayton ceilings for equipment in active forces and the IISS estimate of total equipment holdings.

189. This estimate was provided by the Department of Defense on May 13, 1999. Other estimates often used significantly different numbers.

190. Estimate based on IISS, British Ministry of Defense, and STRATFOR data.

191. *Aviation Week and Space Technology*, July 26, 1999, p. 68.

192. *London Times*, June 24, 1999, Internet edition; Associated Press, June 24, 1999, 0734 and 16:57; Agence France Presse, June 24, 1999.

193. NATO press briefing by General Wesley Clark on September 16, 1999.

194. NATO press briefing by General Wesley Clark on September 16, 1999.

195. The NATO methodology is described in depth by Brigadier General John Corley, the chief the assessment team, during the Clark briefing. He notes that more than 35 people were involved in the study and that the on-site team alone traveled to more than 429 different locations. These comments are taken from the full text of the briefing provided by the Federal News Service on September 16, 1999.

196. Lord Robertson of Port Ellen, Secretary of State for Defense, "Kosovo: An Account of the Crisis," London, Ministry of Defense, October 1999, http://www.mod.uk/news/kosovo/account.

197. Prepared joint statement on the Kosovo After Action Review presented by Secretary of Defense William S. Cohen and Gen. Henry H. Shelton, Chairman of the Joint Chiefs of Staff, before the Senate Armed Services Committee, October 14, 1999.

198. Department of Defense, *Report to Congress: Kosovo/Operation Allied Forces After Action Report*, Washington, Department of Defense, January 31, 2000, pp. 84–85.

199. Department of Defense, *Report to Congress: Kosovo/Operation Allied Forces After Action Report*, Washington, Department of Defense, January 31, 2000, pp. 86–87.

200. For a detailed analysis see Steve Bowman, "Kosovo: US and Allied Military Operations," Congressional Research Service, IB10027, May 21, 1999.

201. The full chronology of events has not been made public, and much of the intelligence available had been discussed only on a background basis. For a good discussion

of the chronology of events, see Blaine Harden, "The Long Struggle that Led the Serbian Leader to Back Down," *New York Times International*, June 8, 1999, pp. A13A-A13B.

202. Interview in the *New York Times*, July 26, 1999, p. A-3.

203. *New York Times*, July 21, 1999, p. A-8

204. This section is based largely on the excellent investigative reporting by Dana Priest in "A Decisive Battle that Never Was," *Washington Post*, p. A-1, September 19, 20, and 21, 1999, and reporting by Steven Erlanger. "NATO Was Closer to Ground War in Kosovo Than Is Widely Realized," *New York Times*, November 7, 1999, p. A-6.

205. Reuters, September 30, 1999, 1158.

206. *Washington Post*, September 19, 1999, p. A-30.

207. Steven Erlanger. "NATO Was Closer to Ground War in Kosovo Than Is Widely Realized," *New York Times*, November 7, 1999, p. A-6.

208. Steven Erlanger. "NATO Was Closer to Ground War in Kosovo Than Is Widely Realized," *New York Times*, November 7, 1999, p. A-6.

209. *Washington Post*, September 19, 1999, p. A-30.

210. *Washington Post*, September 19, 1999, p. A-30.

211. *Washington Post*, June 26, 1999, p. A-1.

212. See Dana Priest in "A Decisive Battle that Never Was," *Washington Post*, p. A-1, September 19, 20, and 21, 1999.

213. Cost figures of $6,000-$14,700 per flight hour have been quote for the B-2. The Department of Defense claims the cost of fuel, consumables and depot supplies averages $5,193 per hour. It claims this cost is roughly equivalent to that of the F-15.

214. *Jane's Defense Weekly*, Vol. 31, No. 24, June 16, 1999, Internet edition, *Washington Post*, June 11, 1999, p. A-1 and A-12.

215. Michael O'Hanlon, "KLA Helped to Turn the Tide," *Defense News*, July 5, 1999, p. 19.

216. *Washington Post*, September 19, 1999, pp. A-27, A-29.

217. See Department of Defense, *Report to Congress: Kosovo/Operation Allied Forces After Action Report*, Washington, Department of Defense, January 31, 2000.

218. Linda D. Kozaryn, American Forces Press Service, "Air Chief's Kosovo Lesson: Go for Snake's Head First," American Forces Information Service, October 26, 1999.

219. *Aviation Week*, November 1, 1998, pp. 33–36.

220. Prepared joint statement on the Kosovo After Action Review presented by Secretary of Defense William S. Cohen and Gen. Henry H. Shelton, Chairman of the Joint Chiefs of Staff, before the Senate Armed Services Committee, October 14, 1999.

221. Department of Defense, *Report to Congress: Kosovo/Operation Allied Forces After Action Report*, Washington, Department of Defense, January 31, 2000, pp. 75–76.

222. Department of Defense, *Report to Congress: Kosovo/Operation Allied Forces After Action Report*, Washington, Department of Defense, January 31, 2000, pp. 46, 75.

223. See Department of Defense, *Report to Congress: Kosovo/Operation Allied Forces After Action Report*, Washington, Department of Defense, January 31, 2000, p. 42

224. Dr. H. C. Uwe Nerlich, "Lessons from Operation Allied Force," IABG, Trier, Germany, November 12, 1999.

225. *Jane's Defense Weekly*, November 17, 1999, p. 11.

226. *Jane's Defense Weekly*, September 1, 1999, p. 29.

227. *Jane's Defense Weekly*, September 1, 1999, p. 29.

228. Department of Defense, *Report to Congress: Kosovo/Operation Allied Forces After Action Report*, Washington, Department of Defense, January 31, 2000, p. 134.

229. Department of Defense, *Report to Congress: Kosovo/Operation Allied Forces After Action Report*, Washington, Department of Defense, January 31, 2000, pp. 6–7.

230. *New York Times International*, May 4, 1999, p. A-12; *Jane's Defense Weekly*, May 12, 1999, p. 4.

231. Military Procurement Subcommittee hearing on lessons learned from the Kosovo conflict—the effect of the operation on both deployed/non-deployed forces and on future modernization plans, October 19, 1999.

232. Department of Defense, *Report to Congress: Kosovo/Operation Allied Forces After Action Report*, Washington, Department of Defense, January 31, 2000, pp. 96–98.

233. Military Procurement Subcommittee hearing on lessons learned from the Kosovo conflict—the effect of the operation on both deployed/non-deployed forces and on future modernization plans, October 19, 1999.

234. See Dana Priest, "A Decisive Battle that Never Was," *Washington Post*, September 19, 20, and 21.

235. There is a minor discrepancy in some of the USAF reporting on the number of B-2 sorties.

236. Cost figures of $6,000-$14,700 per flight hour have been quote for the B-2. The Department of Defense claims the cost of fuel, consumables and depot supplies averages $5,193 per hour. It claims this cost is roughly equivalent to that of the F-15.

237. *Jane's Defense Weekly*, July 7, 1999, p. 3; Associated Press, June 30, 1999, 15:53; Rebecca Grant, "The Kosovo Campaign: Aerospace Power Made It Work," Arlington, Air Force Association, September 1999, p. 19.

238. *Jane's Defense Weekly*, July 7, 1999, p. 3; Associated Press, June 30, 1999, 15:53; Rebecca Grant, "The Kosovo Campaign: Aerospace Power Made It Work," Arlington, Air Force Association, September 1999, p. 19.

239. *Washington Post*, August 2, 1999, p. A-19

240. *Washington Post*, August 2, 1999, p. A-19.

241. See *Aviation Week and Space Technology*, June 14, 1999, pp. 63–73; US Senate Committee on Armed Services, "Senate and House Complete Conference on National Defense Authorization Bill for Fiscal Year 2000," August 6, 1999; House Armed Services Committee, "Summary of Major Provisions S.1059: National Defense Authorization Act for FY2000," Conference Report, August 5, 1999.

242. *Aviation Week and Space Technology*, April 12, 1999, p. 30.

243. Department of Defense, *Report to Congress: Kosovo/Operation Allied Forces After Action Report*, Washington, Department of Defense, January 31, 2000, p. 90.

244. *Washington Post*, July 19, 1999, p. A-15, August 3, 1999, p. A-13.

245. For more detailed discussions of these issues, see Robin F. Laird and Holger H. Hay, *The Revolution in Military Affairs: Allied Perspectives*, Fort McNair, Institute for National Strategic Studies, National Defense University, McNair Paper 60, April 1999; David C. Compert, Richard K. Kugler, and Martin C. Libicki, *Minding the Gap: Promoting a Revolution in Military Affairs*, Fort McNair, Institute for National Strategic Studies, National Defense University, 1999; and Nicholas Florins, "Identity Crisis: Kosovo Experience Prompts European Soul-Searching," *Armed Forces Journal International*, September 1999, pp. 66–70.

246. See the French analysis in Alain Richard, *Les Enseignements du Kosovo*, Paris Ministry of Defense, November, 1999, www.washington/actu/kossovo/actualities/dossier/d36.

247. *Defense News*, August 16, 1999, p. 6; John D. Morocco, "Kosovo Reveals NATO Interoperability Woes," *Aviation Week and Space Technology*, August 9, 1999, p. 32

248. John D. Morocco, "Kosovo Reveals NATO Interoperability Woes," *Aviation Week and Space Technology*, August 9, 1999, p. 32.

249. *Aviation Week and Space Technology*, July 26, 1999, p. 71.

250. The Honorable George Robertson, British Secretary of State for Defense, *Some Preliminary Lessons, Royal United Services Institute Journal*, September 1999, pp. 1–6.

251. Lord Robertson of Port Ellen, Secretary of State for Defense, "Kosovo: An Account of the Crisis," London, Ministry of Defense, October 1999, http://www.mod.uk/news/kosovo/account.

252. The text is excerpted from Secretary Cohen's speech to the International Institute of Strategic Studies at San Diego, California, on September 9, 1999 as reported in www.defenselink.mil/speeches/1999.

253. *Defense News*, August 2, 1999, p. 9.

254. *Jane's Defense Weekly*, September 29, 1999, p. 3.

255. *Jane's Defense Weekly*, September 29, 1999, p. 3.

256. Informal NATO Ministerial, 21 Sept. 1999. Briefing by Secretary of Defense William S. Cohen and Chairman of the Joint Chiefs of Staff General Henry Shelton. (www.nato.int)

257. Informal NATO Ministerial, 21 Sept. 1999. Briefing by Secretary of Defense William S. Cohen and Chairman of the Joint Chiefs of Staff General Henry Shelton. (www.nato.int)

258. *Aviation Week and Space Technology*, May 17, 1999, p. 33.

259. Department of Defense, *Report to Congress: Kosovo/Operation Allied Forces After Action Report*, Washington, Department of Defense, January 31, 2000, pp. 124–125.

260. Department of Defense, *Report to Congress: Kosovo/Operation Allied Forces After Action Report*, Washington, Department of Defense, January 31, 2000, pp. 47–51.

261. Department of Defense, *Report to Congress: Kosovo/Operation Allied Forces After Action Report*, Washington, Department of Defense, January 31, 2000, pp. 26–27, 47.

262. Department of Defense, *Report to Congress: Kosovo/Operation Allied Forces After Action Report*, Washington, Department of Defense, January 31, 2000, pp. 28–29.

263. Department of Defense, *Report to Congress: Kosovo/Operation Allied Forces After Action Report*, Washington, Department of Defense, January 31, 2000, pp. 73–75.

264. Department of Defense, *Report to Congress: Kosovo/Operation Allied Forces After Action Report*, Washington, Department of Defense, January 31, 2000, pp. 48–50.

265. Department of Defense, *Report to Congress: Kosovo/Operation Allied Forces After Action Report*, Washington, Department of Defense, January 31, 2000, pp. 112–114.

266. *Aviation Week and Space Technology*, July 26, 1999, p. 71.

267. Department of Defense, *Report to Congress: Kosovo/Operation Allied Forces After Action Report*, Washington, Department of Defense, January 31, 2000, pp. 90, 92.

268. Military Procurement Subcommittee hearing on lessons learned from the Kosovo conflict—the effect of the operation on both deployed/non-deployed forces and on future modernization plans, October 19, 1999.

269. For a summary description of currently programmed changes in the cruise missile program see "Future Cruise Will Offer Greater Speed, Guaranteed Destinations," *International Defense Review*, 2/2000, pp. 57–62.

270. *Jane's Defense Weekly*, April 21, 1999, p. 5; *Aviation Week and Space Technology*, June 7, 1999, pp. 54–55.

271. *Defense News*, July 12, 1999, pp. 1, 19; *Jane's Defense Weekly*, April 21, 1999, p. 5; *Aviation Week and Space Technology*, June 7, 1999, pp. 54–55.

272. *Jane's Defense Weekly*, April 21, 1999, p. 5; *Aviation Week and Space Technology*, June 7, 1999, pp. 54–55.

273. Colonel A. B. Krasnov, "Aviation in the Yugoslavian Conflict," *Soviet Military Thought*, MTR-No,005, September 1, 1999.

274. Prepared joint statement on the Kosovo After Action Review presented by Secretary of Defense William S. Cohen and Gen. Henry H. Shelton, Chairman of the Joint Chiefs of Staff, before the Senate Armed Services Committee, October 14, 1999.

275. Department of Defense, *Report to Congress: Kosovo/Operation Allied Forces After Action Report*, Washington, Department of Defense, January 31, 2000, pp. 61–63.

276. *Jane's Defense Weekly*, September 8, 1999, p. 4.

277. *Air Force Magazine*, August 1999, p. 25.

278. *Defense News*, September 13, 1999, p. 10.

279. Military Procurement Subcommittee hearing on lessons learned from the Kosovo conflict—the effect of the operation on both deployed/non-deployed forces and on future modernization plans, October 19, 1999.

280. Military Procurement Subcommittee hearing on lessons learned from the Kosovo conflict—the effect of the operation on both deployed/non-deployed forces and on future modernization plans, October 19, 1999.

281. *Jane's Defense Weekly*, September 8, 1999, p. 4; *Defense News*, September 13, 1999, p. 10, September 20, 1999, p. 38.

282. Department of Defense, *Report to Congress: Kosovo/Operation Allied Forces After Action Report*, Washington, Department of Defense, January 31, 2000, pp. iii-iv.

283. See *Aviation Week and Space Technology*, May 31, 1999, pp. 68–69; *Defense News*, June 21, 1999, p. 52.

284. *Jane's Defense Weekly*, December 15, 1999, p. 10.

285. *Aviation Week and Space Technology*, November 15, 1999. pp. 80–81.

286. *Jane's Defense Weekly*, July 7, 1999, p. 38, January 12, 2000, p. 7; *Aviation Week and Space Technology*, July 26, 1999, p. 70.

287. *Aviation Week and Space Technology*, November 8, 1999, pp. 82–83, November 15, 1999, pp. 80–81.

288. *Aviation Week and Space Technology*, July 26, 1999, pp. 70–71.

289. *Aviation Week and Space Technology*, July 26, 1999, p. 70.

290. *Defense News*, July 12, 1999, pp. 4, 20; *Jane's Defense Weekly*, July 14, 1999, p. 3.

291. *Jane's Defense Weekly*, October 6, 1999, p. 3.

292. Department of Defense, *Report to Congress: Kosovo/Operation Allied Forces After Action Report*, Washington, Department of Defense, January 31, 2000, pp. 34–36, 38.

293. Military Procurement Subcommittee hearing on lessons learned from the Kosovo conflict—the effect of the operation on both deployed/non-deployed forces and on future modernization plans, October 19, 1999.

294. Prepared joint statement on the Kosovo After Action Review presented by Secretary of Defense William S. Cohen and Gen. Henry H. Shelton, Chairman of the Joint Chiefs of Staff, before the Senate Armed Services Committee, October 14, 1999.

295. Department of Defense, *Report to Congress: Kosovo/Operation Allied Forces After Action Report*, Washington, Department of Defense, January 31, 2000, p. 39–40.

296. 1st Lt. Dave Huxsoll, "C-17 proves its worth in Allied Force," Aeronautical Systems Center Public Affairs, US Air Force News, Released: 2 July 1999.

297. *Defense News*, October 25, 1999, p. 4; 11.

298. *Jane's International Defense Review*, 10/1999, p. 64; *Jane's Defense News*, October 27, 1999, p. 7.

299. Prepared joint statement on the Kosovo After Action Review presented by Secretary of Defense William S. Cohen and Gen. Henry H. Shelton, Chairman of the Joint Chiefs of Staff, before the Senate Armed Services Committee, October 14, 1999.

300. Military Procurement Subcommittee hearing on lessons learned from the Kosovo conflict—the effect of the operation on both deployed/non-deployed forces and on future modernization plans, October 19, 1999.

301. Department of Defense, *Report to Congress: Kosovo/Operation Allied Forces After Action Report*, Washington, Department of Defense, January 31, 2000, pp. 100–101.

302. For a good summary of US Army expeditionary capabilities, see Colonel Robert B. Killebrew, "Army Force Projection," *Armed Forces Journal International*, September 1999, pp. 90–96. Also see Glenn W. Goodman, "Revolutionary Soldier," *Armed Forces Journal International*, October 1999, pp. 56–63, and Jason Sherman, "Arduous Crusade," *Armed Forces Journal International*, October 1999, pp. 46–55.

303. For an interesting summary discussion, see M. Thomas Davis and Richard Dunn, "Kosovo Should Stir Overhaul of US Army Structure, Policy," *Defense News*, October 18, 1999, p. 57, and Jeffery Record, "Operation Allied Force: Yet Another Wake Up Call for the Army," *Parameters*, Vol. XXIX, No. 4, Winter 1999–2000, pp. 15–24. The best book on the subject remains see Douglas A. Macgregor, *Breaking the Phalanx, A New Design for Landpower in the 21ˢᵗ Century*, Praeger, Westport, 1997.

304. *Jane's Defense Weekly*, October 20, 1999, p. 8, November 3, 1999, p. 3.

305. See interview with General Eric Shinseki, *Defense News*, July 19, 1999, p. 18; *Jane's Defense Weekly*, July 21, 1999, p. 7. For additional data on possible reform of the US Army see Douglas A. Macgregor, *Breaking the Phalanx, A New Design for Landpower in the 21ˢᵗ Century*, Praeger, Westport, 1997 and Colonel Robert B. Killebrew, "Army Force Projection," *Armed Forces Journal International*, September 1999, pp. 90–96.

306. For a good overview of these changes, see Scott Gourley and Bryan Bender, "Designing the Army After Next," *Jane's Defense Weekly*, October 6, 1999, pp. 22–27.

307. *International Herald Tribune*, November 26, 1999, p. 3; *Jane's Defense Weekly*, December 22, 1999, p. 5, January 12, 2000, p. 5.

308. *Defense News*, September 6 1999, p. 52.

309. Department of Defense, *Report to Congress: Kosovo/Operation Allied Forces After Action Report*, Washington, Department of Defense, January 31, 2000, pp. 101–103.

310. *Jane's Defense Weekly*, October 6, 1999, p. 9.

311. Department of Defense, *Report to Congress: Kosovo/Operation Allied Forces After Action Report*, Washington, Department of Defense, January 31, 2000, pp. 40–41.

312. Prepared joint statement on the Kosovo After Action Review presented by Secretary of Defense William S. Cohen and Gen. Henry H. Shelton, Chairman of the Joint Chiefs of Staff, before the Senate Armed Services Committee, October 14, 1999.

313. *Jane's Defense Weekly*, September 28, 1999, p. 7.

314. See the French analysis in Alain Richard, *Les Enseignements du Kosovo*, Paris Ministry of Defense, November, 1999, www.washington/actu/kossovo/actualities/dossier/d36.

315. Prepared joint statement on the Kosovo After Action Review presented by Secretary of Defense William S. Cohen and Gen. Henry H. Shelton, Chairman of the Joint Chiefs of Staff, before the Senate Armed Services Committee, October 14, 1999.

316. Informal NATO Ministerial, 21 Sept. 1999. Briefing by Secretary of Defense William S. Cohen and Chairman of the Joint Chiefs of Staff General Henry Shelton. (www.nato.int)

317. Department of Defense, *Report to Congress: Kosovo/Operation Allied Forces After Action Report*, Washington, Department of Defense, January 31, 2000, pp. 105–106.

318. Department of Defense, *Report to Congress: Kosovo/Operation Allied Forces After Action Report*, Washington, Department of Defense, January 31, 2000, pp. 105–106.

319. Department of Defense, *Report to Congress: Kosovo/Operation Allied Forces After Action Report*, Washington, Department of Defense, January 31, 2000, pp. 106–107.

320. *London Times*, November 23, 1999, p. 14; *Financial Times*, November 25, 199, p. 11; *International Herald Tribune*, November 26, 1999, p. 1; *Economist*, November 20, 1999, pp. 51–52.

321. *Financial Times*, November 25, 199, p. 11.

322. *International Herald Tribune*, November 26, 1999, p. 1.

323. *Jane's Defense Weekly*, November 10, 1999, p. 3.

324. See the French commentary in Alain Richard, *Les Enseignements du Kosovo*, Paris Ministry of Defense, November, 1999, www.washington/actu/kossovo/actualities/dossier/d36.

325. *Jane's Defense Weekly*, November 17, 1999, p. 35.

326. *Jane's Defense Weekly*, October 6, 1999, p. 11.

327. See the report by Ian Kemp, "Peacekeeping at a Stretch," *Jane's Defense Weekly*, July 28, 1999, pp. 18–22. Also, Ed Foster, "Imbalance of Power," *Jane's Defense Weekly*, January 5, 2000, pp. 25–28; *International Herald Tribune*, December 13, 1999, p. 5; *Jane's Defense Weekly*, December 1, 1999, p. 3; Damian Kemp, "The Year of Building Carefully," *Jane's Defense Weekly*, December 11, 1999, pp. 21–25; and *New York Times International*, December 3, 1999, p. A-18.

328. Informal NATO Ministerial, 21 Sept. 1999. Briefing by Secretary of Defense William S. Cohen and Chairman of the Joint Chiefs of Staff General Henry Shelton. (www.nato.int)

329. These points are also supported in the French official analysis of the lessons of the war in Alain Richard, *Les Enseignements du Kosovo*, Paris Ministry of Defense, November, 1999, www.washington/actu/kossovo/actualities/dossier/d36.

330. See Dr. H. C. Uwe Nerlich, "Lessons from Operation Allied Force," IABG, Trier, Germany, November 12, 1999.

331. Department of Defense, *Report to Congress: Kosovo/Operation Allied Forces After Action Report*, Washington, Department of Defense, January 31, 2000, p. 26.

332. *Jane's Defense Weekly*, April 14, 1999, p. 28; *Aviation Week and Space Technology*, May 17, 1999, p. 33.

333. *Defense News*, June 21, 1999, p. 52.

334. *Jane's Defense Weekly*, April 21, 1999, p. 85; *Aviation Week and Space Technology*, April 5, 1999, pp. 26–30.

335. For a good post action report, see Lt. Colonel Phillip C. Tissue, "21 Minutes to Belgrade," *Proceedings*, September 1999, pp. 38–40.

336. *Aviation Week and Space Technology*, May 24, 1999, p. 39

337. Department of Defense, *Report to Congress: Kosovo/Operation Allied Forces After Action Report*, Washington, Department of Defense, January 31, 2000, p. 55.

338. *Aviation Week and Space Technology*, July 26, 1999, p. 68

339. *Jane's Defense Weekly*, September 1, 1999, p. 4.

340. *Aviation Week and Space Technology*, April 5, 1999, p. 31.

341. *Washington Post*, August 2, 1999, p. A-19.

342. US Senate Committee on Armed Services, "Senate and House Complete Confer-ence on National Defense Authorization Bill for Fiscal Year 2000," August 6, 1999; House Armed Services Committee, "Summary of Major Provisions S.1059: National Defense Authorization Act for FY2000," Conference Report, August 5, 1999.

343. Department of Defense, *Report to Congress: Kosovo/Operation Allied Forces After Action Report*, Washington, Department of Defense, January 31, 2000, pp. 122–125.

344. Prepared joint statement on the Kosovo After Action Review presented by Secretary of Defense William S. Cohen and Gen. Henry H. Shelton, Chairman of the Joint Chiefs of Staff, before the Senate Armed Services Committee, October 14, 1999.

345. This section is based largely on interviews and *Aviation Week and Space Technol-ogy*, September 1, 1999, p. 31.

346. Rebecca Grant, "The Kosovo Campaign: Aerospace Power Made It Work," Arlington, Air Force Association, September 1999, p. 15.

347. *Aviation Week and Space Technology*, November 8, 1999, pp. 81–82.

348. *Aviation Week and Space Technology*, November 1, 1999, pp. 33–36.

349. *Aviation Week and Space Technology*, November 1, 1999, pp. 33–36.

350. *Aviation Week and Space Technology*, November 8, 1999, pp. 81–82.

351. *Aviation Week and Space Technology*, November 8, 1999, pp. 81–82.

352. *Washington Post*, November 8, 1999, pp. A-1 and A-10.

353. Prepared joint statement on the Kosovo After Action Review presented by Secretary of Defense William S. Cohen and Gen. Henry H. Shelton, Chairman of the Joint Chiefs of Staff, before the Senate Armed Services Committee, October 14, 1999.

354. Department of Defense, *Report to Congress: Kosovo/Operation Allied Forces After Action Report*, Washington, Department of Defense, January 31, 2000, pp. 53–56.

355. The US Army forces in the field found this to be a particularly serious problem. *Jane's Defense Weekly*, December 1, 2000, p. 8.

356. Department of Defense, *Report to Congress: Kosovo/Operation Allied Forces After Action Report*, Washington, Department of Defense, January 31, 2000, pp. 114–116.

357. Department of Defense, *Report to Congress: Kosovo/Operation Allied Forces After Action Report*, Washington, Department of Defense, January 31, 2000, p. 55.

358. *Aviation Week and Space Technology*, July 26, 1999, pp. 74–75

359. *New York Times*, May 12, 1999, p. A12; *Washington Post*, May 9, 1999, p. A-21; *Aviation Week and Space Technology*, March 29, 1999, pp. 31–33.

360. *Defense News*, June 21, 1999, p. 54.

361. *Jane's Defense Weekly*, September 8, 1999, p. 38.

362. Department of Defense, *Report to Congress: Kosovo/Operation Allied Forces After Action Report*, Washington, Department of Defense, January 31, 2000, pp. iii-iv.

363. *Aviation Week and Space Technology*, August 23, 1999, p. 30.

364. Military Procurement Subcommittee hearing on lessons learned from the Kosovo conflict—the effect of the operation on both deployed/non-deployed forces and on future modernization plans, October 19, 1999.

365. *Air Force Magazine*, August 1999, p. 24.

366. *Aviation Week and Space Technology*, September 6, 1999, p. 88.

367. *Aviation Week and Space Technology*, April 12, 1999, pp. 26–27.

368. These points are also supported in the French official analysis of the lessons of the war in Alain Richard, *Les Enseignements du Kosovo*, Paris Ministry of Defense, November, 1999, www.washington/actu/kossovo/actualities/dossier/d36.

369. *Jane's Defense Weekly*, September 29, 1999, p. 3.

370. *Jane's Defense Weekly*, November 10, 1999, p. 3.

371. Informal NATO Ministerial, 21 Sept. 1999. Briefing by Secretary of Defense William S. Cohen and Chairman of the Joint Chiefs of Staff General Henry Shelton. (www.nato.int).

372. Dana Priest, "Tension Grew With Divide Over Strategy," *Washington Post*, September 21, 1999, p. A-16.

373. *Air Force Magazine*, September, 1999, pp. 43–47; Dana Priest, "Tension Grew With Divide Over Strategy," *Washington Post*, September 21, 1999, p. A-1.

374. Dana Priest, "Tension Grew With Divide Over Strategy," *Washington Post*, September 21, 1999, p. A-16.

375. See the author's detailed analysis in Anthony H. Cordesman and Abraham R. Wager, *The Lessons of Modern War, Volume IV: The Gulf War*, Westview, Boulder, 1996, pp. 373–677.

376. The author explored this issue in depth during a visit to China in August 1999.

377. *Jane's Defense Weekly*, September 8, 1999, p. 37.

378. *Jane's Defense Weekly*, October 6, 1999, p. 3.

379. *Aviation Week and Space Technology*, May 17, 1999, pp. 56.

380. Department of Defense, *Report to Congress: Kosovo/Operation Allied Forces After Action Report*, Washington, Department of Defense, January 31, 2000, pp. 92–96.

381. *Jane's Defense Weekly*, June 23, 1999, p, 9.

382. These points are also supported in the French official analysis of the lessons of the war in Alain Richard, *Les Enseignements du Kosovo*, Paris Ministry of Defense, November, 1999, www.washington/actu/kossovo/actualities/dossier/d36.

383. Military Procurement Subcommittee hearing on lessons learned from the Kosovo conflict—the effect of the operation on both deployed/non-deployed forces and on future modernization plans, October 19, 1999.

384. Department of Defense, *Report to Congress: Kosovo/Operation Allied Forces After Action Report*, Washington, Department of Defense, January 31, 2000, pp. iii-iv.

385. The US is also considering development of a min-JDAM. *Jane's Defense Weekly*, December 15, 1999, p. 15.

386. The text is excerpted from Secretary Cohen's speech to the International Institute of Strategic Studies at San Diego, California, on September 9, 1999 as reported in www.defenselink.mil/speeches/1999.

387. Prepared joint statement on the Kosovo After Action Review presented by Secretary of Defense William S. Cohen and Gen. Henry H. Shelton, Chairman of the Joint Chiefs of Staff, before the Senate Armed Services Committee, October 14, 1999.

388. For a more detailed description of the JASSM program, see "Successful JASSM Flight Spurs Renewed Marketing Push," *International Defense Review*, 2/2000, p. 6.

389. *Aviation Week and Space Technology*, November 1, 1999, pp. 33–36.

390. Department of Defense, *Report to Congress: Kosovo/Operation Allied Forces After Action Report*, Washington, Department of Defense, January 31, 2000, p. 92.

391. Department of Defense, *Report to Congress: Kosovo/Operation Allied Forces After Action Report*, Washington, Department of Defense, January 31, 2000, p. 92.

392. Department of Defense, *Report to Congress: Kosovo/Operation Allied Forces After Action Report*, Washington, Department of Defense, January 31, 2000, pp. 92–96.

393. *Air Force Magazine*, August 1999, p. 24.

394. *Jane's Defense Weekly*, November 17, 1999, p. 10.

395. *Aviation Week and Space Technology*, September 6, 1999, p. 88.

396. *Jane's Defense Weekly*, November 17, 1999, p. 11.

397. *Defense News*, September 20, 1999, p. 38; *Jane's Defense Weekly*, September 8, 1999, p. 8, December 1, 1999, p. 5.

398. *Jane's Defense Weekly*, September 8, 1999, p. 8; US Senate Committee on Armed Services, "Senate and House Complete Conference on National Defense Authorization Bill for Fiscal Year 2000," August 6, 1999; House Armed Services Committee, "Summary of Major Provisions S.1059: National Defense Authorization Act for FY2000," Conference Report, August 5, 1999.

399. *Jane's Defense Weekly*, November 17, 1999, p. 10.

400. *Jane's Defense Weekly*, April 7, 1999, p. 3; *Defense News*, July 12, 1999, p. 1; *Aviation Week and Space Technology*, May 17, 1999, p. 56.

401. *Jane's Defense Weekly*, August 4, 1999, p. 27; *Defense News*, November 1, 1999, p. 3.

402. Assemblee Nationale, Rapport d'Information, "Le cout de la participation de la France aux operations menees en vue du reglement de la crise au Kosovo," presente par Jean-Michel Boucheron, No. 1775, July 1, 1999, pp. 28–29.

403. Prepared joint statement on the Kosovo After Action Review presented by Secretary of Defense William S. Cohen and Gen. Henry H. Shelton, Chairman of the Joint Chiefs of Staff, before the Senate Armed Services Committee, October 14, 1999.

404. See Dr. H. C. Uwe Nerlich, "Lessons from Operation Allied Force," IABG, Trier, Germany, November 12, 1999. Frank Bekkers, "Kosovo and the Strategic Defense Review in the Netherlands," Policy Support MOD, TNO Defense Research, November 1999.

405. *Jane's Defense Weekly*, August 4, 1995, p.27.

406. *Aviation Week and Space Technology*, April 12, 1999, pp. 24–25; *Jane's Defense Weekly*, July 14, 1999, p. 3.

407. *Aviation Week and Space Technology*, July 26, 1999, p. 68.

408. *Aviation Week and Space Technology*, April 5, 1999, pp. 26–32.

409. *Aviation Week and Space Technology*, May 17, 1999, p. 32.

410. Informal NATO Ministerial, 21 Sept. 1999. Briefing by Secretary of Defense William S. Cohen and Chairman of the Joint Chiefs of Staff General Henry Shelton. (www.nato.int).

411. *Jane's Defense Weekly*, August 25, 1999, p. 5.

412. *Jane's Defense Weekly*, April 7, 1999.

413. See Dennis Gormley and Thomas Mahnken, "Smart Weapons Limitations: Enemy Armed with WMD May Not Be Deterred," *Defense News*, September 13, 1999, p. 15.

414. Department of Defense, *Report to Congress: Kosovo/Operation Allied Forces After Action Report*, Washington, Department of Defense, January 31, 2000, pp. 33–34, 121.

415. *Air Force Magazine*, August 1999, p. 60.

416. *Washington Post*, April 21, 1999, p. A-1.

417. Prepared joint statement on the Kosovo After Action Review presented by Secretary of Defense William S. Cohen and Gen. Henry H. Shelton, Chairman of the Joint Chiefs of Staff, before the Senate Armed Services Committee, October 14, 1999.

418. Rebecca Grant, "The Kosovo Campaign: Aerospace Power Made It Work," Arlington, Air Force Association, September 1999, p. 16.

419. *Jane's Defense Weekly*, August 4, 1999, p. 4.

420. *Jane's Defense Weekly*, November 17, 1999, p. 15.

421. *Aviation Week and Space Technology*, November 1, 1999, pp. 33–36.

422. These points are also supported in the French official analysis of the lessons of the war in Alain Richard, *Les Enseignements du Kosovo*, Paris Ministry of Defense, November, 1999, www.washington/actu/kossovo/actualities/dossier/d36.

423. Department of Defense, *Report to Congress: Kosovo/Operation Allied Forces After Action Report*, Washington, Department of Defense, January 31, 2000, pp. 108–109, 116–117.

424. Prepared joint statement on the Kosovo After Action Review presented by Secretary of Defense William S. Cohen and Gen. Henry H. Shelton, Chairman of the Joint Chiefs of Staff, before the Senate Armed Services Committee, October 14, 1999.

425. Jim Garamone, "Predator Demonstrates Worth Over Kosovo," American Forces Press Service, September 12, 1999.

426. Military Procurement Subcommittee hearing on lessons learned from the Kosovo conflict—the effect of the operation on both deployed/non-deployed forces and on future modernization plans, October 19, 1999.

427. *Jane's Defense Weekly*, July 21, 1999, p. 6.

428. *Jane's Defense Weekly*, September 1, 1999, p. 30.

429. *Aviation Week and Space Technology*, September 6, 1999, p. 89

430. Department of Defense, *Report to Congress: Kosovo/Operation Allied Forces After Action Report*, Washington, Department of Defense, January 31, 2000, pp. 56–57.

431. See Dr. H. C. Uwe Nerlich, "Lessons from Operation Allied Force," IABG, Trier, Germany, November 12, 1999. Frank Bekkers, "Kosovo and the Strategic Defense Review in the Netherlands," Policy Support MOD, TNO Defense Research, November 1999; Alain Richard, *Les Enseignements du Kosovo*, Paris Ministry of Defense, November, 1999, www.washington/actu/kossovo/actualities/dossier/d36.

432. *Jane's Defense Weekly*, September 1, 1999, p. 30; *Defense News*, November 1, 1999, p. 8.

433. *Jane's Defense Weekly*, September 1, 1999, p. 30; Assemblee Nationale, Rapport d'Information, "Le cout de la participation de la France aux operations menees en vue du reglement de la crise au Kosovo," presente par Jean-Michel Boucheron, No. 1775, July 1, 1999, p. 12.

434. For a good overview of the potential of UAVs, see Mark Hewish, "Coming Soon: Attack of the Killer UAVs," *Jane's International Defense Review*, 9/1999, pp. 30–37, "Briefing: Autonomous Weapons," *Jane's Defense Weekly*, February 9, 2000, pp. 22–26; and David Mulholland, "New US Radar Increases Possibilities of UAVs," *Defense News*, September 20, 1999, p. 20.

435. *Aviation Week and Space Technology*, July 26, 1999, p. 74; *Jane's Defense Weekly*, September 1, 1999, p. 30.

436. *Aviation Week and Space Technology*, August 23, 1999, p. 30.

437. These points are also supported in the French official analysis of the lessons of the war in Alain Richard, *Les Enseignements du Kosovo*, Paris Ministry of Defense, November, 1999, www.washington/actu/kossovo/actualities/dossier/d36.

438. *Jane's Defense Weekly*, April 19, 1999, p. 4, June 10, 1999, p. 10; *Aviation Week and Space Technology*, June 7, 1999, pp. 55; *Defense News*, April 19, 1999, p. 1, April 26, 1999, p. 1.

439. *Defense News*, June 14, 1999, p. 1.

440. *Jane's Defense Weekly*, September 8, 1999, p. 37.

441. *Jane's Defense Weekly*, December 22, 1999, p. 28.

442. For a more detailed discussion of many of these issues, see Commodore Tim Lawrence, *Humanitarian Assistance and Peacekeeping: An Uneasy Alliance*, London, Royal United Services Institute for Defense Studies, Whitehall Papers Series, no. 48, 1999.

443. The key resolution is Resolution 1244 (1999) which was adopted by the Security Council at its 4011th meeting on June 10, 1999. Other related resolutions include 1160 (1998) of 31 March 1998, 1199 (1998) of 23 September 1998, 1203 (1998) of 24 October 1998 and 1239 (1999) of 14 May 1999. The agreements affecting the end of the war also include the Military Technical Agreement between the International Security Force ("KFOR") and the Governments of the Federal Republic of Yugoslavia and the Republic of Serbia of June 9, 1999; and the undertaking of demilitarization and transformation by the UCK of June 20, 1999.

444. *International Herald Tribune*, November 11, 1999, p. 4; it should be noted that these totals differ radically from the scare-oriented atrocity reporting NATO sometimes stooped to during the war. Secretary Cohen, for example, referred to "about 100,000 military-aged men" as missing and said, "they may have been murdered" in May 1999. *Newsweek*, November 22, 1999, p. 28.

445. *Washington Post*, August 4, 1999, p. A-18.

446. *Washington Post*, September 16, 1999, p. A-17; *New York Times*, September 14, 1999, p. A-3; NATO KFOR press briefing on Kosovo, September 13, 1999 (www.nato.int).

447. *Washington Post*, February 17, 2000, pp. A-21 to A-27.

448. *Washington Post*, February 9, 2000, p. A-14; *New York Times*, March 2, 2000, p. A-1; *New York Times International*, September 29, 1999, p. A-10, December 10, 1999, p. A-12, February 18, p. A-3.

449. For a more detailed discussion of these issues, see Steven Rattner, Chairman and Michael B.G. Froman, Project Director, "Promoting Sustainable Economies in the Balkans," Council on Foreign Relations Task Force Report, New York, 2000.

450. *International Herald Tribune*, September 29, 1999, p. A-10.

451. *Jane's Defense Weekly*, September 29, 1999, p. 5.

452. *Jane's Defense Weekly*, September 29, 1999, p. 5.

453. *Washington Post*, September 19, 1999, p. A-27; *New York Times*, March 2, 2000, p. A-1.

454. *New York Times*, July 29, 1999, p. A-1; July 30, 1999, p. A-3.

455. The UN force has not come close to raising its $325 million annual budget. NATO refused SACEUR's request for 700 additional men in February 2000. *New York Times International*, March 4, 2000, p. A-6.

456. *Washington Post*, October 5, 1999, p. A-11.

457. *International Herald Tribune*, November 22, 1999, p. 7.

458. See Steven Rattner, Chairman and Michael B.G. Froman, Project Director, "Promoting Sustainable Economies in the Balkans," Council on Foreign Relations Task Force Report, New York, 2000.

459. *New York Times*, July 31, 1999, p. A-3; *Economist*, July 31, 1999, p. 53.

460. *Washington Post*, September 24, 1999, p. A-1.

461. David F. Gordon, National Intelligence Council, "Global Humanitarian Emergencies and Projections: 1999–2000, August, 1999," Washington, National Intelligence Council, August 1999.

462. Robert DeVecchi and Arthur Helton, "Are We Asking Too Much of the UN," *Washington Post*, September 19, 1999, p. B-1.

463. "Remarks by the President to the 54th Session of the United Nations General Assembly," September 21, 1999. Text taken from the White House page on the Internet.

464. "Secretary General Presents His Annual Report to General Assembly," Press Release SG/SM/7136 GA/9596, September 20, 1999.

465. For an interesting summary discussion of some of the different views involved over these issues, see James Kitfield, "Not-So-Sacred Borders," *National Journal*, November 20, 1999, pp. 3386–3387.

About the Author

ANTHONY H. CORDESMAN holds the Arleigh A. Burke Chair in Strategy at the Center for Strategic and International Studies, and is a special consultant on military affairs for ABC News. The author of numerous books on international security issues, he has served in senior positions for the Secretary of Defense, NATO, State Department, Department of Energy, and the U.S. Senate.